NATIONAL
SECURITY
AND
AMERICAN
SOCIETY

National Security Studies Series

Sponsored by the National Security Education Program
of New York University, in cooperation with
The National Strategy Information Center

Editorial Board

NATIONAL SECURITY AND AMERICAN SOCIETY

Theory, Process, and Policy

edited by

FRANK N. TRAGER

PHILIP S. KRONENBERG

PUBLISHED FOR THE NATIONAL SECURITY EDUCATION PROGRAM
BY THE UNIVERSITY PRESS OF KANSAS
Lawrence/Manhattan/Wichita

FOREWORD

During the academic year 1969–1970, the National Security Program of New York University, in cooperation with the National Strategy Information Center of New York City, sponsored a series of conferences for college and university faculty members interested in the teaching of national security, defense policy, civil-military relations, defense economics, and related areas. Out of these conferences grew a number of projects designed to extend and improve academic education and scholarly research in the national security field.

Prominent among these projects is a National Security Studies Series under the general editorship of Professor Frank N. Trager of New York University. *National Security and American Society: Theory, Process, and Policy* is the first publication in the Series to appear. This volume is designed as a reader for an introductory course in national security affairs. It attempts a broad overview of the major components of the national security system as it operates in the contemporary United States. In addition, the first section contains three original essays on the nature of national security studies in the academic environment.

Subsequent publications in the near future will include books and monographs on various aspects of national security education. Their working titles are:

1. *American Defense Policy Since 1945: A Preliminary Bibliography*, compiled by John Greenwood and Robin Higham, edited by Geoffrey Kemp, Clark Murdock, and Frank L. Simonie.

2. *Nuclear Proliferation: Phase II*, edited by Robert Lawrence and Joel Larus.

3. *Model Syllabus for Courses in National Security*, edited by T. Alden Williams and David Tarr.

4. *The Statistics of the U.S.-Soviet Military Balance, 1945–1972*, by Geoffrey Kemp and Clark Murdock.

5. *Annotated Bibliography of Congressional Hearings on United States Defense Policy, 1945–1972*, by Geoffrey Kemp.

This Reader, together with the forthcoming works in the Series, will present a comprehensive set of teaching materials for the national security studies field.

CONTENTS

3 The National Security Policy Process

4 Strategy in the National Security Process

5   Societal Impacts of the National Security Process

ix

INTRODUCTION

There is always something a bit presumptuous about trying to edit a collection of works by other scholars into a form that can be labelled a "reader." The editors of such an enterprise confront risks in at least two areas: their selections may not be representative of the field of scholarship or of the scholars whose contributions have been selected, and they may not tap issues that are of interest to the current generation of students of the field. We accepted both of these risks in preparing this reader because we feel that they are necessary given the conceptual scope we have attempted. Our basic purpose is to provide the student with the means to grasp the important range of issues and processes at work in national security affairs in the 1970s.

Several working premises were used to accomplish this end. First, aware that few areas of scholarship are value-free, we felt that the intellectual controversies and central issues which characterize the field of national security studies are of interest to students. The priorities of inquiry which are embodied in the questions we ask in a given field are influenced by the way we define the field and reciprocally have implications for social policy. An informed student will want to address these issues when he contemplates the complex realm of national security. Second, we decided to enlarge the scope of the reader beyond consideration of a single focus, such as defense policy or strategy. Upon surveying a number of edited collections in this field, we concluded that they too often emphasized one facet of national security affairs without providing the means for acquiring perspectives on the broader social processes involved in national security. Third, we chose to emphasize materials written in the mid-1960s or later where possible, although uneven coverage of topics in the scholarly literature led to some exceptions. In some cases, we reproduced essays of a pre-1960 vintage because of their essential conceptualization of a particular topic. Otherwise, we have cited important earlier works in the Selected Additional Readings which follow each section of the book. In all we surveyed several hundred books and articles before making a final choice. The task of exclusion because of space, among other things, created its own order of problems, readily perceptible to anyone in the field.

Section I of this reader consists of three original essays prepared expressly for this volume. Each essay examines the kinds of orienting definitions and issues that characterize the scholarship in national security studies. Taken together, these essays represent three alternative or contrasting interpretations of the scope of the national security field. Although it may still be an overstatement to award the label of "field" to national security studies—in the sense that economics or political science or international relations are fields—nonetheless, there are a number of questions and concepts which are shared by scholars who have an interest in national security affairs so that a certain terrain of scholarship can be identified. This terrain—its premises, perspectives, and controversies—is central to the essays in Section I.

Section II is concerned with a range of historical and theoretical perspectives on the purposes of war and armed defense and the values which underlie the concept of national security. The issues raised in these selections are "traditional" in many respects. However, their apparent lack of novelty should not obscure their importance. The legitimacy and nature of violence between states as well as the magnitude of manpower and resources mobilized for national defense raise these issues to a level of utmost importance. No society can long tolerate either ineffective defenses or unwarranted acts of war.

The remaining three parts of the volume are intended to provide a conceptual grounding in the broad sweep of the policy process in national security affairs. The conduct of national security affairs is not to be characterized as a highly systemized and straightforward set of steps that provide both a clear sense of policy direction for a government and an efficient sequence of instrumental choices which insure maximization of the national interest. Rather, national security policy involves a very large-scale and very complex system of actions taken by myriad institutional actors that generate many intended and unintended consequences. Hence, our focus in national security affairs is on a continuous policy process. Sections III, IV, and V endeavor to illuminate the major elements and actors in the ongoing process of formulating, implementing, and assessing national security policy.

Section III is addressed to the formulation and modification of national security policy. Of particular interest are the various inputs that help shape the substance of national security policy. These include the structure of policy decision-making, technological factors, the role of systems analysis, and the impact of nongovernmental inputs into policy-making, such as the press, multinational corporations, and social change.

In Section IV the focus on the policy process shifts from the input side to the output side, with special emphasis being given to strategic thought and policy implementation. The role of strategy as a major facet of policy implementation and the nature and theory of strategy are examined; attention is also given to the strategy of deterrence which undergirds the contemporary United States strategic posture. Selections in Section IV also include consideration of limited war and of approaches to the pursuit of national security objectives without resort to military force.

Finally, Section V emphasizes the consequences for society of the actions taken in the implementation of national security policy. The outputs of the national security system allocate a variety of costs and benefits among the different sectors of American society. Section V considers the opportunity costs of defense spending to taxpayers and social programs, and the economic concentration that seems to develop from these expenditures. The implications of secrecy and a variety of other issues which arise from the national security process and affect the quality of American society are explored. Not the least of these areas is the nature of military professionalism. How we use our military and the resultant implications of their professional self-concept for civil-military relations are important consequences of the national security process.

At the end of each Section we have listed a few Selected Additional Readings, each with a brief annotation. These are intended as a starting point for students wishing to explore further any of the topical issues covered in this volume. Additional good material is to be found in those parts of the source works for this reader that have not been reproduced here. We also suggest that the student consult John Greenwood, *et al.*, *Preliminary Bibliography on American Defense Policy Since 1945* (Lawrence: University Press of Kansas, 1973) for a much fuller source of national security material.

In a period of less self-criticism and, perhaps, less self-accusation, a reader on national security and American society could well afford to concentrate on any one of the topics we have introduced above. Such tunnel vision is clearly inappropriate in the decade of the 1970s. American society is engaged in yet another period of reappraisal of its national priorities and the institutional mechanisms which serve them. Military and national security policies have central roles to play in this examination. We have therefore tried to respond to the spirit of this dialogue by developing a comprehensiveness in the range of topics encompassed in this volume of readings.

Any success we may have achieved in moving toward this goal is due in no small measure to our research assistants at New York University and Indiana University who toiled many long hours in helping us screen the literature and who proposed a number of highly useful critical suggestions: Frank L. Simonie, Dorothea A. Schoenfeldt, and Wendell Lawther. We are also indebted to administrative assistants Mary Parker and Marilyn King for their invaluable help in getting this manuscript into printable form.

FNT
PSK

1 | NATURE AND SCOPE OF NATIONAL SECURITY STUDIES

Introduction

An initial reaction of students to a discussion of the nature, scope, and analytical methods of an academic field may be, "These are things that professors talk to other professors about!" One can sympathize with this response. On the surface, it is difficult to see the relationships between issues of scope and method and issues of substantive concern. The substance of national security is heady indeed: questions of war and peace, vast expenditures of blood and treasure, global alliances, grand strategy, crisis decision-making, militarism. What do theoretical models and the defining concepts of a field of study have to do with these?

The scope and methodology of a field of study provide an agenda of the things that are considered important to understand and suggest the means that will lead to understanding them. For example, if the study of national security revolved only around an attempt to understand how to wage successful wars, the result would be a systematic bias in our knowledge which might well exclude an awareness of the consequences of war and plausible alternatives to the use of interstate violence.

The study of national security is in a period of exciting change which reflects the dramatic events in the real world of international relations and public policy-making that it seeks to make comprehensible. The field of national security draws upon the approaches and insights of a number of traditional academic disciplines, especially the social and behavioral sciences. A relative newcomer in comparison to the traditional academic fields, the

items on the agenda of national security studies have grown impressively in the past two decades. To its long-standing interests in military affairs and defense policy have been added topics which bear on national security in less obvious but increasingly important ways: natural resources, international communication, the diffusion of technology, and domestic political violence, to mention several.

The three essays in this section were written especially for this book in order to illuminate some of the rich conceptual issues and analytical questions that are embodied in the contemporary study of national security. Each essay takes a different "cut" at interpreting the important issues of scope and method in the field. Hopefully, their combined effect will be to convey some of the excitement of this emergent field of study and provide a better foundation for profiting from the readings in the other sections of the book.

The essay by Klaus Knorr, "National Security Studies: Scope and Structure of the Field," develops two frameworks for the study of national security. Both focus on issues surrounding the nature and use of military power. The National Framework examines factors that influence military potential and decisions to mobilize and use military strength. The International Framework explores the nature and international distribution of military power, the causes of international conflict and approaches to their resolution, factors involved in decisions to use force internationally, and some of the conditions affecting the utility of using force. Knorr views these twin frameworks as alternative ways of looking at the reality of national security. He asserts that the frameworks are comprehensive in that they can accommodate any significant issue in the study of national security, including those of a normative nature.

The second essay, "Interorganizational Politics and National Security: An Approach to Inquiry" by Philip S. Kronenberg, proposes the use of the Interorganizational Politics Model as a framework for analyzing the process of national security. He makes the point that organizations are political in nature and offers the concept of "interorganization" as a basis for analyzing the complex interactions among the participants in national security activities. Kronenberg suggests that two types of interorganizational behavior—the parabureaucratic and the parapolitical—can provide a basis for comparing national security processes; he derives a number of hypotheses which can assist in explaining these processes. Kronenberg applies the Interorganizational Politics Model to several phases of national security pol-

icy-making and indicates some of the implications of the model as an aid to the policy-maker.

"An Introduction to the Study of National Security," by Frank N. Trager and Frank L. Simonie, proposes a working definition of national security:

> National Security is that part of government policy having as its objective the creation of national and international political conditions favorable to the protection or extension of vital national values against existing and potential adversaries.

The essay examines the significance of this conception of national security and gives particular attention to the nature of government policy, the function of vital national values, and the factors involved with "interests" which provide linkages between national values and the techniques of national security operations. The authors also discuss the role played by the "means" of national security, especially military force, in the study of national security affairs. They conclude by emphasizing the need to understand the end purposes of national security and to avoid the tendency to become distracted by less central concerns.

National Security Studies:
Scope and Structure of the Field

KLAUS KNORR

INTRODUCTION

This paper attempts to do precisely what its title implies: to indicate the scope and structure of a still rather inchoate field of studies and a subject of teaching. National security is a field of study in the same sense that modern urban studies is such a field, like it drawing on several academic disciplines. This paper does *not* present a course outline. A course or a seminar outline must be sensitive to several factors which are irrelevant to defining the scope of a field, namely the peculiar capabilities and interests of the instructor, the ability and interests of students, and the curricular relation of a course to others offered at the same institution of higher learning. The substantive and normative interest of teachers and students—in terms of overall focus, emphasis and deemphasis—changes over time and is often affected by the contemporary nature of their particular country's national security problems.

Except for briefly noting them, I will deliberately bypass the semantic and definitional problems generated by the term "National Security." The main problems are (1) the negative connotations which the term evokes in much of today's academic world; (2) the non-traditional meanings which the novice may attribute to the term, e.g., considerations of *domestic* rather than international security; (3) the fact that the state activities with which national security studies are concerned may pursue other than strictly security goals, including objectives which tend to jeopardize military security; and (4) the profound problems of definition which Arnold Wolfers and others have identified, that is to say, the problems of making the term analytically operational and of setting forth criteria for evaluating national security.[1] Among the main problems are the assumptions that a sense of national security is ultimately a subjective matter and that security does not lie only, or even primarily, in the conventional means (i.e., armed forces) but also in the way these means are employed and in the purposes for which they are used.

As do most practitioners, I am using the term "National Security" simply as a rather unsatisfactory label for a field of study whose boundaries and chief structural features remain to be defined. In approaching this task I am aware that, in this case as in others, authorship is, at least up to a point, inevitably personal. Different authors may prefer different approaches and jargon for illuminating this somewhat protean field of study with which we are concerned. Inevitably there is also an arbitrary element in fixing the boundaries of the field since the human reality in which the practitioners in the field are interested is, more or less, directly, connected with all other sectors of human reality. One may choose boundaries to encompass a larger or smaller territory. Very narrow boundaries will make our explanations excessively superficial and fragmentary.

5

At the other extreme, we would sacrifice focus and all the advantages of specialization which, after all, give rise to the organization of academic fields. In all these matters of choice, I let myself be guided by what seem to me to have been the preferences of the majority of practitioners in the field, abroad as well as in the United States, except for drawing boundaries which are more inclusive than most *individual* students or teachers of the subject seem to prefer. I am concerned with what a *collectivity* of practitioners are doing, with what they appear to regard as the core area of the field. Individual practitioners will often draw narrower boundaries than I have done in many directions, following their personal interest and competence, in order to cross the proposed boundary in one particular direction. But they differ in the particular direction in which they prefer to roam.

I take "National Security" to be an abbreviation of "National *Military* Security," and I take this term to denote a field of study concerned *primarily* with the generation of national military power and its employment in interstate relationships. Yet any state's military security results, of course, not only from military means but also, as already pointed out, from what is done with them and from the complementary employment of other means of influence. If this is the central focus, we study a specific instrumentality of policy or mode of behavior, including their resource base, purpose and consequence. The kinds of actors whose behavior is the subject of interest are, as we will see, national or sub-national actors, depending especially on whether we are looking at the interstate or at the intrastate level.

Limitation, if only by emphasis, is of course the price we pay for any choice of focus. We give up inclusiveness in order to obtain the advantages of concentration and specialization of effort. For instance, if we wanted to study with equal emphasis all phenomena suggested by the term "national security," we would have passed on to the study of foreign policy or international relations as a whole. Yet the student of national military security may well choose the analysis of non-military instruments as a subsidiary focus (see B.4 (c) in the following framework), and relate their use to that of military means. He will be aware of the fact, for instance, that the fashioning of a very strong military posture, and its aggressive use, may under certain circumstances reduce national "security" either by provoking other states to arm or by generating a degree of domestic division which will tend to undermine the strong posture.

It is likewise easy to think of studies whose focus cuts across, and only partly overlaps, the focus on which I have settled. For example, a sociologist may want to study the military as a profession just as he may want to study the medical and legal professions. Similarly, the anthropologist or economist may study segments or aspects of cultural or economic reality that appreciably touch on but do not exhaust the selected focus. Such scholars can greatly contribute to the understanding of particular national security problems. But their purpose is apt both to fall short of and to go beyond our chosen focus. Thus, the sociologist studying the armed forces of a particular society, or comparatively of a number of societies, may be uninterested in how their military capabilities compare internationally. He may be interested in the use of these forces for causing domestic order or oppression, or their activities in aiding economic development, or in achieving the political and cultural integration of a population beset with deep ethnic or other cleavages.

The phenomena on which we have chosen to focus have, of course, been an important part of human reality at least since the first civilizations began to flourish in different parts of the world some eight thousand years ago—important that is, in terms of the rise and fall of communities (whether tribal agglomerates, city states or empires), in terms of inter- and intra-community order and destruction, and in terms of the diffusion of races, religions, systems of government, technology, etc. It is clear that the various conditions which determine the production, use and consequences of military strength have been in virtually continuous flux, sometimes exhibiting recurrent and sometimes new patterns of activities and relationships. The reality in our focus is an ever-changing phenomenon and must be studied as such. Static analysis has its place, but it does not address itself to many of the most interesting questions.

To study problems of national security need not, of course, mean that we *like* the reality we want to understand, that we approve of it, or wish to preserve it. Surely the economist need not like business cycles in order to subject them to analysis. However, in the contemporary world, particularly in the economically most advanced countries, there is a strong, and perhaps growing, aversion to the kinds of coercion and physical destruction, and to the instruments employed in military coercion and destruction. Normative interests in this subject matter run ac-

cordingly high. Normative concern is apt to induce particular choices of subject matter in research and particular substantive emphases in teaching. It is nevertheless efficient—and, I believe, sound academic ethics—to preserve the classical distinction between descriptive and normative analysis. There is nothing wrong with proceeding from description to prescription. Indeed prescription without a basis of descriptive knowledge is usually unproductive in terms of modifying the larger reality, though not of course in satisfying the emotional orientation of the prescriptor. And a descriptive bent that shrinks from progressing to normative questions neglects a type of scholarly interest and certainly frustrates the interest of the academic *qua* citizen. As members of the *academic* world, however, we should know as best we can when we are doing the one or the other. This is not to say, of course, that a normative focus can dispense with descriptive analysis as solid scholarship.

In the following, the main concern is with descriptive knowledge and in theories based thereon. Only at the end will I take note of the normative perspective. This disproportion does not express any belief that the normative enterprise is less important; it simply reflects my understanding of where intellectual disorder in the field is mostly lodged.

OUTLINE OF THE FIELD

In outlining the scope and structure of our field of study, I will first present a summary but, I believe, complete scheme and then follow with a somewhat more detailed, though only illustrative, treatment of the parts. I hope to present enough structure to make it possible for the reader to fill in further detail of special interest to him.

A. NATIONAL FRAMEWORK

1. Military Potential

a. economic, technological, scientific resources
b. administrative capabilities
c. political and cultural factors
2. Decision to Mobilize and Use Military Strength
a. substance of decision-making: objectives, policy analysis, choice
b. modes of decision-making:
—range of actors and values
—formal institutions
—informal influence structure

3. The Armed Forces and Their Use (potential or actual)
   a. size, structure, weapons, strategy and doctrine, skill, morale
   b. military strength relative to other armed forces for various missions and in different environments and situations—defense, deterrence, aggression, intervention
4. The Normative Perspective
   This framework can be used for focusing on:
   a. the national security effort of any one state (e.g., the U.S.) or
   b. international comparative analysis.

B. INTERNATIONAL FRAMEWORK

1. Nature of Military Power
   a. direct force vs. coercion
   b. putative vs. actualized military power
   c. processes and mechanisms of conversion
   d. conversion models
2. International Distribution of Military power (putative)
   — hierarchy—alliances—balance of power
3. International Conflicts
   a. causation of international conflicts
   b. causation of military coercion and war
   c. types of resolution
4. Decisions on Using Force Internationally
   a. costs and benefits
   b. rational and non-rational modes of decision-making
   c. nonmilitary coercion and non-coercive influence
5. Conditions of Utility
   — technological, political, economic, social and cultural conditions affecting the costs and benefits of using force
6. The Normative Perspective
   — improving security, justice, wealth and other values by

a. restraining military power and its use in international order
   — reducing frequency and destructiveness of war (arms control and disarmament, collective security, etc.)
b. modifying the existing international order.

These twin frameworks are alternative ways, different in perspective and possibly in emphasis, of looking at the same reality. Although they represent different levels of analysis, logically all the items listed under A could be incorporated with B and vice versa. In the following exposition—which is to clarify and illustrate and to avoid pedantry—I will not demonstrate this in detail.

THE NATIONAL FRAMEWORK

A.1. Whether we focus on one state or (comparatively) on several, we are concerned here with national abilities to mobilize, and decisions to employ, "military strength" defined as national military capabilities. As long as none of the essential parts of these problems is left out, it does not matter where one starts in order to conceptualize the subject matter (the sequence could be reordered). I begin with military potential, i.e., the foundations of military strength, the assets available to a nation which can be allocated to its military sector to a greater or lesser extent for producing military strength. These assets can be variously categorized and differentiated. But they involve three major components.

First, there are economic resources which can be divided, as economists customarily do, into land, labor and capital, and which are understood to include science and technology essential to technological innovation. All these factors have their quantitative and qualitative aspects, e.g., states differ in size and structural composition of manpower, as in the quantity and quality of scientific resources at their command. In comparing states from this point of view, size of population and stage of economic and technological development, and hence level of productivity, are especially critical factors. Second, once an assortment of these resources has been diverted to the military sector, the amount and kind of mobilized military strength produced depends on the skill with which the inputs are employed to yield outputs. This transformation involves the efficiency of decisions regarding all parts of the mobilization process, e.g., what kind and structure of military forces and equipment, military R & D (Research and Development), military strategy and doctrine, military recruitment, training, and indoctrination, etc. are to be produced? The efficiency of such decisions depends on various management skills and techniques, including more recently operations analysis, cost effectiveness studies, PPBS (Planning-Programming-Budgeting-System), simulation, forecasting methods, etc. Third, the political decisions on the level and composition of resources to be allocated to the military sector depend obviously on situational conditions (e.g., the opportunities perceived at any time for using military forces, or their build up, whether defensively or aggressively). But these decisions also depend on a kind of political and cultural potential for building and using national military strength. The factors which make up this potential are antecedent to the development of the international factors. As I have shown in *Military Power and Potential* (1970) this involves (a) a nation's basic propensity to mobilize and use military strength internationally, a propensity which, as historians have called it, tends to make nations more or less warlike; (b) the predisposition to support the national community when under some challenge, i.e., the sense of national solidarity which often has affected the generation of military strength; (c) the

public disposition to accept government decisions on foreign policy and military matters as authoritative and hence binding; (d) support for military efforts from members of the public who have a direct and *specific personal* interest in the mobilization and use of military strength. Needless to stress, all these attitudes are variables, differing between nations and within nations over time, in scope and intensity. And also needless to emphasize, the effect of these antecedent attitude complexes depends upon their distribution in terms of effective political influence in the population concerned. Obviously, cleavages in these matters, particularly when politicized, are a very critical factor, whether they are between classes, generations, religious and ethnic groups, etc. In sum, these factors are part of a society's political culture which, though it may change over time, usually does so gradually.

A.2. (a) Assuming that the "national interest" has been defined authoritatively (see A.2 (b)), government decisions to mobilize or use military strength for resolving international conflicts result from *situational factors* as well as from the predispositional factors referred to above. Regarding decisions to employ force, I refer to B.4. Decisions to build, maintain or decrease mobilized military strength involve some sort of evaluation of expected benefits and costs to the extent that these decisions are made rationally; and the perception of relevant situational factors—in both the external and internal environment—go to the essence of such decision-making. Ideally, leaders will define a set of preferred future events (in matters of "national security"), evaluate the forces in the environment which favor or oppose such "security" outcomes, identify those forces capable of manipulation by available capabilities, estimate the costs involved in manipulation as well as the probabilities of success, and arrive at a satisfactory policy conclusion. Of course, the benefits in the set of preferred events may involve many different values (e.g., deterrence, conquest, domestic tranquility); and so also do the costs. (I am not referring only to *economic* costs but to *all* value losses involved in mobilizing national military strength, including possibly domestic political disunity, restrictions of freedom imposed on members of the armed forces, the risk of causing potentially hostile powers to increase *their* military forces (i.e., arms race), etc. The range of the true opportunity costs can be very broad indeed. In reality, actual decision-making is more or less rational—another variable—(even if we disregard errors resulting from poor information and faulty prediction); and it is important to consider the various deviations from rational decision-making recently set forth by Graham Allison.[2]

A.2. (b). Societies have various institutional arrangements for making decisions to mobilize and maintain military strength, the basic structure depending on the nature of the political regime (e.g., the formal involvement of President, National Security Council, Congress, etc., in the United States). These *formal* constitutional arrangements only coincide more or less with the *actual* power and influence structure which determines policy decisions of this kind. Different interested members of the government, elites, and public may differ in their perception and assessment of the relevant situational factors (as also in the antecedent dispositions mentioned earlier), in their estimate of costs and benefits (to themselves, their class, their political party, their country), and in the policy choice at which they arrive. Their conception of the "national interest," and of the social values to be protected or promoted at various costs, will diverge more or less. Their influence on decisions corresponds to the political influence which they want and are able to exert on matters of this

kind. Of special importance in this respect are also various relevant bureaucracies and professional groups— their influence, their internal decision-making processes, and their interest conflicts and preferences. Political coalitions which favor one choice or another will involve, and may cut across, the military, civilian bureaucracies, political parties, and so on. The impact of military leadership is obviously significant; and problems of civilian-military relations, civilian control over the military, and "military-industrial" complexes are highly pertinent realities in this connection.

A.3. The armed forces which are the outcome of the processes identified above invite comparative study with those of other states, allies or potential opponents, with reference to different objectives and strategies (e.g., nuclear deterrence), different environments, and different international situations.

A.4. The matter of national security studies—as subject to some intellectual order in the foregoing—raises normative questions in virtually every component. By way of example, the bearing of political culture on the military potential of states patently does so. Do we want our society to be warlike as defined? Should we push a growing proportion of our resources for technological innovation away from the military sector in order to improve our capabilities for accomplishing other social tasks? Similarly, in the evaluation of policy choices related to international situations raising questions to the use of military strength, should we revise the relative weight heretofore attributed to various value gains and costs? Is military success worth the costs which war and threat-making entail? Should we care to participate in international balance-of-power activities, or in collective security operations, for the sake of protecting potential victims of foreign aggression? Should we resort to force in order to defend or secure economic advantages? Should we set the human costs of military conscription higher than we have done in the past? Or on another track, to what extent should we control bureaucracies and the military if they make and press *their* choices in terms of past rather than present or newly emerging realities? To what extent should we impose moral considerations on the conduct of the military, and of military operations?

It is also clear that these kinds of normative problems in turn pose questions of feasibility or, to put it more generally, of costs in terms of sacrificing appreciable values in order to gain others. For instance, are we prepared to risk enhanced threats to our security by educating ourselves to be less warlike in a world in which large populations are not subjecting themselves to a similar process of political civilization? In what ways can this inherent conflict of self-interest be reconciled? A second example: how much of a decline in expected security are we ready to accept in order to cut military budgets? Or third, are we prepared to take on the risks of maintaining a professional army in order to free our young from compulsory military service? Or, finally, should we work toward an international order maintained to a much greater extent than is the case at present by internationally agreed-upon norms and internationally collective decision-making?

While this framework lends itself to studying the national security activities and problems of any particular country, it clearly also facilitates and invites international comparison, e.g., comparisons of military industrial potential, relevant political culture, the use of planning techniques, modes of civilian-military relationships, and so forth. Indeed, comparative study is an indispensable method for evaluating the behavior and performance of any one society.

THE INTERNATIONAL FRAMEWORK

The international approach is concerned with establishing patterns of how various national actors, or types of actors, relate to one another in promoting national security objectives.

B.1. Perhaps the major obstacle to a more sophisticated understanding of a military power, used internationally, is the chaotic mess which characterizes even the best theoretical literature on power and influence generally.[3] It is important that power in its various forms, bases, and consequences is carefully conceptualized.[4]

B.1. (a). Military strength can be used for two distinct purposes: first, for simply taking or defending something of value by sheer physical force; and second, for threatening an actor with physical punishment verbally or by physical violence. The essential difference is that in the second use military power is employed coercively, that is, to influence an opponent, and in the first use it is not. The first use presents little conceptual difficulty. Outcomes are determined by the relative military strength of the two parties; and as it succeeds (if it does so) military strength becomes military power, that is to say, the power to hold or to take. In the second use, military strength becomes military power to the extent that another actor's behavior is affected.

B.1. (b). Some theorists regard military power *as a means* to exert influence coercively, while other theorists equate military power with achieved influence, with an *effect*. The difference is important. It lies at the root of such phenomena as that a state with a great superiority in ships and divisions is powerless in particular situations vis-à-vis an inferior opponent. I therefore distinguish between *putative* and *actualized* military power. A state's putative power consists of its military forces, its military potential, and its military reputation (i.e., its reputed readiness to resort to force when vital interests are crossed by the actions of another state). Actualized military power equals achieved influence on the behavior of other states. In a way, putative power is a means, something in the possession of an actor; actualized power is an effect, something that takes place in another actor. Actualized power is always situational. The failure to heed this crucial distinction leads to a lot of confusion.

B.1. (c). There are three processes or mechanisms through which putative military power can be transformed into actualized power: first, military conflict, including war; second, the threat of military action; third, the anticipation by a government that the government of another state may resort to the use of its military strength if what it regards as its interests are crossed. In the third mechanism—which is the most important in terms of frequency of influence achievement—putative power is actualized even though no attempt is made to *exert* influence.

B.1. (d). Given this conceptual apparatus (which can be readily complicated in order to make further distinctions), it is possible to develop theoretical models of conversion. That is to say, one can identify and order the variable conditions which determine whether, or to what extent, putative power will be converted into actualized power. Such analysis is especially useful because it clarifies the operation of variables other than that of relative military strength, such as bargaining skill, degree of rationality, and relative will and commitment which, in turn, depend on the value of the stakes involved in the conflict and the probability of success which the actors attribute to alternative choices of action. (The nuclear deterrence model is simply one of several.)

B.2. The foregoing analysis leads logically to a study of the international distribution of putative military power at any one time or as a phenomenon changing over time. Questions of hierarchy—the distinction between great, middle and small powers—of hegemony and spheres of influence, of alliances and blocs, of multi-state balance of power versus bipolar power relationships call for analysis in this respect. Furthermore, regional structures can be distinguished from global structures. Finally, relations of putative military power can be differentiated in terms of different military capabilities (e.g., nuclear versus conventional) or of suitability for different types of conflict (e.g., counterinsurgency versus conventional war). These distinctions point to the situational character of actualized power.

B.3. Over time, and in relation to other identifiable conditions (e.g., state of economic development and technological advance, or the configuration of the international power structure), the stream of interstate conflicts changes in volume and intensity, and also in terms of suitability for resolution by military means. In this connection, it becomes relevant to study systematically the kinds of goals or values (e.g., religion, political ideology, economic gain, domestic unity, or military power itself) on behalf of which actors are willing to resort to military force. Or, to put it differently, the problem of the causation of war becomes at this point an interesting field of study.[5]

B.4. (a). It is possible and instructive at this stage to design models which identify and relate the variable conditions that together determine decisions on the interstate use of force. Similar to the process discussed under A.2. (a), to the extent that actors proceed rationally, they identify and evaluate choices of action (though not necessarily exhaustively) in terms of the information available to them and perceived to be relevant. What is essentially involved is a cost-gain calculus, touching on many different kinds of costs and benefits, undertaken in the light of more or less adequate information and usually true uncertainties. In addition to purely military considerations, the value of the stakes (which may, of course, differ for a set of antagonists), the credibility of threats, the costs of threatening or fighting, including the risk of being beaten, the support of national publics and other states (allies) are the principal variables. And it is to be noted that as soon as a threat is made or executed, additional values enter the stakes, e.g., the value of a state's military reputation (i.e., the *future* value of its threats), or the value of a society, moral reputation abroad, or of damage to a society's moral self-image, etc. (To show the linkage of the two frameworks in one more instance, decisions to produce and maintain military strength could also be analyzed under B.4 (a).)

B.4. (b). Deviations from the rational model of decision-making are a subject of interest as noted under A.2. It is especially important to identify the variable conditions under which these deviations occur, more or less, and to clarify the consequences of deviations. They are involved in both crisis and pre-crisis decision-making.

B.4. (c). Military coercion is used rarely without simultaneous resort to other means of coercion (e.g., economic) and to non-coercive sources of influence (e.g., offers of cooperation). The composition of the influence "package" depends upon the relative availability and the relative costs and advantages of different forms of influence at any one time and in any one situation. On the other hand, the effectiveness of different forms of influence will vary between countries at any one time (e.g., relations between friendly versus relations between hostile states), and will also change over time. This variability affects the frequency with which military power is used.

B.5. The utility of military power —expected or gauged in retrospect—is subject to modification because of changes in the magnitude of either

costs or gains. As I have pointed out in *On the Uses of Military Power in the Nuclear Age* (1966), strong evidence suggests a diminution in the value of economic objectives on behalf of which military power has been employed frequently in the past, while a new wave of quasi-religious commitments (in terms of political true believership) may tend to increase the value of military conflict. On the other hand, there have been significant changes in the costs of using military power, e.g., the normatively diminished legitimacy of war except for self-defense or the enormous destructive capacity of nuclear weapons. There are even beginnings of a global sense of community or solidarity, expressed for instance in evidence of transnational loyalties and commitments, that affect the utility of military coercion, or of all kinds of coercion (technically speaking, this amounts to a rise in the costs of coercion). On this focus, it is possible to relate systematically all kinds of changes in the environment (technological, economic, political and moral) to the conditions and consequences of military power.

B.6. The approach through the international framework lends itself to posing the same kinds of normative considerations which we noted with reference to the national framework. Thus, even if we are prepared to use military force for defense against aggression, do we ever want to use it coercively? These considerations also involve the question of what kind of a world we want to live in as far as military power is concerned. What are the relative values of international violence and justice with reference to different configurations of interest? What sort of institutions do we need if we want to reduce the generation of conflict and its resolution by violence or by any kind of coercive means?

And again, normative concern and innovation raise problems of feasibility and costs. If we know (or think we know) what a preferred international order looks like, how can we get there, if at all? Which are the feasible and hence interesting or relevant utopias?

In this connection the entire problem area of international arms control and disarmament calls for systematic analysis. How can arms races be avoided or moderated? How can the outbreak of war (all kinds or particular kinds of war) be minimized if not prevented? And how, if war breaks out nonetheless, can its destructiveness be curtailed? Finally, such normative demands on the management of interstate power pose the question not only of whether the workings of existing international order can be improved in specified respects but also of whether the existing system is at all viable over the long run. What alternative orders can there be and by which routes can they be approached? What advantages are we likely to exchange for what sorts of drawbacks?

CONCLUDING REMARKS

I believe that *all* problems relevant to "national security" can be accommodated in the two frameworks I have outlined. This inclusiveness may not be immediately apparent because the summary statement of the conceptual schemes is terse, and the non-summary part is illustrative rather than exhaustive. I eschewed exhaustiveness largely for the practical reason of achieving convenient brevity. But I did so also because the elaboration of the framework can be undertaken on different levels of detail. A progressively differentiated or total job would be a daunting task. And, as I indicated before, wherever the boundary lines are drawn, in the direction of richer elaboration, there are always adjoining problem areas on the periphery—until finally nothing human is left out—which individuals may wish to follow up in all their interlinkage in keeping with their special interests.

As indicated in the Introduction, one deliberate limitation involves restriction to interstate conflict, and also to the classical forms of interstate violence. This is proper. But even within this limitation, domestic strife is a relevant subject for study in various analytical places. Thus, domestic conflict affects the military potential of states, and the mobilization of potential. Domestic conflict may engender international conflicts either because insecure rulers seek the solidarity-increasing effects of a military effort or because governments decide for various reasons to intervene or counter-intervene in internal wars abroad. As a result, military capabilities for such intervention may become an interesting factor, as does the effect of revolutions on the international balance of power. I need hardly emphasize that these phenomena raise a host of normative questions.

Any comprehensive conceptual scheme for the study of the "national security" world, as here defined, evidently calls for multidisciplinary study. There is work appropriate to all academic disciplines. This is not to say that any researcher or teacher in the field must become personally multidisciplinary. Although any achievement in this direction surely redounds to the power of analysis and teaching, this would be an excessive standard. Nor must he combine with others in order to attain multidisciplinary competence collectively. Whenever feasible such collaboration is, to be sure, worth exploring. But experience shows that it is hard to achieve true integration of vision and effort in any collaborative relationship or in a committee. The natural thing is for individuals to teach, or do research, about those aspects or parts of the entire complex which their professional competence suggests. An economist may want to study economic aspects of military potential or mobilization. The expert in American government may wish to turn to constitutional structure and political processes involved in decisions on the production or use of military power. The international-relations specialist will wish to include the analysis of military power relationships in his efforts. On the normative side, the jurist may want to examine certain restraints on the exercise of military power. Sociologists, anthropologists and psychologists may turn to aspects susceptible to the tools of their discipline. But they will all profit, and collectively generate cumulative knowledge more efficiently, if they turn to their specialties with a general knowledge of how their particular subject fits into the overall framework.

I cannot resist a special word, indeed a non-specious pleading, for the uses of history. I am deeply impressed by the fact that shallow historical knowledge produces distorted and superficial views of the contemporary world. For example, I am astounded by the frequent observation that we are right now at a turning point of history, in a transition to a totally new era, etc., when it is overwhelmingly obvious that the entire history of civilized man, stretching back as far as our records go, has been an incessant series of change, turning points, and transition periods. All that we can possibly claim as distinct is that change has become accelerated. To give one more example, many people today are interested in, if not desirous of, an overarching cooperation between the two nuclear superpowers; some even envisage a global co-dominium. I am not concerned here with whether such a development is desirable. But if one wants to study the problem seriously, one might want to note that bipolar patterns of superpower have emerged repeatedly in history. They have never been stable for long, as has indeed proved no other power configuration. But co-dominium between a pair of superpowers has never proved feasible. If this is so, one may want to allow that this is a very difficult, perhaps impossible, pattern to achieve, and one may want to form hypotheses on why this is so. By way of a third example, history shows interesting recurring associations between certain types of military organization and certain types of government. There are indeed many acute contemporary problems germane to our field of study whose appreciation would benefit greatly from the presence of a historical perspective.

In conclusion, as I hope to have demonstrated, the presented set of frameworks permits dynamic as well as static analysis, the development of macro- and micro-theory, and normative as well as descriptive enterprise.

POSTSCRIPT

Several readers of the foregoing paper made interesting comments in which three themes preponderate.

First, they expressed distaste for the term "National Security." I fully share this feeling and continue wondering if "International Security" would not be a better term. But there is no obviously better term by which to refer to the field we have delineated; and it is hard to change the practice of decades.

Second, there is the question of whether the field of "National Security" should not be extended to include also problems of *domestic* security; and it is suggested that such an extension would produce more interest in the subject at contemporary universities and colleges. I appreciate these feelings but think it unwise to extend the meaning of the label in that direction. (Scholars are naturally perfectly free to structure their teaching and research as they see personally fit.) Of course, several *alternative* foci are available. Thus, we could concentrate on "conflict" (regardless of setting); or on "security" (regardless of setting); or on "armed forces" whether employed for national or international purposes. And it would be interesting if some scholars with appropriate inclination and equipment would turn to any of these directions. However, if we did so as a more or less institutionalized group, we would be migrating to different fields, requiring different (or only very partially overlapping) conceptual frameworks, empirical materials, and skills. Under ambitious interpretations, some of these foci would end up encompassing all of politics, domestic and international.

I believe that we are better off if we stick to the above framework because it is in line with what most academic practitioners are actually doing and because there is virtue in a narrower degree of concentration. Moreover, as I indicated, the framework lends itself, for anyone feeling claustrophobia, to making excursions in all directions.

Third, I have been taken to task for not having placed more, if not exclusive, emphasis on the sorts of questions which have excited the academic community in the United States in the wake of the war in Vietnam. In fact, it has been suggested that I am a "conservative" or even a "reactionary." I do not think I am either. In any case, I visualized my task as an essentially descriptive one, to suggest a possible order for the activities that teachers, students and researchers have engaged in, whether descriptively or normatively, in other countries as well as in the United States. In doing so, it is true, I was concerned not only with what has happened academically over the past few years but over a longer period of time, including the recent past. To have done otherwise would have been to embrace parochialism—a restriction to the academic scene in the United States at one moment in history. I did not exhibit my personal normative commitments.

NOTES

1. Arnold Wolfers, *Discord and Collaboration, Essays in International Politics* (Baltimore, 1962), Chap. X.

2. "Conceptual Models and the Cuban Missile Crisis," *American Political Science Review* (September 1969).

3. Compare, for example, the following three excellent writings: Harold D. Lasswell and Abraham Kaplan, *Power and Society* (1950); Robert A. Dahl, "Power," *International Encyclopedia of the Social Sciences* (1968), vol.

12; Carl H. Friedrich, *Man and His Government* (1963), chaps. 9–11.

4. In my *Military Power and Potential* (chap. I) I have begun with formulating a theory of military power. In the following I am drawing on the ideas developed in that chapter.

5. For further clarification see, for instance, Dean G. Pruitt and Richard C. Snyder, *Theory and Research on the Causes of War* (1969).

Interorganizational Politics and National Security: An Approach to Inquiry

PHILIP S. KRONENBERG

NATIONAL SECURITY STUDIES: THE SEARCH FOR AN APPROACH

The nature and scope of the study of national security rests on two questions: *What* is to be studied?—the kinds of events, programs, and policies to which one gives the label "national security"; and *how* is it to be studied? —the analytical approach used to understand events, programs, and policies, once the "what" decision has been made. Many who study national security provide a central role to the military as a definitional boundary. However, numerous other students of public policy, foreign relations, and international politics also emphasize nonmilitary elements in their concept of national security. On the premise that national security is what students of the subject want to study, I will leave that issue to others and move to the second question.

My purpose in this essay is to propose an approach to the study of national security: the Interorganizational Politics Model. I will discuss the analytical features of this model and explore its applications to the study of policy and certain contemporary issues in national security affairs.

ANALYTICAL MODE: NORMATIVE AND EMPIRICAL

There are two kinds of decisions to be made when considering approaches to inquiry: analytical mode and analytical framework.

Analytical mode is the orientation toward value assumptions which will be made in research. We can divide studies into two rough categories according to analytical mode: normative (concerned with recommending what *should* be done in national security programs and policies), and empirical (concerned with describing and explaining what *is* actually done and its consequences).

Normative studies begin with certain assumptions about goals, values, or objectives and then proceed to assess a particular situation in order to decide what actions should be recommended in order to achieve the particular goals, values, or objectives desired. For example, a normative study concerning the decision to establish an all-volunteer army might begin with goal assumptions about the numbers and skills of officers and men required—given certain estimates of the policy commitments that could demand deployment of these troops. The study might then analyze the factors that are likely to influence the ability of the armed forces to recruit and retain the requisite number of volunteers over a specified period

17

of time. These factors could include the pay and benefits needed to attract and keep in service the required numbers of volunteers of different ranks and specialties. Another factor is the willingness of Congress and the public to support the appropriations necessary to provide these pay and benefits. Factors involving the disciplinary practices of the military might be examined to see if modifications may be required to provide a more attractive life style. On the basis of the evaluation of these and other factors, the study would make a series of recommendations which, if implemented, would be likely to accomplish the desired goal.

Empirical studies, on the other hand, begin with a particular condition or set of events which the analyst wishes to understand, define the important elements of the condition or set of events, describe them and their relationships, and then offer some explanations which account for the findings of his analysis. For example, an analyst may want to determine the relationships between various types of fringe benefits for servicemen and patterns of retention after a first enlistment. He would use an analytical model to specify the important variables that describe different kinds of fringe benefits and retention patterns, propose some testable hypotheses based upon the model which define expected relationships and their probable causes, collect the data needed to test these hypotheses, and evaluate his findings. Or an empirical study might be made of the processes that led the President to adopt the policy of ending conscription and developing an all-volunteer military force. Again, the analyst would adopt a model which would let him identify the important variables that shape the behavior of actors in the policy-making process, develop and test the hypotheses which aid in explaining the process, and collect and analyze his data.

In practice, much of the national security literature engages in both normative and empirical inquiry. Although the two categories of analytical purpose are distinct, they are often found in the same study. Their combination may be misleading when the purpose of inquiry is alleged to be an objective empirical study but the author masks his value biases and merely arrays facts which conveniently support his normative interests or goals. But basically such combinations of the normative and empirical are quite justifiable and useful.

Research which is concerned with major issues of national security policy requires the integration of the normative and the empirical. Decisions of high policy, involving recommendations for what *should* be done, demand careful attention to empirical realities.

Normative and empirical analyses are essential to each other. Policy proposals which advocate certain norms but ignore careful empirical assessments of actual cause-effect relationships are naïve at best and dangerous at worst. The most lofty policy objectives will be frustrated if efforts to accomplish them are based upon faulty or incomplete assessments of actual conditions. On the other hand, empirical research is also dependent upon normative considerations. Research in the national security field tends to be problem-oriented. Seldom are empirical studies initiated which are not motivated by some problem or issue.

CONTENDING ANALYTICAL FRAMEWORKS

Whatever may be the substantive purpose of research—strategic posture, force levels, reserve policy, balance-of-payments problems—a decision has to be made about the analytical framework to be used. The term "analytical framework"—often used interchangeably with terms like "theoretical scheme," "conceptual framework," or "model," among others—means a set of basic definitions, premises, and important variables used to describe the phenomenon to be studied, and a set of hypotheses which aid in explanation.

Thomas R. Dye[1] has identified six distinct analytical frameworks in the area of public policy analysis: systems theory, elite theory, group theory, rational decision-making theory, incrementalism, and institutionalism. James N. Rosenau,[2] focusing on the field of foreign policy, delineates frameworks somewhat differently and includes approaches emphasizing factors such as geography and other nonhuman characteristics of a nation, war potential, public opinion, elite characteristics, and national images.

The existence of these and other contending approaches to the question of how we describe and explain events in national security affairs adds to the burden of students who seek to understand the field. But the costs are worth it. Each analytical framework has distinctive advantages and, as might be expected, rather specific limitations. The quest for a single unifying framework that will both identify all critical factors *and* explain their behavior is very much a utopian enterprise, worthy but improbable.

The important fact to note about contending approaches to the study of national security is that they represent alternatives that make a difference. Different analytical frameworks emphasize the importance of different factors when examining a given aspect of national security behavior and offer different explanations for the patterns that are uncovered. Graham T. Allison illustrates this point in his account of the Cuban missile crisis of 1962.[3] Allison analyzed the missile crisis using three different analytical frameworks. Model I, the Rational Policy Model, conceives of events in foreign affairs as actions chosen by a nation or national government—portrayed as a rational, unitary decision-maker—that will maximize strategic goals and objectives. Model II, the Organizational Process Model, views events in international

politics as being the result of the actions taken by governmental organizations in response to the decisions of government leaders. This Model argues that most of the actions of organizations are based on a set of previously established procedures which leaders trigger when they make decisions. Model III, the Governmental (Bureaucratic) Politics Model, sees the actions of governments in international politics as being a result of the compromise, conflict, and confusion of officials who have diverse interests and unequal influence. That is, these decisions and actions are political results of bargaining along regularized channels among officials of the government rather than the results of efforts by officials to solve problems. Having used these three approaches, Allison learned that not only did the three models produce different explanations of the same happening, they also produced different explanations of rather different occurrences.

Different analytical frameworks provide different "lenses" with which to look at national security. Because different lenses may help sharpen our focus on certain aspects of national security and blur our view of other aspects, we must select the approach to be used with a clear sense of its limitations as well as its strengths. There may be wisdom in using several approaches. Allison judges that the three models used in his analysis complement each other and enrich the findings of his study. But research which draws upon several frameworks increases the complexity of conducting and evaluating the analysis. And there is the added danger that the use of several theoretical approaches may result in an unintended analysis of different phenomena instead of a deeper analysis of the same phenomenon. The costs and risks of using various analytical approaches must be assessed with care and with attention to the purposes and benefits sought from their use.

The purpose in proposing the Interorganizational Politics Model in this essay is not to suggest that Interorganizational Politics is superior necessarily to other approaches, but rather to offer it as an alternative. As is true of any analytical framework, the value of the approach can best be judged by its utility for those who might attempt to apply it.

The following pages will, first, discuss the principal concepts, hypotheses, and limitations of the interorganizational politics perspective; second, demonstrate the implications of this perspective as an approach to understanding the national security policy process; and finally, examine some tentative applications of the model to several national security policy issues and suggest some conclusions about interorganizational politics as an approach to inquiry.

INTERORGANIZATIONAL POLITICS AS AN ANALYTICAL FRAMEWORK

Ours is an organizational society in which all of the important decisions and actions in public life occur in the context of organizations. This fact constitutes the rationale for the Interorganizational Politics Model. This model proposes that the important decisions, events, and problems in national security can be described systematically and explained usefully by examining the behavior within and among organizations concerned with national security. The Senate Armed Services Committee, the XVIII Airborne Corps, the Office of Secretary of Defense, the White House Office, the Central Intelligence Agency, the RAND Corporation, the United States Navy, and the Joint Chiefs of Staff are all examples of such organizations. Some organizations, like the United States Navy, are very large and complex and include a number of component organizations. Others, like the Joint Chiefs of Staff, are simple, small-scale organizations which formally involve only a small number of people.

ORGANIZATIONS AND POLITICS

We tend to think of organizations in mechanistic terms, viewing them as systems of bureaucratic cogs and wheels that produce products or perform services and generally operate in predictable conformity to the intentions of their designers and managers. This sterile image of organizations, whether applied to bureaucratic organizations like our infantry battalion or to non-bureaucratic organizations like the Senate Foreign Relations Committee, obstructs our awareness that organizations are *political* in nature. They are political both in their internal workings and in the ways they interact with the individuals and organizations in their environment. Politics involves much more than elections and political parties. When individuals acquire and use power by making others dependent upon them, they are engaged in politics. These power-dependency relationships—politics—are characteristic of much of the behavior within and among organizations. Careers are advanced or destroyed, important policy commitments are adopted or rejected, battles are won or lost. Organizations use and abuse power in myriad ways as they make decisions, enforce preferences, and generate important consequences for their members and the larger society.

It is tempting to focus our attention on a single organization, such as the Department of Defense. However, as important as any particular organization may be, there are many situations where we would overlook critical aspects of national security if we limited our analysis to one organization. Few decisions of importance in national security rest with a single organization. Even the solitude of Presidential decisions is immersed in a swirl of prior consultations, observations, and risks which involve or take into account other organizations. We must think not only of organizations but of *interorganizations* as well. An interorganization is a cluster of components from several separate organizations which together shape national security as a result of their cooperative and conflictive interactions. Therefore, our approach requires a model that is sensitive to interorganizations and their organizational components as well as the political facets of their behavior.

ORGANIZATION AND INTERORGANIZATION: SOME CONCEPTUAL DISTINCTIONS[4]

An organization, for the purposes of this essay, is a purposive, partial, cooperative social system which exercises limited authority over the internal activities of organizational participants and acquires resources and disposes of its output of products or services based upon the legitimacy it is able to maintain in important parts of its environment. It is purposive in that it pursues limited stated objectives. It is a partial social system in that its activities—in terms of time and scope—involve only a part of the daily activities of organizational participants. It is a cooperative social system in that its proper functioning assumes cooperation among organizational participants. Its boundary as a separate organization is defined by the specified reach of its authority over the activities of organizational participants. The most important elements outside the organizational boundary are the organizations that comprise its "task environment."[5] Every organization depends upon its task environment for support in the form

of legitimacy, resources, and disposal of its output. Every organization stakes out a set of claims on its task environment for this support of functions and resources; these claims constitute that organization's "domain." Its ability to sustain acceptance of the legitimacy of these claims regarding domain by these other organizations is "domain consensus."[6]

Organizations tend to be composed of subunits because of technological constraints (which require that tasks be performed in certain sequences), physical constraints (limits of human endurance or of space), and cognitive constraints (limits on the individual's mental capacity to calculate all risks, explore all alternatives, and acquire and process all relevant information— Simon calls this "bounded rationality"[7]). These constraints produce a division of labor in organizations, which not only divides tasks among organizational participants, but also divides the entire organization into subunits. In unitary organizations subunits have little autonomy. Other organizations, such as General Motors or the Department of Defense, are "federal organizations"[8] in which the organization is a virtual holding-company composed of fairly autonomous subunits.

Despite the relative autonomy of subunits in federal organizations, they are not the same as an interorganization. Like an organization, an interorganization is a purposive, partial, social system. But it differs in two important respects: conflict and authority.

Conflict is a basic premise of interorganizations. Separate organizations are necessary when there are conflicting values in society and each of these conflicting values is desired. Different organizations for different values facilitate the protection of these several values in spite of the conflict that may ensue. For example, even though the relations between the Federal Bureau of Investigation and a critical newspaper may be conflictive, the existence of these separate organizations facilitates both internal security and freedom of the press. If the conflict between them is ameliorated by structural integration—making each a "cooperative" subunit of the same organization—the result may be that one of these values is sacrificed, as when a police agency seizes control of a newspaper.

Authority is concerned with the right to command and the duty to obey. But in an interorganization there is no "right to command"; the superordinate-subordinate relationship is absent. What gives interorganizational leadership the leverage to achieve cooperation from separate and essentially conflictive organizations? The answer is a kind of "marriage of convenience" that can be called *supradomain*. Recall that organizational domain means an orientation on the part of organizational elites toward other organizations with respect to certain functions and the resources needed to accomplish these functions. Supradomain is likewise an orientation by organizational elites in terms of other organizations with respect to functions and resources. The difference is that in an interorganization, organizational elites are staking out a joint claim, the elites acknowledge that they—and subunits of their organizations—are involved with other organizations in sharing a social function, like national security, and the resources needed to support it.

Elites are members of separate organizations who have high status roles in their respective organizations. Acknowledgment by elites—in each organization associated with an interorganization—of sharing the social function and the supporting elements is reflected in (1) their expression and elaboration of official goals which are directed toward support of the shared function, and (2) their assignment of people to interfacing roles which have responsibilities for monitoring and representing each organization's commitment to the shared function.

An example may enhance the clarity of this necessarily tortured syntax. There is in the federal government a collection of interacting independent formal organizations known as the "intelligence community." Harry Howe Ransom comments on this formal interorganization:

> A score of government agencies today are engaged in foreign intelligence work in one form or another. But the principal members of the national intelligence community are the National Security Council and its staff adjunct, the Central Intelligence Agency; the Department of Defense, whose intelligence functions are performed by the armed services, the Joint Staff, and the National Security Agency; the Department of State; the Atomic Energy Commission; and the Federal Bureau of Investigation.[9]

The appropriate supradomain here is the social function of national security intelligence and the organizational elements and resources involved in its collection, direction, production, evaluation and interpretation, dissemination, and security. The elites of each of the organizations mentioned by Ransom see their organizations as having a share in this supradomain. Of course, the boundaries of the formal interorganization that encompass the intelligence supradomain tend to incorporate specialized subunits and personnel rather than entire organizations: not the Department of State but its Bureau of Intelligence and Research; not the Department of Defense but the Defense Intelligence Agency and the Office of Naval Intelligence, among others. And the personnel in ONI know that they—together with DIA and State's Bureau of Intelligence and Research, among others—share an involvement with the intelligence function in a system of authority, responsibilities, conflict, and cooperation.

WHAT IS IMPORTANT?

One task of a model is to provide a language with which to talk about the object of study. The variables of the Interorganizational Politics Model introduced below constitute a checklist of the most important characteristics of organizations *and* interorganizations. They apply to both types of systems so that we can highlight some differences between the two and still develop common explanatory hypotheses to account for what we find in the process of national security.

1. *Goals.*[10] What are the official goals: general statements of purpose set forth in enabling documents, charters, annual reports, other public statements? What are the operational goals: decisions about alternative ways of achieving official goals and the priority of multiple goals, actual operating politics, unofficial goals pursued by various subunits? How are these goals factored or subdivided?

2. *Authority Structure.* How specific are assignments of responsibility? On what grounds are the rights of different key individuals and organizational components to exercise authority made legitimate? Over what specific objects is there a right to exercise authority (people, resources, information, etc.)? How is authority distributed?

3. *Communications Structure.*[11] What is the pattern (direction and distribution) of communications in the interorganization? On what criteria are messages filtered? How intense, stable, and frequent are the flows of information? On what bases and by what means do messages cross the boundaries among organizations?

4. *Control Structure.*[12] Who actually controls events in the interorganization and has the power (if not the right or authority) to compel compliance with his or their preferences and to influence the premises of decision-making? How is the capacity to control events distributed? What means (normative, utilitarian, or physical sanctions and rewards) facilitate the capacity of various components or interface leaders to control events? What

principal events were controlled during the process? Is there conflict among those who control events; what are the bases of the conflict?

5. *Task Structure.*[13] What principal types of technology are employed: long-linked (characterized by serial interdependence, e.g., tank assembly line); mediating (characterized by pooled interdependence involving the linking of environmental actors, e.g., combat operations center); or intensive (characterized by reciprocal interdependence involving the application of techniques to an object which requires feedback from the object itself, e.g., the Executive Committee of the National Security Council during the Cuban missile crisis)? How routinized or nonroutinized are the techniques being used?

6. *Environment.*[14] With what environmental organizations does the interorganization interact? What are the reasons for this interaction (resources, information, domain concerns)? How dependent is the interorganization upon each of these other organizations? Has a stable supradomain consensus been established among the interorganizational components; between the interorganization and its environment? Is there conflict or cooperation in the typical interactions of the interorganization with environmental organizations? What are the reasons for this? How stable are the interorganization-environment interactions?

7. *Leadership Strategy.* Do important organizational elites attempt to sustain, reduce, or expand the access and participation of subordinates, superiors, peers, and outsiders in defining objectives, determining the means employed to move toward these objectives, and assessing the results of interorganizational objectives? Do interface leaders, who link the components of the interorganization, endeavor to expand or suppress the conflictive tendencies among components?

POLAR EXAMPLES: PARABUREAUCRATIC AND PARAPOLITICAL IDEAL-TYPES

The patterned interaction of two or more interdependent individuals, where they have some defined expectations about the functions of each other, is an organization. Similarly, an inter-organization is the patterned inter-action of two or more interdependent components of different organizations which have mutual expectations about the functions of each other. The relationships among the variables discussed in the preceding section can be described in terms of ideal-types.

The theoretical literature on organizations describes the patterned interaction of single organizations in terms of bureaucratic and nonbureaucratic ideal-types. Ideal-types are descriptions of behavior patterns which accentuate several elements of reality that are integrated into a single analytical portrait. The purposes of ideal-types are to provide a basis for comparison and a set of expectations about the relationships among important variables. We may never find a situation in the real world that fits precisely the pattern of characteristics found in an ideal-type, but we can expect a close approximation in individual cases.[15] The bureaucratic ideal-type portrays a highly rational and objective hierarchical organization with well-defined tasks and division of labor that operates with machine-like efficiency; the non-bureaucratic ideal-type[16] visualizes a loosely structured team-like organization with fluid definitions of tasks and responsibilities and no permanent hierarchy.

The bureaucratic and nonbureaucratic ideal-types highlight the polar characteristics of the variables under consideration; each variable in fact would form a continuum if measured in terms of a large number of actual organizations. But the variables are dichotomized at their polar extremes in order to serve the purposes of the ideal-types, which is to accentuate and differentiate major patterns.

Ideal-types can also be developed to reflect patterns found in interorganizations. What follows is a description of two ideal-types, the *parabureaucratic* and the *parapolitical,* which include variables shared by both organizations and interorganizations. The use of common variables facilitates efforts to develop an integrated framework for analysis and explanation. A useful analytical framework should allow us to move easily between the similarities shared by the organizational and inter-organizational levels without obscuring the key differences between levels. These ideal-types describe the relationships among the structural variables: authority, communications, control and tasks. Goals, leadership, and environment will be discussed in the next section which deals with theoretical premises.

Ideal-Type Interorganizations

Parabureaucratic	Parapolitical
1. Authority Structure:	
a. Specification of rights and responsibilities for each position. Elites determine assignments to authoritative positions.	a. Specific rights and responsibilities de-emphasized; instead, the emphasis is placed on the broader obligation of each actor to contribute and assume authority to the extent that his skills are relevant to current needs.
b. Stable hierarchical distribution of authoritative positions.	b. Fluid network distribution of authoritative positions with shifting centers of authority.
c. Legitimate exercise of authority tends to be specialized as to type of object (people, resources, and information).	c. Legitimate exercise of authority is open-ended as to type of object.

Parabureaucratic	Parapolitical
2. Communications Structure:	
a. Communication is vertical and bidirectional in a hierarchical pattern.	a. Communication is lateral and multidirectional in a network pattern.
b. Information is concentrated at the upper levels of the authority structure.	b. Information widely distributed throughout the authority network; some concentration at the current authority center.
c. Messages are filtered and channeled on the basis of job criteria associated with specific authoritative positions.	c. Messages are filtered and channeled on the basis of actors' skills and the demands of current problems.
d. Information flows are stable.	d. Information flows are mixed.
e. Style of communication is similar to that found in superordinate-subordinate relationships.	e. Style of communication is similar to that found in advisor-advisee relationships.
3. Control Structure:	
a. Local influentials have greater access to control mechanisms.	a. Cosmopolitan influentials have greater access to control mechanisms.
b. Control is distributed hierarchically.	b. Control is distributed throughout the network with shifting centers of dominance.
c. Utilitarian means are primary bases of compliance.	c. Normative means are primary bases of compliance.
d. Conflict is limited and resolved by authoritative decisions of those in superordinate positions.	d. Conflict is moderate to high and resolved by collegial bargaining.
4. Task Structure:	
a. Clearly defined tasks.	a. Poorly defined tasks.
b. Tasks are routine and performed in a stable working situation.	b. Tasks are nonroutine and performed in an unstable working situation.
c. Long-linked or mediating technologies.	c. Intensive technologies.

The parabureaucratic and parapolitical ideal-types reflect approximate analogues to bureaucratic and nonbureaucratic systems. That is, a parabureaucratic interorganization reflects routinized decisions, rationality, and mechanistic structure. A parapolitical interorganization, on the other hand, is characterized by nonroutine decisions, affectivity, and fluid or organic structure.[17]

BASIC PREMISES AND HYPOTHESES

The variables discussed earlier identify and describe the most important factors at work in interorganizational politics. The two ideal-types give us a basis for anticipating and comparing alternative patterns of relationships among these variables. That is, we would expect to find that interorganizations and their organizational components (subunits) will tend to resemble one or the other of these two patterns. But what premises about social behavior are at the foundation of these ideal-type relationships and what hypotheses might help us account for the actual patterns of interorganizational politics that we find in the arena of national security?

The theoretical literature concerning organizational behavior is too vast and diverse to summarize in this essay. But several working premises and hypotheses can be derived from the literature in order to refine our expectations about national security phenomena and help us account for the patterns that emerge.[18] I have defined earlier in this essay a number of key concepts, introduced premises that are basic to the Interorganizational Politics Model, and proposed some hypotheses. What follows will highlight some key premises and hypotheses that can be used as a basis for discussing the relationships among individual, organizational, and interorganizational behavior in the model or used to refine hypotheses that can be tested empirically.

1. Individual Behavioral Premises
  a. Individuals are rational in that

they pursue self-interest and make choices on the basis of subjective utility functions. When making choices among perceived alternatives, they will choose the alternative which yields higher perceived utility.

b. There are cognitive limits on individual rationality; that is, individuals are subject to bounded rationality which limits their ability to acquire and process information, calculate risks, and identify and evaluate alternatives and their consequences.

c. Individuals avoid uncertainty and dislike ambiguity.

d. Individuals seek satisfactory (good enough) solutions to problems rather than maximum (best possible) solutions.

2. Organizational Hypotheses

a. Organizations sustain themselves by maintaining contributions-inducements equilibria: they balance the demands they impose upon those who make *contributions* to organizational needs with sufficient *inducements* to maintain their contributions.

b. Organizations consist of coalitions of individuals. Coalitions tend to conform to the formal boundaries of subunits.

c. Every organization has one coalition which is dominant. Composition of the dominant coalition will change in response to environmental and technological uncertainties.

d. Changes in organizational dependencies threaten some coalitions and make others possible.

e. Organizations have internally inconsistent goals; they engage in quasi-resolution of conflict. Organizations factor (subdivide) organization goals into subgoals and assign the subgoals to subunits. Because subunit goals may not be consistent with official goals

of the total organization, latent conflict persists.

f. Organizations avoid uncertainty by emphasizing short-run or pressing problems at the expense of planning and the development of long-run strategies.

g. Organizations are neither curious nor do they seek to understand. Instead, they engage in problemistic search; that is, they search for new information or new alternatives in order to control deviant behavior or to solve problems. They do not search until a "fire" breaks out.

h. Information processing in organizations is characterized by uncertainty absorption. As information is passed from subunit to subunit, inferences are drawn from the evidence and the inferences rather than the evidence are then transmitted to the next subunit. These successive editing steps involving selective perceptions guided by individual and subunit goal commitments lead to considerable distortion.

i. Organizations will act to protect the technological requirements for accomplishing organizational goals from environmental contingencies.

j. When organizations commit future control over resources in exchange for present solutions to contingencies, they limit their ability to adapt to future change.

k. Organizations in stable task environments seek to demonstrate fitness for future support by demonstrating historical improvement.

l. Organizations in dynamic task environments seek to demonstrate fitness for future support by scoring favorably on assessment criteria in relation to comparable organizations.

m. To the extent that boundary-spanning actors can contain environmental contingencies and to the extent that the contingencies are important to the organization, the individual is powerful in the bargaining process. (Boundary-spanning actors link the organization with its task environment.)

3. Interorganizational Hypotheses

a. Organizational coalitions are components of interorganizations.

b. Every organization is likely to be oriented to several supradomains and to provide components (its subunit coalitions) to several interorganizations. Since a given organization may have orientations toward many societal functions (e.g., national security, air transport, mass communications) and related supportive resources which could be shared with other organizations, we can characterize organizations as having multiple overlays of different supradomains.

c. The more an orientation toward a supradomain is shared by elites from different organizations, the greater the degree of supradomain consensus.

d. Interface leaders—actors who link the boundaries among the components of an interorganization—who broaden access to participation, bring in new people and new ideas, and stimulate opportunities for confrontations of viewpoints will stimulate innovation within interorganizations.

e. Conflict-expanding interface leaders promote shifts towards the parapolitical ideal-type.

f. Conflict-constraining interface leaders promote shifts toward the parabureaucratic ideal-type.

LIMITATIONS OF THE MODEL

It is both premature and presumptuous for me to comment on the limitations of the Interorganizational Politics Model: premature because the relative newness of the model means that it has not had the advantage of much criticism nor has it been tested extensively in empirical research; presumptuous because my readers are fully capable of identifying its shortcomings without the benefit of my help. I will risk these two hazards and suggest several limitations that are evident to me.

First, the hypotheses need further refinement and operationalization before they can be subjected to the rigorous testing needed for development of the model.

Second, further conceptual refinement and empirical testing of the model requires a more empirically rooted concept of social function. Social function is the foundation upon which the notion of supradomain rests and, indeed, is the glue that holds together the idea of an interorganization. At this time, there is no conceptual basis or empirical referent that is entirely satisfactory for identifying an exhaustive list of social functions. The number of social functions and the meaning of each is limited only by the creative ability of man to manufacture terms and describe their referents. For example, just one social function—national security—has defied the efforts of scholars to reach a consensus on its definition. Social theorists have provided us with little more than broad and imprecise concepts of social function.

Third, the level of an interorganization may make a difference in the resulting patterns of behavior. For example, the informal suspension of hostilities between the front-line units of opposing armies may yield different patterns than the interactions which characterize the military-industrial complex in the United States. The size or number of participants in an interorganization also may make a difference. The hypotheses do not account for such variations.

Fourth, there is the danger that analogies drawn from individual, organizational, and interorganizational levels may obscure important differences.

Finally, I have drawn upon hypotheses and concepts from a variety of kinds of organizational studies. It is possible that my process of derivation may have obscured some basic differences in the meaning of these concepts. I have tried to minimize this possibility by drawing upon studies from a shared theoretical tradition.

POLICY PROCESS AND INTERORGANIZATIONAL POLITICS

The Interorganizational Politics Model requires much refinement in the way of conceptual development, the formulation of testable hypotheses, and rigorous application to the study of national security. This is a very early statement of the model. Its potential rests on the case that can be made for its utility in facilitating understanding of the vast complexity of national security affairs. A modest first cut can be made at exploring the implications of the model by using it to examine the national security policy process.

There is probably no area of public policy that is as important—in terms of manpower, money, and resources—or evokes as much public controversy as national security. Nor is any area of public life as difficult to analyze. Part of the analytical problem is the extreme secrecy that surrounds many of the important deliberations involving national security. Far more important than secrecy, however, is the bewildering complexity and pervasiveness associated with this process. The President, Congress, FBI, Veterans Administration, Department of State, the huge Department of Defense and the armed forces, state militia, and aerospace and defense industries constitute only a partial list of the numerous participants in national security policy. Every institution in American society has linkages into this policy process. Some commentators view this system of national security-related organizations—the Military Industrial Complex—as the dominant institution in the United States. And some other observers argue that "American society does not contain a military-industrial complex conceived of as an entity, but is rather best conceived of as *itself* a military-industrial complex."[19]

The Interorganizational Politics Model can be used to analyze the policy process in the context of five elements: (1) goals and value protection, (2) policy elaboration, (3) strategy and implementation structure, (4) programming, and (5) societal impacts and feedback. These elements may be thought of as tasks which are performed by an interorganization as a contribution to the formulation or implementation of national security policy. They are not to be viewed as sequential stages or phases of the policy process. If someone were to seek to impose a kind of comprehensive rationality on the policy process, it might make sense to place these elements in serial order. But the reality of national security policy does not reflect such ordering. To one degree or another, these elements are simultaneously operative throughout the national security system.

The organizational components actually involved in the activities associated with each element would depend upon the specific policy issue being handled by a given interorganization. Policy consideration of surveillance of civilian political candidates by military intelligence units might include: Subcommittee on Constitutional Rights, Senate Judiciary Committee; Washington Chapter, American Civil Liberties Union; the Civil Rights Division, Department of Justice; and the Counter-Intelligence Analysis Division, Headquarters U.S. Army, to name a few possibilities. My discussion of the policy elements will draw broadly from various substantive areas of national security in order to illuminate the model rather than focus on a particular policy issue.

These comments about the elements of policy process will indicate some expectations about the relevance of the ideal-types for each element. The operating characteristics of each element reflect somewhat different requirements that can be related to the parabureaucratic and parapolitical types. Also, the characteristics of the elements suggest a number of implications for the explanatory power of the model.

GOALS AND VALUE PROTECTION

The clusters of national priorities within the society make claims on the authoritative decision-making apparatus of the political system. It is with this element that the maximum expression of the conflictive traits of interorganizations are likely to be found. The conflicting values of the various organizational components concerned with national security will be brought to bear in order to facilitate the protection of these several values. The interorganizational patterns involved in this element are likely to be highly parapolitical. Decisions typically are nonroutine; interpersonal relations are characterized by affectivity; and the interorganizational structure will be fluid and shifting.

If this element exists in the context of crisis, supradomain consensus may be subject to deterioration with emphasis on short-run expedients. This being the case, a heavy burden will fall to interface leadership to maintain the interorganization and to move toward appropriate decisions. Conflict and uncertainty about supradomain consensus may promote problemistic search but freeze innovative choices. Wilensky argues that "the greater the costs and risks or uncertainty and the more significant the changes in method and

goals involved, the more intense is the search for information. But the stronger, too, is the weight of established policy and vested interests."[20]

The protection of the values implicit in the goal choices made set a foundation upon which the policy process acquires operational meaning. These goals and priorities give a sense of direction to interface leaders who are entrusted with political responsibility for national security and become a general standard against which to measure the performance of the given interorganization.

POLICY ELABORATION

This element is the source of activity from which public goals and general plans for action become concrete as an interorganizational response to the converging imperatives of political demands, expressions of policy support, and feedback from ongoing programs. The interorganizational pattern of this element is essentially parapolitical although hints of parabureaucratic traits become visible, generally limited to the communications structure. It is around this policy element that appropriations and program authorizations begin to be hammered out in hearings; and informal exchanges among legislative aides, agency staff, and interest group representatives put flesh on the bones of general policy commitments. At this point the interactions among organizational components become most integrated; but they may begin to promote conflict with other subunits within each respective organization.

This element tends to operate at what might be characterized as the "assistant secretary level," where the leaders of subunits from various organizations negotiate the plans, resource requirements, and mission responsibilities that will be assumed by their organizations. This element probably reflects a maximum level of supradomain consensus. However, a gap may emerge between supradomain consensus and domain consensus. The fact that there is a stable supradomain consensus which checks conflict and change among the subunits of different organizations comprising an interorganization does not mean that other subunits in each organization are not changing their commitments or beginning to perceive threats to their domains. These events can in turn stimulate conflict or alter the relationships among the organizations. The goal inconsistencies in every organization which are attributable to the quasi-resolution of conflict phenomenon can reinforce this problem. Interface leadership in this instance focuses more attention on conflict-constraint within organizations than on interorganizational maintenance tasks.

STRATEGY AND IMPLEMENTATION STRUCTURE

The business of this element centers on the rationalization of the plans and resources that have been designed, organized, and assigned to give operational expression to the national security policies that have been enunciated. One facet of this task is to evaluate the extent to which the action strategies (strategic policy, force planning, R & D, assistance, arms limitations, etc.) conform to the expectations of policy. Second is the issue of how well the organizational arrangements which are planned to implement policy are designed to mesh with and facilitate strategic plans. A third task related to this element arises out of the relationship between strategy and structure: have efforts to implement policy adequately calculated the political and structural prerequisites for the successful application of alternative strategies?

This element is a mixture of the parabureaucratic and parapolitical ideal-types. The strongest inroads by parabureaucratic traits lie in the area of control: the interorganizational control network tends to break down.

Efforts by interface leaders and interorganizational components to align general policies (which are subject to various interpretations) with the specifics of strategies and structures (to which organizations have made explicit commitments) is likely to be viewed by organizational elites as challenges to their organizational domain. Interface leadership enters a delicate mode of activity. For example, staff from the Government Operations Committee of the Senate and the Office of Management and Budget begin to probe a cost overrun on the development of a new strategic weapon; the contractor and the Air Force view this as unwarranted interference in their shared domain. The problemistic search syndrome caused the contractor and the Air Force to ignore certain symptoms to which the others were sensitive. Consequently, interface leadership had to tighten the reins and try to limit organizational discretion.

PROGRAMMING

The tasks here focus on the organizational processes at work in the daily conduct of national security programs. Of central importance is the analysis of factors which facilitate or inhibit the successful adaptation of these programs to changing professional, technical, and political demands in the operating milieu of those in organizations who have program responsibilities. Symbols and sources of diffuse normative support for programs, maintenance of support by policy-makers, feedback from clientele and adversaries, professionalism, technological innovation, and diffusion of decision-making innovations all have impact for those engaged in the programming element.

Programming likely attains the maximum degree of parabureaucratic characteristics that is possible, given the nature of interorganizations. Routinized decisions, instrumental rationality oriented very explicitly toward stated goals, and a mechanistic structural pattern are to be expected. This routinization of decision-making and the mechanistic structural characteristics also imply high congruency between organizational domain and the supradomain of the interorganization. Such tight control by interorganizational leaders would not be possible without the perception on the part of organizational elites that domain claims and supradomain claims were complementary, if not reinforcing. Interface leaders—who may be the elites of the more powerful organizations in the national security system—would probably attempt to restrict participation by "outsiders" in programming, to recruit or promote people wedded to the local orthodoxy, and to restrain the visibility of new ideas. This will reinforce the orderliness and predictability of interorganizational behavior up to the maximum of supradomain consensus.

SOCIETAL IMPACTS AND FEEDBACK

This element is concerned with the principal consequences of the operation of the policy process for social, political, and economic institutions and how and with what effect these consequences are communicated to other elements of the national security policy process.

The complex nature of the tasks encompassed by this policy element requires a highly parapolitical type of interorganization. Supradomain consensus is likely to be unstable. The extent of its instability will depend upon the strategies adopted by interface leaders and the configuration of the environment which the interorganization must confront.

Given the limits of supradomain consensus, we may expect that interface leadership will broaden access to participation in decision-making, bring in new people and new ideas, provoke opportunities for the confrontation of viewpoints. While this mode of leadership strategy will be destabilizing, it will also promote the adoption of innovations within the policy process.

The environment of an interorganization consists of symbols, individuals, and other organization-interorganization clusters. The most important part of the environment of an interorganization is its configuration: the level of connectedness or interdependence it has with the organizations in its environment. Drawing upon the notion of the causal texture of organizational environments found in Emery and Trist,[21] we can identify four types of configuration. Type 1 is the *placid, randomized environment* in which organizations are unrelated or, at most, loosely related. Such organizations can exert little influence on others so they are not likely to be destabilizing. Type 2 is the *placid, clustered environment* in which many organizations are connected with each other. This environment is slightly destabilizing because the interorganization will have to calculate the unanticipated consequences of their action. Type 3 is the *disturbed-reactive environment* and is moderately destabilizing because environmental organizations interact as competitors which are motivated to hinder other organizations. Finally, Type 4 has a texture of *turbulent fields*. This makes for a highly destabilizing environment because it is characterized by a gross level of uncertainty and, increasingly, the threat of the unexpected is constant.

THE MODEL AND POLICY ADVICE

The preceding section provided some indications of the application of the Interorganizational Politics Model as an aid in understanding the *process* of national security policy. Hopefully,

further refinements of this model will lead to more adequate grounds for describing and explaining the process.

What of the *substance* of national security policy? Can the model shed light on the problems and alternatives that are to be faced and provide a basis for advising policy-makers? The answer is yes, but there are two important qualifications. First, the model cannot select the basic norms that should be used to guide the decisions of policy-makers. These are choices to be made by the political processes of the society and are clearly outside the scope of an empirical model. Second, it cannot predict specific events and thereby eliminate uncertainty from the deliberations of policy-makers. Like all other social science models, it deals with statements of tendencies or probabilities.

The value of the model for the substance of policy is that it places a tool in the hands of the policy-maker that helps him do two things. First, it helps him see the interconnectedness of the organizations that help shape his choices and receive the impacts of those same choices. He becomes aware that a far larger number and variety of organizations have a stake in his decisions. Policy decisions are made in the light of certain value premises—rooted in the goals of the decision-maker and his perceptions of the goals of those who will feel the impact of his decisions—and certain informational premises. The latter is a product of the efforts of the policy-maker to search out data to guide his decision together with the information provided by others who have an interest in the choices made. The model can stimulate the policy-maker to reassess these premises in response to his new awareness that his decisions involve a much more extensive and complex network of interested participants.

A second payoff for the policy-maker who uses the model is that it helps sensitize him to the systematic biases that are built into the interorganizational network in which he operates. He is alerted to the rigidities of para-bureaucratic systems, the potential for information distortion, the latent conflict between organizational elites and

interorganizational components, and the predisposition to focus on the short-run and ignore longer-term planning, among others.

The model also provides some analytical leverage on the substance of specific policy problems. For example, the role of the military in American society has been a source of growing concern in the past ten years or more. Fears of militarism, arguments that excessive defense spending deprives domestic programs of resources, and claims that a military-industrial complex rules the country have characterized public debate in recent years. Whatever the validity of these charges, the point is that our institutional response to this issue has tended to rely upon the tradition of formal civilian control of the military. The premise supporting this response is that militaristic norms are confined to one large organization, the military services. As long as the members of that organization are kept in check by their civilian "bosses," we are in no danger. The Interorganizational Politics Model raises doubts about the civilian control thesis. The model is sensitive to the network of interorganizational relationships among military and civilian organizations which lend support to military norms. The model facilitates questions about the factors that reinforce the interpenetration of military and civilian sectors and helps identify strategies to cope with these boundary problems.

To sum up, the Interorganizational Politics Model appears to be useful as a partial guide to the assessment of substantive policy issues. Policy-makers need substantive advice at two levels. At one level, their concern is with the evaluation of very specific decisions such as weapon systems and force levels. Cost-benefit analysis and other decision technologies are useful here. It is at the other level that the model comes into play. Here three broader political questions interest the policy-maker. First, is there an occasion for policy-making at this time? The model helps answer this question due to its attentiveness to shifting coalition relationships which affect the state of supradomain consensus. Second, he is interested in the political consequences for himself of choosing among different alternatives. The model recognizes the impermanent character of support for the multiple goals that are sustained by the interorganization. His decision might disrupt that support and also jeopardize his role as an interface leader. The third question asks if he can achieve the impact he intended by choosing a particular policy alternative. This is a matter of his securing control over access to appropriate organizational components and being sufficiently powerful vis-à-vis those components to gain support for the goals embodied in the new policy decision. The model is useful here because it guides him in examining the structures of interorganizational authority and control in order to ascertain the opportunities they provide to accomplish desired impacts.

NOTES

1. Thomas R. Dye, *Understanding Public Policy* (Engelwood Cliffs, N.J.: Prentice-Hall, 1972).

2. James N. Rosenau, *The Scientific Study of Foreign Policy* (New York: The Free Press, 1971), pp. 96–97.

3. Graham T. Allison, *Essence of Decision: Explaining the Cuban Missile Crisis* (Boston: Little, Brown and Company, 1971).

4. This conceptualization was developed originally in Philip S. Kronenberg, "Micropolitics and Public Planning: A Comparative Study of the Interorganizational Politics of Planning," Ph.D. dissertation, University of Pittsburgh, April 1969.

5. William R. Dill, "Environment as an Influence on Managerial Autonomy," *Administrative Science Quarterly*, 2 (March 1958), 409–443.

6. Sol Levine and Paul E. White, "Exchange as a Conceptual Framework for the Study of Interorganizational Relationships," *Administrative Science Quarterly*, 5 (March 1961), 583–584.

7. Herbert A. Simon, *Models of Man: Social and Rational* (New York: John Wiley & Sons, Inc., 1957).

8. Herbert A. Simon, Donald W. Smithburg, and Victor A. Thompson, *Public Administration* (New York: Alfred A. Knopf, 1950), pp. 268–270.

9. Harry Howe Ransom, *Central Intelligence and National Security* (Cambridge, Mass.: Harvard University Press, 1958), p. 94.

10. The considerations regarding goals are based to a large degree on Charles Perrow, "Analysis of Goals in Complex Organizations," *American Sociological Review*, 26 (December 1961), 854–866.

11. An important source of ideas about this variable is Harold L. Wilensky, *Organizational Intelligence: Knowledge and Policy in Government and Industry* (New York: Basic Books, Inc., 1967).

12. Concern with this variable is based heavily on two works of Amitai Etzioni: *A Comparative Analysis of Complex Organizations: On Power, Involvement, and Their Correlates* (New York: The Free Press, 1961); and "Organizational Control Structure," in James G. March, ed., *Handbook of Organizations* (Chicago: Rand McNally & Company, 1965), pp. 650–677.

13. Conceptualization of this variable is based on Tom Burns and G. M. Stalker, *The Management of Innovation* (London: Tavistock Publications, 1961); Charles Perrow, "A Framework for the Comparative Analysis of Organizations," *American Sociological Review*, 32 (April 1967), 194–208; and James D. Thompson, *Organizations in Action: Social Science Bases of Administrative Theory* (New York: McGraw-Hill Book Company, 1967).

14. Dill first coined "task environment." William R. Dill, "Environment as an Influence on Managerial Autonomy," *Administrative Science Quarterly*, 2 (March 1958), 409–443.

15. Max Weber, *The Methodology of the Social Sciences*, trans. and ed. Edward A. Shils and Henry A. Finch (Glencoe, Ill.: The Free Press, 1949), p. 90.

16. Larry Kirkhart, "Toward a Theory of Public Administration," in Frank Marini, ed., *Toward a New Public Administration: The Minnowbrook Perspective* (Scranton: Chandler Publishing Company, 1971), 156–161.

17. The essence of these two ideal-types goes back to a long tradition of roughly similar distinctions which can be traced at least to Ferdinand Tönnies, *Gemeinschaft und Gesellschaft* (Leipzig: 1887; Berlin: K. Curtius, 1926); later published in English as Ferdinand Tönnies, *Community and Society*, trans. Charles P. Loomis (East Lansing, Mich.:

Michigan State University Press, 1957). Three contemporary sources that bear the earmarks of the same tradition, from which I draw heavily for the list of parabureaucratic and parapolitical characteristics, are Burns and Stalker, *loc. cit.*; Burton R. Clark, "Inter-organizational Patterns in Education," *Administrative Science Quarterly*, 10 (September 1965), 224–237; and Perrow, "A Framework for the Comparative Analysis of Organizations," *loc. cit.*

18. These premises and hypotheses are derived, in large measure, from a core of theoretical works on organizational behavior: Richard M. Cyert and James G. March, *A Behavioral Theory of the Firm* (Englewood Cliffs, N.J.: Prentice-Hall, Inc., 1963); James G. March and Herbert A. Simon, *Organizations* (New York: John Wiley & Sons, Inc., 1958); and James D. Thompson, *Organizations in Action* (New York: McGraw-Hill Book Company, 1967).

19. Jerome Slater and Terry Nardin, "The Concept of a Military-Industrial Complex." Paper presented at the 1971 Conference of the Inter-University Seminar on Armed Forces and Society, Chicago, November 19, 1971, p. 5.

20. Wilensky, *op. cit.*, p. 78.

21. F. E. Emery and E. L. Trist, "The Causal Texture of Organizational Environments," *Human Relations*, 18 (February 1965), 21–32.

An Introduction to the Study
of National Security

Frank N. Trager
Frank L. Simonie

INTRODUCTION

The phrase "national security," as Arnold Wolfers long ago pointed out, is an "ambiguous symbol."[1] Although Wolfers made this observation about the government policy area called "national security," it could be applied with equal force to the growing academic field of national security studies. There has never been any real consensus among national security specialists and students as to just what intellectual territory lies within their field of interest. There are some topics like deterrence strategy and civil-military relations that nearly everyone agrees should be "in." Other more recently suggested topics like a general theory of political violence and revolution or domestic political coercion are still controversial. An expanding field has begun to cover so much academic ground—so many topics, sub-topics, and sub-sub-topics— that we are in danger of losing any corporate identity that national security studies may have built up over the past twenty-five years. The systematic study of national security phenomena may become seriously retarded through failure to define a coherent field of inquiry. The purpose of this essay is to suggest one approach to the study of national security. We do not expect to produce consensus where none has existed before, but hopefully we will contribute to a dialogue on the definition of national security studies that

may eventually result in some organization in the field.

The phrase "national security" refers both to a political-administrative process carried on by the governments of nation states and to the academic study of that process. While our purpose here is to describe the field of study, we cannot in any meaningful way divorce the study from the actual process. Without the process itself there would be nothing to study. We must, therefore, try to determine just what the basic nature of the national security process is and why it exists. We will then have a starting point, at least, for developing a coherent academic subject.

Our method is both pedagogically and substantively traditional. We will offer a working definition of the national security process and follow it with an elaboration of the important concepts in the definition. Since these central concepts are at the heart of the national security problem, we can define the field of study by including anything that is directly related to the central concepts. All else may be considered outside the field.

Substantively, our definition is based on four fundamental assumptions. First, we believe the independent nation state will continue to exist as the primary unit in international politics. Second, each nation state engages

35

in a more or less continuous assessment of its position in a world composed of many competing nation states. Each state will develop policy—which we call national security policy—to deal with its friends, its enemies, and potentially threatening situations.

Third, this policy is composed of ends and means; that is, each state tries to determine the kind of international system it would like to have and how such a system can be constructed. Our working definition will be concerned mostly with the ends of national security, though the means are obviously an important part of the subject. The means, or some of them, have been treated with relative thoroughness in national security studies as they exist now. This is, in fact, part of the current conceptual problem in the field. An overemphasis on the technique and details of national security operations has obscured the purpose of maintaining a national security system in the first place. We, therefore, feel that the first and most important question students of national security must try to answer is, "What is the ultimate objective of national security policy?"

Fourth, national security policy is mostly concerned with relations among independent nation states. But what of domestic problems like revolution, violent struggles for power, or *coups d'état*? Internal disorders can range along a spectrum from petty crime to full scale civil war. Most of this spectrum is obviously not a part of the national security process or national security studies. Yet, as we move toward the upper end of the spectrum, many domestic situations become indistinguishable from international conflicts and thereby take on the characteristics of national security problems. We suggest here two criteria for the inclusion of domestic conflict within the national security process. First, the ultimate objectives at stake in the conflict should be the same as those national security seeks to protect against foreign adversaries. The means employed in such a conflict should also be the same as would be employed against a foreign threat of similar scope and magnitude. Second, there is the special case of foreign involvement in internal politics. This may take many forms ranging from espionage to material support for insurrectionary movements. A borderline case is foreign financial support for domestic political parties or interest groups which may or may not be legal in any given country. All forms of foreign involvement tend to magnify internal unrest beyond its intrinsic importance and may create a serious threat to national security which did not exist before. This makes the foreign involvement situation pre-eminently a problem of national security.

THE ESSENCE OF NATIONAL SECURITY

We now turn to the concepts we believe are central to both the reality and the study of national security. As a working definition we propose the following:

National security is that part of government policy having as its objective the creation of national and international political conditions favorable to the protection or extension of vital national values against existing and potential adversaries.

The central concepts in this definition should be readily apparent, but some of their implications perhaps are not. It is necessary, therefore, to develop the central concepts in some detail.

GOVERNMENT POLICY

The first and simplest point to be made about national security is that it is a function of government, especially of central government. Since the passing of privateers and trading companies[2] who were chartered by governments, all operations directly concerned with national security have been carried on by governments. No private corporations work independently in the national security field, although in capitalist countries they may sell goods and services to government for use in national security. But there are no private entrepreneurs in national security.

In no other area of policy is the national government monopoly so complete. The decentralized, semi-private patterns evident in other areas of political life, particularly in the United States, are not duplicated in national security. In social welfare, for example, government programs at all levels share the field with private charitable institutions and foundations. In the American education system local governments predominate with some financial assistance from the federal government. There is also a large admixture of private schools and colleges. And, although delivery of the mail is usually thought of as a government monopoly, even the postal service shares its duties with private telegraph, parcel, and messenger services. Only national security has been concentrated exclusively in the hands of the central government.

Indeed, one school of political theory, derived from Thomas Hobbes, maintains that the original purpose of the social contract establishing the state was to release man from "that miserable condition of Warre" which derived from his fundamentally brutal nature.[3] Protection from domestic and foreign threats to security could be achieved only when a people created some sovereign authority to wield the power of the sword. The other functions of government have been added from time to time because government already existed and was organized to get things done on a national scale.

Whether or not one accepts the Hobbesian view, it is indisputable that central governments have always been tremendously concerned with protection of their peoples from foreign and related threats or with extension of national values abroad. There are two probable explanations for this. First, as we have seen, the central government has a natural and, today, an unchallengeable monopoly over national security. This means that the central government bears sole responsibility for achieving the objectives of the national security system. If the government fails in this responsibility, the nation itself may cease to exist in a political or even physical sense. There is no one else to carry the burden.

Second, history deals harshly with those governments that are unsuccessful in the pursuit of national security. They may be destroyed from without by some enemy state as was the French Third Republic. Or they may be overthrown from within as was the German Second Empire.[4] In either case the nation will have a new regime, probably one that can convince its subjects it will make more effective efforts to protect national values.

The overwhelming importance of central government in the national security process makes essential the study of the institutional apparatus through which governments carry on their national security functions. In national security the relationship between policy and administration is reciprocal and often quite complex. In one sense administrative structures are the creatures of policy; or to be more precise they are organized so as to best carry out the kinds of policy decisions governments anticipate in the foreseeable future. In another sense, however, administrative forms—organization and working procedures—have a major influence on the substance of policy. At every level of a complex organization, policy is subtly altered or modified as functionaries impose their own interpretations on the decisions and directives handed down from above. And, of course, the ability of the organizational structure to pass relevant data up to higher levels quickly and accurately will have an important effect on high level perceptions of situations and the impact of policy.

Underpinning the entire political-administrative framework are the legal and social premises on which organizations are based in any given social system. In the United States broad principles like the diffusion of power among competing groups and the desirability of decentralization sometimes result in a national security policy that is vague and inconsistent. The President must share power with both houses of Congress and with the courts. Even within the executive branch, policy-making is decentralized among the White House staff, the State Department, civilian defense officials, and the uniformed military. The military themselves are divided into four services with partially competing goals, interests, and policy proposals. In the U.S.S.R., Britain, or Germany different patterns of power relationships exist. A general familiarity, at least, with the political-administrative systems of those countries is necessary to understand their national security policies.

VITAL NATIONAL VALUES

The ultimate purpose of national security is to protect or extend certain national values which are considered "vital." In this sense "values" are taken to mean the most fundamental principles on which the social, political, and physical existence of the state are based. They may be derived from law, religion, the customs followed by independent states over time, or simply from human psychology. Such values are "vital" if their elimination or radical alteration would substantially change the character of the state or the political system within which it operates. The kinds of values a nation holds will, in theory, have a decisive influence on the shape of its international political and military posture.

The basic problem with a values-oriented approach to national security is that values are hard to define in the abstract and harder still to discuss in concrete terms. Values are vague political concepts because they can be so fundamental or so general as to mean everything or nothing. Often they are only dimly perceived and understood by the leaders who must base policy on them. Many ordinary citizens, possessing only a semi-conscious awareness that what is ultimately good for the country is good for themselves also, cannot articulate the fundamental values of their political existence. Despite these difficulties it is possible to identify a set of vital national values which appear and reappear with great frequency in the international arena. These values are found in different forms and with different emphases from country to country. The basic theme in each remains relatively constant, however.

The most common of the national values whose protection is the goal of national security is simply survival. Survival in one form or another is high on the list of values of nearly every independent country in history. One searches in vain for examples of independent countries that did not wish to survive. Austria at the time of the *Anschluss* in 1938 did voluntarily vote to surrender sovereign status, but Austrian sovereignty had been a construct of the victors at Versailles in the first place. When the allies recreated Austria after 1945, the Austrians gratefully accepted return of their sovereignty as a way of escaping the Nazi stigma. If any countries in history have not wished to survive, their desire has gone unrecorded. Such a country would probably soon pass out of existence as an independent political unit.

Survival, however, is not a simple unambiguous concept. Survival can mean different things to different people in different times; there are several forms of survival which might form the basis of a national security policy. Sheer physical survival—that is, assuring that the people of a society will continue to exist and live in some kind of proximity as an identifiable group—is the most fundamental. This type of survival was especially pressing as a basic value in the ancient world when entire defeated populations were put to the sword or sold into slavery. A failure of national security under those circumstances was likely to be fatal to citizens and governments alike. As populations increased during the medieval period, however, it became progressively less possible for a conqueror to think about killing or enslaving all the inhabitants of a defeated country. Survival as an ultimate value was amalgamated with other values and came to mean much more than simple physical survival. There is now a possibility, however, that the introduction of the nuclear weapon with its enormous destructive capability will cause a reversion to the earlier form of survival on the part of some states. Until an adequate defense against ballistic missiles is developed, we must reckon with the possibility that large populations on both sides in nuclear wars might be completely annihilated along with all their property. Since 1945, sheer physical survival has once more become relevant to the structure of national security values.

As we noted above, survival usually takes on other attributes besides sheer physical survival. This is commonly expressed in terms of ensuring the continuation of some other important values along with physical survival. These values—items of human experience regarded as necessary or desirable—become an acceptable or accepted consensus within a national social system. They are, by consent in a country such as the United States, institutionalized as highly regarded forms of social and political organization. For example, the language of the United States Declaration of Independence, the Preamble and first ten amendments of the Constitution describes the basic structure and functions of government in the American system and enumerates the rights—in our terms, the values—of the citizen under law. These include a government of limited powers, free elections, personal liberties such as speech and religion, the legal safeguards usually associated with the concept of due process of law, and others. In other states and social systems survival may involve protection of an institutionalized theory of social and economic development; maintenance of the political supremacy of a certain class, religion, or racial group; continuation of a ruling dynasty or oligarchy; there are many others. In each of these cases, survival means survival of an entire constellation of basic values.

This broader somewhat normative conception of survival can cause a serious dilemma for the national security process because it may conflict at some points with the requirements for physical survival. In other words, there may be a question whether national survival includes survival of the particular regime or type of regime in power.[5] There are three possible resolutions to this problem: 1) physical survival is paramount and all other values are subordinate; 2) the particular regime in power may be sacrificed as long as its replacement maintains the general character of the old regime (democratic, socialist, Marxist, etc.); and 3) the particular regime in power must be saved at all costs. In both the second and third possibilities, survival of other values achieves status equal or superior to physical survival. In both cases, statesmen may have to make the choice between risking physical annihilation and sacrificing a particular form of government or particular regime.

There is no easy way to choose among these three alternatives. Though there have been regimes willing to sacrifice themselves for the sake of a more basic form of survival (Czechoslovakia in 1938–39 and 1968), and regimes that have passed peacefully out of existence (the U.S. Confederation in 1789, the

Italian Monarchy in 1946), most regimes tend to identify themselves closely with the societies they rule. Governments will usually go to great lengths to perpetuate themselves and the basic principles on which they rest. Both conservative powers and ideologically based revolutionary governments are likely to organize national security policy around the goal of maintaining themselves in power. In 1918, Lenin was willing to sacrifice the Ukraine and a large part of European Russia at Brest-Litovsk[6] in order to save Bolshevik rule in the part of Russia that was left. Hitler ordered a suicidal struggle to the end in 1945, even though the war was clearly lost, on the theory that if the German people could not defend National Socialism they did not deserve to survive. It is therefore probably wise in the assessment of any national security situation to assume that a regime in power, as distinct from its people, will make every effort to preserve itself intact even if this entails the surrender of other national security values. The people at large may or may not be in accord with this view. Even if powerful groups within a country are willing to sacrifice their regime, they may share other values with it and be willing to collaborate on most issues.

The often used phrases "political independence" and "territorial integrity" can be viewed as variations of the survival value. Rare is the country that will voluntarily surrender its own political sovereignty even though other values remain unimpaired. The exceptional case of Austria has already been mentioned. Other examples may be the American annexation of Texas in 1845, the absorption of the south German states into a German Empire in 1870, and the formation of the United Arab Republic in 1958. In all three instances political independence gave way to a drive for national or cultural unification.[7] Conversely, there are obviously hundreds of examples of countries making extreme efforts to maintain not only their internal value systems but their status as sovereign states as well.

Of lesser but still major importance is the matter of territorial integrity. Each sovereign political unit exercises its jurisdiction over a particular, more or less well-defined portion of the earth's surface. A loss of part of this territorial segment is actually a partial loss of both survival and political independence. Such a loss may achieve a symbolic significance far greater than the intrinsic worth of the land itself. A people that is forced to cede part of its traditional territorial base is likely to feel itself violated or dismembered. If there is any reasonable expectation of regaining the lost territory, irredentism will become a value of considerable importance in the national security process. France after 1871 and Germany after 1918 actively sought the recovery of provinces lost through military defeat even though those provinces were relatively unimportant parts of their national territories. Other irredentisms, including China's claim to part of Siberia, continue to play an active role in the national and international security arena. Conversely, Germany since 1945 has apparently put aside hope of regaining its territory east of the Oder, just as Mexico harbors little expectation of reconquering California and Texas, or Finland of regaining the Karelian Isthmus. Territorial irredentism is not now part of the national security structure of those three countries.

The vital national values we have so far discussed as goals of the national security process are basically conservative and defensive. Except for the matter of regaining lost territories (which may be regarded as a return to a former status), they imply a policy of maintaining or protecting some presently acceptable condition. Our working definition of national security, however, refers to the "protection or extension" of vital national values. The "extension" half of this phrase involves different kinds of national values than the "protection"-oriented values. Rather than the maintenance of a presently acceptable *status quo,* countries with "extension" values seek a change in the international situation to conform with the inherent principles of their value systems. A policy based on such values is offensive and aggressive, though not necessarily aggressive in a military sense.

The most common kind of extension value in history is simple territorial imperialism, a drive by one state to dominate another in order to enjoy the intrinsic benefits—population, resources, markets, loot—of the conquered territory. Or the benefits of empire may be indirect—prestige, enhanced power, glory, strategic advantage.

A second major type of extension value is ideological imperialism, the drive to spread, through political means (i.e., propaganda, subversion, infiltration, military force) some "true faith" beyond the borders of its original homeland. This kind of value is found most commonly in countries that have recently undergone political and social upheaval or in countries that are recent converts to some universalistic belief system. Characterized by catchy slogans, vivid symbols, and a deeply felt passion to convert the unbeliever, ideological imperialism is perhaps the least predictable and most dangerous kind of national value. Practitioners of ideological imperialism may even for a time subordinate national survival to the ultimate triumph of their faith, thus making it difficult to deter them from violent excesses of missionary zeal. Expansionary values in national security are not usually held to the exclusion of the more conservative, protection-oriented values. They usually appear in conjunction with the conservative values, but the possible combinations make assessment of an expansionist country's national security policy complex.

If we were to build a Weberian ideal-type of the perfect national security system, every aspect of policy and operations would be logically and demonstrably derived from a well-articulated, consistent basic value structure. All details of military doctrine, for example, would flow clearly and unambiguously from a stated goal of physical survival (or regime survival, ideological imperialism, or some other value). Unfortunately for the student, this kind of policy-making rarely occurs in the real world.

The complexity of most nations deprives their governments of internal political power sufficient to create such a monolithic organization of the national security process. Even the totalitarian states of the twentieth century have proved themselves unable to organize national security completely in accordance with their officially proclaimed values. A democratic country like the United States with a theory of government calling for a decentralization of power finds it much more difficult than the totalitarian or authoritarian state. And, of course, as Czechoslovakia has discovered on three occasions in this century, small states may be physically unable to carry out a national security policy consistent with their national values.

To point out the disparity between theory and practice in the relationship between national values and national security is not at all to contradict the general proposition that such values are the real and proper goals of the national security process. In the final analysis all national security operations and programs are justifiable only through their contribution to the pursuit of such values. The United States government's failure to retain popular support for the Vietnam War is traceable, in part at least, to its inability to demonstrate to many people a direct relationship between the war and vital national values.

Obviously, in order to relate any country's national security policy and operations to basic values we must be able to determine just what those values are and what priority the country assigns to each. This is no easy task. As we noted above, values are likely to be poorly articulated, couched in very general terms, or turned into slogans with a high emotional content. Historical analysis of a country's national security policy development may provide a realistic picture of its basic national value structure. Observing behavior patterns of governments over time may provide other clues. In most cases, however, we are forced to rely on the official proclamations of governments about the values they intend to pursue. Even here the possibilities for miscalculation are great. Though superficially it would seem logical for governments to make their intentions in international relations as clear as possible, there are several reasons why they do not always do so.

First, the official pronouncements of a government about the values it considers most vital may conflict with foreign beliefs about that government's true motives. There is always a tendency to believe the worst about a potential adversary and to interpret all his statements in terms of that pessimistic belief. Marxist ideology tends to persuade communists that capitalist governments are only political expressions of the economic exploitation of one class by another. Maintenance of this exploiting position is seen as the prime value behind the national security policies of capitalist states. Western claims to the contrary are discounted as trickery, maneuvers, or lies. On occasion this process works the other way; that is, one government will credit a rival or adversary with more laudable values than it actually possesses. Some British political leaders of the 1930's believed that Hitler was only a misunderstood nationalist who wanted to regain the territories Germany had lost at Versailles in 1918. This opinion was influential in persuading Prime Minis-

ter Neville Chamberlain to accede to the Munich Agreement of 1938.

Second, a government may believe that an adversary's stated national security values are not the same as those held by the common citizens of that country. This leads to the often unrealistic declaration that the trouble is only with the adversary's government and not with its people. All problems between the two countries would be settled quickly if only that troublesome regime could be gotten out of the way. The adversary's citizens are depicted as victims of the evil machinations of their own government. The result of this type of thinking may be a gross underestimation of the adversary's intentions and capabilities.

Third, governments sometimes deliberately try to obscure their national values as well as confuse opponents about the methods they intend to use in pursuing them. The purpose of such maneuvering is to provide additional flexibility in the conduct of foreign policy, but it may also cause difficulties by encouraging other countries to fear the worst. Fearing the worst, they may prepare for the worst or even decide to strike first.

Fourth, there may be no consensus within a country as to what sort of ultimate values to pursue at any given time or what methods to use in pursuing them. This applies especially in countries that are undergoing domestic social and political change. In democratic countries where there is no official ideology against which values can be tested, values and the official proclamations of values tend to shift with the shifting domestic political balance. This is frequently only a matter of emphasis and not a wholesale replacement of one set of values by another. But relatively minor shifts of emphasis may have a profound effect on a country's national security policy. The pendulum swing between isolationism and internationalism in United States domestic opinion has had profound repercussions in international power relationships, leading, for example, to a withdrawal of American military forces from the Asian mainland in 1945–50. This contributed directly to the outbreak of the Korean War.

We have far from exhausted the subject of national values as the foundation of national security. We have in fact little more than touched on some of the difficulties of dealing with the problem. Hopefully, however, we have also called attention to the primary role of national values in the development of national security policy. Any serious study of national security policy and administration must be placed in the context of values, the ultimate objectives of national security. Although values cannot be the sole concern of national security studies, they are the indispensable first step. Too many otherwise competent efforts in the field have either ignored values entirely or assumed the existence of coherent value structures which might not exist in reality. It is to be hoped that this condition will change in favor of a greater concern with the ultimate purposes of national security, and not simply the technique to be used in getting there.

THE CREATION OF POLITICAL CONDITIONS

Our working definition has identified basic values as the central concept in national security. At the same time we have said that values are often abstract and ambiguous, couched in the most general terms. They are, thus, unsuitable as guidelines for the day to day conduct of national security policy. More concrete, intermediate objectives, which we shall call "interests," are necessary as connecting links between basic values and the techniques of national security operations.

Both values and interests are basically political in character. Survival as a national security value, including simple physical survival, implies some organization of the survivors into a political system even if it is a political system imposed by a conquering enemy. The political or societal nature of values like survival of the regime, territorial integrity, political independence, territorial imperialism and ideological imperialism is even more apparent. If these ultimate values are in fact "protected or extended," there will be international political ramifications. Similarly, if national security fails, the basic results will be political. Interests, as integral parts of values, can be no less political than the values themselves. The political objectives in war are the most familiar kind of national security interests, but similar political objectives exist as interests in all national security operations. Such interests are basic parts of a country's domestic and foreign policy positions and should be chosen with a view toward maximizing the possibilities of protecting or extending ultimate values. Thus, the most significant fact about any national security operation is the effect it will have on achieving its political objective, the securing of some interest. This is the basis of Clausewitz's famous dictum that war is only a continuation of politics with an admixture of other means. War, like other less violent types of national security operations, is a means undertaken by political leaders in their pursuit of important interests and through them of basic values.

The most important feature of interests, then, is that they are by themselves insufficient to justify any kind of national security operation, especially one involving the use of military force. As we use the term here, interests are presumed to be intermediate steps in the pursuit of fundamental values. They are not ends in themselves, as are values, but only contributions to the achievement of those ends. All governments identify and assign priorities to numerous interests they feel are important to their national security. Familiar examples of important security interests would include Britain's interest in control of the seas in the nineteenth century, America's interest in keeping European powers out of Latin America (as expressed in the Monroe Doctrine), and the Soviet interest in maintaining control over communist regimes in East Europe.

Like values, interests are complex and often confusing. Any student of politics can list a variety of interests advanced by his own and other governments. These can usually be placed in some sort of rank order with the top priority interests often referred to as "vital." While "vitality" of an interest is by no means an empirically verifiable concept, as a rule of thumb we might say that an interest becomes vital when the government that advances it is prepared to threaten or actually wage war over it. And, of course, the relative importance of an interest in a country's national security policy structure is subject to change as changing circumstances alter perceptions about international political relationships.

The ranking of interests, vital or otherwise, is, thus, an uncertain enterprise. Opportunity, capability, estimates of the responses by other national regimes, and intentions of friend and foe all play shifting roles in the framing of national security policy. For these reasons security interests, vital or otherwise, are at best transitory. Usually they represent only a regime's present view of itself as an actor in the international arena.

Another serious problem with interests is that over time they can become so familiar that they begin to take on a life of their own apart from the values they were intended to support. Continuous reassessment of interests is necessary but can be lost as policy decisions once considered only expedient become institutionalized through the creation of formal organizations designed to administer them. Pressure arises to maintain certain interests as policy objectives even when changing circumstances make this course less

relevant or counterproductive. This process introduces into national security policy a historical and operational rigidity which is difficult to overcome. Conversely, governments may suddenly reevaluate their own national interests and as a result embark upon unexpected actions. Paradoxically, a single government may pursue both rigid and rapidly changeable interests at the same time. This kind of policy may in turn lead to misperceptions or miscalculations by other powers about what national values that government really intends to pursue.

The relative weight attached to like interests, in terms of their contribution to pursuit of national values, is so variable from country to country that generalizations are difficult. While control of the seas was considered an interest vital to the survival of the British Empire in the nineteenth century, it lapsed as such when Britain decided to decolonize in 1946–47. On the other hand, freedom of navigation (including maritime trade) was not nearly so important to Imperial or post-World War I Germany. But Germany was willing to go to war in 1914 to prevent the dismemberment of the Austrian Empire at the hands of the Russians. We can only conclude that in addition to what we have called basic values—the existence of the state itself, physical survival, survival of the regime, political independence, territorial integrity, and the rest—there is a secondary class of national security objectives called interests which may under changing circumstances achieve a high priority position in the national security process. It is necessary to identify and assess the importance of both values and interests as objectively as we can in order to understand the national security policy of any given country.[8]

A logical relationship between the ends and means in national security begins to take shape. Ultimate values are the controlling force. Intermediate political objectives—interests—are selected to create conditions favorable to the growth of ultimate values. National security operations are the means of achieving these political objectives and should be closely controlled to maximize their political effect. This, of course, describes the ideal situation. In the real world the national security process is never so neat and tidy. Adversaries will have ultimate values in opposition to one's own. Most political objectives will not be fully realized but will have to be compromised because most countries do not have the capability of controlling every aspect of the situation. Unforeseen circumstances may arise. And, most important, the internal national security process is so complex, involving so many interrelated political, military, economic, technical and other factors, that it is virtually impossible to coordinate every detail in every ongoing operation. Problems of administering the U.S. Defense Department alone have filled many scholarly volumes as well as a number of high level government studies.

Despite these acknowledged difficulties we must continue efforts to understand national security in terms of what it is trying to accomplish as well as how the process works in practice. The most important problem in national security remains—in the nuclear age as in the past—the proper relation of ends to means. In practice this involves difficult choices of political objectives, like whether to give military assistance to a foreign government that is friendly toward us but whose domestic policies are repugnant to our own values; whether to allow economic contacts with unfriendly states in the hope of developing better relations through trade; whether to defend with military force if necessary, small countries that are not necessarily our friends simply because they are enemies of our enemies; when to make and break alliances; when to make war and how to make peace; the list is ongoing. And each case also involves selection of weapons and methods of employing them that are suitable to the political objectives. It is the task of national security studies to analyze and understand these problems both from our own perspective and from the perspective of third countries.

THE MILITARY FACTOR IN NATIONAL SECURITY STUDIES

Our working definition of national security has identified three main elements: government policy, basic values and intermediate political objectives. We have alluded only indirectly to the specific means of national security including the generation and use of military power. We have not meant to suggest that the means are unimportant in national security studies; on the contrary, the means are obviously of crucial significance since without adequate means no nation can hope to realize any of the values or intermediate objectives we have discussed above. We must, therefore, turn to a brief discussion of the means of national security, and particularly the role of military force, in national security studies.

The means of national security have traditionally been identified with the great issues of military power, national defense, war and peace. Before the French Revolution military power far overshadowed all other available tools of national security. Indeed, the terms "war" and "national security" were practically synonymous. Since then the growth of mass society under the impact of industrialization and social democracy has wrought profound changes in the means of executing national security policy. While armed force remains the single most important

—and certainly the single most expensive—weapon of national security, there is now a collection of means available for use in national security operations. These include economic assistance, technological research and development, a variety of propaganda and communications techniques, psychological operations, and space exploration as well as the traditional weapons of diplomacy, alliances, and military power.

The rise of these non-traditional means has added a new dimension to national security in the twentieth century. Policy-makers must try to blend the various means as well as possible in order to avoid political results that may be useless or even harmful to national security goals. This is a Herculean task which no government has been able to master completely. Below the ranks of the major powers not every country possesses a full range of national security weapons. Only the United States and the Soviet Union have active space exploration programs, though the long range consequences for national security of permanent stations or settlements away from the earth are incalculable. Japan and Germany, the world's third and fourth ranking economic powers, have—as yet—no nuclear weapons. Psychological operations—a low cost weapon system—are not well appreciated in most countries of the West, and certainly not in the United States. The impact on national security of rapidly expanding international economic, cultural, and social contacts is but poorly understood. The administrative mechanisms for command and control of these various means are often rudimentary, and the means themselves usually have a technical content which is difficult for laymen to understand.

The significant factor in each type of national security weapon remains the same, however. That factor is the contribution each can make toward the creation of desired international political conditions. This opens fertile new fields for academic research. The creation, employment, and coordination of nonmilitary means in national security and their relation to formal organizations designed to administer them are relatively untouched areas. Contributions from disciplines other than the traditional military, political, and economic specialties would be fruitful. Of particular value might be inputs from fields like organization theory, general systems theory, and history (beyond traditional military history). And, in all cases, a greater understanding of the connecting links among policy, organization, objectives, and values is urgently needed.

The special position of military power within national security means that a large proportion of academic national security must be devoted to the study of military policy and military organizations. Many of the best scholarly works in the national security field have been concerned with the nature and purposes of military power. Unfortunately, this phase of the national security process is still surrounded by emotional controversies that tend to obscure the fundamental realities of national security in the twentieth century. At one emotional extreme are those who see military power as the sole means for preserving the security of the nation; at the other extreme are those who would eliminate military power altogether as a method of pursuing national security values. Neither view is compatible with the definition of national security we have proposed. National security is concerned first and foremost with values and with the political conditions in which those values can flourish. Because of its potentially destructive consequences military power is used only when failure to do so would result in an intolerable sacrifice of some vital national value. The obvious criterion is the relative weights of the endangered values and the risks involved in deciding for war. This is the most critical decision any policy-maker in the national security system of any country will ever have to make.

Thus, except in a tactical sense, there are no purely military solutions to national security problems, nor are there any purely military victories in war. All military solutions and all military victories and defeats are instrumental events. They are political in origin and final consequences. While the general is concerned primarily with gaining the military objective before him—that is, with conduct of the war itself—the statesman must always concentrate his attention on the peace to follow the war. The nature of that peace will determine the success or failure of the war itself.

In a rational system of national security, neither the condition of war nor peace can in itself be a national security value. Even if no thought is given to political consequences by a country engaged in war, political consequences will arise, and they will be more important than the war itself. The same is true of peace which can always be attained quite easily by refusing to defend vital national values. Here, too, the political consequences will be more important than the peace

itself. The political situation in Asia, for example, would be quite different today had the United States decided not to enter the Vietnam War. Whether that situation would be better or worse from an American national security viewpoint is a matter of judgment. That there would be a political difference is indisputable. In short military power is a tool, a tool most countries would prefer not to use. But in the world of practical affairs, the tool will be used whenever the projected losses are judged to be greater than the risks of the war itself.

The scholarly approach to national security should reflect these fundamental propositions. The study of national security is not simply the study of military institutions. It is rather the study of the use of particular means, one of which is military force, in the pursuit of political objectives. National security studies focused exclusively on military phenomena would be sterile because they do not answer the question "why?" This would be a fatal defect in today's atmosphere of questioning traditional assumptions. Although continuous reassessment of military postures and organization will be necessary, we hope this will be carried on within a broader conceptualization of the field.

CONCLUSION: WHITHER NATIONAL SECURITY STUDIES?

This essay has not attempted to present a comprehensive survey of the field of national security studies, nor have we presented an outline of subtopics or a model syllabus for the typical national security course. Such efforts, while interesting intellectual exercises, usually fail to make an impact on the structure of the field because individual scholars will design their research and teaching activities in accordance with their own interests and areas of competence.

What we have tried to do here is define the center or core of national security studies and encourage each in-

dividual to relate the details of his own work to that core. The field can thus be expanded and contracted accordion-like to fit each particular situation. This approach to security studies lacks something in neatness and precision, but it does realistically reflect the disciplinary structure of American education and the interdisciplinary nature of national security studies. Rather than compartmentalize national security within its own air tight academic boundaries, we would prefer to see more intellectual input from relatively untapped sources such as comparative analysis, organization theory, history, and the physical sciences. In each case, however, analysis of national security related phenomena must be linked to the central concepts that underlie the entire national security problem.

The most pressing need in national security studies is, in fact, a greater effort to understand these central or core concepts. The issues surrounding values, goals, and political objectives in national security have received far too little attention in the past decade. Weapons systems, defense budgets, military organization, the domestic social impact of national security systems, and even military strategy have been discussed, dissected, and analyzed as though they exist in a vacuum with no relationship to the ultimate objectives of national security policy. As a result we have amassed a great quantity of scholarly, in a sense monographic, material that should be integrated in planning the reforms in American national security that seem inevitable in the immediate future. We must now examine in much greater depth the end purposes of national security, not only in the United States but in adversary, friendly, and neutral countries as well.

The study of national security seems to be on its way toward a root position in the university curriculum. As long as academics are interested in teaching and research in the field—and there is a growing number with such an interest—work will be done. It remains now to improve the quality of our work and move toward a better conceptual integration of the entire range of national security phenomena.

NOTES

1. Arnold Wolfers, *Discord and Collaboration* (Baltimore: Johns Hopkins Press, 1962), p. 47.

2. See Holden Furber, *John Company at Work: A Study of European Expansion in India in the Late Eighteenth Century* (Cambridge: Harvard University Press, 1951). H. H. Dodwell, ed., *Cambridge History of India*, vols. 5, 6 (Cambridge: Cambridge University Press, 1929, 1932).

The U.S. Constitution gives to Congress the power to issue letters of "Marque and Reprisal." See Article I, Section 8.

3. Thomas Hobbes, *Leviathan* (New York: Washington Square Press, 1964), p. 115. See all of Chapters 13 and 17.

4. Losing a major war has often been an invitation to domestic rebellion. Revolution may not only replace the regime with one more capable of protecting national values, but may replace the value structure as well. See, for example, Chalmers Johnson, *Revolution and the Social System* (Stanford: Hoover Institution, 1964), especially pp. 13–17.

5. By "regime" we mean a formal institutional arrangement for the government of a country. In the past century the United States and Britain have each had one regime; Ger-

many has had five (Empire, Weimar Republic, Third Reich, Allied occupation, Federal Republic); France has had four (Third Republic, Vichy-German occupation, Fourth Republic, Fifth Republic); Russia, three (Empire, Provisional Republic, Soviet Union), etc. A simple change of rulers or dynasties does not qualify as a change of regime if the basic institutional structure remains the same.

6. This would constitute a partial loss of physical survival.

7. It is also interesting that Texas, Bavaria, and Syria all tried at a later time to secede from that greater national federation. Only Syria was successful, and even Syria has rejoined a new federation with Egypt.

8. The discussions of values and interests have been derived in part from A. O. Lovejoy. See his "Terminal and Adjectival Values," *Journal of Philosophy*, XLVII, No. 21 (1950), 593–608; and *Reflections on Human Nature*, Lecture III (Baltimore: The Johns Hopkins Press, 1961), pp. 67–127. Simply put, terminal values are desired as goals; they are the "ends of actions." Adjectival values are desired as roles; they are the "qualities of adjectives as agent."

2 | PERSPECTIVES ON NATIONAL SECURITY, DEFENSE, AND WAR

Introduction

This section is concerned with the values that underlie the concept of national security and with the role of armed conflict in securing these values. Although defining and identifying national values may belong more to the realm of philosophy than to the practical applications of governmental policy, since they are the ultimate objectives of the national security process values and their implications must be confronted before we can proceed to other aspects of the subject. The relationships between values and all facets of national security should be borne in mind through the remaining sections of this book.

The first three selections deal with values, interests, and objectives in national security policy. In "Power, Glory and Idea," Raymond Aron discusses possible answers to the question, "Why do political units want to impose their wills on each other?" Material advantage, prestige, and ideological aggrandizement are offered as fundamental values with the caveat that moral and material objectives are usually inseparable. Bernard Brodie's "Vital Interests: By Whom and How Determined" discusses the intermediate level political objectives that form the basis of day to day government policy. "Vital" interests are those for which a government is prepared to take some serious military action. But interests, whether vital or not, are the product of policy-making by fallible human beings. They have, therefore, a certain subjective content and are based on less than unanimous agreement about the importance of specific situations. Finally, Seyom Brown's "The Irreducible National Interest and Basic Premises about World Conditions" tries to identify the "national interest" of the United States and deduce from it specific ground rules for the implementation of foreign policy. Brown argues that debate over foreign policy in the post-1945 world has centered on contending methods of reaching ultimate goals that have remained relatively constant throughout.

The next four selections attempt to place the phenomenon of organized state violence—war—in its proper position within the national security process. As the selections indicate, there is no fixed agreement on the purposes and nature of war. The four excerpts from Karl von Clausewitz's famous work *On War* develop the theory of war as an instrumentality of politics. War should be used rationally by a state's political leadership in the pursuit of political objectives. Clausewitz's theory of the primacy of political objectives can apply as easily to the nonmilitary instruments of national security as to war itself. "Causes of War," from Quincy Wright's monumental *A Study of War*, presents a sociological interpretation of the basic causes and functions of war. War may result from a disequilibrium among many factors, some of them based on a non-rational acceptance of valued symbols. Certain destabilizing factors, such as a lag between political and economic change, have often brought about wars in the past. Wright feels that a voluntary world federation may be the best way to prevent war. Klaus Knorr, in "Military Power: Nature, Components and Functions," focuses on the use of military power for coercive purposes in international politics. Military power may be exercised through war, threats, or simple recognition by other states that military power exists and can be used. The author specifies the conditions for effective use of military power and then points out the increased costs for using military power that have resulted from the development of nuclear weapons. In "The Nature of Modern War" Marshal V. D. Sokolovsky presents the Marxist-Leninist concept of war as a complex social phenomenon—as a violent form of political and class conflict. Three basic types of war in the modern world are theoretically possible: world wars, small imperialist wars, and wars of national liberation.

The final two selections are concerned with the problem of militarism. The short Introduction from Gerhard Ritter's *The Sword and the Scepter* provides a succinct definition of "militarism" and distinguishes between militarism and the "craft of war." Militarism is a condition in which war has become an end in itself rather than a means to achieve ends laid down by statesmen. In the last selection, Alexis de Tocqueville offers a subjective and paradoxical proposition about the causes of militarism. Reflecting on the early development of democratic societies, Tocqueville asserts that democratic nations are usually desirous of peace while their armies wish for war. Tocqueville ascribes this to the low status of military officers in democratic society and to the competition for higher positions within the army itself. It is only through war that ambitious officers can gain advancement and prestige, so they will constantly try to drag their countries into military adventures.

Power, Glory and Idea

or

On the Goals of Foreign Policy

Raymond Aron

Political units seek to impose their wills upon each other: such is the hypothesis on which Clausewitz's definition of war is based and also the conceptual framework of international relations. At this point, one question arises: why do political units want to impose their wills upon each other? What goals does each of them desire and why are these goals incompatible, or seem to be so?

If we focus on the moment at which a generalized war breaks out, it is easy to indicate, with more or less precision, the goals chosen by each of the states in conflict with the others. In 1914 Austria-Hungary sought to eliminate the threat that the southern Slav claims posed to the dualist monarchy. France, which had consented to the annexation of Alsace-Lorraine without acknowledging the fact morally, discovered intact and ardent, on the day the first cannon thundered, the will to restore her lost provinces to the mother country. The Italians claimed lands that once belonged to the Habsburg empire. The Allies were virtually no less divided than their adversaries. Tsarist Russia wanted possession of Constantinople and the Dardanelles, whereas Great Britain had constantly opposed such ambitions. Only the German danger incited London to agree, secretly and on paper, to what it had stubbornly refused for over a century.

Perhaps the Reich inspired its rivals with even greater alarm because its war goals were not known. At the moment of its first successes, these goals seemed grandiose and vague. Leagues and private groups dreamed of the "African belt" or of *Mittel Europa*. The general staff, as late as 1917–18, demanded the annexation or occupation of a part of Belgian territory for strategic reasons. A dominant power which does not proclaim definite objectives is suspected of unlimited ambitions. Provinces (Alsace-Lorraine, Trieste), strategic positions (the Dardanelles, the coast of Flanders), religious symbols (Constantinople), such were the explicit stakes of the conflicts among the European states. But simultaneously, the result of the conflict would determine the relation of forces, the place of Germany in Europe and of Great Britain in the world. Is it possible to distinguish, in an abstract analysis of general scope, the typical goals which states aim at and which set them in opposition to each other?

ETERNAL OBJECTIVES

Let us start from the schema of international relations: the political units, proud of their independence, jealous of their capacity to make major decisions on their own, are rivals by the very fact that they are autonomous. Each, in the last analysis, can count only on itself.

What then is the first objective which the political unit may logically seek? The response is furnished by Hobbes in his analysis of the *state of nature*. Each political unit aspires to survive. Leaders and.led are interested in and eager to maintain the collectivity they constitute together by virtue of history, race, or fortune.

If we grant that war is not desired for its own sake, the belligerent power that dictates the peace terms at the end of hostilities seeks to create conditions guaranteeing that it need not fight in the immediate future and that it may keep the advantages gained through force. We may say that in the state of nature, every entity, whether individual or political unit, makes *security* a primary objective. The more severe wars become, the more men aspire to security. In Germany, too, from 1914 to 1918, there was speculation as to the best methods to insure the nation's definitive security by disarming certain of its adversaries or occupying certain key positions.

Security, in a world of autonomous political units, can be based either on the weakness of rivals (total or partial disarmament) or on force itself. If we suppose that security is the final goal of state policy, the effective means will be to establish a new relation of forces or to modify the old one so that potential enemies, by reason of their inferiority, will not be tempted to take the initiative of an aggression.

The relation between these two terms—*security* and *force*—raises many problems. On a lower level we may first observe that the maximization of resources does not necessarily involve the maximization of security. In Europe, traditionally, no state could increase its population, its wealth and its soldiers without exciting the fear and jealousy of other states, and thereby provoking the formation of a hostile coalition. In any given system there exists an *optimum of forces;* to exceed it will produce a dialectical reversal. Additional force involves a relative weakening by a shift of allies to neutrality or of neutrals to the enemy camp.

If security were, by evidence or necessity, the preferential objective, it would be possible to determine rational behavior *theoretically*. It would be necessary, in each circumstance, to determine the optimum of force and to act in consequence. A more serious difficulty appears as soon as we raise questions as to the relation between these two objectives, force and security. We concede that man, whether individual or collective, desires to survive. But the individual does not subordinate all his desires to his desire for life alone. There are goals for which the individual accepts a risk of death. The same is true of collective units. The latter do not seek to be strong only in order to discourage aggression and enjoy peace; they seek to be strong in order to be feared, respected or admired. In the last analysis, they seek to be powerful—that is, capable of imposing their wills on their neighbors and rivals, in order to influence the fate of humanity, the future of civilization. The two objectives are connected: the more strength he has, the less risk a man runs of being attacked, but he also finds, in strength as such and in the capacity to impose himself upon others, a satisfaction which needs no other justification. Security can be a final goal: to be without fear is a fate worthy of envy; but power, too, can be a final goal: what does danger matter once one has known the intoxication of ruling?

But on this level of abstraction, the enumeration of objectives still does not seem to me to be complete: I would add a third term, *glory*. In the essay entitled "On the Balance of Power," David Hume explains the behavior of the Greek city-states in terms of the spirit of competition rather than the calculations of prudence: "It is true, that Grecian wars are regarded by historians as wars of emulation rather than of politics; and each State seems to have had more in view the honor of leading the rest, than any well-grounded hopes of authority and dominion." Opposing *jealous emulation* to *cautious politics,* Hume thus formulates the antithesis that we shall call the *struggle for glory* and the *struggle for power.*

When the struggle is joined, there is a danger that military victory in itself will become the goal, causing political objectives to be forgotten. The desire for *absolute victory,* that is, for a peace dictated without appeal by the victor, is often more the expression of a desire for glory than of a desire for force. Dislike of *relative victories,* that is, of a favorable peace negotiated after partial successes, derives from the *amour-propre* that animates men once they measure themselves against each other.

It might be objected that glory is merely another name or another aspect of power: it is, so to speak, power recognized by others, power whose fame spreads across the world. In a sense this objection is valid and the three objectives might be reduced to two: either the political units are in quest of security and of force, or they seek recognition by imposing their wills, by gathering the conqueror's laurels. One of the two goals, force, is material, the other is moral, inseparable from the human dialogue; it is defined by grandeur, consecrated by victory and the enemy's submission.

The ternary division, however, seems to me preferable because each of the three terms corresponds to a concretely defined attitude while it also expresses a specific notion. Clemenceau sought the *security,* Napoleon the *power,* Louis XIV the *glory* of France (or each his own).[1] In 1918 any rational chief of state would have proposed the same goal: to spare France the recur-

rence of a war as severe as the one that an immense alliance had just brought to a favorable conclusion. Napoleon, at least after a certain date, dreamed of ruling Europe: he was not content with the honor of being universally celebrated as a great war leader; even Clausewitz's homage—"the God of war himself"—would not have satisfied him. He was ambitious for reality, not for appearances, and he knew that in the long run no state commands others if it does not possess the means of constraining them. Louis XIV probably loved glory as much as power. He wanted to be recognized as the first among monarchs, and he made use of his force in order to seize a city and fortify it, but this half-symbolic exploit was still a way of showing his force. He did not conceive of a disproportionately enlarged France, furnished with resources superior to those of her allied rivals. He dreamed that the names of Louis XIV and of France would be transfigured by the admiration of nations.

This first analysis would be more dangerous than useful if it were not filled out by another. Indeed, if we abide by these abstract notions, we will be inclined to dismiss glory as irrational,[2] to condemn the indefinite accumulation of force as contradictory (the loss of allies more than offsetting, at a certain point, the increase of one's own forces). From this angle, we would arrive at the allegedly unique objective of security. Let us abandon such abstract analyses and consider a political unit—that is, a human collectivity occupying a fragment of space. If we suppose that this collectivity is comparable to a person, with an intelligence and a will of its own, what goals is it liable to choose?

A collectivity occupies a certain territory: it can logically consider the surface of the earth at its disposal as too small. In rivalry among peoples, the possession of space was the original stake. Secondly, sovereigns have often estimated their greatness according to the number of their subjects: what they desired, beyond their frontiers, was not territory, but men. Lastly, the armed prophet is sometimes less anxious to conquer than to convert: indifferent to the wealth of the earth and what it contains, he does not calculate the number of his workers or soldiers; he seeks to spread the true faith, he wants the organization corresponding to his interpretation of life and of history to encompass gradually all of humanity.

Here again, this ternary series seems to me complete. All the goals that states determine for themselves, in historical circumstances, necessarily refer to one of the three terms we have just listed: *space, men* and *souls*. Why should societies fight if not to extend the territory they cultivate and whose wealth they exploit, to conquer men who are alien today, slaves or fellow citizens tomorrow, or to insure the triumph of a certain idea, whether religious or social, whose universal truth the collectivity proclaims simultaneously with its own mission?

Concretely, these objectives are difficult to separate. Unless he exterminates or drives out the inhabitants, the conqueror takes possession of both space and the men who occupy it. Unless conversion takes place by the mere force of proselytism, the prophet does not disdain to govern men before administering the salvation of souls. It remains no less true that in certain cases the three terms are distinct: the Crusaders first sought to liberate the Holy Land, not to convert the Moslems. The Israelis wanted to occupy the Palestinian space that had been the Kingdom of David, they were not interested in either conquering or converting the Moslems of Palestine. The sovereigns of monarchical Europe collected provinces—land and men—because the power and prestige of princes was measured by possessions. As for the conversion of the infidel, perhaps it has never been the exclusive goal of any state. Only unarmed prophets dream of pure conversion, but, as Machiavelli said, they perish. Though states are sometimes prophetic, they are always armed. Not that an idea is an instrument or a justification of the desire to conquer space or men. In the minds of religious or ideological leaders, the triumph of the faith, the spread of an idea, may be conceived, in all sincerity, as the true goal of action. It is in the eyes of the unbelievers that this goal seems a camouflage for imperialism: historians and theoreticians, also unbelievers, adhere all too easily to this cynical interpretation.

What are the relations between the abstract series and the concrete series? It would be as arbitrary to subordinate the second to the first as to decree the opposite. The increase of space, the augmentation of material and human resources are, certainly, elements of security and power, sometimes even the objectives of glory. This does not mean that the conquest of a province can never be desired for itself. The French did not regard the return of Alsace-Lorraine to the mother country as a means to some ulterior goal, but as a good in itself, which required no other justification. Without Alsace-Lorraine, France was mutilated: with Strasbourg and Metz, she recovered her integrity. Down through the centuries, regions and cities and the men who populate them have assumed a historical significance, a symbolic value. The question is no longer whether the Moslems of Palestine or the Israelis could have found elsewhere a territory as fertile and resources that would have been equal or superior. It was here, around the Sea of Tiberias and on the plain of Jerusalem, it was here and in no other place on the planet that certain Jews (who no longer believed in God and in the "covenant") wanted to create anew a collectivity that would proclaim itself the heir of a semi-legendary past.

In our times, no guarantee of order and justice suffices to disarm national claims: active minorities leading various populations seek to belong to the political unit of their choice. The Cypriots wanted a fatherland, which could not be Great Britain or the British Empire: fair administration, autonomy, a relatively high standard of living—nothing could compensate for the absence of a political community. Of the two aspirations, not to be uprooted and not to be deprived of a fatherland, it is the first that has ultimately yielded in Europe: transfers of populations have in a sense signified the primacy of the nation over the territory.

In each series, abstract or concrete, the third term, *glory* or *idea,* stands apart. Not that these two terms correspond to each other: on the contrary, glory is an empty notion, and exists only in human consciousness, perhaps especially in the consciousness of the man who desires to possess it. The man "full of glory" is the man who is satisfied with the idea that he believes others have of him. Therefore it is precisely the "vainglorious" man who is a character of ridicule. Even if he is not mistaken as to the sentiments he inspires, the man "full of glory" should be unaware of his fortune or indifferent to it in order to be entirely worthy of it. But thereby, the goal itself retreats progressively as he approaches it. Never will the exploits performed satisfy the doubts of the man who aspires to glory.

An idea—whether it is Christianity or communism, the divinity of Christ or a certain organization of society—is, on the contrary, quite definite. Perhaps the inquisitors will never be sure of the sincerity of conversions. Perhaps the members of the Presidium will never eliminate the "capitalist" tendencies of the peasants, perhaps deviations will always appear, continually renewed upon the expulsion of the preceding deviationists. At least an idea has a specific content, whereas glory cannot be grasped since it is linked to the dialogue of men.

Yet in essence this objective too is situated in infinity. Where truth is concerned, nothing is done so long as something remains to *be* done. The religions of salvation have a universal vocation, they are addressed to humanity since they are addressed to each man. Once a prophet takes arms to propagate them, his enterprise will never know an end unless it covers the entire planet. Wars for glory and wars for an idea are human in a different way from wars for land and its riches. Crusaders are sublime and dangerous. The nobles who fight for prestige can never be through fighting. If the goal is to conquer in order to be recognized as a conqueror or to conquer in order to impose the truth, it suffices that the determination to win be the same on each side for the violence to proceed to extremes. The most humane wars in origin are also, frequently, the most inhumane, because they are the most pitiless.

Hence we are tempted to constitute a third ternary series which, following the Platonic model, would be that of body, heart and mind. Whether it is a question of land or men, of security or force, the stake is ultimately material: the political units seek to enlarge their space or to accumulate resources in order to live free of danger or with the means to avert it. But neither security nor force satisfies the aspirations of communities: each desires to prevail over the others, to be recognized as first among its rivals. Political units have their *amour-propre,* as people do; perhaps they are even more sensitive. Hence they sometimes prefer the intoxication of triumph to the advantages of a negotiated peace. Sometimes the desire for glory will be satisfied only by the diffusion of an idea, of which each community wants to be the unique incarnation. The mind, finally, animates the dialectic of violence and drives it to extremes, once it links its destiny to that of a state, that is, of a human collectivity in arms.

Of course, the demand for security and force also leads to extremes. In the last analysis, a political unit would feel entirely safe only if it had no further enemy, in other words, if it had been enlarged to the dimensions of a universal state. But the desire for security and force does not transform itself into a demand for unlimited power, unless *amour-propre* or faith arouses and finally overwhelms the calculations of interest. Anxious only to live in peace, neither Pyrrhus nor Napoleon nor Hitler would have consented to so many certain sacrifices in the hope of an uncertain gain.

Conquerors have sometimes justified their undertakings in terms of the prosperity their people would enjoy after victory. Such Utopias served as an excuse, not an inspiration. These leaders desired power as an instrument of their glory, with a view to the triumph of an idea for its own sake, never in order that men might know "the good life."

HISTORICAL OBJECTIVES

Like the theory of power, this theory of objectives has a suprahistorical value, while it also permits us to comprehend historical diversity. The objectives of states refer, in every century, to the terms of the two ternary series or even, if one prefers the simplified formula, to the three terms of the last abstract-concrete series. But many circumstances—of military or economic technique, of institutional or ideological origin—intervene to limit and specify the objectives statesmen actually select.

Let us start with the first term, the most constant stake of human conflicts: space. At the dawn of history as on the threshold of the Atomic Age, human groups dispute the territory on which some are established and which others desire. Collectivities distribute territory among their members and legalize individual ownership. But the sovereignty of the collectivity itself over the whole of the territory is not thereby admitted by the other collectivities. During the first millenniums of the historical phase, the tribes retreated before the invaders from the east, to become conquerors in their turn with regard to the populations settled farther west. The horsemen of the steppes established their dominion over the sedentary populations and created hierarchic societies, the warriors constituting a superior class superimposed upon the mass of laborers.

In modern times the struggle for land has lost its primeval simplicity and brutality, but is no less cruel when it breaks out. Israelis and Palestinian Moslems cannot form a single collectivity and cannot occupy the same territory: one or the other is doomed to suffer injustice. In North Africa the French conquest of the nineteenth and twentieth centuries signified partial expropriations from the Berber or Arab populations, the French settlers receiving lands belonging to tribes, villages or families. Tunisian or Moroccan independence brought about a more or less rapid expropriation of French colons. The Algerian War, in a sense, had as its stake the land that both Moslems and French regarded as their own, and upon which they were temporarily obliged to coexist, both demanding sovereignty—the former under the banner of independence, the latter under that of integration.

For the French who were established across the Mediterranean, Algeria was the land on which their fathers lived, and therefore, so to speak, the fatherland. But for France, what has been, what is the significance of Algeria? Why had France[3] desired, since 1830, to extend her sovereignty over a territory which she had never occupied in the course of past centuries? It is difficult to answer, because the very statesmen or military leaders who determined and executed the conquest either did not know why they acted or else were divided as to their motives.

Some emphasized the threat of the Barbary Coast pirates to navigation, and the security that possession of the Algerian coast would assure to Mediterranean shipping. Let us say that they emphasized a *military motive*. Others favored the possibilities of colonization and hinted at a French Empire of a hundred million men on both shores of the Mediterranean. Let us say that they dreamed of an *enlargement of French space* and an *increase of French population*.[4] During the last years Frenchmen cited the many economic advantages of French sovereignty over Algeria, which constituted a reserve of manpower, a customer of and purveyor to the metropolitan economy, a source of raw materials and, particularly since 1956, of petroleum. Let us say that *economic advantages* are invoked here. In other words, this example permits us to discern the three typical arguments in favor of conquest: *military or strategic importance, spatio-demographic advantage, spatio-economic profit*.

Each of these arguments is subject to the law of change. The military, demographic or economic value of a territory varies with the techniques of combat and production, with human relations and institutions. The same positions are or are not strategically important, depending on the state of international relations (with the Russian army established two hundred kilometers from the Rhine, the old frontier between Germany and France is of no significance in military terms), and on armament (the Bosphorus and the Suez Canal have lost most of their value since they are too easily "closed" by atom bombs, too easily "crossed," too, by air transport). With Algeria independent, the security of Mediterranean shipping will not be threatened by the Barbary pirates.

The demographic argument is presented in two radically different forms. Space is still precious when it is empty or sparsely populated. We cannot overestimate the historical influence of the fact that after the sixteenth century Europeans had at their disposal the empty spaces of America. In the nineteenth century, when mortality was diminishing and the old birth rate was being lowered only slowly, millions of Englishmen, Germans and Scandinavians, then Italians and Slavs were able to cross the Atlantic and occupy the immensities of North America. Numbering sixty-five thousand at the period of the Treaty of Paris, there are now over five million French Canadians, less than two centuries later. Even today, if the objective of states is that their populations should "increase and multiply," the occupation of empty space is the ideal means (whence the—truly diabolical—temptation to empty space in order to reserve it for the victors: Hitler would not have resisted the temptation).

On the other hand, the occupation of an already populated space raises problems that vary according to the centuries. Princes once tended to measure their greatness by the number of their provinces and their subjects. When the number of men increased, so did that of laborers and soldiers. In the centuries when underpopulation, a shortage of men, was feared, the extension of sovereignty over inhabited lands passed for advantageous or beneficial. This traditional conception was called into question by the liberal economists, according to whom commerce could and should ignore frontiers. The assumption of sovereignty imposed administrative expenses upon the metropolitan country without affording it any additional profit.

The anti-colonial argument of the liberals, which had wide influence in England in the last century, but did not prevent the expansion of the British Empire, was opposed by the apparent soundness of traditional ideas and several phenomena originating in the industrial era. How could anyone doubt that conquest was profitable, a proof and symbol of greatness, when it was cheap in military terms and when the metropolitan country found in its empire both raw materials at low prices and protected markets? Imperialists and the Marxists were fundamentally in agreement as to the benefits of the colonies: higher rates of profit, guaranteed outlets for manufactured products, insured supply of raw materials. The only difference between the two lay in the judgment of value set upon the enterprise and the goal attributed to it. Marxists denounced an exploitation that was, in their eyes, the cause and goal of imperialism; the imperialists justified by its civilizing mission an enterprise whose advantages for the colonizing state they were not ashamed to proclaim.

The liberal argument again found an audience after the Second World War, following the convergence of political motives and economic motives. Either the colony did not include a European population, in which case the principle of equality of peoples established the right to independence. Or else the colony included a European population, in which case the principle of individual equality forbade treating the natives as inferiors, and led to the power of the greater number—that is, of the indigenous peoples—by means of universal suffrage.

The imperial state discovered, at the same moment, that a "civilizing mission" was expensive when taken seriously. Certain individuals, certain companies benefited from the colonial situation, but the balance-sheet for the collectivity ceased to be positive, insofar as the creation of an administrative and educational infrastructure and the improvement of the standard of living figured among the obligations of the metropolitan country.

Between the *advantage* of possessing the territory and the *cost* of assuming responsibility for its popula-

tion, the European states, Great Britain first of all, have chosen decolonization (or, more precisely, Great Britain has chosen, France has gradually been forced to choose). The transfer of sovereignty involved diplomatic and military risks: instead of commanding, the ex-imperial state was henceforth obliged to negotiate. The military forces of India were no longer at the service of British interests in the Middle East. But, on the military level too, the abandonment of sovereignty was less costly than a war against nationalism. France has been weakened more by the Indo-Chinese War than it would have been by an agreement with Ho Chi Minh, concluded in 1946. Great Britain would have been weakened more by resistance to Indian nationalism, even had such resistance been victorious over a generation, than it has been by the transfer of sovereignty to the Congress Party and the Arab League.

However summary, these analyses have permitted us to define two of the fundamental factors in the historical transformation of goals: *the techniques of combat and production* change and, thereby, modify the strategic value of positions, at the same time that the economic value of various natural and human resources of the territory, in other words *the modes of organization of collectivities,* authorize or exclude, in every period, certain modes of domination. Conquerors, down through the ages, have rarely acknowledged that victory imposed duties to a greater degree than it conferred rights. Superiority of arms was equivalent to the superiority of a civilization. The conquered were always wrong, and subjection seemed the legitimate sanction of defeat. The chapter in which Montesquieu deals with conquest already belongs to an age in which the judgment of arms no longer passed for the just verdict from the tribunal of history or Providence.[5]

The doctrine of empires depends on concepts involving relations among governed and governing, and among various populations, even more than on concepts involving war and the privileges of force. When citizenship was limited to a small number within the city-state, when only nobles bore arms and owned laborers as property, no limit could rationally be set on the enterprises of conquest: the number of subjects and slaves could increase without a proportionate increase in the number of citizens. The ruling people remained free to accord or refuse citizenship—the Roman Empire long tolerated a considerable number of populations subject to Rome, but not integrated within the Roman civilization. Similarly, the kings of France and Prussia were persuaded to increase their forces as their territories enlarged and the number of their subjects increased. It was assumed that the desire of men to obey one master rather than another did not count and, most of the time, did not exist. The religious conflicts that had drenched Europe in blood confirmed the merits of the old political wisdom: it is best to keep men from meddling in their own business. In order to re-establish peace in Europe, it had been necessary to order each and every man to believe in the truths of the Church acknowledged by the prince.

The case was altered after the French Revolution, when two new ideas gradually won men's minds: the juridical equality of the members of the collectivity; the aspiration of the governed to belong to a community of their choice, a community of their own.

The first idea, carried to its logical consequences, implied the elimination of the distinction between victors and vanquished within the collectivity, as of the distinction between orders, i.e., between nobles and commoners. "Thus a conqueror who reduces a conquered people to slavery ought always to reserve to himself the means (for means there are without number) of restoring that people to their liberty."[6] In the democratic age, we would say that imperial domination finds its outlet either

in accession to independence on the part of the conquered populations, or in the integration of the colonies with the metropolitan country in a multinational (more or less federal or centralized) complex. The choice itself between these two outcomes is determined less by the desires of statesmen than by the nature of the metropolitan country. It is difficult for a strictly national state, like France, to become the nucleus of a multinational community. A state with universal pretensions, like the Soviet State, can attempt a policy of integration on a grand scale.

The second idea, intimately related to the first, is that self-determination of the governed *cannot* be repressed, and *should not* be constrained by force. The national idea, it is true, oscillates between two formulas, that of nationality embedded within the historical, if not the biological, being of populations, and that of the voluntary decision whereby each man (or each group) must determine the political collectivity to which he (or it) will belong. According to the first formula, Alsace was more or less German in 1871; according to the second, it was French.

The national ideal is not entirely new, nor did the authentic citizens of the city-states or monarchies obey just any prince. However, even the nobles could pass from the service of one sovereign to that of another without creating the scandal of treason. The extension of citizenship to all members of the collectivity profoundly transformed the meaning of the national idea. If all the subjects became citizens, or if the citizens refused to obey just any master because they sought to participate in the state, political units could no longer take for their objective the conquest of just any territory or just any population. Moreover, the violation of this prohibition was generally "punished" by the difficulty and the cost of governing recalcitrant populations.

In other words, the concrete objectives that political units choose do not evolve with the techniques of combat and production alone, but also with historical ideas associated with the organization and government of the collectivities. In the long run a state does not apply two philosophies, one internally, the other externally. It does not keep both citizens and subjects under its orders indefinitely. If it seeks to keep subjects externally, it will end by turning its own citizens into subjects.

The concrete objectives of states, in a given period, are still not precisely defined by the *state of techniques* (of combat and of production) and *historical ideas*. We must also take into account what we shall call, with the theoreticians of international law, *custom*. The conduct of states with regard to each other, the procedures they consider legitimate, the cunning or the brutality from which they abstain, are

not directly determined by the organization of the army or of the economy. Strategic-diplomatic conduct is a matter of custom. Tradition bequeaths, from generation to generation, great or remote goals which statesmen sometimes refuse to forget, against all reason. In 1917, when the government of the Third Republic, in a secret agreement with the Tsar's government, upheld the Russian claims to the Dardanelles as compensation for Russian support of its own claims to the left bank of the Rhine, the *custom of bargaining* and *traditional natural frontiers* prevailed over the techniques and ideas of the period. Perhaps economic and ideological rationality prevail over the habits of the past and the passions of circumstances, but they prevail only in the long run.

NOTES

1. Which does not exclude the fact that each also desired the objectives suggested by the two other terms.

2. It would be wrong to do so; man does not live by bread alone.

3. When we use such an expression we personify a political unity, we introduce no particular metaphysic: it is clear that men, in the name of France, have taken the decision. But the very object of [*Peace and War*] implies that we consider states as endowed with intelligence and will.

4. "May the day soon come when our fellow citizens, close-pressed in our African France, will overflow into Morocco and Tu-

nisia, and finally establish that Mediterranean empire which will not only be a satisfaction for our pride, but which will certainly, in the future state of the world, be the last resource of our greatness." This text occurs at the end of *La France nouvelle*, by Prévost-Pradol.

5. "It is a conqueror's responsibility to repair a part of the harm he has done. I therefore define the right of conquest thus: a necessary, legitimate but unhappy power, which leaves the conqueror under a heavy obligation of repairing the injuries done to humanity." (*L'Esprit des lois*, X, 4.)

6. *Ibid.*, X, 3.

Vital Interests:
By Whom and How Determined?

BERNARD BRODIE

At any one time, the United States is committed to a set of strategic policies aimed at supporting or implementing certain purposes usually designated by the term "vital interests." One often hears a good deal of glib talk about our "vital interests," as if the speaker knew exactly what they are or ought to be. Yet vital interests are not objective facts fixed in nature. They are instead the products of fallible human judgment, on matters concerning which agreement is usually less than universal. Was it a vital interest in 1962 that Soviet intermediate range ballistic missiles (IRBMs) be kept out of Cuba? If so, why was it not considered a vital interest also to keep Soviet troops and surface-to-air missiles (SAMs) out? One type was held permissible, the other not. The judgment in each instance was President Kennedy's, and in each he had ample support but by no means universal concurrence. Some feared he demanded too much; others were sure it was not enough.

It is obvious that prevailing conceptions of American vital interests, which are effectively those held by the Administration in power, have changed drastically with time, especially over the three decades since we entered World War II. With closer scrutiny, we can see them continue to change before our very eyes. In some instances, we know that if yesterday's decision on vital interests could be called back, it would be changed. And yet, we are not talking about mere gossamer. Some interests will be vital beyond any shadow of doubt. In other instances, the conception of what is vital may be subject to debate, but we should bear in mind what the debate is about. It is not about what should be regarded as trivial, but rather about what should be regarded as having that peculiar and special importance denoted by the word "vital."

Let us, therefore, attempt to explore, first, what we mean by "vital interests," and by whom and how they are determined; and second, how we go about deciding what strategic policies are required by those interests. Inasmuch as our military *capabilities* have much bearing on what we decide to regard as vital interests—a small power must obviously be much more restrained in its conception of vital interests than a superpower—we must regard the relationship between our foreign policies and our military power as being inherently reciprocal.

By definition, which is to say by customary usage, our "vital interests" are those interests against the infringement of which we are prepared to take some kind of serious military action. We should observe that by this definition we exclude many issues of genuine and even important national interest. Thus, while nations have had what they called tariff or trade wars, that is,

From *Strategy and National Interests: Reflections for the Future* by Bernard Brodie. Copyright © 1971 by National Strategy Information Center, Inc. Reprinted by permission of the publisher.

retaliations in kind for what were deemed to be discriminating or otherwise offensive trade practices, they have rarely if ever fought genuine military wars over such issues. Marxian and neo-Marxian theorists to the contrary notwithstanding, historical evidence over the past two centuries overwhelmingly discredits the notion that conflicts of economic interest are an important cause of war, let alone the primary cause.[1] A war, especially what promises to be a great war, is always certain to be far more costly than any strictly economic issues could possibly justify (unless the latter genuinely relate to the question of survival); and while this fact does not by itself prove the assertion of the preceding sentence, it is nevertheless not as foreign to the appreciation of the decision makers as the theorists like to imagine.

If economic and various other important interests are excluded, however, what do we include in the notion of "vital interests?" For a nation not bent on expansion, the answer usually is that vital interests concern those issues which are deemed to affect the survival or security of the nation, meaning security specifically against military attack. Obviously, a nation ready to resort to aggression to gain its ends is expanding its conception of vital interests to include those objectives which it wants badly enough to be prepared to fight for them. As a matter of record, however, aggression has more often than not been justified by its perpetrator on the ground that it was allegedly necessary to the ultimate security of the state, and this allegation has sometimes been sincerely meant. However, inasmuch as the United States is clearly not now, and has not for a long time been bent on territorial expansion of any kind—a posture universally approved by its citizenry—we may dismiss from our present consideration those interests which are not somehow conceived of as defensive, that is, in some manner concerned with security.

It is clear enough what we mean by national security when we are considering a direct military attack upon our own territories. This is normally the only kind of national security that very small nations can afford to let themselves be concerned about—though for the sake of such security, even they will sometimes join alliances which in principle require them to be concerned about other frontiers besides their own. Great nations, however, and especially what we now call superpowers, will often be concerned with what they deem to be threats to the national security which are much more distant in space, time, and even in conception than the kind of direct attack on home territories described above.

By saying that the threat may be more distant "even in conception," we mean the following: in some situations viewed as menacing, considerations of appropriate response tend towards emphasizing the national responsibility rather than the national peril. A superpower like the United States does have unique (though far from unlimited) capacities to influence events throughout the world, and its leaders would be remiss in their duties if they did not regularly seek to exercise that influence in a manner calculated to enhance the nation's long-term interests, meaning above all its security interests. If that exercise of influence takes the very serious form of military intervention, the citizenry will certainly demand assurance that the purpose is indeed to enhance security; they will invariably receive that assurance, and normally it is quite sincerely meant. Certainly that has been true of our interventions both in Korea and in Vietnam. In both cases, it is fair to say, even the supporters of our intervention admitted that the peril to the United States was neither immediate nor direct. They did, however, hold it to be real—which is one of the respects in which their opponents in each case differed from them.

There is not only a considerable range of threats but also a wide range of military actions for dealing with those threats. This range of actions reflects varying degrees of conviction about whether our national security is essentially involved, or about the immediacy of the threat. The view that communism must be contained wherever in the world it threatens to expand, especially when that expansion is by aggressive military action, will stimulate a very different American response in Central Asia from what it will in some special areas like Western Europe or Cuba. When the Chinese Communists were attacking Indian outposts in the Himalayas in 1962, the Kennedy Administration contented itself with rushing arms to India by aircraft. But the response we were making at the very same time to the action of the Soviet Union in placing IRBMs in Cuba was of an entirely different order of magnitude.

Another variable worth noting has to do with the degree of real risk estimated to be inherent in a commitment. It is easy to offer a guarantee against external aggression to a country which is in little, if any, danger of attack anyway. It has long been a cliché that the young American republic which promulgated the Monroe Doctrine was depending upon the shield of the British Navy. It is also true, however, and at least equally important, that by that time the countries of Europe which could still be called great powers—and Spain was no longer such—had no particular interest in expanding their holdings in the New World. Even Napoleon III's meddling in Mexico was tentative and timid. This does not imply that the Monroe Doctrine was ineffective; it only says that the burden it had to carry was not excessively heavy.

By the same token, guarantees have often been advanced on the supposition that the guarantee itself (or alliance) would sufficiently dissuade the potential aggressor so that it would never have to be fulfilled. Undoubtedly there was much of that attitude behind the exuberance with which the Truman Administration committed the United States to all the countries protected by the North Atlantic Treaty of 1949 as well as by other alliances of the time. Why else should we have included Norway in that treaty, and later Turkey? Norway especially was much too small to be a useful ally; it had a common frontier with the USSR, but that frontier was in the far north, and the Soviet Union had never shown much interest in it. To be sure, we are talking here not about the basic justification for NATO, but rather about one idea among the mix of ideas that went into the formulation of the original plan for that alliance, and which certainly helps to account for its extension to weak, peripheral nations.

It should, however, be said about this idea that while historically it has often worked, it has sometimes failed spectacularly. It was the idea by which the principle of collective security under the League of Nations Covenant was rationalized. It was reiterated over and over again throughout the 1920s and early 1930s that if only nations would agree upon this principle, they would never have to deliver. But Mussolini in his attack on Ethiopia in 1936 showed that this was not true; after a feeble attempt at sanctions, the League of Nations security system collapsed. It was undoubtedly because Mussolini sensed the weakness of the guarantee that he was ready to flout it.

Our reference above to the Monroe Doctrine should remind us of the enormous role of traditions and slogans in delimiting vital interests. British diplomacy was dominated for three centuries by the concept of maintaining the "balance of power" in Europe. Almost as strong and as ancient was the slogan that British security depended upon maintaining the freedom of the Low Countries. The function of such traditions is twofold. First, they save considerable wear and tear on the analytical powers of men in high office, who are thereby spared the necessity of reevaluating each threat as it presents itself; and second, by making the response of the offended state more predictable, they serve as a warning to the potential aggressor. The possible penalty, however, is very great. The slogans that make up the traditions by which "vital interests" are determined are very likely to outlive whatever justification they originally had.

It is sometimes alleged that access to certain raw materials, especially from nearby sources, constitutes a "real" vital interest. They are indeed such if the power concerned insists on so regarding them, but there is no reason to assume that there is something inherently objective about such a determination. A power like the United States, with its enormous fund of domestic raw materials, and with its technological resources for making synthetics and for finding substitutes for various scarce materials, is not likely to win foreign assent to the proposition that access to Venezuelan oil or Chilean copper, for example, is vital to its existence. Pre-World War II Japan made such a claim with respect to what it called its East Asia Co-Prosperity Sphere, and it was the refusal of the United States to go along with this notion that produced war between them.

In recent times, international tolerance for such claims has sharply declined. When Britain and France took military action against Egypt in 1956 because President Gamal Abdel Nasser nationalized the Suez Canal, they quickly discovered that the rest of the world regarded their action as anachronistic and intolerable. The pressure imposed upon them, especially by their chief ally, the United States, obliged them to desist—after which it became abundantly obvious that the transfer of control over the Canal through nationalization made no discernible difference

to the general commercial or strategic interests of Great Britain and France. Apart from the quite insignificant question of the value of the shares of the company previously operating the Canal, the question of control was adventitiously exposed to being not only not vital but not even important.

The more distant or indirect the threat that is alleged to affect our national security, the more controversial is the question whether it actually does warrant a military response, and if so, what kind. In this respect, we have witnessed—for example between 1939 and 1945, and again between 1965 and 1970—remarkable changes in the climate of American opinion concerning the range and scope of adversary actions warranting a direct military response. The first of these time frames represented a period of United States emergence from isolationism, and the second appears (at this rather short range) to represent, certainly not a return to isolationism, but nevertheless a distinct turning away from an attitude that incorporated a fairly ready acceptance of intervention.

Our entrance into the Korean War in June-July 1950, after Communist North Korea invaded the non-Communist South, was a kind of action that appeared entirely appropriate at the height of the "cold war" era; but it seemed quite foreign to the mood of 1970, the era of the Nixon Doctrine,[2] when the only significant debate over President Richard M. Nixon's policy of withdrawing American soldiers from Vietnam concerned the question whether the rate of withdrawal was fast enough. At this writing, it is too early to assert conclusively that the latter change represents a turning point with long-term implications, rather than merely a temporary pause. But if the present writer may be permitted a prediction based on his appraisal of the current scene, he would hold that the change appears very definitely to be a long-term one. For one thing, our frustrations in Vietnam, and the resulting perturbations and divisions within the United States, have cast a new light on the real capabilities of the country for this kind of intervention, especially when it is based on the draft. We have also learned a good deal—the hard way—about the uncertainties of estimating the various kinds of risk involved (including the political risk to the President who makes the decision), and also the total costs (including social and political as well as economic costs), as against the likely effectiveness of any action to shore up a partner who is weak not only materially but also politically.

To be sure, future situations will have distinctive characteristics. Not all of them will involve jungle fighting against a small but determined and skillful opponent. Still, the nation has lost a certain innocence about appraising future situations that are at all comparable to Vietnam, however distinctive their characteristics may be. We have also learned the wisdom of the late President Dwight D. Eisenhower's extreme reluctance to consider undertaking an intervention alone. Even though we might be carrying a disproportionate burden, the cooperative participation of other powers, as in Korea, places the entire operation in a different moral light both in our own country and in the world outside. But in this respect, too, the times have changed; it is very difficult to imagine in the future the kind of joint enterprise in furtherance of a United Nations "police action" against an aggressor that we witnessed in the Korean War.

All this does not mean the end of American military intervention abroad.

One must, however, be alive to the likelihood that we have seen the end of the kind of lightheartedness that went into American talk about "putting out brush fires" wherever they might occur. It is already becoming difficult to recall that mood, represented, for example, by Mr. McNamara's request for a fleet of "fast logistic ships" (subsequently denied him by Congress) which was supposed to facilitate such fire-fighting. Among the things we have learned is that restraint in the application of force—in order to keep that application compatible with its purpose—may make the force applied ineffective for its purpose. Thus, to grant sanctuary and to withhold tactical nuclear weapons may be correct policy, but such restraints have to be recognized as being costly, possibly very costly, in military effectiveness. For the future, this is bound to mean not fewer limitations upon the use of force, but rather fewer occasions for applying force under circumstances requiring restraint.

Having thus considered how variable and subjective are those interests which we call vital, we must nevertheless be clear that we cannot dispense with the basic concept. Some interests are quite unambiguously vital. The perennial problem for the leaders of a superpower like the United States is to determine the outer boundaries of what is truly vital, and in more practical terms to decide—under the whole range of relevant circumstances prevailing at the time—what kinds of threat indicate what kinds of response. To be able to make these decisions even reasonably well—the proof being mainly in the outcome—is to display statesmanship in foreign and strategic affairs.

NOTES

1. Four books on this subject may be regarded as classics, having, among other things, remained in print for an extraordinarily long time. First is the small volume by the British economist Lionel Robbins, *The Economic Causes of War* (London: Jonathan Cape, 1939). Important and relevant historical research is contained in two books by American economist-historians, Herbert Feis, *Europe the World's Banker, 1870–1914* (New Haven:

Yale University Press, 1930); and Eugene Staley, *War and the Private Investor* (Chicago: University of Chicago Press, 1935); and also in the book by the American historian William L. Langer, *The Diplomacy of Imperialism* (New York: Knopf, 1935).

2. Much ambiguity attaches to what President Nixon meant when he first enunciated the so-called "Nixon Doctrine" on the island of Guam in July 1969, and in his further elucidation of his foreign policy objectives in February 1970, reprinted by the Government Printing Office under the title, *U.S. Foreign Policy for the 1970's, A New Strategy for Peace.* The basic message for our allies in the Western Pacific seems to have been that they should henceforward not depend on the kind of assistance with fighting manpower that we contributed to Vietnam, but that they may continue to depend on us for support in military materiel. But see Earl C. Ravenal, "The Nixon Doctrine and Our Asian Commitments," *Foreign Affairs,* January 1971.

The Irreducible National Interest and Basic Premises About World Conditions

Seyom Brown

National interest is more important than ideology.
John F. Kennedy

Between the lofty reiteration of outworn platitudes and the glib profession of radical alternatives are found the deepest and most persistent reasons for basic United States foreign policy. Those who fear the smallest concession to criticism will topple the whole edifice of postwar foreign policy, and those who are trying to topple it with adolescent iconoclasm, mistake the clichés for the underlying concept of the national interest. This underlying concept was indeed the source of many policy formulations—particularly the rhetoric—now regarded as Cold War clichés. But the concept antedated the Cold War and will likely outlast it. It set the boundaries to and had much to do with shaping the character of the foreign commitments and programs of each of the Administrations described [here]. Without his profound appreciation of this same underlying concept John F. Kennedy would not have been able to accomplish as much as he did in his efforts to pry loose the barnacled formulations of the fifteen years previous to his Presidency. And only such an appreciation will allow current and future national leaders to face squarely the awful choices ahead.

The concept of an irreducible national interest is imprecise, but essential, and deeply rooted in the American political experience.

Each of the men whose constituency has been the national electorate have been intensely aware that they were bound by an historical, Constitutional, and current political obligation to service, first and foremost, at least two basic objectives of the national society: its physical survival; and the perpetuation of something called the American Way of Life—in the familiar words, "to secure the blessings of liberty to ourselves and our posterity."

Although it was fashionable in some circles during the years 1959 to 1961 to debate the proposition "Better Dead than Red" or its converse, highly placed officials were reluctant to enter into the speculative discourse, however morally instructive. The Presidential view of the matter has been constant from Truman to Johnson: the primary task is to assure that such a choice never has to be made. Foreign commitments and national security programs have been constrained by firm insistence from the White House that *both* survival and the non-totalitarian condition of the nation are to be placed ahead of all other objectives.

A third imperative with almost as much compelling force upon highest

From Seyom Brown: *The Faces of Power*, New York: Columbia University Press, 1968. Reprinted by permission of the publisher.

policy levels has been the injunction to promote the general welfare, or the economic well-being of the whole society. From the vantage point of the Presidency, there is a good deal of political steam in the passion of the populace to have its liberties and eat well too.

The highest officials, in their need to erect their foreign policies on the bedrock of historical consensus, often attempt to show how their actions derive from these Constitutional and constant political imperatives: we seek today, as we did in Washington's time, explains President Johnson, "to protect the life of our nation, to preserve the liberty of our citizens, and to pursue the happiness of our people. This is the touchstone of our world policy."[1] Such resounding claims are more than ritualistic bell-ringing. They are reflective of Johnson's perception that the least common denominator of political demand, from the national constituency at large, is that the President pursue *simultaneously* the nation's interest in its own survival and those conditions which allow for the perpetuation of the nation's essential sociopolitical patterns.

This perception is sustained by the dominant themes of debate between the two great political parties. The party in opposition will often accuse the party in the White House of sacrificing too much of one basic value in the service of another. But the premises of critic and defender alike are that all of the basic values—survival, liberty, and economic well-being—can and ought to be pursued at the same time; and that this irreducible triumvirate of interest must not be subordinated to other considerations.

Thus, the strongest criticisms by Democrats against the Eisenhower Administration involved the charge that the nation's defense requirements were being neglected because of a slavish pursuit of a balanced budget. The President, also fending off those in his own party who wanted to reduce defense expenditures still more, defended the existing size and structure of the armed forces with the argument that "to build less would expose the nation to aggression. To build excessively, under the influence of fear, could defeat our purposes and impair or destroy the very freedom and economic system our military defenses are designed to protect."[2]

The concept of an irreducible national interest provides no specific guidance for its implementation—therefore the debate. The point is that, in the offices of ultimate national responsibility, the concept is considerably more than a cliché. Too vague to determine programs and specific commitments, it nonetheless constrains the range of policy choices. Although the concept is dependent for its programmatic expressions upon the particular Administration's definition of the essential American liberties (how much freedom of enterprise? how much freedom of speech?), premises on what makes the economy tick, and analyses of the capabilities and intentions of potential foreign adversaries, the basic Presidential impulse to lead the nation away from situations where ultimate choices between survival, liberty, and welfare have to be made is in large measure responsible for the central thread of continuity in foreign policy from Truman to Johnson.

No less important a reason for the continuity in foreign policy from Truman to Johnson has been the persistence of the view that the primary threats to this irreducible national interest are the spread of International Communism and another world war. The constancy as well as the changes in foreign policy which have occurred may be read as the theme and variations of the basic objective of avoiding one of these threats without bringing on the other. The two prongs of this basic objective are derived from a set of premises about world conditions, and what these conditions seem to require of the United States in order to perpetuate itself and its Way of Life. This set of critical premises—those which have persisted in top policy levels over the past twenty years and have had a pervasive impact on specific commitments and actions—can be stated as follows:

A. The Soviet Union is motivated (how strongly is a variable) to be the dominant world power, and eventually to fashion the world into a single political system based on the Soviet model. The premise that the Soviets are motivated only to secure their society against outside interference has never been bought at the highest levels of the United States government since the Second World War. However, there has been constant questioning, and occasional diplomatic probing, to determine the extent to which the actions of the Soviets to implement expansionist motives are constrained by their perception that such action may place the security of the Soviet Union in danger and/or take away from their ability to achieve domestic economic and social goals. There apparently has been increasing receptivity in White House and State Department circles, since the Cuban missile crisis, the Test Ban, and the widening of the Sino-Soviet split, toward the premise that the Soviets have seen the futility of expansionist adventures and would now like to turn their energies to domestic development tasks.[3] But varying interpretations are made of the presumed Soviet constriction of their external power drive. It may, as some analysts suggest, be the natural result of the maturing of their sociopolitical system—a supplanting of the revolutionary leadership by a bureaucratic generation most interested in efficiency and political stability. Or, it may be primarily the result of the application of the Leninist stratagem of "two steps forward, one step backward," in the hope that a relaxation of international tension now will lead to a slackening in the West, during which

time the Soviet Union will be tending to the reorientation of its economy and technology in preparation for the next phase of hostile competition. There are many versions of these theses, each suggesting a somewhat different set of United States policy responses and initiatives to the Soviet Union. . . . For present purposes it is only necessary to take note of this turbulence beneath the surface constancy of the basic premise that the Soviets would be expanding if we, the United States, were not containing them. The desirability of containing the Soviets at least within their present sphere is not in question; but the appropriate role for the United States in this containment function has increasingly become a central issue of policy.

B. Another critical premise underlying the observed constancy in foreign policy from Truman to Johnson has been that in another world war the United States would quickly become a prime target for mass destruction. Early in the period the technology of warfare, plus the obvious strategies deduced from the new technology, were seen to be bringing about a situation in which the United States could not become involved in war against its largest rival without thereby placing the lives of millions of American civilians in jeopardy. By 1948 there was consensus among United States scientists and military planners that it would be only a matter of a few years before the Soviet Union developed such a capability. In the interim the Soviet Union could compensate for its strategic inferiority vis-à-vis the United States (we could already reach the Soviet Union with weapons of mass destruction from our overseas bases) by holding "hostage" the urban populations of Western Europe. By the mid-1950s Soviet thermonuclear developments plus great improvements in their long-range strategic bomber fleet made the vulnerability of the continental United States in a world war an operating premise of military planners and top foreign policy officials. The avoidance of another world war was seen to be equal in importance to preventing the expansion of Communism. "Deterrence" became for a time the magic word, presumably eliminating the potential conflict in priority between preventing strategic attack on the United States and containing the Soviets. But the pursuit of peace could no longer be dismissed as mere rhetoric. World peace, meaning basically the avoidance of general war between the United States and the Soviet Union, had become irrevocably an *essential* policy objective—that is, a necessary means of preserving the irreducible national interest.

C. Yet prevailing premises about the distribution of international power since the Second World War would not allow the pursuit of world peace to take *precedence* over the containment of Communism. The war had left the Soviet Union surrounded by power vacuums where previously it had been hemmed in by constellations of great power. The only source of great countervailing power now was the United States. Therefore, the desire to prevent the extension of Soviet power (assuming the Soviets wanted to expand the territorial basis of their power) carried with it a responsibility for the United States to make its power available to dissuade or block the Soviets. At first, the United States tried to dissuade the Soviets from expanding by appeals to the spirit of the Grand Alliance and the decent opinions of mankind as reflected in the United Nations Charter (there was no expectation that the collective security machinery of the United Nations could be used as a coercive instrument against the Soviet Union). Under the immediate postwar assumption that the Soviets, requiring foreign capital for reconstruction, were anxious to maintain the goodwill of the West, the Truman Administration early tried by tough talk alone to induce the Soviets into a more benign posture. But as it appeared that Stalin was more anxious to take advantage of opportunities to expand his territorial base than to maintain the goodwill of the West, the Truman Administration soon began to seek means of redressing the local imbalances of power around the Soviet periphery. At first, these efforts were concentrated in economic and social measures to reconstruct wartorn Europe and Japan. But Soviet military power plays against Iran, Turkey, Greece, and Czechoslovakia brought into prominence at the White House level premises of the critical effect of military balances, local and global, on the Soviets' propensity to expand. The Berlin blockade of 1948 apparently sealed the case for Truman, and Secretary of State Acheson was given the go-ahead to make explicit in the North Atlantic Treaty the unequivocal commitment of United States military power to counter any Soviet attempts to exploit their military superiority in Europe. In exchange for this commitment of American power the West Europeans were expected to work urgently to build up their own military power, so that the burden would not fall disproportionately on the United States. The willingness to forego even our commitment to world peace, if indeed that were necessary to prevent the Soviets from forcibly adding unto themselves the vast power potential of Western Europe, was by 1949 an explicit premise of United States foreign policy. Such explicitness was possible with respect to Western Europe because its fall to the Soviets could be defined as tantamount to "surrender." The Soviets would become the dominant world power, and could eventually overpower the United States itself.

D. Thus, the "balance of power" became the critical concept for determining the priority to be given in any specific situation to containment of Communism or the avoidance of world war, should these two objectives appear impossible to pursue at the same time. Each of the four postwar Administrations have agreed on at least this much: if a Communist success in a given conflict would critically undermine the power of the non-Communist world to dissuade the Communist world from further advances, then, presumably, the balance of power itself was at stake, and, since, by extension, this meant the survival of the United States, there was no question of where the national interest would lie. In such situations, peace would have to give way temporarily to the active containment of Communism, even if the temporary breakdown of peace would place the United States in danger of direct attack.

E. But none of these premises provided sufficient advance guidance for basic policy in situations where the overall U.S.-Soviet power balance was not thought to be immediately at stake. If the Soviets were only making a limited grab, would it be worth a world war to frustrate them? What if another Communist nation were attempting to extend its power—would we, should we, automatically equate such an attempt with an increment to the Soviet side of the global balance of power? In global balance of power terms, how should we regard the coming to power *within* nations of supposedly indigenous Communist movements? The fact that the United States, through successive Administrations, has not been able to answer such questions *in principle* in advance of unfolding situations has been in large measure responsible for some of our major policy crises over the past two decades. The decision not to bring our coercive power to bear to prevent Mao Tse-tung's victory over Chiang Kai-shek; the expenditure of blood and treasure in Korea to rectify the gross miscalculation of the Soviets that we would not be willing to intervene there to oppose aggression; the Truman-MacArthur controversy; the great debate over "massive retaliation" vs. "flexible response," and particularly

its expression in NATO policy; the Quemoy and Matsu crises of the 1950s; the Bay of Pigs, the Cuban missile crisis, and the chronic problem of how to deal with Castro; the Dominican military intervention of 1965; and, of course, Vietnam—all of these have produced as much dissensus as consensus in the nation, precisely because of the existence of varied concepts of international "power."

There has been constancy at one very important level of analysis and policy. Premises of the irreducible national interest, and basic assumptions about world conditions have given persistence to the two-pronged objective of attempting to prevent the spread of International Communism and to prevent the outbreak of a Third World War. As perceived by those responsible for the conduct of United States foreign policy, this has meant primarily influencing the Soviets and the Communist Chinese not to try to expand their territorial base, and influencing other nations to pursue policies that would enhance their resistance to control by these two Communist giants.

But, the major issues have been over means, not objectives. The problem has been essentially a problem of *power*. The difficult question has been what *kinds* of power—what capabilities —are needed to accomplish the agreed upon objectives of the nation. . . .

The objectives of containing Communism and preserving peace do not exhaust the range of objectives animating United States foreign policy since the Second World War. These have been emphasized first, however, because they have been generally accepted during the period as practically inevitable derivatives from the irreducible national interest of survival in a non-totalitarian condition.

The nation has also considered itself committed to interests of a more altruistic nature, and much of the story of the past two decades centers on attempts to reconcile the requirements of implementing these altruistic interests with the requirements of self-preserva-

tion. But again, the major arbiter of choice has proven to be the concept of the global balance of power.

NOTES

1. Address by President Johnson to The Associated Press, April 21, 1965, in the *New York Times,* April 22, 1965.
2. State of the Union Message by the President, January 5, 1956.
3. See, for example, Walt W. Rostow, "The Third Round," *Foreign Affairs* (October 1963), pp. 1–10.

On War

KARL VON CLAUSEWITZ

ABSOLUTE AND REAL WAR

The Plan of the War comprehends the whole Military Act; through it that Act becomes a whole, which must have one final determinate object, in which all particular objects must become absorbed. No War is commenced, or, at least, no War should be commenced, if people acted wisely, without first seeking a reply to the question, What is to be attained by and in the same? The first is the final object; the other is the intermediate aim. By this chief consideration the whole course of the War is prescribed, the extent of the means and the measure of energy are determined; its influence manifests itself down to the smallest organ of action.

. . . [T]he overthrow of the enemy is the natural end of the act of War; and . . . if we would keep within the strictly philosophical limits of the idea, there can be no other in reality.

As this idea must apply to both the belligerent parties, it must follow, that there can be no suspension in the Military Act, and peace cannot take place until one or other of the parties concerned is overthrown.

. . . [T]he simple principle of hostility applied to its embodiment, man, and all circumstances out of which it makes a War, is subject to checks and modifications from causes which are inherent in the apparatus of War.

But this modification is not nearly sufficient to carry us from the original conception of War to the concrete form in which it almost everywhere appears.

Most Wars appear only as an angry feeling on both sides, under the influence of which, each side takes up arms to protect himself, and to put his adversary in fear, and—when opportunity offers, to strike a blow. They are, therefore, not like mutually destructive elements brought into collision, but like tensions of two elements still apart which discharge themselves in small partial shocks.

But what is now the non-conducting medium which hinders the complete discharge? Why is the philosophical conception not satisfied? That medium consists in the number of interests, forces, and circumstances of various kinds, in the existence of the State, which are affected by the War, and through the infinite ramifications of which the logical consequence cannot be carried out as it would on the simple threads of a few conclusions; in this labyrinth it sticks fast, and man, who in great things as well as in small, usually acts more on the impulse of ideas and feelings, than according to strictly logical conclusions, is hardly conscious of his confusion, unsteadiness of purpose, and inconsistency.

But if the intelligence by which the War is decreed could even go over all these things relating to the War, without for a moment losing sight of its aim, still all the other intelligences in the State which are concerned may not be able to do the same; thus an opposition arises, and with that comes the

From *On War* by Gen. Karl von Clausewitz, Book VIII, chapters 2, 3, 6. Translated by Col. J. J. Graham. Edited by Col. F. N. Maude.

necessity for a force capable of overcoming the inertia of the whole mass—a force which is seldom forthcoming to the full.

This inconsistency takes place on one or other of the two sides, or it may be on both sides, and becomes the cause of the War being something quite different to what it should be, according to the conception of it—a half-and-half production, a thing without a perfect inner cohesion.

This is how we find it almost everywhere, and we might doubt whether our notion of its absolute character or nature was founded in reality, if we had not seen real warfare make its appearance in this absolute completeness just in our own times. After a short introduction performed by the French Revolution, the impetuous Buonaparte quickly brought it to this point. Under him it was carried on without slackening for a moment until the enemy was prostrated, and the counter stroke followed almost with as little remission. Is it not natural and necessary that this phenomenon should lead us back to the original conception of War with all its rigorous deductions?

Shall we now rest satisfied with this idea, and judge of all Wars according to it, however much they may differ from it—deduce from it all the requirements of theory?

We must decide upon this point, for we can say nothing trustworthy on the Plan of War until we have made up our minds whether War should only be of this kind, or whether it may be of another kind.

If we give an affirmative to the first, then our Theory will be, in all respects, nearer to the necessary, it will be a clearer and more settled thing. But what should we say then of all Wars since those of Alexander up to the time of Buonaparte, if we except some campaigns of the Romans? We should have to reject them in a lump, and yet we cannot, perhaps, do so without being ashamed of our presumption.

But an additional evil is, that we must say to ourselves, that in the next ten years there may perhaps be a War of that same kind again, in spite of our Theory; and that this Theory, with a rigorous logic, is still quite powerless against the force of circumstances. We must, therefore, decide to construe War as it is to be, and not from pure conception, but by allowing room for everything of a foreign nature which mixes up with it and fastens itself upon it—all the natural inertia and friction of its parts, the whole of the inconsistency, the vagueness and hesitation (or timidity) of the human mind: we shall have to grasp the idea that War, and the form which we give it, proceeds from ideas, feelings, and circumstances which dominate for the moment; indeed, if we would be perfectly candid we must admit that this has even been the case where it has taken its absolute character, that is, under Buonaparte.

If we must do so, if we must grant that War originates and takes its form not from a final adjustment of the innumerable relations with which it is connected, but from some amongst them which happen to predominate, then it follows, as a matter of course, that it rests upon a play of possibilities, probabilities, good fortune and bad, in which rigorous logical deduction often gets lost, and in which it is in general a useless, inconvenient instrument for the head; then it also follows that War may be a thing which is sometimes War in a greater, sometimes in a lesser degree.

All this, theory must admit, but it is its duty to give the foremost place to the absolute form of War, and to use that form as a general point of direction, that whoever wishes to learn something from theory, may accustom himself never to lose sight of it, to regard it as the natural measure of all his hopes and fears, in order to approach it *where he can, or where he must.*

That a leading idea, which lies at the root of our thoughts and actions, gives them a certain tone and character, even when the immediately determining grounds come from totally different regions, is just as certain as that the painter can give this or that tone to his picture by the colours with which he lays on his ground.

Theory is indebted to the last Wars for being able to do this effectually now. Without these warning examples of the destructive force of the element set free, she might have talked herself hoarse to no purpose; no one would have believed possible what all have now lived to see realised.

Would Prussia have ventured to penetrate into France in the year 1798 with 70,000 men, if she had foreseen that the reaction in case of failure would be so strong as to overthrow the old balance of power in Europe?

Would Prussia, in 1806, have made War with 100,000 against France, if she had supposed that the first pistol shot would be a spark in the heart of the mine, which would blow it into the air?

INTERDEPENDENCE OF THE PARTS IN WAR

According as we have in view the absolute form of War, or one of the real forms deviating more or less from it, so likewise different notions of its result will arise.

In the absolute form, where everything is the effect of its natural and necessary cause, one thing follows another in rapid succession; there is, if we may use the expression, no neutral space; there is—on account of the manifold reactionary effects which War contains in itself, on account of the connection in which, strictly speaking, the whole series of combats follow one after another, on account of the culminating point which every victory has, beyond which losses and defeats commence—on account of all these natural relations of War there is, I say, only *one result,* to wit, the *final result.* Until it takes place nothing is decided, nothing won, nothing lost. Here we may say indeed: the end crowns the work. In this view, therefore, War is an indivisible whole, the parts of which (the subordinate results) have no value except in their relation to this whole. The conquest of Moscow, and of half Russia in 1812, was of no value to Buonaparte unless it obtained for him the peace which he desired. But it was only a part of his Plan of campaign; to complete that Plan, one part was still wanted, the destruction of the Russian Army, if we suppose this, added to the other success, then the peace was as certain as it is possible for things of this kind to be. This second part Buonaparte missed at the right time, and he could never afterwards attain it, and so the whole of the first part was not only useless, but fatal to him.

To this view of the relative connection of results in War, which may be regarded as extreme, stands opposed another extreme, according to which War is composed of single independent results, in which, as in any number of games played, the preceding has no influence on the next following; everything here, therefore, depends only on the sum total of the results, and we can lay up each single one like a counter at play.

Just as the first kind of view derives its truth from the nature of things, so we find that of the second in history. There are cases without number in which a small moderate advantage might have been gained without any very onerous condition being attached to it. The more the element of War is modified the more common these cases become; but as little as the first of the views now imagined was ever completely realised in any War, just as little is there any War in which the last suits in all respects, and the first can be dispensed with.

If we keep to the first of these supposed views, we must perceive the necessity of every War being looked upon as a whole from the very commencement, and that at the very first step forwards, the Commander should have in his eye the object to which every line must converge.

If we admit the second view, then subordinate advantages may be pursued on their own account, and the rest left to subsequent events.

As neither of these forms of conception is entirely without result, therefore theory cannot dispense with either. But it makes this difference in the use of them, that it requires the first to be laid as a fundamental idea at the root of everything, and that the latter shall only be used as a modification which is justified by circumstances.

*   *   *

Theory demands, therefore, that at the commencement of every War its character and main outline shall be defined according to what the political conditions and relations lead us to anticipate as probable. The more that, according to this probability, its character approaches the form of absolute War; the more its outline embraces the mass of the belligerent States and draws them into the vortex—so much the more complete will be the relation of events to one another and the whole, but so much the more necessary will it also be not to take the first step without thinking what may be the last.

OF THE MAGNITUDE OF THE OBJECT OF THE WAR AND THE EFFORTS TO BE MADE

The compulsion which we must use towards our enemy will be regulated by the proportions of our own and his political demands. In so far as these are mutually known they will give the measure of the mutual efforts; but they are not always quite so evident, and this may be a first ground of a difference in the means adopted by each.

The situation and relations of the States are not like each other; this may become a second cause.

The strength of will, the character and capabilities of the Governments are as little like; this is a third cause.

These three elements cause an uncertainty in the calculation of the amount of resistance to be expected, consequently an uncertainty as to the amount of means to be applied and the object to be chosen.

As in War the want of sufficient exertion may result not only in failure but in positive harm, therefore, the two sides respectively seek to outstrip each other, which produces a reciprocal action.

This might lead to the utmost extremity of exertion, if it were possible to define such a point. But then regard for the amount of the political demands would be lost, the means would lose all relation to the end, and in most cases this aim at an extreme effort would be wrecked by the opposing weight of forces within itself.

In this manner, he who undertakes War is brought back again into a middle course, in which he acts to a certain extent upon the principle of only applying so much force and aiming at such an object in War as is just sufficient for the attainment of its political object. To make this principle practicable he must renounce every absolute necessity of a result, and throw out of the calculation remote contingencies.

Here, therefore, the action of the mind leaves the province of science, strictly speaking, of logic and mathematics, and becomes in the widest sense of the term an *Art*, that is, skill in discriminating, by the tact of judgment among an infinite multitude of objects and relations, that which is the most important and decisive. This tact of judgment consists unquestionably more or less in some intuitive comparison of things and relations by which the remote and unimportant are more quickly set aside, and the more immediate and important are sooner discovered than they could be by strictly logical deduction.

In order to ascertain the real scale of the means which we must put forth for War, we must think over the political object both on our own side and on the enemy's side; we must consider the power and position of the enemy's State as well as of our own, the character of his Government and of his people, and the capacities of both, and all that again on our own side, and the political connections of other States, and the effect which the War will produce on those States. That the determination of these diverse circumstances and their diverse connections with each other is an immense problem, that it is the true flash of genius which discovers here in a moment what is right, and that it would be quite out of the question to become master of the complexity merely by a methodical study, it is easy to conceive.

In this sense Buonaparte was quite right when he said that it would be a problem in algebra before which a Newton might stand aghast.

If the diversity and magnitude of the circumstances and the uncertainty as to the right measure augment in a high degree the difficulty of obtaining a right result, we must not overlook the fact that although the incomparable *importance* of the matter does not increase the complexity and difficulty of the problem, still it very much increases the merit of its solution. In men of an ordinary stamp freedom and activity of mind are depressed, not increased, by the sense of danger and responsibility; but where these things give wings to strengthen the judgment, there undoubtedly must be unusual greatness of soul.

First of all, therefore, we must admit that the judgment of an approaching War, on the end to which it should be directed, and on the means which are required, can only be formed after a full consideration of the whole of the circumstances in connection with it: with which therefore must also be combined the most individual traits of the moment; next, that this decision, like all in military life, cannot be purely objective, but must be determined by the mental and moral qualities of Princes, Statesmen, and Generals, whether they are united in the person of one man or not.

*   *   *

WAR AS AN INSTRUMENT OF POLICY

Having made the requisite examination on both sides of that state of antagonism in which the nature of War stands with relation to other interests of men individually and of the bond of society, in order not to neglect any of the opposing elements—an antagonism which is founded in our own nature, and which, therefore, no philosophy can unravel—we shall now look for that unity into which, in practical life, these antagonistic elements combine themselves by partly neutralising each other. We should have brought

forward this unity at the very commencement if it had not been necessary to bring out this contradiction very plainly, and also to look at the different elements separately. Now, this unity is *the conception that War is only a part of political intercourse, therefore by no means an independent thing in itself.*

We know, certainly, that War is only called forth through the political intercourse of Governments and Nations; but in general it is supposed that such intercourse is broken off by War, and that a totally different state of things ensues, subject to no laws but its own.

We maintain, on the contrary, that War is nothing but a continuation of political intercourse, with a mixture of other means. We say mixed with other means in order thereby to maintain at the same time that this political intercourse does not cease by the War itself, is not changed into something quite different, but that, in its essence, it continues to exist, whatever may be the form of the means which it uses, and that the chief lines on which the events of the War progress, and to which they are attached, are only the general features of policy which run all through the War until peace takes place. And how can we conceive it to be otherwise? Does the cessation of diplomatic notes stop the political relations between different Nations and Governments? Is not War merely another kind of writing and language for political thoughts? It has certainly a grammar of its own, but its logic is not peculiar to itself.

Accordingly, War can never be separated from political intercourse, and if, in the consideration of the matter, this is done in any way, all the threads of the different relations are, to a certain extent, broken, and we have before us a senseless thing without an object.

This kind of idea would be indispensable even if War was perfect War, the perfectly unbridled element of hostility, for all the circumstances on which it rests, and which determine its leading features, viz., our own power, the enemy's power, Allies on both sides, the characteristics of the people and their Governments respectively, . . . are they not of a political nature, and are they not so intimately connected with the whole political intercourse that it is impossible to separate them? But this view is doubly indispensable if we reflect that real War is no such consistent effort tending to an extreme, as it should be according to the abstract idea, but a half-and-half thing, a con-

tradiction in itself; that, as such, it cannot follow its own laws, but must be looked upon as a part of another whole—and this whole is policy.

Policy in making use of War avoids all those rigorous conclusions which proceed from its nature; it troubles itself little about final possibilities, confining its attention to immediate probabilities. If such uncertainty in the whole action ensues therefrom, if it thereby becomes a sort of game, the policy of each Cabinet places its confidence in the belief that in this game it will surpass its neighbour in skill and sharpsightedness.

Thus policy makes out of the all-overpowering element of War a mere instrument, changes the tremendous battle-sword, which should be lifted with both hands and the whole power of the body to strike once for all, into a light handy weapon, which is even sometimes nothing more than a rapier to exchange thrusts and feints and parries.

Thus the contradictions in which man, naturally timid, becomes involved by War may be solved, if we choose to accept this as a solution.

If War belongs to policy, it will naturally take its character from thence. If policy is grand and powerful, so also will be the War, and this may be carried to the point at which War attains to *its absolute form.*

In this way of viewing the subject, therefore, we need not shut out of sight the absolute form of War, we rather keep it continually in view in the background.

Only through this kind of view War recovers unity; only by it can we see all Wars as things of *one* kind; and it is only through it that the judgment can obtain the true and perfect basis and point of view from which great plans may be traced out and determined upon.

It is true the political element does not sink deep into the details of War. Vedettes are not planted, patrols do not make their rounds from political considerations; but small as is its influence in this respect, it is great in the formation of a plan for a whole War, or a campaign, and often even for a battle.

For this reason we were in no hurry to establish this view at the commencement. While engaged with particulars, it would have given us little help, and, on the other hand, would have distracted our attention to a certain extent; in the plan of a War or campaign it is indispensable.

There is, upon the whole, nothing more important in life than to find out the right point of view from which things should be looked at and judged of, and then to keep to that point; for we can only apprehend the mass of events in their unity from *one* standpoint; and it is only the keeping to one point of view that guards us from inconsistency.

If, therefore, in drawing up a plan of a War, it is not allowable to have a two-fold or three-fold point of view, from which things may be looked at, now with the eye of a soldier, then with that of an administrator, and then again with that of a politician, &c., then the next question is, whether *policy* is necessarily paramount and everything else subordinate to it.

That policy unites in itself, and reconciles all the interests of internal administrations, even those of humanity, and whatever else are rational subjects of consideration is presupposed, for it is nothing in itself, except a mere representative and exponent of all these interests towards other States. That policy may take a false direction, and may promote unfairly the ambitious ends, the private interests, the vanity of rulers, does not concern us here; for, under no circumstances can the Art of War be regarded as its preceptor, and we can only look at policy here as the representative of the interests generally of the whole community.

The only question, therefore, is whether in framing plans for a War the political point of view should give way to the purely military (if such a point is conceivable), that is to say, should disappear altogether, or subordinate itself to it, or whether the political is to remain the ruling point of view and the military to be considered subordinate to it.

That the political point of view should end completely when War begins is only conceivable in contests which are Wars of life and death, from pure hatred: as Wars are in reality, they are, as we before said, only the expressions or manifestations of policy itself. The subordination of the political point of view to the military would be contrary to common sense, for policy has declared the War; it is the intelligent faculty, War only the instrument, and not the reverse. The subordination of the military point of view to the political is, therefore, the only thing which is possible.

If we reflect on the nature of real War, and call to mind . . . , *that every War should be viewed above all things according to the probability of its character, and its leading features as they are to be deduced from the political forces and proportions,* and that often —indeed we may safely affirm, in our days, *almost* always—War is to be regarded as an organic whole, from which the single branches are not to be separated, in which therefore every individual activity flows into the whole, and also has its origin in the idea of this whole, then it becomes certain and palpable to us that the superior standpoint for the conduct of the War, from which its leading lines must proceed, can be no other than that of policy.

From this point of view the plans come, as it were, out of a cast; the apprehension of them and the judgment upon them become easier and more natural, our convictions respecting them gain in force, motives are more satisfying, and history more intelligible.

At all events from this point of view there is no longer in the nature of things a necessary conflict between the political and military interests, and where it appears it is therefore to be regarded as imperfect knowledge only. That policy makes demands on the War which it cannot respond to, would be contrary to the supposition that it knows the instrument which it is going to use, therefore, contrary to a natural and indispensable supposition. But if policy judges correctly of the march of military events, it is entirely its affair to determine what are the events and what the direction of events most favourable to the ultimate and great end of the War.

In one word, the Art of War in its highest point of view is policy, but, no doubt, a policy which fights battles instead of writing notes.

According to this view, to leave a great military enterprise, or the plan for one, to *a purely military judgment and decision* is a distinction which cannot be allowed, and is even prejudicial; indeed, it is an irrational proceeding to consult professional soldiers on the plan of a War, that they may give a *purely military opinion* upon what the Cabinet ought to do; but still more absurd is the demand of Theorists that a statement of the available means of War should be laid before the General, that he may draw out a purely military plan for the War or for a campaign in accordance with those means. Experience in general also teaches us that notwithstanding the multifarious branches and scientific character of military art in the present day, still the leading outlines of a War are always determined by the Cabinet, that is, if we would use technical language, by a political not a military organ.

This is perfectly natural. None of the principal plans which are required for a War can be made without an insight into the political relations; and, in reality, when people speak, as they often do, of the prejudicial influence of policy on the conduct of a War, they say in reality something very different

to what they intend. It is not this influence but the policy itself which should be found fault with. If policy is right, that is, if it succeeds in hitting the object, then it can only act with advantage on the War. If this influence of policy causes a divergence from the object, the cause is only to be looked for in a mistaken policy.

It is only when policy promises itself a wrong effect from certain military means and measures, an effect opposed to their nature, that it can exercise a prejudicial effect on War by the course it prescribes. Just as a person in a language with which he is not conversant sometimes says what he does not intend, so policy, when intending right, may often order things which do not tally with its own views.

This has happened times without end, and it shows that a certain knowledge of the nature of War is essential to the management of political intercourse.

But before going further, we must guard ourselves against a false interpretation of which this is very susceptible. We are far from holding the opinion that a War Minister smothered in official papers, a scientific engineer, or even a soldier who has been well tried in the field, would, any of them, necessarily make the best Minister of State where the Sovereign does not act for himself; or, in other words, we do not mean to say that this acquaintance with the nature of War is the principal qualification for a War Minister; elevation, superiority of mind, strength of character, these are the principal qualifications which he must possess; a knowledge of War may be supplied in one way or the other. France was never worse advised in its military and political affairs than by the two brothers Belleisle and the Duke of Choiseul, although all three were good soldiers.

If War is to harmonise entirely with the political views and policy, to accommodate itself to the means available for War, there is only one alternative to be recommended when the statesman and soldier are not combined in one person, which is, to make the Commander-in-Chief a member of the Cabinet, that he may take part in its councils and decisions on important occasions. But then, again, this is only possible when the Cabinet, that is, the Government itself, is near the theatre of War, so that things can be settled without a serious waste of time.

This is what the Emperor of Austria did in 1809, and the allied Sovereigns in 1813, 1814, 1815, and the arrangements proved completely satisfactory.

The influence of any military man except the General-in-Chief in the Cabinet is extremely dangerous; it very seldom leads to able vigorous action. The example of France in 1793, 1794, 1795, when Carnot, while residing in Paris, managed the conduct of the War, is to be avoided, as a system of terror is not at the command of any but a revolutionary government.

We shall now conclude with some reflections derived from history.

In the last decade of the past century, when that remarkable change in the Art of War in Europe took place by which the best Armies found that a part of their method of War had become utterly unserviceable, and events were brought about of a magnitude far beyond what any one had any previous conception of, it certainly appeared that a false calculation of everything was to be laid to the charge of the Art of War. It was plain that while confined by habit within a narrow circle of conceptions, she had been surprised by the force of a new state of relations, lying, no doubt, outside that circle, but still not outside the nature of things.

Those observers who took the most comprehensive view ascribed the circumstance to the general influence which policy had exercised for centuries on the Art of War, and undoubtedly to its very great disadvantage, and by which it had sunk into a half-measure, often into mere sham-fighting. They were right as to fact, but they were wrong in attributing it to something accidental, or which might have been avoided.

Others thought that everything was to be explained by the momentary influence of the particular policy of Austria, Prussia, England, &c., with regard to their own interests respectively.

But is it true that the real surprise by which men's minds were seized was confined to the conduct of War, and did not rather relate to policy itself? That is: Did the ill success proceed from the influence of policy on the War, or from a wrong policy itself?

The prodigious effects of the French Revolution abroad were evidently brought about much less through new methods and views introduced by the French in the conduct of War than through the changes which it wrought in state-craft and civil administration, in the character of Governments, in the condition of the people, &c. That other Governments took a mistaken view of all these things; that they endeavoured, with their ordinary means, to hold their own against forces of a novel kind and overwhelming in strength—all that was a blunder in policy.

Would it have been possible to perceive and mend this error by a scheme for the War from a purely military point of view? Impossible. For if there had been a philosophical strategist, who merely from the nature of the hostile elements had foreseen all the consequences, and prophesied remote possibilities, still it would have been practically impossible to have turned such wisdom to account.

If policy had risen to a just appreciation of the forces which had sprung up in France, and of the new relations in the political state of Europe, it might have foreseen the consequences which must follow in respect to the great features of War, and it was only in this way that it could arrive at a correct view of the extent of the means required as well as of the best use to make of those means.

We may therefore say, that the twenty years' victories of the Revolution are chiefly to be ascribed to the erroneous policy of the Governments by which it was opposed.

It is true these errors first displayed themselves in the War, and the events of the War completely disappointed the expectations which policy entertained. But this did not take place because policy neglected to consult its military advisers. That Art of War in which the politician of the day could believe, namely, that derived from the reality of War at that time, that which belonged to the policy of the day, that familiar instrument which policy had hitherto used—*that* Art of War, I say, was naturally involved in the error of policy, and therefore could not teach it anything better. It is true that War itself underwent important alterations both in its nature and forms, which brought it nearer to its absolute form;

but these changes were not brought about because the French Government had, to a certain extent, delivered itself from the leading-strings of policy; they arose from an altered policy, produced by the French Revolution, not only in France, but over the rest of Europe as well. This policy had called forth other means and other powers, by which it became possible to conduct War with a degree of energy which could not have been thought of otherwise.

Therefore, the actual changes in the Art of War are a consequence of alterations in policy; and, so far from being an argument for the possible separation of the two, they are, on the contrary, very strong evidence of the intimacy of their connection.

Therefore, once more: War is an instrument of policy; it must necessarily bear its character, it must measure with its scale: the conduct of War, in its great features, is therefore policy itself, which takes up the sword in place of the pen, but does not on that account cease to think according to its own laws.

Causes of War

QUINCY WRIGHT

Wars arise because of the changing relations of numerous variables—technological, psychic, social, and intellectual. There is no single cause of war. Peace is an equilibrium among many forces. Change in any particular force, trend, movement, or policy may at one time make for war, but under other conditions a similar change may make for peace. A state may at one time promote peace by armament, at another time by disarmament; at one time by insistence on its rights, at another time by a spirit of conciliation. To estimate the probability of war at any time involves, therefore, an appraisal of the effect of current changes upon the complex of intergroup relationships throughout the world. Certain relationships, however, have been of outstanding importance. Political lag deserves attention as an outstanding cause of war in modern civilization.

POLITICAL LAG

There appears to be a general tendency for change in procedures of political and legal adjustment to lag behind economic and cultural changes arising from technological progress. The violent consequences of this lag can be observed in primitive and historic societies, but its importance has increased in modern times. The expansion of contacts and the acceleration of change resulting from modern technology have disturbed existing power localizations and have accentuated the cultural oppositions inherent in social organization. International organization has not developed sufficiently to adjust by peaceful procedures the conflict situations which have arisen. This lag is related to the usual lag of value systems behind scientific and technological progress, accounting for the great transitions in civilizations . . . .

War tends to increase in severity and to decrease in frequency as the area of political and legal adjustment (the state) expands geographically unless that area becomes as broad as the area of continuous economic, social, and cultural contact (the civilization). In the modern period peoples in all sections of the world have come into continuous contact with one another. Although states have tended to grow during this period, thus extending the areas of adjustment, none of them has acquired world-wide jurisdiction. Their growth in size has increased the likelihood that conflicts will be adjusted, but it has also increased the severity of the consequences of unadjusted conflicts. Fallible human government is certain to make occasional mistakes in policy, especially when, because of lack of universality, it must deal with conflicts regulated not by law but by negotiation that must function within an unstable balance of power among a few large units. Such errors have led to war.

War tends to increase both in frequency and in severity in times of rapid technological and cultural change because adjustment, which always involves habituation, is a function of time. The shorter the time within which such adjustments have to be made, the greater the probability that they will prove inadequate and that violence will result. War can, therefore, be attributed either to the intelligence of man manifested in his inventions which increase the number of contacts and the speed of change or to the unintelligence of man which retards his perception of the instruments of regulation and adjustment necessary to prevent these contacts and changes from generating serious conflicts. Peace might be kept by retarding progress so that there will be time for gradual adjustment by natural processes of accommodation and assimilation, or peace might be kept by accelerating progress through planned adjustments and new controls. Actually both methods have been tried, the latter especially within the state and the former especially in international relations.

Sovereignty in the political sense is the effort of a society to free itself from external controls in order to facilitate changes in its law and government which it considers necessary to meet changing economic and social conditions. The very efficiency of sovereignty within the state, however, decreases the efficiency of regulation in international relations. By eliminating tensions within the state, external tensions are augmented. International relations become a "state of nature." War therefore among states claiming sovereignty tends to be related primarily to the balance of power among them.

Behind the power equilibrium are others, disturbances in any of which may cause war. These include such fundamental oppositions as the ambivalent tendency of human nature to love and to hate the same object and the ambivalent tendency of social organization to integrate and to differentiate at the same time. They also include less fundamental oppositions such as the tendency within international law to develop a world-order and to support national sovereignty and the tendency of international politics to generate foreign policies of both intervention and isolation. Elimination of such oppositions is not to be anticipated, and their continuance in some form is probably an essential condition of human progress. Peace, consequently, has to do not with the elimination of oppositions but with adequate methods of adjusting them.

The lag of adjusting procedures behind a change of conditions is a general cause of war. The persistence of this lag is due in part to the actual or presumed service of war to human groups. War has been thought (1) to serve sociological functions, (2) to satisfy psychological drives, (3) to be technologically useful, and (4) to be legally rational.

SOCIOLOGICAL FUNCTIONS OF WAR

Animal warfare is explained by the theory of natural selection. The behavior pattern of hostility has contributed to the survival of certain biological species, and consequently that behavior has survived. In the survival of other species other factors have played a more important role.

Among primitive peoples, before contact with civilization, warfare contributed to the solidarity of the group and to the survival of certain forms of culture. When population increased, migrations or new means of communication accelerated external contacts. The warlike tribes tended to survive and expand; furthermore, the personality traits of courage and obedience which developed among the members of these tribes equipped them for civilization.

Among peoples of the historic civilizations war contributed both to the survival and to the destruction of states and civilizations. Its influence depended upon the stage of the civilization and the type of military technique developed. Civilized states tended to fight for economic and political ends in the early stages of the civilization, with the effect of expanding and integrating the civilization. As the size and interdependence of political units increased, political and economic ends became less tangible, and cultural patterns and ideal objectives assumed greater importance. Aggressive war tended to become a less suitable instrument for conserving these elements of the civilization. Consequently, defensive strategies and peaceful sentiments developed, but in none of the historic civilizations were they universally accepted. War tended toward a destructive stalemate, disintegrating the civilization and rendering it vulnerable to the attack of external barbarians of younger civilizations which had acquired advanced military arts from the older civilization but not its cultural and intellectual inhibitions.

In the modern period the war pattern has been an important element in the creation, integration, expansion, and survival of states. World civilization has, however, distributed a singularly destructive war technique to all nations, with the consequence that the function of war as an instrument of integration and expansion has declined. Efforts to break the balance of power by violence have increasingly menaced the whole civilization, and yet this balance has been so incalculable that such efforts have continued to be made. Atomic weapons may have deprived war of any social function and made its consequences more calculable.

PSYCHOLOGICAL DRIVES TO WAR

Human warfare is a pattern giving social sanction to activities which involve the killing of other human beings and the extreme danger of being killed. At no period of human development has this pattern been essential to the survival of the individual. The pattern is a cultural acquisition, not an original trait of human nature, though many hereditary drives have contributed to the pattern. Of these, the dominance drive has been of especial importance. The survival of war has been due to its function in promoting the survival of the group with which the individual identifies himself and in remedying the individual problem arising from the necessary repression of many human impulses in group life. The pattern has involved individual attitudes and group opinion. As the self-consciousness of personality and the complexity of culture have increased with modern civilization, the drive to war has depended increasingly upon ambivalences in the personality and inconsistencies in the culture.

A modern community is at the same time a system of government, a self-contained body of law, an organization of cultural symbols, and the economy of a population. It is a government, a state, a nation, and a people.

Every individual is at the same time subject to the power and authority of a government and police, to the logic and conventions of a law and language, to the sentiments and customs of a nation and culture, and to the caprices and necessities of a people and its economy. If he fights in war, he does so because one of these aspects of the community is threatened or is believed by most of those who identify themselves with it to be threatened. It may be that the government, the state, the nation, and the people are sufficiently integrated so that there is no conflict in reconciling duty to all of these aspects of the community. But this is not likely because of the analytical character of modern civilization which separates military and civil government, the administration and the judiciary, church and state, government and business, politics and the schools, and religion and education. Furthermore, it may be that the threat is sufficiently obvious so that no one can doubt its reality, but this is seldom the case. The entities for whose defense the individual is asked to enlist are abstractions. Their relations to one another and the conditions of their survival are a matter of theory rather than of facts. People are influenced to support war by language and symbols rather than by events and conditions.

It may therefore be said that modern war tends to be about words more than about things, about potentialities, hopes, and aspirations more than about facts, grievances, and conditions. When the war seems to be about a particular territory, treaty, policy, or incident, it will usually be found that this issue is important only because, under the circumstances, each of the belligerents believed renunciation of its demand would eventually threaten the survival of its power, sovereignty, nationality, or livelihood. War broke out in 1939, not about Danzig or Poland, but about the belief of both the German people and their enemies that capacity to dictate a solution of these issues would constitute a serious threat to the survival of the power, ideals, culture, or welfare of the group which submitted to this dictation.

Even more remote from the needs of the individual and the state was the bearing of a campaign to expand the Roman frontier into Gaul, the Moslem frontiers into Africa, the Christian frontiers into Palestine, or the Communist frontier into central Europe. The meaning of Rome, of Islam, of Christendom, or of communism had to be understood by a considerable public. The importance of such increases in territory, population, and glory had to be inculcated by education of all those influencing policy, even though the prospect of immediate rewards to the active participants was obvious.

In the modern situation far more conceptual construction is necessary to make war appear essential to the survival of anything important. War, therefore, rests, in modern civilization, upon an elaborate ideological construction maintained through education in a system of language, law, symbols, and values. The explanation and interpretation of these systems are often as remote from the actual sequence of events as are the primitive explanations of war in terms of the requirements of magic, ritual, or revenge. War in the modern period does not grow out of a situation but out of highly artificial interpretation of a situation. Since war is more about words than about things, other manipulations of words and symbols might be devised to meet the cultural and personality problems for which war offers an increasingly inadequate and expensive solution.

TECHNOLOGICAL UTILITY OF WAR

The verbal constructions which have had most to do with war in the modern period have been those which center about the words "power," "sovereignty," "nationality," and "living." These words may be interpreted as attributes, respectively, of the govern-

ment, the state, the nation, and the people. By taking any one as an absolute value, the personality may be delivered from the restlessness of ambivalence and from the doubts and perplexities which arise from the effort to reconcile duty to conflicting institutions and values, particularly in times of rapid change. Although the relation of war to the preservation of any of these entities requires considerable interpretation, the validity of the interpretation varies with respect to the four entities.

The power of the government refers to its capacity to make its decisions effective through the hierarchy of civil and military officials. In a balance-of-power structure of world politics even a minor change in the relative power position of governments is likely to precipitate an accelerating process, destroying some of the government elites and augmenting the power of others. If a government yields strategic territory, military resources, or other constituents of power to another without compensating advantage, it is quite likely to be preparing its own destruction. The theory which considers war a necessary instrument in the preservation of political power is relatively close to the facts. The most important technological cause of war in the modern world is its utility in the struggle for power.

The sovereignty of the state refers to the effectiveness of its law. This rests immediately on customary practices and on the prestige and reputation for power of the state rather than upon power itself. Sensitiveness about departures from established rules about honor and insult to reputation has a real relation to the preservation of sovereignty. A failure to resent contempt for rights or aspersions on prerogatives may initiate a rapid decline of reputation and increase the occasions when power will actually have to be resorted to if the legal system is to survive. Thus in the undeveloped state of international law, self-help and the war to defend national honor had a real relation to the survival of states prior to the nuclear age.

Nationality refers to the expectation of identical reactions to the basic social symbols by the members of the national group. It has developed principally from common language, traditions, customs, and values and has often persisted through political dismemberment of the group. Although national minorities have usually resisted the efforts of the administration and the economic system of the state to assimilate them, these influences may in time be successful. Thus, the use of force to preserve the power of the government and the sovereignty of the state which supports a given nationality may be important to the preservation of the latter. War, however, has been less useful to preserve nationality than to preserve power or sovereignty.

Living refers to the welfare and economy of a people. The argument has often been made that war is necessary to assure a people an area sufficient for prosperous living. Under the conditions of the modern world, this argument has usually been fallacious. The problem of increasing the welfare of a people has not depended upon the extension of political power or legal sovereignty into new areas but rather upon the elimination of the costs of war and depression, improvements in technology and land utilization, and a widening of markets and sources of raw materials far beyond any territories or spheres of interest which might be acquired by war. Population pressure, unavailability of raw materials, and loss of markets are more often the effect of military preparation than the cause. Although it is true, in a balance-of-power world, that economic bargaining power may increase with political power, yet it has seldom increased enough to compensate for the cost of maintaining a military establishment, of fighting occasional wars, and of impairing confidence in international economic stability. Through most of modern history people, even if conquered, have not ceased to exist and to consume goods. Efforts toward economic self-sufficiency and toward the forced migration, extermination, or enslavement of conquered peoples have, however, added to the reasonableness of conventional war for the preservation of the life of peoples.

Modern civilization offers a group more alternatives to war in most contingencies than did earlier civilizations and cultures. Resort to war, except within the restricted conception of necessary self-defense, is rarely the only way to preserve power or sovereignty and even more rarely the only way to preserve nationality or economy. War is most useful as a means to power and progressively less useful as a means to preserve sovereignty, nationality, or

economy. That economic factors are relatively unimportant in the causation of war was well understood by Adolf Hitler:

> Whenever economy was made the sole content of our people's life, thus suffocating the ideal virtues, the State collapsed again. . . . If one asks oneself the question what the forces forming or otherwise preserving a State are in reality, it can be summed up with one single characterization: the individual's ability and willingness to sacrifice himself for the community. But that these virtues have really nothing whatsoever to do with economics is shown by the simple realization that man never sacrifices himself for them; that means: one does not die for business, but for ideals.

LEGAL RATIONALITY OF WAR

Which of the entities for which men fight is most important for men? Is there any criterion by which they may be rationally evaluated? Political power has been transferred from village to tribe, from feudal lord to king, from state to federation. Is it important today that it remain forever with the national governments that now possess it? The transfer of power to a larger group, the creation of a world police, under an international organization adequate to sanction a law against aggression, appears a condition for eliminating a major cause of war.

Legal sovereignty also has moved from city-state to empire, from baronial castle to kingdom, from state to federation. To the individual the transfer of authority over his language and law to a larger group, although it has brought regret or resentment, has assured order, justice, and peace in larger areas and has increased man's control of his environment, provided that authority has been exercised with such understanding and deliberation as to avoid resentments arising to the point of revolt.

Nationality, in the broadest sense of a feeling of cultural solidarity, has similarly traveled from village to tribe, city-state, kingdom, nation, empire, or

even civilization; but when it has become too broad, it has become too thin to give full satisfaction to the human desires for social identification and distinctiveness. There is no distinctiveness in being a member of the human race. Few would contemplate a world of uniform culture with equanimity. Geographical barriers and historic traditions promise for a long time to preserve cultural variety even in a world-federation, though modern means of communication and economy have exterminated many quaint customs and costumes. The need of cultural variety and the love of distinctive nationality suggest that a world police power is more likely to be effective if controlled by a universal federation than by a universal empire.

The area from which individuals have obtained their living has expanded from the village to the tribal area to the kingdom and empire, until, in the modern world, most people draw something from the most remote sections of the world. This widening of the area of exchange has augmented population and standards of living. Diminution of this area, such as occurred when the Roman Empire disintegrated into feudal manors, has had a reverse effect. The economist can make no case for economic walls, if economy is to be an instrument of human welfare rather than of political power, except in so far as widespread practices on the latter assumption force the welfare-minded to defend their existing economy by utilizing it temporarily as an instrument of power.

It may be questioned whether a rational consideration of the symbols, for the preservation of which wars have been fought, demonstrates that they have always been worth fighting for or that fighting has always contributed to their preservation. The actual values of these entities as disclosed by philosophy and the actual means for preserving them as disclosed by science have been less important in causing war than popular beliefs engendered by the unreflecting acceptance of the implications of language, custom, symbols, rituals, and traditions.

Military Power:
Nature, Components & Functions

Klaus Knorr

When sovereign nation-states pursue interests which clash with those of other states, and take action to achieve the most satisfactory (or least unsatisfactory) outcome of the resulting interstate conflict, they will usually attempt to exert influence on each other's behavior. Some of the means they will use for this purpose are coercive; that is, they are threats or actions aimed at depriving the other party of something it values, such as territory, independence, peace, trade, prestige, or self-respect. Means are non-coercive when one government offers another the continuation or an increment of something it values, such as diplomatic and military support, cessation of hostilities, financial aid, or export markets. Threats are made and benefits offered in order to produce certain intended effects on the behavior of the addressee. A wants B to do X, or to refrain from doing Y; therefore A threatens B with punishments or offers him rewards. However, governments may also influence other states without offering rewards or using coercion. They may be able to do so by giving information, for example, by explaining the purposes or implications of their own policies which contributed to the conflict, for these may have been misunderstood. Coercive and non-coercive means, and information, may be used simultaneously in various combinations.

Throughout recorded history, sovereign states have employed military power as one means of coercion, usually in combination with other means of influence. However, military power can be used for other than coercive purposes. It has been, and can be, used to take or defend something forcibly, for example a city or province, or to exterminate an enemy. In this case, no attempt is made to influence the opponent. The object is simply to take or withhold something from him by sheer force.[1] Sufficient military strength, and the will to use it, is all that is needed to achieve the objective. When military force is employed in war, it is often, if not usually, for both purposes; that is, to take or defend some objects forcibly, and—by threatening the opponent with further destruction—to influence him toward terminating hostilities on certain terms, or toward accepting surrender.

Even when military power is used as a means of influence, its employment is not always coercive. It can be used in order to offer utilities to another state, as when an alliance is proposed. Our focus, however, will be on the use of military power to threaten some other state with disutilities, or to inflict actual violence on it, since the employment of power as a benefit to one state rests on the possibility of its use as a means of coercion against another.

In applying this focus, the use of military strength is not regarded as

Reprinted by permission of the publisher, from Klaus Knorr: *Military Power and Potential* (Lexington, Mass.: D. C. Heath and Co., 1970).

standing in contrast to the employment of diplomatic negotiation or other government communications. The use of force is only part of the process of reconciling interstate interests when they are in sharp conflict, and even then the resort to force is a matter of choice. Where the choice to use force is made, the aim is usually agreement. The weight of military force is thrown into the scales when other communication is expected to lack sufficient impact.

Since the purpose of this chapter is to introduce the examination of military potential . . . , its scope is restricted accordingly. The following discussion will concentrate on the military power, putative and actualized, of single states vis-à-vis other single states. However, this analysis could be extended readily in several directions. As indicated by frequent references to foreign support and the possibility of third-party intervention, the analysis could be extended to cover military power relationships between groups of states. It could be extended further to consider the impact of different patterns in the international distribution of power, such as the classical balance-of-power system, or the bipolar pattern which emerged following World War II. Finally, it could be extended by examining the role of military power, putative or actualized, when it becomes effective in conjunction with other means of international influence, whether coercive or noncoercive. Such an extension would open the way to a study of crisis bargaining.

THE CONCEPT OF MILITARY POWER

Like all means of influence, the concept of military power as a capacity for exercising coercion is not as clearcut as it looks on first notice.[2] If power is defined as the ability to affect behavior, the concept can then be interpreted in two alternative ways, each of which captures a different aspect of reality. One interpretation equates power with actual influence. Power then exists only as influence is achieved, and is measurable only in terms of visible changes in behavior patterns. We will call this *actualized power*. According to the second interpretation, power is the *ability* to coerce in order to exercise influence. In this meaning, power is only the potential cause of behavioral changes; it preexists the actual achievement of influence. We will call this *putative power*. Actualized power is generated in the influence process and exists only within a specific relationship between states. Putative power is something which pertains to particular states; it is something they possess, and which they may use or not use. Putative power is a means; actualized power is an effect. Henceforth, when we simply refer to military power, we mean putative power which, however, is a capacity for taking or defending objects forcibly as well as a means to exercise coercion.

The notion of power does not specify purely unilateral power by one state over another. Most power relationships are characterized by some degree of reciprocity. Hence, when we speak of A exerting power on B, we refer to net power.

MECHANISMS OF EFFECTIVENESS

There are three mechanisms through which the military power of one state may affect the behavior of other states. One mechanism is resort to war—that is, organized violence between collective groups, especially state-organized forces—to the extent that hostilities have the purpose of affecting the opponent's behavior (*i.e.,* to the extent that the object of force is not simply seizure or denial of a valuable object). The second mechanism is the *threat* of military action, including war, or of the expansion of ongoing hostilities. The third is through the *anticipation* by states that another state may proceed to use its military forces in the event of a serious dispute.

This third mechanism is very important in the relations of states since its operation is less discontinuous and more pervasive than actual warfare or the use of specific military threats. A government, in shaping its policy to-ward a state perceived to be not only militarily superior but also apt to use its military force, will take these conditions tacitly into consideration even though no specific military threat has been uttered. It will simply reject, or not even consider, certain choices of action. If this happens, the military power of the stronger state has been effective in influencing the behavior of other states even without deliberate attempts to do so. The putative power of the superior state has then become actualized.

CONDITIONS OF EFFECTIVENESS

In inquiring further into the nature of military power, both putative and actualized, we begin, for reasons of expository convenience, by discussing the third mechanism of effectiveness first, and then the second and first. In the analysis which follows, we will look into the military power relationships between two states, A and B.

According to the third mechanism of anticipated force, State B may be influenced by its expectation that, if it does X rather than Y, State A may with some probability resort to its military power. But exactly what determines A's putative military power? This results from three factors: its actual military capabilities, its capacity for increasing these capabilities in a crisis, and its military reputation.

The effectiveness of a state's military forces or capabilities depends on their size, composition, equipment, logistical reach, and availability for new application. Military forces are not a homogeneous entity with which different states are endowed in varying amounts. As will be examined in more detail below, states may have forces more suitable for some modes and theaters of war than for others. For example, a state may possess a strong capability to deter a nuclear attack by another state but lack strong forces for waging conventional combat. Or its forces may be strong for defense of its territory but lack of the logistical capacity for large-scale operations in far away places. Thus, the very composition of a nation's armed forces conditions the scope of its military power. Even though a state has impressive armed forces, they may be partly, or wholly committed to certain uses and, to that extent, unavailable for different types of conflict. Regarding new uses of military strength, only those forces count which can be allocated for them. In general, the armed forces of great military powers have larger size, more versatility, wider geographic reach, and are capable of greater, and more varied expansion than those of lesser military powers. But sheer scarcity of resources places limitations even on the capabilities of great and wealthy military powers.

Related to the size, equipment and reach of a state's military forces is its military potential, that is, its ability to increase these forces in a crisis or in war. States differ in the magnitude and composition of resources convertible into military capabilities, in the speed and versatility with which conversion can take place, and in the degree to which governments are able to commit resources to this purpose.

But although military forces, both actual and potential, are vital conditions of military power, military forces and putative military power are not the same thing. Armies, air forces, and navies are instruments of military power—capabilities from which power may be derived. They are a necessary but not a sufficient condition of military power. Another essential condition is a state's recognized willingness to employ military force on behalf of interests it deems important enough to justify the costs of such employment. In short, this power rests also on A's military reputation—an intangible asset —which is based, in turn, on its previous military and crisis behavior, and on the absence of new evidence which would counsel a discounting of past behavior. The more readily a state has resorted to force in the past, in general or in specifically relevant situations, the more credible that it will do so in the future. However, events such as changes in government or political regime can lead to revisions in a state's military reputation.

If such is the nature of A's putative military power, it becomes actualized when B anticipates a possible military threat by A if it (B) undertakes a course of action sharply countering some sufficiently vital interests of A. The actualization of A's power also depends upon additional factors, indicated by the following questions with which B's government will be concerned.

1. What are the chances that A will proceed to a military threat in the course of the dispute which will ensue?

2. What sort of threat will it be?

3. How vulnerable militarily are we to it?

4. What kind of support can we expect, or manage to evoke, at home and abroad?

5. How does the value of our intended action compare with the risks of receiving a military threat?

This list indicates the conditionality of A's actualized power; and such conditionality explains why, even though states perceive and consider differences in their military power, militarily weak states have usually had considerable freedom of action in countering the interests of stronger states. Thus, although A may be a strong military power in its region, the geographic reach of its military forces may be small, and hence will not impress small powers located at a considerable distance. But even if A is a world military power, a small State B may be substantially invulnerable to its military force either because the coercive exercise of such force is too costly to A when considering the broad range of possible conflicts of interest and/or because B can count on support from a militarily powerful ally.

This consideration brings us to the second mechanism through which a state's military power may become effective in affecting another's behavior, namely the use of a military threat. Assuming a severe conflict between A and B, and assuming furthermore that all other means of influence have been exhausted, the effectiveness of a military threat by A against B would depend upon:

1. The estimate of B's government of
   a. the balance of interests at stake, *i.e.*, the disutility of the threatened action compared with the disutility of compliance,
   b. the probability that A will proceed to execute its threat in the event of noncompliance,
   c. the character of domestic and foreign support for alternative courses of action.

2. The skill of A's and B's governments in the bargaining process.

3. The propensity of B's government to accept military risks and to behave rationally.

This list of factors specifies the conditions under which the effectiveness of A's threat, and hence the actualization of its power, will vary from total to zero. The first of these is self-explanatory. The second may be important since specific military threats are usually made in the course of an intense diplomatic confrontation; within this crisis context, the effectiveness of a military threat depends to some extent on its timing, nature of delivery and similar characteristics which can be chosen with greater or lesser skill. Similarly, the way in which a threat is received, and the response to it in terms of procrastination, evasiveness, appeals for reconsideration, or counter-threats may affect its success. The choice of such responses is also subject to the skill of leadership.[3] In regard to the third condition listed, the propensity to accept military risks and to approach crisis situations rationally are important since government and military leaders differ in these respects.[4] Some leaders have a stronger propensity to act rationally than others, and some are more inclined than others to run risks.

This model, as all models in this chapter, could be made more complex by differentiating various sub-variables for each of the listed factors. For example, B's estimates of relevant conditions depend on its power of perception, that is, the accuracy of its information and its ability to interpret this information. B's estimate of the probability that A will execute its threat depends on B's perceptions of the military means available to A for executing the threat, on the support A is likely to receive at home and abroad, and on A's previous record of resorting to force.

In turn, the willingness of A's government to make a military threat against B depends chiefly on the following factors:

1. The estimate of A's government of
   a. the value of the gains it hopes to obtain from the threat compared with the costs of making the threat,
   b. the effectiveness of the threat on B,
   c. the strength or nature of domestic and foreign support of, or opposition to, the threat.

2. A's propensity to accept military risks and behave rationally.

This list of factors specifies the conditions under which A's willingness to resort to a military threat will range from extremely high to zero. The list could be greatly lengthened by differentiating between different gains and costs. Thus, the gains which State A hopes to secure involve the issue or issues at stake in the conflict with B that gave rise to the considered use of coercive power. But as soon as A resorts to a military threat, other values may come into play, for example, the immediate value of giving confidence to an ally. They may also include more diffuse future benefits resulting from a reputation for the forthright or cautious use of military power. If we focus on A as a particular government or regime, rather than as a state acting through a government, the gains may involve an increase in domestic power or other such benefits, including perhaps personal glory, to which its leaders may be attracted.

On the other side, the costs of employing a military threat may also touch on many different values. Among these costs, as perceived and evaluated by A's government, may be unfavorable domestic and foreign responses. If a threat is widely held to be clumsy, a nation's or a government's reputation for finesse may decline. If a threat is widely regarded as unjust or brutal, their moral reputation may suffer. For example, by the 1960's, and even earlier, the expectation of such costs tended to inhibit nuclear powers from employing their nuclear arms against a state without such weapons. A military threat may be illegal under the UN Charter and provoke action because it is regarded as a threat to peace. In addition, a threat may lead to counterthreats by third states. One possible cost of a threat is that it may be defied. The very act of defiance may do damage to the threatening state's reputation as a powerful country. And if the threat is defied, there are also the costs of either making good the threat, including the costs and risks of war and foreign intervention, or the costs, in terms of reputation, of having one's bluff called.

It follows from our model that actualized military power is usually dependent on asymmetries in the costs of making threats and in the values at stake, as estimated by the two disputing governments, and in the prospect of foreign military support. This holds true when, as is often the case, there are small or no differences in the propensity to accept risks or behave rationally. The values at stake, the costs of making a threat, and the prospects of support from third states are more likely to vary. For instance, it is consistent with the above model that a State B may make a military threat against a State A which possesses substantially greater putative military power, and this not because B's leaders are irrational or have an extremely high propensity to accept military risks. They may do so, of course, in the event they have effective military backing from a third power with which A is reluctant to tangle; but they may also do so because the issue at stake, perhaps only moderately important to A, is absolutely vital to B; and it is possible that some of the costs of using a military threat—for example, domestic and foreign criticism—are smaller for the weaker than for the stronger military power.

Turning to war as a mechanism through which A's instrumental military power may affect B's behavior, the outcome will normally be decided by the decisions of the two governments to continue or to terminate hostilities at various stages of the conflict. For both governments, the main considerations will be their estimates of:

1. the military prospects of victory, stalemate or defeat,

2. the value of the stakes involved (which, however, may differ appreciably from those that led to crisis and war),

3. the various costs of inflicting and suffering further military violence,

4. the strength of domestic and foreign support, and the possibility of foreign intervention on either side,

5. the other party's evaluation of these conditions.

Again, these factors determine State A's actualized military power over B which, making allowance for B's actualized counterpower over A, is a net effect in terms of influence. It is obvious that the sooner B offers to terminate the war, and the more willing it is to do so on A's terms, the greater is A's actualized military power. But this analysis makes it clear that the terms of conflict settlement do not reflect merely the balance of tested military strength between A and B. It calls attention to other variable factors in the equation. Certainly actual military power does not result only from the possession of military forces, or a superiority in such capabilities; it also results from the will to put these forces, or this superiority, to use. In other words, it is crucially the result of purpose, determined by the stakes of the conflict, and of readiness to bear the various costs of employing force, including the risk of intervention by other states. The equation, which could be further complicated by the introduction of subvariables, shows, furthermore, that to measure actualized military power in the concrete instance would be a formidable and, as it seems safe to conclude in most cases, a prohibitive task.

It is clear from the foregoing that the transformation of putative military power into actualized power is subject to several variable conditions. It is also clear that, depending on the concatenation of these conditions, the transformation of putative into actualized power may be great or small, and under some extreme circumstances may even approach zero. Nevertheless, other factors remaining the same, actualized or actualizable military power will be the greater, the more potent is a state's putative power.

CHANGES IN POWER GAINS AND COSTS

In applying the model we have developed, it is interesting to note that the gains a state may obtain by employing military power are subject to modification over time as the governing criteria for evaluating such gains change. It is observable, for instance, that the traditional attraction of territorial conquest has waned in recent decades, particularly for the technologically more advanced nations. This has happened largely, though not only, because alternative avenues to increased wealth and power have been recognized as more productive.[5]

Even more conspicuous has been an increase in the costs of using military force.[6] This change has occurred partly because standards of valuation have changed; for example, the individual's welfare counts for more than it used to count in many societies, and his sacrifice is therefore held justified only if the nation's stakes are very high. Partly, the increase in costs has occurred because the aggressive use of military power has lost legitimacy, as is evidenced in the United Nations Charter. And, in part, costs have mounted because modern military technology has supplied nuclear weapons capable of inflicting unprecedentedly massive destruction against which there is thus far no adequate defense. This condition has rendered war between nuclear powers too costly for virtually any conceivable purpose. This does not mean that such military power has become useless. On the contrary, it is the threat of inflicting such unprecedented damage on an opponent which surely acts as a coercive means of influence and deters any adversary from launching an attack, or even from bringing about conflicts which might escalate to the strategic nuclear level. Moreover, when intense crises occur between nuclear powers, bargaining moves which increase the risk of nuclear war—a risk in which both parties share—are employed deliberately in order to secure a relatively favorable outcome of the crisis. As has been observed, these contests have become less a contest of military strength—of which at present each great nuclear power possesses enough to devastate the homeland of the other, even if attacked first—than a contest of nerve and will.[7] As we have seen above, the outcome of such a contest depends mainly on the values at stake to each opponent, and on their propensity to accept military risks and to act rationally.

Nevertheless, the rise in the costs of employing military power means that its usability has declined recently, especially for the great military powers; and this decline tends to diminish its utility. Furthermore, in examining the uses of military power, a distinction can be made between the purpose of deterrence and the purpose of "compellence."[8] Both are coercive uses of military power, but deterrence employs a threat in order to keep an opponent from doing something he might otherwise be tempted to do, while compellence employs a threat in order to make him do something which he would otherwise not choose to do. Given this distinction, it may be observed that the rising costs of employing military power has caused the usability of force for compellence to decline more than for deterrence.

To complete this part of the analysis, the use of putative military power simply for the purpose of taking or holding an object of interstate contention by sheer force, a use of force involving no attempt to influence an opponent, depends upon a more limited set of conditions than those indicated in connection with military coercion. In order to make use of military power for this purpose, a state must have the required capabilities and the will to use them, and this positive will is determined by the net balance of prospective gains over cost and the propensity to accept military risks and act rationally. The effectiveness of military power in this kind of application is governed by the relationship of the opposing military forces in the theater of war, and the relationship between each side's will to fight and to continue fighting; this latter relationship, in turn, depends in part on each government's estimate of the other's will to continue the war. Of course, both the will to fight and the outcome are also subject to the intervention, actual or threatened, on the part of third states.

Furthermore, the disposition of states to use force for this purpose is conditioned by the kinds of changes in the valuation of gains, and in the costs of resorting to military power, which were discussed above.

Statesmen think in terms of both putative and actualized military power even though they do not use these terms. If they are concerned with the employment of military power in the course of crisis bargaining, they will necessarily consider the conditions, prospects and consequences of its effectiveness in particular situations. Their perceptions of such power situations may be awry, and their ability to predict may be unreliable; but they will be compelled to consider the variable conditions which may determine the outcome of an international conflict.

NOTES

1. For the most lucid exposition of this distinction, see Thomas C. Schelling, *Arms and Influence* (New Haven: Yale University Press, 1966), Ch. I.

2. Cf. Robert A. Dahl, "The Concept of Power," *Behavioral Science*, II (1957), pp. 201–215; John C. Harsanyi, "Measurement of Social Power, Opportunity Costs, and the Theory of Two-Person Bargaining Games," *Behavioral Science*, VII (1962), pp. 67–68; William H. Riker, "Some Ambiguities in the Notion of Power," *The American Political Science Review*, LVIII (1964), pp. 341–349; Jack H. Nagel, "Some Questions About the Concept of Power," *Behavioral Science*, XIII (1968), pp. 129–137.

3. The element of skill tends to rise in importance if we relax our simplifying assumption that means of influence other than military coercion have been exhausted. If, as is usually the case, other means of influence, whether noncoercive or coercive, continue to be available to the contending governments, then skill in concerting their employment carries especial weight in the outcome of military threats.

4. Donald L. Harnett, Larry L. Cummings, and G. David Hughes, "The Influence of Risk-Taking Propensity on Bargaining Behavior," *Behavioral Science*, XIII (1968), pp. 91–101.

5. Cf. Klaus Knorr, *On the Uses of Military Power in the Nuclear Age* (Princeton: Princeton University Press, 1966), Ch. II.

6. *Ibid., passim.*

7. Cf. Schelling, *Arms and Influence*, Ch. II.

8. *Ibid.*, pp. 69 ff.

The Nature of Modern War

V. D. SOKOLOVSKY

One of the primary problems in the theory of military strategy is the study and determination of the nature of wars, their strategic and technical peculiarities. The correct, scientific solution of this problem is mainly possible on the basis of a Marxist-Leninist analysis of the historical conditions of social development, which makes it possible to establish what the socio-political essence and the causes and conditions of the origin of war are, and what material base is required to conduct it.

Only a scientific understanding of the nature of future war can enable the civilian and military command to direct the construction of the armed forces without error and rationally to solve the problems of preparing the country as a whole for war with an aggressor.

In the present situation, proper foreknowledge of the nature of the initial period of a war has become exceptionally important for the solution of the theoretical as well as the practical problems of military strategy. The effect of armed conflict during this period upon the course and outcome of modern war will differ in principle from its effect on past wars. Therefore, important new demands are now being made on the armed forces, the country, and the people.

THE MARXIST-LENINIST MEANING OF THE NATURE OF WAR IN THE MODERN ERA

The problem of the essence of war is decisive in solving the principal theoretical and practical problems of military strategy. It is of paramount importance in explaining the nature of any actual war. An exhaustive answer to this question is contained in the tenets of historical materialism, in the Marxist-Leninist study of war, and in the most important program documents of the Communist and Workers' parties determining their theoretical, political, and practical activities under modern conditions. The military events of our age are convincing proof of the Marxist-Leninist concept of the essence of war and the causes and conditions of its origin.

This thesis requires special emphasis because in recent years, due to the aggravation of the international ideological struggle, the revisionists and dogmatists of various schools of thought, inspired by imperialist reactionary forces, have greatly intensified their attack on Marxism-Leninism, attempting to prove that it has become obsolete and does not correspond to modern historical conditions of social development. These attacks touch directly on military and political questions. In the West, the military ideologists of imperialism have more actively propagandized various "new" military and philosophical theories—which correspond to the interests of imperialist monopolies and which are used to justify aggressive wars under the banner of anti-Communism.

Marxism-Leninism teaches that war is a socio-historical phenomenon occurring at a definite stage in the development of human society. It is an extremely complex social phenomenon, and it is possible to reveal its essence only by using a uniquely scientific method: Marxist-Leninist dialectics. Lenin stated that "dialectics requires a comprehensive study of a given social phenomenon in its development, and reduction of the external phenomenon to its fundamental motives—to the development of industrial forces and to the class struggle."[1]

The experience of history shows that even the largest world war, no matter how all-encompassing it may be, represents only one side of social development; it is entirely dependent on the course of this development and on political relationships between classes and countries.

Lenin stressed that *war is part of a whole, and this whole is politics.* He also stated that war is a continuation of politics and that politics also "continue" during war. This thesis of Lenin is extremely important: It notes the bourgeois theory of the universal, all-absorbing nature of war, of the "class peace" during war; it explains that during war politics are continued—i.e., class relations, the class struggle in all its forms and by all its methods (ideological, political, economic, etc.) do not cease.

The correct understanding of these principal theses allows the essence of war to be disclosed. "As applied to wars," wrote Lenin, "the main thesis of dialectics . . . consists of the fact that war is simply a continuation of politics by other (namely, forcible) means. And it was always the point of view of Marx

and Engels that every war was a continuation of the politics of interested powers—and of the various classes within them—at a given time."[2] It is known that the statement "war is simply a continuation of politics by other means" was made by the German military theoretician Clausewitz. Lenin, however, introduced an important correction—the phrase "namely, forcible" —which radically changed the statement of the problem. Here it must be stressed that Marxist-Leninists always meant by "forcible means," as applied to military action, the methods of armed conflict, the armed forces, and the military organization as a whole in time of war. Engels, in his work *The Theory of Coercion,* wrote that coercion is at the present time represented by the army and the navy. He explained that coercion is a political act. Coercion in relations between countries, says Khrushchev, is war.

Starting from these Marxist-Leninist theories, it can be said that war is armed coercion, organized armed conflict between the various social classes, states, groups of countries and nations, in order to achieve definite political goals.

Classes, countries, and nations always strive in peacetime to attain their goals by using the most diverse means and forms of conflict: ideological, political, economic, etc. When contradictions are seriously aggravated, they resort to the use of the methods and forms of armed conflict—to war.

All this shows that war is only one form of political and class conflict. Lenin said, in particular: "Civil war is the most acute form of class struggle, when a series of economic and political clashes and battles, being repeated, accumulated, widened, and sharpened, reaches the stage of conversion of these clashes into armed conflict."[3] Another of Lenin's concepts is that "in known periods of acute economic and political crisis, the class struggle develops into direct civil war—i.e., armed conflict."[4]

Lenin's statement that war is a continuation of politics by other, forcible methods means that war is not equivalent to policy in general, but makes up only a part of it and that policy, beside war, has available a large arsenal of various nonforcible methods which it can use for achieving its goals without resorting to war. Under present conditions, this theory guides the Communist Party of the Soviet Union and the Soviet Government in their appeals to the Western powers to solve all international issues by negotiation and not by war.

The theory of Soviet military strategy takes into consideration the other side of the problem, namely, that as opposed to other political methods, war has its own special character. In order to conduct a war, a special system of military organization is created, weapons for armed conflict produced, and combat methods developed. The waging of war itself has always represented a specific form of human activity, when each side directed its efforts toward the destruction of the other, toward capture of enemy territories or defense of its own territory, striving thereby to attain its political goals.

The present era is characterized by an enormous increase in the productive forces of society, which have brought about the appearance of new superpowerful and long-range means of destruction, and also by radical changes in the conditions of political struggle brought about by the formation of a world system of socialism. Under these conditions, the political aims of participants in a future world war will be achieved not only by defeat of armed forces, but also by the complete disorganization of the enemy's economy and by lowering the morale of his population. *Therefore, the essence of war as a continuation of politics by means of armed violence and the specific character of war appear today more clearly than in the past, and modern means of*

coercion assume ever-increasing importance.

Thus armed conflict has now become an even more specific form of human activity. This is stipulated by the following facts. First, huge masses of people are drawn into a modern war due to the growth of armed forces and the wide recruitment of the civilian population to solve a number of military and semimilitary problems in guarding the rear areas of the country. Secondly, the complexity of modern mass weapons demands special military knowledge and skills. And, finally, modern war requires, as never before, the utmost strain on the economy in order to provide the needs of war and, simultaneously, a powerful military industry, and a special material, scientific, and technical base created for the satisfaction of war needs.

In spite of its drawing into war hundreds of millions of people, however, war is only one side of social life, a special form of the political and class struggle, while social development, the interrelations of classes, countries, and nations are phenomena immeasurably broader than war. Therefore, it is fully understandable that no world ("total" or "global") war can encompass all of these phenomena. And, during war, an uncompromising class struggle must go on simultaneously. This means that confusion and identification of two such social phenomena as war and the class struggle, war and politics, is not permissible.

This was always the Marxist-Leninist concept of these problems. It remains in force also under present conditions.

Meanwhile, in various foreign military publications there have recently appeared statements that to consider war a continuation of politics by forcible means is invalid, that not only military forces, but also various "nonmilitary" means of conflict (ideological, political, psychological, economic, financial, commercial, diplomatic, scientific, technical, subversive, etc.) must be considered as means of conducting war. On the basis of these assertions, it is concluded that war is a struggle by all the methods of politics, a "complex" of all its means and forms of conflict. Thus war is equated with politics and the class struggle as a whole.

The military ideologists of imperialism cannot but take into account the fact that the outcome of a world nuclear war unleashed by the imperialists would inevitably lead to the death of capitalism as a social system. Fear for the fate of capitalism, and fear of their people who oppose wars, force these ideologists to seek ways of justifying war, as if it were no longer violent. The British military theoretician Liddell Hart, in his book *Strategy*, asserts that means of war must now include not only the armed forces, but also various "nonmilitary" means of warfare: economic pressure, propaganda, diplomacy, subversion, etc.

The Yugoslav revisionists also keep pace with the military ideologists of imperialism. In his slanderous book, *Socialism and War*, E. Kardelj tries in every way to whitewash the aggressive policy of American imperialism and to conceal the real source of the war threatening the world. Despite the historically proven teachings of Marxism-Leninism, he does not consider war as a continuation of politics by forcible means and ignores the connection between war and the class struggle.

War as a social phenomenon, as the extreme means of accomplishing the policies of certain classes and countries, is not isolated from the other phenomena of social life. The experience of modern wars shows that in starting them, countries strive for maximum mobilization of their resources to achieve victory. Once it comes to war, said Lenin, then everything must be subordinated to the interests of war.

The role and importance of various methods and forms of conflict with which political aims are accomplished are not constant. In peacetime or wartime, they vary according to the situation. During war, the fundamental, decisive means are the armed forces. All others are primarily for assisting the armed forces and the other military formations created by the widespread enlistment of the people in order to achieve political aims through armed coercion.

It is obvious that only armed conflict is a sign of war; its beginning and end determine, in fact, the beginning and end of war.

It must be emphasized again that Lenin saw the essence, the specific character of war in the continuation of politics by violence, by armed conflict and military action.

It was precisely as a result of military action, of armed conflict and violence—and not of "nonmilitary" and "indirect" action—that 10 million people were killed in World War I and over 20 million wounded. World War II took almost 50 million lives. Many countries suffered colossal material losses. In the Soviet Union alone, more than 70,000 villages and 1,710 towns were completely or partially destroyed and burned.

This is the reality that reflects the essence of war as armed conflict. A future war, in which the basic means of violence would be nuclear weapons, weapons of mass destruction, would lead to immeasurably greater casualties and destruction.

As a result of the rapid development of industry, science, and technology, the means of conducting war have become so powerful that the chances of attaining the most decisive political goals by war have enormously increased. This means that to count upon "nonmilitary" means of conflict in a future war does not correspond to the methods of warfare or to the laws of development of war. The attempts of certain Western ideologists to propagandize "nonmilitary" methods for conducting war are designed to veil the horrors of a nuclear war and to divert the attention of the mass of the people from the preparations for war by imperialist forces.

The teachings of Marxism-Leninism on war were creatively developed in the resolutions of the Twentieth, Twenty-first, and Twenty-second Congresses of the Communist Party of the Soviet Union, the new Program of the CPSU, documents of the conferences of the Communist and Workers' Parties, and statements made by Khrushchev and other prominent party and state figures in the Soviet Union and the countries of the socialist camp. Of especially important value are the statements on the nature of the modern era, the categories of wars, the absence of fatal inevitability of wars and the possibilities of preventing world war, the peaceful coexistence of countries with different social systems, the military function of a socialist country under present conditions, the development of the peaceful socialist system and the further degradation of imperialism, the outcome of a future war in favor of socialism, and the means of conducting war.

The concepts of coexistence between two world systems, which were developed by the Communist Party, have great value for correct understanding of the fundamental problems of war.

"Peaceful coexistence," said Khrushchev at the meeting of workers of Novosibirsk, October 10, 1959, "must be correctly understood. Coexistence is a continuation of the conflict between two social systems, but *by peaceful means without war. . . .* We consider this an economic, political, and ideological struggle, *but not a military one.*" [Emphasis supplied by the editors of the English language version.]

The entirely clear and principled logical conclusion that the concept of "war" does not include peaceful, "non-military" means of combat stems from this.

Especially important are Khrushchev's statements on the means of conducting war. Appearing at the National Press Club in Washington on September 16, 1959, he said, on the question of disarmament, that the best and most reliable method of making war impossible was to establish conditions for all countries without exception so that they did not stockpile weapons—in other words, to solve the problem of disarmament.

At his appearance at the United Nations General Assembly on September 18, 1959, Khrushchev, treating this problem in more detail, said that if countries disarmed completely and had no means of conducting war—i.e., no nuclear or rocket weapons, armies, navies, or air forces—then all international problems would be solved not by the force of arms, but by peaceful means. With the destruction of weapons and the abolition of armed forces, no material possibility would remain for any policy but peace.

In summing up all that has been said, it should be emphasized that: 1) war is violence in the relations between states; 2) the armed forces of states are meant to be means of violence and warfare; and 3) Lenin's concept of war as a continuation of class politics by forcible means and the concept of war as armed conflict to attain definite political aims remain in force even in the present era.

Bourgeois ideologists, by denying the class nature of politics and war, always strive to show politics as an expression of the common interests of a country and its people.

Modern ideologists of imperialism and their agents in the international workers' movement—the revisionists—contradict the reformist theory of "class peace," deny the class struggle, and distort the Marxist-Leninist concepts of war, defense of the socialist homeland, and proletarian internationalism.

American bourgeois ideologists and

reformists announce, in particular, that modern American capitalism is not the capitalism about which Karl Marx wrote, but rather a popular, humane, and peaceful type of capitalism.

Yugoslav revisionists assert that modern bourgeois countries have a superclass nature, that they protect the interests of all classes, and that their policy is universal.

The Program of the CPSU states that the defenders of the bourgeois system, striving to hold the masses in spiritual captivity, adopt new "theories" that mask and embellish the exploitative nature of capitalism. They believe that modern capitalism has changed its essence and that it has become "people's capitalism," in which classes disappear and class contradictions are erased. In reality, the development of modern capitalism proves the correctness of the Marxist-Leninist teachings on the growth of contradiction and antagonism in capitalist society.

Certain military writers attempt to prove that in the capitalist world today, the entire country and the whole people wage war, and that under present conditions, war has been transformed into a conflict of one armed nation with another, each directing all their military, labor, and spiritual forces toward defeat of the enemy.

All these theories depart from objective reality, conceal the class contradictions of modern capitalism and mask both the real essence of war and its contradictory class nature. Lenin wrote in 1914: "War in our time is the people's war. From this truth it follows not that it is necessary to drift in the 'popular' current of chauvinism, but that in wartime, class contradictions continue to exist."[5]

In order to prove this Leninist thesis by contemporary facts, it is sufficient to use only the example of the United States—the richest country in the capitalist world. During the last war, there was a vast strike movement in that country. In 1941, there were 4,288 strikes involving 2.4 million people; in eleven months of 1943, there were 3,425 strikes in which 3.5 million people participated; and in 1944, there were 4,956 strikes, with 2.1 million participants.

The refusal of a group of capitalists to re-equip their enterprises for the manufacture of war material also attests to the "unity" of the American people and the nation in war time. "Capitalists," writes William Z. Foster, "even arranged the peculiar 'Italian strike' and continued it until the government accepted their usurious conditions."[6]

The experience of imperialistic wars attests to the fact that the actual unity of the people in those wars is unthinkable. As regards just wars, the position is different. Speaking of the causes of the victories of the Soviet Government over external enemies during the period of foreign intervention and the Civil War, Lenin stated that more people than ever before were enlisted for an active part in the war and that "in no single political regime was there even one-tenth of the participation aroused by the Soviet regime."[7] This was confirmed to an even greater extent by the experience of the Great Patriotic War of the Soviet Union against Hitler's Germany.

The position of Marxism-Leninism on the class nature of wars, on the continuation of politics by other means, is a fundamental assumption for Soviet military strategy. It allows for the correct solution of the basic problems in training the armed forces for war against an aggressor; it makes it possible to reveal the nature of modern wars and the methods for conducting them; and it also allows for the solution of other important problems in the theory and practice of strategy.

WARS OF THE MODERN ERA AND THE CONDITIONS
AND CAUSES OF THEIR ORIGIN

Marxism-Leninism teaches that it is impossible to understand a given war without understanding the era. The characteristics of the modern era have been deeply, scientifically and universally treated in such important documents of our day as the Declaration and Appeal of the Conference of Representatives of the Communist and Workers' Parties of 1960, the speech by Khrushchev at the Fifteenth Session of the General Assembly of the United Nations, and the Program of the Communist Party of the Soviet Union adopted at the historic Twenty-second Congress of the CPSU. These outstanding theoretical and political documents allow a correct understanding of the true nature of modern wars, of the conditions of their origin, and the ways in which they develop.

Lenin's approach to the characteristics of the era is that all great events of history can be correctly understood only when considering them from two points of view: (1) from the point of view of the struggle between two fundamental historical trends—capitalism and socialism; and (2) from the specific historical development of these opposing forces, i.e., the natural growth and consolidation of the positions of socialism.

At the beginning of the twentieth century, capitalism was a unique, all-encompassing system, and it ruled the international arena, unleashed war at its discretion, and caused revolutionary uprisings. In these conditions, Marxism-Leninism correctly stated the problem of the "era of imperialism, wars, and revolution."

The Great October Socialist Revolution opened a new era in the history of mankind, an era of the destruction of capitalism and the consolidation of Communism. The victory of the socialist revolution in Russia was directly connected with World War I. The outcome of World War II was a series of socialist revolutions in European and Asian countries, which led to the formation of the world socialist system.

Today, the countries of the world socialist system occupy over 26 per cent of the territory of the world and make up about 35 per cent of its population. They have huge natural wealth, produce almost one-half of the world's grain supply, and account for over one-third of the industrial production. Soon the socialist countries will provide over half of the world's industrial production. In industrial output per capita, the world socialist system as a whole has already caught up with the world capitalist system. The socialist method of production demonstrates its obvious supremacy over that of capitalism. The balance of power in the international arena is now in favor of socialism, and this predetermines the course and nature of international relations.

The most important factor now is the national-liberation revolution, destroying the colonial system of imperialism. The international revolutionary movement of the working class is growing.

The Program of the CPSU states that the present era—the fundamental pattern of which is the transition from capitalism to socialism—is one of *conflict between two opposite social systems,* an era of socialist and national liberation revolutions, an era of the downfall of capitalism and the liquidation of colonialism, an era of the *victory of socialism and Communism on a world-wide scale.* The international working class and world socialism are the focal point of the modern era.

In characterizing the modern era, Marxist-Leninists stress the fact that this is not an era of imperialism and war, but the era of the decay of imperialism as a world system. This is fundamental in explaining the basic problems of war and peace.

Imperialism has entered a period of decline and death in our time; it has lost its sway over most of mankind. Now the main direction of mankind's historical development is determined by the world socialist system.

World War I and the Great October Socialist Revolution began the general crisis of capitalism. During World War II and the socialist revolutions in a number of countries, the second stage of the crisis of capitalism began. Today, world capitalism enters a third stage.

One expression of this crisis is the further, unprecedented strengthening of militarism. The imperialist countries have built up huge armed forces on which they spend the greater part of their state budgets. The imperialist countries have become militaristic countries.

During one generation of imperialism, mankind was drawn into two world wars in which millions of people were killed. Another world war, caused by international reactionaries, would bring about the deaths of hundreds of millions of people and the devastation of cities.

Under present conditions, as a result of the lack of uniformity in capitalism's development, the economic, political, and military center of imperialism has moved from Europe to the United States. American monopolistic capital has taken over the main sources of raw materials, the markets, and the spheres of application of capital; it has created an unproclaimed colonial empire and become the strongest world exploiter. American imperialism today plays the role of a world gendarme against democracy and revolution and has unleashed aggression against people who are fighting for their independence.

The American monopolists and their British and French allies in NATO have again aided the rise of West German imperialism. Thus, a dangerous breeding ground for war, a breeding ground for new aggressive power has been created in the center of Europe.

In the Far East, where the American monopolists are reviving Japanese militarism, another dangerous breeding ground for war is being created.

The Near and Middle East must be considered among the most likely regions for the unleashing of aggressive imperialist wars. Here there are great conflicts between the colonial rulers and the people fighting for independence. Korea is also a likely place, inasmuch as considerable armed forces are maintained in South Korea, especially by the United States; there is also Taiwan, which is occupied by the United States and which instigates provocative action against the People's Republic of China; finally, there is Vietnam, where, as a result of the American imperialists breaking the Geneva Agreements, the Government of South Vietnam constantly aggravates relations with democratic North Vietnam.

Thus, Soviet military strategy must take into consideration the possibility of new wars of conquest unleashed by imperialist aggressors at diverse points on the globe.

It is impossible to exclude the possibility of *wars between imperialist, capitalist countries.* The fact of the matter is that the capitalist world is torn by deep contradictions. There is a savage competitive battle for markets, for spheres of application of capital, and for sources of raw materials. And the battle has become more savage as the number of territories dependent on capital are reduced. The contradictions between the principal imperialist powers are growing—Anglo-American, Franco-American, Franco-German, German-American, Anglo-German, and Japanese-American. Political crises arise periodically in the imperialist military blocs.

In this connection, it is not without interest to refer to the experience of the past. Former Nazi General Kammhuber today occupies the post of

Inspector of the West German Air Force. In an article entitled "The Art of War," published in one of the West German magazines, he wrote that if Nazis had had the atomic bomb, they would have completely destroyed Britain and France and won World War II. It must be assumed that today there is no guarantee that the Bonn revanchists, once they had obtained atomic weapons, would not use them against their partners in NATO, Britain and France. As R. Edwards, the British labor leader, writes in the brochure "America—Ally or Boss?," the West German revanchists are persuading the United States that there are too many Communists in France and too many socialists in Britain, and that therefore Britain and France are very unstable allies. This is advanced as one argument for giving the West German Army atomic weapons—so that in emergency, it could "neutralize" England and France.

Our era is characterized by the universal historic victories of the international revolutionary movement of the working class. In capitalist countries, social forces are building up to ensure the victory of socialism. These countries are constantly shaken by class struggle. The ruling circles suppress strikes by using the armed forces. The imperialists create military blocs and bases not only for the fight against the socialist countries, but also to defeat revolutionary workers' movements and movements for national liberation.

Marxism-Leninism teaches that socialist revolutions are not necessarily connected with war, although both the world wars unleashed by imperialists brought about socialist revolutions. The great aims of the working class can be accomplished without world war, without civil war, by peaceful means. However, when the exploiting classes resort to coercion, it is necessary to remember the possibility of nonpeaceful transition to socialism. And this means that revolutionary wars and peoples' uprisings are not to be excluded.

The modern era is characterized by one great national liberation revolution after another.

The imperialists use every effort to maintain their rule in colonies. They employ all possible means: colonial wars, economic pressure, subversion, conspiracy, terror, and bribery.

The colonialists do not grant independence voluntarily. Therefore, colonies are freed by stubborn conflict, including armed conflict. As long as imperialism and colonialism exist, *national liberation and revolutionary wars are unavoidable.*

Socialist, national liberation, anti-imperialist, and peoples' democratic revolutions, vast peasant movements, the struggle of the masses against fascist and other tyrannical regimes—all are merged in a general world revolutionary process undermining the foundations of the imperialist camp.

Revolution cannot be imposed from without; it arises as a result of the deep internal and international contradictions of capitalism.

Together with other Marxist-Leninist parties, the Communist Party of the Soviet Union states in its Program that its international duty is to summon the peoples of all countries to rally and mobilize all internal forces for action and, relying on the power of world socialism, to prevent the interference of imperialists in the affairs of the people of any country. The CPSU also has an international duty to aid countries in winning and strengthening their national independence, and to assist all nations fighting for the complete destruction of the colonial system.

The choice made by nations that have thrown off the yoke of colonialism —to take the capitalist or noncapitalist road—is made by themselves; it is their internal affair. But given the present balance of power in the world arena and the possibility of support from the world system of socialism, the peoples of former colonies can solve this problem in their own interests.

All these Marxist-Leninist teachings are starting points for a correct understanding of the socio-political essence of modern war.

Studying the nature of these wars, Soviet military strategy starts with the fact that in the present era, the following basic categories of war are theoretically possible:

World war between the imperialist and socialist camps, which—if not prevented—would be, in political essence, a decisive armed clash of two opposing world systems. Such a war would be aggressive, rapacious, and unjust on the part of imperialism and a liberating, just, revolutionary war on the part of socialism.

Small imperialist wars on a local, limited scale, started by the imperialists for the purpose of suppressing national liberation movements and for maintaining colonies. Small, local wars are also possible between imperialist countries. All these wars are aggressive and unjust on the part of imperialism.

National liberation, civil, and other popular wars, for the repulse of the aggressive, predatory attacks of the imperialists and for freedom and independence. These wars are just, liberating, and revolutionary.

The Communists were always the most resolute enemies of world wars, as well as of wars in general. Wars are needed only by the imperialists for the capture of foreign territories and to enslave the peoples.

The CPSU and the entire Soviet nation have always been the first to oppose any and all aggressive wars (wars between capitalist countries as well as local wars intended to hinder national liberation movements) and they consider it their duty to support the sacred struggle of the oppressed peoples and their just wars of liberation against imperialism. It is understandable that the causes and development of such wars will differ on each occasion.

There will be a sharp distinction between the military-political and strategic aims of the participants, and also between the ways and means of conducting these wars. This poses a serious problem in the development of the theory of military strategy: to study and analyze the problems of modern war not in general, but as applied to a given concrete instance.

The distinguishing characteristics of the present era allow the Marxist-Leninists to pose the problems of war and peace in a new way.

The Twentieth Congress of the CPSU concluded, on the basis of the basic change in the balance of power between the two world systems and in the international situation as a whole, that since the world socialist camp has been transformed into a powerful political, economic, and military force and the forces of peace throughout the entire world have been strengthened, war is not a fatal inevitability.

Developing this position, the Twenty-first Congress of the CPSU resolved that even before socialism is victorious throughout the world and even when capitalism is still preserved in part of the world, there is a real possibility of eliminating world war from the life of society. This conclusion is based on the fact that fulfillment of the Seven-Year Plan for building a Communist society which the Congress adopted will exert a strong influence on the entire international situation; lead to the consolidation of the forces of peace and the weakening of the forces of war; cause enormous changes not only in our country but throughout the world; and bring about a decided shift in world economics in favor of socialism. Economics, as is well known, is the main field of competition between socialism and capitalism.

The Twenty-second Congress of the Communist Party defined the general strategic line for the U.S.S.R. in the near future, the period of the extensive building of Communist society.

The main problems of this period are the creation of the material and technical bases of Communism; the most complete satisfaction of the needs of the people; and further strengthening of the Soviet Union's economy and defenses. During this period, we must catch up with and surpass the capitalist countries in production of consumer goods. The fundamental problem of the forthcoming Seven-Year Plan is the maximum gain of time in the world economic competition between socialism and capitalism.

In the area of international relations, the Twenty-second Congress defined a consistent foreign policy directed toward maintaining peace and security on the basis of the Leninist principle of peaceful coexistence among nations of differing social systems. The Congress pointed out the necessity of ending the "Cold War" and of easing international tension—also of universally strengthening the world socialist system and the friendship of fraternal nations.

In the present age, the struggle for peace and for gaining time demands above all the steadfast strengthening of the military power of the Soviet Union and the entire socialist camp by developing industrial power and by the continuous growth of its material and technical base. The historic necessity of solving this vitally important problem is due to the fact that as long as imperialism exists, the economic basis for war is preserved, and reactionary forces representing the interests of capitalist monopolies will continue to aim for military adventures and aggression. Our military strategy must take into consideration the fact that, despite the presence and weight of factors ensuring the preservation of peace, there remains a danger of aggressive wars unleashed by imperialists against the socialist countries, primarily against the U.S.S.R.

The Program of the CPSU stresses that the imperialist camp is preparing a terrible crime against mankind—a nuclear war that could cause untold destruction to countries and peoples. The problem of peace and war has become a problem of life or death for hundreds of millions of people.

This is why the CPSU and the Soviet Government consider it their main task to prevent nuclear war. This problem is real, since the united forces of the powerful socialist camp, the peace-loving nonsocialist countries, the international working class and everyone who defends the cause of peace are interested in its accomplishment. Socialism, having outstripped capitalism in the most important branches of science and technology, has placed in the hands of the peace-loving peoples powerful weapons for restraining imperialist aggression.

When considering the conditions of the origin and the nature of modern wars, Soviet military strategy starts first from the existence and the struggle of two world social systems: socialism, traveling along the path of building Communism and conducting a policy of peace; and capitalism, which has entered upon the third stage of its decay and which is conducting an aggressive policy aimed to unleash new wars.

Peaceful coexistence between the two world systems is a continuation of the class struggle of these opposite systems on an international scale. But this is a conflict by peaceful means and without the use of violence. But in spite of the fact that the socialist camp is conducting a policy of peaceful coexistence, the imperialist bloc may undertake an adventurous attempt to achieve its aggressive aims by force of arms—i.e., by war.

The main source of the military threat is the aggressive policy of American imperialism, which reflects the desire of United States capitalist monopolies for world domination.

The aggressive course of imperialist foreign policy is expressed in the constant opposition of the ruling circles of the United States and other countries in the aggressive military blocs to the peaceful settlement of international problems, to the liquidation of the aftermath of World War II; it is also expressed in the so-called policy liberation for the countries of Eastern Europe, in the continuous arms race, the stockpiling of nuclear weapons, the establishment of missile, air, and naval bases around the countries of the socialist camp, and in the intensified preparation of the armed forces and the future theaters of operations for nuclear war. The Western powers attempt to draw all new countries into the existing aggressive groups such as NATO, SEATO, CENTO, and into new united blocs under the control of the U.S.A. directed against the socialist camp.

This aggressive course manifests itself in the ever-increasing militarization of science and economics, in the intensification of the political and economic enslavement of underdeveloped countries, in the striving to preserve the remnants of colonial rule by force of arms, and in the systematic provocation of military conflicts in various parts of the globe, including the territories of the socialist camp. The aggressive nature of imperialism is also expressed in ideological preparation for another war under the pretense of fighting Communism.

The arming of West Germany by the ruling circles of the United States, the restoration of her military economy, and the equipment of her forces with nuclear missiles are especially dangerous for the world. In Western Europe and other areas, the aggressive imperialist blocs maintain strong armed forces in the immediate vicinity of the borders of the socialist countries, have many air and naval bases available, and are building more and more nuclear-missile bases clearly directed against the Soviet Union and other socialist countries.

In accordance with the imperialist policies of the Western powers, the leaders of their armed forces and the general staffs are forming detailed plans for a military attack on the Soviet Union and other countries of the socialist camp. The aims of these plans clearly demonstrate their aggressive nature.

This indicates that the danger of military attack on the Soviet Union is not declining. Moreover, in the 1960's, the danger of a world war has become especially acute. War against the U.S.S.R. and other socialist countries can be unleashed by direct attack on them, or as a result of some local aggressive war against one of the non-socialist countries if it is against the basic interests of the socialist countries and creates a threat to peace in the world. In either case, the start of war by an aggressor will obviously lead to a new world war in which the socialist countries will be on one side and the imperialist and capitalist countries on the other. An overwhelming majority of all countries will be drawn into such a war. It would indeed have the character of a war of world coalitions.

Certain nonsocialist countries might join the socialist camp in a future war, especially during it. The possibility of forming a coalition of countries with different social and political structures is supported by the experience of World War II, when the Soviet Union and individual capitalist countries formed an antifascist coalition.

War between the socialist and capitalist camps would be an extreme means of solving the historic problem of armed conflict between the socialist and capitalist social systems.

Soviet military strategy clearly expresses the thesis that the class nature of such a war would predetermine the extreme resolution of the political and military aims on both sides. In addition, the widespread use of weapons of mass destruction would give the war an unprecedentedly destructive character. Our armed forces must be prepared for such a grim, intense, and exceptionally violent war.

In a new world war, the imperialist bloc would strive for the utter defeat of the armed forces of the socialist states and the liquidation of their political system, establishing instead capitalist systems and the enslavement of these countries.

The Soviet Union and the countries of peoples' democracy would be forced, in order to protect their socialist achievements, to adopt the no less decisive aims of the total defeat of the enemy's armed forces, and simultaneous disorganization of his home front, suppression of his will to resist, and assistance to the peoples to free them from the yoke of imperialism.

When evaluating the real balance of all the political, economic, and military power of the two world systems, our military strategy considers that the socialist camp has everything at its disposal for the successful repulse of an attack by any aggressor and for his complete defeat. The basis for this conclusion is the complete and final victory of socialism in the Soviet Union, the strengthening of the unity of the socialist countries, the development of their economy, science, technology, and military power. In addition, in its just struggle against aggressive forces, the socialist camp can count on active support from colonial and dependent countries in the courageous struggle against imperialism and colonialism, and also on the support of the peoples of the capitalist countries, who are deeply concerned with the preservation of peace. Our evaluation of the military and strategic situation of both camps as a whole shows that the position of the socialist camp is considerably more advantageous and ensures victory in the case of aggression.

It is entirely clear that, in this decisive world war, both gigantic military coalitions would use mass armies as well as all the powerful and long-range weapons available; the most decisive methods would be employed. An enormous strain on the moral strength of the people and on the economy of the country would be required to conduct such a war.

It follows that the Soviet Government, all the countries in the socialist camp, and their armed forces must be ready for a world war—primarily for a war against a militarily and economically powerful coalition of imperialist powers. The most probable and, at the same time, the most dangerous means of unleashing war against the socialist camp would be by surprise attack.

At the same time, the armed forces of the socialist camp must be prepared for small-scale wars that could be unleashed by the imperialists. The experience of such wars that have arisen during the postwar period shows they are conducted by methods that differ from those used in world wars. Therefore, Soviet military strategy calls for a study of the means of conducting such wars in order to prevent them from developing into a world war and in order to achieve a quick victory over the enemy.

In order to understand correctly the conditions for the origin of wars, it is necessary to distinguish the causes of wars and reasons for their outbreak.

The causes of modern wars lie in the operation of the law of non-uniformity and the spasmodic nature of economic and political development in the capitalist countries, in the contradictions within the capitalist system, and in the imperialists' struggle for world domination. The direct cause of wars in the present age is the aggressively imperialistic and rapacious nature of the policy of the United States and other strong capitalist countries, primarily directed against the Soviet Union and the other countries of the socialist camp.

The most diverse events may serve as occasions for unleashing war. Experience shows that the ruling classes of aggressive imperialist countries usually resort to direct fabrication of reasons for attack. At the present time, this problem is considerably complicated by the great likelihood of a so-called accidental origin of a war. Due to the arms race, there is serious danger that even a small error by state leaders could lead to a new war.

Nuclear weapons can be launched not only on the command of a government but also at the discretion of individuals at the control panel.

Careless operation of radar systems can cause an incorrect interpretation of instrument readings, and this could lead to the beginning of military activities. Incorrect understanding of an order or the mental disorder in the case of an American pilot flying a bomber armed with nuclear warheads could cause the bombs to be dropped on the territory of another country. Faults in electronic equipment of combat nuclear-missile systems could also lead to war. All this requires the greatest vigilance by our armed forces, our government, and political and military leadership so that war is not allowed to start by accident.

These are the fundamental problems relating to the categories of war and to the conditions and causes of its origin at the present time.

NOTES

1. Lenin, *Works*, XXI, 193–94.
2. *Ibid.*, XXI, 194–95.
3. *Ibid.*, XXVI, 2.
4. *Ibid.*, II, 192.
5. *Ibid.*, XXI, 23.

6. William Z. Foster, *An Outline of the Political History of America* (Moscow: Publishing House for Foreign Literature, 1955), p. 614.
7. Lenin, *op. cit.*, XXXI, 467.

The Sword and the Scepter

Gerhard Ritter

The problem of militarism is the question of the proper relation between statesmanship as an art and war as a craft. Militarism is the exaggeration and overestimation of the military, to a degree that corrupts that relation. Militarism is encountered whenever the pugnacious aspects of diplomacy are one-sidedly overemphasized and the technical exigencies of war, real or alleged, are allowed to gain the upper hand over the calm considerations of statesmanship.[1] Viewed in this light, "militarism" appears as the diametric opposite of "pacifism"—taking that term to mean an attitude renouncing resort to arms on principle and in all circumstances, i.e., at best acknowledging conflict by word, by purely intellectual means.

Yet this opposition, however clear it may be in theory, cannot be translated into practice. The realities of history record many militarist states, while radically pacifist states are seen only exceptionally, and even then but fleetingly. Without an adequately secured system of universal supranational law a national policy of radical pacifism could be maintained only at the risk of self-destruction; and survival is the basic instinct of all living things and of states as well.

Hence militarism has a much better claim to political realism than pacifism, which—at least from our present experience—carries political weight not as a general policy put to the practical test, but rather as an ideology that may be widely professed on an individual basis and thereby serve to erode a country's military potential. There are, to be sure, "peace-loving" governments, side by side with "militarist" ones; but there are none that can be called "pacifist." A predilection for peaceful settlements, moreover, cannot be described as extreme in the sense of a fundamentally bellicose orientation. It is rather an indispensable element of true statesmanship.

Accordingly, the problem of militarism cannot be made plain without a picture of what the proper relation between statesmanship and war should be. We have spoken of war as a craft rather than an art, although the conduct of war is indeed as much an art as is the government of states, and in no way inferior. (Awareness of this is reflected in the fact that successful generals usually rate many more public monuments than successful statesmen!) Yet it is part and parcel of sound public order that the military function remain subordinate to over-all government. The Prussian military theoretician Clausewitz 120 years ago reduced this to a formula that has since been unendingly reiterated: War is the continuation of diplomacy by other means.

He was stating nothing new. The principle had long been recognized by monarchial governments and their ministers. War was purely a profession, a craft. Armies were to be regarded merely as instruments of statecraft, to be used as sparingly as possible, and only for very definite, clearly delimited ends. The essence of militarism is best

understood in the reversal of this formula in the twentieth century by General Ludendorff and his ilk. "Politics
subserves the conduct of war," runs the
brusque statement; or even: "Sound
policy is the continuation of war by
other means in peacetime."[2] This was
the theory on which Adolf Hitler subsequently based his policy—with the
devastating consequences that are all
too well known.

A long road had to be traversed
before this reversal was effected, and it
is our object to trace its main stages.
But first the problem of militarism—i.e.,
the question of the proper relation between statesmanship as an art and war
as a craft—requires discussion at greater
length. Quite evidently it is not enough
to say that war is to be regarded merely
as a means of diplomacy. This is no
more than a truism—if diplomacy is
viewed solely as a struggle for power.

It is a fact that military history
offers numerous instances of vehement
quarrels between political and military
leadership in wartime, between government and army high command. We
read of the conflict in Athens over the
Sicilian Expedition of Alcibiades; of
serious disputes, both in Rome and in
Carthage, during the Punic Wars; of
Prince Eugene's fights with the War
Council at the Vienna Court; of objections to Metternich's policy of appease-
ment by Blücher's headquarters; of serious disagreements between Bismarck
and Moltke, and of even more serious
ones between Ludendorff and Beth-
mann Hollweg that shook the government to its foundations—to cite but a
few of the better-known examples.

How explain all these conflicts if
diplomacy (as a struggle for power) and
war are basically one and the same
thing? Are they nothing more than
"misunderstandings," owing to poor
jurisdictional demarcation, conflicting
ambitions, lack of political and military
skill? One would have to draw this
conclusion, from a reading of traditional military history which deals out

praise and reproof with the greatest
assurance and usually judges that the
best solution is to combine government
and generalship in one hand. But is
this not even more of a truism? It is
true that outwardly the soldier king
seems to solve the conflict, especially if
he is a great captain and at once a
statesman of genius like Alexander,
Caesar, Frederic the Great, or Napoleon. But who can say whether within
these men the same conflicting elements
that are usually embodied in different
personalities may not be at war with
each other? Above all, when that happy
union is absent, whose claim has absolute priority in war? Or can there be
no such priority, on principle, everything depending upon the whims of
history?

To pose the question is to point a
finger at the fact that of the two opposing concepts, diplomacy and war, only
one is unequivocally definable—namely,
war, the clash of arms. Diplomacy is
not a clear-cut thing, despite the efforts
of theoreticians in the service of National Socialism to equate the "concept
of diplomacy" outright with the
"friend-foe relation," the element of
fighting. If this equation were valid
there should be no existential conflict
between state and army leadership, and
recorded instances of such conflicts
would have little historical interest.
They would be at best examples of
human failure, of lack of political sense;
and history would offer us nothing but
the monotonous spectacle of endless
struggles for power among states.

But diplomacy is in truth not a
clear-cut thing. It carries a dual meaning with which the mysterious demoniac quality that hovers over all political history is closely associated—as is
the infinite, inexhaustible variety of actual political life, of the true history
of states.

Wherever the state makes its appearance in history it is first of all in
the form of a concentration of fighting
power. National policy revolves around

the struggle for power: the supreme political virtue is a ceaseless readiness to wage war with all its consequences of irreconcilable enmity, culminating in the foe's destruction, if necessary. In this view political and military virtue are synonymous—*andreia, virtus,* manliness, valor, will power, a disposition to take clear-cut action, a sense of dedication, rigid self-discipline and, where necessary, discipline imposed on others, a sense of honor that is instantly aroused, a resolve to carry every conflict to its ultimate conclusion whatever havoc that may wreak.

So powerful can this destructive drive be that in the heat of battle the moral standards without which an orderly society is impossible, without which there can be no rule of law or peace, are severely shaken. The vehemence of this force increases with the violence of the action, the unleashing of passions, the imminent danger of destruction for the contending parties. Fighting for one's life, one is little inclined to pay heed to the conventions of civil life. All is fair in war: every ruse is permissible. The application of brute force is limited only by considerations of its countereffects, the permanent destruction it may bring on, not least in the moral values of the participants. Such considerations, at the very least, are far more effective than those of humanity and law. A similar law of nature holds outside war as well. In the great power struggles among nations, as in their internal partisan strife, what restrains public men from completely ignoring the civil conventions is far less a sense of the moral force of those conventions than fear of endangering their own power, reputation, and credibility. For command of moral trust is a power factor of the first order.

In any event, the ethics of war, first detailed with unequivocal, relentless, and even brutal clarity by Machiavelli,[3] are altogether different from those of peaceful society. Indeed, in large measure the two are diametrically opposed. Yet fighting power is not the whole of the state, whose ends are not nearly so simple and clear cut as those of an army. Real conflicts between military and political policy are never confined to jurisdictional disputes between soldiers and statesmen, nor can they be solved by technical or organizational measures such as "unified leadership" or "close liaison" between military and political command. No, such conflicts tend to reach into the very heart of the political sphere.

For even more than to prevail in war, it is essential to the idea of the state to be the guardian of peace, of law and order. Indeed, this is the highest, the proper end of policy—to harmonize conflicting interests peaceably, to conciliate national and social differences, to establish law on a firm foundation, to promote human welfare, to overcome selfish private and class goals by education in public service and civil integrity to the end of creating true national and international communities.

From this point of view, an altogether different set of mainly political virtues is deemed to be in the public interest—strict law-abidingness, social responsibility, mutual assistance, a willingness to compose differences. Manliness may have been one political ideal of ancient Greece, but so were justice, moderation, and piety; and the ancient Roman philosophy of Sallust placed *moderatio* and the *justum imperium* beside *virtus* and *audacia* as cardinal virtues. Politics as "the art of the possible," moreover, is always dependent on the skillful conciliation of conflicts, the harmonization of interests, if there is to be a true political community of people living together in tolerable conditions. Theory is of little use in achieving these ends. The problem always has to be solved in practice.

Historically there have been very different solutions, in keeping with the basic orientation of the statesmen concerned and the objective situation in which they found their countries.

There have been stormy times that knew no peace, when decaying orders left only a legacy of chaos from which new power centers formed with difficulty, in savage ferment; times dominated by ruthless soldiers and power-hungry politicians, like the feud-ridden late middle ages in Germany and the incipient Renaissance in Italy. In such times military ability, the *virtù* of Machiavelli, is everything, and the peaceful work of the legislator is held in disdain. The only thing that is sought, admired, grasped with the ruthless mailed fist is the success of the moment. None is concerned with the smoking ruins, the destruction of moral, spiritual, and material values in the fighting, so long as power for conquest prevails. At such times there is no true conflict between sword and scepter, for politics is all struggle and nothing but struggle.

But once the chaotic ferment has quieted and given birth to a new order, that order strives to perpetuate its dominion. The peaceful elements in political life re-emerge and seek to confine the instincts of war. War becomes an exceptional state instead of the rule. Instead of its heroism being admired, its bloody shambles is recognized for what it is, a national disaster.[4] If it becomes unavoidable every effort is made to curb its internal dynamics, to shorten it, to limit its aims, to streamline and humanize it as much as possible, or at least to confine its horrors to a strictly limited number of preferably professional combatants, to prevent the unleashing of murder and rapine by strict military discipline. These are times when statesmanship displays its greatest zeal, to keep war instincts even in the midst of crisis from getting the better of calm political reason as expressed in terms of a permanent peaceful order.

That is the time when real conflict arises between political and military command. The army may demand commitment of every resource to achieve final victory, while the statesmen begin to calculate whether such a commitment is still worthwhile. Or the army may insist on draining its triumph to the dregs, while the statesmen seek to conciliate the enemy by generous treatment, to make a friend for tomorrow of the foe of yesterday. Or the strategists may counsel against neglecting any occasion to destroy the enemy forces, while the statesmen may fear destruction of permanent values, undesirable political side effects, the stiffening of the enemy's resolve against peace. Or the generals may wish to trust only in the tested, tangible, and visible effects of physical force, while seasoned politicians prefer to operate with psychological warfare or diplomatic efforts which, while less certain, are also less costly and risky. In general terms such conflicts arise whenever immediate military ends fail to coincide with political goals—which, however, may very well include impressive successes in the field.

These conflicts take on their full gravity only when both considerations are accepted with equal seriousness—the need of the struggle for power and the restoration and preservation of an enduring peaceful order. Neither in high policy nor in high strategy is there a set of ready-made rules and regulations, a patent solution that can be learned and taught, any more than there are convenient rules in private morality that prescribe the proper conduct in every crisis—whether or not the demands of self-preservation outrank those of altruism, brotherly love, and society. Conscience alone, from its irrational depths, can resolve these conflicts. The realities of moral life are made up almost exclusively of such conflicting claims, as shown by daily experience.

And what is true of the individual is repeated at a higher level in the life of the state. Here the stakes may be the lives of millions, yet every crucial decision ultimately amounts to a risk taken without rational certainty about the demands of the hour; and rather than being taken on rational grounds these decisions seem to stem usually from political instinct—or perhaps it is more accurate to say that they are based on the total character of the men who have to make them, on whether they incline more to armed action or to peaceful construction.

The statesman, in any event, is forever torn between the demands of concentrated fighting power and those of peaceful and enduring order, as between Scylla and Charybdis, and must seek a firm footing between the two. One might even say that his historic stature depends directly on his taking both claims with the utmost seriousness —the need for the struggle for power as a means to create and preserve an enduring peaceful order as the ultimate goal—on his bridging them in action rather than evading them.

This at least is true of the great states of history, especially the great continental powers whose situations and traditions permit no escape into neutrality in foreign affairs. Noncombatant neutrality, a pure policy of law and welfare—these have been vouchsafed only certain marginal and insular states which, owing to special circumstances, were able to maintain themselves beyond the sphere of great power decisions. Citizens of the great powers envy this exemption, unattainable to them. Within their countries true statesmanship can exist only when the sense of power, the readiness to wage war, is combined with a determination to maintain order.

This ideal, alas, is the rare exception and history is full of attempts at evasion. The devout provincial sovereigns of Germany in the sixteenth and seventeenth centuries, for example, desired only to be peaceful rulers, free of military ambition, content to care for their patrimony and the eternal salvation of their subjects. But if we fail to note any conflict between a policy of war and peace here, it is only because

these petty principalities, huddling under the protection of the Holy Roman Empire, had no real power. They were only partially states in the modern sense. For the rest they were little more than large personal estates. They certainly never intruded into the sphere of high policy.

The reality of history is just as barren of the extremist military ruler— with no sense whatever for the tasks of enduring peaceful order—as it is of the purely peaceful prince. True, there have been political activists for whom other affairs of state came far behind the concentration of fighting power— one need think only of Charles XII of Sweden, of Louis XIV, and above all of Napoleon. It is no accident that Napoleon's extreme activism with its demoniac unleashing of military power on a grandiose scale elicited an equally monomaniacal antagonist, Metternich, the great champion of order conceived of in purely static terms and the founder of the most durable peace our continent has known since the middle ages.

Yet the limitations of his achievement are plainly seen. He sought to preserve a form of law and order which the passage of time itself was undermining from within. New vital forces were arising and the dynamic militant policy of Bismarck did them far better justice. In Bismarck's person both elements were joined in a rare combination—the will to power and the striving for an enduring peaceful order, national self-assertion, and a sense of European responsibility. Yet even here the mixture can scarcely be called ideal, for there can be no question that Bismarck's combative will power was much more strongly developed than his sense of law and justice. In domestic affairs particularly he shows up as the lordly aristocrat, forever locked in a battle for power with the political parties. He never knew how to harness their ambitions to the service of the nation, replacing partisan strife with a higher integration of forces. But when one takes a close look at the heroes of history, one finds no ideal figures; and despite everything the phenomenon of true statesmanship may be studied in Bismarck to better effect than in almost any other figure in our history. After Hitler, the most extreme of all activists and militarists, we Germans have become doubly aware of that fact.

The strongest impression from such a study is the tremendous importance of *Staatsraison*—that higher political wisdom without which no state can truly flourish. Properly understood—and considered apart from the special historical coloration the term took on during its origin in the sixteenth and seventeenth centuries[5]—such political wisdom is neither mere skill in grasping the advantage of one's own side nor a mere appreciation of "reasons of state," the inexorable necessities of political life. Nor is it a transition from the natural or primitive pursuit of power to a more idealistic conception of law and culture, a mere rationalization of the power struggle serving to enlighten blind power instincts. A policy is not necessarily statesmanlike, informed by true political wisdom, merely because it proves itself particularly shrewd and adaptable, i.e., an effective means of practical power politics, in the sense of a clever opportunism capable of correctly assessing the needs of the moment, or because it employs particularly effective methods in the struggle for power. Nor does a statesmanlike conduct imply the idealistic pursuit of cultural ideals that power is to subserve.

A statesman in the higher sense never allows his inalienable responsibility for creating, preserving, and securing a true and therefore enduring order of society to be diluted by the passions, triumphs, and emergencies of the power struggle. For that reason it is germane to statesmanlike thinking to remain forever aware of the unique character of any war situation, to realize that there are limits that cannot be transgressed without risk of destroying enduring moral values beyond repair, without alienating and dehumanizing the very combatants. A statesman in the higher sense is a leader who even in the heat of battle never for a moment neglects to ask himself what the real issue is, how the world is to look afterward. What is the new order toward which we are drifting? Unless the struggle is to be perpetuated, it must lead to a new communal order—not only among the states but among the classes and individuals of each state—an order with a chance of enduring. That chance accrues only to the kind of order that is viewed as a society based on true morality, not one that is foisted on the people. It must be seen to be sound, in keeping with the actualities of life, the true national and social needs, and the balance of power. In the proper sense, therefore, higher political wisdom turns out to be moral reason. It has two aspects: clear, statesmanlike insight into the realities of the situation, the sure political eye without which no political task succeeds; and an unfailing awareness of moral responsibility that is not drowned out by even the fiercest din of battle.

It is this true political wisdom that can in practice overcome the insoluble antinomy of power struggle and peaceful order, for the power struggle then becomes only a means to create an enduring peaceful order. Political wisdom alone invests the diplomatic power struggle with moral justification, not considerations of "culture" and "cultural ideals," vague concepts quite unsuitable for the comprehension of political problems. It is true that political wisdom is never clear enough and strong enough to hold down all the blind, intemperate, destructive passions of the combatants. Indeed, there is no social order that would meet all the criteria of true justice, if only for the reason that life keeps moving ahead; hence law and order cannot prevail forever, for new claims stand against old, the natural interest of one against that of the other. But this lesson from history is no more than what experience teaches us about the kind of human inadequacy that marks all life. Great political power struggles bring home to us with particular clarity the fact that life forever moves on the borderline where the human will and human capacity collide with superhuman forces, with the powers of destiny that often defy control.

When we now look back at the starting point of our consideration of the subject, we see that any proper analysis of the many conflicts between state and army leadership necessarily leads us into the central problem of policy in general. It would be very tempting to trace the history of such conflicts within the total context of history. A comparison of analogous events occurring in the several states of Europe should reveal their innermost structure to our eyes. But first things first. An analysis of our own Prussian and German past has priority. German readers of today need scarcely to be told how urgent this task is. It goes to the very heart of our political self-examination; and the present study, begun and in its first major part concluded during the Second World War, never pursued any other aim. It sought to help answer the question that gnawed at us even then: How did the German people, for centuries among the most peaceful nations of the West, come to be the terror of Europe and of the world, acclaiming a violent adventurer who will live on in history as the destroyer of the old order of Europe? The origins and growth of what is today called Prussian militarism were to be laid bare, unhampered by ingrained prejudices rooted in our national history—but also without the prejudices which a foreigner, proceeding from altogether different political premises, might naturally be expected to bring to them.

Militarism is one of the vaguest and hence most confusing catchwords of our day. The distinction between the military profession proper and militarism is being more and more obscured. It is not appreciated that they differ as much as do character and truculence, steadfast and enlightened self-assertion and head-long recklessness, loyalty and slavish submission, genuine power and brute force. We have already discussed the kind of militarism that falsifies policy because it completely misreads the essential and foremost purpose of all social order.

This is what we set out to fathom: how was the proper relation between statesmanship as an art and war as a craft almost completely reversed in Germany; or to put it another way, what was the road that led from political war to warlike politics? It is a road that at the same time led from a professional army to a nation in arms. Both are closely associated, but they are not the same. There is a difference between an armed and a militarized nation.

Today the German people have surrendered all their traditions, even that of a nation able to defend itself. Unlike 1918, many today look on our military past as a haunting nightmare from which they would escape forever. Others wince as they look back on so many blunders in our history. Still others may ask whether it is still worthwhile for us today to discuss statesmanship and war in the historical sense, since in the age of world powers, mass democracy, and the atom bomb, both political wisdom and the craft and profession of war have changed so completely that the concepts and standards prevailing in the nineteenth century and at the beginning of our own seem obsolete. War itself seems to have become unsuited as an instrument of high policy, now that its destructive power has reached the point of threatening all life. We may well ask whether there can any longer be a statesmanship able to control the demons of war once they have been unleashed.

Yet precisely because this may be true, a historical analysis of what led us into this abyss is doubly necessary. We do not know what the future will bring; but we plainly sense that we are living in an iron age in which the world is haunted by a specter of war more terrible than at any time in history. After the great European wars of the past, occurring each time during the early part of the eighteenth, nineteenth and twentieth centuries, there was always hope that enduring peace might be achieved. Today mankind is farther away from such hopes than ever.

All this, in my view, lends special urgency to our theme. Without insight into history there can be no true understanding of the present and its problems. Such insight cannot be gained by politically oriented journalism but only by careful and patient examination of the original sources.

NOTES

1. On origin and usage of the term "militarism" in the various countries, see H. Herzfeld, "Der Militarismus als Problem der neuen Geschichte," in *Schola*, Vol. 1, No. 1 (1946), pp. 41ff.

2. E. Ludendorff, *Der totale Krieg* (1935), p. 10; General Alfred Krauss, "Die Wesenseinheit von Politik und Krieg als Ausgangspunkt einer deutschen Strategie," in *Deutschlands Erneuerung*, Vol. 5, No. 6 (1921), p. 324.

3. See my book, *Machtstaat und Utopie. Vom Streit um die Dämonie der Macht seit Machiavelli und Morus* (3rd ed.; 1943), or more recent editions under the title: *Die Dämonie der Macht* (6th ed.; Munich, 1948); also my study, "Machiavelli und der Ursprung des modernen Nationalismus," in *Vom sittlichen Problem der Macht* (Berne, 1948), pp. 40–90.

4. I am here but opposing the two extreme cases. There are, of course, a thousand intermediate forms that preponderate numerically.

5. When C. Schmitt, in *Positionen und Begriffe im Kampf mit Wiemar—Genf—Versailles,* 1940, p. 52, notes that "we are today far removed from *ratio* and *status* [in the sense of the seventeenth century] this does not argue against the need for true *raison d'état* in general. Without real political wisdom sound policy is impossible even in the age of modern mass democracy.

Why Democratic Nations Are Naturally Desirous of Peace, And Democratic Armies of War

Alexis de Tocqueville

The same interests, the same fears, the same passions which deter democratic nations from revolutions, deter them also from war; the spirit of military glory and the spirit of revolution are weakened at the same time and by the same causes. The ever-increasing numbers of men of property,—lovers of peace, the growth of personal wealth which war so rapidly consumes, the mildness of manners, the gentleness of heart, those tendencies to pity which are engendered by the equality of conditions, that coolness of understanding which renders men comparatively insensible to the violent and poetical excitement of arms,—all these causes concur to quench the military spirit. I think it may be admitted as a general and constant rule, that, amongst civilized nations, the warlike passions will become more rare and less intense in proportion as social conditions shall be more equal.

War is nevertheless an occurrence to which all nations are subject, democratic nations as well as others. Whatever taste they may have for peace, they must hold themselves in readiness to repel aggression, or in other words they must have an army.

Fortune, which has conferred so many peculiar benefits upon the inhabitants of the United States, has placed them in the midst of a wilderness, where they have, so to speak, no neighbours: a few thousand soldiers are sufficient for their wants; but this is peculiar to America, not to democracy.

The equality of conditions, and the manners as well as the institutions resulting from it, do not exempt a democratic people from the necessity of standing armies, and their armies always exercise a powerful influence over their fate. It is therefore of singular importance to inquire what are the natural propensities of the men of whom these armies are composed.

Amongst aristocratic nations, especially amongst those in which birth is the only source of rank, the same inequality exists in the army as in the nation; the officer is noble, the soldier is a serf; the one is naturally called upon to command, the other to obey. In aristocratic armies, the private soldier's ambition is therefore circumscribed within very narrow limits. Nor has the ambition of the officer an unlimited range. An aristocratic body not only forms a part of the scale of ranks in the nation, but it contains a scale of ranks within itself: the members of whom it is composed are placed one above another, in a particular and unvarying number. Thus one man is born to the command of a regiment, another to that of a company; when once they have reached the utmost object of their hopes, they stop of their own accord, and remain contented with their lot.

From *Democracy in America* by Alexis de Tocqueville. Translated by Henry Reeve.

There is, besides, a strong cause, which, in aristocracies, weakens the officer's desire of promotion. Amongst aristocratic nations, an officer, independently of his rank in the army, also occupies an elevated rank in society; the former is almost always in his eyes only an appendage to the latter. A nobleman who embraces the profession of arms follows it less from motives of ambition than from a sense of the duties imposed on him by his birth. He enters the army in order to find an honourable employment for the idle years of his youth, and to be able to bring back to his home and his peers some honourable recollections of military life; but his principal object is not to obtain by that profession either property, distinction, or power, for he possesses these advantages in his own right, and enjoys them without leaving his home.

In democratic armies all the soldiers may become officers, which makes the desire of promotion general, and immeasurably extends the bounds of military ambition.

The officer, on his part, sees nothing which naturally and necessarily stops him at one grade more than at another; and each grade has immense importance in his eyes, because his rank in society almost always depends on his rank in the army. Amongst democratic nations it often happens that an officer has no property but his pay, and no distinction but that of military honours: consequently as often as his duties change, his fortune changes, and he becomes, as it were, a new man. What was only an appendage to his position in aristocratic armies, has thus become the main point, the basis of his whole condition.

Under the old French monarchy officers were always called by their titles of nobility; they are now always called by the title of their military rank. This little change in the forms of language suffices to show that a great revolution has taken place in the constitution of society and in that of the army.

In democratic armies the desire of advancement is almost universal: it is ardent, tenacious, perpetual; it is strengthened by all other desires, and only extinguished with life itself. But it is easy to see, that of all armies in the world, those in which advancement must be slowest in time of peace are the armies of democratic countries. As the number of commissions is naturally limited, whilst the number of competitors is almost unlimited, and as the strict law of equality is over all alike, none can make rapid progress,—many can make no progress at all. Thus the desire of advancement is greater, and the opportunities of advancement fewer, there than elsewhere. All the ambitious spirits of a democratic army are consequently ardently desirous of war, because war makes vacancies, and warrants the violation of that law of seniority which is the sole privilege natural to democracy.

We thus arrive at this singular consequence, that of all armies those most ardently desirous of war are democratic armies, and of all nations those most fond of peace are democratic nations: and, what makes these facts still more extraordinary, is that these contrary effects are produced at the same time by the principle of equality.

All the members of the community, being alike, constantly harbour the wish, and discover the possibility, of changing their condition and improving their welfare: this makes them fond of peace, which is favourable to industry, and allows every man to pursue his own little undertakings to their completion. On the other hand, this same equality makes soldiers dream of fields of battle, by increasing the value of military honours in the eyes of those who follow the profession of arms, and by rendering those honours accessible to all. In either case the inquietude of the heart is the same, the taste for enjoyment as insatiable, the ambition of success as great,—the means of gratifying it are alone different.

These opposite tendencies of the nation and the army expose democratic communities to great dangers. When a military spirit forsakes a people, the profession of arms immediately ceases to be held in honour, and military men fall to the lowest rank of the public servants: they are little esteemed, and no longer understood. The reverse of what takes place in aristocratic ages then occurs; the men who enter the army are no longer those of the highest, but of the lowest rank. Military ambition is only indulged in when no other is possible. Hence arises a circle of cause and consequence from which it is difficult to escape: the best part of the nation shuns the military profession because that profession is not honoured, and the profession is not honoured because the best part of the nation has ceased to follow it.

It is then no matter of surprise that democratic armies are often restless, ill-tempered, and dissatisfied with their lot, although their physical condition is commonly far better, and their discipline less strict than in other countries. The soldier feels that he occupies an inferior position, and his wounded pride either stimulates his taste for hostilities which would render his services necessary, or gives him a turn for revolutions, during which he may hope to win by force of arms the political influence and personal importance now denied him.

The composition of democratic armies makes this last-mentioned danger much to be feared. In democratic communities almost every man has some property to preserve; but democratic armies are generally led by men without property, most of whom have little to lose in civil broils. The bulk of the nation is naturally much more afraid of revolutions than in the ages of aristocracy, but the leaders of the army much less so.

Moreover, as amongst democratic nations (to repeat what I have just remarked) the wealthiest, the best educated, and the most able men seldom adopt the military profession, the army, taken collectively, eventually forms a small nation by itself, where the mind is less enlarged, and habits are more rude than in the nation at large. Now, this small uncivilized nation has arms in its possession, and alone knows how to use them: for, indeed, the pacific temper of the community increases the danger to which a democratic people is exposed from the military and turbulent spirit of the army. Nothing is so dangerous as an army amidst an unwarlike nation; the excessive love of the whole community for quiet continually puts its constitution at the mercy of the soldiery.

It may therefore be asserted, generally speaking, that if democratic nations are naturally prone to peace from their interests and their propensities, they are constantly drawn to war and revolutions by their armies. Military revolutions, which are scarcely ever to be apprehended in aristocracies, are always to be dreaded amongst democratic nations. These perils must be reckoned amongst the most formidable which beset their future fate, and the attention of statesmen should be sedulously applied to find a remedy for the evil.

When a nation perceives that it is inwardly affected by the restless ambition of its army, the first thought which occurs is to give this inconvenient ambition an object by going to war. I speak no ill of war: war almost always enlarges the mind of a people, and raises their character. In some cases it is the only check to the excessive growth of certain propensities which naturally spring out of the equality of conditions, and it must be considered as a necessary corrective to certain inveterate diseases to which democratic communities are liable.

War has great advantages, but we must not flatter ourselves that it can diminish the danger I have just pointed out. That peril is only suspended by it, to return more fiercely when the war is over; for armies are much more impatient of peace after having tasted military exploits. War could only be a remedy for a people which should always be athirst for military glory.

I foresee that all the military rulers who may rise up in great democratic nations, will find it easier to conquer with their armies, than to make their armies live at peace after conquest. There are two things which a democratic people will always find very difficult,—to begin a war, and to end it.

Again, if war has some peculiar advantages for democratic nations, on the other hand it exposes them to certain dangers, which aristocracies have no cause to dread to an equal extent. I shall only point out two of these.

Although war gratifies the army, it embarrasses and often exasperates that countless multitude of men whose minor passions every day require peace in order to be satisfied. Thus there is some risk of its causing, under another form, the disturbance it is intended to prevent.

No protracted war can fail to endanger the freedom of a democratic country. Not indeed that after every victory it is to be apprehended that the victorious generals will possess themselves by force of the supreme power, after the manner of Sylla and Caesar: the danger is of another kind. War does not always give over democratic communities to military government, but it must invariably and immeasurably increase the powers of civil government; it must almost compulsorily concentrate the direction of all men and the management of all things in the hands of the administration. If it lead not to despotism by sudden violence, it prepares men for it more gently by their habits. All those who seek to destroy the liberties of a democratic nation ought to know that war is the surest and the shortest means to accomplish it. This is the first axiom of the science.

One remedy, which appears to be obvious when the ambition of soldiers and officers becomes the subject of alarm, is to augment the number of commissions to be distributed by increasing the army. This affords temporary relief, but it plunges the country into deeper difficulties at some future period. To increase the army may produce a lasting effect in an aristocratic community, because military ambition is there confined to one class of men, and the ambition of each individual stops, as it were, at a certain limit; so that it may be possible to satisfy all who feel its influence. But nothing is gained by increasing the army amongst a democratic people, because the number of aspirants always rises in exactly the same ratio as the army itself. Those whose claims have been satisfied by the creation of new commissions are instantly succeeded by a fresh multitude beyond all power of satisfaction; and even those who were but now satisfied soon begin to crave more advancement; for the same excitement prevails in the ranks of the army as in the civil classes of democratic society, and what men want is not to reach a certain grade, but to have constant promotion. Though these wants may not be very vast, they are perpetually recurring. Thus a democratic nation, by augmenting its army, only allays for a time the ambition of the military profession, which soon becomes even more formidable, because the number of those who feel it is increased.

I am of opinion that a restless and turbulent spirit is an evil inherent in the very constitution of democratic armies, and beyond hope of cure. The legislators of democracies must not expect to devise any military organization capable by its influence of calming and restraining the military profession: their efforts would exhaust their powers, before the object is attained.

The remedy for the vices of the

army is not to be found in the army itself, but in the country. Democratic nations are naturally afraid of disturbance and of despotism; the object is to turn these natural instincts into well-digested, deliberate, and lasting tastes. When men have at last learned to make a peaceful and profitable use of freedom, and have felt its blessings,— when they have conceived a manly love of order, and have freely submitted themselves to discipline,—these same men, if they follow the profession of arms, bring into it, unconsciously and almost against their will, these same habits and manners. The general spirit of the nation being infused into the spirit peculiar to the army, tempers the opinions and desires engendered by military life, or represses them by the mighty force of public opinion. Teach but the citizens to be educated, orderly, firm, and free, the soldiers will be disciplined and obedient.

Any law which, in repressing the turbulent spirit of the army, should tend to diminish the spirit of freedom in the nation, and to overshadow the notion of law and right, would defeat its object: it would do much more to favour, than to defeat, the establishment of military tyranny.

After all, and in spite of all precautions, a large army amidst a democratic people will always be a source of great danger; the most effectual means of diminishing that danger would be to reduce the army, but this is a remedy which all nations have it not in their power to use.

Selected Additional Readings

Aron, Raymond. *On War.* New York: Norton, 1968.

A treatise on war in the nuclear age; the author concludes that atomic weapons have not radically altered the trend of international politics.

Bramson, Leon, and George W. Goethals. *War: Studies from Psychology, Sociology, Anthropology.* Rev. ed. New York: Basic Books, 1968.

A collection of articles—many from historical sources—that seek to probe the nature of war as a phenomenon of human behavior.

Cunliffe, Marcus. *Soldiers and Civilians: The Martial Spirit in America, 1775–1865.* Boston: Little, Brown, 1968.

A history of American attitudes toward military policy and the American military tradition in the pre-Civil War period; analyzes the origins of such American phenomena as the citizen-soldier and the opposition to a standing army.

Fuller, J. F. C. *The Conduct of War, 1789–1961.* New Brunswick: Rutgers University Press, 1961.

Analyzes the impact of the French, Industrial and Russian revolutions on war; stresses the political nature of war and the need to relate military operations to clearly defined political objectives.

Hoffmann, Stanley. *The State of War: Essays on the Theory and Practice of International Politics.* New York: Praeger, 1965.

An exposition of the Hobbesian view of international politics as a "state of war" based upon historical development and political philosophy.

Kinter, William R., and Harriet Fast Scott, trans. and eds. *The Nuclear Revolution in Soviet Military Affairs.* Norman: University of Oklahoma Press, 1968.

A collection of translations from the Soviet military press discussing Soviet thinking on problems of nuclear strategy and the relationship of nuclear war to political objectives.

Knorr, Klaus. *On the Uses of Military Power in the Nuclear Age.* Princeton: Princeton University Press, 1966.

Argues that the destructive power of nuclear weapons has made military force less useful and less legitimate as a means to pursue traditional values such as territorial conquest.

Morgenthau, Hans J. *In Defense of the National Interest.* New York: Knopf, 1951.

Argues that foreign policy and operations must be geared to a realistic assessment of the "national interest" and that there is no antithesis between national interest and moral principles.

Nef, John U. *War and Human Progress.* Cambridge: Harvard University Press, 1950.

A study of the interrelations between war and industrial civilization; argues that industrialism has removed many of the restraints on war that grew up in the eighteenth century.

Osgood, Robert E. *Ideals and Self-Interest in America's Foreign Relations.* Chicago: University of Chicago Press, 1953.

A historical interpretation of American attitudes toward world politics in the twentieth century emphasizing the conflict between idealism and a realistic assessment of national interests.

Osgood, Robert E., and Robert W. Tucker. *Force, Order, and Justice.* Baltimore: Johns Hopkins University Press, 1967.

Analyzes the "role and rationale" of force in international politics in the current age and suggests trends that may point toward a more tolerable control of force in the future.

Preston, Richard A., Sydney F. Wise, and Herman O. Werner. *Men in Arms: A History of Warfare and its Interrelationships with Western Society.* Rev. ed. New York: Praeger, 1962.

The development of warfare in its social and political setting from ancient times to the present.

Pruitt, Dean G., and Richard C. Snyder. *Theory and Research on the Causes of War.* Englewood Cliffs: Prentice Hall, 1969.

A collection of essays by contemporary political scientists on methodology in the study of war, the causes of war, and the restraints on use of violence by governments.

Ropp, Theodore. *War in the Modern World.* Rev. ed. Durham, N.C.: Duke University Press, 1962.

An excellent history of warfare from the fifteenth century to the present, emphasizing the interrelationships between political, economic, and social developments and the conduct of war.

Waltz, Kenneth N. *Man, the State, and War: A Theoretical Analysis*. New York: Columbia University Press, 1954.

A far-ranging probe into the causes of war based upon three major themes: the nature of human behavior, the internal structures of states, and anarchy in the international system.

Wolfers, Arnold. *Discord and Collaboration: Essays on International Politics*. Baltimore: Johns Hopkins University Press, 1962.

Contains sixteen essays on the nature of international politics, the goals of foreign policy, and the role of national security in the modern world.

3 | THE NATIONAL SECURITY POLICY PROCESS

Introduction

The preceding section focused upon the concept of national security and examined the value implications of national security, especially as they bear upon ideas of war, defense, and the proper role of military power. This section is concerned with the formulation and modification of public policies that relate to the function of providing for national security. Although most national security resources are absorbed by the military, it must be recognized that the national security function itself involves more than military force and that national security policy evolves in the context of a complex range of national policy considerations, both foreign and domestic.

The development of national security policy involves the participation of (1) a number of executive and legislative agencies which together constitute the national security system of the government, and (2) sources of influence on national security policy that are outside of government, such as public opinion, the mass media, and various types of interest groups. Each of these structural components of the national security system performs a set of key tasks in the formulation and modification of policy. Laurence Radway, in "Forging the National Position," examines the role of Congress and the Executive in this process. An underlying assumption is that among these officials there is a basic unity of ideology which makes the national security system operate more by consent than conflict. The tactics for influencing national security policy by each of the branches of government and the leaders within them are treated. In a related analysis, "Strategic Programs and the Political Process," Samuel P. Hunt-

ington explores the relationships between executive and legislative branches of government with respect to the planning of military programs. Huntington develops his analysis in terms of a distinction between congressional "legislation" and executive "legislation."

Policy leaders have introduced technological innovations which have substantial political content into the national security process. This issue is the concern of the next two selections. Paul Y. Hammond analyzes the political functions of the planning, programming, and budgeting system (PPBS) adopted by the Department of Defense under the McNamara leadership. He compares and contrasts traditional management techniques with the McNamara innovations in terms of three political functions: bureaucratic rationalization in the military establishment, risk and role distribution in the making and implementing of military policy, and self-legitimization within the military establishment and in relation to other elements of the government and political system. Technological change related to military hardware, on the other hand, may not have the consequences for policy-making that have been suggested by some observers. Bernard Brodie, in "Technology, Politics, and Strategy," argues that weapons engineering innovations and changes in systems analytic techniques do not have such a drastic impact on the higher levels of national security policy and strategic planning.

The next two selections provide a more detailed view of the nature of systems analysis and present some limitations associated with its application to national security policy-making. "Principles and Procedures of Systems

Analysis," by E. S. Quade, surveys the craft of military systems analysis, identifying its essential characteristics, typical phases of analysis, and limitations. James R. Schlesinger, in "The 'Soft' Factors in Systems Studies," probes more deeply into these limitations. He is concerned particularly with the tendency to neglect to incorporate the so-called "soft" political and social variables into systems analyses and the inappropriate use of such analyses by policy-makers.

The final three selections in this section examine important nongovernmental factors in the environment of the national security system which help shape national security policy. "The Influence of the Press," by James Reston, assesses the impact of the press upon American foreign policy, an impact which the author feels is often exaggerated. He examines the press as an ally

and critic of the government and explores its relations with Congress and the foreign diplomatic corps. Raymond Vernon, in "Multinational Enterprise and National Security," examines the nature of large-scale multinational corporations and explores the implications for national security of their operation. One important conclusion that he reaches is that there will be a reduced role for multinational corporations as instruments of national strategy. The last selection, "The United States: Social Change and Military Power" by Klaus Knorr, is an assessment of the impacts of social change and the reactions of public opinion to the Vietnam War upon the future generation and use of American military power. At issue in his analysis is the future relationship between American political will and military strength.

Forging the National Position

Laurence I. Radway

A brief recapitulation may be helpful here. America's responses to a changing world environment emerge from the interactions of the President, the remainder of the executive branch, Congress, and the private sector. In this process, to a degree rarely approached in domestic affairs, the initiative rests with the President and his senior political and career advisers; Congress and the private sector play only subordinate roles.

POLICY FORMATION IN THE EXECUTIVE BRANCH

The key executives are not only members of legally constituted administrative agencies but also of more amorphous geographical and functional communities which cut across agency lines and often embrace elements outside the executive branch itself. Five such functional communities have been described in order to point up perspectives, concerns, or values which influence whole sets of foreign policy decisions; and attention has been drawn to factors which strengthen or weaken the influence of a group or community. Here it is useful to note that power also varies with the issue at stake. No community, no agency, is equally interested or equally influential in all foreign or military problems. In a crisis over Berlin, diplomats and warriors are likely to carry more weight than scientists or economists. But the latter are certain to play major roles in debates over future weapon systems.

THE BEDROCK OF UNITY

The fiercely combative process by which foreign and military policies are made has been well described by scarred participants.[1] But when American experience is viewed in comparative perspective a larger truth emerges, namely that impressive bonds of unity exist among the very actors whose alarums and excursions appear to indicate irrepressible conflict. . . . [T]his unity is itself an important by-product of American egalitarianism. Since the colonial era distinctive social values and a distinctive social structure have generated a pervasive sense of national identity, an enormous pride and satisfaction in "the American way of life," and quite extraordinary support for basic social, economic, and political institutions, including the constitutional system. Even when particular public policies are debated heatedly, as they so often are, the spectrum of popular opinion is relatively narrow. For ordinary citizens do not differ so much in ideology, nor are they so disposed to argue ideologically, as their counterparts in European democracies.

Moreover, since government is not the exclusive province of a small upper class, there is a good deal of job-hopping between Washington and the law offices, universities, foundations, and business firms. Such occupational mobility permits the government to keep in closer touch with, and to enjoy a firmer basis of support in, the country as a whole. Rarely, for example, does one encounter in America the deeply rooted mutual suspicion which marks relations between Japanese professors and their government. Finally, it should be noted that a few senior officials are also highly mobile *within* the executive branch. Job transfers enable them to acquire a sympathetic understanding of the perspectives of two or more competing agencies. The result has shrewdly been called "coordination by shuffling."[2] At lower levels, especially in the State and Defense Departments, mutual understanding is further promoted by exchange programs and by cross-training in the war colleges. For all these reasons a remarkable similarity in underlying convictions unites and restrains even those executives who take greatest pride in their rugged individualism. Competitive pluralism in institutions but something approximating monism in ideology—this is the true secret of the American foreign policy process.

The existence of a bedrock of unity explains the special style of policy-making during serious national crises. When a grave security threat arises, presidential leadership is accepted almost automatically. Pressures and counterpressures do not vanish. They continue to operate, not only in horizontal relationships among peers, but in vertical relationships between the President and his subordinates. Yet the instinct to follow the chief executive is also strong: many who doubt the wisdom of his course choose to remain silent; many who cannot remain silent express themselves with unwonted restraint. In short, policy-making in crisis is better distinguished by cooperation than by conflict; bargaining for once yields place to command and to freely offered consent.

INEVITABLE CONFLICT

Within this framework of national unity the foreign policy process exhibits its celebrated turbulence. Disputes are inevitable, if only because the substantive issues are so intractable. With whom, for example, should the United States cooperate in emerging nations? With pro-American but repressive oligarchs? Or with left-wing neutralists who enjoy popular support? Should a Communist regime be tolerated in the Caribbean? Under what conditions, if any, should the United States make first use of nuclear weapons? Should the President try to gain southern votes for foreign aid by ordering the sale of surplus cotton to Italy at bargain prices? Suppose this deprives Egyptian growers of Italian markets and drives their government to barter cotton for Soviet tanks? Should the United States cancel production of weapon "A" if it finds weapon "B" cheaper and better, *and* if cancellation seriously weakens a major allied government which has told its people that its defense plans are based on weapon "A"?

Reflection on such questions suggests several conclusions. One is that policy-makers have to balance conflicting values—peace, survival, efficiency, democracy, self-determination, prosperity. A second is that they must satisfy, or at least not enrage unnecessarily, multiple constituencies—allies, neutrals, the American public, and even unfriendly nations. A third is that action must often be taken when essential factual information is missing and when there is room for argument about whether proposed measures will have desired results. A fourth is that the response of particular officials will be influenced by professional perspectives and legal responsibilities that cause them to exaggerate some dangers while they ignore others.

The likelihood of contention is also increased by factors that are distinctly, if not uniquely, American. Foreign policy functions are performed by many organizations, some with a right to be consulted, all with a right to speak, most with a sizeable staff, a substantial budget, and a devoted coterie of beneficiaries and admirers in Congress, in the press, or at the "grass roots." Buttressed by such institutional resources, the experienced official judges emerging issues not only on their merits but in terms of the power his organization is likely to win or lose vis-à-vis other organizations. He plays two roles simultaneously. As an American he strives conscientiously to promote the national interest. As a bureaucrat he strives to protect the jurisdiction, or the "legitimate interests," or the traditional prerogatives of "State" or "the White House" or "the Joint Chiefs," as the case may be.

In a model hierarchy, superior officers can close arguments by issuing orders. But in the United States power is diffused vertically as well as horizontally. Occasionally, especially in the military establishment, Congress gives formal authority to subordinate officials in an effort to weaken the control of the Secretary of Defense or the President. In other cases superiors possess authority but refrain from using it. To a degree unknown in less egalitarian societies, for example, it is considered legitimate for major initiatives to be taken by so-called "action officers," or "Indians," several rungs down the administrative ladder. In the words of a French officer assigned to the NATO naval headquarters at Norfolk, Virginia:

> Here one rarely receives higher guidance regarding the position to adopt. Ideas do not circulate from top to bottom but from bottom to top. Problems move from section to section. Each man comments.[3]

In still other cases superiors are deterred from using authority because they fear the displeasure of Congress or of powerful private critics. Egalitarianism produces an anti-authoritarian bias which makes it risky for officials to try to make their way simply by "pulling rank." In addition, many subordinates are highly respected for their technical expertise. For all these reasons, even the President will not lightly overrule his principal military advisers. Finally —and this distinguishes national security affairs from some domestic questions—when the stakes are high, the nagging doubt that he may be wrong prompts many a conscientious official to allow dissenters to carry their case to still higher authority.

TACTICS IN THE MARKET

Such a policy arena both invites and rewards political dexterity. Officials must know how to develop support, inside and often outside the executive branch, if their proposals are to be considered carefully. They court allies in an effort to build a coalition that will impress the President or the Congress, not to speak of their own agency heads. They trade favors or offer them freely to build up credits for the future. They solicit endorsements from private experts or dignitaries. They describe new ventures in glowing terms. Alternatively, in order to forestall criticism, they may try to conceal them or to plead that they will be only temporary. Under pressure, they are usually prepared to negotiate a compromise by modifying the substance of their position or by restating it so ambiguously that opponents are able to accept it. Such work calls for attributes that are highly developed in the legal profession: a special sensitivity to jurisdiction, together with the capacity to advocate, to negotiate, and to draft documents. This is one reason why lawyers are often found in top foreign and defense policy posts.

Opponents of policy proposals also build coalitions, trade support, and negotiate compromises. If they lose, moreover, the American system probably gives them more opportunities to appeal the verdict than any other system on earth. The effort to utilize such opportunities sometimes results in "end runs" to Congress and "leaks" to the newspapers. The advocate who has lost or who anticipates losing in councils of the executive branch seeks to outflank the other side by carrying his cause to Capitol Hill, to the press, or directly to friends in the private sector. Defeats and victories in the executive branch are not necessarily final. For this reason the path of policy does not run straight ahead: it "zigs and zags, reverses itself, and then moves forward in incremental steps."[4]

But even during this continuing war of maneuver, the importance of underlying agreement can be appreciated by recalling that there is more than a difference of degree between an "end run" and a coup d'état, or between appeals for the intervention of a columnist and appeals for the intervention of a foreign power. Compromise is considered respectable not only because no man is deemed to have a monopoly on truth and not only because the best test of an idea is thought to be its power to gain acceptance in competition with opposing ideas, but because, win, lose, or draw, participants usually sense that they will be able to "live with the result"—and that they will be allowed to live with it! Although the clamor of debate in Washington may seem to suggest the onset of civil disorder, it conceals a massive consensus; where so many sellers compete so vigorously in offering much the same merchandise, strident tones and a leonine bearing are necessary merely to be noticed at all. Sharp exchanges can be tolerated, indeed they are often encouraged, precisely because it is assumed that intransigence or fanaticism are unlikely. The resultant process resembles a major sports event crossed with an advertising campaign.

THE PRESIDENT AND "SUPERCOORDINATORS"

Presidents differ widely in their insistence on harmony. President Eisenhower strove mightily, but not always successfully, to insure that his admin-

istration would present a united front. President Roosevelt welcomed feuds because he thought they ensured that major issues would be brought to him for settlement. In his view, splits among subordinates increased, rather than decreased, his power. But whatever their attitudes toward interagency conflict, modern Presidents must try to hold the foreign policy reins in their own hands. They struggle to control a process in which they have to bargain with or outmaneuver underlings and in which execution often falters because some officials drag their feet and others are too obtuse to move fast. The need to keep control determines to whom Presidents are prepared to delegate power and in what forum they wish debates to be conducted.

Occasionally suggestions are advanced that Presidents should seek aid by delegating foreign policy powers to the Vice-President, to a second, appointive Vice-President, or to a superior official who might be called "First Secretary of the Government." But Presidents are likely to be wary of such proposals. The Vice-President, for example, is often chosen because he belongs to a different wing of the President's party. A ticket that appeals to different groups may help win an election, but it increases the odds that the President and Vice-President will disagree on substantive issues. Such disagreement can be awkward, since the President cannot remove the Vice-President from office. Moreover, just as the President is likely to view any "supercoordinator" as a potential rival, so his proud department heads are likely to resent him as an intermediary between themselves and the chief executive.

Instead of delegating foreign or military functions to individuals with exceptional authority, Presidents have turned in four other directions. Occasionally they have sought the advice of private citizens, who are less likely to view new proposals as a rebuke for past performance or as a threat to future status. More often they have utilized the National Security Council, the White House staff, or the State Department as mechanisms, partly competitive and partly complementary, for developing and supervising *government-wide* policy.

THE NATIONAL SECURITY COUNCIL

The National Security Council is an interagency committee chaired by the President. It was created by Congress in 1947, in part as a reaction to President Roosevelt's untidy administrative habits, including his alleged vulnerability to the views of the last man to get his ear. In the last two generations, however, Washington has tended to oscillate between devotion to tidiness and devotion to creativity, and critics of NSC often charge it with being insufficiently innovative, especially during crises. More important for present purposes, some Presidents have apparently feared that NSC might limit rather than enhance their power. After all, its creation was inspired not by the President but by his competitors, namely department heads and the Congress. Its minimum membership—the Vice-President, the Secretaries of State and Defense, and the Director of Emergency Planning—was fixed by Congress; and although the President is free to invite others to attend, few participants are likely to share his special sensitivity to the domestic economic and political values that have to be balanced against national security goals. There is no doubt, also, that some of the original advocates of NSC were admirers of British government, that they sought to "modify the Presidency as an institution" and to replace that institution by a system in which power rested in the Cabinet as a collegial body.[5] The hope was that NSC would give its advice in a way that the President could not safely ignore.

This conception was uncongenial to President Truman. Personal taste and political instinct led him to the Jacksonian concept of the President as a "tribune of the people." For this reason he chose not to call many meetings of the National Security Council, and when it did convene, he sometimes absented himself to underscore the point that it was purely advisory to him. On the other hand, modern history had made Republican leaders more skeptical of a strong, personalized presidency, and long experience with the Army staff system had induced President Eisenhower to view leadership as a corporate or institutional endeavor. In his administration, therefore, NSC was given new life. Its meetings were prepared more thoroughly. Agenda items and discussion papers were circulated in advance, the latter usually being prepared by a subordinate "planning" committee. Participants were also briefed in advance by their own "special assistants for NSC affairs." The meetings themselves tended to be both more frequent and larger. Intelligence briefings and other formal presentations often preceded the period of free discussion. When the President approved an NSC paper or otherwise reached a decision on any matter that had been under discussion, a subordinate "operations coordinating" committee was charged with the responsibility of assuring that the decision was executed.

Under President Kennedy the pendulum swung back. NSC met less often. Its two subordinate committees were abolished. More use was made of *ad hoc* working groups, luncheon meetings, and task forces, reporting to the President or a member of the White House staff. President Johnson continued this approach, which seems also to be preferred by the State Department. Like other participants, the State Department is acutely aware of the tactical advantages and disadvantages of any particular forum. To the extent that its representatives can take the lead in some other forum, State will often prefer it to NSC, where, despite having what is frequently a paramount interest, State tends to meet other agencies on a basis of formal equality.

WHITE HOUSE STAFF

The use of specially trusted presidential assistants in foreign affairs can be traced back at least as far as the service of Colonel House in the Wilson administration. The fact that there has been such a steady stream of them since 1940—Harry Hopkins, Averell Harriman, Gordon Grey, Robert Cutler, McGeorge Bundy, and Walt Rostow—suggests that such assistants have become a permanent part of our actual constitutional system.

The functions of such men are as varied as Presidents wish. They may spark ideas, collect data and suggestions, draft speeches, or "ride herd" on agencies to see that presidential decisions are executed. They save the President's time by making little pieces of paper out of big ones. Some act as personal emissaries in delicate negotiations abroad or in Congress. Almost all help prepare the President for his endless round of meetings with agency heads, legislators, reporters, and foreign potentates, advising him what each caller is likely to say, what he is likely to mean, what the President may wish to say in return, what commitments have already been made, and what other interests are likely to be affected.

From the President's standpoint, the most important fact about White House staff members is that they are peculiarly and uniquely *his* men. In the kaleidoscopic universe of Washington they are somewhat more likely to view matters from his special perspective. He alone selects them, defines their power, and controls their destiny. And while they do not have behind them the intellectual resources of a great department, by the same token they are less tied to past policies and freer of departmental bias, supported

as it often is by members of Congress and by private groups. For these reasons Presidents tend to rely increasingly on White House assistants when they seek to assert themselves in foreign affairs. For the same reason, department heads are likely to be on guard against any tendency of an assistant to insert himself in the line of command between themselves and the President.

Relations between the White House staff and regular departments were especially delicate early in the Kennedy Administration. The Joint Chiefs of Staff and their chairman were put in an awkward position by the appointment of Maxwell Taylor, a distinguished and senior general officer, as the President's personal adviser. The State Department was placed in a comparable position when McGeorge Bundy and other energetic men were given foreign policy assignments in the White House. No less than four such aides operated in the field of Latin American affairs, and although they did much to reshape the Latin American policy of the United States, they also overshadowed the Assistant Secretary of State for Latin America. The latter subsequently resigned.

STATE DEPARTMENT RELATIONSHIPS

By tradition, the Secretary of State outranks other Cabinet members, and although his authority in foreign affairs is far less than the President's, his interests in that subject are substantially as broad. Moreover, they are broader than the interests of any other department head. Hence State has always felt it had a right and a duty to supply guidance to other agencies when the latter ventured into foreign affairs. In practice, . . . State's influence varies, depending on the preferences and the power of the President, and of the Secretary. Its influence also varies with the particular agency with which it is dealing.

It is useful to divide such agencies into at least three categories. First are those which work exclusively in foreign affairs and which are, in effect, satellites of the State Department. These include the Agency for International Development, the Peace Corps, the Information Agency, and the Arms Control and Disarmament Agency. The first two are actually semi-autonomous components of the Department, and all four could plausibly become integral parts of it if it were to evolve into a superdepartment like the Pentagon. Even now the head of the disarmament agency has a dual status as an adviser to the Secretary of State, while the chief of the Information Agency serves simultaneously as a member of the Secretary's staff.

A second category consists of departments like Commerce, Agriculture, and Treasury. Although they may have profound influence on foreign trade, international commodity prices, or the balance of payments, their foreign affairs functions are distinctly subordinate to their domestic functions. Moreover, they enjoy independent political support. In an issue over which they feel deeply, to the extent that they look anywhere in the executive branch for direction, they are likely to look to the President, not to the Secretary of State.

In a third category is the Defense Department. Its institutional ties with State, and the personal relationship between the two Secretaries, are of paramount importance in the conduct of foreign relations. The proper balance between the diplomats and military establishments can be upset by either party. Diplomats may pursue goals which the armed forces are too weak to attain, or military leaders may deploy their forces in ways that force the diplomat's hand. The views of the two bodies often conflict, and many recent policy decisions have been determined by the relative influence of one or the other. During a crisis over Laos in 1962, the Defense Department wanted either massive intervention or complete withdrawal, while the State Department proposed limited military steps coupled with an effort to neutralize the land. Here the State Department position prevailed.[6] In Vietnam, especially after 1961, most Pentagon officials sought a military solution, while most State Department officials, especially Far East specialists, sought to subordinate military measures to political and social programs. Here, according to the testimony of a former Assistant Secretary of State, the Defense Department position prevailed.[7]

STATE DEPARTMENT TACTICS

It has been noted that the State Department keeps a wary eye on White House foreign affairs specialists and that the Secretary of State is less likely to wish to conduct important business in the "town meeting" atmosphere of the National Security Council than in private conversation with the President. In recent years the State Department has also made efforts to strengthen its influence vis-à-vis the Defense Department. So that it might comment on their probable impact on foreign relations, it has asked to be kept informed about war plans, covert operations, weapons systems, force levels, the defense budget, and military aid programs. It has also assigned political advisers (called POLADS) to generals and admirals commanding major military forces outside Washington. It has asserted the right to review, and if necessary to censor, speeches by military and other officials to insure their conformance to its definition of the foreign policy of the country. It has created the Office of Politico-Military Affairs to maintain liaison with the Joint Chiefs of Staff and other Pentagon units. Moreover, it has secured explicit statements from the President, attesting its primacy in foreign affairs. In 1961, for example, Congress was notified that:

> The President does not wish any question to arise as to the clear authority and re-

sponsibility of the Secretary of State, not only in his own Department, and not only in such large-scale related areas as foreign aid and information policy, but also as the agent of coordination in all our major policies toward other nations.[8]

If such a sweeping mandate is to have force, the State Department must be granted a dominant voice in interagency deliberations. A notable effort to give it this special status was made in 1966, when President Johnson assigned to the Secretary of State a part of *his own power* to exercise "overall direction" of interagency activities overseas. To help the Secretary exercise these powers the President established a permanent steering committee, called the Senior Interdepartmental Group, composed of officials who controlled the principal departments engaged in overseas functions. Its members included the Deputy Secretary of Defense, the heads of the intelligence, economic aid, and information agencies, the chairman of the Joint Chiefs of Staff, and the Special Assistant to the President for National Security Affairs. The distinctive feature of this committee, however, was that the Under Secretary of State was designated as "executive chairman" with authority to "decide" all matters on the agenda. Counterpart groups, chaired by regional Assistant Secretaries of State with comparable powers, were established for five geographical areas of the world.

Despite the resolute language of the President's directives, the primacy of the State Department is not assured. The very order that gave its Under Secretary authority to "decide" issues on the agenda of the Senior Interdepartmental Group contained some illuminating fine print. One clause exempted overseas military commanders, to whom the line of control runs from the President, as commander in chief, through Defense rather than State. Another clause in effect authorized agencies to appeal to the President if the State Department's decision was unacceptable to them. This merely ac-

knowledged the truth stated bluntly by Dean Acheson, "No Cabinet officer can direct other Cabinet officers."[9]

THE COUNTRY TEAM

Relations between an ambassador and other agencies abroad resemble those between the Secretary of State and the same American agencies in Washington. Indeed, the Senior Interdepartmental Group was modeled on a similar mechanism abroad, the so-called "country team." The ambassador, who represents not only the State Department but the President, is the captain of this team in the sense that he is authorized to "coordinate" the activities of all United States agencies in his country. He supervises not only the activities of the major foreign affairs agencies but also the work of officials in such fields as immigration, customs, public health, education, shipping, and agriculture. These officials often have their own channels for reporting to Washington, their own sources of funds, and their own systems for assigning, rewarding, and disciplining personnel. But most ambassadors regularly hold staff meetings and resort to other administrative devices to insure that the foreign policy views of the State Department are respected.

Although the country team includes military attachés and military missions which train or equip foreign armed forces, it does not oversee the activities of American operating forces under a field commander. For a time certain activities of the CIA were also excluded from its supervision, but this is no longer the case. There are, however, special problems in the relation between an ambassador and CIA personnel in the field. These problems are less common in the case of agents under "loose" cover, who are often assigned to the embassy staff and whose identity is known not only to that staff but to key officials in the host government. They are more common in the case of agents under "deep" cover, who may be engaged in activities which governments do not ordinarily acknowledge. Apparently an ambassador is sometimes informed of such activities in general rather than specific terms. Again, the matter may be so sensitive that the ambassador is the only man in the embassy who is informed.

Finally, there are cases in which the embassy, although fully informed, happens to disagree with officials of other American agencies which have their own lines of communication to Washington and to bureaucrats and politicians in the host country. The embassy may advocate land reform where the United States economic aid mission, perhaps directed by an ex-businessman opposed to "socialism," fears that such a measure will impair rice production. The embassy may wish to work with the local finance minister to limit defense expenditures in an effort to curb inflation, even as the American military aid chief is working with the defense minister to improve what both regard as a dangerously weak army. Or the ambassador may disagree with the CIA station chief over which rising local politicians are most worthy of American support. In recent years such issues, which often parallel similar interagency conflicts in Washington, have split "country teams" in such places as Korea, Laos, and South Vietnam.

EXECUTIVE-LEGISLATIVE RELATIONS

Executive-legislative relations further illustrate the tactics of executive branch leaders, who are the "insiders" in the policy process; at the same time, they shed light on the capabilities and limitations of the most important "outsiders," the members of Congress.

BUTTER AND BIPARTISANSHIP

Presidents spend much time "buttering up" key members of Congress. Receptions, special briefings, and breakfast conferences for majority and minority leaders are now Washington routine. But in some cases a President goes much farther. He may take a legislator into the inner sanctum in which his closest advisers are discussing highly sensitive matters; in this way William Fulbright (D., Ark.), chairman of the Senate Foreign Relations Committee, learned of the plan to topple Fidel Castro in 1961. He may encourage a ranking minority member to lead in the development of a new national position, the classic example being the role of Senator Arthur Vandenburg (R., Mich.) in shaping military and economic policy toward Europe after World War II. He may include minor-ity and majority leaders in delegations to international meetings, such as the San Francisco Conference on the United Nations Charter.

These less conventional gestures are but special cases of the general tendency of Presidents to seek broad national support for potentially controversial foreign policy ventures. Another example of this stratagem is the appointment of members of the opposition party to top posts. As World War II neared, for example, President Roosevelt appointed Republicans to be Secretary of War and Secretary of the Navy. President Kennedy's Republican appointees included the Secretary of Defense, the Secretary of the Treasury, his special assistant for national security affairs, two successive directors of the CIA, an ambassador to Vietnam, and a special assistant for disarmament. He also called upon former President Eisenhower, former Secretary of State Herter, and Governor Rockefeller for help on aspects of foreign economic policy.

The fact that such gestures have been more common in Democratic administrations may simply mean that the bitter partisan debate which culminated in Senate rejection of the Versailles Treaty and the League of Nations was a traumatic experience for the Democratic party. At any rate, two of its members, each of whom suffered his only major electoral defeat in 1920, subsequently became the architects of bipartisanship in foreign affairs. They were President Roosevelt and his Secretary of State, Cordell Hull. It may also be significant that many of the Democrats who developed the techniques of bipartisanship (not only Secretary Hull but Secretary Byrnes and Presidents Truman, Kennedy, and Johnson) had themselves served in Congress. But the more important point, surely, is that major innovation in foreign affairs tended to occur under Democratic Presidents because they occupied the White House in most of the years since 1932. Although President Eisenhower, too, engaged in bipartisan consultation with congressional leaders, Democrats felt greater need to seek public confidence by widening discussion to include members of the opposition.

A useful general theorem is evident. In many foreign and military policy issues it is possible to determine whether the President or a particular agency chief is satisfied with his position and his prospects—in colloquial terms, whether he is "sitting pretty" or "on the make." For example, a President who is simply trying to preserve a neutral course during an Arab-Israeli confrontation probably holds the upper hand with his critics. If so, he has little incentive to stimulate discussion of his policy by Congress or the public. On the contrary, he will try to discourage debate by disciplining lower ranking officials who have the temerity to express doubt about his policy or by appealing for bipartisan support in what is really an effort to inhibit critical comment. To be "on the make," on the other hand, is to be unhappy about existing policy or uncertain of one's ability to launch new policies. "Insiders" in this position have every incentive to bring "outsiders" into the act in order to increase their power as well as to share responsibility for the new policy. Thus careful overtures to Congress would precede any presidential request for a large appropriation for a new economic aid fund to be supervised by the United Nations. Likewise, long and patient discussion with Congress would undoubtedly precede any such step as recognition of Communist China. In both cases, direct appeals are likely to be made to the public and opinion leaders in an effort to light a fire under Congress.

CONGRESS' HARD-NOSED PERSPECTIVES

When an administrative agency seeks Congress' attention, it often does so because it has suffered a defeat at the hands of the President, the Bureau of the Budget, or some other executive agency or agencies. It seeks to reverse the verdict by appealing it to the legislature. This stratagem may also be used by a bureau or faction which has lost the first round within an agency. In the early history of the Atomic Energy Commission, officials who did not agree with its chairman sometimes sought support from Congress' Joint Committee on Atomic Energy. Each military service has at some time appealed to Congress to restore budget items cut by the Secretary of Defense. Admiral Rickover appealed to Congress when he believed that the Navy was neglecting the atomic submarine program; Air Force General LeMay appealed when he felt that a proposed test ban treaty endangered national security.

To a degree, these appeals are made simply because agencies are shrewd enough to capitalize on the historic institutional rivalry between Congress and the President. Because the great prize in this rivalry is the federal bureaucracy, members of Congress in turn are shrewd enough to sense that they may be able to enhance their own influence by increasing disunity in the bureaucracy. Their obvious gambit is to try to divide and rule by limiting the supervisory authority of superiors (hence outcries against both a "Prussian" general staff and a civilian "czar" in the Pentagon), by vesting statutory authority and funds directly in subordinates, and by encouraging or tempting the latter to appeal decisions made by their superiors.

The more important reason for appeals to Congress is that its perspectives on foreign and military policy are likely to differ from the President's; and although these differences are often slight by the standards of other countries, they may well loom large enough in the eyes of a disappointed underling to justify a modest effort at insubordination. By and large, Congress is more nationalistic than the President, more intent on retaining every last drop of American sovereignty, more inclined to drive hard bargains with friends and to take a hard line with enemies, and more solicitous of the interests and the conventional ideology of American business. Administrative officials who share these hard-nosed views are likely to find a sympathetic hearing on Capitol Hill.

Congress' relative coolness toward the needs of friendly countries is illustrated by its prohibition of the sale of surplus military supplies to France and England in 1940 unless the Chief of Naval Operations and the Chief of Staff certified that such sales were essential to American defense. Later, when it enacted more generous Lend-Lease legislation, Congress retained the right to terminate the program at any time by joint resolution. In more recent years the result of Congressional influence over economic aid policy has been less aid, more loans and fewer grants, and more loans repayable in dollars rather than in soft currency. Congress has regularly called upon western Europe to carry more of the aid burden. It is

vexed if recipients fail to acknowledge their appreciation and furious if they "bite the hand that feeds them." Skeptical of aid to neutralists, it has been even more critical of aid to Communist states, or to countries which trade with Communist states, or to those which expropriate American-owned property without "just compensation."

Prior to World War II, when it sensed no threat to national security, Congress was largely indifferent to military needs. In both hot and cold wars, however, Congress leans toward military techniques of national policy; it looks more indulgently on the armed forces than on the State Department, USIA, or AID; and it is more reluctant to make drastic reductions in the military budget. Indeed, economy myths to the contrary notwithstanding, Congress has more than once appropriated funds for the armed forces which the President has refused to spend. It has tried ·to increase and to prevent the President from decreasing the size of the Marine Corps; it has lobbied for new generations of manned bombers; it has pressed for faster progress in the space program; it has demanded more ambitious and expensive missile and countermissile programs. On one notable occasion the chairman of the Joint Chiefs of Staff was taken to task in a Senate hearing because he was allegedly too easily persuaded by the conservative economic views of the Secretary of the Treasury.

Cynics may look to specific constituency interests to explain this behavior or to the fact that as late as 1965 one out of six or seven members of Congress was a member of the Ready Reserve of the armed forces. But it is likely that more fundamental political forces have been at work. While the recruitment of presidential aspirants has combined with the working of the nominating convention and the Electoral College to give relatively great influence to voters in the major metropolitan areas, the recruitment of members of Congress, the historic operation of the districting system, and the rules of seniority have combined to give disproportionate power to legislators from small towns and rural areas, especially in the South and Midwest. Voters in these districts have tended to be less cosmopolitan and more fundamentalist in their outlook, and congressmen hear from them daily.

NUANCES AND COALITIONS

Congress, of course, is not a monolith. The generalizations just made do not fit the Senate as closely as the House of Representatives. They fit particularly poorly the Foreign Relations Committee, which attracts more than its share of liberal senators. Basking in the attention they receive from the State Department, members of this committee regard themselves as more knowledgeable and more "responsible" than other senators, let alone members of the House. In their sensitivity to the foibles of allies and the clamor of neutrals, they are much more likely to resemble the President and Secretary of State. At times, to be sure, the entire committee or its chairman have been severely critical of the administration. Senator Fulbright, for example, protested bitterly against escalation in Vietnam. But since 1945 the committee has most often acted as the Administration's loyal agent within Congress.

Quite a different impression is produced by the House Appropriations Committee. Operating through subcommittees, which review budget requests in closed session, this fearsome body prides itself on being the chief champion of the economy-conscious American taxpayer. Its subcommittees on the State Department and on the Agency for International Development have been openly skeptical of programs administered by those organizations and not a little contemptuous of their personnel.

Still another nuance is evident in the Armed Services Committees of Congress. Here one is more likely to encounter "cold warriors," men with the acutest sense of the Communist menace, the greatest impatience with neutrals (e.g., India), the greatest desire to negotiate from positions of strength, and, accordingly, the greatest determination to maintain large armed forces equipped with the best that money can buy. Their members tend to serve as spokesmen for the professional officer corps, some of whose retired personnel are employed on their staffs. Similar views, and a similarly protective attitude toward its administrative "constituency," are evident in the special "watchdog" committee that oversees the CIA. This body serves primarily to ward off criticism of the CIA or intrusion into its affairs by less sympathetic members of Congress.

These examples suggest the range of views in Congress and the opportunities that exist for conflict between committees, houses, and voting blocs. They also make clear why components of Congress form part of the functional communities described earlier. It should be evident that executive-legislative relationships do not consist only, or even primarily, of relationships between the President and Congress. More often they consist of arrangements in which the State Department, for example, works closely with *some* members of the Foreign Relations Committee, or in which Treasury and Budget Bureau officials find themselves working with appropriations committees to prevent budget increases gratuitously recommended by *some* members of an armed services committee in cahoots with *some* elements within the Pentagon. In these informal, constantly shifting coalitions it is not quite enough to say that executive branch officials "use" legislators or that the latter "use" their administrative allies. The larger truth is that they all use each other. Their alliances are formed for mutual aid. The formation of such alliances permits policy participants to follow their most deeply held convictions about the national interest while preserving a due regard for self-interest and institutional interest.

THE FORCE AND EFFECT OF CONGRESS

There remains the question of power. How much of it does Congress, and various parts of Congress, have? Or, better, what kinds of power does it have? Over what kinds of issues?

Many answers to these questions begin by bewailing the absence of information and expertise on Capitol Hill. But this deficiency should not be exaggerated. Besides information supplied by personal staff, committee staff, and the Library of Congress, members get masses of data from hearings and investigations, not to mention juicy items supplied in confidence by disgruntled bureaucrats. Committees vie with administration experts by contracting for their own specialists from universities and other private research centers. It is no longer unusual to find multi-volume studies of Latin America or foreign aid prepared under congressional auspices. Undoubtedly there is much highly classified data that members do not possess, but in many cases this is the result of a self-denying ordinance rather than of inability to get access; there are some things members feel uneasy about knowing.

In the matter of job experience, members who have served on foreign or military affairs committees for fifteen or twenty years are not necessarily less well informed than political executives who have taken leaves of absence from their law firms to serve the government for three or four years, or than military or foreign service officers who rotate between Washington and a miscellany of overseas stations at similar intervals. Congress has more than its share of veterans. When Dean Rusk took office in 1961, one third of the members of the Senate Foreign Relations Committee greeted him as the *seventh* Secretary of State with whom they had cooperated.

GENERALS WITHOUT TROOPS

Despite its knowledge and experience, Congress is clearly the junior partner, the reactive rather than active element, in the foreign policy establishment of the government. It operates primarily as a limit-setting mechanism. Only rarely does it take and hold the initiative in the evolution of truly major foreign policy. An example of the exceptional instance was its leadership in the 1930's, when it enacted neutrality legislation which President Roosevelt thought unwise. In many cases, however, what appear to be Congressional initiatives are actions really inspired by administration officials who prefer not to reveal their role.

Why is Congress so often found responding to administrative initiatives rather than the other way around? One reason is that in fast-moving diplomatic situations Congress' information, even if ample, tends to come late. The State Department, alerted by its overseas "troops," has defined the nature of the problem, formulated the major options, and, probably in consultation with other agencies, decided, or nearly decided, what course to adopt—all before Capitol Hill is more than aware of the problem.

This is only one of the prices Congress must pay for not possessing its own administrative apparatus. If, for example, most legislators desired a détente with Communist China, they could neither force such a policy upon an unwilling President nor carry it out themselves. Congress does not negotiate with foreign leaders; it lacks even the basic constitutional authority to require others to do so.

Moreover, Congress cannot organize its own members into an effective hierarchy. The difficulty here stems from its nature as a college of peers. Congress is composed of successful politicians, all of whom are formally equal in authority and most of whom are less impressed by threats of punishment or promises of reward than even the more incorrigible individualists in the bureaucracy. A comparison with the administration is particularly revealing at this point. Foreign policy functions are now widely diffused in both the executive and legislative branches. In a simpler age they were concentrated mainly in the Department of State, on the one hand, and in the Foreign Relations Committee, on the other. But such is the interpenetration of nations today, so pervasive their mutual impact, and so total their efforts to cope with one another, that foreign affairs touch the guts and sinews of every nation. Accordingly, not only do most executive agencies deal with international issues, but so do more than one half of the committees of Congress. In addition to committees already named, these include the ones concerned with space and science, the merchant marine, agriculture, immigration, interior and insular affairs, banking (Export-Import Bank), commerce (oil), revenue (tariff), public works (St. Lawrence Seaway), and many others.

But here the parallel between the two branches ends; for in Congress the mechanisms to coordinate and direct this diffuse committee activity are woefully weak. The rule of seniority permits leadership within a committee, but no single committee has a jurisdiction broad enough to encompass the major interests—diplomatic, scientific, economic, and military—which must be represented and reconciled. No single leader is authorized to issue orders. Indeed, few legislative leaders possess both great interest in foreign affairs and great power over them. With some notable exceptions, the recent lords of Capitol Hill like Alben Barkley, Everett Dirksen, Lyndon Johnson, Joseph Martin, Sam Rayburn, and Robert

Taft have fixed their attention on domestic rather than international problems. In other words, those congressmen who have had more power have had less interest; those who have had more interest have had less power. Only in the President has the marriage between interest and power been complete. Only he, in coming to grips with the diffusion of responsibility and with the wonderfully independent barons who hold it, can call upon a White House staff, a Budget Bureau, a National Security Council, and a Department of State.

CONGRESSIONAL POWERS

Given its handicaps, it is understandable that Congress should normally be content to exercise its power to consent, its power to criticize, revise, or veto, and its power to deter.

Sometimes the act of consent precedes an administration decision; sometimes it follows. Sometimes it is performed voluntarily; sometimes in response to a specific request. Pursuant to such requests, Congress agreed to approve the use of force under specified conditions in the Middle East, in the Formosa Straits, and in Vietnam. Presidential decisions received strong support after the fact in the Pearl Harbor, Korean, and Cuban missile crises. In such cases the grant of consent is an exercise of power in the sense that it has important political consequences. Especially if given by a significant majority and after thoughtful consideration, Congressional approval signifies agreement between the two political parties. This creates or strengthens consensus among private citizens. At the same time, it unites them with their government. But if Congressional action is to have this effect, Congressional discussion must formulate problems in terms that private citizens can understand, even if this means exaggerating, oversimplifying, or even misstating the issues.

It is more exciting, of course, when

Congress exercises its power to criticize, revise, or veto. Members are skilled in probing cross-examination designed to uncover weaknesses in administration proposals or extravagance in agency budgets. They mount investigations to expose waste, inefficiency, corruption, or folly. Why were we taken by surprise at Pearl Harbor? Was it wise to fire General MacArthur? Are we letting the Russians win the space race? The missile race? Why do we give military aid to Latin American dictators? Why does the State Department choose to operate its language school on the Riviera? Why must we feel obligated to preserve the territorial integrity of the Congo?

Some questions raise issues of general policy; others are highly specific. Some are asked in public, others in private. Some are put without hope of immediate effect but in the expectation that criticism now may lay a basis for change later if present policy is found wanting. Others are essentially part of a lobbying campaign directed at the administration. The Joint Committee on Atomic Energy, for example, operates as a kind of self-appointed interest group on behalf of nuclear power, urging the development of superbombs, small nuclear devices for riflemen, warheads for sea-borne missiles, counter-missile weapons, and nuclear-powered warships or aircraft. Still other questions lead directly to amendments or substitute proposals developed by Congress itself. Reservations are attached to a treaty; proposed selective service or immigration bills are revised drastically; a rider increasing the size of the Air Force is attached to an appropriation bill; funds for the Voice of America are slashed.

A special word needs to be added about the nay-saying power of particular committees. For at least three reasons the House Appropriations Committee is the most feared. One is that it is a highly coveted committee whose members enjoy such prestige that their decisions are not lightly challenged by their colleagues. A second is that the precise dollar limitations it imposes cannot easily be circumvented. Statements designed to confine or prohibit certain functions are sometimes so general or ambiguous that ingenious agency lawyers can frustrate Congressional intent; but this is harder to do with numbers. Third, of the two appropriations committees, it is the House's that traditionally acts first and wields the heavier axe; its Senate counterpart tends to restore part of what has been cut.

Finally, other committees may seek to veto agency action outright. For example, armed services committees have requested the Pentagon not to dispose of military real estate without their permission. They have also asked chiefs of service not to promote more than a given number of individuals to general or flag officer rank without securing their permission. In 1964 the agriculture committees drafted a bill which gave them the power to veto proposed uses of foreign currency acquired through the sale overseas of surplus farm products. Needless to say, the constitutionality of these claims can be challenged. But it is sometimes not politic to challenge them, and if pressed informally, they can be quite effective.

Congress is probably most influential, however, when it works silently and invisibly within the nervous systems of the President and his chief advisers, dissuading them from actions which might provoke a hue and cry on Capitol Hill—in a word, when it exercises its power to deter.

In this century the Senate has rejected no ambassadorial nomination and only two treaties.[10] It doesn't have to. The fear that it might is enough to persuade Presidents to withdraw nominations that promise to be unacceptable; to permit reservations to be attached, or amendments to be drafted, to treaties that would otherwise be unpalatable; or, what is still more significant, to refrain from submitting such nominations or such treaties in the first place. To the senior departmental official, the possibility of a Congressional investigation and the certainty that his activities will be subject to review in the course of annual appropriations hearings serve as a constant constraint. Before venturing on a dangerous path, he is likely to sound out key congressmen informally or to test reactions by an inspired "leak" to the press, a "trial balloon" in the form of a statement which can, if necessary, be repudiated on the ground that it was not authorized.

Since the recriminations over "who let the Reds take China?" the Far East policy of the United States has been heavily influenced by the prospect of hostile Congressional and public reaction should any more of that part of the world—especially South Korea, Taiwan, or South Vietnam—fall under Communist control. Likewise, to preclude an attack on his foreign aid program so savage as to constitute a vote of no confidence, the President may submit a smaller program than he would like. He may also choose to submit a nuclear test ban agreement in the form of a treaty, even though in principle he could evade the Senate by calling it an "executive agreement." Why should he embarrass his supporters and enrage his opponents in the Senate? Their power to deter, like that of the Strategic Air Command, rests on their capacity for massive retaliation *at times and places of their own choosing*. Their target need not be the test ban agreement. It can be the State Department budget or a housing or civil rights program dear to the administration's heart. It can also be the coming election.

THE TENDENCY TO AGREE

Just as it was necessary to ask why Congress seldom takes the lead, so it is now necessary to inquire why Congress rarely exercises to the full its power to thwart or emasculate administration initiatives. Since Pearl Harbor, Congress has rarely blocked truly major national security measures proposed by the President. Why?

One reason, already suggested, is that the anticipation of its reactions has deterred Presidents from courses that Congress might find intolerable. Another reason is that Congress, too, anticipates and avoids unfavorable reactions—in this case, of the public. Members are slow to challenge the President if they have reason to think that their constituents will agree with *him* rather than with them. But the most important reason is that members of Congress have felt it *unnecessary* to repudiate the administration of the day. By and large, they and the administration take the same view of the Cold War, of the dilemmas of emerging nations, of the trends in Europe, and of the appropriate American responses. The reason that Congress rarely repudiates the President is that it agrees with him. Its agreement is not total. Attention was called earlier to Congress' characteristically "hard-nosed" views. The weary and bruised deputy assistant secretary is likely to be obsessed by them. But he is simply too punch-drunk to seek consolation from the larger perspective. The truth is that Congress ordinarily lacks the desire to knock him right out of the ring.

Conceivably, irreconcilable conflict between the branches would be more common if legislators of the President's party had no sense of partisan obligation or if no senator identified himself with any of the functional communities that so often bridge the gap between the administration and Capitol Hill. But even when the opposition controls one or both houses of Congress, as in 1946–1948 or in much of the Eisenhower administration, cooperative relationships are the rule in national security affairs. This is the result of *natural* rather than *contrived* bipartisanship. Congressmen and political executives do not think alike because one has cajoled or coerced the other. They think alike because they are alike. Especially when in Washington, they read the same press, go to the same parties, live in the same neighborhoods, attend the same churches, and send their children to the same schools. When the President and his Secretaries of State and Defense agree on a military budget, a senator is unlikely to try to cut it 50 to 60 per cent, not only because he, too, is impressed with the prestige and expertise of such eminent authority, but because he probably shares their view of the world. Nor is he likely to try to raise the budget 50 or 60 per cent, because on the question of taxes, spending, debt, and inflation, he is likely to share the assumptions of the Treasury, the Bureau of the Budget, the Federal Reserve Board, and the Council of Economic Advisers.

THE OCCASION OF DISSENT

There are, nonetheless, both exceptional and common cases in which Congress challenges the administration vigorously. The exceptional cases are those in which Congress believes that the public shares its concern that the President is moving too fast or too slowly. Examples are Wilson's fight for the League of Nations, President Roosevelt's effort to move more resolutely against the Axis powers between 1937 and 1941, and probably President Eisenhower's effort to minimize the significance of Soviet space and missile achievements in the late 1950's. If President Truman had tried to prevent demobilization in 1945, or if President Kennedy had attempted to appease Castro in 1962, they might well have encountered comparable opposition.

Also in the category of unusual cases are those in which the administration is indecisive. In 1954 President Eisenhower had conflicting advice about Indochina. The Vice-President, the Secretary of State, and some senior military men urged the use of American forces to relieve the French. The British and the Army chief of staff disagreed. In this situation, Congressional leaders helped turn the tide by raising many questions about the enterprise when their views were sought by the President. An analyst of this episode has noted astutely that Congress, if pressed, might well have passed a resolution authorizing intervention to avoid compromising the President's stature as a world leader. But prudence, which induced the President to solicit Congressional views in the first place, also counseled that he not ask for open support after so many doubts, reservations, and misgivings had been expressed privately.[11]

The *common* cases are those in which Congress' own access to the bureaucracy is at stake or in which a proposed foreign or military measure clearly allocates burdens or benefits between one group of Americans and another, or between Americans and foreigners. As noted above, members of Congress like to deal directly with subordinate officials. If the two sides discover that they have a common interest, congressmen will support and protect their administrative allies, even against the latters' hierarchical superiors. The legislative leader, bloc, or committee which has woven such a web of relationships will fly to arms against any President or department head who tries to destroy it by manipulating budgets, jurisdictions, assignments, reassignments, or promotions. The greatest resentment will be expressed if an effort is made to censor or muzzle subordinate officials to whom congressmen put direct questions. This is why one can see a Secretary of Defense sitting patiently in a legislative chamber while his senior military subordinate openly disagrees with him on the need to invest more in defenses against ballistic missiles. During hearings over the relief of General MacArthur, when a chairman of the Joint Chiefs of Staff refused to answer questions about his conversations with the President, a special Senate committee debated for long hours whether to cite him for contempt of Congress.

BENEFITS AND BURDENS

Congress is most likely to reveal a mind of its own on foreign or defense matters that raise issues of domestic politics. No legislator can afford the charge that his constituents are not getting their "fair share" of contracts, airfields, Nike missile sites, armories, or chances to serve in a National Guard outfit. When a bill was introduced to create an Air Force Academy, the question that most excited Congress was not the probable future of airpower but the probable location of the institution. Whose state was going to get this plum? And who would control appointments? In 1967 two defense issues before the country were whether to strengthen missile defenses and whether to revise the draft rules. The administration had a position on each. In the first, it was almost inevitable that its negative stand would prevail unless there were a perceptible change in the world balance of power or in the balance of forces within the executive branch. In the case of the draft law, nothing so momentous was required. Congress simply rewrote the administration's proposal. Apart from relatively technical questions involved in the missile defense issue, a major difference was that the draft issue obviously involved the cutting of pie. Some Americans were going to be called, others not. The question was, "Which ones?"

Just as congressmen want to maximize benefits and minimize burdens for their constituents vis à vis other constituents, so they want to do this for their country vis à vis other countries. This explains why Congress supports legislation to require aid recipients to purchase what they need in the United States and to transport their purchases in American ships; why it is reluctant to defray more than its "fair share" of the United Nations budget; why it opposes "give-away" programs unless what

is being given away is surplus farm produce; and why it resists reductions in tariff or immigration barriers which are likely to depress prices or wages in Waltham, Massachusetts, or Seattle, Washington. In such instances, as in those which involve domestic interests alone, the number of actively participating legislators varies with the issue at stake. Efforts to revise an administration bill in order to give special benefits to a particular industry are likely to be confined to a single committee or bloc; speed and silence are the time-honored tactics for such a "closed" political process. But measures which raise issues of distributive justice for large numbers of citizens are likely to provoke extended debate on the floor and full comment in the press.

CONSEQUENCES OF CONGRESSIONAL ACTIVISM

Although in the end Congress is the junior partner in foreign and military affairs, its members tend to have ampler resources and to display greater vigor in their use than their counterparts in any other major country. This activism both weakens and strengthens the United States abroad and has both divisive and unifying effects at home. On the one hand, foreign governments are not always certain who is speaking for America or whether a particular stand taken by the State Department will subsequently be undercut on Capitol Hill. On the other hand, the astute American negotiator can employ the prospect of Congressional displeasure to explain why he cannot do what the other government wants him to do or why the other government had better do what *he* wants it to do.

On the home front, Congressional activism may exacerbate the rivalry between the Army and Air Force, encourage an economic aid administrator to maintain his distance from the State Department, or plant doubt in the public mind about whether the President's Asian policy accords with the national interest. Moreover, the mere fact that policy must run legislative as well as executive hurdles increases the likelihood that it will incorporate compromises at the cost of internal inconsistency or wishful thinking about how much can actually be accomplished with the means made available.

On the other hand, a policy that runs these hurdles with great success, as the Marshall Plan did, is not vulnerable to every small shift of opinion. The disappointed administrator who has managed to appeal to Capitol Hill may win part of his case; at least he knows he has had yet another day in court. When photographs are taken of the President signing the bill, the opposition leader who has contributed to the result may emerge smiling with a President's pen. The debate as a whole will have given the country something to mull over. The result is likely to be a wider measure of agreement than a merely executive process, or a wholly passive legislature, would be able to foster.

NOTES

1. See, for example, Roger Hilsman, *To Move a Nation* (Garden City, N.Y.: Doubleday & Co., Inc., 1967), pp. 7–9.

2. Kenneth N. Waltz, *Foreign Policy and Democratic Politics* (Boston: Little, Brown & Co., 1967), pp. 131–133.

3. Laurence I. Radway, "Military Behavior in International Organizations," in Samuel P. Huntington, ed., *Changing Patterns of Military Politics* (New York: The Free Press of Glencoe, Inc., 1962), p. 109.

4. Hilsman, *op. cit.*, p. 5.

5. Paul Hammond, "The National Security Council as a Device for Interdepartmental Coordination: An Interpretation and Appraisal," *American Political Science Review*, LIV (December 1960).

6. Hilsman, *op. cit.*, pp. 146–151.

7. *Ibid.*, chapters 28–34.

8. Letter from McGeorge Bundy to Senator Henry M. Jackson, September 4, 1961, in Henry M. Jackson, ed., *The National Security Council* (New York: Frederick A. Praeger, Inc., 1965), p. 278.

9. Dean Acheson, "The President and the Secretary of State," in Don K. Price, ed., *The Secretary of State* (Englewood Cliffs, N.J.: Prentice-Hall, Inc., 1960), p. 39.

10. For this and other examples cited in this section, see William P. Gerberding, *United States Foreign Policy: Perspectives and Analysis* (New York: McGraw-Hill Book Co., 1966), pp. 32–37.

11. *Ibid.*, pp. 31–32.

Strategic Programs and the Political Process

SAMUEL P. HUNTINGTON

STRUCTURE, STRATEGY, AND PROCESS

The complexity and diversity of military policy are reflected in the processes through which is it made. Three categories of governmental groups are concerned with military policy. The Administration includes the elected and politically appointed leaders of the executive branch: President, Vice President, agency heads, secretaries, undersecretaries. Bureaucratic groups include the Foreign Service, the military services, the civil servants in all bureaus and agencies. Together the Administration and the bureaucracy make up the executive. The third category exists in Congress and includes primarily the members of the Foreign Affairs, Foreign Relations, Science and Astronautics, Aeronautical and Space Sciences, and Armed Services committees, the Military Appropriations subcommittees, and the Joint Committee on Atomic Energy. Within the executive branch the groups are arranged in two overlapping structures. In the hierarchical structure, all officials and agencies are in theory arranged in superior-subordinate relationships in the classic pyramid culminating in the President. Superimposed upon the executive hierarchy is a second, conciliar structure. It includes many interdepartmental and interagency boards and committees, the most important of which are the National Security Council and the Joint Chiefs of Staff. The hierarchical structure of the executive provides a vehicle for vertical communication be-

tween superiors and subordinates; the conciliar structure supplements this and also provides a formal means for lateral communication among agencies or officials at similar levels in different hierarchies.

These officials and bodies play different roles in the determination of different military policy issues. Deterrent commitments may take the form of force deployments ordered by the President, treaties negotiated by the executive and ratified by the Senate (NATO, SEATO), joint declarations of Congress passed on the recommendation of the executive (Formosa resolution, Eisenhower Middle East doctrine), or statements by the President or Secretary of State (Dulles' September, 1958, warnings on the offshore islands). Action commitments or interventions are made by the President in consultation with the Secretary of State, the military chiefs, and other executive officials. In the decisions on the Berlin crisis and Korea in the Truman Administration, congressional leaders apparently were informed after the executive branch had determined policy. In the Indochina and Lebanon crises in the Eisenhower Administration, congressional leaders were informed before final action by the President, and in the Indochina crisis in the spring of 1954 the doubts of the congressional leaders (together with those of the British) apparently persuaded the Administration to reverse its inclination

From Samuel P. Huntington: *The Common Defense.* New York: Columbia University Press, 1961. Reprinted by permission of the publisher.

to intervene. In each case, however, the final decision on peace or war always rested with the President, and presidential decisions were not formally ratified by Congress. The military and diplomatic conditions of the mid-twentieth century made obsolete the congressional declaration of war. In a small-scale intervention or limited war a congressional declaration was unnecessary and undesirable; in a general war it would, in all probability, be impossible.

Structural issues of military policy are usually handled through what might be termed the domestic legislative process. Proposals usually originate in the executive branch or in advisory groups close to the executive branch. They are advanced through the executive hierarchy, modified, and eventually approved by the appropriate secretaries, the Budget Bureau, and the President. They are then recommended to Congress as Administration measures and referred to the Armed Services committees or other congressional bodies, which hold hearings and act upon them: substantially approving the Administration's recommendations, amending them significantly, or at times rejecting them. The action of the committees is usually approved by their respective houses; the differences are ironed out in conference; and the measure becomes law. In this process the President, the leaders of the Administration, and, usually, the heads of the President's party in Congress act as legislative leaders, focusing the attention of Congress on the proposals which they support and compelling Congress to act upon them in one way or another. The decisions on their proposals, however, are made in the committees and houses of Congress, and the political processes of arousing support or opposition are directed toward these multiple decision-making foci in Congress.

Between 1945 and 1960 the major issues of structural policy were resolved through this process. These included the organization of the military establishment and the individual services,[1] military pay scales and the conditions of service and retirement,[2] conscription and military training,[3] the disciplinary law of the services (Uniform Code of Military Justice, 1950), and basic policy on procurement (Armed Services Procurement Act, 1947). Although they involved strategic issues as well as structural ones, major policies concerning the reserves (Armed Forces Reserve Act, 1952; Reserve Forces Act, 1955) were also determined in a similar manner. For much of the period between 1947 and 1960, the House Armed Services Committee maintained subcommittees which specialized in pay and promotion matters, material and procurement, reserve policy, and real estate and construction. The members of these groups developed a recognized expertise in their subjects. There "is no man on this committee, or in Congress," the Republican chairman of the Armed Services Committee declared in 1953, "who knows more about it [personnel] than Mr. Kilday"—the ranking Democrat on the personnel subcommittee.[4] Similarly, Representative Overton Brooks, chairman of the reserves subcommittee, was the acknowledged congressional expert on reserves. On these structural issues the congressmen and senators acted with competence and authority. They did not hesitate to revise or to reject Administration measures. UMT legislation was repeatedly turned down, organizational proposals to centralize authority in the Pentagon weakened, pay legislation reworked. On these matters, the executive proposed and Congress disposed.

The process of policy formation on strategic programs differs significantly from both the familiar processes of congressional legislation of domestic policy and executive decision in foreign affairs. It tends to be executive in locale but legislative in character. In the formulation of strategic programs the need for legislation is recognized by an executive agency or by some skill group (nuclear physicists) or consulting group close to the executive branch. The agency develops proposals to deal with the new problem. It arouses support for them among other executive agencies, congressional bodies, and, possibly, some nongovernmental groups and foreign governments allied with the United States. Opposition develops from some of these agencies and groups. Alternative solutions to the problem are proposed; in some cases, the existence of the problem or the need to do anything about it may be denied. A process of negotiation, bargaining, and conflict ensues among the various executive agencies and groups. Many of these efforts to arrive at a compromise take place in the budgetary process, the Joint Chiefs of Staff, and the National Security Council. Eventually, an agreement is reached among the interested agencies, it is approved by the President, and it is then implemented by the executive branch. Sometimes the presidential decision is announced to the public, or the implementation of the decision reveals the fact of decision, or an executive official dissatisfied with the decision finds means of expressing his dissatisfaction. Discussion and debate flare up in Congress and the press. The Administration attempts to suppress evidence of dissension in the executive ranks. Its leaders either refuse to confirm the fact that a decision has been made, refuse to comment on it, defend it when challenged, or, perhaps, if the criticism has been particularly widespread and effective, modify the policy in practice while staunchly defending it in debate. Eventually the discussion subsides and the executive agencies continue to implement the policy, modified or unmodified, while controversy and interest turn to other issues.

In one sense, in American government there are no final decisions. Almost every decision by one body or in one forum can be appealed to another body or another forum. It is possible, however, to speak of "effective decisions," of decisions which in the normal process of politics settle the issue, at least temporarily; because although the possibility of appeal exists, it is seldom exercised. In this sense, effective decision on structure rests in Congress, and effective decision on strategic programs rests in the executive.

A significant gap thus exists between the theory and practice of the Constitution. Few constitutional principles are more firmly established than that which gives Congress the final say on the size and composition of the nation's armed forces. The "whole power of raising armies," Hamilton declared, "was lodged in the *Legislature,* not in the *Executive* . . ." The authority of the President as Commander in Chief "would amount to nothing more than the supreme command and direction of the military and naval forces, as first General and admiral of the Confederacy; while that of the British king extends to the *declaring* of war and to the *raising* and *regulating* of fleets and armies,—all which, by the Constitution under consideration, would appertain to the legislature."[5] Later commentators emphasized again and again the authority of Congress over all aspects of military policy.[6] The President could command only the forces which Congress placed at his disposal. After World War II, however, the division of authority between Congress and President no longer coincided with the division between policy and command. The great powers of Anglo-American legislatures over the size and composition of the armed forces, so bitterly fought for in the seventeenth and eighteenth centuries and so carefully inscribed in the Bill of Rights, the Mutiny Acts, the Declaration of Independence, and the Constitution of 1787, had faded away. The loss of power by Congress, however, did not necessarily mean an equivalent increase in the power of the President. Congress lost its power not to the President but to the executive branch. Just as power to legislate strategic programs was at one time, at least in theory, shared by President and Congress, so it is now, very much in practice, shared by the President and a variety of agencies within the executive branch.

In the post-World War II period, the executive determined the overall level of military effort and the strategy by which it was shaped. The executive decided whether the Air Force should have 95 or 137 wings, the Army 14 or 24 divisions, the Navy 200 or 400 warships. The fundamental decisions to maintain a massive nuclear retaliatory force, to construct a continental defense system, and to develop or not to develop forces for conventional limited wars were all made in the executive branch. The decisions on whether to build hydrogen bombs, "super-carriers," long-range jet bombers, intermediate-range intercontinental ballistic missiles, nuclear-powered submarines and planes were also executive decisions. This is not to say that congressional groups played no role in these decisions. In a variety of ways they could influence them, and in some cases compel the Administration to pay a high price to get what it wanted. But they could not make the decisions. The effective, final "yes" or "no" rested with the executive branch.

In addition to individual legislative acts on specific problems, three regular pieces of executive legislation dealt with strategic programs in general. The annual NSC paper, "Basic National Security Policy," a brief document of about twenty-five pages, contained "a broad outline of the aims of U.S. national strategy and a more detailed discussion of the military, political, economic, and domestic elements to support the overall national strategy."[7] Much of this document did not change from year to year. Nonetheless it did reflect shifting emphases in pol-

icy. The first of the series, NSC 68, in 1950 provided the framework for the Korean War rearmament. In 1951 the paper stressed continental defense and civil defense, and in 1952 new efforts in the Middle East and southern Asia, although in neither year were the programs fully implemented. In 1953 the Eisenhower Administration adopted the New Look, NSC 162, reducing military spending and increasing the emphasis upon nuclear weapons. In 1954 nuclear weapons were again stressed. The 1955 paper shifted away from nuclear weapons and massive retaliation, recognizing the emergence of mutual deterrence and the need to have forces for limited wars. In 1957 and in 1958 the stress was on the stabilization of defense expenditures.[8]

The JCS counterpart to the NSC annual policy paper was the Joint Strategic Objectives Plan, which annually defined the military programs required three years in the future. It "estimates the military requirements for cold, limited, or general war, and includes a determination of the military forces together with their dispositions and employment necessary to implement the military strategy derived from the 'Basic National Security Policy.' "[9] In the Eisenhower Administration, the Basic National Security Policy paper was usually formulated in May. It then became the basis for the third regular piece of executive legislation: the annual formulation of force requirements by the military chiefs, which, when approved by the Administration, became the grounds for the appropriation and expenditure requests by the military services in the executive budgetary process ending in December.[10] Through these three mechanisms the Administration and the executive agencies annually shaped the strategic programs of the government.

In many, if not most, areas of domestic policy, statutory authorizations prescribe fairly explicitly and in detail the amounts of money which are authorized to be appropriated for various projects. As a corollary, the appropriation of funds for any project which has not received prior statutory authorization is subject to a point of order in Congress. Before 1961, however, except for military aid, military public works, and a few weapons, little legislation existed to guide the Appropriations committees in acting upon the military budget. General authorizations, of course, furnished the legal basis for Army, Navy, and Air Force appropriations, but in most cases no statutory authorization existed for the specific programs which the military might be pursuing at any particular moment. The same statutes could furnish the legal base for a budget of $15 billion or $50 billion. As a result, military programs were in effect authorized through the machinery of the JCS and the NSC. In 1953 the Eisenhower Administration initiated the practice of including cost estimates in a financial appendix to NSC papers. This was the executive equivalent of the congressional practice of requiring legislative authorization before money can be appropriated for support of a program.[11] Only in military policy were programs involving the expenditure of billions of dollars determined in the executive rather than through the traditional process. The decision to have a national highway program requiring the eventual expenditure of $20 billion, for instance, was legislated in the normal way through Congress. The decision to have a continental defense program involving a comparable level of expenditures was made through executive processes: the Joint Chiefs of Staff, advisory committees, the National Security Council, and the President. The only significant exceptions to the pattern of executive decision were reserve force levels and military public works. Here Congress played a more aggressive and assured role than it did on weapons and the size of the active

forces. Even so, the final power to say "no" rested with the executive.

Congressional incapacity to determine force levels and strategic programs is frequently attributed to the lack of proper information and technical competence on the part of congressmen. This may indeed be a factor, but it is only a contributory one. In the first place, it is striking, as one acute observer has noted, "how well informed some members of Congress are" on foreign and military policy.[12] Congressmen who have specialized in military affairs for a decade or more are at least as knowledgeable and competent as most Administration officials. In addition to all the informal sources and mechanisms by which strategic information is fed to Congress from competing services and departments, well-established formal procedures also exist to provide the principal congressional groups with basic information on existing and proposed strategic programs. Nor is the problem of classified information a significant one. Congressmen do receive classified information in briefings and appropriations hearings, and the amount of additional security information required to enable them to reach conclusions on major strategic programs would not be substantial. Much information on the considerations for and against an executive decision on a strategic program comes out after the decision is made. Presumably the release, officially or informally, of the same information to Congress before the decision was made would not involve any greater security risk except as it might require greater revelation of the Administration's assumptions and intentions. In addition, the more important a policy issue is, the less important becomes detailed technical information and the more relevant become broad judgments on goals and values, i.e., political judgments, where presumably the congressman's competence is greatest. Yet congressmen themselves, as Lewis Dexter has pointed out, often tend to view broad questions of general military policy as "technical" and therefore beyond their competence, although they do not hesitate to probe thoroughly and to render judgments concerning highly specialized and detailed questions of military administration.[13]

Congress is unable to play a decisive role in strategic programs not for technical reasons but for political ones. In the late 1930s, when the country was split over isolationism vs. interventionism, Congress actively considered and, at times, rejected strategic programs (naval base construction on Guam). The Administration was then moving toward a foreign policy which did not command general support until after the outbreak of the war in Europe. In the late 1940s, on the other hand, a general consensus among people, Congress, and Administration quickly emerged on the need to maintain whatever military programs were required to prevent the expansion of Communism. With a few exceptions members of Congress did not espouse conflicting foreign policies with conflicting implications for strategic programs. General agreement on the goals of policy meant that controversy centered on the relative usefulness of alternative programs to achieve those goals. The groups primarily interested in these issues were the agencies of the executive branch.

The initiation and elimination of programs and the apportionment of resources among them, nonetheless, remain political decisions involving competing interests and groups. The military programs have to be weighed against each other, against conflicting interpretations of the security threats and military requirements, against the needs of domestic and nonmilitary foreign policy programs, and against tax revenues and the requirements of fiscal policy. No congressional committee is competent to do this, not because it lacks the technical knowledge, but because it lacks the legal authority and

political capability to bring together all these conflicting interests, balance one off against another, and arrive at a compromise or decision. This can only be done by bodies before which or in which all the conflicting interests can be brought together. The issues of whether the federal government should build schools or regulate the internal affairs of labor unions are contested by coalitions of private interest groups. The issue of whether the federal government should build greater limited war capabilities is contested by the Army, Navy, Air Force, Marines, Defense Department, State Department, Budget Bureau, Treasury, and a few other officials. The diversity of interests is just as great as on many domestic policy issues, but the interested groups are almost entirely executive agencies. Moreover, they do not function, as often is the case in domestic policy, as representatives of other interests outside the government. They are more principals than agents, and they trade on their own account. They are not adequately represented in any single congressional body. The Armed Services, Appropriations, Ways and Means, Finance, Foreign Relations, Foreign Affairs, and Atomic Energy committees all participate in the process. No congressional body gets more than a partial view of the interests involved in the determination of any single major strategic program. Every congressional action in military affairs is to some extent *ex parte*. Consequently, congressional bodies may become advocates of particular programs, but they lack sufficient political competence to determine an overall program. The key interests can only be brought together in the executive branch. If "the group interests work out a fair and satisfying adjustment through the legislature," Bentley wrote in 1908, "then the executive sinks in prominence . . . when the adjustment is not perfected in the legislature, then the executive arises in strength to do the work . . . the growth of executive discretion is therefore a phase of the group process . . . "[14]

After World War II congressional groups rarely prevented the Administration from going ahead with a strategic program which it deemed necessary. Although not perhaps obsolete, like the Crown's veto over legislation, the veto power of Congress over military programs certainly was dormant. At times in the past Congress formally legislated and limited military programs through unit and personnel authorization, appropriations, and the authorization of weapons development. As instruments of control and elimination, these have fallen into disuse. Throughout the nineteenth century Congress established by legislation the number and type of regiments and other units permitted the Army. This practice came to an end in 1920. Before World War II Congress legislated the maximum personnel strengths of the services, although the appropriated strengths seldom approximated the authorized strengths. In 1945, General Marshall and other representatives of the executive branch appeared before Congress as supplicants, pleading for congressional approval of the force levels which they believed necessary. Once the Cold War began, however, Congress ceased to exercise a negative over executive force level recommendations. In the 1946 debates hardly a member of Congress challenged the validity of the executive goal of a 1,070,000-man Army; what they debated was whether such a force could be maintained through volunteers or whether continuation of selective service was required. In the Selective Service Act of that year Congress accepted Administration recommendations and set ceilings, effective July 1, 1947, of 1,070,000 men for the Army, 558,000 for the Navy, and 108,000 for the Marine Corps. In 1948, after the establishment of the independent Air Force and in response to the spring crisis of that year, Congress authorized a strength of

837,000 enlisted men for the Army, 666,882 enlisted men for the Navy and Marine Corps, and 502,000 officers and men for the Air Force. After the start of the Korean War Congress first suspended these ceilings and then established a general ceiling of 5 million military personnel on all the armed services. At the peak of the Korean War mobilization, however, the strength of the services amounted to only 3,600,000, so this high overall ceiling had little practical effect on policy. The suspension of the individual service ceilings was renewed in 1954, 1957, and 1959. "These ceilings," as Senator Russell explained, "apply in normal times, when we are not engaged in either hot wars or cold wars, to the Armed Forces of the United States."[15] In effect, Congress ceased to set the maximum personnel strengths for the services.

Similarly, throughout the dozen years after World War II, except when confronted by similar competing programs, Congress never vetoed directly a major strategic program, a force level recommendation, or a major weapons system proposed by the Administration in power. In 1908 Congress did not hesitate to slash in half Theodore Roosevelt's requests for battleships. After World War II the chairman of the House Appropriations Committee fought a lonely and unsuccessful battle against the Navy's requests for Forrestal-class carriers. During the Cold War Congress was simply not going to assume the responsibility for weapons selection. The most that congressional groups could do was to use their veto authority to compel the executive to make a choice.[16] In addition, while the practice of congressional authorization of (as well as appropriation for) the warships of the Navy had been well established in earlier years, this practice did not initially carry over to airplanes and missiles. In 1959 the Armed Services committees asserted their right to authorize airplane and missile procurement.[17] Their first exercise of this power in 1961, however, suggested that it would seldom be used to veto executive requests. Nor did Congress ever eliminate programs or weapons, with one partial exception (the Navy's second nuclear carrier), through the failure to appropriate the funds recommended by the executive. While the Appropriations subcommittees did not hesitate to decide structural issues through the budget, they usually avoided strategic ones. Almost regularly, of course, Congress reduced the *total* military appropriations request, but it almost never did so in a manner which seriously affected a major strategic program. The relative inviolability of the military estimates throughout this period was striking when compared with the appropriations requests for nonmilitary security programs, such as foreign aid and civil defense, and for many domestic programs. Between 1950 and 1958, for instance, Congress reduced military appropriations requests by roughly 3 percent; during the same years foreign aid requests were reduced by about 18 percent. A strong tradition in Congress, stemming in part from the experience of the Committee on the Conduct of the War dur-ing the Civil War, holds that Congress should not interfere in wartime strategy. During the Cold War congressmen have also felt ill-equipped to be responsible for the military security of the country. They have generally recognized and accepted the decisive role of the executive in formulating strategic programs. The areas of congressional responsibility, the chairman of the Senate Military Appropriations subcommittee argued, are essentially structural: "the four M's . . . money, men, material, and management." Never, he proudly declared, has "Congress cut Defense Department requests so as to impair the carrying out of the overall strategic concepts of the establishment." The Armed Services committees may have subcommittees on personnel and real estate, the Appropriations subcommittee panels on the Army, Navy, and Air Force; but the congressional bodies do not have special groups concerned with strategic deterrence, continental defense, or limited war. "God help the American people," Senator Russell once said, "if Congress starts legislating military strategy."[18]

*   *   *

CRITICISMS OF THE STRATEGY-MAKING PROCESS

Curiously enough, the location of the point of decision on strategic programs in the executive rather than in Congress has occasioned only sporadic criticism from American commentators. Instead, dissatisfaction has focused upon the importation into the executive branch of the processes and characteristics of policy-making common to the legislative branch. The most common criticisms are: 1) National security policy has lacked unity, coherence, and a sense of direction; decisions have been made upon an *ad hoc* basis, uninformed and unguided by a common purpose; 2) National security policies have been stated largely in terms of compromises and generalities; clear-cut alternatives have not been brought to the highest level for decision; 3) Delay and slowness have characterized the policy-making process; 4) The principal organs of policy-making, particularly the NSC, have not been effective vehicles for the development of new ideas and approaches; they tend to routinize the old rather than stimulate the new; 5) The procedures of policy-making tend to magnify the obstacles and difficulties of any proposed course of action; 6) The above deficiencies are primarily the product of government by committee, particularly when the members of the committee necessarily represent the interests of particular departments and services.

To remedy these deficiencies, the critics urge reducing the role of committees and enhancing the role of individual executive decision-makers, developing more effective, farsighted, and more powerful executive leadership, imbuing the executive branch with a greater sense of purpose and direction, and, in general, rationalizing the structure of the executive to achieve a greater correspondence between organization and purpose.[19]

Almost all these allegations of fact are accurate. The strategy-making process *is* slow, prone to compromise, given to generalities, strewn with reefs and shoals, and unlikely to produce clear-cut, coherent, and rational policies. Judgments of the effectiveness of a policy-making process, however, must be based upon at least two criteria. In strategy, as elsewhere, meaningful policy requires both content and consensus. Strategic policies, like statutes or treaties, are both prescriptions for future action and ratifications of existing power relationships. A strategy which is so vague or contradictory that it sets forth no prescriptions for action is no strategy. So also, a strategy whose prescriptions are so unacceptable that they are ignored is no strategy. Consensus is a cost to each participant in the policy-making process, but it is a prerequisite to any policy.

Critics raise two issues. First, is the "better" policy, however defined, more likely to be the product of a single responsible official or agency or the product of negotiation and compromise among a number of officials and agencies? The answer depends largely upon whether one thinks that the policy views of the single responsible official or agency will coincide with one's own policy views. The Framers of the Constitution, believing that it was wiser not to take chances, devised a remarkably complex system of dividing power and responsibility. Bagehot, on the

other hand, argued that the American Constitution was based "upon the principle of having many sovereign authorities, and hoping that their multitude may atone for their inferiority."[20] The question of who was right need not be answered here. The second issue raised by the critics is the more relevant one: To what extent is policy made through a single responsible official or agency feasible in the American system of government? Madison not Bagehot wrote the Constitution. In the course of a century and a half, constitutional pluralism has been supplemented by socio-economic pluralism and bureaucratic pluralism. One can accept the premise of the critics that greater purpose, unity, and direction are needed for a good policy, but one must also accept the fact of American politics that agreement among a number of groups and agencies is needed for any policy. One perceptive critic, for instance, has argued that ". . . the conclusions of both the Joint Chiefs of Staff and the National Security Council reflect the attainable consensus among sovereign departments rather than a sense of direction."[21] Some measure of departmental consensus, however, is essential to any policy. If it is a good policy, it will also have direction and purpose. But the direction can only be a product of the consensus, not an alternative to it. Professor Morgenthau has struck directly to the heart of the problem and argued that:

The policy decisions of the Executive Branch of the Government, like the decisions of the business executive or any decision an individual must make in his private affairs, are fundamentally different from the legislative decision. The latter is supposed to represent divergent interests brought to a common denominator or one interest which has won out over the others. The executive decision is supposed to be, first of all, the correct decision, the decision which is more likely than any other to bring forth the desired result.

The committee system is appropriate for the legislative process, and it is not by accident that it originated and was institutionalized there. The executive decision requires the mind and will of one man who, after hearing the evidence and taking counsel, takes it upon himself to decide what is the right action under the circumstances.[22]

"Divergent interests," however, exist within the executive as much as within Congress. Lower taxes, domestic welfare programs, balanced budgets, massive retaliation, limited war, foreign assistance—these are only a few of the foreign and domestic goals and needs represented by executive agencies. That the conflict among them takes place within the executive branch of government does not make that conflict any less real or the values at stake any less important.

Committees have proliferated within the executive branch precisely because the "committee system is appropriate for the legislative process." At times, of course, the President does act against the advice of his associates. Major decisions on strategic programs, however, can seldom be the result of the "mind and will of one man." Like major decisions on domestic programs in Congress, they require the participation and consent of many men representing many interests. If the negotiation and bargaining do not take place in committees, they take place outside them. On the principal issues which come up within the executive branch, there is no single "correct decision." There may, indeed, be no decision at all if the interests involved cannot discover some basis of agreement; the form which that agreement may take is as unpredictable as the final version of a bill in the legislative process in Congress. In the executive as in Congress, the major problem is not to discover rationally what is required to bring forth "the desired result" but rather to reconcile conflicting views of what results are desirable. The problem of consensus always exists, and there are costs involved in winning support for any policy proposal or decision. Many practices which critics properly deplore

because they weaken the content of policy contribute directly to the development of a consensus for policy.

The political and legislative character of the strategy-making process also casts a different light on the argument that the NSC and JCS have failed to initiate new policy proposals. As one observer of the domestic legislative process has commented, "Very little legislation ever originates within a legislature."[23] Hence, it is to be expected that original contributions and policy proposals would come from the service staffs rather than the Joint Staff, which functioned as a negotiating agency. In view of the significance of this function for the NSC, the JCS, and their subordinate bodies, the absence of originality among them hardly seems so crucial. Similarly, as the critics argue, the committee system facilitates the raising of objections to any particular proposal. If a function of the committee, however, is to elicit consent, to devise the policy upon which all can agree, the airing of all major objections to that policy becomes an essential part of the process.

Just as much of the early criticism of Congress stemmed from failure to appreciate the political roles of that body, so much of the criticism of the NSC and JCS stems from the application to these bodies of nonpolitical standards. In the past, it has been assumed that through investigation and debate all members of a legislative body should arrive at similar conclusions as to where the public interest lay. More recently, conflict within a legislature has been viewed as normal rather than reprehensible, and policy thought of as the result, not of a collective process of rational inquiry, but of a mutual process of political give and take. Analyses of Congress seldom criticize it now because of the conflicts and disagreements among its members. To a considerable extent, however, the JCS and the NSC are judged by the earlier theory: in them disagreement is still considered inherently evil. As one naval officer wryly commented: "How curious it is that the Congress *debates,* the Supreme Court *deliberates,* but for some reason or other the Joint Chiefs of Staff just *bicker!*"[24]

Significantly, next to the supposed lack of agreement among the Joint Chiefs, those aspects of their operation which receive the greatest criticism are precisely their mechanisms for reaching agreement: delay, devolution, referral, platitudinous policies, compromise, logrolling. Assuming agreement among the Chiefs to be natural and rational, the critics have almost as little use for artificially produced agreement as they have for the inherent tendencies toward disagreement. At the same time the Chiefs are criticized because they can not resolve major issues, they are also criticized because they do resolve them through the classic means of politics.

Much criticism of strategic decision-making fails to appreciate the tenuous and limited character of hierarchical authority in American government. Reacting against the prevalence and visibility of horizontal bargaining, the critics almost unanimously advocate the abolition of committees and the strengthening of executive controls. In temporary periods of emergency and crisis presidential coordination may partially replace the normal bargaining processes.[25] But no presidential laying on of hands can accomplish this on a permanent basis. Decisions on strategic programs are simply too important to be fitted into a symmetrical and immaculate model of executive decision-making. Clarifications of the chain of command and legal assertions of formal authority may reduce bargaining, but they can never eliminate it. Each of the three reorganizations of the military establishment after 1947 purported to give the Secretary of Defense full legal authority to control his department and yet each succeeding Secretary found his control circumscribed. The

existence of counterparts to the NSC and JCS in almost every other modern state suggests that the causes which have brought them into existence may be pervasive and inherent in the problems with which they deal.

The problem of legislating strategy is the dual one of producing both content and consensus. The problem can be solved neither by denying its complexity nor by looking for relief in institutional or administrative reforms which are not based upon underlying political realities. The abolition of committees or a reduction in their importance, for instance, may not necessarily strengthen executive leadership. What strength the administrative hierarchy does retain is at least partially derived from the fact that it does not have to bear the entire burden of bargaining, that much of the responsibility for developing a consensus within the executive establishment has been transferred to horizontal mechanisms such as the NSC and the JCS. The emergence of these committees in the executive branch was, in part, an effort to avoid the problems and difficulties of bargaining along the vertical axis. Abolition of the committees would transfer many questions now resolved by negotiation among bureaucratic equals back to the administrative hierarchy to be resolved by negotiations between an administrative superior and a multiplicity of subordinates. The result could overload the hierarchy, increase the ambiguities and misunderstandings resulting from the confusion of hierarchical and bargaining roles, and dissolve still further the authority of the superior over his subordinates.

"Nobody stands sponsor for the policy of the government," one critic has written. "A dozen men originate it; a dozen compromises twist it and alter it; a dozen offices whose names are scarcely known outside of Washington put it into execution." These words sum up the case against the strategy-making process. They were written, however, by Woodrow Wilson in 1885.[26] The new criticism of strategy-making falls into a classic pattern of criticism of American governmental processes. The ideas, fears, goals, and even phrases of the strategic reformers echo those not only of Wilson, but those of the progressives in the first part of the twentieth century, the devotees of economy and efficiency of the 1920s, and, most particularly, the complaints of the liberal reformers of the 1930s and 1940s on domestic policy and economic planning. In each case, the critics concluded that certain critical policy needs demanded prompt, coherent action, and that the governmental machinery was incapable of giving these needs the priority which they deserved. The targets of the liberal reformers and the strategic critics were the same: the dispersion of power, the absence of sharply defined alternatives, the dangers of stalemate. The liberal critics saw policy as the product of compromise among pressure groups with narrow interests; the strategic critics see it as the product of compromise among agencies and departments with narrow purposes. The liberal criticism complained that political parties cohered only long enough to produce an electoral majority at the polls; the strategic criticism argues that the policy-making committees cohere only long enough to produce a unanimous report. The old criticism argued that the absence of disciplined and responsible parties prevented the voters from making a clear choice between sharply different policy proposals; the new criticism argues that the proliferation of committees prevents executive officials from making a clear choice between sharply different policy proposals.

The liberal criticism wanted to organize the majority so that it could work its will despite interest groups, local bosses, and the constitutional separation of powers; the strategic criticism wants to organize the executive so that presidential leadership can over-

ride semi-autonomous departments, parochial interests, and bureaucratic inertia. The principal reforms advocated by the old critics were responsible parties, modification of the separation of powers, and presidential leadership. The principal reforms advocated by the new critics are elimination of committees, vitalization of the chain of command, and presidential leadership. What the old criticism found inadequate in Congress, the new criticism finds inadequate in the executive.

The prophecies of economic calamity by the old critics proved erroneous and their demands for reform superfluous. The American people moved out of the depression without resorting to constitutional reform, disciplined parties, or cabinet government, and even in the face of a gradual decline in the effectiveness of presidential leadership from its high point of 1933–1935. This was due more to fortuitous circumstance, which moderated and redirected the challenge, than to the demonstrated ability of the governmental system to meet the challenge. The economic challenge disappeared in World War II and was replaced by the strategic challenge. The likelihood of fortuitous circumstance's moderating or eliminating the latter appears reasonably remote.

Criticism of strategy-making is thus the latest phase in a prolonged confrontation or dialogue between American intellectuals and reformers and American political institutions. It is directed at the appearance in the strategy-making process of characteristics pervasive in American government. On the one hand, the critics express the need to recognize new policy imperatives, to establish priorities, and to reflect felt needs in an adequate manner and with a sense of timeliness. On the other hand, the persistent and pervasive dispersion of power and authority in American government insures the representation of all claims but the priority of none. The criticisms of the strategic reformers go to the very roots of the governmental system. In many ways they are much more profound than the critics themselves seem to realize. The condition which they protest is not a passing one, the product of particular men or events. The defects which they highlight are not easily remedied by exhortations to unity, assertions of executive authority, or changes in personnel or Administration. They are endemic to the political system.

THE SCOPE OF STRATEGY-MAKING

THE PUBLICS OF STRATEGY

Strategy-making is carried on largely within the executive, and the consensus arrived at, if any, is primarily an executive one. The consensus is often tenuous and tentative. Repeal or modification of an Administration decision usually faces fewer procedural and institutional obstacles than repeal or modification of an act of Congress. Groups which are not fully satisfied with the policies developed within the executive branch are tempted to express their dissatisfaction and appeal their cases to groups outside the executive branch. Although the effective power of decision on strategy rests with the Administration, the possibility always exists that external forces could impose such high political costs for adherence to a decision that the Administration would prefer to reverse it. The world outside the executive branch is a continuing potential threat to executive strategic decisions. Hence, the activity of the Administration is more often devoted to defending a policy which has been decided upon than advocating a policy which has yet to be adopted.

In the traditional legislative process, an issue is debated first within the executive and then publicly within and about Congress. All the debate contributes directly or indirectly to shaping the final product: to pushing the legislation through without change, amending it in one direction or another, or defeating it entirely. In strategy-making, predecision debate among the various executive agencies and related groups (and, in some cases, foreign governments) also contributes directly to shaping the measure. Once the decision is made by the President and the NSC, this debate subsides. Once the decision becomes known, however, to nonexecutive agencies and groups, the postdecision public debate begins. The likelihood of such debate may affect executive policy-makers before they decide, but their anticipation of public reactions often is, at best, an informed hunch and, at worst, a rationalization that the public will not accept policies which they do not accept themselves. Public debate of a strategic decision may also affect its implementation and may influence subsequent decisions. Coming after the initial decision, the debate conceivably may undermine the decision but it cannot constructively shape it.

The public debate usually is triggered either by the official announcement of the policy decision (hydrogen bomb, massive retaliation) or by the public dissent from the decision by an executive official or group (airpower sufficiency, missile gap). Often public announcement and public dissent occur almost simultaneously. Some dissent within the executive branch is a *sine qua non* to public debate of the decision outside the executive branch, and on major policy issues this *sine qua non* is almost never absent. Executive dissenters not only aid the opponents with information and arguments, but also assure them that they are not completely "on the outside," and making criticisms which are irrelevant or quite detached from reality. Outside criticism of Administration policies can be effective only if it is supplemented by inside opposition. Inside opposition to Administration policies can be effective only if it is supplemented by outside criticism.

The tentative quality of the executive consensus is enhanced by the uncertain interest and influence of nonofficial groups.[27] In other policy areas, strong private groups link the policymakers within government to the publics outside government. They mobilize and structure opinion and interests. For most of the period between 1945 and 1960, however, strategy-making lacked a large stable system of private interests through which public opinion could be formulated, directed, and structured. Toward the end of this period a limited system of private interests in strategy was beginning to emerge. The alumni of executive branch positions concerned with military affairs were growing in number. Private scholars and experts were responsible for a rapidly expanding literature on strategic issues. Many university centers, other private research groups, and specialized journals focusing upon the problems of war and peace had come into existence. Interservice competition had stimulated the development of a variety of organizations and interests about each of the services. Scientists and other technical specialists outside the government participated more regularly in the consideration of strategic problems. Industrial and regional interests became more conscious of their stakes in defense programs. The emergence of this private system of interests was a natural result of the disequilibrium in military policy. Nonetheless, in 1960, the system of private interests was still uncertain and fragmentary. The outside individuals and groups concerned with strategy were all closely associated with the executive branch, and strategy-making was still dominated by executive officials. Individual outside experts experienced considerable frustration in attempting to play a positive role in the bureaucratic process. The other concerns of service-oriented groups often tended to obscure the debate of strategic problems. The books and articles on strategy were often seized upon as weapons in the intra-executive struggle, playing more of an instrumental than a creative role. The economic interests of the industrial concerns—potentially the most powerful of the outside groups—usually did not extend to major strategic issues. The companies tended to accept the decisions on basic strategy and then, within that framework, compete for contracts for their products and services. It is doubtful, for instance, that the aircraft industry—more involved with military policy than any other industrial complex—influenced the decision on massive retaliation or even that it played an important role in determining the size of the Air Force.[28] In the future, the influence of some outside interests in the formulation of strategy probably will increase. Between 1945 and 1960, however, their role was distinctly peripheral.

Throughout most of the Truman and Eisenhower Administrations, strategic programs received only occasional attention from the general attentive public: the leading quality media of communication, interest groups such as the major business and labor organizations which have concerns with most areas of public policy, congressmen not on the military committees, and the like. Groups and media with broad interests in public policy often feel much more confident in expressing themselves on foreign policy issues than on strategic programs. The AFL-CIO and the American Farm Bureau Federation, for instance, not only take stands on most issues of domestic policy, but also on the key issues of foreign policy such as ratification of the UN Charter or the North Atlantic Treaty.

What interest does the AFL-CIO or the AFBF have, however, in massive retaliation, continental defense, the adequacy of limited war forces, the relative merits of a minimum deterrent versus a counterforce strategy? The implications of strategic programs for specific domestic interest groups are often obscure, and tradition holds that military questions are technical and outside the competence of all but a few.

Public debate can most easily come to grips with issues which are simple and discrete: to pass or not to pass a bill, to ratify or not to ratify a treaty, or to intervene or not to intervene in Korea, Indochina, Formosa. The issues relating to strategic programs, however, are complex and continuing, seldom simple and dramatic. As Roger Hilsman suggests, efforts are regularly made to dramatize issues in simple quantitative terms: Should the Air Force have 48 or 70 wings, more or less planes than the Soviet Union?[29] Inevitably, however, most program issues decided within the executive branch are less dramatic. The question is allocating an extra hundred million dollars to one multi-billion dollar program or to another, and the decision is complicated by the fact that it must be related to earlier and later decisions involving similar issues. The same problem will come up the following year and the year after that. Issues are seldom resolved; they are simply rendered tolerable. As a result, they arouse little interest outside a small number of groups composing the attentive public.

Strategic programs thus differ significantly from the structural areas of military policy, which have reasonably stable systems of concrete interests whose views must be taken into consideration in the policy-making process. UMT legislation activates veterans, educational, religious, farm, and labor organizations; reserve legislation, the various reserve and National Guard organizations; personnel legislation, the military welfare groups and retired officers' groups. The public of strategy, however, goes through an accordian process of expansion and contraction. The expression, "The public won't stand for it," is frequently heard in discussions of military policy as executive officials attempt both to predict nonexecutive reaction and to invoke their predictions to support the policy of their choice. . . . In contrast, one rarely hears the phrase, "The public won't stand for it" in connection with agricultural policy, resources policy, or labor policy. In these areas, the structure of interests concerned with policy is relatively stable, the limits within which those groups primarily concerned can make policy are reasonably well-defined, and the demands which the semi-autonomous policy-making areas impose on the political system as a whole are reasonably constant, expected, and accepted. The instability of the strategy public is characteristic of an area where policy is in a state of disequilibrium and change. Instability in the public of military policy goes hand-in-hand with instability in its substance.

PARTISANSHIP AND STRATEGIC PROGRAMS

The normal process of legislation in American government goes through phases of debate, consensus, and decision. This same process goes on, more or less, in executive development of strategy. So far as public debate is concerned, however, the process is more one of decision, debate, controversy. The occurrence of the debate after the decision leaves little room for the constructive discussion of the issues, the narrowing of the points of contention, the gradual development of a consensus. Instead, since the decision has been made, discussion tends to polarize opinion. Opponents of the Administration can only criticize; they have little expectation of being able to improve. Supporters of the Administration, on the other hand, may have doubts about the policy but they too are prevented from improving it and become committed to its defense in the form in which it was made. The Administration has little direct interest in the debate. Discussion can only restrict its freedom of action in carrying out the policy. In domestic policy, the course of the debate sets the character of the policy. In strategy, the character of the policy sets the course of the debate.

Party voting in Congress prevails on some issues of domestic legislation. On other issues, however, the coalitions cut across party lines: sectional blocs, congressional committees, economic groupings, personal cliques, ideological affiliations often are significant in the legislative process.[30] In particular, successful legislation usually requires a wide degree of consensus within the committee which is responsible for it. An effective committee, in the long run, is not divided along party lines. The Armed Services committees and the Military Appropriations subcommittees take great pride in their nonpartisan approach to the structural issues of military policy. On these issues, Democrats and Republicans respond similarly to the demands of farm groups, reserve organizations, industrial lobbies, and veterans organizations.

On major issues of foreign policy a different pattern of bipartisanship has existed. Instead of the natural bipartisanship of policy legislation within Congress (because other affiliations are more significant to congressmen than partisan ones), formal, artificial procedures have been developed for consultation between congressional leaders of both parties and Administration leaders. The prevalence and usefulness of these procedures has apparently varied considerably, but if an Administration wishes to utilize them, particularly in moments of crisis, they are normally available. Bipartisanship in foreign policy thus tends to come from above, the conscious product of collaboration between executive and legislative leaders.[31] Bipartisanship on domestic policy, however, tends to come from below, the natural outgrowth of sectional and economic divisions which cut across party lines.

Strategic program determination falls somewhere between the artificial bipartisanship of foreign policy and the natural bipartisanship of domestic policy. The process of strategic program decision-making inherently encourages partisanship. Developed primarily within the executive, strategic programs are a rare instance in American government: the responsibility for policy belongs clearly to one party; the other party is clearly excluded from responsibility. Political leaders argue that national defense is above partisanship, but the record of debate and voting on strategic programs suggests that strong pressures exist in the opposite direction. When confronted with an Administration decision on weapons or force levels, the natural tendency of the opposition party members is to react negatively. The absence of other groupings with easily identifiable interests in major strategic issues enhances the importance of party groupings. Lacking clear-cut constituency or other interests, a congressman is more likely to react to an Administration decision on strategy in terms of his general attitude toward the Administration rather than in terms of the specific merits or demerits of the Administration's policy. Moreover, the inhibitions which restrict congressional criticism of the more strictly foreign policy actions of the Administration do not have the same effect on strategic programs. After the President's March, 1959, speech on the Berlin crisis, for instance, congressional Democrats unanimously endorsed his strong declaration of American intentions to stay in Berlin. The other portion of his speech, however, dealing with the defense budget, was vigorously criticized by many leading Democrats as an inadequate response to the crisis.

Thus, public debate over strategic programs is largely the result of opposition party attacks upon Administration policy. In the debates over massive retaliation, sufficient airpower, the missile gap, limited war, the lines were fairly sharply drawn between the Administration and its party supporters in Congress and the opposition party leaders. In strategic program decisions, the United States almost has a form of semi-parliamentary government.[32]

If the distinction between strategic and structural issues suggested above is valid, a marked difference should exist between the degree of partisanship in congressional votes on strategic matters and votes on structural issues. Table 1 shows this to be the case.

TABLE 1. Partisanship on Controversial Military Policy Issues, 1946-1960

Partisan Cleavage	Amendments To Increase Appropriations	Other Appropriations Votes	Selective Service	UMT-Reserve	Pay	Organization	Total Issues
				Type of Issue			
Sharp cleavage	11	7	....	6	1	4	29
Moderate cleavage	....	4	2	4	....	3	13
Little cleavage	1	5	18	5	8	3	40
Total issues	12	16	20	15	9	10	82

NOTE: Controversial issues are those in which more than 10 percent of one party was in a minority. Sharp cleavage means an index of likeness of less than 50; moderate cleavage, index of likeness, 50–65; little cleavage, index of likeness, 65–100. The index of likeness is calculated by subtracting the percentage of "yes" votes cast by one party from the percentage of "yes" votes cast by the other party, and subtracting the result from 100. See Julius Turner, *Party and Constituency: Pressures on Congress* (Baltimore, 1951), pp. 36–38, 69–71.

Amendments increasing funds in the military appropriations bill give Congress almost its only opportunity to record itself formally on major issues involving strategic programs.[33] Sharp cleavages between the parties occurred on over 90 percent (11 out of 12) of the votes in this category, and on slightly over 40 percent (7 out of 16) of the votes on other appropriations issues. In contrast, in no category of structural issue were there sharp cleavages on more than 40 percent of the votes. Sharp cleavages occurred on 64.3 percent of the total votes on appropriations but on only 20.4 percent of all the votes on structural issues. The appropriations votes made up 34.1 percent of the total number of votes in the analysis, but they furnished 62.1 percent of the votes on which there were sharp cleavages. Thus, partisanship is less on structural issues, where the decisive roles rest with Congress and its committees, than on strategic issues, which come before Congress in the form of budgetary recommendations to implement policy decisions already made in the executive branch. The relatively high degree of partisanship in voting on strategic programs undoubtedly in part reflects differences in the constituencies of the two parties.[34] It is also, however, in part the result of the process of strategic decision-making which makes these decisions the responsibility of a single party. In effect, only those nonbureaucratic forces, ideas, and groups which can express themselves through the party in control of the executive branch are in a position to influence significantly the determination of strategic programs.

THE ADMINISTRATION'S DEFENSIVE ROLE

Both the Truman and Eisenhower Administrations, as different as they were otherwise, have been criticized for not exercising "leadership" in national security policy. In each case, it is alleged, the President failed to take the initiative in bringing strategic issues to the people, in arousing support for foreign and military policy proposals, and in educating the public to its responsibilities in the nuclear age. Clearly, this criticism assumes that the President should play the same leadership role in strategic matters that he does in domestic legislation. In the latter, the President must be the source of energy for his program; it is usually in his interest to dramatize the issue, broaden public concern with it, and take the lead in presenting the case for it to as many groups and in as many forums as possible. The concept of presidential leadership is that of Theodore Roosevelt, Wilson, FDR, rallying support for a legislative program being urged upon a recalcitrant Congress. In the strategy-making process, however, the President's role is very different, and the domestic model is inapplicable. In strategy, the President and his Administration have no reason to desire public debate and many reasons to fear it. The decision has been made; the policy is being implemented. The expansion of the public concerned with the policy can only lead to pressure to change it in one way or another and to the exploitation of the issue by the opposition party. While executive dissenters from Administration policy—the Crommelins, Ridgways, Gardners, Taylors —attempt to expand the public concerned with strategy, the Administration's role is defensive: to protect the balance of interests, the policy equilibrium which has been arrived at within the executive, against the impact of profane forces and interests outside the executive.

The interest of an outside group in any particular aspect of strategy, its efforts to shift the emphasis from one program to another or to correct an inadequacy or deficiency in one portion of the military effort, inevitably appears to the Administration as a threat to the entire strategic balance, involving the reopening of all the issues which have been laboriously settled. Mr. Cutler put the case very bluntly:

> There is another seamlessness in our complex world: the fabric of our national defense. Perhaps the most potent argument against public disclosure of secret projects or of short-falls (which inevitably always exist) in any one aspect of our national defense is that such disclosure builds up a Potomac propaganda war to rectify that defect or over-finance that project. But if you devote larger resources to one area of national defense, you are apt to imbalance the rest.[35]

Other members of both Administrations have shared Mr. Cutler's fears. When President Truman impounded the extra funds which Congress voted for the Air Force in 1949, for instance, he declared that this money "must be viewed in the light of total national policies and it must be evaluated in terms of our present commitments, . . . the effect of large military expenditures on our economy, . . . security needs in the light of our foreign policy and the economic and fiscal problems facing us domestically."[36] Similarly, in the formulation of NSC 68, George Kennan was concerned over the consequences of revealing its general policies to the public. He predicted, not entirely inaccurately, that the balance which the members of the Administration saw as desirable would be upset, that military programs would get priority over economic programs, and that military programs related to the massive deterrent would get priority over those designed to deal with less drastic contingencies. "If you tell Congress nothing," Forrestal quoted Reston as saying, "they go fishing; . . . if you tell them all, they go wild."[37]

The fear which executive leaders have of the impact of external influences on national security policy decisions is, in their own terms, a legitimate one. In the abstract, it can even be argued that while it is rational to debate the merits of one possible strategic balance over another, any balance put together with some consideration for all the elements entering into the picture is to be preferred to a mauled and disrupted strategy, the product of the pulling and tugging of a variety of groups with limited concerns and *ex parte* interests. The problem is that once the executive has produced a strategic program no other groups can approach it as a whole. They can change parts of it, but they cannot change it systematically in terms of an alternative strategy which they prefer. The realization of its incapacity to legislate a strategic program as a whole is one reason why Congress usually treats the military budget as gently as it does.[38] In cold outrage, Stewart Alsop quotes one NSC member as declaring, "Policy decisions of the National Security Council are not a fit subject for public discussion."[39] Yet, in a sense, the official is right. Once the decision is made, the time for debate is past. If it is to make a positive contribution to the shaping of policy, discussion must come before the decision, not after it.

Taken singly, persuasive and compelling cases can be made for more limited war forces, civil defense, military aid, antisubmarine forces, long-range missiles—not to mention domestic programs, a balanced budget, and tax reduction. To produce favorable action toward any one of these goals, its proponents must build up support, arouse interest, inspire publicity, reach influential congressmen and journalists, and utilize all the other techniques of political persuasion. The interest of the supporters of each program is to widen the public concerned with that program. The job of the Administration, on the other hand, is to impose discipline, restraint, and balance. The strategic balances themselves—between security programs and domestic programs, military ones and nonmilitary ones, among Army, Navy, and Air Force, massive deterrence, continental defense, limited war—are hardly merchandisable commodities. The Administration may well have struck the best balance possible, but inevitably every one on the outside will have a different perspective. The Administration can win the point, but it can seldom really win the debate. It can only attempt to discourage debate.

The new techniques of presidential leadership are directed primarily to developing and preserving consensus within the executive branch. While congressional groups are the targets of the old forms of presidential leadership in domestic policy, executive groups are the targets of the new forms of presidential leadership in strategy. These "defensive" weapons of presidential leadership are as important to the Administration in the determination of strategic programs as the familiar "offensive" techniques are in the promotion of domestic legislation in Congress.

1. *Restrictive information policies.* Both Administrations tended to restrict the flow of information to the public. As the Moss Subcommittee investigations amply demonstrated, the technical requirements of military security hardly justified many actions which were taken. Supplementing the technical needs of security, the demands of consensus building within the executive branch lead the Administration to attempt to curtail the flow of information out of the executive branch. The limitation of the flow of information to that which makes a "constructive contribution" to the mission of the Defense Department is a normal reaction of an Administration trying to prevent releases "destructive" of the policy consensus it is attempting to develop.

2. *Suppression of leaks.* The establishment of broad policies limiting the flow of information out of the executive branch inevitably leads to circumvention and evasion. The pressures upon the dissenting executive officials to make their dissent known outside the executive branch are just as strong

as the pressures on the Administration to maintain a united front. Hence the phenomenon of the "leak" has become a common, although unofficial, governmental practice. Presidents may express their disapproval in the strongest terms, but staff officers and commanders will still find means of getting to sympathetic newsmen and congressmen. The services, Truman observed, "wanted to boast openly of their top-secret achievements. I directed that the strictest measures be taken to stop these leaks to the press by anyone in the government." "This leakage," Eisenhower declared, "is something that's got to stop."[40] Yet, just as it was natural for the Administration to classify as "confidential" General Ridgway's retirement letter expounding his views, so also was it natural for the *New York Times* to acquire and publish the letter.

3. *Minimizing of Soviet achievements.* The leaders of both Administrations tended to minimize the significance of Soviet achievements in weapons and foreign policy. This was in part due to a fear of public hysteria which might upset the policy plans of the Administration. In the case of the Soviet atomic bomb, the Administration took the lead in breaking the news to the public to soften the impact of the news. In 1955, on the other hand, the Administration, apparently from the same motive, was slow in releasing any official statement on the new Soviet aircraft. Similarly, in 1957 the Administration knew of the Soviet ICBM tests before the Russian announcement in August and had been warned of the imminence of a Soviet satellite launching. In each case, however, the Administration refused to reveal its information to the American public, and when the announcements were finally made by the Russians, Administration leaders (with a few exceptions) minimized their significance. Throughout both Administrations, the American people were assured either that new Soviet develop-

ments were unimportant or that they had already been taken into account by existing American policies. Significantly, not once did either Administration attempt to seize upon a Soviet technological advance as a means of intensifying or expanding the American military effort. When some changes in program were made, as in 1955 and 1957, they were more a reaction to the congressional and public reaction to the Soviet achievement than a direct response on the part of the Administration itself.

4. *Minimizing American deficiencies.* Once the Administration has adopted a program its natural tendency is to obscure any deficiencies in it both to protect its own reputation and, as Mr. Cutler suggests, to prevent the unbalancing of the program by efforts to remove the deficiencies. In addition, of course, a strong case can always be made for obscuring any deficiencies in American military strength because of the effects their revelation would have on enemies, allies, and neutrals. The public exposure of a deficiency may at times be necessary to remedy it; its exposure, however, may also enable the enemy to capitalize upon it. Inevitably, if forced to make a choice, an Administration tends to choose silence rather than self-criticism. In general, the Administration attempts to maintain an air of calm assurance, an imperturbable facade.

5. *Reluctance to make formal pronouncements on strategic programs.* Both Presidents Truman and Eisenhower only addressed the country on national security programs when they were compelled to answer criticism or when they desired to push through Congress measures on which that body retained the power of final approval. The hesitancy about publicizing the implications of NSC 68 in the spring of 1950, the abandonment of Operation Candor in 1953, the effort to suppress General Ridgway's statement of his views in 1955, the refusal to reveal the

contents of the Gaither Report in 1957, all indicate a desire to shy away from a general public debate of military force levels and weapons.

The contrast between the Administration's roles in strategic programs and in structural measures is clearly seen in President Eisenhower's two addresses to the nation after sputnik, in October and November of 1957, and his speech on behalf of his defense reorganization plan in the spring of 1958. The former were defensive in character: the President had no alternative but to defend the past record of his Administration. On the other hand, his speech on reorganization was advocatory, a plea to Congress and the public to support his proposed reforms. The general tone of the post-sputnik speeches was reassuring; that of the reorganization plea was demanding. Both were reasonably successful in achieving their purposes. The sputnik talks calmed the public and encouraged the feeling that no substantial increases in the defense program were necessary. The reorganization speech was followed by a marked change in public attitudes toward Pentagon reform, and directly helped the presidential recommendations in Congress.[41]

Public debate and questioning of strategic programs may also be reduced by distracting public attention from these issues. By proposing major changes in structural policy the Administration may shift the debate to issues for which Congress rather than the Administration is primarily responsible. In 1947 and 1948, when Congress was urging the Administration to increase the strength of the Air Force, the Administration proposal of UMT forced Congress to assume responsibility for limiting the trained manpower reserve. In 1955 the Eisenhower Administration's reserve forces legislation shifted attention away from the second stage of the New Look. In 1958 the Administration's proposals for reorganization and military pay increases dis-

tracted attention from the state of the strategic programs. In this instance, the insufficiency of some programs could hardly be denied. By identifying interservice competition and lack of effective centralized authority in the Defense Department as contributing causes to the deficiency, however, the Administration successfully compelled Congress to assume partial responsibility by enacting the Administration's reorganization proposals.

6. *Restriction of testimony before congressional committees.* The problem of the freedom of executive officials (and particularly military officers) to express their views before congressional committees when those views conflict with the policy of the Administration is an extremely difficult one.[42] The problem comes up in two different forms. With normal legislation, such as a reorganization bill or a military pay bill, where the effective power of decision rests with Congress, the process of consensus development within the executive branch usually does not proceed as far as in the instances where the policy decision is made within the executive. Consequently, dissenting executive officials are freer to express their views before the congressional committees. The Administration will, of course, attempt to discourage such activity—witness Secretary McElroy's rebuke of Admiral Burke in the 1958 reorganization debate—but the logic behind Congress' hearing all views on a proposal upon which it must make the final decision is fairly overwhelming. The Administration usually is more anxious to cover up expression of executive dissents from Administration strategic programs where the final power of decision rests with the Administration. In these cases the expression of military dissent before Congress cannot be justified on the grounds that it is essential to help Congress make a decision. Indeed, if the dissents come after the formulation of Administration policy, they can be justified only

in terms of the pressures and incentives which they might generate to get the Administration to alter its policy. If they come before the Administration has determined its course of action, they are even more vigorously resisted by the Administration as attempts to limit its freedom of action and prejudice its decision. Both the Truman and Eisenhower Administrations tried to define as broadly as possible the obligation of military officers to support Administration programs before Congress.[43]

LEGISLATIVE LEADERSHIP IN STRATEGY

In the traditional legislative process, interest groups and executive agencies originate proposals, the President integrates them into a legislative program, Congress debates, amends, and decides. In the executive legislative process, executive officials and related groups originate proposals, and the President and Secretary of Defense, working through the mechanisms of the NSC and JCS, debate, amend, and decide upon them. Who, however, plays the role of legislative leader? Who winnows out the various ideas and proposals in the light of an overall set of priorities or grand strategy and then integrates these proposals into legislative programs which can then be discussed, amended, and ratified? Paradoxically, it is in executive leadership of legislation that the executive legislative process is weakest. In a hierarchy, ideas and proposals presumably bubble up from below; individual executives decide on programs and proposals, rejecting some, approving others and pushing them along to the next higher level. The highest executive makes decisions; he does not formulate proposals to present to some other body.

The concept of a superior executive official drafting a program and submitting it to a committee of subordinates for approval is not generally accepted; on the contrary, it is the function of the committee of subordinates to formulate the program and submit it to the executive for approval. Hence, the issue: Who leads the subordinate committee? Throughout the decade after World War II this problem was never absent from the operations of the NSC and the JCS. If the President or the Secretary is the final decider or ratifier of strategic programs, one of two things happens: initiative comes from a variety of uncoordinated sources and the committee is never confronted by an integrated legislative program; or some other body or official drafts such a program and presents it to the committee, which then discusses, amends, and decides upon it and presents recommendations to the President and Secretary. The problem in the executive legislatures is to develop something comparable to the dialectic of proposal and decision which exists between the President and Congress in domestic legislation. The body which has the final decision on policy issues should not also have complete and exclusive control over its own agenda. Otherwise the temptation to avoid the tough issues becomes almost irresistible. In presenting his legislative program to Congress, the President often compels Congress to face up to issues which it would be happy to avoid. In the executive legislative process, the problem has been to develop sources of initiative and leadership which can compel the NSC and the JCS, the President and the Secretary of Defense, to face up to issues which they might just as well wish to avoid, and to present the strategic legislatures with general strategic programs initially drawn up from a broader viewpoint than that which they are collectively capable of producing.

Congressional groups are able to seize upon specific issues and proposals which might be lost in the executive machinery and bring them up to the top where the principal executive decision makers must come to grips with them. Congressional groups cannot, however, perform the function of legislative leadership. Necessarily, they deal with only parts of the whole picture. Similarly, ad hoc committees and study groups, such as the Finletter Commission, the Lincoln Summer Study Group, the Killian Committee, or even the Gaither Committee, can help to prompt an executive decision on a particular policy proposal, but usually they cannot develop an overall strategic program. Largely recruited from outside the government and limited in existence to a year or so at the most, these groups serve as temporary stimuli but not as continuing leaders. Even when the group develops a broad concern with a wide variety of defense policy problems (as the Gaither Committee did), its inevitable termination means that it is in a poor position to force an Administration to make a clear decision on its proposals (much less make a favorable decision) as long as the Administration wishes to temporize and avoid them. Congressional committees and citizens' committees thus may be able to focus attention upon a particular policy issue, but they lack either the scope or the longevity to play a continuing role as effective legislative leaders.

Other difficulties hamper the ability of executive groups to play leadership roles. The stress upon the concept of "civilian control" inhibits both military and civilians. The military tend to accept as fixed the existing political and economic assumptions of policy. Apart from the Chairman of the Joint Chiefs of Staff, the military leaders themselves have "parochial" concerns. Consequently, they usually lack the scope to come forth with a broad, balanced defense program, and, frequently, they feel that this is not their responsibility. The initiative for a general reappraisal of defense programs and strategy seldom has come from the military. . . . The stress on "control"

in civilian control also discourages civilian initiative, and encourages reliance upon the allocation of resources rather than the definition of goals as the means of insuring civilian supremacy. The prevailing concept of "civilian control" thus fits in perfectly with the idea that the executive decision-maker is a judge rather than a leader, that it is his function to say yes or no to programs proposed by others rather than to originate programs himself. Civilian control is rarely thought of in terms of policy leadership in the formulation of military programs.

Critics of both the NSC and the JCS have regularly stressed the desirability of greater initiative and leadership from above by the President and the Secretary of Defense. They have often urged the enlargement of the NSC staff so that it could play a policy-formulating role rather than simply a coordinating and processing role. They have also advocated a civilian-military policy staff for the Secretary of Defense. The inherent difficulties of placing responsibility for both the formulation of policy proposals and the final decision on policy proposals on the same agency have prevented much development along this line. The problem is: Who can propose an overall policy without committing the Administration? The President is in a poor position to do this. In actuality, the leadership of the strategic legislatures has fallen to members of the legislatures: the Department of State in the NSC and the Chairman of the Joint Chiefs. The problem has perhaps been less acute in the NSC than in the JCS. After 1950 the President kept in close contact with the operations of the NSC; not until 1959 was a regularized procedure developed for the participation of the Secretary in the deliberations of the JCS. In addition, the presumption of absolute equality which existed with respect to the services in the JCS did not prevail in the NSC. Instead, the State Department was recognized as the first among equals. The primacy of the Department of State among cabinet departments has long been recognized by tradition and statute. In both the Truman and Eisenhower Administrations roughly three-quarters of the papers considered by the NSC originated in the State Department. Until the Vice-President was added to the NSC in 1949, the Secretary of State chaired the NSC deliberations in the absence of the President. In addition, until 1960 the Under Secretary of State chaired the Operations Coordinating Board. For a decade, during the most critical years of the Truman and Eisenhower Administrations, the Department of State was headed by two individuals who combined sustained tenure in office with the highest confidence of and closest relations with the President. Mr. Acheson and Mr. Dulles also brought to the deliberations of the NSC superior minds, great force of character, and unusual skill in articulation and debate. All these factors combined to give the Secretary of State a position of leadership in the operations of the National Security Council. On the other hand, the Secretary of State can never be more than first among equals under the President. Conceivably, as Herman Kahn has urged, if backed by an expanded staff, the Special Assistant to the President for National Security Affairs could become the "party leader" in the National Security Council.[44]

The high premium placed upon the formal equality of the service representatives precluded a similar development in the Joint Chiefs. However, the normal absence of the Secretary of Defense from JCS deliberations permitted the emergence of a separate chairmanship. Although the position of chairman was not formally established until 1949, since their creation in 1941 the Joint Chiefs have almost always had a chairman in practice, and from 1949 down through 1958 the powers of the Chairman grew steadily. In 1953 and again in 1958 his authority

over the Joint Staff was increased, and, particularly during the incumbency of Admiral Radford (1953-1957) the Chairman played an active and creative role in formulating strategic ideas and plans. Under Radford, as General Taylor put it, the Chairman came "to be a sort of party whip . . ."[45] The principal limitation on his development of this role rested in the character of the Joint Staff. While the Chairman himself was divorced from and independent of service interests, the staff upon which he had to rely was not. Despite the efforts which were made to stimulate a "joint" outlook on the part of the Joint Staff members, their future careers still lay with the services, and the principle of equal representation of the services strengthened the assumption that the members had some representative responsibilities. The replacement in 1958 of the committees in the Joint Staff with a more strict system of executive hierarchical control in the long run would help the Chairman of the Chiefs to play a more independent role as a legislative leader.

Just as the desirability of greater leadership from the presidential level in the formulation of NSC policy has been urged, so also it has been frequently argued that the Secretary of Defense should play a more active role in the initial development of policy proposals in his department. Secretaries Forrestal and Lovett and other informed observers urged the creation of a policy staff, usually to be composed of both civilian and military personnel, to enable the Secretary to play this role. Such a staff would, at the least, give him an independent source of advice, and, at the most, enable him to be a leader in making strategic decisions.

In due course, either the leadership functions of the Secretary of State and the Chairman of the Joint Chiefs will become more fully recognized and clarified, or the Special Assistant and Secretary of Defense will develop the staff facilities necessary to perform these functions. This development would not only facilitate consensus but would also probably improve the content of strategic decisions. The form in which issues are presented for decision affects the nature of the decision. The problem in the executive legislative process is not the presence of bargaining but rather the point at which bargaining starts. Bargaining cannot be eliminated, but the development of more effective leadership organs in the NSC and JCS would limit it and focus it. The starting point would become not three separate proposals advanced by three separate departments but one set of proposals advanced by the legislative leaders. The requirements of consensus might still cause those proposals to be torn apart tooth and limb, but, at the very least, the clear visibility of the mutilation would have certain restraining effects. It has had them in Congress.

A striking feature of the past dozen years has been the extent to which expressions of alarm at the decline of presidential leadership have occurred simultaneously with expressions of alarm at the growth of executive power. This apparent paradox simply reflects the fact that the very ability of the executive to make the crucial decisions on strategic programs has undermined the ability of the President to lead. The more the President becomes, at least in theory, the judge, the less he can be the advocate. This shift inevitably has had its effect upon the personal role and influence of the President. The President's ability to lead in the process of congressional legislation is a very real one. No one else can focus attention on a legislative program, arouse support, dramatize the issues, as effectively as he. He can, if he so desires, almost monopolize this role. His power to decide strategic issues within the executive branch, however, is more difficult to exercise and to monopolize. To be sure, the President appoints the members of the NSC and

the JCS, and they are theoretically only his advisers. No policy exists until he has approved it. Yet in part this is a myth to preserve the appearance of presidential decision-making.

The President does not override unanimous or near-unanimous recommendations of his advisers much more often than he vetoes acts of Congress. The theory that the President makes the decisions, in short, serves as a cloak to shield the elaborate processes of executive legislation and bargaining through which the policies are actually hammered out. As a decision-maker, the President may, in many respects, have less influence on strategic programs than as a legislative leader he has on domestic policy in Congress. The leadership function is personal to him. Decision-making he shares with a variety of groups in the executive branch. The development of stronger sources of legislative leadership in strategy within the executive branch, however, would enhance the power of the President "as a court of last appeal" on strategic programs.[46]

In discussing the processing of papers through the NSC machinery Robert Cutler raises the issue: "[A]re we to let in the public while this preparatory work goes on? Are the propagandists of one view or another to be given the opportunity to argue the pros and cons in the press?" His answer is a resounding "No!" It is based upon the concept that in the process of strategy-making, "nothing has happened" until the President "has approved a policy recommendation made to him by the National Security Council . . ." All the arguments and advice before this "are personal to the Chief Executive . . ."

It is my concept [Mr. Cutler declares] that all papers, all considerations, all studies, all intelligence leading to the formulation of national security policy recommendations to the President, are the property of the Chief Executive. They are his working papers; they have no other standing to be recognized. Only he can dispose of them.

This argument is buttressed by the claim that a decision by the President on national security is of the same order as the decision of a corporation executive on plant location:

> While the staff of a business executive is working up a problem to present to him, the working papers and the preliminary views which fluctuate and change in successive conferences are kept under lock and key. If this confidential procedure is sensible for decision-making in business, surely it is doubly so in matters of national security which affect the lives of our people and the survival of the Republic.[47]

To question Mr. Cutler's views it is not necessary to invoke democratic theory as to the possible *right* of the people in a democracy to be informed of the considerations which go into national security policy. The problem is rather the conflict between the rationale and reality. The concept that "nothing has happened" until the President has approved an NSC recommendation is a legal fiction. The fact is that by that point almost everything in the policy-making process has happened. Mr. Cutler's argument amounts to saying that nothing has happened in the domestic legislative process until the President has signed a bill into law or that nothing has happened in the judicial process until the Supreme Court has rendered a decision on appeal. The theory is one of pure presidential decision; the actuality is executive agencies hard at work legislating strategic programs. The representatives of these agencies no more function simply as personal, confidential advisers to the President than the witnesses in a congressional hearing function as personal, confidential advisers to the committee. They act as representatives of the interested groups, and, it might be argued, it is precisely the claims which they make and the compromises which they arrive at which should be opened as far as possible to public view.

The struggle between the Administration, attempting to capitalize upon its advantages of hierarchy, and the subordinate executive agencies, attempting to appeal to a broader forum is a continuing one, as much a part of the system of strategy-making as the struggle between President and Congress is a part of the governmental system in general. The Administration can never be sure of its policy so long as potential sources of opposition exist outside the executive branch, and the executive agencies can never expect to exercise a greater influence on the policy outcome so long as the public statement of their views comes after rather than before the Administration decision. Policy on a controversial issue can be free of tentativeness and certain of support only when it emerges from a process in which all the potentially interested groups have an opportunity to make a contribution. Public interest in strategic program decisions, knowledge of the considerations entering into those decisions, and discussion and contribution to the making of the decisions depend upon the revelation of conflicting views within the executive branch before the Administration makes its decision. Nongovernmental groups, and even nonexecutive groups, can seldom originate policy proposals and alternatives, but they can consider those espoused by responsible executive groups, make clear the implications of the proposals for themselves and other groups in society, and indicate the extent to which they are willing to support one against another.

The opening up of policy proposals for more extensive debate before an Administration position is reached might have several results. It would enable congressional and public groups to play a more effective and recognized role in the discussion of policy alternatives. It would broaden the consensus supporting the policy which is finally adopted. It would remove the need and the opportunity for dissident executive groups to appeal their cases to the public after the decision. It would minimize post-decision debate and lessen doubt about the finality of the presidential action. It would mitigate many of the defects of the policy-making process which disturb the critics. One effect of congressional lobbying has been to bring issues to the top and compel a personal and explicit presidential decision on them. Broader public debate of strategic issues would, in all probability, have the same effect. The attention and the interest which would be aroused on particular strategic issues would compel them to be resolved by presidential decision. Greater publicity and more participation by nonexecutive groups in strategy-making might also restrain the tenden-

cies toward "horse trading" which exist within the executive. It might both enhance the roles of public and congressional groups and, at the same time, strengthen the hand of the President. In addition, the sense of purpose which the critics have found lacking in the policy-making process, if it is to be developed at all, can only be developed from society at large. Common purpose can only emerge out of broadly based policy discussion and widespread participation in the policy-making process. It cannot be decreed from on high. Broadening the scope of the policy consensus may well go hand-in-hand with improving the quality of the policy content.

NOTES

1. For example, National Security Act, 1947; Security Act Amendments, 1949; Reorganization Plan No. 6, 1953; Defense Department Reorganization Act, 1958; Navy Organization Act, 1948; Army Organization Act, 1950; Air Force Organization Act, 1951.

2. For example, Officer Personnel Act, 1947; Army and Air Force Vitalization and Retirement Equalization Act, 1948; Career Compensation Act, 1949; Uniformed Services Pay Increase Act, 1952; Reserve Officer Personnel Act, 1954; Career Incentive Act, 1955; Military Pay Act, 1958.

3. For example, Extension of World War II Selective Service, 1946; Selective Service Act, 1948, and extensions, 1950, 1954, 1959; Universal Military Training and Service Act, 1951; universal military training bills, 1947, 1948, 1952.

4. *Organization of the Armed Services Committee*, Hears./HR CAS/83C1/1953, p. 2.

5. *The Federalist* (Modern Library ed.), No. 24, p. 148, No. 69, p. 448.

6. See, e.g., Howard White, *Executive Influence in Determining Military Policy in the United States* (Urbana, Ill., 1924), p. 44; Clarence A. Berdahl, *War Powers of the Executive in the United States* (Urbana, Ill., 1921), p. 101.

7. Gen. Maxwell D. Taylor, *The Uncertain Trumpet* (New York, 1960), pp. 81–82. I have adapted this discussion of the annual executive "legislation" from Taylor, *ibid.*, pp. 21–22, 80–87.

8. *Ibid.*, pp. 26–27, 29, 57–65; Paul H. Nitze, "The Need for a National Strategy," Address, Army War College, Carlisle Barracks, Pa., Aug. 27, 1958; Paul Y. Hammond, "NSC

68: Prologue to Rearmament," and Glenn H. Snyder, "The New Look," MSS to be published in Warner R. Schilling, Paul Y. Hammond, and Glenn H. Snyder, *Making National Security Policy: Three Case Studies* (New York, 1962).

9. Taylor, *Uncertain Trumpet*, p. 85.

10. *Ibid.*, pp. 22, 85–87; *Organizing for National Security*, Hears./USS GOC SC on National Policy Machinery/86C2/1960, p. 795.

11. See *Organizing for National Security: Selected Materials*, Cmte. Print/USS GOC SC on National Policy Machinery/86C2/1960, pp. 26–28. Apparently, however, the annual "Basic National Security Policy" paper does not have a financial appendix. Taylor, *Uncertain Trumpet*, p. 82.

12. Roger Hilsman, "Congressional-Executive Relations and the Foreign Policy Consensus," 52 *American Political Science Review* (Sept. 1958), 725.

13. Lewis A. Dexter, "Congress and the Formation of Military Policy" (paper read at the American Association for the Advancement of Science, Dec. 31, 1958, Washington, D.C.), pp. 12–13; E. L. Katzenbach, Jr., "How Congress Strains at Gnats, Then Swallows Military Budgets," 11 *The Reporter* (July 20, 1954), 31–35.

14. Arthur F. Bentley, *The Process of Government* (Evanston, Ill., 1949), p. 359.

15. 103 *Cong. Record* (June 10, 1957), 8592. For the relevant statutes, see 60 Stat. 341 (1946), 62 Stat. 605 (1948), 64 Stat. 321, 408 (1950), 65 Stat. 88 (1951), 66 Stat. 282 (1952), 68 Stat. 27 (1954), 71 Stat. 208 (1957), 73 Stat. 13 (1959). See also Charles H. Don-

nelly, *United States Defense Policies in 1958*, H. Doc. 227/86C1/1959, pp. 72–73.

16. See, e.g., the actions of the House and Senate committees in the Bomarc-Nike dispute. *New York Times:* May 14, 1959, p. 15; May 24, 1959, p. 1. S. Rept. 434/86C1/1959, pp. 1–3.

17. The Army and Air Force Authorization Act of 1949, 64 Stat. 321, did authorize for the Air Force 24,000 aircraft or 225,000 airframe tons, whichever its Secretary deemed most in accordance with the purposes of the act. For perceptive analyses of the "Russell Amendment," Military Construction Authorization Act, 1959, 73 Stat. 302, I am much indebted to unpublished papers by Raymond H. Dawson, "Legislative Authorization of Weapons Programs: Congressional Intervention on Defense Policy," and Bernard K. Gordon, "The Military Budget: Congressional Phase."

18. Sen. Russell, *New York Times,* Mar. 15, 1953, p. 17; Sen. Chavez, "Influence of Congress on Military Strategy," 103 *Cong. Record* (Jan. 14, 1957), 598. See also *Unification and Strategy,* H. Doc. 600/81C2/1950, pp. 33–35, and Richard W. Hatch, *Notes on Congress and the National Interest: 1945–1951* (Massachusetts Institute of Technology, Center for International Studies, May, 1957), pp. 30–32.

19. Many papers on the policy process have been brought together in *Organizing for National Security: Selected Materials,* Cmte. Print/USS GOC SC on National Policy Machinery/86C2/1960. For criticisms see particularly the comments of Messrs. Rostow, Kintner, Kissinger, Morgenthau, and Senator Jackson.

20. Walter Bagehot, *The English Constitution* (London, 1949), p. 202.

21. Henry A. Kissinger, *Nuclear Weapons and Foreign Policy* (New York, 1957), p. 407.

22. Hans J. Morgenthau, "Can We Entrust Defense to a Committee?" *New York Times Magazine,* June 7, 1959, in *Selected Materials,* Cmte. Print/USS GOC SC on National Policy Machinery/86C2/1960, p. 162.

23. A. L. Moffat, "The Legislative Process," 24 *Cornell Law Quarterly* (1939), 224, quoted in George Galloway, *The Legislative Process in Congress* (New York, 1955), p. 4.

24. Vice Admiral H. E. Orem, "Shall We Junk the Joint Chiefs of Staff?" 84 *U.S. Naval Institute Proceedings* (Feb. 1958), 57.

25. Robert A. Dahl and Charles E. Lindblom, *Politics, Economics, and Welfare* (New York, 1953), chap. 13.

26. Woodrow Wilson, *Congressional Government* (Boston, 1885), p. 318.

27. See G. A. Almond, "Public Opinion and National Security Policy," 20 *Public Opinion Quarterly* (Summer 1956), 372.

28. See G. M. Lyons, "The New Civil Military Relations," 55 *American Political Science Review* (Mar. 1961), 59–61; S. P. Huntington, "Recent Writing in Military Politics: Foci and Corpora," to be published in Huntington, ed., *Changing Patterns of Military Politics*; G. M. Lyons and Louis Morton, "School for Strategy," 17 *Bulletin of the Atomic Scientists* (Mar. 1961), 103–6; "Defense Spending Lobby," 19 *Congressional Quarterly* (Mar. 24, 1961), 463–478; Henry A. Kissinger, *The Necessity for Choice* (New York, 1961), chap. 8.

29. Hilsman, 52 *Amer. Pol. Science Review* (Sept. 1958), 736–37.

30. See Arthur N. Holcombe, *Our More Perfect Union* (Cambridge, Mass., 1950), pp. 152–55; David B. Truman, *The Congressional Party: A Case Study* (New York, 1959), chaps. 3, 5, 7.

31. See, in general, H. Bradford Westerfield, *Foreign Policy and Party Politics: Pearl Harbor to Korea* (New Haven, 1955), *passim*; Cecil V. Crabb, *Bipartisan Foreign Policy: Myth or Reality* (Evanston, Ill., 1957), chaps. 7, 8.

32. "Several members of the Congress occupying important foreign policy positions feel that the United States is moving toward the 'British system,' as they interpret it, in foreign policy. Congress is playing more the roles of critic, reviewer and supporter of executive-initiated policies. Increasingly, these men do not regard the anticipated trend with alarm. Indeed, they express the thought with mild enthusiasm." Holbert N. Carroll, "Congressional Politics and Foreign Policy in the 1960's," Paper presented at the Annual Meeting, American Political Science Association, New York, N.Y., Sept. 8–10, 1960, p. 12 (footnotes omitted).

33. See Samuel P. Huntington, *The Soldier and the State* (Cambridge, Mass., 1957), pp. 423–27.

34. . . . The analysis here is designed only to show the tendency toward partisanship in strategy as compared with other military policy issues, not to analyse the substance of the party positions.

35. Robert Cutler, "The Seamless Web," 57 *Harvard Alumni Bulletin* (June 4, 1955), 665.

36. *New York Times,* Oct. 30, 1949, quoted in Stephen K. Bailey and Howard D. Samuel, *Congress at Work* (New York, 1952), p. 381.

37. Walter Millis, ed., *The Forrestal Diaries* (New York, 1951), p. 444.

38. See, e.g., Rep. Plumley's remarks, 95 *Cong. Record* (Apr. 12, 1949), 4433.

39. *New York Herald Tribune,* Mar. 30, 1956, p. 10.

40. *New York Times,* Dec. 8, 1956, p. 1; Harry S. Truman, *Memoirs* (Garden City, N.Y., 1956), II, 291–92.

41. See Samuel Lubell, "Sputnik and American Public Opinion," 1 *Columbia University Forum* (Winter 1957), 15–21; *New York Times:* Apr. 10, 1958, p. 1; Apr. 18, 1958, pp. 1, 8; May 29, 1958, p. 1; May 31, 1958, p. 1; June 7, 1958, p. 9; June 12, 1958, p. 17.

42. See E. L. Katzenbach, Jr., "Should Our Military Leaders Speak Up?" *New York Times Magazine,* Apr. 15, 1956, pp. 17 ff.; Huntington, *Soldier and State,* pp. 412–18.

43. *Military Establishment Appropriation Bill, 1948,* Hears./HR CA SC/80C1/1947, p. 631; Gen. J. L. Collins, "The War Department Spreads the News," 27 *Military Review* (Sept. 1947), 17–18; Lt. Gen. James M. Gavin, *War and Peace in the Space Age* (New York, 1958), p. 171; *New York Times,* Jan. 15, 1959, p. 19.

44. See Herman Kahn, *On Thermonuclear War* (Princeton, 1960), pp. 581–82.

45. Taylor, *Uncertain Trumpet,* p. 110.

46. Henry L. Stimson and McGeorge Bundy, *On Active Service in Peace and War* (New York, 1947), p. 516.

47. Cutler, 57 *Harvard Alumni Bulletin* (June 4, 1955), 684.

A Functional Analysis
of Defense Department Decision-Making
in the McNamara Administration

PAUL Y. HAMMOND

In 1961 the Defense Department, under a new Secretary of Defense, Robert McNamara, began a major management revolution, based on a set of methods and techniques which came to be called a programming, planning, and budgeting system (PPBS). Few, if any, of the techniques were new. Their revolutionary impact depended upon (1) the high degree of development or sophistication to which some of them (e.g., cost and program analysis) had been driven, and (2) the relatively high degree of integration achieved in the new "system," so that, for example, decisions about current operations can be taken in the light of their effect on programs four or five years in the future, and decisions about future goals can be taken with their implications for present operations specified.

In August, 1965, President Johnson announced his plans to develop comparable management systems in other executive departments. The progress of this effort has been uneven. But it is clear that PPBS is going to be with us for a while.[1] This article is an attempt to assess its effect on the bureaucratic politics of the Defense Department.

The principal method used is functional analysis.[2] A more common method in the literature of public administration is a less theoretical and more detailed analysis of political relationships. Such attention to political detail is warranted by the importance of the subject. But the case studies that result often concentrate on the shape and flow of political transactions without dealing explicitly and systematically with the raison d'être of the agency under consideration. Even the more formally structured studies of administrative organizations that use the methods of social psychology commonly do not examine the agency's overall purposes.

The literature on administration has long grappled with the problem of giving appropriate weight to the formal structure and purpose of the organization. Obviously, to take either formal structure or purpose on its face is to be insufficiently empirical. To ignore them, on the other hand, is also to neglect relevant data, particularly since bureaucrats use formal structure and purpose frequently as tools. A distinguishing feature of bureaucratic politics, that is to say, is the prominent role which structural arrangements and authoritative goal prescriptions play in the process. Functional analysis has been used here in an attempt to strike a balance between process descriptions and means-ends analyses.

Briefly, my thesis is that the tradi-

From the *American Political Science Review*, vol. LXII (March 1968). Copyright © 1968 by the American Political Science Association. Reprinted by permission of the publisher and the author.

tional military requirements process has fulfilled certain political or institutional needs, that these needs still exist, explaining its survival in certain areas, particularly in NATO, but that the new policymaking processes have been able to perform these functions remarkably well. In effect, the political functions which the administrative process must perform for military policy-making explain in part both the survival of old and the success of new processes.

THE FUNCTIONS OF TRADITIONAL REQUIREMENTS GENERATION PROCESSES

The political functions that the administrative process must perform for military policymaking can be divided, somewhat arbitrarily, into three main ones: (1) bureaucratic rationalization in the military establishment, (2) risk and role distribution in the making and implementing of military policy, and (3) self-legitimization within the military establishment and in relationship to other elements of the government and the political system. Suppose we look first at the way the traditional requirements process has performed these functions.

1. *The Rationalizing Function.* To be rational, one must overcome two obstacles. One's propositions must be logically consistent with each other and each must correspond with the real world. For bureaucracies, three standards of rationality cope with these obstacles in different ways. They are radical rationality, procedural rationality, and liberal or transactional rationality.

Radical rationality attacks the cognitive obstacles directly, postulating criteria and applying them to the substance of policies. It persuades and legitimizes on the basis of shared values. In any given context, however, the radically rational position begs the questions about how to establish criteria scientifically. Radical empiricism is a variant of radical rationality. It postulates the validity of empirical (not necessarily organizational) methods by which to acquire and analyze data. One might refer to it as scientific due process.

Procedural rationality appeals to some self-evident or widely accepted standards of organizational or administrative due process, such as deliberation and clearance, information gathering and processing, authority, subordination, and responsibility. Administrative due process can rely upon agreement about more tangible things having to do with how things ought to be done.

The third form, liberal or transactional rationality, is a special case of the second: due process for extreme skeptics in a pluralistic and liberal culture. Skeptical of prevailing standards of administrative due process, it falls back upon the generic political processes of the classical liberal market place. It is more individualistic than administrative due process. Of the three forms of rationality, it may beg the fewest questions, although it assumes rationality in individual behavior.[3]

The rationalizing function is a reciprocal process with several phases. In one it articulates and clarifies objectives and methods (in the course, presumably, of generating the rationale which will explain and win support for them). In another phase it tests the validity of articulated ends and modifies them accordingly. In still another, it adapts, in turn, methods and means to ends or objectives. Rationalizing is concerned with the propriety and probity of ends and the appropriateness of means. A bureaucracy performs the rationalizing function in several ways. It seeks consistency by requiring agreement among various offices on the nature of problems and how to deal with them: the internal clearance process. It may, in addition, expose policies to less structured examination. It seeks factual accuracy, or correspondence, through similar procedures. Viewed in this light, a rationale is an attempt to explain ends and means with reference to each other. The rationalizing function can be described in terms of the policymakers who perform it, the procedures they follow, the content, scope, political weight, factual accuracy and logical rigor of the rationale they produce, and the changes they make in adapting practice to rationale.

Since World War II the traditional military requirements determination process[4] has helped bolster central authority in all the services and the Defense Department and prevent Congress from taking significant initiatives. It may seem sensible to assign the central office responsible for military operations the authority to determine the kinds of military forces that it needs. In the United States, however, this arrangement has not existed until recently. Before World War II the supporting bureaus in both the Army and Navy had been inclined to take it upon themselves to decide what kinds of weapons and forces to make available for operations, quite apart from what the operations wanted. One therefore cannot consider the authoritative, centralized determination of requirements a "traditional" process. The propensity to concentrate efforts on means-oriented objectives is doubtless found in other complex organizations, but it is probably peculiarly acute in military ones which spend most of their time preparing for but not performing their pay-off function.

In this pluralistic setting, what I have called the traditional requirements generation process had a rationalizing effect in two respects. First, it gave a prominent voice in specifying what the overall capabilities of the whole military establishment should be to those military officers most directly concerned with the pay-off func-tion.[5] By doing so, it raised the chances that the definition and choice of military tasks or objectives would be valid.

Second, since the wartime role of the military chiefs dictated that at all times they be at or near the center of the military organization, giving them the main voice in determining military requirements had the effect of centralizing authority in the military service departments and throwing more weight onto ends-oriented interests over means-oriented interests.

It should be noted that the criterion of rationality here amounts to what we might call administrative due process: the distribution of authority so as to give sufficient weight to the views of the people who are most closely identified with the pay-off function. One does not attempt to test the wisdom or validity of their collective findings by scrutinizing the deductive and inductive methods by which they have arrived at their conclusions. Avoiding that task may be only for economic reasons. It can also be in order to accommodate an essentially romantic view about judgment that intuition can come closer to the truth than can formal—and hence explicit, articulate, and communicable—analytical procedures.

The traditional military requirements notion may be regarded as the supporting doctrine for an authoritative due process arrangement. It replaces, for example, the idea that shipbuilders know best what kinds of ships to build for the fleet, or supply corpsmen what kind of war materiel to provide the combat forces. It does not, however, concern itself with the criteria for deciding *what kinds* of ships to build or materiel to procure. It is concerned with procedures, roles, and authority, with who should decide, not with substance. Issues of substance were raised only within this procedural framework.

Before unification, each service chief was the principal determiner for his service of short-term posture requirements. The Joint Chiefs of Staff accommodated military interests with each other. In the fifties, with the establishment of unified commands, and the conferring of command responsibility on the JCS, a second channel for generating military requirements came into effect. Both originate among the operating forces. But one goes up the chain of command, reaching the Joint Chiefs of Staff through the headquarters of a unified command. The other shifts to the supporting service, reaching the JCS through the service chief.

Specifications for weapons capabilities to guide research and development do not always reach the joint arena. Unless they involve weapons for joint use, requirements are usually stipulated by the service chief. The decision to take a developed weapon into production, which could be regarded as a "qualitative" requirement decision, is in fact handled as a quantitative requirement, since it must be linked to particular force postures. In this form it concerns the JCS.

The rationalizing function includes both the generation of ideas and their explication—enough to link perceptions of objectives and purposes to force capabilities and postures. Explication and elaboration may also expose these ideas and linkages to critical examination.[6] The military requirements generation processes have not been very successful in performing this function. Even the special deference accorded the JCS has not made it conspicuously successful in performing the function by developing and adapting strategic objectives, strategic concepts, and force postures to each other. The Secretary of Defense stepped into a vacuum of unexplicated strategic concepts and obsolete strategic doctrine when he assumed an important formal role in performing the rationalizing function.

Concepts which could define policy issues and derive alternative resource needs and programs have not

been the conspicuous output of the JCS. Rather than encouraging the JCS to rationalize in this manner, the traditional generation process may suppress the explanation of concepts and their systematic use by confirming the military as an authority whose decisions, though unexplained, should be deferred to. Deference to military requirements decisions has served at least to protect the military establishment from external probings about the reasonableness of military programs, but without assuring effective internal handling of problems.

2. *The Distribution of Risks and Roles.* The processes used to determine military requirements distribute political risks and establish administrative and political roles. The ranking military authorities cannot guarantee national security against external threats. The effort to get them to do so helps distribute political responsibility for national security. If at any time since World War II the Joint Chiefs of Staff had been willing to specify without qualification a politically acceptable level of military effort as sufficient to insure the national security, the administration would have shared to the maximum the internal political burdens of the national security effort. In fact, however, never have the Chiefs gone that far. Usually, they have shifted the burden back or avoided it by setting military requirements above politically acceptable levels, by failing to agree upon a common military posture, or upon the nature and extent of the threat, and by qualifying their guarantees. Despite the protective capabilities thus manifest, or perhaps because of them, until the 1960s the JCS have usually been under continuous heavy pressure to bear the political burdens of military force requirements.

Roles are at stake here as well as risks. The incentive to unload responsibility onto the military, which any incumbent administration experiences, depends upon their prestige, nonpartisan status, professionalism, and limited identity with the incumbent administration—factors which make the military capable of bearing them. The political commitments involved in the military program—the demands it makes on resources and manpower, the overseas entanglements that are a part of it, and the involvement of national prestige—all may be considered political burdens in the form of costs and risks. Risks, of course, involve opportunities. The military may run political risks (or assume other political burdens) in order to acquire wanted resources.

Yet, it may be prudent to limit political risks. Not all wanted resources will be granted anyway, and, if necessary, risks can always be assumed later, when the gains as well as the risks are more certain. Whether or not they have carried the political burden in peacetime, the military can be expected to reap the benefits of political risk-bearing in times of high ·national security threat anyway. To the extent that they understand this, military authorities are discouraged by their understanding from assuming political burdens in peacetime. In a similar way the prospect of later payoffs to the military at their expense may discourage political authorities from reducing their political burdens by loading them onto military authorities.

The government must decide upon a military program and win support for it. The more that elective officials can make the military do these things, the less burdensome the program is to them. Yet, the military can carry the political burden only to the extent that they do not appear to be either aggressive interest claimants or captives of political authority. They are not captives in the degree that they can limit their commitments and state their differences with civil authorities.

The traditional procedures both pinpoint and obscure responsibility. When an administration tries to push more political burdens onto the military, and they actively resist, much confusion can result. When, as is more often the case, both military and civil authority groups are divided into factions with alliances that include each other, the distribution of risks is a chaotic process, to say the least.[7] The jostling that has occurred in using the traditional requirements generation process since World War II indicates that it has performed this function very imperfectly.

3. *Legitimization.* When military requirements are generated according to the traditional rules, or appear to be, they carry a presumption of legitimacy with them, winning deference for the incumbent administration's military policies and programs from Congress and from other outside groups. Probably the requirements process has performed the legitimizing function the most satisfactorily, although there have been difficulties with it, also. They seem to fall into three areas. The first involves budget-program-planning discrepancies within the military establishment.

Before McNamara, strategic military planning, military programming, and the annual military budget-making all took place quite independently of each other. The problems of this disjunction among the core policymaking activities of the military establishment could have been isolated and clarified if each process occurred without reference to the other, or had each consistently taken the others into account. But neither has been the case. Each was performed with an eye on the other, but an eye which produced unexplained and varying accommodations.

This was the consequence for quantitative requirements. For qualitative requirements, the ramifications went much further. Knowing that many feasible and valuable weapons projects would have to be dropped eventually, the Defense Department during the fifties adopted cumbersome procedures to see that the dropping occurred as early as possible. This was done both to save resources and to assure that a new weapons system was eliminated before it had acquired a political base for itself.[8]

The second area of difficulty concerns authority and consent problems within the Defense Department. Legitimization is valuable to an organization because it reduces the cost of compliance. In the Defense Department consent and support depend heavily upon the political feasibility of alternatives. Whenever it has been easy to persuade powerful Congressmen to support one's minority position in the Defense Department, it has been relatively easy to obstruct central Defense Department authority. Legitimized policies bolster central authority by increasing the cost of risks of advocating alternatives.

The third area of difficulty is the greater prestige and perceived value which military activities and needs have enjoyed over nonmilitary ones in foreign relations. Military legitimization has often provided an umbrella for many nonmilitary parts of foreign policy. The result may be that military instruments in foreign policy get too much attention in comparison with nonmilitary instruments. Certainly during the time when the military umbrella worked the most effectively, in the early 1950s, much criticism was leveled at the administration in these terms.

THE McNAMARA ADMINISTRATION: FROM AUTHORITATIVE ROLE-PLAYING TO PROGRAM ANALYSIS

The McNamara administration both replaced and modified the traditional ways of military decision-making. Without describing changes in detail, it should be helpful now to compare the way the program-generation process McNamara installed performs the three functions which the military requirements setting processes used to perform.

1. *The rationalizing function.* One of the most impressive achievements of the McNamara reforms is the tight linkage which has been achieved between the five year program and the current annual budget.

The five year program introduced the use of systems analysis, upon which, in turn, cost-effectiveness analysis and program budgeting have heavily depended. They are the backbone of an impressive system for relating means and ends.

The management techniques of the McNamara administration work best when they can address problems some distance in the future. Systems analysis, in the experience of some hardware engineers, works much better in designing new systems than in adapting old ones. Perhaps management problems are comparable. To be effective in the general designing of alternatives, the analytical methods which have been built into the budgetary system need to be able to address problems up to five years or more in advance.[9]

Similarly, systems analysis, used as a management technique, works best when it can design resources and postures for "set-piece" operations. As one might expect, then, the emphasis in military management has come to be on these techniques to the neglect of improvisation, institutional learning and marginal or incremental adaptation.

Systems analysis has held the initiative in defense management for six years. In the research and development sector, the Directorate of Defense Research and Engineering had become a powerful agency by 1961. Since then it has lost its predominance to the Office of the Assistant Secretary of Defense for Systems Analysis, the primary agent in OSD for exploiting these techniques. The "opportunity approach" to research and development used normally in DDR&E may be more flexible, but it is less thorough in the exploration of trade-offs in a technological environment of rapidly increasing possibilities than are the decision analysis techniques which are exploited by OSD(SA). It is a fair estimate that the latter persuades the Secretary of Defense more often than does DDR&E on major research and development questions.

For a brief period after the Comptroller's office was split into two parts it looked as though OSD(SA) would be faced with a new competitor. When Robert N. Anthony, a former Harvard Business School professor, took charge of the older elements of the Comptroller's office, as Defense Comptroller, there was some hope that the fiscal management function could draw from (and to some extent pioneer) modern business comptrolling practices to produce adaptive capabilities within the Office of the Secretary of Defense which could exploit the flexibilities of incremental decision-making. The promise of such a development is that it would be a supplement to existing programming methods, an alternative to the analytical constructs of systems analysis.[10] In fact, however, Anthony's office has become almost wholly absorbed with a formidable and necessary task with less profound implications. It amounts to turning the cost estimates which have served as the basis for the programming, planning and budgeting system into cost accounts—developing, that is to say, a budget and an accounting system for operations which corresponds to the programming and planning categories now used.

From the beginning of Anthony's effort, the difference in perspective between his office and OASD(SA) has been apparent. There may yet be some rivalry ahead for the two offices in OSD. If that rivalry, or something else, can raise the capacity of the Defense Department to improvise and learn in the process of operating, it will have expanded the rationalizing capabilities of contemporary management methods.[11]

Explication can expose ends and means to critical scrutiny and clarify their relationship to each other. The heavy emphasis on the explication of major program decisions provides a body of data and doctrines by which to orient and indoctrinate audiences within the Defense Department to the military program, to explain and defend it before external audiences, like the Congress, and hence to evaluate it. The heavy emphasis of the McNamara reforms on the articulation of reasons and criteria is more than an effective defense mechanism. It is also a procedural inducement to be rational in the same way that written judicial opinions, because they are carefully prepared statements of the reasons why, encourage judges to deliberate carefully. Theoretically, the defense program budget, linked to systems analysis methods for the exposition of major defense policy issues, establishes common frames of reference for discussion throughout the military establishment and establishes what kinds of data to extract and collect. This is in effect a "scientific" commitment to a rational organization discourse.

According to the market place or transactional approach, critical discussion must be entirely open. There must be no appeal to authority.

Of course, other procedural standards have been applied to defense policy-making. The main alternative is a closed authoritative system. It is similar to the traditional process. It asserts that military judgment is esoteric and deserves a privileged position in the market place of ideas as well as in the policy clearance process for specified authorities who possess it. In some degree every professional group claims that its professional talents involve esoteric knowledge. It cannot claim special status without doing so. The scientific norm of open inquiry without appeal to authority is in fact applicable only *within* privileged groups. Pursued to its ultimate conclusion it argues for a wholly unstructured arena.

The Defense Department under Secretary McNamara hardly went that far. While the changes he instigated have widened the participation of department officials in the development of military policies by denying to certain professional military groups the privilege of deciding without explaining, the decision-making process remains highly structured. The Secretary of Defense not only decides major policy issues, but decides as well which issues, in what form, will be addressed. He holds the initiative in the establishment of the frames of reference for data selection and analysis, chooses many of the issues at controversy, and specifies the criteria by which they will be decided. More people may participate in Defense Department policymaking than before. Yet the modifications of the McNamara administration brought the major issues into fewer hands.

Fewer participants, or centralization, does not necessarily mean greater procedural rationality, even in a military establishment where assumptions about rationality tend to favor authoritarian models. These changes have also been costly to Congressional participation in defense policymaking, a change which may be, but is also not necessarily, more rational. I have suggested elsewhere that Congressional politics tends to give advantage to correspondence rationality, defined as accurate perceptions of the real world, while the more unitary an administrative structure is, the more administrative politics depends upon consistency as its standard of rationality.[12]

It follows that the more pluralistic administrative politics are, the more resources they will devote to achieving accurate perceptions of the real world, even at the expense of internal consistency. OSD is heavily committed to standards of internal consistency, insofar as they can be given practical meaning. That, in any case, is the premise on which military requirements generation procedures mainly rest. The management reforms of the incumbent administration, then, have established strong controls over the internal policy dialogue. According to this line of reasoning, the Defense Department is strong on internal consistency, but quite possibly at the expense of that untrammeled dialogue and debate which tend to promote accurate depictions of and adaptations to external conditions.

2. *The Distribution of Risks and Roles.* Across the range of major policy issue areas, the Secretary of Defense assumed a larger role and commensurately greater political burdens. If something goes wrong with the F-111, if the Russians deploy an effective antiballistic missile defense before the United States does, if there are materiel shortages in Vietnam, if we lose our strategic superiority, McNamara (and his successors) could be blamed.[13]

Undeniably, the distribution of roles and powers, of risks and political burdens, is clearer now than it has ever been in the past. The Joint Chiefs of Staff are no longer the major determiners of defense programs. It is now the Secretary of Defense who takes responsibility, as he should, for a program which must necessarily be a balancing of risks and costs. He can shift responsibility on the margins. But the main political risks, and the main political defenses within the Defense Department, remain his. Role and risk distribution have been clarified by concentration.[14]

The value of this clarification is demonstrated by the relationship of the

Secretary of Defense to the Joint Chiefs of Staff in the present administration. The Secretary of Defense has taken over some important functions from the Joint Chiefs with surprisingly little opposition. First reactions were somewhat militant, but the militancy of the JCS has much subsided. One could conclude that the Chiefs have lost gracefully, but considering the persistence and skill with which they had previously protected their prerogatives, a further explanation may be needed. Probably more than one might have expected, they are content in their reduced role because it involves commensurately reduced responsibilities. There is, at any rate, a certain unprecedented equitableness in the changed status of the JCS which they may recognize.

The assumption by the Secretary of Defense of political risks and responsibilities is not the only factor which produced JCS assent to reduced political status. Another major factor has been what Warner R. Schilling has termed the "shower of dollars"—the increase in Defense Department expenditures under McNamara, as indicated by Table 1.

TABLE 1. Total Department of Defense Expenditures 1959–1967[a]

1959	41,223
1960	41,215
1961	43,227
1962	46,815
1963	48,252
1964	49,760
1965	46,173
1966	54,409
1967	66,950[b]
1968	72,300[b]

[a] Excluding military assistance, nuclear weapons and materials, and defense support expenditures. Figures, in millions of dollars, taken from *Budget of the United States Government for Fiscal Year Ending June 30, 1968* (G.P.O., 1967), p. 456.
[b] Estimated.

As these figures indicate, during the period when most of the McNamara revolution was being carried out—in the first two years, say, of the Kennedy Administration—the services had increasing resources to distribute. The management techniques—including the economizing ones, were instigated in an expansive environment. Where the management policies of McNamara really pinched, as with the forced marriage of several aircraft system requirements into the TFX, or with the negative responses to the advanced manned bomber, or the delayed procurement of anti-ballistic missiles, the contentment of the services with the prominence of OSD has been less impressive.

These money matters explain a great deal. But we should not lose sight of the fact that the McNamara administration did change things in the Defense Department to an unprecedented degree. No one previously has come close to changing major functions and processes so much. There have been "showers of dollars" before, in 1950–51, and, of course, in the early 1940s, to take the major instances. But neither of these showers was used to consolidate civilian power in the military establishment. Unquestionably it was easier, politically, to win control in a period of expansion. The opposition had less to rally around. But technically it was much harder. McNamara's consolidation of power was an impressive managerial achievement in taking advantage of political opportunities.

At least four improvements seem to be related to the clarification of roles and risks that was a part of the McNamara reforms. (1) The Defense Department has become more responsive—compared with the State Department, strikingly more responsive—to needs perceived in the White House.[15] (2) The new delineation of authority and responsibility is more protective of the military professionals. (3) OSD has held the initiative more in dealing with changes in the military policy environment than it did previously. (4) The new distribution of risks and roles, implemented in part by the integrated

planning, programming, and budgeting procedures, has focused defense
policies more on issues and less on roles
and personalities than it used to.

3. *The Legitimizing Function.*
The defense policy and management
innovations of 1961–1967 performed remarkably well the legitimizing functions for policy, perhaps because of the
particular combination of authorita-
tiveness and open rationality which
seem to have been associated with them.
Within the Defense Department, as
outside it, the McNamara administration won early respect for its competence. As one might expect of an administration which modifies the status
and rewards of powerful interests, the
McNamara administration was not
spared criticism, or avoided deserving
it; but rarely did it come close to being
discredited on any particular issue.[16]
Moreover, holding control of the services to the extent that it did while
carrying out major modifications of
their forces and methods demonstrates

that it could cope with external as well
as internal pressures.

The McNamara administration did
not encourage its external critics to
think that they could ally with dissatisfied segments of the Defense Department in order to criticize its central
authority. At the same time, the vigor
with which it defended itself in Congress enhanced its authority within the
Defense Department by giving confidence to subordinates that they would
be supported if they were loyal, and by
indicating that the challenges from
outside could only have a limited effect.
Effective legitimizing inside and outside
the military establishment thus reinforced each other.

The last seven years have seen less
appeal than before to military authority to legitimize established policies
both inside and outside of the Defense
Department. Internally, the change of
tone reflects the greater capacity of OSD
to compel compliance with general policies through the integrated program-
planning-budgeting procedures.

THE McNAMARA ADMINISTRATION: PAST AND PROSPECTIVE TRENDS

So far I have looked at the changes
wrought by the McNamara management revolution for their effect on the
political functions performed by military policymaking procedures. My purpose has been to establish a basis for
evaluating the claims about rationality
in behalf of the major changes in relationship to their political environment and functions. In an effort to
carry the analysis of political factors
further in that direction I will look at
two hypothetical developments and
then take a final look at the rationality
problem.

1. *Limited Military Engagement
with Increasing Political Burdens.* Let
us suppose that over the next five to
ten years the United States will continue to make increasing commitments
of military power and political prestige

in Southeast Asia. Maybe the war in
Vietnam will be settled in our favor:
Then suppose other military challenges
arise in the area.

The mounting military effort
would impose mounting political burdens on the U.S. Government to go
along with mounting expenditures.
More and more questions would be
raised both inside and outside the government about means and ends. Official Defense Department presentations
would carry less weight in legitimizing
military policies.

What effect would such a prolonged but limited military effort have
on the policy and management reforms
achieved in the past few years? On the
one hand, one might expect it to
weaken the newer analytical methods
and strengthen the role of traditional

military judgment in defense policy-making. The growing military effort would enhance the prestige of traditional military command channels and the role of traditional requirements generation. One should expect greater reliance on professional military judgments about how to fight the war and less reliance on analytical methods under the direction of civil authorities. In part the shift could be the result of greater pressures from Congress and the public which would force the shift in roles and political risk distribution, and modify the way the administration would seek legitimization. Congressional probes of military establishment activities in wartime rarely concern themselves with the discrediting of military operational command authority. More often they look for failures in support efforts. During the Korean War, and recently with respect to Vietnam, Congress showed much interest in the possibility of an ammunition shortage.[17] The internal environment, showing the effects of the conflict, would enhance the role of the military authorities (the Joint Chiefs of Staff and the major operating commands in the field) at the expense of the civilians in OSD who have gained so much prominence in recent years.

In part, this shift would reflect changes in the tasks performed in the military establishment. Growing military commitments would increase the importance of managerial and operational adaptiveness at the expense of middle range planning. Five-year programs would be less important than how given capabilities would be adapted to cope with immediate and continuing problems. Rationality in the military establishment would come to be defined less in terms of internal consistency and more in terms of the accurate depiction of and accommodation to the real world of the combat situation.

In this environment, not only might more systems analysis be employed under military command channel sponsorship, but analytical and managerial capabilities under the control of OSD might be enhanced, particularly if these capabilities could compete successfully with the military in making operations and programs more adaptable. If OSD could respond by developing in the Comptroller's office the management control techniques which would do that, OSD might continue to hold the initiative.

In effect, the growing burdens of war could become an opportunity for further modifications in Defense Department management controls, providing policy implementation techniques which could be made equal to the burdens that would have to be imposed on them. They would, it seems fair to say, have to undergo considerable development to do that. But if they did so successfully, the pay-off could be high: enhanced Defense Department capabilities to learn and adapt military efforts in the course of implementing policies generated through the new analytical techniques now used.

The argument in favor of continued civilian initiative in reshaping the Defense Department turns in part on propositions suggested by the experience in Vietnam that internal war imposes heavy demands for innovation on military capabilities, that the efforts to meet these demands requires reinforcement or support from outside the operational command channels, and—what may be the most important proposition --that the largest apparent need for innovations involves military *and* civil capabilities for dealing with an environment described better by the behavioral sciences than the physical or biological sciences. If this is the case, then civilian-generated innovations would be in much demand in the hypothetical case under consideration, whether they came from outside or within the military establishment. If OSD should respond to the opportunity, its role would grow in developing more adaptive military capabilities and generating parallel nonmilitary capabilities for use where the military ones are not applicable, or to compete with military capabilities where their predominance is in question.

It may be too much to expect problems of this nature as they appear in Vietnam to be solved by improved management analysis and implementation techniques. Probably no amount of further sophistication in systems analysis or "management control" techniques can overcome the effects of the White House's granting priority to military instruments there. On the other hand, Vietnam may now be demonstrating the profound need for a learning and "steering" capability which PPBS in the Defense Department has not provided.

2. *The Cold War Extended.* The second hypothetical case is a continued period lasting one or more decades in which the United States would experience no direct military engagement, yet would continue to perceive sufficient military threats to require the maintenance of a substantial military capability.[18] As a result, on the general strategic level present military policies would be maintained, their success measured in deterrent value, not in the achievement of disarmament.

One of the effects claimed for the cold war has been that it enhances the dominance of the Presidency over the Congress in making and implementing military policy. This hypothetical extension of the cold war might not further Presidential dominance because it might offer the White House, through OSD, few new opportunities to maintain the initiative. The major gains in economizing may now be behind us and further gains are too hypothetical to be taken seriously. If the Secretary of Defense should be willing to assume political burdens as much as he could, he might be able to maintain a working relationship with Congress in which his political risk assumption and role-

playing were the basis for continued Congressional support. Yet if his opportunities for taking initiatives proved to be low, it may well be that he could not continue effectively to assume risks and win legitimization for his initiatives.

In the hypothetical case of a continuing cold war, one should anticipate continued centralization, with an emphasis on internal consistency at the expense of three things: efforts to reexamine the relevant premises about the real world, the development of more adaptive capabilities in the implementation of policy, and the propensity of the organization to explore and generate new options. In all three ways, options would be lost or buried in the administrative processes of the Defense Department.

3. *Actual and Potential Trends.* These sharp contrasts in the hypothetical future draw attention to at least three important indicators of trends in the new defense management arrangements. The first and most important is the policy-making and management initiative of OSD.

If, as I have suggested, the character of the management revolution in the Defense Department has depended upon OSD's taking and maintaining the initiative in the definition of policy issues, the distribution of risks, the legitimization of policy, and in the further rationalization of structures and processes, then it follows that the loss of initiative could mean changes in all of these phenomena. The character of existing structures and processes, the sources of political leadership for military affairs, the basis for public support of defense policy, and the direction of management efforts in the Defense Department could all change if executive initiative is lost. That is why OSD initiative is such an important indicator.

The initiative which would have to be sustained seems to be composed of the high risk-assumption propensities of

OSD, combined with very considerable adaptive and innovative capabilities. Two possible component indicators of the latter have been a demonstrated capacity to extract new kinds of information from sectors of the defense establishment, and evidence of innovative momentum, such as new attacks on cost/effective or strategic program analysis problems.

In general, the maintenance of initiative after seven years is impressive. OSD continues to assume risks and to generate new questions and analytical answers. Innovation has been institutionalized in internal OSD capabilities and through a variety of contractual relations with private industry. Large cost analysis tasks remain unfinished which hold much promise. Still, it would not be hard to imagine a lagging of OSD initiative great enough to have a significant effect on the functioning of the Defense Department. In the end, the maintenance of initiatives may depend, as it has so much in the past, on OSD's setting and pursuing major, concrete objectives.

The most promising next set of objectives might be to reach out beyond the new policy-making arrangements and develop new policy implementation techniques. Systems analysis has not provided the way to adapt military capabilities while they operate in close relationship to an uncertain but rich environment.[19] These new techniques should try to do so.

A second indicator—or rather, set of indicators—would be the components of a political support-winning strategy for any Secretary of Defense, for they would indicate the extent that he has adopted or found his way to one. Secretary McNamara played a role of unprecedented prominence in national policy debates for someone in his position. His administration was a striking combination of executive initiative-taking, energetic defensiveness in Congressional relations, and political dependence upon the White House. His

administration required the defense establishment to assume large political risks and a comparatively prominent political role. The performance may have been impressively successful; but in relationship to the political burdens assumed, the political support was not abundant. Much depended upon its finite limits.

The war in Vietnam shows all the signs of becoming an increasingly prominent national political issue. If it is comparable to the fall of China as a foreign policy issue, with the incumbent administration held responsible and the Congressional parties taking care to disassociate themselves from the administration, this relationship between McNamara's assumption of political risks and the limited political consent and support upon which he depended may come to have an increasingly important bearing on the development of military programs. From the viewpoint of the incumbent administration, it might then appear that changes had been pushed too fast or too far, and that more external support should be generated and existing support demonstrated. In that event, some retrenchment in the recent management revolution would be likely. These may be extreme and unlikely outcomes, yet something less would be a trend worth noticing. Any change in the efforts of OSD to win approval for the administration's military policies would be an important indicator of that trend.

The third indicator to watch is centralization. It is also an important trend in its own right. We can infer from the foregoing depiction of political functions that the side effects from centralizing decision-making in the Office of the Secretary of Defense will vary, depending upon the way political risks are handled and how much executive initiative is maintained. In particular, the more one exploits a given political base, the more he increases the potential costs of centralization in two ways, by pushing the organization into

defending the status quo and by encouraging it to suppress options,
hedges, and innovations.

These observations can be explained with reference to transactional
rationality by looking at the incentives
of OSD to conform with prevailing
standards of procedural and radical rationality—standards which include the
exploration and explanation of unex-
amined premises, the openness of communications, the opportunity for competitive analysis, the clear distribution
of risks and responsibility. Three statements summarize the arrangement of
relevant incentives:

> 1. Where the payoffs for OSD instigated
> program changes based on cost/effectiveness
> and systems analysis are high, the quality
> of the analysis will be high and the pro-
> pensity of OSD to assume risks and accept
> responsibility will also be high.
>
> 2. Where the payoffs are high, but the
> political risks associated with them increase,
> OSD will be encouraged to obscure respon-
> sibility and degrade the integrity of the
> analysis.
>
> 3. Where payoffs are low, and political
> costs high, but decisions must be made,
> analysis will lose its integrity and become
> a tool of management interests.

The point of this survey is that the
first situation may have existed and
continue to exist in the Defense Department, but the trend has been toward
the second and third combinations—the
increase in political risks and the re-

duction of payoffs achievable by the
techniques of rational analysis. I have
suggested that the first statement will
remain applicable, to the extent that
OSD maintains the initiative, so that
payoffs in programs will stay high and
the political costs of risk and responsibility bearing will be held down. I have
also indicated that rising costs could
handicap the maintenance of initiative
and increase the political costs and
risks to OSD—a phenomenon which already can be observed to some degree.

What might happen if the U.S.
military program were to be reduced
—in conformity with disarmament arrangements or in unilateral response to
changed perceptions of threat, for example—might be equally discouraging.
The services would become more res-
tive, their political supporters more
critical of particular OSD economy
measures, though still committed to reductions in general. OSD could not
score well with a general economy program and would cause outright hostility in many particular cases. These are
circumstances in which the pressures
and temptations to degrade the policy
debate would be brought to bear from
all sides. The level of debate might
not sink as low as it did in 1949 or
1954–55, but any degradation would
have serious consequences. The utility
of present management methods is particularly sensitive to quality.

CONCLUSION

In 1960 I wrote:

> In all the major fields of defense or-
> ganization it is evident that the shortcom-
> ings of the business approach have been
> perceived. In some, it has led to a search
> for program—for some way to formulate
> general policies—which will provide more
> adequate guidance to management efforts.
> Whenever a solution has been considered,
> however, it has been rejected because it
> challenged the prerogatives of the Joint
> Chiefs of Staff as the determiners of the
> military ends for which the military estab-
> lishment exists.[20]

Sooner than I thought possible the
Defense Department had a "program."
What made the difference was a new
administration which assumed the task
of generating programs and objectives
by imposing radically rationalistic programming, allocation, and operational
techniques.

I have laid stress on the prospects
that the initiative which OSD held
under McNamara will be sustained.
Holding the initiative depends upon

both internal and external conditions. I have taken an optimistic view of the internal ones here, referring to some prospects for further innovation. But we ought to consider some less attractive eventualities. If initiative is sustained, we can expect some additional achievements in defense management and policymaking. We can also expect that the rate of innovation will be sustained, in turn sustaining the capacity to adapt to a changing political and technological environment. But against these prospects, we must measure the very considerable propensities of any large and highly centralized organization to kill its own capacity to innovate or change. By now, the issue may well be whether the Defense Department can survive its own success.

The relations of the Defense Department with external conditions I approached through two alternative views of the future, the cold war continuing peacefully, and the expansion of limited war somewhere, such as Southeast Asia. The first threatened to produce executive stagnation, which could be particularly harmful to the validity of military programs. The second could make Defense Department programs increasingly vulnerable to political attack, and that could produce stagnation and its consequences, too. That may be an important danger posed by the domestic political effects of the war in Vietnam; they would not, so far as I can tell, be the effects anticipated in Hanoi.

We have come to depend heavily for the quality of the defense program upon the quality of executive leadership and management in OSD. In

order to get the quality of programs that we want, there may be no other choice. The McNamara reforms were carried out and worked effectively because OSD was able to take and keep the initiative and thus expand its dominating position in military policymaking outside of the Defense Department as well as inside it. Reduced OSD dominance over external policy-making competitors would mean, conversely, reducing effectiveness within the military establishment, including reduced ability to generate options and innovations. In fact, the first quality OSD would lose by retrenching on the exercise of its authority would probably be its adaptability.

Put in these terms, it should be evident that we are back where we started, with a military program generation process which must defend its actions not "on the merits" but over issues of institutional integrity. That is why, in the end, the case for the new policies and methods of defense policymaking cannot be made on the grounds that they rest on more satisfactory concepts of rational decision-making. Rather, a more inclusive standard must be applied. I have specified three political functions which a military program decision process must perform, and argued that it performs them at least as well as its predecessor did. Functional analysis can be altogether too general and too detached to be much use in evaluating organization behavior and output. But it can bridge the gap between transaction-oriented political analysis and end-means oriented systems analysis, as this study is intended to show.

NOTES

1. The President's press release and related documents are now compiled in Senate Government Operations Committee, *Planning-Programming-Budgeting: Official Documents,* Committee Print, 90th Cong., 1st Sess. (1967).

2. For an evaluation of structural-functional analysis as a method in social anthro-

pology see John Beattie, *Other Cultures: Aims, Methods and Achievements in Social Anthropology* (London: Cohen & West, 1964), ch. 4. A thoughtful but rambling evaluation somewhat closer to home is Theodore L. Becker, "Judicial Structure and Its Political Functioning in Society: New Approaches to Teaching and Research in Public Law," *Journal of Politics*, 29 (May, 1967), 302–333.

3. Aaron B. Wildavsky deals with a comparable distinction in his "Political Implications of Budgetary Reform," *Public Administration Review*, 21 (Autumn, 1961), 183–190. Wildavsky's *The Politics of the Budgetary Process* (Boston: Little, Brown, 1964), is a clearly delineated example of a process description.

4. For an excellent normative statement about the traditional military requirements determination process see House Armed Services Committee, *Hearings on Military Posture*, 88th Cong., 1st Sess. (1963), 361.

5. The balance all too often went too far in that other direction in wartime, when administrative doctrine dictated giving the military commander *anything* he asked for without challenge. Since it was, of course, impossible to do that, the field commander could be his own enemy. Pershing, for example, though anxious to get American aircraft onto the Western Front in World War I, was, by his frequent changes in major specifications a principal cause of delays in getting production under way: see I. B. Holley, Jr., *Ideas and Weapons* (New Haven: Yale University Press, 1953), pp. 67–79.

6. One would expect that the more the rationalizing process is unified, the more it normally will produce mutually consistent explanations based on agreed suppositions about the real situation, while the more pluralistic the process the more it would reflect disagreement about which data depict the real world.

7. Glenn Snyder has described with illuminating detail how misleading the claims of unanimous JCS endorsement were for the "New Look" elements of the fiscal 1955 budget: see W. R. Schilling, P. Y. Hammond, and G. H. Snyder, *Strategy, Politics, and Defense Budgets* (New York: Columbia University Press, 1962), esp. pp. 418–440, 486–491.

8. House Appropriations Committee, *Supplemental Appropriation Bill*, 1957, H.R. Report No. 2638, 8th Cong., 2nd Sess. (July 7, 1956), 11–12.

9. Of course, the major reason why one pushes the program budget out five years into the future is not to accommodate the convenience of systems analysis but to achieve the economies of long range programming.

10. Robert N. Anthony has stated the case for what he calls management control, which he distinguishes from operational control, in his *Planning and Control Systems: A Framework for Analysis* (Boston: Harvard Business School, 1965), esp. ch. 3. The book cannot be taken as analogous to C. J. Hitch and R. N. McKean, *The Economics of Defense in the Nuclear Age* (Cambridge, Harvard University Press, 1960), in relationship to Charles J.

Hitch's appointment as Defense Comptroller in 1961, although the comparison with Anthony's appointment may be revealing. The Hitch-McKean volume is a set of essays representing an already existing capability. Anthony's book is an effort to formulate and clarify the tasks for developing a capability. Hitch's task was to apply a set of analytical capabilities which had already reached impressive proportions; Anthony's task, if the analogy holds, is to develop the general capabilities as well as apply them.

11. Congress must approve changes in the budget and accounting system. For OSD's efforts to win this approval, see House Appropriations Committee, H.R. Report No. 349, *Defense Appropriations for Fiscal 1968*, 90th Cong., 1st Sess. (1967), pp. 6–7; Senate Appropriations Committee, S. Report No. 494, *Appropriations for Fiscal 1968*, 90th Cong., 1st Sess. (1967), p. 22; the Secretary of Defense's letter to Rep. George H. Mahon, Chairman, House Committee on Appropriations, August 7, 1967; the Secretary of Defense's Memorandum to Secretaries of the Military Departments, Subject: "Tests of Budgeting and Accounting Systems," August 9, 1967; Department of Defense Position on Amendment Adding Sec. 641 to H.R. 10738, Approval of Accounting and Budgeting Systems, August 19, 1967; *Congressional Record*, 113 (August 18, 1967), S. 11842–4, and (August 21, 1967), S. 11923–5; and House Appropriations Committee, H.R. Report No. 595, *Conference Report on H.R. 10738*, 90th Cong., 1st Sess. (August 23, 1967).

12. "Foreign Policy Making and Administrative Politics," *World Politics*, 17 (July, 1965), 660.

13. I do not mean either that blaming them would take care of the matter or that no one else would be blamed. Here I am only concerned with their assumption of political responsibilities and risks.

14. It is not entirely obvious, however, how much the clarification of role and risk distributions represents an asset. If the Secretary of Defense can be held responsible for everything, that may be clear, but it is not very practical. For discussion of this problem in broad democratic representational context, see Robert A. Dahl, *A Preface to Democratic Theory* (Chicago: University of Chicago Press, 1956), ch. 2.

15. The case against the State Department has been given wide publicity by Arthur M. Schlesinger, Jr., *A Thousand Days* (Boston, Houghton Mifflin, 1965), pp. 406, 410–413, 446–447, 513, 681, 1016.

16. Still the closest, probably, is its source selection for the development and manufacturing of the F–111.

17. E.g., Senate Armed Services Commit-

tee, *Ammunition Shortages in the Armed Services,* Hearings; *Investigation of Ammunition Shortages in the Armed Services,* Interim Report; and *Investigation of Ammunition Shortages in the Armed Services,* 2nd Report, all in 83rd Cong., 1st Sess. (1953), and *Status of Ammunition and Air Munitions,* Hearings, 89th Cong., 2nd Sess., 1966.

18. I am not concerned with the likelihood of these two conditions existing together —the continued perception of major, low probability threats and the continued lack of much military engagement.

19. Systems analysis can design flexibility beforehand for a hypothetical future, given sufficient lead time. For a price, it can build in different capacities beforehand. But it cannot tell someone how to evaluate unfolding events in order to establish new criteria by which to use the capacities it designs.

20. *Organizing for Defense* (Princeton: Princeton University Press, 1961), p. 315.

Technology, Politics, and Strategy

BERNARD BRODIE

I

The original title of this paper was to be, rather grandly, "Strategy and Technology," but after I had somewhat rashly accepted the invitation to write it, the question arose: what can now be said on the subject of technology and strategy that is both significant and new? I do not wish to strain for novelty, but neither do I wish to waste the readers' time. The opportunities for concocting fresh generalizations in this area are not what they once were.

Some twenty-seven years ago I published a book which, in so far as it was not simply a history of the major naval inventions of the past hundred years, presented the basic argument that changes in the instruments of war which appear to be simply tactical can be so far-reaching as to have large strategic and political effects.[1] I thought when I published it that there was some novelty in the idea, but that thought may have been illusory even then. Today the point would be obviously and ludicrously banal. The literature dealing directly or indirectly with the relationship of technology to strategy has, especially since World War II, been very considerable, and much of it has been quite good. In this present company I have to remember that one of the more recent examples of that literature was Adelphi Paper No. 46, entitled *The Implications of Military Technology in the 1970s,* which contains six of the eighteen papers delivered at this Institute's Ninth Annual Conference at Elsinore in 1967.

But merely to refer to the vast amount of pertinent literature is certainly to understate the influence which preoccupation with technology has had on our recent strategic thinking. The whole impressive development of systems analysis and of related techniques, especially in the United States, has fostered the notion that selection of future weapons systems for appropriate development and deployment represents most of what there is to modern military strategy. I suspect that the former American Secretary of Defense, Mr. Robert S. McNamara, tended automatically to think in such terms. Military history, which used to be the main acknowledged source of strategic insight—Clausewitz and Mahan are examples—has been enormously down-graded in favour of the new analytical techniques. Except for economics the modern social sciences have had only a peripheral influence.

As you may by now guess, I shall use this circumstance as the basic challenge in this paper, and I shall be emphasizing mainly the limitations of technology in strategy, and also the limitations of the study of technological trends as a means of acquiring strategic insights. The time is indeed over-ripe for considering these limitations. Vietnam is almost too conspicuous an example of technological superiority having inadequate payoff and of the modern techniques to which I have referred proving irrelevant. Over the past year, incidentally, I have witnessed two instances where a remark like the one I have just made provoked in each case the retort that systems analysis could not have been proved inapplicable in Vietnam because it has not been tried—the implication being that an appropriate trial might produce some very far-reaching results. In each case the person making that retort was a distinguished member of the strategic intellectual fraternity. I feel that such a reply reflects either a profound misunderstanding of what has been happening in Vietnam, or a stubborn refusal to distinguish between the areas of consideration where systems analysis is applicable and indeed invaluable and those in which it has little or no relevance. I suspect it reflects both.

II

One of the first points I should like to make is that the speed and extent of technological change have not usually been closely coupled with the strategic and political implications of the relevant changes. Some technological advances may be so earth-shaking in their consequences that subsequent ones, however more sophisticated individually and impressive in the aggregate, cannot but be of diminished significance relative to the original device. The outstanding example is the weapon which introduced the nuclear age, the original fission weapon tested at Alamagordo in 1945 and used in that year at Hiroshima and Nagasaki.[2] A corner was turned in those few months which vastly separates the world before those events from the world after them. Against the bursting flash of the first A-bomb, the later much larger thermonuclear weapons and all their associated gear are of distinctly lesser importance.

Let me develop this example further. At the end of the first decade of the nuclear age, that is about 1955, a condition had settled upon us which in most essential respects is the same as that in which we find ourselves now and which involved changes much greater in their political implications than were to derive from the second decade of that age, ending about 1965. I will also venture the prediction that the second decade will prove more significant than the third, in which we now live, even though the changes occurring in this third decade are far-reaching enough.

At the end of the first decade there was fairly general understanding among statesmen that major war must be avoided at almost all costs. Notice I do not specify thermonuclear war but simply major war between powers possessing large nuclear capabilities, because no one is entitled to have, and practicing statesmen seem not to have ever had, any abiding faith in our abilities to control or avoid escalation from nonnuclear to nuclear war between such powers. We might observe, however, that at the end of this first decade the ideas were already developing that were subsequently to constitute a theory of limited war, the existence of which has in itself had enormous political consequences—including on the negative side, I regret to say, helping to get the United States involved in the Vietnam war.

At the end of the second decade the most important achieved realization was that the balance of terror was really not delicate, that is, that the expectation of being able to make a surprise attack against the major opponent with near-impunity was most unlikely ever to be entertained by leaders of either of the super-powers. This second decade, embracing the shift from fission to fusion weapons, included also great developments in ballistic missiles of all ranges, and vast increases in the stockpiles of all nuclear weapons and their delivery systems. As it happened, missiles lent themselves to passive protection and to concealment in a way that aircraft did not—or at least appeared not to among those responsible for operating them. The result of this latter change was enormously to reduce the fear of surprise attack, a fear which persisted halfway through the second decade of the nuclear era and which was in itself by far the single most important factor that would have made for swift escalation to nuclear war in the event of a really serious break in the peace between the superpowers. The dominant military concern for those powers in the earlier period was with getting one's own delivery vehicles moving in time in order to avoid their being destroyed on the ground. The coming of underground silos and *Polaris* submarines greatly reduced that anxiety, though this reduction of fear was also vitally assisted by various political and psychological influences, including simply the experience of having lived for years under a regime of strong mutual deterrence—during which process one may also get to know the enemy much better and to fear him less.

For reasons I have already hinted at, I am not able to be seriously disturbed by such new technologies as MIRV or as Ballistic Missile Defence (BMD). The latter in its present American form we call the *Sentinel* system. MIRV has been called potentially destabilizing because it tends to alter in favour of the attacker the cost in offensive missiles of destroying retaliatory missiles—that is, it seems to put "surprise attack" back in business. From the strictly technological side, I should expect that if the individual components of the MIRV system acquire the accuracy they will need to make them a real threat to heavily hardened retaliatory missiles, there will be some options open to the defender which will enable him to restore some large measure of his defensive integrity—assuming he moves not altogether too laggardly with the times.

Much more to the point, the patterns of thought and of emotional response with which governments have become imbued as a result of living with nuclear deterrence are undoubtedly capable of surviving very large perturbations in the style of the weaponry which originally induced them. The frequent use of the phrase "unacceptable damage" conceals the fact that no one knows what the phrase means quantitatively to anyone, and no one will know, for almost any phase of nuclear technology henceforward, just how limited the attacks upon oneself can be made to be. So far the trend in potential destructiveness has steadily gone up, and only a most drastic reversal would really be meaningful. Under such circumstances, it will continue to require a very great deal of motivation for one great nation to think of attempting to destroy another. An enemy one has lived with a long time has after all proved that it is possible and perhaps not even seriously inconvenient to live with him. The Chinese seem not to fear and have no real reason to fear preventive action by the United States, whose nuclear superiority is not only wholly commanding but, unlike the situation *vis-à-vis* the Soviet Union prior to 1950, expressed also in huge capabilities.

I do not expect that we should ever be indifferent to changes which might threaten sharply to reduce the retaliatory capability of American nuclear power against our major opponent or opponents. However, I do expect that if such changes should appear to impend, our threshold of panic would remain rather high—partly, I suppose, but only partly, because we would expect an alert and provident defence organization to be anticipating these changes by appropriate technological measures. Since 1945 the United States' record in this respect, though flawed, is not one of neglect. If, however, such anticipation failed to bring the retaliation factor quite back to its previous high level, I should expect the defence communities on both sides to become quickly adjusted to being adequately deterred with other patterns of potential attack and response. That awful phrase "assured destruction" will inevitably still count for a lot in a world which will have more nuclear weapons in it than already exist today.

Similarly, the BMD has been accorded vast potentiality for both good and evil, but it seems to me likely to be enough limited in its future technical effectiveness as to have little consequence other than adding huge additional expense to the weaponry systems that accomplish nuclear deterrence. U.S. Senator Frank Church has been quoted somewhere as having called it potentially the most expensive sieve in history. An article in the March 1968 edition of *Scientific American* by Dr. Richard L. Garwin and the enormously respected Dr. Hans A. Bethe (reprinted in the August 1968 issue of *Survival*) describes some of the ways in which the system can be defeated. Perhaps it has shaken some in the American defence community whose high expectations of the *Sentinel* system seemed to me at the very least one-sided. The story of how that confidence became so inflated in the first place is itself interesting and significant, and is unfortunately the kind of story that rarely gets properly told in print. To do it requires someone with the requisite exposure, the necessary freedom, and the appropriate talent for interpreting and describing human behaviour in a technological environment. Professor R. V. Jones of Aberdeen University is one of the few who have enjoyed such a combination of opportunities and abilities.

I have myself seen only the outer edges of the BMD enthusiasm, and all I can bear witness to is the fact that people who have access to the classified information needed to make a rounded evaluation of the system are by no means immune to highly subjective judgments. Many tend to be particularly prone to a desire to see put in service highly sophisticated and novel weaponry mostly because they have been working on it for a long time. I might add that Drs. Garwin and Bethe are particularly merciless about the proposal for a so-called "thin" BMD defence against China, as is also Dr. Donald G. Brennan, who unlike Garwin and Bethe, strongly advocates a *large* BMD system.

I will not pretend to know much more than is in the public domain about the *Sentinel* system. I will only say that the arguments made for that deployment, and especially for the thin defence against China only, seem to me to be transparently full of flaws both in logic and in the reliability of the applied data. They certainly do not take into account the vital points made by Garwin and Bethe, as well as others. The simple fact that the *Spartan* exo-atmospheric missile alone will cost between one and two million dollars each, and is easily confused by decoys, is enough to suggest to me that although the case for deploying it *may* be substantial, it can hardly be overwhelming in technical terms alone, even before some negative political considerations are taken into account. Of course, the presently available BMD system will improve, especially if we avoid or postpone as long as possible that deployment which tends to freeze designs, but so will the means of defeating it.

Both MIRV and BMD represent an extraordinarily high degree of technological sophistication but, as I have already suggested, they do not compare with the original A-bomb in their effects on the whole pattern of deterrence. Their appearance stems from and in turn induces a good deal of costly competition—possibly avoidable in part by international agreement, tacit or formal. Also, because of their effects on the total costs of nuclear capabilities, they will tend, when and if deployed, to maintain the exclusiveness of the super-power club.

That last observation suggests, however, a contrary idea which is possibly worthy of being called a second "major point." We have become accustomed, largely through the thinking fashioned over a long period of American denunciation of French nuclear ambitions, to conceiving of very high thresholds of expense below which it makes no sense to have or to aspire to a nuclear capability.

A very few nuclear weapons, perhaps even one, in the hands of either Israel or the UAR could be of very great significance in the Middle East, even though deliverable only by fighter aircraft. The effects of possession by one side or the other would not be symmetrical, and mutual possession would have still different and possibly even favourable effects, though I should certainly not have enough confidence in the possibility to want to see it tried out in practice.

Still on the subject of meaningful thresholds of nuclear power: I admit to finding it somewhat difficult in my own thinking to find a convincing utility for the French nuclear effort on its present scale of activity, but I might find it at least as difficult to justify those additional conventional military forces that could be purchased and maintained with the same money. One of the common fallacies of our time is that nuclear forces are inevitably expensive and conventional forces are by comparison cheap. It certainly matters how much and what kind of each one is talking about. Well-equipped ground divisions or naval forces are certainly not cheap, and the one sure thing President de Gaulle could accomplish by sacrificing his nuclear power to buy more divisions is please the Americans —which is clearly not his main endeavour in life. Anyway, he would not get many more divisions.

The same people who have made the most of that alleged threshold have often expressed a fear of proliferation —I think appropriately, though somewhat inconsistently. Some of them have also displayed a fear of the Chinese nuclear capability which seems to me to be entirely disproportionate to the true menace of that capability, and which is anyway entirely inconsistent with their arguments about the nullity of French nuclear power. The reasoning which shows the French being shatteringly overwhelmed if they dare raise the threat of their nuclear power against the Soviet Union, not to mention the United States, which figures in the "all azimuths" plan, described by General Ailleret before his untimely death, applies just as cogently to the case of China. Nevertheless, China's potential for mischief is for some reason—somewhat obscure so far as the manifest argument goes—supposed to be sufficient to warrant the construction of the thin missile defence referred to above.

We notice here a certain disorderliness of thinking that goes on above those levels which all would agree are appropriate for the application of cost-effectiveness or systems analysis. What was the basis for justifying the projection of the thin BMD system partly on the ground that China was a less *responsible* adversary than the Soviet Union so far as concerned the use of military force? On what evidence and whose expert analysis was this finding based? Political judgments of such character and importance can be carefully weighed and evaluated by persons of the appropriate political expertise and sensitivity, but the patterns for doing so systematically seem not yet to be established in government practice. The Chinese have said and done many foolish things, but where have they shown the tendency to mad abandon in their use of military force beyond their frontiers which is presupposed by those who advocate the thin defence—the justification of which must also presuppose a form of Chinese nuclear missile attack that is technologically primitive, i.e. *sans* decoys. At least one student of Chinese affairs has, apparently without major dispute from colleagues in his field, cogently argued the case that the Chinese Communists have always shown appropriate circumspection and indeed caution in the external use of military power.[3]

None of this would matter very much if the thin BMD defence would really stay as thin and as cheap as some of its advocates claim, but if the recent restatement by Mr. Clifford of Mr. McNamara's proposal and the Senate support thereof do not actually prod the Russians into the appropriate arms-control agreement—which the Russian response to the Senate's voting the funds gives us some reason to hope it may—then there are several reasons for predicting with relatively high confidence that the thin defence would soon become a thick and enormously expensive one, and that it would probably have mischievous political consequences as well.

III

My third major point concerns a phenomenon, related to the one just discussed, which is very well-known but is very far from being well understood. We have witnessed, for what is surely the first time in history, a huge development and growth of outlandishly powerful weapons systems which are sealed off from use but not yet from utility. How much are they really sealed off from possible use? What utility do they nevertheless continue to have? When provided in the lavish manner in which they are provided and developed in the United States, strategic nuclear forces are exceedingly costly. If we should add a large anti-missile defence to our existing anti-bomber defence and retain our offensive nuclear capabilities in anything like the configuration that they have today, the cost of maintaining both the offensive and defensive sides of the strategic nuclear capability in the United States may come to approximate what we are currently spending each year on the Vietnam war. We could bear it, but who should want to?

I have been writing so far only of strategic capabilities, but we also have tactical nuclear capabilities which, according to official reports, are already large and still growing and which appear to be sealed off from use to only a slightly lesser degree than the strategic nuclear weaponry. Everyone, of course, agrees that for the United States huge expenditures on these tremendous and all-too-powerful forces are indispensable. The debate of some few years ago on the question of minimum or finite deterrence seems to have petered out—or rather to have been replaced by a debate on the question of whether it is really necessary or even meaningfully advantageous to maintain a substantial numerical superiority over the Soviet Union if that country should choose to challenge our existing superiority, as she appears to have been doing of late. The jargon of debate has given us such barbaric terms as "overkill," "assured destruction," and several similar unappetizing word figures. On the whole, however, I would submit that on these issues there has been much dogmatism but little searching inquiry. How much are all these weapons systems really sealed off from use in war, and under what situations might they become unsealed? Almost everyone seems to be agreed that the cement should be very strong indeed, but should it mean effectively a promise of non-use under almost any circumstances? If so, the utility of these systems-in-being will inevitably be much diminished, and that utility is presently high. They make major war between the super-powers and between their respective alliance systems certainly much less likely than without them and perhaps critically so.

The vital question, however, is: how much utility have these capabilities exerted in deterring much lesser conflicts? This is the area in which I feel we have sustained a real failure in our efforts to understand the issues. All the diplomatic pressure by the United States on her allies since 1961 to build up their conventional forces, slackened within the last two or three years only because the allies refused to heed these admonitions and demands (and recently resumed, or rather exhumed, in the wake of the Czechoslovakian misfortune) has been based on the assumption that our large nuclear capabilities had inadequate utility in deterring less than major wars and were not even proof against the occurrence of major wars on the conventional level. Much of this pressure was not simply an attempt to interpret probabilities but rather to strengthen that cement which would keep nuclear capabilities totally and completely out of use. Many relevant propositions have been urged simply as articles of faith, with a minimum of hard, cold analysis. A simple and familiar example will serve to clarify my meaning. What was essentially a leading question was often put in the form: Suppose the Russians and their allies make a massive attack on Western Europe without using nuclear weapons? This was presumed to be enough to justify building up large conventional forces. Hardly anyone, however, asked and then proceeded to work on the quite researchable question: is it at all possible for the Russians to think of doing such a thing in the face of American and allied forces possessing huge nuclear capabilities?

To be sure, analyses in areas of this kind do not yield hard and fast figures, which can be neatly portrayed in graphs on charts. Those who produced numbers on charts have enjoyed a better hearing in recent years than those who were merely reflective and who asked relevant and penetrating questions. My friend and former colleague at RAND, Dr. Amrom Katz, has said that the trouble with charts is that one can present only data on them, usually in the form of numbers, and that therefore the motivation to produce charts tends to become an incentive to gather data because of their availability rather than because of their relevance.[4]

Thus, while we have relatively rigorous and disciplined thinking at the mostly tactical levels at which systems analysis is applicable, the tolerance for sloppy thinking appears to be at least as great as ever the moment we spill over into those areas of inquiry where systems analysis, by common agreement among the best practitioners of the art (e.g., Charles J. Hitch), has no real applicability. As it happens, these are the areas where we find all the really tough and important strategic and political questions. I am assuredly not suggesting that the questions that the new quantitative techniques help to solve are not important, I am suggesting rather that generally they prove to be of much less importance than the questions which normally are answered out of the simplest kind of intuition and bias. The point would not be worth making except that I do happen to believe that a great deal more rigour *is* possible in what are significantly enough often called the "soft" areas.

To be sure, the appearance of a new problem—and the questions of choice which arose following World War II with respect to new weapons systems had the dimensions of an historically new problem—had a greatly stimulating effect in producing a new kind of skill. People who had the requisite training for developing into systems analysts might not have become interested in strategic questions at all if these new problems, and the research institutions for solving them, had not come forward. On the other hand, a prestige factor has been involved, and what should have been supplementary talent tended in fact to become pre-emptive of the field of strategic study. Under the seven critical years of the regime of Mr. McNamara, something like the effect I am describing took place in the United States.

The demands for figures, and for new ways of using computers, are relatively easily met. I understand that something called music is now being composed by computers. No doubt I should try to hear some before passing judgment on it, but I always have felt that both the composing of and the listening to music were a deeply personal kind of communication. The fact that machines have now intruded into this process suggests to me only that it has become extremely fashionable to find new and additional ways—the farther out the better—of exercising these machines. One is always interested in useful work, but not in make-work projects.

NOTES

1. Bernard Brodie, *Sea Power in the Machine Age,* Princeton: 1941.

2. It is, of course, now well-known that the Nagasaki bomb was the same (implosion-type) as that tested at Alamagordo and that the Hiroshima bomb was different, but for the purposes of this paper the difference is inconsequential.

3. David P. Mozingo, "Containment in Asia," *World Politics,* April 1967, pp. 361–377. Reprinted in *Survival,* July 1967.

4. Amrom H. Katz, "The Short Run and the Long Walk," *Air Force,* June 1967.

Principles and Procedures of
Systems Analysis

E. S. QUADE

INTRODUCTION

The RAND Corporation has produced analyses of national security problems for quite a number of years—in fact, since World War II. Although collectively we have learned a great deal that should be useful to anyone attempting to analyze such problems, we have not yet learned enough to supply a sequence of steps or rules that, if followed mechanically—by the numbers, so to speak—would automatically guarantee solutions that will stand the tests of time. In the main, this so because military systems analysis is to some extent still an art—or at least a craft—rather than a form of engineering or an exact science. It is not, like statistics or physical chemistry, say, a body of knowledge and skills that can be acquired largely without becoming involved in particular applications.

Now, of course, some techniques of an art—even some of the most important ones—can be taught, but not by means of fixed rules which need only be followed exactly. Thus, in our analyses, we must sometimes do things that we think are right but cannot really justify or even check in the output of the work. We must accept many subjective judgments as inputs, and we must present answers based partly on judgment to be used as a basis for other judgments. Hence, a discussion of "how systems analysis is done" must content itself with indicating some guidelines, some principles, and some illustrative examples.

THE ESSENCE OF SYSTEMS ANALYSIS

If systems analysis is largely "art" and "judgment," what does the "analysis" contribute? . . . [T]o a large extent systems analysis is successful in areas where there is no accepted theoretical foundation (defense planning is an example), precisely because it is able to make a more systematic and efficient use of expert judgment than can its alternatives. The essence of the method is to construct and operate within a model—an idealization of the situation appropriate to the problem. Such a model . . . introduces a precise structure and terminology that serve primarily as a means of communication. As such, it enables the participants to make their judgments concretely, and, through feedback—which, in the previous example, would be the outcomes predicted by the planning factors—it helps the analysts, the experts, and the decisionmakers to arrive at a clearer understanding of both the problem and its context.

To keep the discussion from be-

From *Systems Analysis and Policy Planning: Applications in Defense,* edited by E. S. Quade and W. I. Boucher. Copyright © 1968 by the RAND Corp. Reprinted by permission of the RAND Corp. and American Elsevier Publishing Co.

coming too abstract, we will attempt to illustrate the points we intend to make by reference to the following hypothetical example:

Suppose a new, lighter-payload missile system is being advocated to replace or supplement the Minuteman. It would make use of the Minuteman silos and other ground facilities. Supporters claim that it will be more reliable and much more accurate and that these advantages far outweigh its somewhat higher cost and lower payload. Assume also that although development is advanced, several variants are possible, and that a decision should be made soon whether or not to freeze the design and plan procurement.

How can we proceed with an analysis to provide advice on this decision?

THE ALTERNATIVES

Before we answer this question, we might examine briefly the alternative sources of such advice. One of the most common, unfortunately, is pure intuition. It is in no sense analytic, since no effort is made to structure the problem or to establish cause and effect relationships and operate on them to arrive at a solution. The intuitive process is to learn everything possible about the problem, to "live with it," and to let the subconscious provide the solution. Someone using this method does not feel any obligation to show how he arrived at the solution.

Between pure intuition, on the one hand, and systems analysis, on the other, there are other sources of advice that can, in a sense, be considered analytic, although the analysis is ordinarily less systematic, explicit, and quantitative. One alternative is simply to ask an expert for his opinion. What he says can, in fact, be very helpful, if it results from a reasonable and impartial examination of the facts, with due allowance for uncertainty, and if his assumptions and chain of logic are made *explicit,* so that others can use his information to form their own considered opinion. But an expert, particularly an unbiased expert, may be hard to find. National security problems—even those like our example, which is one of the simpler types—are complex and what should be done depends on many widely different disciplines. An expert's knowledge and opinions are likely to be more valuable if they can be formulated in direct association with other experts. This suggests systems analysis, for, as remarked above, that approach, with its models and feedback, is essentially a device for providing a framework for the systematic and efficient employment of the knowledge, judgment, and intuition of the available experts.

Another way of handling a problem is to turn it over to a committee. Now, although there is no reason why a committee cannot engage in systematic analysis, this is not likely to happen. Committees are much less likely than experts to make their reasoning explicit, since their findings are usually obtained by bargaining—by the effort to reach a consensus or an acceptable compromise. How this effort can affect originality, precision, and efficiency hardly need be mentioned. This is not to say that a look by a "blue ribbon" committee into our missile problem might not be useful, but its greatest utility is likely to be in the critique of work done by others.

Answers obtained from experts working individually or as a committee depend largely on subjective judgment. *So do the answers obtained from systems analysis.* As one writer has put it:

Subjectivity is inherent because of the essential content of political values in public policy questions. Public policy by definition pertains to human conduct—the behavior and relations among men in political society. Because of its human impact pub-lic policy—and strategy in particular—can-not be free of questions of political value and hence cannot be decided except through the exercise of human judgment. The ingredient of human judgment—be it only the simplest kind of intuition—is there-fore an essential part of any study of policy, no matter how analytical. Judgment can be aided and augmented by the techniques of scientific analysis, but it can never be supplanted.[1]

But the analytic approach, in contrast to its alternatives, provides its answers by processes that are accessible to crit-ical examination and can be retraced by others, who can modify them more or less readily on the basis of their own judgments as errors appear or as new information becomes available.

However, no matter whether the advice is supplied by an expert, a com-mittee, or a formal study group, an *analysis* of a problem of choice involves . . . the objectives; the alternatives for attaining them; the costs, or what we must give up; the models, which allow us to see the costs of the alternatives and the extent to which they attain the objectives; and finally, the criteria, which tell us what alternatives to choose.

We now turn to the process by which these elements are identified and the analysis carried out.

THE PROCESS OF ANALYSIS

The process of systems analysis represents a conscious attempt to ex-tend the approach and methods—and, ideally, the standards—of the "hard" sciences into areas where controlled experimentation is seldom possible. Unfortunately, some people have ex-aggerated the significance or success of this attempt, and we find them saying such things as that systems analysis and operations research are really nothing more than the "scientific method" ex-tended to problems outside the realm of pure science. Leaving aside the question whether there is anything that might be called *the* scientific method, what such statements must mean, in part, is that the analysis advances (by iteration or successive approximation) through something like the following stages:

FORMULATION (The Conceptual Phase)	Clarifying the objectives, de-fining the issues of concern, limiting the problem.
SEARCH (The Research Phase)	Looking for data and rela-tionships, as well as alterna-tive programs of action that have some chance of solving the problem.
EVALUATION (The Analytic Phase)	Building various models, using them to predict the consequences that are likely to follow from each choice of alternatives, and then com-paring the alternatives in terms of these consequences.
INTERPRETATION (The Judgmental Phase)	Using the predictions ob-tained from the models and whatever other information or insight is relevant to com-pare the alternatives further, derive conclusions about them, and indicate a course of action.
VERIFICATION (The Scientific Phase)	Testing the conclusions by experiment.

All analyses involve these five ac-tivities to some extent, but often the fourth is done largely by the policy-maker and the last must be done in-directly, if at all. There is a class of problems—our missile comparison is an example—in which verification may be possible in principle, but the costs of an actual test would certainly be too high. Thus, if we want to estimate what damage our missiles might do to the Soviet Union, the best we can do is use simulation to devise a vicarious experiment.

The process of analysis may be represented as in Fig. 1. Here the ac-tivities appear neatly separated. This is seldom the case, however, for to one degree or another they all occur simultaneously. In our missile comparison, for example, the prescription for carrying out the work might run as follows:

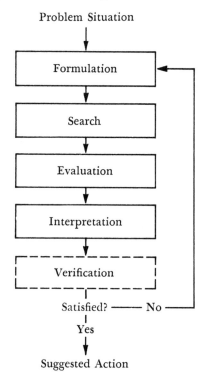

Fig. 1. Activities in Analysis.

1. Define and limit the problem. Are we helping to make a force posture decision or is the decision really only one of whether or not to continue a promising development?

2. Classify the objectives or goals that one hopes to attain with the system being considered. Are we striving for deterrence to prevent a nuclear attack on the United States or are we striving for an even more comprehensive deterrent?

3. Forecast the political and military environment in which the systems are to operate. Do we need to consider scenarios in which the war starts as a result of the degeneration of a crisis situation, or deliberate escalation, or, as is often done, solely an attack "from out of the blue"?

4. Determine ways to measure the degree of attainment of the goals or objectives. This requires us to identify the mission to be assigned the missiles.

5. List and define the alternative systems that offer some reasonable hope of accomplishing the objectives, and select appropriate criteria for choosing among these systems.

6. Choose the approach. Shall we compare the systems for a fixed budget or shall we first fix the mission requirement? Do we start with a computer model or a manual war game?

7. Formulate a scheme for working out the dollar costs that takes account of changes in operating philosophy and development time. Explore the nonmonetary costs. Are there significant resource restraints or are there undesirable side effects that interfere with programs?

8. Examine the risks and timing in the development. Are we seeking to advance the state-of-the-art or merely to improve current capabilities?

9. Compare the systems. Do the important differences stem from unresolvable uncertainties about the future state of the world, or are they matters of engineering?

10. Perform sensitivity analyses by varying key parameters across a range of values, to see that major uncertainties are thoroughly explored.

11. Consider the factors that we have so far not taken into account, and test them against various assumptions where we think we have some knowledge of what the outcome should be.

12. Decide what we can really recommend on the basis of the analyses.

13. Document our work. This should include the rationale and assumptions, more than a mere summary.

Some of these steps are clearly part of problem formulation, others belong in the domain of the comparison, and still others might be classified as part of the interpretation stage. The search stage, as is typically the case, permeates the whole process and is especially difficult to isolate as a separate activity. If, however, we stand back from the clutter of the real world, there are several points we can usefully make about the process of analysis as it appears in each of the activities named in Fig. 1. Let us take them in turn, beginning with "Formulation."

FORMULATION

Formulation implies an attempt to isolate the questions or issues involved, to fix the context within which these issues are to be resolved, to clarify the objectives, to discover the variables that are operative, and to state relationships among them. These relationships may be extremely hypothetical if empirical knowledge is in short supply, but they will help make the logical structure of the analysis clear. In a sense, formulation is the most important stage, for the effort spent restating the problem in different ways or redefining it clarifies whether or not it is spurious or trivial and points the way to its solution.

The process of formulation is highly subjective. We must, for example, consider what evidence will be meaningful and significant to the decisionmaker we are trying to help. Thus, in our missile comparison, will it be sufficient to compare the new missile with the Minuteman alone, or must other missiles or even manned bombers be considered? Will it be adequate to make the comparisons in a U.S. second strike situation? Greater reliability and accuracy may show to more advantage in wars initiating in other ways. Are we helping to make a force posture decision or should we really only be trying to demonstrate that we have a promising development that should be continued for its growth potential alone?

The tendency all too frequently is to accept the client's original statement of what is wanted, and then to set about building a model and gathering information, scarcely giving a thought to whether the problem is the right problem or how the answer will contribute to the decisions which it is meant to assist. In fact, because the concern is with the future, the major job may be to decide what the policy-maker should want to do. Since systems studies have resulted in rather important changes, not only in how the policy-maker carries out his activity, but in the objectives themselves, it would be self-defeating to accept without inquiry the customer's or sponsor's view of what the problem is.

But how is the analyst to know that his formulation of the problem is superior? *His only possible advantage lies in analysis.* That is, the process of problem formulation itself has to be the subject of analysis. What this means is that, using the few facts and relationships that are known at this early stage and assuming others, the analyst must simply make an attempt to solve the problem. It is this attempt that will give him a basis for better formulation. He always has some idea as to the possible solutions of the problem; otherwise, he probably should not be working on it, for his analysis might prove to be too formal and abstract.

Let us consider a classic example. For fiscal year 1952, Congress authorized approximately $3.5 billion for air base construction, about half to be spent overseas. RAND was asked to suggest ways to acquire, construct, and maintain air bases in foreign countries at minimum cost. The analyst who reluctantly took on this problem regarded it at first as essentially one of logistics. He spent a long time—several months, in fact—thinking about it before he organized a study team. Although he had little of the information needed to make recommendations, he was able to see the problem in relation to the Air Force as a whole. He came to the conclusion that the real problem was *not* one of the logistics of foreign air bases, but the much broader one of *where and how to base the nation's strategic air forces and how to operate them in conjunction with the base system chosen.* He argued that base choice would critically affect the composition, destructive power, and cost of the entire strategic force and thus that it was not wise to rest a decision about base structure and location merely on economy in base cost alone. His views prevailed and he led the broader study, the results of which contributed to an Air Force decision to base SAC bombers in the continental United States and use overseas installations only for refueling and restaging.[2] An Air Force committee later estimated that the study recommendations saved over $1 billion in construction costs alone. In addition, it sparked a tremendous improvement in strategic capability, particularly with regard to survival, and stimulated a good deal of additional research on related questions.

In analysis, the problem never remains static. Interplay between a growing understanding of what it involves now and might involve in the future forces a constant redefinition. Thus, the study just mentioned, originally conceived as an exercise to reduce costs, became in the end a study of U.S. strategic deterrent policy. Its recommendations led to a major reduction in SAC vulnerability; that costs were also reduced was secondary.

Primarily as the result of discussion and intuition, the original effort to state a problem should suggest one or more possible solutions or hypotheses. As the study progresses, these original ideas are enriched and elaborated upon—or discarded—and new ideas are found. The process of analysis is an *iterative* one. Each hypothesis serves as a guide to later work—it tells us what we are looking for while we are looking. As a result, the final statement of the conclusions and recommendations usually rests on a knowledge of facts about the problem which the analyst did not have at the start. In the early stages it is not a mistake to hold an idea as to the solution; the error is to refuse to abandon such an idea in the face of mounting evidence.

It is important to recognize that anything going on in one part of an activity, organization, or weapon system is likely to affect what goes on in every other part. The natural inclination in problem-solving is to select a part of the problem and analyze it separately, or to reduce the problem to one that looks manageable. "Many scientists owe their greatness not to their skill in solving problems but to their wisdom in choosing them."[3] Systems analysis, however, does not offer us this freedom, at least not at the outset. We have to solve the problem that exists. It calls for us to extend the boundaries of the problem as far as required, determine which interdependencies are significant, and then evaluate their combined impact.

But even for small-scale problems, the number of factors under consideration at any one time must be reduced until what is left is manageable. In systems analysis, the complexity of the full problem frequently far outruns analytic competence. To consider in detail anything like the complete range of possible alternative ways to deliver weapons on strategic targets may be impossible. The use of suitcases or automobiles as delivery systems does not belong in our missile comparison. Fortunately, the vast majority of alternatives will be obviously inferior, and can be left out without harm. The danger is that some alternative better than the one ultimately uncovered by the analysis might be left out. Thus, although constraints must usually be imposed to reduce the number of alternatives to be examined, this should be done by preliminary analysis, not by arbitrary decree. Moreover, such constraints should be flexible, so that they may be weakened or removed if it appears in later cycles that their presence is a controlling factor. In analyzing our missile system, for example, we do not simultaneously seek to determine the ideal ground support weapon for the Tactical Air Command or the ratio of medical corpsmen to cooks in the base support battalion. We call such a restriction of the problem a "suboptimization."

The necessity for suboptimization compounds the difficulties in the selection of criteria and objectives. It is inevitable that not all decisions can be made at the highest level or by one individual or group; some must be delegated to others. Analysts and decisionmakers must thus always consider actions that pertain to only a part of the military problem. Other choices are set aside temporarily, possible decisions about some things being neglected and specific decisions about others being taken for granted. What is crucial is that the criteria and objectives for the suboptimization be consistent with those that would apply to the full problem.

*   *   *

It is commonly supposed that goals should, and can, be set independently of the plans to attain them. Yet there is considerable evidence that operationally significant objectives are, more often than not, the result of opportunities that possible alternatives offer rather than a source of such alternatives. For one thing, it is impossible to select satisfactory objectives without some idea of the cost and difficulty of attaining them. Such information can only come as part of the analysis itself. For another, only some of the possible consequences of different alternatives can be anticipated before the analysis. The newly discovered consequences may then become goals. Thus, for example, the invention of a near-perfect system for continuous peacetime strategic reconnaissance might, in some circumstances, make a first strike to disarm the enemy an objective worth considering.

In fact, a characteristic of systems analysis is that solutions are often found in a set of compromises which seek to balance and, where possible, to reconcile conflicting objectives and questions of value. It is more important to choose the "right" objective than it is to make the "right" choice between alternatives. The choice of the wrong alternative may merely mean that something less than the "best" system is being chosen. Since we must frequently be satisfied with at most a demonstration that a suggested action is "in the right direction," this may not be tragic. For, as we shall see, such a demonstration may be the best that can be done anyway. But the wrong objective means that the wrong problem is being solved.

The choice of the objective must be consistent with higher, or national, objectives. Since these are seldom operationally defined, however, the analyst has a great responsibility to exercise care and good judgment. In our missile comparison, for instance, if we choose as an objective one that puts a great premium on keeping collateral damage and civilian casualties low, we bias the analysis toward the more accurate missile. Since in the example we are attempting to determine whether or not to replace a current capability with a more accurate one, we should select deterrence as our objective, measuring it proximately by the total mortalities inflicted, for accuracy is not so significant here. We then can argue *a fortiori* that if the lighter payload shows up better given this objective, then the case for it is all the stronger.

At some stage we must decide on a specific approach to the problem. The essence of the questions with which systems analysis is concerned is uncertainty, not only about economic, technical, and operational parameters—which can be serious but are to a large extent under our control and somehow appear limited—but also about future environments or contingencies. It is almost impossible to forecast what these might be, let alone to predict what an enemy might do about them. Hence, except in very narrowly defined problems, we must look for an approach to the analysis which offers a hope of producing something constructive in spite of the great uncertainties.

A point of view that has evolved from bitter experience runs something like the following. An attempt to determine a sharp optimum or the unique best solution in a problem having largely indeterminate parameters, some subject to enemy influence, is probably doomed to failure. The goal instead should be to find and recommend a system that is close to the optimum for the expected circumstances, but, at the same time, is to a large degree insensitive to many uncertainties—specifically, a system that might work well under many widely divergent contingencies and could even give some sort of reasonably satisfactory performance under unexpected and thus possibly catastrophic circumstances. This characteristic is probably what the military man intends when he speaks of "flexibility."

It is helpful here to recall that the primary purpose of systems analysis is to advise a decisionmaker, help answer his questions, sharpen his intuition, and broaden his basis for judgment. In practically no case should we expect to "prove" to the decisionmaker that a particular course of action is uniquely best. The really significant problems are just too difficult and there are too many considerations that cannot be handled quantitatively. If we insist on a strictly quantitative treatment, we are likely to end with such a simplified model that the results will be almost meaningless, or arrive too late to be useful to the decisionmaker.

These observations suggest two rules of thumb:

1. Throughout the inquiry, it is well to look for *gross* differences in relative costs and effectiveness among the alternatives and, specifically, for differences of the sort that have a chance of surviving many likely resolutions of the various uncertainties and intangibles. Thus, in comparing future systems, the question to address is which systems have a *clear* advantage, rather than that of precisely how much better one is than another. Something of this attitude no doubt underlies a motto of the Systems Analysis Office in the Office of the Secretary of Defense: "It is better to be roughly right than exactly wrong."[4]

2. All comparisons should be made with the uncertainties in mind. A choice between missile systems, therefore, must depend on a careful investigation of a wide range of enemy offensive and defensive capabilities. But this is not enough. When, as in our example, a proximate criterion must be used —the capability of the force to inflict mortalities being supposed to substitute for deterrence—the effort must be made to test with criteria other than the one used for preliminary screening. Moreover, the performance of the alternatives must be considered under a variety of contingencies that involve major changes in the environment— those due, say, to political acts or actions that depend on human caprice.

SEARCH

The search phase is concerned with finding both the alternatives and the data, or evidence, on which the analysis is to be based. It is as important to look for new alternatives (and evidence to support them) as it is to look for ways to compare them. Obviously, if we have no alternatives or no ideas about them, there is nothing to analyze or to choose between. If in the end we are to designate a preferred course of action, we must have discovered earlier that such a course exists.

In military analysis, many facts are hard to come by. The actual operational performance of future missiles in combat, for instance, cannot be predicted with any great degree of certainty by purely theoretical studies. Nor, for that matter, is it very likely that an individual systems analyst modeling a weapon system will be thoroughly familiar with all the aspects of the system and its environment. For these reasons, systems analysis must depend a good deal more on informed judgment than do most types of engineering. The analyst must be assisted by others, civilian as well as military, and depend on their judgment, not only for facts, but for opinions about the facts. Of course, it may not always be possible to recommend a course of action even when the facts are known, but it is a knowledge of them which makes a solution possible.

One aspect of the search stage that will be emphasized . . . is the role of component or supporting studies—scientific, engineering, and cost—in systems analysis. A sensible answer to broad questions obviously requires a great many facts at hand, and these supporting studies are designed to provide them. Thus, in our example, the feasibility of the alternative missiles, or the range of force postures in which they might be imbedded, may hinge primarily on discovering the trade-offs between such engineering parameters as range, payload, and accuracy and how these affect the cost, effectiveness, and availability of the missiles. It is here that most of the man-hours invested in a study must go. As a result, it is largely the technical competence found in his associates in engineering and science that may account for an analyst's successes. Certainly, this is the case at RAND. One might get the idea . . . that systems analysis is done mainly by men with their feet on a desk, men once described as "pipe-smoking, tree-full-of-owls types." And this may sometimes be the case; but typically it takes a lot of detailed individual research, conferences, and traveling by engineers, cost analysts, economists, political scientists, operations analysts, and other specialists to produce an analysis that makes a useful contribution.

The search for data can, of course, be endless, since in principle the uncertainties of most planning problems can never be completely eliminated. When should the theoretical analysis begin? What proportion of effort should be devoted to empirical research? D. M. Fort offers these suggestions:

> . . . the proper balance between theoretical analysis and fact-gathering depends on the problem. It is important, of course, to get the facts on the proper subject; a preliminary theoretical analysis can be very useful to this end, in pointing out what information is lacking and most needed. Much effort can be and often is wasted gathering the wrong data, for failure to do the necessary theoretical homework first. On the other hand, much effort is also wasted applying sophisticated analytical techniques to inadequate data, trying to make silk purses out of sows' ears. Physical experiments and data gathering in general are expensive; making plans and decisions in the face of uncertainty, even if aided by the best possible systems analysis, can also be very expensive. A proper balance may well call for much more emphasis on fact-gathering than has been customary.[5]

Expert opinion must be called upon when it is necessary to use numerical data or assumptions that cannot be based on theory or experience —when, say, we want to obtain something like an estimate of the guidance accuracy of our new missile in the presence of counter-measures that have been conceived in theory but have not yet been developed. . . .

EVALUATION

In order to choose among alternatives, a way to estimate or predict the various consequences of their selection must exist. This may be as elementary as calling on the intuition of a single expert, but the more formal process of using a model or a set of models usually leads to better results. The role of the model in systems analysis is to provide a way to obtain cost and performance estimates for each alternative. Sometimes these estimates are obtained from a single over-all model—say, an elaborate computer program which combines into a single computation all the various submodels for determining dollar cost, reliability, lives lost, targets destroyed, and so on. At other times, consequences of different types are obtained separately by a wide variety of processes—gaming, computation, or political analyses.

*   *   *

Consider our example of how to advise a decisionmaker on a substitute for the Minuteman. A typical military systems analysis such as this usually takes one of two forms. In the first, some level of military effectiveness (the objective) is fixed and an attempt is made to determine the alternative which will attain the desired effectiveness at minimum cost. In the second, the budget level is fixed and we seek to maximize effectiveness. Suppose we decide to take this latter approach.

To carry out the analysis, a specifically dated budget must be assumed and, using various models, the forces attainable with that budget must be worked out. This task, which is by no means simple, requires a cost model. In part, this model is constructed by measuring the purchase price not only of the various weapons and vehicles involved, but also of the whole materiel and manpower structure. The costs must take into account the entire system of utilization, extended over a period of time prolonged sufficiently to reflect the important factor of peacetime maintenance. It takes a great deal of research and sophisticated knowledge to cost a system that does not yet exist.

Next, an environment and a mode of war initiation must be specified. Rather than base the analysis on a set of assumptions forced reluctantly from some consultant political scientist, an analytic scenario might be useful. Such a scenario starts with the present state of the world and shows, step by step, how one or more future situations might evolve out of the present one and how, in those situations, war might begin.

To carry on from here, a step-by-step procedure, called the campaign model, is used to work out what the war outcomes might be. Then, finally, some criterion or payoff function is used to weigh the various war outcomes and determine a preference ordering of the alternatives.

This process may break down at almost any stage. Some problems are so ill-structured and the cause and effect relationships so poorly understood that we cannot build a model with any feeling of confidence. When this is so, we cannot work out the consequences of adopting the various strategies or compare outcomes. The alternative is then to use a model which compares the salient characteristics of the possible strategies. This is the "consumers' research" approach, in which experts or "potential users" rate the alternatives. Again, of course, some way is needed to bring the various ratings together—a problem we have already looked at, but not when value judgments were involved. We will consider this in greater detail in a moment, for the same type of difficulty arises even when we can, in one sense or another, compute the outcomes.

It should be emphasized that, for many important problems, we are in fact unable to build really quantitative or even formal models. The most obvious function of a model is "explanatory," to organize our thinking. What counts, therefore, is not whether the model was mathematical or was run on a computer, but rather whether an effort was made to compare alternatives systematically, in terms as quantitative as possible, using a logical sequence of steps that can be retraced and verified by others.

Usually, we can go beyond this

bare minimum, and although we may not be able, at least initially, to abstract the situation to a mathematical model or series of equations, some way can generally be found to represent the consequences that follow from particular choices. Simulation, for example—the process of imitating, without using formal analytic techniques, the essential features of a system or organization and analyzing its behavior by experimenting with the model—can be used to tackle many seemingly unmanageable or previously untouched problems where a traditional analytic formulation is at least initially infeasible. Operational gaming—that is to say, simulation involving role-playing by the participants—is another particularly promising technique, especially when it is desirable to employ several experts with varying specialties for different aspects of the problem. Here the game structure—again a model—furnishes the participants with an artificial, simulated environment within which they can jointly and simultaneously experiment, acquiring through feedback the insights necessary to make successful predictions within the gaming context and thus indirectly about the real world.

Getting back to our example, suppose there is general agreement (highly unlikely!) that the model accurately reflects the real situation and that the calculations are valid. Suppose further that, for a particular set of assumptions (about such things as the way war begins, the strength and disposition of the enemy forces, and so on), the expected or average "war outcomes" as computed by the model are those shown in Table 1.

Of course, many other outcomes might have been computed or estimated from war gaming exercises that took other considerations into account—flexibility, contributions to our limited war capabilities, and so on. But given what we have, how does one decide which alternative to prefer? Fif-

TABLE 1. Hypothetical War Outcomes for Three Alternatives

	Alternatives		
Expected War Outcomes	A	B	C
Number of Enemy Targets Destroyed	80	100	150
Hours to Destroy 50 Enemy Targets	1	2	4
U.S. Lives Lost (millions)	20	25	50
Cost to the Enemy to Cut His Losses by 50 per cent ($ billions)	3	12	180

teen years ago the rule was: Pick the system which destroyed the most targets for the given cost. Today we realize we must be interested in the other outcomes as well—some of which we cannot compute. One unrecommended way to determine a preference a priori is to use a payoff function which takes only the various numerical outcomes into account.[6]

A single decisionmaker would probably operate differently. He need only make up his mind, arguing with himself—thinking, for example:

"C should be chosen. The potential threat it represents means that the probability of war will be reduced practically to zero and the cost to the enemy to counter it will collapse his economy."

Or, alternatively:

"A is best. The primary purpose of these systems is to create a threat of unacceptable damage; 80 targets are as good as 150 for this purpose. C is too threatening; it leaves the enemy no choice but to attack."

In the usual case, there are a number of decisionmakers. The process changes accordingly, for what is needed is a collective judgment from them and the experts on whom they lean for advice.

Whenever possible, of course, this judgment should be "considered" judgment; that is, supplemented by inductive and numerical reasoning and made explicit. But it is judgment nonetheless.

How, then, might we apply group judgment to the problem of choosing one of the systems A, B, and C? We might seek a consensus by using one of several methods that allow us to pool the judgments of experts when faced with factual value uncertainty. The Delphi technique is a possibility. Another is simply to ask each of our decisionmakers or experts to fill in an array such as the one illustrated in Table 2. After the experts had estimated the military worth of the various considerations relevant to the decision—using, say, a number between 0 and 10—we could then work out a numerical measure.[7]

TABLE 2. A Framework for Evaluating Alternatives

Consideration	Rating of Alternatives		
	A	B	C
Targets Destroyed	—	—	—
Time to Destroy 50 Targets	—	—	—
U.S. Lives Lost	—	—	—
Cost to Enemy	—	—	—
Intra-War Deterrence Capability	—	—	—
False Alarm Security	—	—	—
Flexibility	—	—	—
Growth Potential	—	—	—

In addition to uncertainty as to the outcomes as listed in such a table, and moral or value uncertainty as to which combination of outcomes would be preferable, this problem also presents uncertainty as to the state of the world and the actions of the enemy. (This further complicates our problem, for we would have a display such as Table 1 for each contingency.) But even if we went no further than to display systematically the opinions and judgment of a single decisionmaker for his own use, the exercise would be likely to help him. If the quantitative judgments of others are presented along with their arguments, they should be still more valuable, even though we might not make use of feedback to bring the various judgments more nearly to a consensus.

These, then, are some of the general notions the analyst cannot ignore. In a certain sense, specifically in their application to the problem of building models, they can be reduced to two heads: questions involving quantification or the treatment of uncertainty. . . . [W]e may content ourselves here with a simple example that points out what is meant by the explicit treatment of uncertainty. Its problems are, of course, intimately associated with those of quantification.

A farmer must decide what crop or crops to plant without knowing whether the weather will be wet, moderate or dry. An analysis is performed to help him decide. A popular approach is employed in which the analysis is repeated in turn for each of the three distinguishable types of weather, in each case determining the best crop to plant for that type of weather. Considering all possible crops, it is found that for wet weather corn would be best, for moderate weather oats would be best, and for dry weather wheat would be best. The principal results presented to the farmer consist of the findings concerning the best crops in the three types of weather, the best yields achievable in each contingency (i.e., the wet-weather yield of corn, the moderate-weather yield of oats, and the dry-weather yield of wheat), and estimates of the probabilities of wet, moderate and dry weather. The implication is that the farmer ought to make his choice from the "preferred" crops, corn, oats or wheat, or perhaps a combination of these to provide some all-weather insurance.

The farmer is not satisfied with the analysis, however. He points out that the analysis tells him what crop he should plant if he knew for certain what the weather would be, but he doesn't see how this helps him to decide what to plant when he doesn't know what the weather will be, except for the weather probabilities. He would like to know, for example, what will happen if he plants corn and the weather turns out moderate or dry, and similarly for the other crops. The analyst therefore prepares a two-way contingency table, showing for each of the three "preferred" crops the yields in wet, moderate and dry weather. Yields for various mixtures of these crops are also shown in the various types of weather. It is found that each of the three crops is rather narrowly tailored for that type of weather in which it is best, and gives disastrously poor yields in other types of weather. Oats, for example, gives poor yields in wet or dry weather, but very good yields in moderate weather. The farmer can insure against disaster by planting a mixture of corn, oats and wheat, thereby obtaining a fair overall yield whatever the weather.

The farmer is still not satisfied, however. The contingency table does give him the information he wants on the three "preferred" crops, but he would like to see the same information for some other crops, even though they have been ruled out as "inferior" in the analytical optimization. The analyst obligingly expands the contingency table to show the yields of various other "inferior" crops in wet, moderate and dry weather. At this point it is noted that cane, which is inferior to corn in wet weather, inferior to oats in moderate weather, and inferior to wheat in dry weather, gives a "pretty good" yield in all types of weather, providing better all-weather insurance than can be achieved with any combination of the three "preferred" crops. This particular farmer, having a pronounced aversion to risk, decides that of all the crops he prefers the weather-yield pattern of cane over that of any other crop or combination of crops. Another farmer, looking at the same table, might prefer to take somewhat more of a chance on alfalfa, another "inferior" crop shown to give a rather good yield in wet or moderate weather but a poor yield in dry weather. Still another might prefer to take a greater chance on corn, but not necessarily because it was one of the "preferred" crops in the original analysis.[8]

The first approach described above, which determines which of the farmer's various options is "preferred" for each situation or specific set of assumptions about the uncertain factors, is far from uncommon in actual applications of systems analysis. It is useful in indicating some of the systems that merit consideration by the decisionmaker or planner. It can be worse than useless, however, if it leads him to limit his attention only to those "preferred" systems.

The approach that evolves toward the end of the example has the advantage of not ruling out systems that ought to be considered. It has the disadvantage, however, of not ruling out very many systems at all, for it eliminates only those systems which are "inefficient"; that is, systems which are inferior or at most equal to other systems in *all* situations or for *all* assumptions about uncertain factors. Some means must be found to narrow the list further. This may require going beyond the bounds of strictly quantitative analysis, by such expedients as eliminating systems or uncertainties by direct application of the analysts' judgment or that of experts on whom he might call.

> Whatever approach is used in narrowing down the list of systems to be presented to the customer, the approach should be described as explicitly as possible. The presentation should include, among other things, a contingency table, showing for each system its performance and cost in each of the various relevant situations and/ or for each set of assumptions about the uncertain factors. Digesting this information and using it in making decisions or plans puts a heavy burden on the decisionmaker or planner, but it can't be helped. Systems analysis does not relieve the customer of the responsibility for facing the uncertain consequences of his decisions or plans; it can, however, help him face uncertainty with a better appreciation of the relevant considerations than he might otherwise have had.[9]

Why is quantification desirable? Some aspects of problems of choice in national security require numbers; others do not. When a quantitative matter is being discussed, the greatest clarity of thought is achieved by using numbers instead of avoiding them, even when uncertainties are present. Only in rare cases is it possible to make a convincing comparison of alternatives without a quantitative analysis.

> What is at issue here really is not numbers or computers versus words or judgment. The real issue is one of clarity of understanding and expression. Take, for example, the statement "Nuclear power for surface ships offers a major increase in effectiveness."
>
> Precisely what does that mean? Does it mean 10 per cent better or 100 per cent better? When that sort of question is asked a frequent answer is, "It can't be expressed in numbers." But it has to be expressed

with the help of numbers. Budgets are expressed in dollars, and nuclear power costs more than conventional power. If nuclear power costs, say 33 per cent more for some ship type, all factors considered, then, no matter what the budget level, the Navy and the Secretary of Defense have to face the choice of whether to put the nation's resources into four conventional or three nuclear ships, or for a larger budget, eight conventional or six nuclear ships, and therefore whether by "major increase" is meant more than 33 per cent, about 33 per cent, or less than 33 per cent. Because the Secretary of Defense has to make the decision in these terms, the statement "major increase" is not particularly helpful. It must be replaced by a quantitative analysis of the performance of various missions, leading to a conclusion such as "Nuclear power for surface ships offers something between X and Y per cent more effectiveness per ship. Therefore, $1 billion spent on nuclear powered ships will provide a force somewhere between A and B per cent more or less effective than the same dollars spent on conventionally powered ships.10

Some variables are difficult to quantify, either because they are not calculable, like the probability of war, or because no satisfactory scale of measurement has yet been devised for them, like the effect on NATO solidarity of some unilateral U.S. action. This sometimes leads either to their neglect, for they tend to be ignored, or to their being recognized only by modifying a solution reached in fact by manipulating quantified variables. Thus, when the problem arises of using the model to recommend an action, the analyst may have trouble weighing these variables properly: the effect of the quantitative variables is built in, while that of the nonquantitative ones may be easily lost in the welter of qualitative considerations that must be taken into account.

As we have already seen, certain variables can be eliminated, either because they are irrelevant or trivial in their quantitative effects or because they have roughly the same effect on all the alternatives under consideration. The second explanation is the more important. Indeed, the fact that many

variables fall into this category makes analysis possible. If the results were *not* insensitive to all but a relatively small number of variables, analysis would have to yield completely to guesses and intuition. *The point is that this insensitivity must be discovered.* Sometimes logical reconnoitering alone is sufficient, but usually analysis is required, possibly with arbitrary values assigned to the variables we are unable to calculate.

If nonquantitative variables are not to be neglected without mention or dismissed with some spurious argument, such as the one that they act in opposite direction and hence cancel out,11 then how are they to be treated? The usual method is the one mentioned a moment ago—to attempt to take them into account through modification of the solution rather than to incorporate them into the model. But this in itself represents a particular method of quantification, for, by altering the solution to take account of the previously omitted variables, the analyst is implicitly valuing them. Since we nearly always have some insight into the range of values that a factor might take, we can, in many cases, assign it an arbitrary value and observe the effect on the solution.

In the general process of investigating a problem and gathering data about it, the analyst will have developed ideas of what considerations are likely to be most influential in determining the possible courses of action. To construct a model, he uses these insights—which actually represent crude preliminary models—and conducts pencil and paper experiments to illuminate their implications. Analysis, being iterative, is self-correcting; as the study goes on, early models are refined and then replaced, so that the behavior of the relationships being investigated is represented with greater accuracy.

For most phenomena, there are many possible representations; the appropriate model depends as much on the question being asked as on the phenomena about which it is asked. A town can be modeled by a map if the question being asked is how to walk from A to B; but if the question is how to speed up the flow of traffic between the same two points, a much more elaborate model may be needed. The point is that there are no "universal" models—that is to say, no one model that can handle all questions about a given activity.

"Working" the model, trying out various strategies and concepts of operation, is the closest systems analysis comes to scientific experimentation. Deductions based on operating with the model frequently suggest new directions of effort. That is to say, starting with the relatively few parameters that characterize a system in terms of the model, it is sometimes possible to show that changing them would improve the performance of the system as measured by the model, which, in turn, might suggest corresponding improvements that could be made in the real system as it performs in the real world. In this way, working the model contributes to system design.

It is also important to go outside the model, to contemplate changes that violate its assumptions, and thereby perhaps achieve a better model. But whether or not one model is better than another does not depend on its complexity or computability, but solely on whether it gives better predictions. Unfortunately for systems analysis, but possibly fortunately for the world, this test is not usually an operational one when military problems are being considered.

INTERPRETATION

At this stage, not only does the analyst attempt to interpret his work, but so does the sponsor or the decisionmaker. Thus, the real world gets into the iterative cycle again, possibly to counteract its always imperfect mapping onto the model and, hopefully, to produce better answers.

As we remarked earlier, good criteria can only be found by working with the problem; that is, they cannot be developed a priori. Ends and means interact. Are the criteria good? What are the costs? What is the state-of-the-art? Are the objectives attained? Judgment must tell us whether we need to modify these things and run through another cycle or not.

Suppose the study has been done properly. Say the assumptions are reasonable, the chain of reasoning logical, the judgments as to the various inputs sound. This does not mean that the analysis is ended. As we have seen, the outcomes obtained from a model must be interpreted in the light of considerations which may not have been adequately treated by the model. Thus, in our example, the decisionmaker (or, for that matter, the systems analyst) may have established the requirement that a follow-on Minuteman worth considering have the capability to assure the destruction of, say, 95 per cent of a certain target list under a particular range of contingencies. But many questions occur. Perhaps the minimum cost of achieving this capability for all alternatives is too high; maybe the tasks of deterrence and limiting damage to the United States which we are trying to assure with our damage capability could be better done by spending less on strategic forces and more on air defense. The 95 per cent measure of effectiveness may be too high, or too low. Someone must translate the percentage of target destruction into its implications in terms of more meaningful criteria, such as the balance of military forces, the will to continue fighting, and the effect on our diplomacy. We can never know these things fully. For indicating the attainment of such vaguely defined objectives as deterrence or victory, it is even hard to find measures that point in the right direction. Consider deterrence, for instance.

It exists only in the mind—and in the enemy's mind at that. We cannot use some "scale of deterrence" to measure directly the effectiveness of alternatives we hope will lead to deterrence, for there is no such scale. Instead, we must use such approximations as the potential mortalities that we might inflict, or the industrial capacity we might destroy. Consequently, it is clear that, even if a comparison of two systems indicates that one could inflict 50 per cent more casualties on the enemy than the other, we cannot conclude that this means the system supplies 50 per cent more deterrence. In fact, since in some circumstances it may be important not to look too threatening, we can argue that the system capable of inflicting the greatest number of casualties may provide the least deterrence!

The solution to a problem that has been simplified and possibly made amenable to mathematical calculation by drastic idealization and aggregation is not necessarily a good solution of the original problem. But even if the model and its inputs are excellent, the results may be unacceptable. The reason is obvious: Major decisions, in the field of military policy, are part of a political as well as an intellectual process. To achieve efficiency, considerations other than those of cost-effectiveness are important—discipline, morale, *esprit de corps,* tradition, and organizational behavior. The size, composition, location, and state of readiness of forces influence our foreign policy and the freedom of action we have. They also have a major impact on our domestic economy and public morale. The men who must somehow integrate these factors with the results of the study must necessarily deal with much that is nonquantitative, and their results may differ.

It is important for the user of analysis to distinguish between what the study actually shows and the recommendations for action the analyst makes on the basis of what he, the

analyst, thinks the study implies. Some experienced and successful users of analysis hold even stronger views:

> Simply said, the purpose of an analysis is to provide illumination and visibility—to expose some problem in terms that are as simple as possible. This exposé is used as one of a number of inputs by some "decision-maker." Contrary to popular practice, the primary output of an analysis is not conclusions and recommendations. Most studies by analysis do have conclusions and recommendations even though they should not, since invariably whether or not some particular course of action should be followed depends on factors quite beyond those that have been quantified by the analyst. A "summary" is fine and allowable, but "conclusions" and "recommendations" by the analyst are, for the most part, neither appropriate nor useful. Drawing conclusions and making recommendations (regarding these types of decisions) are the responsibility of the decision-maker and should not be pre-empted by the analyst.[12]

When new minds—the decision-maker's, for example—review the problem, they bring new information and insight. Even though the results obtained from the model are not changed, recommendations for action based on them may be. A model is only an indicator, not a final judge. While the analysis may compare the alternatives under a great many different assumptions, using various models, no one would expect the decision to be made solely on the basis of these comparisons alone—and the same would hold even if an immensely more complicated version of the study were to be carried out.

When should an inquiry stop? It is important to remember that, in problems of national security, inquiry is rarely exhaustive. Because it is almost always out of the question to collect—much less process—all the information that is required for exhaustive analysis, inquiries are partial, and the decision-maker must get along without the full advantage of all the potentiality of systems analysis, operations research, and the scientific approach. Inquiries cost money and time; as we suggested earlier, they can cost in other values as well. They can cost lives; they can cost national security. This is not to say that some costs cannot sometimes be ignored; the point is rather that paradoxes arise if we allow ourselves to forget that almost all inquiries must stop far, far short of completion either for lack of funds or time, or a justification for spending further funds or time on them.

For these reasons, an analysis is usually far from finished when it is briefed to the decisionmaker or even when it is published. There are always unanswered questions that could be investigated further, even though the need for reporting requires a cutoff. And the decisionmaker's questions and reactions will usually involve an extension of the study.

Since we must often give our advice before we are fully ready, we may be wrong on occasion. But one cannot do useful work in the field of defense analysis unless he is willing to accept uncertainty. If, in the judgment of the analyst and those who use his analysis, the alternative ranked highest by the criterion is good enough, the process is over; if not, more and better alternatives must be designed or the objectives must be lowered. Analysis is helpful in reaching a policy conclusion only when the objectives are agreed upon by the policy-makers. In defense policy in particular, and in many other cases as well, objectives are not, in fact, agreed upon. The choice, while ostensibly between alternatives, is really between objectives, and nonanalytical methods must be used for a final reconciliation of views. Although the consequences computed from the model may provide guidance in deciding which objectives to compromise, such decisions are not easily made, and judgment must in the end be applied.

NOTES

1. Col. Wesley W. Posvar, "The Realm of Obscurity," in *American Defense Policy*, prepared by Associates in Political Science, United States Air Force Academy, The Johns Hopkins Press, Baltimore, Md., 1965, p. 224.

2. For the full report, see A. J. Wohlstetter, F. S. Hoffman, R. J. Lutz, and H. S. Rowen, *Selection and Use of Strategic Air Bases*, The RAND Corporation, R-266, April 1954. A nontechnical account of this study appears as Chapter VI in Bruce L. R. Smith's *The RAND Corporation: Case Study of a Nonprofit Advisory Corporation*, Harvard University Press, Cambridge, Mass., 1966.

3. E. Bright Wilson, Jr., *An Introduction to Scientific Research*, McGraw-Hill Book Company, Inc., New York, 1952, p. 1.

4. But one RAND analyst notes that even the discovery that the quantitative differences among the alternatives are insignificant can have a considerable value to the decisionmaker. "This is especially true if sensitivity analyses have been made . . . [and] the final results are still within relatively narrow ranges. Given results of this kind, the decisionmaker can be less concerned about making a mistake regarding the quantitative aspects of the problems, and he may then feel somewhat more comfortable about focusing more of his attention on the qualitative . . . considerations."

(G. H. Fisher, *The Analytical Bases of Systems Analysis*, The RAND Corporation, P-3363, May 1966, p. 14.)

5. D. M. Fort, *Systems Analysis as an Aid in Air Transportation Planning*, The RAND Corporation, P-3293-1, March 1966, p. 10.

6. For example, confining ourselves to the four war outcomes we have listed, we might say: Pick the system for which the product of the number of targets destroyed and the logarithm of the cost to the enemy, divided by the product of the number of lives lost and the time to destroy 50 targets, is greatest. Using this payoff, the analyst would reach these results:

$$A: (\ 80 \log_e \quad 3)/20 \ = 4.4$$
$$B: (100 \log_e \ 12)/50 \ = 5.0$$
$$C: (150 \log_e \ 180)/200 = 3.9$$

This indicates that B should be the choice. But the use of such a function is extremely arbitrary; it might be just as absurd to use the square root instead of the logarithm of the cost to the enemy. The values for A, B, and C would then be 6.9, 6.9, 10.1, respectively. Either payoff function would give a lesser weight to the cost factor than to the other factors involved, but by what logic can we choose such a function? This approach is never satisfactory unless there is a logical argument or empirical evidence to determine the form of the payoff.

7. A very similar approach is advocated by Everett J. Daniels and John B. Lathrop in "Strengthening the Cost-Effectiveness Criterion for Major System Decisions," a paper presented at the October 1964 meeting of the Operations Research Society of America.

8. D. M. Fort, *Systems Analysis as an Aid in Air Transportation Planning*, pp. 12–13.

9. D. M. Fort, *Systems Analysis as an Aid in Air Transportation Planning*, p. 15.

10. Alain C. Enthoven, Assistant Secretary of Defense (Systems Analysis), "Choosing Strategies and Selecting Weapon Systems," *United States Naval Institute Proceedings*, vol. 90, No. 1, January 1964, p. 151.

11. It is not enough to know that two variables act in opposite directions; their quantitative impact must also be estimated.

12. Maj. Gen. Glenn A. Kent, "On Analysis," *Air University Review*, Vol. XVIII, No. 4 (May–June 1967), p. 50.

The "Soft" Factors in Systems Studies

Systematic use of quantitative analyses over the past six years has substantially enhanced the effectiveness with which resources are invested in U.S. military forces. In this limited sense, at least, there is little question that the usefulness of analytical techniques has been amply demonstrated. Yet, in this same period a number of prominent policy failures have occurred, and it is sometimes suggested that some of these failures are attributable to the narrow range of factors incorporated in military systems studies and to the single-mindedness with which the conclusions of such studies are implemented by policymakers. Inevitably the primary concern is with those "soft" social and political factors which admittedly are neglected.

We will deal with three major themes. First, in military systems studies the self-imposed limitation of playing down the broader political factors is defensible up to a point in the attempt to deal with a critical portion of the overall problem. Starting with the accepted "political wisdom" may so corrupt the analysis that one never understands some of the fundamentals. Second, the chief difficulties arise in the transition from these "suboptimized" analytical studies to decisionmaking. In this respect analysts may have been remiss in failing to appreciate the crucial role of bureaucratic structures. Third, all important system studies—even when stated to be limited and "suboptimized"—inevitably incorporate a number of non-technical assumptions, though typically in a tangential and implicit fashion. Without careful examination of the non-technical factors, adopting the conclusions of such specialized studies may be detrimental to national policy.

THE SEMI-ORTHODOX POSITION

Whenever one considers the entire complex of decisionmaking, it is apparent that everything is ultimately related to everything else: the ramifications of a single issue spread out to other issues. What appears at one level to be a precise and dominating objective becomes, as one moves to higher order problems, only one of several alternative inputs, and the choice among them becomes dependent on higher order objectives. The layering and tying of issues makes the *fully complete* analytical treatment of a policy problem infeasible, for there occurs an exponential growth in its complexity and cumbersomeness. In principle, policy formation would require the solution of an infinite number of simultaneous equations, a large proportion of which are unknowable and almost all of which must inevitably lie outside the attention span of a single human mind.

One cannot do everything at once.

From the *Bulletin of the Atomic Scientists*, vol. XXIV (Nov. 1968). Reprinted by permission of *Science and Public Affairs, the Bulletin of the Atomic Scientists*. Copyright © 1968 by the Educational Foundation for Nuclear Science.

To attempt to do so is the road to analytical impotence. The point is to start somewhere: and the most productive place to start is with those elements which are fundamental to the final results and which are relatively easy to manipulate.

In analytical work this is taken to imply the so-called hard elements—hard in the sense of being susceptible to measurement rather than in the sense of being intractable. (In this latter sense the political or organizational factors are undoubtedly the most difficult of all.) One begins with the elements of technology, cost, and—admittedly inadequate—measures of output or effectiveness, for these provide an easy-to-grab handle to the problem. The underlying premise is that the economic factor—seemingly implicit in the phrase, cost-effectiveness—should outweigh political, social, and other factors.

Within the original scope of the analysis, these last are often given zero weight. While such a procedure is clearly acceptable for lower-order instrumental problems, it is apparent that for higher-order strategies or policies it becomes increasingly questionable. For higher-order problems the measure of effectiveness must be based on some broad strategic criteria, in which political or psychological assessments unavoidably play a role. And, even in straightforward hardware studies, the "effectiveness" concept is likely to be tainted by political estimates that make up the overall strategy. It is fervently, if secretly, hoped that these "soft" elements will have a minimum effect on the results.

It is not always recognized that the conventional procedure for delimiting the problem may also help to reduce the risk of gross error. Good reasons do exist for avoiding the soft elements at the outset. Political assessments, for example, are based on opinions which may fluctuate wildly with changes in fashion. What is worse, they may rest on the gossamer support provided by intuition, whose range and variety are limited only by the number of people involved. To the extent that intuitions converge, the focal point tends to be some sort of unchallengeable political myth—impervious to the adjustments required by changing circumstances.

Thus, aside from the difficulty of absorbing political factors into analyses, a powerful reason for exclusion in the early stages is the characteristically low quality of available political inputs. Not only is sophisticated political insight rare, it is usually unavailable to those doing the studies. What is available turns out, frequently as not, to be demonstrably wrong—despite the many evasive techniques used to rationalize past mistakes. When so-called political insight turns out to be a collection of Delphic utterances, subject to "reinterpretation" over time, it becomes a dubious foundation for analysis.

In the realm of the political myth, premature use of political inputs is likely to introduce the type of stodgy or obsolescent ideas produced by "wise men." The classic and frequently derided example is provided by "old China hands," but "old X hands" provides a better clue to the generic case. The underlying premise in such assessments is that the best guide to the future is some mild perturbation of previous experience, sometimes highly limited and subjective. But in a world characterized by high-speed communications, by the ability to mobilize resources rapidly, by changing technologies, and by the possibility of rapid development of impressive new capabilities, reliance on ossified "political wisdom" may lead to irrelevant, and possibly disastrous, conclusions.

The record of achievement by these means is very spotty indeed. To choose one of the most responsible and highly commended examples: the United States' decision to organize NATO was based on some rather obsolescent notions regarding the strength of the European nations and the direct contribution that they could make to the security of the United States. There was a striking failure to anticipate the revolutionary impact that nuclear forces would have on earlier beliefs regarding European defense. Not recognizing how dominant the strategic nuclear balance was to be in both American and European security, the United States attempted to organize European defense in the traditional pattern of the grand coalition. The need for free nations to "stand together" in a sacramental bond against tyranny had been learned by the United States in the two world wars.

Since imitation is the sincerest form of flattery, we may have been flattered by the Soviets' establishing a similar structure in the East, but it has become increasingly apparent that both alliances are façades, barely masking the overwhelming dominance of each by a single partner—a dominance which, in the NATO case, the prevailing political wisdom conspicuously failed to predict and still may fail fully to recognize. Putting aside NATO's political desirability, its military relevance is entirely different from what was anticipated. Over the years the total loss resulting from the misallocation of resources to and within NATO has been impressive, and the waste reflects in no small part the faulty original concepts.

It is a striking case in which more effective forces could have been obtained at far lower cost—if there had been continuing force structure analyses that initially excluded the soft political factors and their accompanying shibboleths.

Though one may reasonably conclude from such experiences that the standard methodology—with its initial concentration on the hard elements—is defensible in principle, it should simultaneously be emphasized that the initial exclusion of the soft factors is not intended to lead to their permanent exclusion. Sensible analysts have always recognized that the deciding factors frequently go beyond those incorporated in the analysis and that the decisionmaker should therefore supplement the original analysis with the excluded considerations in reaching his decision. Analysts do recognize the limitations of analyses. That these limitations have not been typically stressed reflects a common conviction that the real world is overrun with political or bureaucratic pressures making it improbable that analytical efforts will be pushed too far without political review. The danger, it is believed, lies in analysis being ignored rather than sweeping all before it. That the defense may be justified, however, hardly contributes to the elimination of the problem.

BUREAUCRATIC BEHAVIOR

The assumption, made almost casually, that the appropriate adjustments will be done later does represent a serious pitfall in analytical work. There is some element of irresponsibility in ignoring how studies may subsequently be used or manhandled in the bureaucracy. While it is not their primary role, analysts must pay attention to organizational complexities. This might even lead to a more satisfactory accommodation between their own efforts and institutional reality.

There are pressing reasons for studying this problem. Most obvious, in light of the way bureaucracies work, a careful technical study is likely to become a departmental position. The department may regard its responsibilities as limited, and advocate a policy optimized solely for cost, economic, and technical factors. It then assumes that the responsibility for considering other elements lies with other departments. If the bureaucratic position of the first department is sufficiently powerful it may carry the day with its recommendation without receiving the review that the department itself considered necessary. Something of this sort seems to have occurred in the case of Skybolt, where the strongest forces that emerged supported a strictly technical analysis, with insufficient political coordination taking place after the decision.

Increasing the awareness of bureaucratic behavior is important for a more fundamental reason—one which transcends purely internal policymaking and bears upon the threats or the cooperation expected from other nations. In the bulk of systems-analytic work there has been an underlying premise that policy is determined by a single deciding unit. Yet, in developing alternatives for a large organization or in predicting the behavior of other organizations, the assumption is invalid. Within the government the unit to which advice is tendered will typically lack control over the resources included in the study—and may even lack knowledge of the activities and objectives of supposedly cooperating units. The results may be particularly deficient when the advice is tendered either directly or indirectly to a committee of equals or to an alliance. Given the resistance and the bargaining which is inevitable in light of the disparity of objectives, perspectives, and information, the results will diverge sharply from those anticipated on the basis of presumed rationality and single-minded efficiency.

It is remarkable how little serious work has been done on the bureaucratic aspects of national decision-making. On the level of political gossip, almost everyone accepts the importance of factional conflict; we associate particular causes with particular individuals and groups and carefully watch who is rising and falling. Yet, whenever an attempt at prediction is made, it becomes convenient, emotionally satisfying, and possibly bureaucratically

rewarding to fall back on a monolithic interpretation of what that abstraction —"the government"—should or will do. This tendency is even more formidable for the other national actors on the international stage. Whatever their disciplinary backgrounds, analysts typically treat policymaking in other nations as if it were governed by a rational and unified deciding unit.

The reality is quite different. Decisions are nominally made by senior political figures who are harried, have insufficient time to study problems in detail, who are gripped by emotions of their youth or by prior experiences, and who are susceptible to claims made by subordinate groups which are couched in a way to appeal to their prejudices. Below them are a set of mutually jealous and warring bureaucratic groups, clamoring for resources and anxious to protect established preserves. To the extent that they are not closely watched, the subordinate bureaucratic groups will attempt to achieve their objectives quietly or even surreptitiously. Moreover, their capacity for resistance to high-level objectives enunciated from above, but to which they take exception, is breathtaking. Actual programs and allocative decisions will consequently diverge quite sharply from those that would be predicted on the assumption of a rational intelligence. Instead they will be strongly influenced by prejudice, incompetency, and by infighting, deviousness, and bootlegging within the bureaucracies. Changes which appear rational and desirable will be compromised half to death, and the compromises themselves will be slow in coming. Traumatic events—like Sputnik, an initial nuclear detonation, or the invasion of Korea—may speed up the process of change, but the capacity for resistance will remain formidable.

Statements on national policy provide only a superficial and basically misleading indicator of probable change. The decisive battleground in the competition between new proposals and continuing programs is not on the level of ideas but on the level of budgets. New ideas may be accepted in principle (to resist openly may be politically imprudent). The national leadership may believe it has endorsed a new concept and may believe that a program is being implemented. But the place for the established bureaucracies to cut ambitious new programs down to size is in the budgetary infighting. It is a truism that the demand for resources far exceeds the supply. Radical cuts in old programs are rare. In the face of the established programs, which may become masked under imitative labels, it is difficult for a new program to secure and expand upon its Darwinian niche in the budget structure. Even when a program is objectively obsolescent, its established position indicates that it satisfies some deep-seated emotion in the society. New, if fraudulent, stories can be cooked up to play on the old emotions —and thereby to preserve or expand an organization's historical share of resources. New growths find it tough going in a badly weeded garden.

To ignore these realities of bureaucratic life will repeatedly lead the analyst into error. The excuse that "the best laid schemes of mice and men gang aft a-gley" seems singularly inappropriate; the neglect of the real character of the environment implies that the plans may be the worst laid. In this light one might consider a number of historical examples. One fascinating case was the attempt to extract expanded conventional forces from our European allies in the 1961–62 period —with little appreciation of the real structure of NATO or the divergency of interest and attitude among its members or their component bureaucracies including the U.S. military. In fact, given the need to obtain approval from the North Atlantic Council, even obtaining a *formal* change in NATO strategy involves far greater resistance than one would anticipate on the premise that the decision will reflect the members' collective interest.

Considerations of feasibility ought not lead into simple accommodation to the status quo. But analyses might prove to be more useful, if supplemented by an understanding of the organizational barriers to their implementation. Rational resource allocation may be the proper initial benchmark, but study variants should also be prepared which take organizational feasibility into account. Only in this way might one have some confidence in designing alternatives, which are both superior and feasible. The seemingly second-best solution may actually be the preferred one. Without organizational analysis the nominal best may remain the enemy of the good, for reasons more subtle than perfectionism.

OPPONENT RESPONSE

However strong the desire to minimize the role of soft factors, their introduction cannot be avoided in analyses at the highest strategic level. Some measure of effectiveness must be designed to compare alternatives, but any serious measure of effectiveness inevitably becomes tainted by the political or psychological assessments that make up overall strategy. Unless the system being dealt with is purely instrumental, overall systems effectiveness is dependent upon the response of the opponent. Instrumental capabilities are useful in certain specific roles, not in others. Unless an opponent can be disarmed or his powers of resistance crushed, this simple fact must be recognized: it will ultimately be necessary to have to have recourse to policy which, to turn Clausewitz on his head, is a continuation of conflict by other means.

Only when a disarming strategy is feasible, can the application of force remove most of the burden from policy and policy assessment. (Even in such cases there is no indication that to rely completely on force—unconditional surrender—is the wiser strategy; it is only a feasible one.) While such cases are never perfectly clear-cut, they are sufficiently different to be distinguishable from those in which policy assessment becomes the heart of the problem. To cite a straightforward example: in the fifties a nuclear war waged against the Soviet Union might have sufficiently disarmed the Soviets that they would have become susceptible to our pressures. However, the buildup of Soviet forces in the sixties has been such that we must carefully consider how the Soviets might employ their residual forces. As a result, any projection of a nuclear war and any plan for conducting such a war must rest on a highly subjective assessment of enemy responses.

Of more immediate concern, in an engagement such as that in Vietnam, we should now be painfully aware that relying on military analyses which ignore the organization and psychology of the foe and of the population he desires to control is likely to be the basis of continuing self-deception. It has become almost a bromide that in Vietnam "the political factor is dominant." Yet, consider the unsatisfactory set of mechanical indicators of military performance—and the inconsistent way in which these mechanical criteria are applied.

To be sure, neither these specific criteria nor overall performance in Vietnam should be blamed on serious analytical efforts. Vietnam reflects more the *absence* than the *failure* of analysis. From the standpoint of systems analysis, it represents almost an anthology of classic errors. Sub-analytic urges of a highly traditional sort have encouraged conceptualizing the war as one of attrition—and of *manpower* attrition at that. The existing indicators reflect this faulty image. To choose a single example, the use of "body count" has been intended to provide hard evidence of enemy mortalities—though some question persists regarding the count's accuracy. (The circumstances are hardly such as to invite careful statistical procedures.) Nonetheless an estimate can be made of relative casualties, and this is presumed to be a revealing figure.

Several questions may be raised. First, why is the ratio of casualties supposed to be dramatically revealing, yet the ratio of costs (in Vietnam alone) has no significance at all? (On other issues such as ABM deployment, cost ratios are presumed to indicate what is worthwhile or not worthwhile for Americans or for Russians.) Currently in Vietnam cost ratios may favor our opponents at something like 15:1, a level which certainly has been regarded as precluding other lines of activity. While in this case we may prefer to ignore cost ratios, we would be ill advised to assume that other members of the international audience are similarly ignoring these unfavorable ratios.

Second, more is involved than sacrifices alone. It is apparent that when something is sufficiently important to us we are prepared to jettison calculations on cost ratios. Since their undertakings are important to them, our opponents in Vietnam may be equally prepared to disregard *casualty* ratios. They may be buoying up their spirits by contemplating cost ratios, and gloating over the number of dollars it costs us for each dollar that they invest. For example, a table which appears in *The People of Vietnam Will Triumph! U.S. Aggressors Will be Defeated!* (Peking: Foreign Languages Press, 1965) indicates the brilliant victories against the imperialists through the destruction of planes, ships, vehicles, trains, and structures. One moral is clear: the valuations placed by each side of the outcome are more important than ratios, per se. High valuation of an objective may make unfavorable cost ratios inconsequential, whereas low valuation may make the cost favorable ratios wholly unsatisfactory.

Third, ratios alone are a poor indicator of overall sacrifices. Even in terms of casualties it is scale rather than loss ratios that is critical. It is absolute losses that determine how long the insurgent forces can maintain the size, cohesion, and effectiveness of their units. To analyze staying power is a tricky problem involving estimates of motivation, dedication, and inherent capacity of enemy manpower. And these too are essentially soft factors.

Similar issues crop up with respect to European defense. Differences regarding strategies both within the United States and among the members of NATO reflect in large part different assessments of the potential foe. The present complacence in Europe reflects the position, held more strongly there than here, that the Soviets are just not very aggressive and the detente is here to stay. An earlier, widely advertised European opinion regarding a strategy of immediate nuclear response reflected a particular view of Soviet character and Soviet ambitions. It was held that the Soviets would put sufficient credence in the threat to be deterred. The Americans have been more inclined to fear that the Soviets could be adventurous, and, since this was a possibility, we are more eager to obtain capabilities that we would not be afraid to use or that would not necessarily crumble. Part of European resistance to the buildup of conventional forces, and European disinclination to accept American manpower and equipment estimates, reflect a vastly different picture of the consequences of an engagement in Central Europe. European experiences with multi-national forces have not been reassuring. Some NATO members recall that Allied forces on the Western front in 1940 were equal in number to the German forces, yet they were simply swept away. With basic disagreement regarding the potential of one's own side and the foe, it is hardly surprising that different strategic judgments are reached.

At a higher level of violence, suppose the United States were forced to consider retaliation against Soviet territory—because of an invasion of Europe, for example. Should a time-urgent attack be inaugurated against the main elements of the Soviet strategic forces or should one start with very modest, essentially demonstrative, attacks, hoping that the Soviets will cease their provocation? Perhaps the critical element is whether one believes that a heavy time-urgent attack would automatically trigger Soviet retaliatory forces against our cities—and whether a much lower-level attack would or would not elicit the same Soviet response. These questions are difficult, not only because Soviet intentions remain obscure and little light is shed on them by Soviet declarations, possibly issued with intent to deceive, but also because the Soviets themselves may not know how they should behave in such a contingency. Knowing your enemy becomes particularly challenging if the enemy does not know himself.

Strategy depends on the image of the foe. At one time the accepted image of the Soviets seemed close to "commie rats who only understand force." Since the Kennedy years it has become more fashionable to accept an image in which the Soviet opposite numbers of our more optimistic officials are just as urbane, as civilized, and as intent on the eradication of differences. Neither of these images, however, would seem fully to represent the character of Soviet society. Soviet behavior, no less than our own, is subject, not only to gradual alteration over time, but to oscillation as well. For the foreseeable future, we would be as ill advised to base our policies on the belief that the Soviets are inherently peace-loving, as on the premise that they are inherently and ideologically aggressive.

Such shifts in the assessment of the

foe are likely to have considerable impact on decisions—even research and development decisions. For example, certain types of weapons development have been rejected because of the intuitive feeling of the decisionmaker that such capabilities would create arms control difficulties and intensify the arms race. There is, of course, nothing inherently wrong with basing decisions on such values. What is desirable, however, is that decisions not be made intuitively, and that political assumptions be analyzed explicitly—in relation to the relevant data and conditions—rather than accepted implicitly. Higher-level analytical efforts normally suggest specific decisions which should be scrutinized on the basis of their political implications. Yet, in moving from a technical analysis to a political decision, it is clearly desirable to go through additional stages of analysis. Before a class of capabilities is rejected as destabilizing, for example, careful analysis should convincingly demonstrate that the arms balance would indeed be upset.

There is a temptation to fuzz up analysis at such controversial points. In political debate one does not wish to admit the existence of speculative imponderables. One prefers to imply that one's opponents are commiting incompetent errors because of an inadequate methodology. Unfortunately, systems analysis has provided something of a façade of pure objectivity for political debate. While insiders know better, systems analysis has been presented to the public as an instrument that somehow "solves" problems. The upshot has been to obscure the unavoidable role of political imponderables in decisionmaking, and to discourage analysts from dealing explicitly with these imponderables.

THE INHERENT RISKS

What this discussion has tried to establish is the expanding risk of applying the semi-orthodox methods of systems analysis as one moves up the ladder from low-level decisions and instrumental capabilities to problems which increasingly involve the total society. The chances that really excellent studies may result in misleading policy decisions increase greatly. But technical studies are not one's sole support; they ought to be fully supplemented by additional studies on policy issues taking into account a wider range of factors. The point of danger, the point to be carefully watched, but also the point of maximum opportunity, is the one at which the transition occurs from analytical studies to decisionmaking.

Even in this phase the role of traditional analysis is not negligible. Their function is to see that appreciation of the technical factors is not washed away in what may become the emotional catharsis of policymaking.

Nonetheless, there are dangers in a partial view, however well grounded in logic. On the big issues a society's response may be erratic, even compulsive, but the elements of change are likely to be interdependent. The analyst's habits of mind, stressing the disentangling or separating-out of supposedly independent factors, may here be irrelevant under conditions that the premise of *ceteris paribus* does not apply. Realism about policies frequently demands that we recognize when hypothetically separate elements are hopelessly entangled. At such times, the analytical intelligence may point to more options than really exist.

When the nation is caught in some situation, an analyst may study certain alternatives with the intent to improve our position—while assuming that we can back off, if the attempt fails. In such cases the analyst, in his search for options, both exaggerates flexibility and underestimates how the actual exercise of an option may reduce flexibility. When a nation is embarked on some course of action, the sucking-in process may be intensified by the search for improvements. Certain policies—the bombing of North Vietnam, for example—cannot be taken up and discarded on an experimental basis. These are not tools alone, but commitments that influence society's subsequent behavior.

That means and ends may be inseparably linked should come as no surprise to those who are as alert to the *systemic* as to the *analytic* aspect of systems analysis. That there is a momentum inherent in political processes is perhaps less obvious, but it illustrates the ultimate need for grappling with the soft elements. Happily, analysis remains in its infancy. There is much to be learned regarding how better to take the soft factors into account. To the extent that such factors cannot be taken directly into consideration, we are forced to reiterate the final dependence on the sophistication of those decision-makers who eventually employ the analyses.

The Influence of the Press

JAMES RESTON

AS ALLY OF THE GOVERNMENT

The influence of the American press on American foreign policy, in my view, is usually exaggerated. Its influence is exercised primarily through the Congress, which confuses press opinion with public opinion; through foreign embassies and the foreign press in Washington, which think we know more about what is going on in the Federal capital than we really do; and through the universities of America, which, ironically, have a kind of intellectual contempt for the press, but read it more avidly, more critically, and probably more accurately than we read it ourselves. No doubt, the press has great influence on American foreign policy when things are *obviously* going badly; it has very little influence, however, when things are going badly but the impending disaster is not obvious and the government is saying, as it usually does, that all is well or soon will be if everybody only has faith and confidence.

Newspapers, radio, and television stations in the United States influence foreign policy mainly by reporting the actions of government. Acts are more powerful than words in this field and news more influential than opinion. Most of the time, reporters are in the distributing business, transmitting the accounts of what Presidents and Secretaries of State do onto the front pages and into the top headlines, where they undoubtedly influence public opinion. Let me make the news, Franklin Roose-velt said in effect, and you can write all the editorials you like against it.

Most of the time, contrary to official mythology, the people who write the news are not the enemies but the allies of officials. They are usually delivering the news as the post office delivers the mail, and when officials and reporters perform this cooperative service, which is what they do most of the time, they are undoubtedly an influential combination.

I remember writing the first detailed story about the government's vague thoughts for a European Recovery Plan in the spring of 1945. It appeared in column one of page one of a Sunday edition of *The New York Times,* leading with the news that the Truman Administration was considering a five-year plan that would cost about $20 billion. Before nine o'clock that Sunday morning, Senator Arthur Vandenberg of Michigan, then Chairman of the Senate Foreign Relations Committee, telephoned me at home. "Either you are wrong," he said, "or this government is out of its mind. Any plan of that size is out of the question."

Yet after a few months of official speeches and explanations, of transatlantic meetings and conferences on Capitol Hill, all of them making front-page news, public support for the plan developed and Vandenberg, with some sympathetic and convivial guidance from Dean Acheson, led the fight to get it through the Senate.

Secretary of State George C. Marshall, who launched the plan that later bore his name, conceded when it was all over that the support of the newspapers and commentators had contributed greatly to its success. "I found, as in almost everything I touched," he said, "it is not so hard to make a general plan; the great problem is how to put that thing over, how you carry it through, and that was the case in this instance."

Much depends, of course, on who makes the news. Senator J. W. Fulbright, one of Vandenberg's successors as Chairman of the Foreign Relations Committee, commanded the news in the spring of 1966 by staging a series of nationally televised hearings that were critical of the Johnson Administration's policy toward Viet Nam and China. The hearings also had some influence on foreign policy for a time, not for but against the Administration's line; however, it is the executive and not the legislative branch of the Federal government that usually dominates the headlines.

Washington reporters also assist the government and influence foreign policy in more oblique ways. For example—though officials seldom like to talk about this—reporters are constantly used to transmit to foreign governments, through press, radio, and television, those official views which the Administration in Washington does not want to put in formal diplomatic communications. One reason for this is that the old diplomacy, with its polite but geometric language, has broken down, and the new diplomacy—part secret, part public, part propaganda—has devised new techniques of communication between governments and peoples.

The notion that the mass of the people of a nation should become deeply involved in foreign-policy questions was regarded in the nineteenth century as preposterous, if not downright reckless. George Canning was probably the first statesman who recognized what he called the "fatal artillery of popular excitation," and Prince Metternich was appalled. He accused Canning of seeking "popularity—a pretension that is misplaced in a statesman."

In fact, the diplomats of the old school were so cautious about arousing popular emotion over foreign-policy questions that they invented a whole catalogue of technical phrases or guarded understatements that enabled them to say harsh things to one another without being impolite or provoking public concern. Thus Harold Nicolson reminds us that Wellington once referred to a bloody massacre as "the transactions complained of." Thus, too, if the British Foreign Office requested, with exquisite politeness, a reply to a note by "six in the evening of September 5," this was recognized in every foreign office in the world, but usually not by the people, as an ultimatum threatening forthwith a military response to the controversy.

All this tidy discretion was overwhelmed by the propaganda of the two world wars and the blunter undiplomatic language of Moscow and Washington in the 1940s. Nevertheless, the problem of transmitting guarded warnings from one government to another remains, and it is the reporters who are very often used to perform this function in the United States today.

When, for example, the French government indicated in 1966 that it intended to withdraw its military forces from the integrated command of the North Atlantic Treaty Organization and force all NATO troops to accept French control or get out of France, the American government, hoping to forestall the move without threatening the French, "inspired" certain news stories through American reporters on the unpleasant consequences of such action by France. The meaning of these news dispatches was perfectly clear to the French government, though they did not bring about a change in French policy.

To cite another example: for over two years, during most of the Kennedy and the first part of the Johnson Administrations, the United States government supported in the North Atlantic Treaty Organization the idea of an international surface fleet armed with nuclear weapons. The crews would be made up of men from various Allied nations but subject to American control over the actual firing of nuclear weapons. This was bitterly opposed by the Soviet Union on the ground that it gave the NATO Allies, including the Germans, "access" to nuclear information and experience. It was also opposed by some members of the Alliance on the ground that it would weaken their national authority without actually giving them equality in an international force.

The opposition from both Moscow and some of the Allies became so strong after President Johnson came to power that he decided to shelve the whole idea in order to reassure the new governments of Harold Wilson in London and Kosygin and Brezhnev in Moscow. Since he did not, however, wish to repudiate formally the position he and President Kennedy had taken in the past, he told a reporter of his plans and allowed him to publish the decision, which was not even known to his own ambassadors in Moscow or the NATO countries at the time of publication. Later, and privately, the report in *The New York Times* was confirmed to governments that requested an explanation. This illustrates one of the official-reporter diplomatic techniques of modern diplomacy, and also demonstrates one of the scientific oddities of the age, namely, that a government is the only known vessel that leaks from the top.

AS CRITIC OF THE GOVERNMENT

The influence of press, radio, and television when they act against the foreign policy of a government, however, is not so powerful as when they are transmitting the government's views and commenting favorably upon them. Occasionally, one or two correspondents may uncover facts that are either unknown to or ignored by the government and, by publishing them, influence the government to investigate the published facts and adjust policy to meet them.

This happened from time to time during the Viet Nam war. For example, when the press reported the careless use of artillery fire and air power in South Viet Nam, leading to unnecessary civilian casualties, the government in Washington issued orders to minimize the element of accident. However, when news reports gave a much more pessimistic account of that war during most of 1963 and 1964 than the government itself was giving, the more optimistic claims of the top officials of the government were believed by most people until both the political and military situations began to collapse.

Much of the time, the influence of the press on foreign policy depends on the attitude of the President toward the press. President Eisenhower was irritated by the press and did not read it carefully. President Kennedy had his troubles with the press and once barred the *New York Herald Tribune* from the White House, but he read the newspapers avidly as a check against the activities of his own government. It was not unusual for him to call his Secretary of State or even one of the regional Assistant Secretaries before eight in the morning to ask for a report on some news account back on page 16 of *The New York Times*. Such attention greatly enhanced the influence of the press during his thousand days in the White House.

The President's attitude toward the press sets the pattern for the rest of his Administration. If he reads the newspapers carefully, his aides will read them to be prepared for that early morning call from the White House. If he likes, trusts, and sees reporters officially and socially, as President Kennedy did, then cabinet members, Foreign Service officers, ambassadors and top civil servants will tend to do the same. This is vital to a free press, for a great deal of the most important news is gathered not from the top of the government but from the experts on various subjects and regions who "brief" the President and the others at the top.

If, on the other hand, the President is known to be hostile to the press or to certain of its leading commentators, he does not have to tell his aides to be wary or to avoid what he regards as his "enemies" in the press. They simply feel it is prudent in their own self-interest to be "in conference" when reporters call or to be extremely cautious and uncommunicative if they do see reporters.

An atmosphere of caution and reserve gradually came to influence the Johnson Administration, for example. The President watched the press even more closely than his predecessor did, but regarded it mainly as a problem rather than as an opportunity. He had the Associated Press and United Press International news tickers in a small cubbyhole off his main office and followed their news files constantly throughout the day. He also installed not one but three television sets both in his office and in his bedroom so that he could watch all three national television networks at once. During the noon and four o'clock news briefings by his White House Press Secretary, Mr. Johnson would occasionally telephone to give his own answer to some question posed a minute before by a reporter, leading the press to the not very remarkable suspicion that the President was listening in on the conference from another room.

One wonders whether President Johnson consciously adopted these habits to dominate the press and to keep his own aides under control. Maybe so, maybe no. Probably he was mainly determined to keep in touch with everything that was going on. Often, he would see an item on the ticker about some citizen in trouble, or even some reporter in an accident, and out of kindness would immediately telephone the family to express his sympathy and to offer his help. He did this once for me when I crashed in a naval airplane in Danang during the Viet Nam war, though his personal enthusiasm for my writings at that or any other time was not unbounded. Yet one effect of his preoccupations with the press and his savage and often cruel comments about members of the press corps to his associates was to curb the flow of the news, perhaps even more than he intended it to do.

Public criticism of government policy can, of course, influence policy, but it tends to do so not through persuading a mass audience but by reaching a much smaller audience in the Congress and the intellectual and communications communities of the nation. The editorial pages of American newspapers still reach a very limited percentage of the newspaper-reading public and, like the television commentators, tend to be dominated by the flow of news coming mainly from official sources.

Never have reporters and commentators reached so many people in America with their news and views as they do now, and had so little power to change the direction of the nation's foreign policy. The television network "stars" reach as many as 26 million viewers a night with their news summaries. They bring in their vivid reports on video tape from all the major capitals and battlefields of the world, and occasionally even bounce them off man-made stars in transoceanic broadcasts, but the reaction of the public in the foreign field is quite different from that in the national field.

Within the nation, reporters have a powerful influence on local and national issues. The local editor is usually a respected leader on community issues. The television reports of racial strife in the American South undoubtedly aroused the conscience of millions of viewers and helped produce the nation-wide protest movements and the legislation that transformed the legal position of the American Negro in the mid-1960s.

In certain situations overseas, modern news reporting arouses Congressional and public opinion sufficiently to influence the President and his aides. News reports and television films of American and South Vietnamese casualties undoubtedly helped encourage resistance to that war. Yet despite the enlarged scope and volume of reports to the American people from abroad, the President has seldom if ever been more free to conduct foreign policy in accordance with his own judgments, and the reasons for this are fairly clear.

The issues of foreign policy are increasingly complex and dangerous. It was easy to have a strong public opinion against getting involved in wars when the mood and tradition of the nation were powerfully isolationist, and easier still to get almost unanimous public support when wars started with an attack on Pearl Harbor or with the movement of enemy armies across recognized international frontiers. Even experts on foreign affairs, however, find it difficult to have dogmatic opinions about what to do when the nation is confronted with wars 10,000 miles from home started by subversion and guerrilla action under ambiguous circumstances carefully calculated by the enemy to confuse and deceive.

A fundamental change has thus occurred in the attitude of the American people toward the government's conduct of foreign policy. In the old days, the people tended to believe the government was wrong until war was actually declared; now, confronted with torrents of confusing and often contradictory information about questions that could lead to war, the tendency is to assume the government is right. I believe the American reporters were nearer to the truth than the published government reports were during the critical periods that preceded the indirect American invasion of Cuba in 1961 and the large American intervention in South Viet Nam in 1965, but the people paid little attention to those reports and the government was free to use its own judgment, which was not brilliant.

It takes some thumping crisis to startle a vast continental nation out of its normal preoccupations with family and work. There is a time problem here that minimizes the influence of newspapers on the public. To be effective, reports on a developing situation have to come considerably ahead of the crisis; but at that time the people are usually not paying attention, and once the crisis breaks, they tend to leave it to the government.

Besides, it is hard for even the most careful reader or listener or viewer to be sure when the reporters are right and when they are wrong, since we reporters are wrong so often. If we tell the readers a mayor is a crook and provide some evidence in support of the claim, they will usually believe us, but if we suggest the Secretary of State is a numskull or the President is a pleasant incompetent, they will usually tell us to mind our manners. Our power is smaller than our reputation. The credit of the American newspapers with the American people for accuracy and good judgment is not high. Everybody knows how often the American voters reject the advice of newspapers in local, state, and national elections: one word from us and they do as they please. And especially in the field of foreign policy, a majority of the people will usually take the government's judgment over that of the newspapers.

THE PRESS AND CONGRESS

What influence the press has on the conduct of foreign policy usually comes indirectly, not through the mass of the people but mainly through the Congress of the United States. The relations between well-informed reporters in Washington and influential Congressmen are quite different from the relations between reporters and officials of the executive branch of the government.

Officials in the White House, the State Department, and the Defense Department, though polite and often friendly, almost always regard the reporter with suspicion. He is potential trouble. Even if the official tells the reporter nothing and puts it off the record as well, which often happens, the mere fact that he is known to have seen the reporter may lead his superiors to blame him for something the reporter prints several days later. Thus, the official is canny, particularly if the President or the Secretary of State happens to be in a waspish mood toward the press, which is the case a good deal of the time.

Congressmen are different. Unlike officials of the executive branch, they live most of the time in the open. They think the good opinion of the press is important to their re-election, which dominates much of their thinking; consequently, they see reporters and some of them even read us. Also, they are always making speeches and, like reporters, looking for mistakes to correct or criticize, especially if they are in the opposition.

Reporters and Congressmen are thus often natural allies. They exchange information in a discreet way, and sometimes in ways that are not so discreet. When the Administration comes to the Congressmen for its money, it has to answer their questions and justify its programs, and in the process it discloses a lot of information which interests the press a great deal. Particularly in these days when so much of foreign policy depends on economic and military appropriations that the Congress must approve, the committee hearings are often a profitable source of news.

How the press, radio, and television reporters use the close association with members of the Congress determines whether their influence is good or bad. Out of the hundreds of thousands of words spoken on a busy day in the committees and on the floor of the two houses of Congress, the reporters must make a selection, and what they select goes not only to all the newspapers and radio and television stations but also over those tickers outside the President's office. Thus the reporters at the White House are constantly conveying the views of the President to the members of the Federal legislature, and the reporters in the House and Senate press galleries are similarly serving as a link between what is happening on Capitol Hill and the President and his cabinet members, who also have news tickers in their offices.

What makes news in a democratic society thus influences policy decisions both in the executive and legislative branches of the government. The politicians at both ends of Pennsylvania Avenue are particularly sensitive to what the reporters select, what is going out on the air and into the headlines, for this often produces strong reactions among the voters outside Washington. In the battle for the appropriation of money, for example, the dramatic news of military requirements tends to get a larger play than the less spectacular news about foreign aid, and this news emphasis on the military undoubtedly helps assure more votes for the armed services than for the foreign aid programs.

The influence of reporters on the conduct of individual members of the House and Senate, particularly the House, is much greater than is generally realized. For example, if reporters tend to play up the spectacular charges or statements of extremists on Capitol Hill and to play down or ignore the careful, analytical speeches of the more moderate and responsible members—as, unfortunately, they do most of the time —this inevitably has its influence on many other members, particularly new members. The latter are naturally trying to establish themselves. They are eager to say things that will get into the news and be read back home before the next election. Accordingly, if the moderate and the serious statements are ignored by the reporters and the spectacular trivialities are emphasized, the new Congressman often draws the obvious conclusion and begins spouting nonsense to attract attention. This is one influence of a popular press in a democracy that merits more attention than it gets.

Multinational Enterprise and National Security

Raymond Vernon

In the past twenty years or so, Americans have been increasing their assets outside the United States faster than those at home. They have been acquiring real estate, securities, bank accounts and going businesses abroad at a rate that has brought the "outside" assets under their control near the $200 billion mark. This aspect of *le défi Américain,* however, has been matched by a countermovement of similar proportions by others. Europeans and Japanese also have been enlarging their holdings outside of their home territories at considerable speed. Their holdings in the United States alone, for instance, have risen to the neighbourhood of $100 billion. As far as the developed countries are concerned, therefore, the interests of their nationals now sprawl untidily over the globe.

Developments of that sort are hardly new in human history. It is no new experience for nations to see their national interests extending well beyond their boundaries. Cases in which sovereigns have been called on to protect the overseas interests of their nationals or have put those interests to work in the name of national security are common enough. But today, there are some differences. One such difference is a question of scale: the size and

extent of the ownership of overseas assets by nationals has dwarfed anything of the kind previously experienced. Another difference is more profound. The conduit for overseas growth has changed.

Today, the principal medium by which outside assets are built up is the multinational enterprise, that is, the enterprise headquartered at home which maintains operating arms of its home business in foreign locations. The assets that are committed by the nationals of one country in another through a multinational enterprise differ from the assets of the traditional international investment. Those of the multinational enterprise are directed and managed day by day according to some business strategy which links those assets to others all over the globe. This is a large step away from the days when the overseas assets of the advanced countries were represented mainly by pieces of paper issued by governments, railways and power plants acknowledging the right of the holder eventually to receive some funds from the issuer. In order to understand the implications of this change for national security, it will help to examine some aspects of the nature of multinational enterprises.

NATURE OF THE MULTINATIONAL ENTERPRISE

For 500 years or more, the sovereign states have occasionally found it useful to create artificial persons; and having created such persons, to endow

them with some of the attributes of natural men, including the right to own and owe, the right to sue and be sued, and—*mirabile dictu*—the right to nationality. Entities such as the British East India Company, the Dutch East India Company, the Hudson's Bay Company and the Massachusetts Bay Colony were familiar examples. These entities represented an extension of the Crown's personality; they were its instruments and its subjects. And it goes without saying that, like natural persons, they were entitled to call on the Crown for protection as needed.

The modern corporation has descended in an unbroken lineage from these early aberrations. But it has managed to acquire some rather extraordinary attributes along the way.

First, the main restrictions that once limited the powers of the corporations have been shed. Until a century ago, the powers of corporations created in the United States and Britain had characteristically been sharply limited by their charters. They were generally confined to certain explicit economic activities, such as banking or canal-building or trading in certain specified areas; their life-span was usually confined to some given period; and the maximum size they could legally attain was generally specified.

By World War I, however, practically all of these restrictions had gone by the boards, both in the United States and Western Europe. By that time, corporations could be formed by practically anyone for practically any purpose without limit of time or size. More important, however, was the fact that corporations by this time had acquired the extraordinary right to own other corporations. With that right established, all sorts of new possibilities were opened up. An enterprising group pursuing a given business strategy could create a separate corporation to perform each different element of the strategy, thus ensuring that their legal accountability was limited and their financial eggs were not contained in a single basket. If their masters so chose, the separate corporations could be made to respond to a common

will, and to provide mutual support. The advantages of separateness and the advantages of agglomeration were brought together in a single institution.

When corporations created in different national jurisdictions were linked together in a single multinational enterprise, the virtues of multiple nationality were added to those of multiple identity. An American entity that enjoyed all the rights and privileges for doing business in the United States could join its resources and relate its strategy with a British entity in Britain, a French entity in France, and so on; and the resulting union, while retaining its compartmentalized multiple identity, could be made to respond to a common purpose and to draw on a common pool of resources.

It would be too gross a simplification to say that each national part of a multinational enterprise acquired the same rights and privileges in the country where it was located as an enterprise that was locally owned. The labyrinthine legal doctrines that were applied when national laws were in conflict, for instance, drew heavily at times on such metaphysical concepts as the location of the "real seat" of an enterprise, that is, the principal decision-making centre.[1] But there were also more obvious distinctions made by many nation states between "our" enterprises and "theirs." Long before World War II, corporations owned by foreigners, even if created under local law, were commonly prohibited from engaging in public broadcasting, in coastwise shipping, in munitions manufacture and in other "sensitive" industries.[2] Besides, when the companies concerned were very large in relation to the economy in which they hoped to do business, it was inevitable that the terms of their entry should be fashioned on an *ad hoc* basis. Accordingly, foreign-owned mining companies, oil companies and large-scale plantation enterprises commonly found it necessary to come to special terms with the host government, involving distinctive rights and distinctive obligations. Still, despite these qualifications, the day-to-day business of foreign-owned subsidiaries was generally conducted around the world on a basis that was not very different from that of locally-owned enterprises.

The experiences of World War II offered a hint that the problem of the nationality of industry might one day arise as a major issue. The question "What is an alien?", which had already arisen in World War I, came back again in stronger form. Should the factories of the German subsidiary of General Electric, located in Germany, be dealt with as if they were owned by a German "national?" And how should the United States classify an American company whose parental links could be traced to a German parent, thence to a Swiss grandparent? To disentangle such issues, the principal allied countries found the need to develop elaborate international agreements which among other things set out some ground rules aimed at defining what was an enemy alien and what not.[3]

While the sovereign states have occasionally found themselves trying to sort out who was whose, the enterprises themselves have not wholly been unaware of some of the advantages of multiple national identity. In wartime, the subsidiaries of foreign-owned enterprises commonly performed their assigned wartime tasks without any overt indication of their foreignness.[4] It was characteristic of such cases that, with a fine indifference to ownership, the local managers put the premises to work for the local war effort, at the same time as bombers carrying the insignia of the parent's government sought diligently to blow them up. In an exceptional case or two, enterprises were also known to try to use their national ambiguity to more explicit advantage, arranging their inter-affiliate relationships so that they could claim to be on the winning side, whatever that side might turn out to be.

Even in situations short of actual warfare, the potentialities of multiple identity have at times proved most attractive. Both Royal Dutch Shell and Unilever, for instance, have carefully developed the dual Dutch-British nationalities of the parent because they have found the ambiguity to be useful. When Sukarno was being beastly to Dutchmen, these enterprises emphasized their British identity. But when someone declares a vendetta against the British, it is the Dutch identity that comes to the fore.

The advantages of ambiguities of this sort have been evident at times not only to the enterprises but also to the governments with which they deal. Governments in power tend to follow a more pragmatic policy at times than the ideology which they publicly profess. Those that are trying to survive in the mercurial politics of the less-developed world sometimes want to tap the resources of a large "American" enterprise without being obliged to acknowledge locally that they are doing business with the ideological enemy. In that case, a little protective colouration, transparent though it may be, is still welcome; doing business with an intermediate company, "European" or "Middle Eastern" in apparent identity, is often an acceptable arrangement, even if the company is obviously owned by an American parent.

Despite the fact that the ambiguousness of the identity of multinational enterprises has not been altogether a drawback for host countries, most countries on balance have felt an increasing need to pierce the corporate veil. In addition to laying special restraints on foreign-owned subsidiaries at the time of their entry, therefore, most have tended to distinguish such subsidiaries in the treatment accorded under local law and regulation. In some cases, these distinctions violated treaty obligations to the contrary, treaty obligations that bind each contracting state to grant non-discriminatory treatment to the local subsidiaries owned by the nationals of the other states. But commitments of that sort were set aside, as various states —impelled mainly by questions of national security or national prestige— strove to reduce the role of foreign-owned subsidiaries in various "key sectors" of the local economy.

Discriminatory treatment has taken many forms. When dispensing research subsidies, for instance, government officials have had a keen eye for the ownership of local enterprises. In view of the national purposes in granting such subsidies, one could hardly have expected the British, the French, or the Japanese, to make such awards impartially; that would mean dispensing research funds not only to the struggling computer companies that are locally owned but also to the local subsidiaries of IBM, GE and Honeywell. Propelled by the same kind of consideration, national governments have developed discriminatory policies in public purchases, in the rationing and subsidizing of local credit, in the admission of foreign technicians and in the screening of corporate mergers and consolidations. Throughout, there has been an attempt to build up locally-owned enterprises at the expense of the foreign-owned contingent.

The United States has not been wholly free of discriminatory practices of this sort. The procurement regulations of the defence agencies have sometimes excluded American corporations whose management or ownership included foreigners. The facilities extended by the United States Government to "American" corporations that invested in less-developed countries, such as insurance against the losses of expropriation and war, have not been available to "American" corporations that were primarily owned by foreigners. On the whole, the United States Government has made less of this sort of distinction than other governments have done. But the lesser use of such practices has been due partly to the fact that the regulatory powers of the American Government have been rather less extensive than those of Europe or Japan. Besides, the United States Government has tried to make a show of tolerance for foreign-owned subsidiaries in the United States in order to increase the tolerance of foreign governments for American-controlled subsidiaries in their countries.

Despite the restraints and roadblocks, however, the multinational enterprise has become more visible. That increased visibility has raised a variety of questions about its relations to the national defence.

PLACE OF THE MULTINATIONAL ENTERPRISE

A penchant for hyperbole has led many who speculate about the future to see the world dominated a few decades hence by several scores of large multinational enterprises. That outcome, however, is still quite remote.

So far, according to the crude statistics covering American-controlled enterprises, there are about 200 large United States parent companies with heavy overseas commitments in manufacturing and raw materials extraction. These enterprises, taken all together, probably account for about one-third of manufacturing sales in the United States proper. Through their subsidiaries and branches, they cover about 6 or 8 per cent of manufacturing sales in the other advanced countries and 10 or 12 per cent in the less-developed countries. In addition, there are many multinational enterprises headquartered in the other advanced countries—notably companies with headquarters in Britain, Germany, France, Italy, Switzerland, the Netherlands, Sweden and Japan. These also contribute considerable amounts both to their own national output and to "foreign" output of manufactured goods and raw materials. By a heroic numerical leap, multinational enterprises can be thought of as embracing one-quarter to one-third of the output of goods in their "home countries" and one-sixth or so of the output in countries that are foreign to the parent.[5]

If there are national security problems embedded somewhere in these operations, they lie not so much in the sheer size of the enterprises as in the kind of activities in which the enterprises specialize.

Take raw materials production. Half a dozen large multinational enterprises are enough to account for three-quarters of the oil that moves in international trade; and a like number would account for about the same proportion of the ores that cross international boundaries to be processed into copper, aluminium, lead, zinc or nickel. The position of the large enterprises in these industries is most commanding at the unfabricated end of the production chain, where size offers the most obvious advantages; and it is least extensive at the last stages of fabrication and distribution. Still, in all these products, the enterprises concerned operate at all levels, moving the product from one affiliate to the next in a complex chain that reflects an extensive degree of vertical integration.

In the field of manufactures, the industries in which large multinational enterprises are to be found are principally those in which unique competitive positions—what economists like to call "barriers to entry"—can be built up and maintained through large expenditures. There are two main strategies conducive to this end: those that emphasize the building up of brand names, as in food products, automobiles and drugs; and those that are based on heavy expenditures in the development of products with unique performance characteristics, as in chemicals and computers. More often than not, the two strategies are found in combination in the same firm.[6]

The propensity of multinational enterprises to concentrate in activities in which entry is difficult means, in effect, that they are heavily represented in the sectors that nations regard as essential to defence. One could go through the familiar drill of reciting the percentages: 40 per cent of Britain's computer industry; 40 per cent of France's telephone and telegraph industry; 100 per cent of Italy's ballbearing industry; and so on. The size of any such figures, however, is arbitrary in some measure, depending on how widely or narrowly one defines an industry.

Whatever the appropriate definition of an industry may be, one is justified in observing that the industries in which multinational enterprises have tended to survive and prosper include those that are prominent in industries producing and processing major raw materials and those that are identified with the forefront of modern industry. These industries occupy a key position in the tense periods before the outbreak of war, to prepare the national economy for hostilities and to signal that state of readiness to the other side. Even where the subsidiaries have been in activities of a more mundane sort, such as food preparations, they have seemed more important in the economy than their simple size indicated, because the marketing strategy of such subsidiaries has demanded an emphasis on distinctiveness.

The operations of the units that make up multinational enterprises have been linked to national security not only because they have tended to cluster in industries that are critical for conventional warfare, but also because they have come to occupy a commanding place in the external transactions of many countries. In a typical year, the United States exports $4 billions or so in the form of direct investment and receives $6 or $7 billions of income from her outstanding direct holdings. In both Britain and the United States, more than a quarter of the exports of manufactured goods consist of transactions between the parents of multinational enterprises and their affiliates. In Latin America, the exports of manufactured goods by foreign-owned subsidiaries, which now well exceeds $500 millions annually, probably represent over 40 per cent of all such exports from the area.[7] As for exports of raw materials by multinational enterprises, these occupy an overwhelming position in the external transactions of some less-developed countries. Saudi Arabia, Iran, Iraq, Libya, Chile and Venezuela are heavily reliant on the continuation of a flow of raw materials from local facilities managed by foreign interests to the overseas affiliates of those same interests. Although there are many things that nations can do without, if necessary, for their national security, foreign exchange is not usually one of them; in the short run, there is almost no substitute for the foreign exchange earnings that exports generate.

The heavy reliance of some countries upon the operations of multinational enterprises in the generation and maintenance of a reasonable balance-of-payment position is a symptom of a much larger problem. For the past ten years or so, international trade and investment have been growing faster than national trade and investment. If multinational enterprises were abolished tomorrow, the odds are that the higher rate of growth in international trade and payments would still continue, albeit in other forms. Measured in gross quantity terms, therefore, most nations are becoming somewhat more vulnerable to external influences.

If multinational enterprises were abolished, however, there would be one difference. Transactions between two affiliates in a multinational enterprise system located in different countries are rather less easily reached by the regulatory devices of a national government than transactions that are undertaken at arm's length between unrelated parties. Although all businesses in the government's jurisdiction could be mobilized for war, whether the businesses were national or multinational, the capacity of the multinational enterprises to make choices among the prospective belligerents in the pre-war disposition of men, money and materials are thought to be far greater than that of the nationals. Accordingly, nations that feel a sense of vulnerability to outside forces as a result of a high level of foreign transactions have that feeling heightened when the transactions are "internal" to the multinational enterprise; and heightened still further when the parent of the enterprise is located on foreign soil.

MULTINATIONALS AS NATIONAL CONTRIBUTORS

Whether or not multinational enterprises pose a challenge at the borders of a nation's territory, the fact remains that they are capable of making useful contributions to national growth and national well-being. In the national security context, one of the more obvious contributions is in the production of *matériel* for the national military establishment. Two questions are raised by that fact: does a country increase its ability to generate defence goods by encouraging the establishment of multinational enterprises in its economy; and, if so, does the country's capacity to produce defence goods through the units of multinational enterprises add anything on balance to its defence?

The treatment of these questions requires a certain intellectual diffidence. One is being asked to compare what actually has transpired with what might have occurred if the complex world had been a different place. Would Germany have been more formidable as an industrial power if she had been less willing to accept the subsidiaries of American enterprises; or France and

Japan more formidable if they had been more willing? Are the Soviet Union and China handicapped by the absence of multinational enterprises? And are Argentina and Brazil more capable of defending their interests because they have admitted many subsidiaries of foreign-owned enterprises?

A few propositions are quite clear. The capacity to produce goods for defence turns heavily on the ability to scan the technology of the world's producers. That scanning can be done in many different ways: by repatriating a few hundred key scientists from the United States and Europe and putting them to work, as China did in the 1950s; by creating licensing links between local firms and foreign enterprises, as Japan and others have done, and using those links not merely to divide up markets but also to secure and exploit information; by appropriating the technology that can be found in scientific periodicals and patent applications or that can be acquired by industrial espionage, as many countries almost certainly do; and, finally, by permitting or encouraging the creation of subsidiaries of multinational enterprises on one's territory, especially enterprises that have some explicit bearing on defence production.

All of these techniques have costs. All of them can "work," in the sense that they can yield information that is more valuable than the national resources used in securing the information; some of them can work remarkably well.[8] In terms of efficiency of communication, however, there is a strong case to be made that detailed industrial information and ways of producing things are more readily transmitted by way of multinational enterprises than by any of the other channels of communication suggested earlier. That heroic conclusion is not in the nature of things; it is rather an empirical generalization, based on patchy observations about costs and performance,[9] and supported here and there by rudimentary propositions about relative efficiency in communication networks.[10]

Of course, once a country assigns a given defence task to a subsidiary of a multinational enterprise located in its country, such as the manufacture and repair of tanks, there is always a risk that the country's logistical planners may stop using other channels for scanning outside sources of information that bear on the manufacture and maintenance of tanks. If one could assume that the multinational enterprise were reliable as a conduit for such information, the delegation of the task of tank manufacture to a subsidiary of such an enterprise might be a sensible national decision. But what if the central management of the enterprise decided systematically to refrain from passing on to its subsidiary certain types of information that were available to the enterprise? Something like this sort of concern, no doubt, troubles the logistical planner of all countries where subsidiaries of multinational enterprises are important producers. It may very well be that there are hard grounds for the concern. But the dimensions of the problem ought to be very clear.

If the wanted information was proprietary information belonging to the multinational enterprise itself, and if the central management of the enterprise was unwilling to provide it to a subsidiary, there is a presumption that the central management will be unwilling to impart the wanted information by any other route. Given the general preference of multinational enterprises to keep their technology under their control as long as it has considerable proprietary value, the assumption is that more will be communicated inside a multinational system than by way of arm's length licensing. The area that national authorities would have to concern themselves about, therefore, was the area of technology that a local facility would have access to if it were not a member of the multinational enterprise. This includes information in the public domain outside the country, or information that could be extracted by espionage from the outside affiliates of the multinational enterprise.

The problem just described cannot be shrugged off. In mitigation of the problem, however, it is worth noting that various studies of the internal structure of American-based multinational enterprises suggest that the barriers to information inside such enterprises are growing less watertight, not more.[11] Most multinational enterprises have been pushing their organizational structures in directions that are aimed at facilitating the inside flow of technical information among constituent units in different countries. As the "foreign" side of the activities of these enterprises has grown, that aspect of the business has been incorporated more and more intimately into the mainstream of the enterprise. The compartmentalizing of useful information on tight geographical lines within the enterprise is becoming less possible.

Today, therefore, information travels more effortlessly across boundaries than ever before. Capital installations, such as chemical process plants, are characteristically designed and constructed by multinational enterprises for multinational enterprises; the construction entity scans the world for ideas and designs, while the using entity applies the results wherever its installation may be. Automobile manufacturers adopt techniques where they find them, moving the needed skills from one market to another; they borrow the latest wrinkles for machining aluminium from the subsidiary with the largest experience, and spread it quickly to the others; or they call upon their multinational suppliers of parts to carry out the needed skills across national boundaries as the occasion arises. National authorities that rely on the subsidiaries of multinational enterprises for critical technological inputs

still need to be sure that the enterprises are receiving what the rest of the system knows and are doing an adequate job of scouring other outside sources. But the authorities also have to maintain that kind of vigilance when they make use of locally-owned facilities for critical defence purposes.

Of course, once some useful information has been moved across a national boundary inside a country, its availability for the national defence is still not wholly assured. One can picture a foreign-owned subsidiary holding back information that would be useful for defence purposes. It would be hard to test whether anything of the sort has occurred in the past. The sort of casual evidence that can be gleaned from business histories suggests that when a nation is under siege—when it is preparing for war or engaged in actual combat—the information which has been transmitted to the local subsidiary is usually at the service of the state to the same degree as if the ownership of the enterprise were in local hands. In World War I and World War II, as nearly as any outsider can judge, the facilities of National Cash Register and Ford in Germany, for instance, were exploited just as effectively as the nationally-owned facilities of their local competitors.

Although foreign-owned subsidiaries may be no less "reliable" as wartime producers than locally-owned enterprises, there is one possibility that each nation will surely want to explore with care. This is the possibility that the plants of multinational enterprises are geared to dependence on outside products to a greater extent than the plants of locally-owned enterprises. Generalizations on that point are a bit dangerous. So much depends on the industry and the country involved. In so far as there is evidence on this point covering industry in the large, it suggests that there is not much basis for such a concern. It is clear that the units of multinational enterprises make a much heavier contribution to international trade as a whole than do national entities. But that is due in considerable part to the selection of industries in which multinational enterprises concentrate, such as raw material processing, automobiles and chemicals. Industry mix aside, the propensity for foreign-owned subsidiaries to engage in international trade is mainly due to a heavier stress on exports, not to heavier stress on imports. According to the limited data, foreign-owned enterprises have depended only a little more than locally-owned enterprises upon foreign sources when acquiring machinery and intermediate products.[12] And some make the assumption that even this modest tendency is to be encouraged because it reflects better market intelligence and leads to higher efficiency.[13]

There is an understandable preference on the part of nations, nevertheless, to keep foreign-owned enterprises out of "sensitive" industries associated with national defence. Nations can accept the support of the foreign-owned enterprises only as long as the efficiency gained by sharing the superior information grid of the enterprise is not offset by other losses. Those losses include not only a fear of reliance on outside sources of materials but also a fear of sharing the information grid with others. Some delicate choices are involved. IBM computers are reluctantly bought and put to work by the defence authorities in other countries for just so long as the substitute "national" product would be substantially inferior; but light submachine guns, ingenious though they may be, can be designed and manufactured by local interests. In this choice, there is always the wistful hope that somehow the foreigner's role can be made less critical or can be dispensed with altogether.

Japan ranks high among the nations that have gone to some lengths to keep foreign-owned industry out of sensitive sectors. The case of Japan is commonly cited for the proposition that such a policy is feasible—that multinational ownership is not important for the efficient transmission of technology, and that the use of licensing can be at least as efficient. But the case of Japan may demonstrate much less. For one hundred years, Japan has doggedly and consistently spent large sums and considerable manpower in an effort to bargain effectively for technology. Her negotiating position has been bolstered by the fact that most of the technology she sought was not very closely held. It has been strengthened also by the fact that Japan's internal market was large, so that access could be used as an effective bargaining counter. Besides, Japan's workforce was literate and disciplined, so it was capable of applying the information it acquired. Finally, prospective licensers in the United States and Europe saw the prospective Japanese licensees as threatening in world markets if they were not tied up with licensing agreements. Conditions of that sort, coming together in one nation, may well be *sui generis*. In fact, Japan herself may be finding this strategy less effective, as her needs for outside technology reach into the more esoteric and closely held fields of proprietary information, and as her needs for access to the markets of others begin to erode the negotiating edge that her control over market access once provided.

If there is any country that is entitled to harbour some doubts about the national security implications of multinational enterprises, it is the United States. The widening horizons of American enterprises, their increasing disposition to use remote overseas facilities for the manufacture of components and intermediate products, raise questions about the internal sufficiency of the American industrial complex. Does Fords' overseas fabrication of the engine and transmission system for its new little *Pinto* make any difference to American security; does IBM's production of computerized office equipment in Europe matter from this viewpoint? On the whole, these are not very serious questions, in view of the size and diversity of the American industrial establishment. But they are questions that a military planner would reasonably ask.

Once asked, the answer to such questions is obscure. It is obscured by the fact that the dispensation of benefits by multinational enterprises is not "zero-sum." Measured in absolute terms, all nations may find their military strength increased by the dispositions of such enterprises. The increased sharing of knowledge across international boundaries may enhance the ability of all nations to build better tanks and guns. Moreover, the fact that some of the nation's facilities form part of a multinational system could mean that the output available for actual warfare would come from a logistical structure that was more widely dispersed, a relevant fact in an era of atomic blackmail or actual atomic warfare.

There is one impact of the growth of multinational enterprises upon defence capabilities, however, that has special significance for the United States. The capacity of the multinational enterprise to increase the manufacturing productivity of a national economy, where that capacity exists, stems from its ability to ingest and apply technical information about products and processes. Although the actual production processes of the multinational enterprise do not always occur on American soil, it is likely that the information-storage centre of the enterprise as well as the administrative apparatus for planning, adapting and controlling the enterprise are located there. In short, the United States is specialized in the management function and its ancillary services. As I read the evidence of industry's role in warfare, organizational capabilities of that sort are more important for the satisfaction of national security needs in emergency situations than are the plants themselves.

Since multinational enterprises probably have somewhat strengthened the military capacity of all the countries in which they operate, when capacity is measured in absolute terms, the aggregate capacity with which an embattled non-Communist coalition would confront a Communist world has probably been increased. (As a corollary, the extension of affiliate multinational enterprises inside the Communist countries probably increases the capacity of those countries, to a degree that trade would not.) Within the portions of the non-Communist world where the multinational enterprises have operated, however, it is hard to say which parties have been strengthened more: whether the gains to the United States have exceeded those of Europe or *vice versa,* whether those of Argentina have outdistanced those of Brazil.

So far, the emphasis has been on multinational enterprises engaged in manufacturing. Enterprises that are devoted to the exploitation of raw materials and to their processing and distribution are thought to have a quite distinctive impact on national security. Oil, of course, is the outstanding case; but copper, aluminium, iron ore and others are also involved. In these cases, the operations of the multinational enterprise are tied to national security by two rather different causal chains.

There is one line of wistful speculation that sees international peace as being related to a satisfactory rate of national economic growth, especially the economic growth in the less-developed nations. Countries that are growing well, according to this view, are less likely to be a cause of difficulties than those that are not. If the operations of multinational enterprises increase the output of oil and ores from remote places, as they almost certainly do, then the multinational enterprises are the agents of stability through growth. Unless their very presence is an irritant, their contribution to the growth of such places may reduce the areas of troubled waters in which national dissidents or outside revolutionaries may be tempted to fish.

The assumption that economic growth reduces the peace-disturbing propensities of the less-developed areas, however, is a doubtful proposition. If there is any relationship between the growth of less-developed areas and their contribution to peace among nations, it is very complex. Nations that have never known much growth and that are living near subsistence levels, such as Burma, Mauritania and Paraguay, are rarely heard from. Those that have grown for a time and then had their growth arrested, such as Egypt and Algeria, can be stormy petrels. Yet those that are growing rapidly, such as Libya, are no less capable of contributing to the world's tensions; indeed Libya's very growth is a basis for her capacity to disturb the peace. The underlying relationships between growth and tension in the less-developed countries, if relationships exist, have yet to be well understood.

If multinational raw material producers cannot claim to contribute to the defence interests of nations by reducing the number of trouble spots on the globe, they can claim another tie to the defence interests of some of the nations in which they operate. The logistical grid of these enterprises is spread very wide; it draws on many sources and serves many markets. Diversity represents an important form of insurance both to selling and buying nations. It reduces the probability that games of national blackmail will succeed: either blackmail by governments that hold the markets, or blackmail by governments that hold the supplies. (Blackmail by those that control the multinational enterprises is also a possibility, of course; but that is a subject for discussion below.)

Of course, if one could picture a genuinely competitive international market in oils and metals as a real alternative to the present oligopoly structure, the existence of such a market might represent even a greater measure of insurance through diversity. If the present oligopoly structure in products of this sort were to weaken, however, it is improbable that big national buyers and sellers would be content to take their chances in an open competitive market. Though such a market reduces the commitment of any buyer to a given source and of any seller to a given market, it introduces the usual uncertainties of price and delivery that are associated with relying on an open market.

The likely alternative to the present oligopoly structure is a set of relatively inflexible bilateral flows between major producers and major consumers, such as Japan has negotiated in iron ore, copper and coal. For instance, if the present international network in crude oil were to be eroded, and if industrial users of crude oil were to be cut off from control of their raw materials, both buyers and sellers would be under strong compulsion to recapture some of the stability they had previously enjoyed. One could picture the national oil companies of Iran, Kuwait, Libya and so on, searching diligently for large scale importers that were in a position to guarantee a stipulated amount of imports over an agreed time period. More than likely, major refiners and petrochemical producers in the advanced countries would be found that were willing to enter into such contracts *faute de mieux*. However, relations created by such a network of bulk purchase contracts would be much less flexible than the internal logistical arrangements that now exist in the large multinational oil enterprises.

The significance of the multinational enterprise as a form of insurance against national blackmail, however, can easily be exaggerated. As far as the advanced countries are concerned, notably the United States and Western

Europe, the power to ward off a blackmail threat, such as the threat of the Arab countries to cut off oil supplies, is probably greater than is popularly supposed.

First of all, comparatively moderate expenditures in the stock-piling of a few key raw materials would reduce such threats to some extent. For instance, one authoritative estimate puts the cost of continuously maintaining a stockpile of six months' oil supply in Western Europe at about fifteen per cent of the current price of such oil.[14] Fifteen per cent may overstate the cost to importing countries, in fact, since the existence of a stockpile in Europe might have the effect of depressing import prices. Ironically, part of what inhibits some public and private organizations from supporting the stock-piling step is just that: the fear of lower prices for oil, not the concern for higher prices. The interests of local high-cost oil producers and coal producers combine with those of the multinational enterprises to resist this "solution" to the national defence problem.

The second sense in which the defence problem may be overstated relates to the ability of raw material suppliers actually to hurt the advanced countries even if stockpiles did not exist. That Europe would be hurt by an abrupt interruption in oil supplies goes without saying; but no one has yet made the careful calculations that are needed to determine the size of the problem. Even without data, it is clear that the American case is less difficult. The United States would encounter no more than transitional difficulty if her oil imports were badly interrupted.

In metallic ores, the problem for the advanced countries is even less serious. In this area, the amount of metal that could be saved by postponing the production of consumer-related hardgoods, automobiles and capital equipment would more than fill any conceivable defence needs.

For all that, the increased sense of psychic comfort that the sourcing patterns of the multinational enterprises provide for the advanced countries is not to be dismissed as a political force.

MULTINATIONALS AS NATIONAL CHALLENGERS

In a discussion of national security interests, it is hard to know where the limits ought to be drawn; in one way or another, directly or indirectly, any aspect of national life can be said to bear on the question of security.

Still, there is no gainsaying that institutions which threaten to be chronic irritants in relations between the states have some bearing on the national security. It is unnecessary to document the point that the operations of foreign-owned enterprises are a repeated source of irritation to the countries in which they operate.[15]

It also seems fairly evident that there is something systematic in the quality and level of such irritation: that American-controlled multinational enterprises, for instance, tend to generate higher levels of tension in host countries than enterprises controlled from Germany, and the Germans higher levels than the Dutch; that the French and the Japanese find such foreign operations less tolerable in their home territory than do the British and the Belgians; that less-developed countries as a whole find the presence (as well as the absence) of such enterprises more nerve-provoking than do the advanced countries; that large enterprises stir more passions than small; and raw material producers more passions than manufacturers.

Elsewhere, I have tried to describe the sources of these tensions and to analyse their causes. In their present context, it is sufficient to concentrate on only one or two of the factors that contribute to the tension-begetting quality of the multinational enterprise.

One element of tension derives from the fact that foreign-owned enterprises are generally seen as outsiders—worse still, outsiders that bring something to the country which the country cannot readily provide for itself: capital or technical capabilities or markets. Even the Swedes are not invulnerable. "Those damned Swedes," says a Canary Islands' expatriate revolutionary, "they own all the hotels, the travel agencies, the buses and the night clubs. And all the stores are run by Hindus. They are the first ones we are going to get rid of."[16]

The sense of dependence on the part of the host government may be tolerable as long as the foreigner's role is seen as complementary to domestic interests, rather than competitive. But whatever the starting position of the foreign-owned enterprise may be, some aspects of its existence eventually are seen by local elements as more competitive than complementary. Government officials who originally felt their position strengthened by having brought the foreign investor to their shores eventually feel their position weakened by being closely identified with foreign interests. Local businessmen who once thought of the foreign-owned enterprise as an attractive customer, a reliable supplier, or a beneficent senior partner, eventually develop the ambition to take over the foreigner's interests completely. The timing of these shifts in attitude varies according to country and culture, and according to quirks of personality and style. But it also depends on more systematic factors, such as the dispensability of the capital or technology or markets provided by the foreigners, as judged through the eyes of the local interests.

Some foreign-owned enterprises, therefore, are less vulnerable than others, especially if they are in a position constantly to bolster their negotiating position by generating expectations in the host country of added capital, technology, or markets which the host country could not provide for itself. The pronounced differences in the seeming vulnerability of the international copper companies as compared with, say, the international aluminium companies, can be attributed to just this factor: as seen by host governments, the copper companies no longer have much to offer in the way of capital, technology, or market access, whereas the aluminium companies appear indispensable for the time being.

In most countries, independent intellectual groups—especially groups that are in a position openly to play the role of the political or ideological opposition—are almost certain to be aligned against the foreign-owned subsidiaries. As part of the opposition, intellectuals tend to see the foreign-owned enterprises as allies of the government in power, yet as allies that constitute the government's Achilles' heel. But the opposition of intellectuals is also based commonly on ideological differences that transcend the political strategies of the moment.[17]

What all these groups share in their reaction to multinational enterprises, however, is a common frustration over the relative strength and flexibility of such enterprises, especially in situations in which the interests of the nation and those of the enterprise are clearly at odds. The strength of the enterprise, as seen through the eyes of local interests, lies in the fact that it operates in many jurisdictions. Accordingly, the enterprise is thought able to shift its locus of activities to a more friendly environment whenever the natives seem hostile.

The local concern over the strength and flexibility of multinational enterprises is not wholly hypothetical. When the Mexicans were being difficult in their negotiations with the foreign-owned oil companies in the 1920s and 1930s, the production of Mexican oil by foreign companies fell precipitously —while the production in more friendly Venezuela nearby was growing at a satisfactory rate. When Mossadegh took over the foreign-owned oil properties in Iran in 1952 and when Ovando repeated the Mossadegh performance in Bolivia in 1969, the oil companies suffered less than the countries that had taken the action; and, in the end, the countries were obliged to come to terms with the foreigners.

Concern over the relative strength and flexibility of multinational enterprises is not confined to oil, and it is not limited to the less-developed countries. American labour complains that the adversary it confronts across the bargaining table is capable of responding to labour's bargaining demands simply by shifting its production to another country—to Taiwan or Mexico or Canada. The French Government is frustrated by the fact that if it lays down harsh terms for licensing a General Motors production facility in Strasbourg, the company can do about as well by setting up a facility in Brussels. The perceived flexibility of the enterprise in adversary situations is a source of the deepest uneasiness for the governments through which it must deal.

Underlying all these reactions—governmental, entrepreneurial, intellectual—is a cultural dimension as well, a dimension that has to be invoked in order to understand the differences in the intensity of the response to multinational enterprises that are found from country to country. The French and Japanese uneasiness from the presence of foreign enterprises stands in contrast to the relatively relaxed (though by no means wholly comfortable) reactions of the British and Germans. The ability of the Ivory Coast to embrace the presence of French companies is not to be construed as evidence of an equal tolerance for German or American enterprises. But even if the cultural dimension were absent, the problem would still remain.

All this adds up to the fact that multinational enterprises can be an irritant—at times, even more than an irritant—in international relations. The very importance of the enterprises to the countries in which they operate adds to their tension-generating capabilities. As long as the importance of an enterprise is perceived by interests in the host country as being very large, the tension may not lead to aggressive action. Such action may occur, however, when the country's need for the foreign-owned enterprise begins to decline, ruffling the waters of international relations.

MULTINATIONALS AS TROJAN HORSES

The most threatening aspect of multinational enterprises by far—the aspect that links the existence of such enterprises intimately to questions of national defence—is the potential role of these enterprises as the agent of foreign governments. Perhaps it is this factor more than any other that explains why host countries are less uneasy about the presence of subsidiaries controlled by Dutch or Swiss parents than of subsidiaries controlled by American or Japanese parents.

The propensity of national enterprises to work in concert with their governments when operating on foreign soil varies greatly from one country to the next. On the one hand, it would be almost inconceivable for a large French enterprise to take any major strategic move abroad without consulting its tutelary ministry in some depth. In similar vein, no large Japanese enterprise could contemplate an overseas adventure of any significance without substantial consultation with the Japanese Ministry of International Trade and Industry and the Bank of Japan. Even if a formal licensing system did not apply in these countries, the consultation would take place in the ordinary course.

By comparison with other large industrial countries, the United States Government exerts comparatively little influence over its enterprises in connection with the operation of their overseas activities. The propensity to avoid *ad hoc* relations with enterprises runs very deep in American law and administrative practice. The usual relationship with such enterprises is arm's length and non-discriminatory. When the American Government has attempted to deviate from that general approach, powerful internal forces have generally arisen to push the relationship back to its customary non-selective patterns. The application of the American system of capital export controls in the 1960s, for instance, began almost on case-by-case basis; but after some months of operation, it has already reverted to the relatively non-selective and non-discriminatory approach that is characteristic of American governmental administration.

To be sure, the American Government is quite capable at times of working abroad through chosen instruments. Industries such as the petroleum industry and the commercial airlines consist of a sufficiently small number of firms and are associated with sufficiently vital interests that the chosen instrument role is sometimes inevitable. In the case of oil, any interruption in foreign supplies is likely to be followed by hurried consultations between the companies and the key government departments. In the case of the airlines, the chosen instrument approach is bolstered and even made necessary by the international system for the allocation of landing rights. Despite exceptions of this sort, however, the generalization holds.[18]

Although the United States Government does not generally have the faculty for close concertment with its overseas enterprises, other countries can hardly be expected to dismiss their fear of Trojan horses from the United States. Even if the behaviour of General Motors or Jersey Standard is only occasionally influenced by the suggestions of the American Government, the consequences of that influence can be more substantial than a fierce and purposeful thrust on the part of the British Government through British Leyland Motors, or by the Italian Government through ENI. Besides, the reserve power of the United States economy behind its selected agent, however large or small that agent may be, seems awesome in its potential force from the viewpoint of the countries being acted upon.

Since foreign nations commonly take it for granted that large American enterprises are in some sense the agents (or the masters) of the United States Government, they tend to assume also that the enterprises will be protected by their government. That expectation is bolstered by recollections of the Marine landings in Mexico and Central America during the second and third decades of this century, and by the unending promotional efforts of the United States governmental apparatus in favour of "free private competitive enterprise."

From time to time, the United States has demonstrated that the concern of other countries is not totally without substance, not even in the current era. Britain, for example, is prevented from selling aircraft to the government of China because the American Government refuses to permit an American parent company to send some indispensable electronic components to its subsidiary in Britain; in that case, a British corporation, created under British law, is prevented by the United States from being responsive to British national policy. Perhaps even more egregious was the case of the IBM computer, involving the government of France. In this instance, the United States Government came to the conclusion that, as a signatory to the nuclear non-proliferation treaty (NPT) it could not permit the parent American enterprise to send computers to its subsidiary in France, because the instruments would have been used in the operation of a nuclear reactor not subject to the Treaty's control. Although the number of publicized cases in which the United States Government has exercised its power in this way comes to only a dozen or two over the past decade, there is no doubt that instances of this sort have been much more common.

The critical question here is not whether the United States was within her rights in these cases but whether other governments felt greatly threatened by the actions. As they saw it, the relationship between, say, IBM in France and its American parent demonstrated the unwisdom, if not the outright danger, of relying on the subsidiaries of American-controlled enterprises. Even though the United States was a signatory to the NPT, France was not. The IBM preemption of the field, including the French market, was seen as the moving cause of French vulnerability. If the computer manufacturer in France had been an independent entity, capable of scanning the world for its components and designs, it might conceivably have produced an inferior computer. But it might also have adopted a technology and a sourcing pattern that kept France free of the potential influence of the American Government. This case, in short, has been taken as concrete evidence for the fact that the multinational enterprise could undermine rather than contribute to the defence of the host country.

The possibility that governments may direct the parents of their multinational enterprises to instruct their overseas subsidiaries to carry out some national objective seems a good deal higher, on its face, for enterprises whose parents are located in certain European countries or in Japan than for those headquartered in the United States. Countries like Australia and Indonesia cannot have failed to feel some internal qualms at the appearance of Japanese ventures in their economies. But the lesser weight of countries such as Japan, rather than their lesser disposition to control, makes their presence appear less threatening than that of the United States.

One small aside, difficult to resist. It should not be supposed that the subsidiaries of multinational enterprises whose parent units are directly owned by governments are more dangerous from the viewpoint of host governments than multinational enterprises that are privately owned. The leading international oil companies of France and Italy are respectively owned by their national governments, and that of Britain has the government as its principal stockholder. As instruments of national policy, however, these companies probably are no more feared than privately-owned enterprises of the same nationality; nor, in all probability, should they be. In the quixotic twists and turns of human behaviour, one finds that the resistant bureaucrat in a publicly-owned enterprise has almost as many ways of fending off directives from government agencies as the bureaucrat in a privately-owned undertaking. The critical dimension, it appears, is not so much the formal nature of the ownership of enterprises; it is rather the complex system of relations between the governmental apparatus and the enterprise apparatus in the economy. Irrespective of patterns of ownership, one can look to the Japanese and the French to maintain the closest control over the operations of their multinational enterprises, while the British and American governments express their authority in much more dilute form.

MULTINATIONALS AS HOSTAGES

Although the development and growth of multinational enterprises pose some novel problems in terms of national defence, they also resurrect some very familiar problems of defence in slightly altered guise. Among the familiar problems is that of dealing with the potential enemy when the enemy holds hostages. Governments of nations in which the subsidiary units of multinational enterprises are located have been tempted at times to use these units as hostages, to ensure the good behaviour of the country in which the parent is based. This is obviously a part of the strategy that Arab guerrillas keep trying to mount in order to separate the United States from Israel and Europe from the United States.

The use and abuse of hostages by adversaries is a subject that invites analyses of consummate complexity. It makes a considerable difference, for instance, whether only one party holds hostages or whether hostages have been exchanged, whether the number and quality of the hostages are large or small, and whether the threat to the hostages is latent or explicit.

As far as the advanced nations are concerned, the hostages that each holds have tended to grow rapidly since World War II, as economic and political interests have overlapped and intertwined. Meanwhile, as the United States has enlarged her commitments in the less-developed world and as Europe has converted its interests from colonial holdings to arm's length investments, the less-developed nations also have increased their supply of hostages.

My judgment is that this development is one of the critical factors which accounts for a new style in the advanced countries on the subject of the protection of overseas investments. The increase in the number of hostages held all over the world reduces the possibility of a net gain for any side in any international conflict. By the end of any such conflict, the loser may have done away with the hostages he held. Clear-cut victories, therefore, are less likely than they ever have been. This is one reason why the United States, Brit-

ain and France would have difficulty being utterly nasty to one another on the subject of foreign investment. It is also one of the reasons why these advanced countries have been following a relatively restrained and muted policy in the protection of their business interests in less-developed countries. Without much protest or demurrer from the United States, Mexico has been able to force the "mexicanization" of American-owned mining companies, Bolivia has nationalized the properties of Gulf Oil, Peru has taken similar steps towards the International Petroleum Company, Chile has nationalized the holdings of the American copper companies and so on. Yet, only in the case of Cuba and only after all the hostages were "destroyed," did the United States unambiguously attempt some punitive action. Britain has reacted in similarly muted measures toward threats and take-overs affecting properties of her nationals in Asia and Africa. France, exposed to like measures in North Africa, has had a similarly restrained response.

However, the reaction of the advanced countries in the protection of their investors' interests in the less-developed world might be a good deal more aggressive were it not for some other factors. One of these is the realization that political leaders in the less-developed countries often need the form of a successful nationalization much more than they need—or want—its substance. As long as these countries lack capital, technology, or foreign markets, they are disposed to find some means of maintaining some of the substance of their old arrangements if they can, even when they alter its form. Sukarno's handling of the nationalized oil companies in Indonesia during the mid-1960s was a classic illustration of the pattern; so was Bolivia's handling of the Gulf Oil nationalization. To the extent that this factor remains, all parties to the dispute are disposed to conduct it in muted terms.

A third factor that has led the advanced countries to apply caution and restraint in the conduct of these disputes is the increased capacity of the less-developed countries to make effective coalitions: coalitions among themselves, or coalitions with the Soviet Union and China. Egypt's handling of her relations with the United States and East Africa's managing of the Tan-Zam Railroad project are illustrative. This capacity for coalition increases the ability of the less-developed countries to threaten with credibility. That fact represents a change of far-reaching importance which deeply affects the economic interests of the advanced countries, including the position that their multinational enterprises are likely to play in matters of national security.

POSSIBILITIES FOR THE FUTURE

It is a tangled skein that links multinational enterprises to the problems of national security. But a few threads are visible and clear.

There has been a trend towards increased economic interdependence among nations; both the advanced countries and the less-developed countries are exposed to that trend, as each reaches outward for more technology, more capital, more labour, more land and more markets. In the process, multinational enterprises have taken a position of increased importance in international economic relations. While that growth has created difficulties, the lopsided nature of the multinational enterprise phenomenon—the fact that American-based enterprises have been so much more important than the enterprises of other countries—has added to those difficulties.

Although multinational enterprises have maintained or extended their position across international boundaries, however, my guess is that their utility and availability as instruments of national security are declining, not increasing.

Part of the reason for the expectation stems from a key assumption stated earlier, the assumption that the United States and other advanced countries are in a relatively poor position to use very vigorous measures in promoting and defending the interests of their overseas enterprises. If that should prove to be the case, then the multinational enterprises themselves are likely to adapt to the fact. Those adaptations, if they occurred, would reduce even further the utility of such enterprises as instruments of national policy. What kind of adaptation is to be anticipated?

History is filled with incidents that attest to the fact that the principal business of business is business. Attachment to a particular flag may be of great importance to some of the individuals associated with the bureaucracy of a multinational enterprise. But the degree to which that attachment is expressed in policy will depend in part on its business utility. This observation carries no pejorative overtones; it does not distinguish business bureaucracies from any other, certainly not from the bureaucracies of government. One of the most universal characteristics of large bureaucracies is their capacity for developing a collective conviction that the steps needed to keep their institution strong are socially justified and socially desirable.

I anticipate that multinational enterprises will respond to that imperative. They will pursue their natural bent—the creative business of moving ideas, money, people and goods in increasing volume across international boundaries—secure in the feeling that they are contributing to social welfare. If my projection is right that governments will be more restrained in the support of the activities of these enterprises, the decline in such support will hardly go unobserved in the board rooms of the enterprises themselves.

One of the major reasons for maintaining a close identification with the government of the parent unit will thereby be weakened. "The world is my oyster," a self-conscious household slogan in many such enterprises, will be one step closer to genuine enterprise policy.

As a matter of fact some of the symptoms of such a trend already are in evidence. It is not wholly accidental that the names of some of the world's leading multinational enterprises are being denationalized, that Food Machinery is now FMC, British Petroleum BP, Badische-Analin Soda-Fabrik BASF and so on. To be sure, some enterprises such as Ford and Coca-Cola, probably do not have the option of diluting their national identity. Others, such as those of the French and the Japanese, will find it difficult on cultural grounds even to contemplate the possibility. But it would be unwise to assume that national associations could not be altered, and less wise still to assume that the alteration will not genuinely affect the self-perception of the enterprise itself.

The ability of an enterprise to dilute its national identification with a single country is determined not only by legal and cultural considerations but also by the nature of the business strategy that the enterprise has accepted. In some industries, such as aluminium and computers, the need for a tightly-controlled international strategy on the part of the firm generally leads the parent to place a high value on exercising very close control over its subsidiaries. Enterprises of this sort will be loath to make organizational changes inside the enterprise that weaken the possibilities for central control. For them, therefore, the use of arrangements that introduce ambiguities in the control apparatus, such as the use of joint ventures or licensing agreements, will be difficult. Enterprises whose strategy requires the continuation of central control, therefore, may have real problems in attenuating the national identity of the system to which the subsidiary belongs. It may be that such enterprises will concentrate their efforts on devices of the sort that Unilever and Royal Dutch/Shell have employed, such as the use of dual national identities and similar arrangements. For some in this category, the possibility of regional holding companies as identity buffers will also exist.

Enterprises that do not need very tight central controls, however, are likely to engage in organizational stratagems that generate greater national ambiguity. Entities that do little international cross-hauling and that sell mainly to local markets will find this an attractive possibility. Joint ventures and management contracts will be used by such enterprises to an increasing extent.

As a result of adaptations of this sort, it is to be anticipated that multinational enterprises will be even less available as instruments of national strategy than has heretofore been the case. If that fact should begin to be clear to the governments of the United States and other advanced countries, the disposition of those countries to draw a line between multinational enterprises that are "ours" and multinational enterprises that are "theirs" may well decline. When that occurs, the willingness to entertain a multigovernmental approach to the control of multinational enterprises will grow. Once that door is opened, the position of the multinational enterprise in international relations will be greatly changed, and the relationship between multinational enterprises and national security will become more attenuated than ever.

NOTES

1. For a recent exploration of this concept, especially as it applies to Europe, see Eric Stein, "Conflict-of-Laws Rules by Treaty: Recognition of Companies in a Regional Market," *Michigan Law Review*, vol. 68, no. 7, June 1970, pp. 1327–54.

2. For summaries of these limitations, see Symposium sponsored by International and Comparative Law Center, Southwestern Legal Foundation, *Rights and Duties of Private Investors Abroad* (New York: Matthew Bender, 1965); D. F. Vagts, "United States of America's Treatment of Foreign Investment," *Rutgers Law Review*, vol. 17, no. 2, winter 1963, pp. 374–404; and, by the same author, "The Corporate Alien: Definitional Questions in Federal Restraints in Foreign Enterprise," *Harvard Law Review*, vol. 74, no. 8, June 1961, pp. 1489–551.

3. Malcolm Mason, "Conflicting Claims to German External Assets," *Georgetown Law Review*, vol. 38, January 1950, pp. 171–99.

4. For characteristic experiences involving subsidiaries of the Ford Motor Company abroad, see Mira Wilkins and F. E. Hill, *American Business Abroad* (Detroit: Wayne State University Press, 1964), pp. 64–87, 311–36. For references to experiences in the US and elsewhere, see D. F. Vagts, "The Corporate Alien," *op. cit.*, pp. 1524 ff.

5. According to some estimates generated by Judd Polk, of the $3,000 billions in goods and services produced annually in the non-Communist world, about $450 billions are produced by enterprises away from their national "home."

6. The reasons why multinational enterprises are found in industries of the sort described are developed at some length in my "Organization as a Scale Factor in the Growth of Firms," in J. W. Markham and G. F. Papanek (eds.), *Industrial Organization and Economic Development* (Boston: Houghton Mifflin Company, 1970).

7. *Survey of Current Business*, October 1970, p. 20.

8. See, for example, G. R. Hall and R. E. Johnson, "Transfers of United States Aerospace Technology to Japan," in Raymond Vernon (ed.), *The Technology Factor in International Trade* (New York: Columbia University Press, 1970), pp. 325–58.

9. A summary of the available evidence will appear in Raymond Vernon, *Sovereignty at Bay: The Multinational Spread of U.S. Enterprise* (New York: Basic Books Inc., 1971). This book is one of a series on the multinational enterprise, financed by a grant of the Ford Foundation to the Harvard Business School.

10. For more on the subject of communication, together with bibliographical references, see my article "Organization as a Scale Factor in the Growth of Firms," *op. cit.*

11. The most extensive study to date of the organizational side of multinational enterprises will appear in a book by J. M. Stopford and L. T. Wells, Jr., shortly to be published by Basic Books as part of the Harvard study of multinational enterprises.

12. G. C. Hufbauer and F. M. Adler, *Overseas Manufacturing Investment and the Balance of Payments* (Washington: US Treasury Department, 1968), pp. 20–28.

13. Sune Carlson, "Some Notes on the Dynamics of International Economic Integration," *Swedish Journal of Economics (Ekonomisk Tidskrift)*, 1970, p. 24.

14. M. A. Adelman, *The World Petroleum Market 1946–1969* (Washington: Resources for the Future, 1971) forthcoming. Other sources argue in the same direction for the United States, albeit on different facts and assumptions; see Cabinet Task Force on Oil Import Control, *The Oil Import Question* (Washington: US Government Printing Office, 1970). Many industry experts have expressed sharp dissent, but they are not in quite as strong a position to be wholly objective on questions of this sort.

15. This analysis is developed at much greater length in my *Sovereignty at Bay, op. cit.*, especially chapters 2 and 6.

16. Quoted in Sanche de Gramont, "Our Other Man in Algiers," *New York Times Magazine*, 1 November 1970, p. 128.

17. This is especially true in Chile, for example, where the opposition to multinational enterprises is based in part on a well-elaborated neo-Leninist view that such enterprises create a relationship of "dependence" between Chile and the more advanced countries, especially the United States.

18. This conclusion is, of course, less than universally shared. For a contrary view, well reasoned and carefully documented, see Ralph Miliband, *The State in Capitalist Society* (New York: Basic Books Inc., 1970), pp. 28–59 ff. See also W. A. Williams, *The Roots of the Modern American Empire* (New York: Random House, 1969).

The United States:
Social Change and Military Power

Klaus Knorr

In his book on *The Limits of Intervention*, Townsend Hoopes suggests that the Vietnamese War "is now recognized as the probable high watermark of America's tidal impulse to political-military intervention in the period following World War II. What course U.S. foreign policy now takes is far less clear than the fact that its failure in Vietnam has arrested the growth of an implicit American universalism, born of our extraordinary effort and exhilarating triumph in the great struggle that began in Europe before Pearl Harbor and ended when the second atomic bomb was dropped on Nagasaki."[1]

Mr. Hoopes, it seems to me, is right. One cannot imagine a future United States militarily intervening abroad as easily as it did in Vietnam. Indeed, it is this recognition which, in retrospect, makes this country's international behaviour over the past 25 years a cause for amazement. For almost two decades prior to World War II dedicated to isolationism, it organized a huge war effort and then assumed, apparently as a matter of course, international leadership in rebuilding order in an exhausted, impoverished and chaotic world. Reading Dean Acheson's account in *Present at the Creation*, one marvels at the casual self-confidence with which American leaders went to work and reshaped—not by any grand design but by a series of improvisations—an international order which, since it naturally reflected and accommodated American wealth and power, invited these men to identify their country's interest with the emerging *status quo*. Perceiving Communist threats as the major challenge to the system, defensive reactions became gradually rigidified into a cold war syndrome of set responses that continued to operate even as the international environment changed and modified the challenge to the *status quo*. The propensity of the bureaucratic-military machine, fashioned in the war against Germany and Japan, to resort to military strength when diplomacy could not prevent encroachments on the new order, required the maintenance of vast fleets and armies at home and abroad, and led to armed intervention in Korea, Lebanon, the Dominican Republic and eventually in Vietnam. In a democratic country, the maintenance of this machine was made possible only by the unstinting willingness of the American people to feed it, with few questions asked, the men and other resources from which its strength was derived. The war in Vietnam has undermined this willingness. It has drained national purpose as well as lives and money.

POWER AND WILL

A major question raised by this change in American behaviour concerns its consequences to the security of the United States and to that of foreign

From *Europe and America in the 1970's, II: Society and Power* in *Adelphi Papers* No. 71. Copyright © 1970 by the International Institute for Strategic Studies. Reprinted by permission.

countries who are its allies, and to the complexion of world order as a whole. As is often the case in the course of severe international conflicts, the original stakes leading governments into them diminish, and the future status of their power position increases in importance in the evaluation of possible outcomes. What has been, for some time now, mainly at stake in Vietnam —and what Presidents and their advisers, unlike their critics, dare not take lightly—is the future value of American threats for intervention, defence and deterrence. Even the nuclear retaliatory threat is involved although to a lesser degree. Like all military threats, its value turns, of course, on other factors as well as the outcome of the Vietnam War. Relative military capabilities— which, incidentally, have been changing drastically over the last two years— are of unquestionable weight. But to the crucial extent that deterrence rests on the credibility of a retaliatory threat, even deterrence on this level may be affected by the war in Vietnam. The supreme value of the threat available to a great Power is not only, or even first of all, that it will be heeded under a large range of circumstances when uttered, but that the power behind it influences the decisions of other governments even though no specific threat has been made. This value results not only from the availability of military forces but also from a nation's military reputation, that is to say, from the widespread anticipation that military strength will be brought into play when the interests of the country concerned are seriously crossed. The value of this threat is largely a matter of imputed will.

Mr. Hoopes, who is a staunch advocate of unilateral American withdrawal from Vietnam, is aware of all this. But he predicts reassuringly that there is nothing much to worry about. He points to the "advantageous truth that mere loss of prestige for a great Power is always transient and usually brief . . . (and) that great Powers quickly recover from blows to their prestige alone, precisely because of their power."[2] Yet, as anxieties in Europe and elsewhere demonstrate, the validity of this prediction is not universally accepted.

Whether or not the United States can recoup her putative military power[3] depends, of course, on the precise nature of the circumstances under which she will finally extricate herself and on what will then happen in the short run in South Vietnam. Suppose, however, that the United States will not, against most betting, somehow still exit as winner and come to enjoy the kind of reputation with which it emerged from the Korean war. In that case, the effect on American power and on the international power structure will depend much more on why the United States failed to win or, more exactly, on how various other governments explain this failure. Few of them, if any, are likely to have already arrived at definitive conclusions. Like most of us, they may as yet be subject more to puzzlement than clarity of perception. But their interest drives them to gain as much clarity as can be managed about so complicated a piece of reality.

Earlier on, before the United States herself tried to win a military victory in Vietnam, she might have been able to extricate herself with her military reputation intact if the President had declared that the country slid into this mess, step by little step, without much forethought; that, upon further examination, he had decided that it was not in our interest to stay; and if the entire nation had stood undivided behind the President's decision. If, in the eyes of the world, the United States had coolly confessed to and corrected a mistake—a type of action admittedly rare among states—her *military* power would not have suffered inasmuch as, historically, military strength and intelligence are understood not to be invariably associated. Somewhat for the same reason,

the United States might even have escaped without great loss of power if it
had been plain to anyone that she had
over-reached herself militarily; that she
attempted to gain a military victory in
a situation in which a military solution
was unfeasible; and if there had been
no lack of support at home. In that
case again, error, not weakness, would
have produced the results.

Both conditions do in fact provide
a partial explanation of the American
misadventure. The manner in which
the United States was gradually sucked
into the Vietnamese morass does not
look like a triumph of foresight. And
it is also fairly clear that American
military intervention consisted of a series of strategic and tactical blunders.
Indeed, to point up briefly the nature
of this mismanagement is not an unnecessary digression, for it greatly affected public reaction in the United
States.

Although the United States did
not suffer military defeat in Vietnam,
she was denied victory because the situation was unsusceptible to a purely
military solution,[4] and because, as an
alien outsider, she could not substitute
for Saigon in supplying the political
conditions of success. Moreover, the
United States applied the wrong military means as a contribution to a solution. Pursuing the will-o'-the-wisp of
military success, she used a fantastic
volume of explosives in order to compensate for poor target intelligence and
unsuitable tactics, instead of acting on
the recognition that the nature of the
civil war (and the public sensitivities
at home) demanded the protection and
"pacification" of the population, and
hence called for *minimization* of civilian casualties.

However, the fact of the matter (at
the time of writing) is that although
the United States was not militarily
defeated on the battlefields and jungle
trails of Vietnam, she was denied success not only by military mistakes and
the resistance of her plucky military

opponents (and their foreign backers
who furnished ample supplies, and
sanctuaries), but also by increasing
public opposition at home—a factor
which gave Hanoi and the Viet Cong
little incentive to seek a compromise
settlement even when they had become
militarily weakened. Indeed, as American public response to the invasion of
the Cambodian sanctuaries revealed,
the United States seemed nearing a
breaking point on the home front. The
genesis of this extraordinary convulsion
would be easy to explain if it has been
a mere consequence of mounting weariness of American casualties and war-
induced financial instability. Such responses undeniably played a part. But
it is abundantly clear that much of
public opposition was rooted more
deeply. Some of it, undoubtedly, resulted from a growing repugnance,
persistently fed by television coverage,
with the endless brutalities of the war.
And there is the question of whether,
ranging still more deeply, there are not
new forces at work in American society
whose impingement was only partly
touched off by Vietnam—forces which
are more fundamental and which may
severely restrict the future political and
military choices of the United States.
To put it more bluntly, are these new
forces coursing through the body politic of a character and influence to finish
off, or at least greatly subdue, the
United States as a military power capable of acting with determination in
making her weight felt beyond her
boundaries?

Before turning to an analysis of
the relevant events in the United States
—events, to repeat, which occurred in
part as a result of, and in part independently from, the war in Vietnam—I
wish to record that I approach the
problem with utter diffidence and suitable misgivings. Having lived through
these events, one is too close to them to
enjoy the vantage point of proper perspective; one is uncomfortably aware
of the many ambiguities in this rapidly

evolving situation; and one is conscious of the fact that, though explanations have been offered, there are too many of them, they are more or less unrelated, and not a few are logically inconsistent.

One fact is indubitable. Behaviour in the United States over the past two or three years manifests attitudes which do impinge on military power. Thomas Schelling's work[5] has greatly sharpened our understanding of the crucial role of will in the exercise of military power. Men and arms count only if there is determination to commit them. Domestic support is a vital prerequisite of such resolve. As I have demonstrated elsewhere[6] in some detail, the potential of societies for generating military strength rests not only on the scale and composition of economic and technological capacity, and the skill to transform such resources efficiently into appropriate military capabilities, it is *also* a function of political will, that is, of the *political* act of allocating men and other resources to the military sector. Regarding both the national production and international use of military strength, the impact of political, social and cultural factors is predispositional as well as situational. It is *situational* to the extent that government, élites and publics perceive the need for generating or employing military strength in response to current stimuli emanating from the external environment. It is a matter of underlying attitudes to the extent that leaders and public are *predisposed*, by historical experience and political culture, to favour or disfavour the solution of international conflicts by means of physical violence or its threat. Among the attitudes—antecedent to the situations raising the question of producing or applying military strength—which affect the mobilization of military power are a sense of national solidarity; a disposition to support the foreign and military policy of government as a matter of course; and the

support of groups whose members have an abiding direct and specific interest in the production and use of military strength. As is evident from historical experience, societies differ appreciably in the diffusion and intensity of these underlying attitudes. It the propensities favouring military power weaken, as when a society is rent by deep cleavages along these lines, the output and exercise of military power will suffer whatever the level of material and skill resources available. Where a society is divided with reference to underlying attitudes or situational response, the outcome depends naturally on the relative political influence of the opposing groups.

This view of the manifold factors involved in the build-up and international use of military strength makes it clear that the "military–industrial complex" is only a part of the picture and that the thesis, upheld by a good many critics, according to which United States involvement in Vietnam followed from the country's domination by the "complex" offers only a very partial and exceedingly facile explanation. To true believers in this doctrine, a conspiratorial interpretation of history is obviously congenial. The kernel of truth in this thesis is trivial. As I already noted, there are in most societies people who profit directly from the maintenance and use of military strength. Such people are numerous in the officer corps and among industrial producers, including workers, with a large stake in the supply of armaments. Their total number is apt to be relatively large in a country maintaining large military forces. Like many other interest groups these people exert influence on government decisions, for example, when governments depend on the expert advice of the military, etc. But the plain fact is that, granting this influence, civilian control of the military has been firmly established in the United States, and the members of the "military–industrial complex" are neither organized for conspiracy nor monolithic in their attitudes and views. It is Presidents Kennedy, Johnson and Nixon, and their respective civilian advisers who have set policy on Vietnam; and if any of them ever felt that their capacity to resist military advice was limited, the limitation resulted from their political understanding that given the attitudes of various publics, refusing military advice and being proven wrong by subsequent events would be courting electoral disaster.

I will now proceed to present some hypotheses designed to explain some of the changes in American society that seem to me to have a bearing on the production and use of military power. These hypotheses can claim no more than plausibility. They will be stated with no particular order of importance in mind since it would be premature to rank them now in these terms. Most of them concern conditions that preceded the Vietnam war as a major public issue, although public reaction to this war—which in many ways did act as a catalyst or accelerator of change —speeded the development, and intensified the expression of phenomena that would otherwise have taken longer to increase in visibility. Indeed, the pressures and tensions providing an impetus to change prior to sharp and wide-spread public reaction to the Vietnam war can be observed, though to lesser degree, in many affluent societies.

'INWARD-TURNING'

A number of students of contemporary life have observed multiplying signs of self-preoccupation or, as they call it, "inward-turning" in the most highly developed countries, in what Kenneth Galbraith has called the "new industrial state," and others have characterized as the post-industrial society. Inward-turning is not the same as isolationism, and it does not mean that the level of transactions with other states, especially other affluent societies, may not be on the rise. It simply means a shift in the balance between domestic and external concerns, reflecting the realization that an increased proportion of politically and economically effective demands must be, and can be, met by internal performance rather than by international action.[7] There are several variations of this hypothesis.

First, while in the pre-industrial world, economic growth and military power were frequently sought and achieved by conquest and colonization, the sources of riches and strength are now realized to lie primarily at home, in domestic saving, investment (especially in human resources) and innovation. Look at Germany and Japan just before World War II; look at them today! This is not to say that international trade is not useful or that autarchy is possible. Size of population, permitting economies of production, facilitate "inward-turning"; and the creation of a Common Market or economic union in Europe can be seen as a way to achieving the scale that makes "inward-turning" possible. Similarly, the sinews of military strength in this age of high technology have become more dependent on domestic capabilities. As I have argued at some length elsewhere,[8] while the benefits of military power applied on behalf of economic objectives have declined, the costs of applying such power, for whatever acquisitive reasons, have risen, chiefly because violent conflict has become more destructive for technological reasons, because several new restraints have reduced the legitimacy of any use of military power, except in defence against aggression, and because resistance to such use has correspondingly risen the world over. This sort of shift in the utility of military power is surely one reason why the middle powers of Europe, and likewise Japan, show little desire for returning to the international power practices in which they indulged with not inconsiderable gusto until not so long ago. Being super-powers, the United States and the Soviet Union remain more susceptible to the temptations of using strength coercively.

Second, society in the new industrial state is finally forced to face that fact that private gain—the primary engine of helter-skelter economic development—is on its way to making life unbearable, and that the excessive neglect of social costs in productive processes is impoverishing the physical and social environment at a cumulative pace. The urgent need to put one's house in order by means of enlarged public expenditures for improving atmosphere, cities, mass transportation systems, etc., again draws public attention inward.

Third, and directly related, the very same factors emphasize attention to internal regulation and local government, to more elaborate planning and organization, and—because of the inertial properties of modern bureaucracies—these activities prosper most when external disturbances can be avoided. Moreover, the extraction of resources for undertaking huge public tasks inevitably breeds conflict and is highly absorbing of political energies since people are not equal in tolerating high levels of self-coercion through political mechanisms. As one author recently put it, the mature industrial state tends towards parochialism and a kind of "self-closure."[9] Thus, as the most desirable objectives are incapable of being gained abroad, the problems of domestic rule loom larger. Foreign policy loses its claim to primacy and tends to be relegated to a subordinate role.

THE PROCESS OF DEMOCRATIZATION

The following proposition can be readily integrated with the self-preoccupation hypothesis. Throughout the history of human civilization, élites (kings, priests, oligarchs, aristocracies, business élites) have claimed a share of wealth and other privileges in compensation for organizing the production of various public goods and services, such as internal and external security, religious experiences and transportation and irrigation systems, and once they achieved the power to fix and extract their rewards, they could rarely resist the temptation to do very well by themselves. But even when their rule was decidedly exploitative—and one cannot blink at the melancholy fact that it often was—they did provide public services—sometimes even the service of restraining particularly offensive forms of exploitation—in the consumption of which populations shared, and which were probably unobtainable without élite rule. Arrow has proved that if the choices of individuals are unconstrained, they are incapable of aggregation into a public choice.[10] Though not necessarily motivated by other considerations than self-interest (even *noblesse oblige* is, after all, self-serving), ruling groups have tended to cultivate time preferences which do not overly discount the future (at least in certain respects) and have been able throughout virtually all of history to constrain the public and make them pay, one way or another, for the generation of public goods. Coercive and non-coercive leadership have been important bases for exercising such constraint. Yet most important has been élite control over socialization, that is, the indoctrination of individuals, particularly in childhood and youth, by which individual utility functions were shaped to conform with what the ruling groups designated as a desirable political culture. They were taught to want what their betters thought best; and effective socialization made élite demands legitimate. In composition, the

output of public goods reflected naturally to a marked degree the tastes of
the élites.[11] Concerns of foreign policy
and military power ranked traditionally very high among the public services
organized by élites. Not rarely this was
no doubt a service from which the
masses of the public benefited, even if
to a lesser extent. But a careful reading
of the history of many wars, usually
written by members of the élite, casts
considerable doubt on the general
identity of élite and public interest in
these matters.

Now, there is no question but that
the mature industrial states are at
present going through a process of democratization.[12] This is, the experts
tell us, what "political modernization"
is all about. Populations are becoming
increasingly mobilized politically. The
expanding scope and rising level of
education, and new ranges of occupational experiences in a technologically
sophisticated world, are providing more
and more citizens in the affluent countries with political competence and,
what is more, with a sense of political
competence. It is now becoming clear
that the gradual *formal* democratization which took place in the most advanced societies during the nineteenth
and twentieth centuries produced *effective* democratization only with a
remarkably long time lag.[13] Until recently, most citizens were content,
largely as a result of effective indoctrination, to accept élite decisions on most
matters, and particularly on matters of
foreign and military policy, as authoritative and hence binding. What is
happening now in these countries, and
especially in the United States, is a
process of more broadly based participation in government decision-making.
Unless these new, effectively enfran-
chized, citizens socialize *themselves* in

order to accommodate the time perspectives required for the production
of needed public goods, the present
crisis of authority may end in progressive decay, and eventual chaos and disorder. In that case, the nostalgic wag
was right who said: "There is nothing
fundamentally wrong with the United
States, except perhaps its people."
However, because of the spread of education, it is more likely that the *content*
rather than the *level* of public goods
will see marked changes. On the basis
of evidence presented below, one might
predict that the international power-
game cultivated by previous élites will
not receive the attention and resources
it used to attract. The political culture
favouring rather indiscriminate military mobilization and conflict is changing. This need not signify that defence
against aggression will lack adequate
resources, but it will almost certainly
mean that the uses of military power
will become more selective. It may
now turn out, after all, that de Tocqueville was prophetic in his conclusions
on democracy and foreign policy. "It
is incontestable that, in times of danger,
a free people display far more energy
than any other. But I incline to believe
that this is especially true of those free
nations in which the aristocratic element preponderates. Democracy appears to me better adapted for the
conduct of society in times of peace ...
Foreign politics demand scarcely any
of those qualities which are peculiar to
a democracy; they require, on the contrary, the perfect use of almost all
those in which it is deficient."[14] And:
"it may be admitted as a general and
constant rule that among civilized nations the warlike passions will become
more rare and less intense in proportion as social conditions are more
equal."[15]

THE AMERICAN INTELLIGENTSIA

No one class of people in the
United States has been as instrumental
as the contemporary intelligentsia, to

use a convenient Marxist concept, in
accounting for the "inward-turning"
orientation, in broadening effective

public participation in determining public policy and, as I will suggest below, in bringing about the youth rebellion.

I mean by "intelligentsia" those people who are occupationally engaged in producing, interpreting, distributing, criticizing and inculcating cultural values, including the values of which political culture is comprised. They are occupied in the school system, including the universities, in the mass media and religious institutions, in publishing books, in the theatre, etc. There are also members of other professions and personnel in the public bureaucracies who identify with the predominant value-system of the intelligentsia. We do not know how many they are but partial statistics (e.g. number of teachers) suggest that they have increased in number with each stage of economic development. Most of them are located outside the business sector. Projections by the U.S. Bureau of Labour Statistics project for "professional, technical and kindred workers" (an overlapping group) a 40 per cent increase between 1961 and 1975, to reach a total of thirteen million by the end of this period.[16] It is a class which obviously occupies a crucial position in the making of opinion and the formation of attitudes.

Unfortunately, there is no statistical evidence for the following characterization of this segment of the population. My remarks are based on my own impression and that of many other observers. Such qualitative material is abundant since this class, which lives by talking and writing, naturally talks and writes a great deal about itself. Like any other class it is, of course, far from uniform, and numerous kinds and shades of opinion are easily produced and readily encountered. What I will be discussing is what seems to me the dominant strain in the more salient expressions of value and policy. Whether it reflects the majority feeling in the group I do not know.

On this precarious basis, then, I venture to say that serious doubt on the merits of the Vietnam War, and opposition and moral revulsion to this war, has come mostly from the American intelligentsia. (I am, at this point, referring chiefly to its more definitely adult age groups.) Our question is: Why has this opposition occurred?

It is the hallmark of any dynamic society—a society in rapid transit from one transition period to another—that individuals and groups undergo fairly frequent changes in their identification with institutions and other groups, and in the level and direction of their political and cultural commitments. The intelligentsia in the industrial state is especially mobile in these respects because many of its members are, occupationally or by intellectual propensity (if not compulsion), committed to social analysis. This is an activity which leads naturally to the questioning of authority in any form. (It is for this reason that perceptive ruling groups have often distrusted the intelligentsia as agents of undesirable change.)

As the history of the United States since the beginning of the century reveals, critics of its institutions and policies have been recruited overwhelmingly from this class. They have tended to go in for muck-raking journalism, *avant-garde* postures, and liberal and radical politics. More recently, they have originated increasingly from the descendants of non-Anglo-Saxon immigrants; and, although many have been absorbed in the establishment, especially its lower reaches, their loyalty to its values is less automatic than contingent upon the performance of the governing élite. The dominant WASP establishment and culture—Victorian residues, Protestant ethic and all—were to many of these people naturally alien, the product of an envied class, and certainly inexpressive of their own outlook and interests.[17] If they seem more alienated now, this is so because their numbers and expressive freedom

have increased. They have been looking askance at some of the social
mechanisms and predispositions that,
traditionally, have tended to favour the
military enterprise. They are in fact
inclined to adopt and express humanitarian and egalitarian values and,
transcending exclusively national loyalties, to apply these values internationally. Given this orientation, they were
particularly sensitive to the exercise of
military coercion and to the endless
slaughter and destruction in which
their country found itself involved in
Vietnam for reasons that were obscure
and, to many of them, flatly objectionable. Most of them might be able to
tolerate the brutality of war, but only
in *extremis*. In short, they are not a
class which finds the easy use of military power respectable and, since they
have ample influence on the media of
communication, they can make their
opposition heard.

   Whether or not one regards all
this with sympathy, as I do, it is clear
that the manifestation of these values
is for this class unrestrained by the
burdens of office and final responsibility, by being forced to heed circumstances which, in a constitutionally
messy world, often obstructs purity of

action. In other words, this class can
afford the luxury of favouring policies
wholly conforming to its dominant
sentiments. This is natural. There are,
however, two further manifestations,
shared by a much smaller proportion,
which is more ominous. One is a tendency of some, to be found especially
at universities, to "lose their cool" and
suspend all reason (though not clever-
ness) when enraged by government action. The events at many university
faculty meetings touched off by President Nixon's (in my opinion, gravely
mistaken) move into Cambodia in April
accentuated this somewhat self-demean-
ing weakness.[18] The other tendency is
to get locked into a world-view which
sees practically all evil concentrated in
Washington and regards all other international actors as more or less benign.
Ho Chi Minh is "beautiful" and so
forth.

   It is hardly necessary to emphasize
that the emerging ethos of the American intelligentsia—which is by necessity
of economic development destined to
increase in number and probably influence—has a direct bearing on the kind
of military posture which the United
States will be able to sustain in the
future.

REBELLIOUS YOUTH

   American youth, to put it mildly,
is an extremely kaleidoscopic phenomenon. I cannot possibly deal with all
its parts, such as the gentle "flower-
children" (on the wane?) or those,
more numerous, that seem to wear little
else than a lot of hair and a basic
frown. They are self-consciously and, I
believe rightly, critical of many features
of contemporary American civilization,
but mostly substitute tentative modes
of life which, though decidedly different, one cannot easily regard as much
of an improvement. Nevertheless, a
sizable proportion of American youth
today rejects the old culture which was
based on the premise of perennial

scarcity in the means for satisfying
human wants, and which therefore
stressed property rights, competitive
achievement, self-discipline, and which
legitimated inequality.[19]

   All these and other manifestations
of the "new culture" impinge on the
question of national power; but it is
impossible now to foresee which the
dominant culture patterns will be. I
must limit myself to that small but
indubitably significant minority which
is politically active. Some of these, representing a tiny sub-culture, are given to
virtually continuous activity (it is their
life!) and in a manner calculated to
draw disproportionate attention. Their

members say that they are dead-set not only against the war in Vietnam but against all established institutions and their outputs which made this war possible and which, they fervently believe, must be eradicated before a better world can arise. What they would put in place of present society they have left totally unclear. Indeed, they regard inquiry along this line as typically repressive.

More important is the far larger group—also mostly college students—who are preparing for careers and enter serious political activity intermittently, that is to say, when specially outraged by some event for which the older generation performing regular institutional roles seem clearly responsible. They pretend to no identification with Mao, Ché Guevara or *El Fatah*. But like the more violent group, they are—as several studies have revealed—by and large the sons and daughters of the American intelligentsia, plus a considerable addition of establishment progeny. They are numerous in the academically better colleges, very bright and mostly hardworking. They share predominantly the political values and disenchantments of the American intelligentsia which has, formally and informally, educated them except that, being youthful, they are disinclined to compromise. They are, as a group, very much against the war in Vietnam, and they are fundamentally anti-capitalist and humanitarian. There are no doubt many reasons why these young people have developed their political attitudes and the strong propensity to act them out. One is sometimes reminded of Bertrand Russell when he said: "A large proportion of the human race, it is true, is obliged to work so hard in obtaining necessaries that little energy is left over for other purposes, but those whose livelihood is assured do not, on that account, cease to be active."[20] But there is more to it than affluence. The basic explanation seems to me simple. They were brought up

that way. It seems now fairly clear that the American intelligentsia (and quite a few members of the establishment who found its values attractive) discarded the traditional child-rearing precepts of the WASP culture and instead welcomed new ideas of progressive education, child psychology, psychotherapy—all in the image of a new kind of family which was less authoritarian, more child-centered, less disciplined, more humanitarian and democratic.[21] Regarding political views and values, therefore, their children, far from acting out the usual inter-generational drama, are following right in the footsteps of their elders. (It is hard to imagine a Dean Acheson reared by a mother doting on Dr. Spock.) There is no question but that the war touched these youngsters very deeply and turned them more sharply against the leaders and institutions they hold responsible for it, than would have happened otherwise. But even without the war—one does not know, but suspects—accepted institutions all around would have been losing authority in their eyes. This is not surprising, for these institutions—marriage, family, church, school, government and business enterprise—proved less and less adapted to a rapidly changing environment. One should not forget that the highly accelerated rate of change in the technologically advanced societies—a rate which is probably insupportable in the longer run—engenders a cataract of social and cultural discontinuities, so that children born after World War II never had the chance to experience a reasonably integrated culture. The trouble, it seems to me, is that their parents did not succeed in mastering change by recreating institutions that would represent a new and viable synthesis of what was good in the past and what was needed in the future. In this, I believe quite excusable deficiency, they failed as socializing agents of society. They helped to polarize society between themselves and the large bulk of the lower classes who are sticking to old ideals. Such parents who cared—as well as another segment who withdrew more or less from all but the routine aspects of child-rearing, leaving their offspring to be socialized mainly by peers and TV—failed as models of identity. This failure is at the bottom of the many juvenile casualties who take to drugs and other forms of "dropping out," eagerly reject some of the old American virtues in favour of instant gratification (sometimes so instant as to almost precede the recognition of a need), glory in narcissistic poses and, even when politically active are attracted primarily by the sensation and pose, rather than the substance, of commitment. The problem of discovering one's identity is very hard for those brought up in a culture that has suffered an excessive loss of stability, and in which the geographic and social mobility of parents permits few enduring connections with place and people.

It is too early to tell how the "young intelligentsia" will work out when their time comes to take over. They labour under various deficiencies, including a rash rejection of history, which condemns them to a more shallow understanding of the human condition than is possible, and often including also a disillusionment with science (and sometimes even rationalism), which will deprive them of some useful modes and tools for solving problems that cannot be evaded. But then, so many of them are just splendid individuals. In some ways, the sensitive young have probably a keener sense of quickly emerging realities than their elders whose most formative experiences were received in a far-away past; and furthermore, these young at last believe without any effort and strain that the human race is fundamentally one.

OTHER GROUPS

I have so far concentrated on a numerically small segment of the American people because I feel intuitively that it holds the key to our problem. In a paper which is already too long, I will refer very briefly to three other groups.

Regarding the Blacks, it is clear that their *subjective* exploitation has sharply increased at the same time that their *objective* exploitation has been diminishing. This fact is weakening American society in terms of divisive passions and activities, and the inclination of many young Blacks to reject the very notion of national solidarity. By and large, they do not regard the war in Vietnam as their war. The vast majority of Blacks, however, want a better place in this society, not to destroy it. And the motives which propel Whites to reduce the objective exploitation of the Negro at a speed which is creditable by any historical standard, are among the most constructive operating in this society. But in this area too, it is hard to foresee the end of the story.

The American establishment, that vaguely defined but undeniable stratum, which has run business, professions and government, and clearly dominated foreign and military policy has lost, it seems to me, the previous sharpness of its performance profile. In conducting foreign affairs, its representatives appear to have lost some of the vigour, wisdom and adaptability which distinguished their predecessors in the 1940s and 1950s. Trapped in a cold-war philosophy that became insufficiently attentive to most aspects of the changing world environment, they led their country into Vietnam. Increasingly aware of this mistake, and sensitive to the divisiveness it bred, increasingly disturbed also by the behaviour of youth, often their own children, at their own *alma maters*, and more recently unsure of their management of the economy, the members of the establishment as a group seem to me currently—and this is very much a personal judgment—to have fallen prey to pessimism, to show signs of some loss of direction, and sometimes even loss of nerve. This development may well prove temporary, but one cannot be sure.

Finally, there is the great bulk of American society, largely composed of "white ethnics" who regard themselves as lower-middle class (or just middle-class), patriotic and firmly dedicated to the old virtues of hard work and self-reliance. They are presumably what President Nixon has called "the silent majority." One has the impression that, by and large, they are puzzled by the behaviour of the establishment, suspicious and a little contemptuous of the intelligentsia, and very hostile to the young New Left, especially the student activists. They are bewildered by the fact that, at times of rapid and tumultuous change, the members of the establishment and the intelligentsia are talking mostly to themselves;[22] and not a few—as the attraction of George Wallace and Vice-President Agnew suggests—are casting about for leaders who talk to *them* and express *their* feelings. Some observers have become alarmed enough to fear a backlash political movement in the name of the old virtues which, though more commendable than the upholders of the "new culture" allow, no longer suffice to cope with the problems of the 1970s. Recent elections and political campaigns certainly bear out that the nation is tending to political polarization. As one public opinion expert put it, the "intellectual and moral strains among the liberal élite groups run directly counter to strains in the white ethnics and other members of middle America."[23] If the right kind of leadership emerges, there is some chance of backward-looking conservative rule.

SOME CONCLUSIONS

Before formulating some tentative conclusions, it may be useful to present some relevant inferences supported by election results and public opinion polls.

(1) At the turn of the year, the majority of the nation regretted involvement in Vietnam, wanted to reduce the country's commitments there, but rejected complete withdrawal as an alternative.[24] According to a Gallup Poll, in May 1970, 56 per cent thought that the United States had made a mistake by sending troops to fight in Vietnam, 36 per cent did not think so, and 8 per cent had no opinion. In April 1968, the respective percentages had been 48, 40 and 12. In October 1952, comparable figures concerning the Korean War, were 43, 37, 20 (as against 20, 65 and 15 in August 1960).

(2) Unsurprisingly, Blacks and women have shown more disenchantment with the war than white males.[25]

(3) As a group, the college-educated have been firm in support of the war and register disproportionately among the staunchest "hard-liners."[26] The large majority of this group is made up of people who are either out of college or are presently at colleges where anti-war sentiment has found little echo.[27]

(4) Persons with advanced graduate training and those attached to the most prominent universities were more "dovish" than the rest of the population.[28]

(5) Sentiment for peace is largely separate from sentiment for the radical peace movement. Nearly two-thirds of those definitely opposed to the war object to the militant protesters.[29]

(6) The radical movement has turned off between 60 and 90 per cent of the American people.[30] More than half of the public blame the Kent State

University killings on the students themselves.[31]

(7) Analysis of election returns during the 1968 Presidential election show that Democrats sympathetic to George Wallace outnumbered those supporting Senator Eugene McCarthy, and that Wallace drew proportionately more voters under thirty than from any other age group.[32]

Facing this fast-changing, ambiguous and largely incoherent phenomenon of American society at this time, nobody can respond to the request for predictive conclusions with any other feelings than acute discomfort and a strong desire for evasive action, which I do not intend to frustrate completely.

(1) Concerning changes in the internal power structure of the United States, the extreme Left, including its junior division has no chance of gaining appreciable power. Its preference for the shock of confrontation prevents it from getting enough allies for the beginning of a significant mass base. The more moderate new Left, largely composed of old and young intelligentsia is not strong enough to dominate American politics through political elections since the bulk of the citizenry remains fundamentally conservative. The best chance of the intelligentsia for increased political influence is some subversion of the establishment class. The formation of a winning coalition which would represent a constructive synthesis of forces dedicated to some of the old American values and to forces pushing in a more democratic, cosmopolitan and humanitarian direction would require political innovators in establishment and intelligentsia who care for and talk with the lower-middle class, as well as the Blacks, and other ethnic minorities, rather than ignore and deplore them and their sensibilities, thus leaving them to the appeals of reactionary demagogues. There is as yet no sign that such a coalition is forming.

(2) The isolationism of the 1920s and 1930s is very unlikely to return. The bulk of the intelligentsia and establishment remain genuinely interested in the outside world. And even though protectionist elements are gathering political strength, American economic interdependence with the outside world, and especially with other advanced economies, will not decline. The activities of the big corporations, particularly also the multi-national corporations, indicate that American banking and business has no taste for economic insularity. National self-preoccupation, however, is apt to increase. Yet this is only a shift of emphasis induced by the need to tackle the urgent domestic problems of which the public has become sharply aware.

(3) American inclination to intervene abroad militarily will certainly tend to decrease, as a result partly of the lesson of Vietnam, partly of a degree of "inward-turning," partly of an increasing perception that military power has lost some of its utility compared with the past, and partly of the fact that the United States seems unable to master the degree of internal unity to sustain the commitments to anything like an imperial role. The Nixon Doctrine is some indication of this changing posture. The immediate question is whether foreign-policy objectives will actually be retrenched in keeping with a lesser appetite for intervention and probably a lesser availability of means for intervention, or whether there will be an attempt, for a time, to base the over-ambitious objectives of the past more on rhetoric than on real commitment. There is also some danger, later on, that Americans will follow their friends in western Europe and simply declare that foreign threats have declined or disappeared, and that diminished United States involvement abroad was therefore realistic. (The problem in the real world is that the phenomenon of threats is subject to change in any direction, and that the perception of such change should be regarded as

an empirical question unbeclouded by wishful thinking.) It would be wrong, however, to write off completely the American capacity for military intervention. Even the present American mood does not justify doing so. Many doves on Vietnam are after all rather hawkish about the Middle East.

(4) There will be greater pressure to limit the defence budget. Over the past two decades, American planners could usually start by defining foreign-policy objectives, then formulate military requirements, and finally present the bill to a benevolent Congress. In the future, budgetary limitations, based on a confrontation of resources with the entire structure of national priorities, are likely to be brought into play at the very outset. I believe it unlikely that the United States will starve the military and, regardless of the outcome of SALT negotiations, that strategic nuclear deterrence will be deprived of essential capabilities. Forces for conventional war, however, will almost certainly continue to be reduced appreciably. And if there is a shift to a professional army, rising expenses per man will exert further pressure towards retrenchment.

(5) There may (and should) be further efforts to seek accommodations with the Soviet Union, and if additional arms-control agreements can be reached without the help of illusions, the world will become a somewhat safer place, though not as yet one in which all swords can be enthusiastically beaten into ploughshares.

(6) The alliance with the Western European nations will in all likelihood survive (although this depends, of course, on whether western Europeans want to co-operate towards this outcome, rather than simply demand it). Americans may become more detached in their feelings about the security of Western Europe, but there is no indication of a massive change of mind. Even the young intelligentsia, the most radical wing excepted, while being bored by NATO and such things, do not question it. NATO apart, the present disillusionment with allies and alliances will probably make itself felt in other parts of the world. But such a development would not be an altogether bad thing.

These conclusions may perhaps add up to too comforting a picture. And they may indeed prove wrong. Mankind has always been capable of producing unpredicted and deeply disturbing events, and if such events occur, they may change the complexion of world and American affairs dramatically. There is the ominous tendency of the peace movement—in the United States as in Europe—to favour drastic changes without any thought of international repercussions. In a world in which the passion for peace is unevenly spread, serious consequences would arise if these movements were successful in the affluent societies alone. Historically viewed, the combination of riches and unwillingness to fight has proved invariably fatal. There is, finally, perhaps the outside possibility that, under the impact of a wave of increasingly bitter controversy, American society, unable to cope with a discontinuous culture, will simply crumble to an extent paralysing it as a power. I regard this as improbable. There are too many signs of constructive effort as well as of decay in this incredibly dynamic society. And in any case, at the time of the American Revolution, when Sir John Sinclair expressed to him his fear that England's decay was approaching the point of signalling imminent collapse, Adam Smith said: "Young man, do not forget that there is a great deal of ruin in a great nation."

NOTES

1. Townsend Hoopes, *The Limits of Intervention: An Inside Account of how the Johnson policy of Escalation in Vietnam was Reversed* (New York: David McKay, 1969), Preface.

2. *Op. cit.*, p. 239. Mr. Hoopes reiterated

this prediction more recently in "Legacy of the Cold War," *Foreign Affairs*, July 1970, p. 613.

3. I find it useful to distinguish between *putative* military power (i.e. military forces, potential and reputation) and *actualized* military power (i.e. actual power achievement). A number of variables determine the extent to which—from zero at one extreme to complete at the other—putative power can be actualized in concrete conflict situations. See my *Military Power and Potential* (Lexington, Mass.: Heath, 1970), Chapter I.

4. Technically, the United States *could* have "won" militarily by having recourse to the most developed military technology, i.e. nuclear weapons. But it would have done so at a price and with results which made this clearly a non-option.

5. Thomas C. Schelling, *Arms and Influence* (New Haven: Yale University Press, 1966).

6. *Military Power and Potential,* especially Chapter V.

7. Visionaries of the "global village" point to the increasing flow of inter-society communication. It is a fact, however, that intra-society communication has increased much more.

8. *On the Uses of Military Power in the Nuclear Age* (Princeton, N.J.: Princeton University Press, 1966), especially Chapters I–III.

9. Rob Paarlberg, "The Domestication of American Foreign Policy," *Public Policy*, XVIII, 1970.

10. Kenneth J. Arrow, *Social Choice and Individual Values* (New York: Wiley, 1951).

11. It will not escape the reader that Karl Marx and his disciples caught some of this. Unfortunately, they state an essentially plain state of affairs in an exceptionally convoluted manner and, for purposes of class antagonism, distorted reality by denying any public benefits organized by the ruling groups.

12. Cf. Karl de Schweinitz, Jr., "Growth, Development, and Political Modernization," *World Politics*, July 1970, p. 530.

13. *Ibid.*, pp. 531–33.

14. Alexis de Tocqueville, *Democracy in America* (New York: Knopf, 1960), Vol. I, pp. 228 and 234.

15. *Op. cit.*, Vol. II, p. 264.

16. Richard Flacks, "Young Intelligentsia in Revolt," *TRANSACTION,* June 1970, p. 54.

17. *Ibid.*, p. 48.

18. For a moving self-criticism concerning these events, see Alexander M. Bickel, "The Tolerance of Violence on the Campus," *New Republic,* 13 June 1970. Mr. Bickel is a liberal of immaculate reputation.

19. Cf. Phillip E. Slater, "Cultures in Collision," *Psychology Today*, June 1970, pp. 31 ff.

20. Bertrand Russell, *Power* (New York: Norton, 1938), p. 9.

21. Flacks, *op. cit.*, p. 48.

22. "I am not persuaded that the élite groups in American society have the humility or the patience or even the personal security necessary to establish, or perhaps reestablish, dialogue with the rest of the nation. There seems to be some extremely important payoff in being alienated from the larger society . . ." Andrew N. Greeley, "The War and Ethnic Groups, Driving off 'The People,'" *New Republic,* 27 June 1970, p. 16.

23. *Ibid.*, p. 15.

24. Philip E. Converse and Howard Schuman, "'Silent Majorities' and the Vietnam War," *Scientific American,* June 1970, p. 20.

25. *Ibid.*, p. 22.

26. *Ibid.*

27. Of the 760 campuses where protests were recorded during the excited days of early May, only one quarter had strikes in which classes were boycotted on a large scale or in which schools were closed. The strongest protest took place at the leading universities. Cf. *New York Times,* 24 June 1970, p. 29.

28. Converse and Schuman, *op. cit.*, pp. 20–24.

29. *Ibid.*, p. 24.

30. Greeley, *op. cit.*, p. 14.

31. *Ibid.*

32. Philip E. Converse *et al.*, "Continuity and Change in American Politics: Parties and Issues in the 1968 Election," *The American Political Science Review*, December 1969, p. 1103.

Selected Additional Readings

Armacost, Michael H. *The Politics of Weapons Innovation: The Thor-Jupiter Controversy.* New York: Columbia University Press, 1969.

This case study examines the role of interservice rivalry in the politics of weapons development.

Art, Robert J. *The TFX Decision: McNamara and the Military.* Boston: Little, Brown and Company, 1968.

A case study of the conflicting roles of military and civilian defense leaders in the development of a controversial weapon system.

Clark, Keith C., and Laurence J. Legere, eds. *The President and the Management of National Security.* New York: Frederick A. Praeger, 1969.

Assesses the major issues of organization and management of national security which confront a new President.

Derthick, Martha. *The National Guard in Politics.* Cambridge, Mass.: Harvard University Press, 1965.

Profiles the changing role of National Guard since 1879, revealing its capacity to adapt itself to changing demands of society.

Enthoven, Alain C., and K. Wayne Smith. *How Much is Enough? Shaping the Defense Program, 1961–1969.* New York: Harper and Row, 1971.

The authors describe—through personal experience—the operation of the Systems Analysis Office in the McNamara period. A strong argument is made for quantitative analysis of defense programs outside the military.

Hammond, Paul Y. *Organizing for Defense: The American Military Establishment in the Twentieth Century.* Princeton: Princeton University Press, 1961.

A comprehensive study of the politics, structure, and management of the defense establishment during the period 1900–1960.

Hitch, Charles J., and Roland N. McKean. *The Economics of Defense in the Nuclear Age.* Cambridge, Mass.: Harvard University Press, 1960.

Explores the application of quantitative economic analysis to defense problems.

Hoopes, Townsend. *The Limits of Intervention: An Inside Account of How the Johnson Policy of Escalation in Vietnam Was Reversed.* New York: David McKay Company, 1969.

Account of the personal factors and political dissent which led President Lyndon B. Johnson to stop the growth of U.S. military involvement in Vietnam, as told by an important insider.

Kolodziej, Edward A. *The Uncommon Defense and Congress, 1945–1963.* Columbus: Ohio State University Press, 1966.

An analysis of Congress's use of its power of the purse to influence military force levels, weapons, and strategic policy in the postwar period.

Millis, Walter, with Harvey C. Mansfield and Harold Stein. *Arms and the State: Civil-Military Elements in National Policy.* New York: The Twentieth Century Fund, 1968.

Explores the course of civil-military relations in the United States, emphasizing the period since World War II.

Raymond, Jack. *Power at the Pentagon.* New York: Harper and Row, 1964.

An insightful journalistic account of the impact on society of the growth of the American military since World War II.

Riddle, Donald H. *The Truman Committee: A Study in Congressional Responsibility.* New Brunswick: Rutgers University Press, 1964.

Traces the role of an important Senate committee and its investigations of American military policy during World War II and the immediate postwar period.

Ries, John C. *The Management of Defense: Organization and Control of the U.S. Armed Services.* Baltimore: Johns Hopkins University Press, 1964.

A study of the concepts that have influenced defense organization. One of the few serious works that argues for decentralization in the Defense Department.

Robinson, James A. *Congress and Foreign Policy-Making: A Study in Legislative Influence and Initiative.* Rev. ed. Homewood, Ill.: The Dorsey Press, 1967.

Points to a progressive contraction of the role of Congress relative to the Executive on problem identification and policy ini-

tiative in the realm of defense and foreign relations.

Roherty, James M. *Decisions of Robert S.
McNamara: A Study of the Role of the
Secretary of Defense*. Coral Gables, Fla.:
University of Miami Press, 1970.

Analyzes the tenure of McNamara as Secretary of Defense in the context of the
different roles and leadership styles of the
men who have managed the Defense Department since 1947.

Schilling, Warner R., Paul Y. Hammond and
Glenn H. Snyder. *Strategy, Politics, and
Defense Budgets*. New York: Columbia
University Press, 1962.

Case analyses of the decision-making processes concerned with determining the
levels of defense programs and the budgets
required for their support. The FY1950
defense budget, NSC–68, and military
policies during the first years of the
Eisenhower Administration are examined.

Smith, Bruce L. F. *The RAND Corporation:
Case Study of a Nonprofit Advisory Corporation*. Cambridge, Mass.: Harvard University Press, 1966.

Studies history of a major "think tank"
and probes its role in the policy process.

4 | STRATEGY IN THE NATIONAL SECURITY PROCESS

Introduction

Section III was concerned with policy making and the determinants of policy in national security. Section IV takes up the operational side of national security, that is, the output of the policy-making process.

In theory, the structure of national security policy is usually broken down into several levels, each of which controls the one next below it. On the uppermost level is *policy* itself which sets the overall political objectives for all national security operations. We have already dealt with policy, in terms of values and interests, in Section II. The next lower level is *national* or *total strategy* (also called at times *grand strategy*) which coordinates and balances the various instruments—military, political, psychological, economic, etc.—that may be used at any one time and establishes their particular objectives. Each instrumentality is controlled by *strategy*, the most familiar being *military strategy*. *Strategy* is the creation and deployment of forces in such a way as to maximize their chances of achieving the objectives established by *policy* and *total strategy*. Actual employment of these forces in combat or in non-military operations is *tactics*, the lowest level in our hierarchy. These levels are far from watertight compartments. They merge into one another gradually, and they do not always carry the same relative importance. But these concepts are useful as analytical tools in trying to determine the relationship of ends to means in national security.

The selections in this section are designed to explore the relationships between these levels of national security policy and their employment in the contemporary context. As an introduction, Michael Howard's "The Classical Strategists" surveys the development of strategic thinking in the western countries from World War II to the present time. Howard concludes that the quality of strategic thought in this period is related both to international relations and weapons technology.

The next six selections deal with the theory of strategy and with strategic theory in the nuclear age. In "A General Survey of Strategy," André Beaufre proposes a definition of the term "strategy" and describes the various major schools and patterns of strategic thought. In "Policy and Strategy," Beaufre outlines the concept of total strategy and argues that the expanded importance of total strategy in the twentieth century has reduced the autonomy of the military instrument. Henry Eccles, in "Strategy," tries to dispel some of the confusion surrounding use of the terms "strategy," "grand strategy," "tactics," "logistics," and "policy."

Strategic deterrence is a particular kind of military strategy that has become vitally important since the introduction of nuclear weapons. Bernard Brodie's "The Anatomy of Deterrence" outlines the major features of deterrence theory. Credibility—making a threat to use nuclear weapons believable within a given political context—emerges as the central problem. Brodie then distinguishes between nuclear forces adequate for deterrence and those necessary to "win the war," arguing that the United States must have sufficient forces to fight a total war if deterrence fails. Raymond D. Gastil's "Alternative Strategies" discusses two basic variations of deterrence theory. Finite deterrence stresses "assured destruction"—the ability to destroy an enemy society in any conceivable circumstance—and ignores the relative sizes of the two contending forces. Balanced deterrence emphasizes damage limitation through invulnerability of forces and deployment of defensive systems to offset the enemy's offensive weapons. The strengths and weaknesses of each theory are discussed, but the author is not fully satisfied with either. Jerome Rothenberg's carefully reasoned article, "The Deployment of Defensive Weapons Systems and the Structure of Deterrence," describes the possible effect of strategic defenses (missile defense, anti-submarine warfare, etc.) on deterrence theory. The author concludes that defensive systems will have a long-run advantageous effect only when an arms control agreement would prohibit an offsetting enemy buildup of offensive forces.

The next two selections deal with less apocalyptic forms of warfare. Robert Osgood's "The Reappraisal of Limited War" discusses the development of western theory on less than all-out nuclear war. The Vietnam experience has caused us to rethink the utility of limited war as a tool of American policy while at the same time the Soviet Union is increasing its own limited war capability. David Galula's "Counterinsurgency in the Hot Revolutionary War" is a succinct description of the policy and methods necessary to defeat guerrilla insurgency. In addition to military successes, the counterinsurgent must politically isolate the insurgent from the population.

The remainder of the articles in this section describe some of the methods of pursuing national security objectives that do not involve direct employment of military force. In "The Psychological Instrument of Statecraft," Robert T. Holt and Robert W. van de Velde argue that psychological operations are an instrument of policy in the same manner as military power. But psychological operations have not been fully appreciated even though they provide a relatively inexpensive means of influencing other states' behavior. The selection from Arnold Horelick and Myron Rush describes how military power may have political effects far beyond its objective capabilities. Differences between Soviet and American approaches to the non-military uses of nuclear power are analyzed and an explanation is offered as to why the Soviets make better use of strategic power than does the United States. Roger Fisher's "Making Threats Is Not Enough" demonstrates the dysfunctions of overreliance on military force. Threats and inflicted pain will not force a foreign government to alter its behavior unless we give them a "yesable" proposition. Finally, the two selections by James E. Dougherty outline the basic issues involved in arms control and disarmament and evaluate the prospects for an arms control agreement in the 1970's. Dougherty concludes that the current strategic picture is changing so rapidly that no firm prediction about successful arms control can be made.

The Classical Strategists

Michael Howard

I

It may help to begin with a definition of "classical" strategy. Liddell Hart
has provided us with one which is as
good as any, and better than most:
"The art of distributing and applying
military means to fulfill the ends of
policy."[1] Whether this remains adequate in the nuclear age is a matter of
some controversy. André Beaufre, for
example, has adumbrated the concept
of an "indirect strategy," to be considered later, which embraces more than
purely military means;[2] but even he
still gives as his basic definition of the
term "the art of the dialectic of two
opposing wills using force to resolve
their dispute."[3] It is this element of
force which distinguishes "strategy"
from the purposeful planning in other
branches of human activity to which
the term is often loosely applied. When
other elements such as economic pressure, propaganda, subversion and diplomacy are combined with force, these
elements may also be considered as
"strategic"; but to apply this adjective
to activities unconnected with the use,
or threatened use, of force would be to
broaden it to such an extent that it
would be necessary to find another word
to cover the original meaning of the
term as defined by Liddell Hart, and as
considered in this paper.

It need hardly be said that students of strategy have generally assumed that military force is a necessary
element in international affairs. Before
World War I, there were few who questioned even whether it was desirable.
After 1918, many regretted its necessity
and saw their function as being to ensure that it should be used as economically, and as rarely, as possible. After
1945, an even greater proportion devoted themselves to examine, not how
wars should be fought, but how they
could be prevented, and the study of
strategy merged into that of arms control, disarmament and peace-keeping.
There the "classical strategists" found
themselves working with scholars of a
different kind; men who believed that
the element of force was *not* a necessary
part of international intercourse, but
could be eliminated by an application
of the methodology of the social sciences. . . . This paper will concern itself
. . . solely with the thinkers who assume
that the element of force exists in international relations, that it can and must
be intelligently controlled, but that it
cannot be totally eliminated. Further,
it is confined to the men who have primarily used the methodology of history
or traditional political science; though
it includes such figures as Schelling and
Morgenstern, who have made considerable contributions in the newer disciplines as well.

The art[4] of strategy remains one of
such complexity that even the greatest
contributors to its study have been able
to do little more than outline broad
principles; principles which neverthe-

less must often be discarded in practice if the circumstances are inappropriate, and which must never be allowed to harden into dogma. Even when these principles appear self-evident, it may be extraordinarily hard to apply them. In World War II "command of the sea" as advocated by Mahan and "command of the air" as advocated by Douhet were certainly necessary preliminaries to the military victory of the Western powers. The problem was how to obtain them with resources on which equally urgent calls were being made for other purposes. The academic strategist could not help the Chiefs of Staff much, for example, in deciding how to allot a limited number of long-range aircraft between the conflicting needs of the strategic offensive against Germany, the war against German submarines, interdiction bombing of German railways, the requirements of the Pacific theatre and support for guerrilla activities in occupied Europe. Operational research and systems-analysis could simplify the problem without ever eliminating it. In the last resort the quality termed by Blackett "the conventional military wisdom"[5] remained the basic factor in making the decision; and that decision was determined by what could be done rather than by what ideally should. The military commander is always primarily conscious of the constraints under which he operates, in terms both of information and of resources. He is, therefore, likely to be impatient with the advice of the academic strategist which may appear to him either platitudinous or impracticable. His decisions must be based at best on educated guesses.

But the academic strategist does have one vital role to play. He can see that the guesses *are* educated. He may not accompany the commander to battle, as Clausewitz expressed it, but he forms his mind in the schoolroom, whether the commander realizes it or not. In World War II the Allied High Command did operate in accordance with certain very definite strategic principles. It is tempting to link these principles with the names of specific theorists: General Marshall's desire for concentration against the enemy army with Clausewitz, General Brooke's desire to enforce dispersal on the enemy with Liddell Hart, the doctrine of the Allied air forces with Douhet: tempting, but difficult to prove. The name of Douhet was virtually unknown in the Royal Air Force.[6] The most eminent thinkers sometimes do no more than codify and clarify conclusions which arise so naturally from the circumstances of the time that they occur simultaneously to those obscurer, but more influential figures who write training manuals and teach in service colleges. And sometimes strategic doctrines may be widely held which cannot be attributed to any specific thinkers, but represent simply the consensus of opinion among a large number of professionals who had undergone a formative common experience.

Of this kind were the doctrines which were generally held in the armed forces of the Western world in the mid-1940s as a result of the experiences of World War II. It was considered, first, that the mobilization of superior resources, together with the maintenance of civilian *morale* at home, was a necessary condition for victory; a condition requiring a substantial domestic "mobilization base" in terms of industrial potential and trained manpower. It was agreed that, in order to deploy these resources effectively, it was necessary to secure command of the sea and command of the air. It was agreed that surface and air operations were totally interdependent. And it was agreed that strategic air power could do much—though *how* much remained a matter of controversy—to weaken the capacity of the adversary to resist. The general concept of war remained as it had been since the days of Napoleon: the contest of armed forces to obtain a position of such superiority that the victorious power would be in a position to impose its political will. And it was generally assumed that in the future, as in the immediate past, this would still be a very long-drawn-out process indeed.

II

The advent of nuclear weapons, to the eyes of the layman, transformed the entire nature of war. But certain eminent professionals suggested that they made remarkably little difference, at least in a conflict between two powers of the size of the United States and the Soviet Union. These weapons obviously would make it possible to inflict with far greater rapidity the kind of damage by which the strategic bombing offensive had crippled Germany and Japan. But the stockpiles of bombs were small—how small is still not known. The bombs were vulnerable to interception; and they had to operate from bases which had to be protected by land armies which would have in their turn to be supplied by sea. All this was pointed out to the general public by, among others, two scientists with long experience in military planning— the British Professor P. M. S. Blackett and the American Dr. Vannevar Bush. Blackett, on the basis of careful calculations from unclassified material, concluded in 1948 that "a long-range atomic bombing offensive against a large continental Power is not likely to be by itself decisive within the next five years."[7] Bush, a figure closely associated with the American military establishment, described in 1949 a conflict barely distinguishable from the last.

> The opening phases would be in the air soon followed by sea and land action. Great fleets of bombers would be in action at once, but this would be the opening phase only. . . . They could undoubtedly devastate the cities and the war potential of the enemy and its satellites, but it is highly doubtful if they could at once stop the march of great land armies. To overcome them would require a great national effort, and the marshalling of all our strength. The effort to keep the seas open would be particularly hazardous, because of modern submarines, and severe efforts would be needed to stop them at the source. Such a war would be a contest of the old form, with variations and new techniques of one sort or another. But, except for greater use of the atomic bomb, it would not differ much from the last struggle.[8]

It was along these lines that planning went forward when the framework of the North Atlantic Treaty Organization was established at the end of the 1940s. Such ideas were legitimate deductions from the then "state of the art." NATO planners had to think what could be done with the weapons they had available, not with those which might or might not be developed in ten years' time. But many scientists and academic strategists, particularly in the United States, were already thinking ahead. Because their views appeared to have no immediate relevance, or because of the pressures of interservice politics, they had little immediate influence on Western policy; and they were usually set out in papers or articles which enjoyed only a limited circulation within the academic world.[9] An adequate account of these seminal discussions would require a separate paper. We can, however, salvage and admire the shrewd insights shown by two thinkers who had already established their reputations in the prenuclear era: Bernard Brodie and Sir Basil Liddell Hart. Both of them, in works published in 1946, made prophecies which twenty years later were to be commonplaces of strategic thinking.

In the final chapter of *The Revolution in Warfare*,[10] Liddell Hart suggested that, failing disarmament, attempts should be made "to revive a code of limiting rules for warfare—

based on a realistic view that wars are likely to occur again, and that the limitation of their destructiveness is to everybody's interest." "Fear of atomic war," he wrote, "might lead to indirect methods of aggression, infiltration taking civil forms as well as military, to which nuclear retaliation would be irrelevant. Armed forces would still be required to fight 'sub-atomic war,' but the emphasis should be on their mobility, both tactical and strategic."

The great armies of the past would be irrelevant to the needs of the nuclear age. Liddell Hart did not, at this stage, consider the problems and contradictions of limited war, including the possibility which emerged fifteen years later, that it might be necessary to have large conventional forces precisely in order to keep war limited.

Neither did he explore the implications and requirements of deterrence. Brodie, however, with his collaborators in the Yale Institute of International Studies' publication *The Absolute Weapon*, did exactly this, and with remarkable prescience. Much that he wrote was to become unquestionably valid only with the development of thermonuclear weapons, but his insights were none the less remarkable for that. He rejected, for example, the whole concept of a "mobilization base." "The idea," he wrote, "which must be driven home above all else is that a military establishment which is expected to fight on after the nation has undergone atomic bomb attack must be prepared to fight with the men already mobilized and with the equipment already in the arsenals.[11] More important, he outlined the concept of a stable balance of nuclear forces.

> If the atomic bomb can be used without fear of substantial retaliation in kind, it will clearly encourage aggression. So much the more reason, therefore, to take all possible steps to assure that multilateral possession of the bomb, should that prove inevitable, be attended by arrangements to make as nearly certain as possible that the

aggressor who uses the bomb will have it used against him . . .
> . . . Thus, the first and most vital step in any American programme for the age of atomic bombs is to take measures to guarantee to ourselves in case of attack the possibility of retaliation in kind. The writer in making that statement is not for the moment concerned about who will *win* the next war in which atomic bombs are used. Thus far the chief purpose of our military establishment has been to win wars. From now on its chief purpose must be to avert them. It can have almost no other useful purpose.[12]

Not until thermonuclear weapons had been developed and the Soviet Union had shown itself to possess an inter-continental delivery system did the U.S. Joint Chiefs of Staff accept Brodie's logic; though it is significant that shortly after the publication of this work Brodie joined the newly formed RAND Corporation, where with the support of the U.S. Air Force the full implications and requirements of his ideas, and others current in the United States academic community, were to be exhaustively studied. The first western government to adopt the concept of "deterrence" as the basis of its military policy was that of the United Kingdom in 1952; very largely thanks to the thinking of Marshal of the Royal Air Force, Sir John Slessor, the then Chairman of the Chiefs of Staff.[13]

Giving a late account of his stewardship at Chatham House in 1953, Slessor was to say:

> The aim of Western policy is not primarily to be ready to win a war with the world in ruins—though we must be as ready as possible to do that if it is forced upon us by accident or miscalculation. It is the prevention of war. The bomber holds out to us the greatest, perhaps the only hope of that. It is the great deterrent.[14]

This doctrine of "the great deterrent" was to unleash within the United Kingdom a debate which foreshadowed that set off in the United States by the comparable "New Look" strategy which Mr. Dulles was formally to unveil there in January 1954. Among its earliest and ablest critics were the men who, four years later, were to be primarily responsible for the foundation of the Institute for Strategic Studies: Rear-Admiral Sir Anthony Buzzard, Mr. Richard Goold-Adams, Mr. Denis Healey, and Professor P. M. S. Blackett. In its public presentation by Ministers and senior officers, the doctrine of "massive retaliation" provided its critics in England with an even easier target than it did in the United States. No official distinction was made between the use of Bomber Command as a first-strike force in response to a Soviet "conventional" invasion of Western Europe and as a second-strike force to retaliate after a Soviet nuclear attack. In face of the growing strength of Soviet nuclear-strike forces, the first role appeared to lack political, the second technical, credibility. Liddell Hart had already pointed out in 1950 that defence against nuclear weapons would be credible only if accompanied by massive civil-defence measures of a kind which no government showed any sign of being prepared to carry out.[15] Britain's military leaders indeed at first assumed that the civilian population might be induced to grin and bear the nuclear holocaust as cheerfully as they had endured the German blitz. The inhabitants of areas which contained no protected installations, suggested Slessor, "must steel themselves to risks and take what may come to them, knowing that thereby they are playing as essential a part in the country's defence as the pilot in the fighter or the man behind the gun."[16] This attitude presumably remained the basis of British official thinking until the acquisition of the *Polaris* missile system gave the United Kingdom a second-strike weapon which was technically if not politically credible. The validity of this thesis however gave rise to widespread doubts, and not only among the members of the Campaign for Nuclear Disarmament. In a famous lecture to

the Royal United Service Institution in November 1959, after Mr. Duncan Sandys had, in two Defence White Papers, laid yet greater stress on the importance of "the deterrent," Lieutenant-General Sir John Cowley was to ask a question unusual for a senior serving officer:

> The choice of death or dishonour is one which has always faced the professional fighting man, and there must be no doubt in his mind what his answer must be. He chooses death for himself so that his country may survive, or on a grander scale so that the principles for which he is fighting may survive. Now we are facing a somewhat different situation, when the reply is not to be given by individuals but by countries as a whole. Is it right for the Government of a country to choose complete destruction of the population rather than some other alternative, however unpleasant that alternative may be?[17]

As a coherent theory of strategy in the traditional sense, the doctrine of deterrence by the threat of massive retaliation, in the simple form in which it was set out by the British and American governments in the early 1950s, is not easy to defend, and its exponents tended at times to use the vocabulary of exhortation rather than that of rational argument in their attempts to justify it. But three points should be noted if we are to appreciate their standpoint. First, the British Chiefs of Staff from the beginning saw Bomber Command as a supplement to rather than a substitute for the United States Strategic Air Command, with the task of striking at targets of particular significance for the United Kingdom. Its strategic utility and its credibility as a deterrent were thus to be judged within the context of the Western deterrent force as a whole.[18]

Second, it was an attempt, like the American "New Look" two years later, to solve the problem—and one far more difficult for the United Kingdom than for the United States—of maintaining an effective military force in a peacetime economy. The burden of rearmament assumed in 1950 had proved not only economically crippling but politically unacceptable; and since the political objective of the United Kingdom was the maintenance, *virgo intacta,* of the *status quo* in Europe, a policy which imposed the maximum penalty for *any* violation of that *status quo* was not so irrational as it appeared. For the United Kingdom not one inch of Western Europe could be considered negotiable.

Third, as British officials repeatedly said later in the decade, "The Great Deterrent" existed not to fight but to deter war: "If it is used, it will have failed." This argument was open to the rejoinder that a strategy which was not militarily viable was not politically credible, but this rejoinder is by no means conclusive. The concept of "deterrence" takes us out of the familiar field of military strategy into the unmapped if not unfamiliar territory of political bargaining, where total rationality does not invariably reign supreme. Schelling and others were only then beginning their studies of "the strategy of conflict"; but even without the help of game-theory techniques, it could be reasonably argued that, even if there was only one chance in a hundred that a political move could really be met by the threatened nuclear response, that chance would be an effective deterrent to any responsible statesman.[19] "The most that the advocates of the deterrent policy have ever claimed for it," said Slessor in 1955, "is that it will deter a potential aggressor from undertaking total war as an instrument of policy, as Hitler did in 1939, or from embarking upon a course of international action which obviously involves a serious risk of total war, as the Austrian Government did in 1914.[20]

Certainly the British advocates of the "deterrent policy" in the 1950s did not underrate the continuing importance of conflicts which would *not* be deterred by nuclear weapons. Liddell Hart repeatedly pointed out that nuclear stalemate would encourage local and indirect aggression which could be countered only by conventional forces; a lesson which British armed forces tied down in operations from Cyprus to Malaya had no need to learn. Faced with the double burden of deterring total war and fighting small ones, it was natural enough for British strategists to adopt the doctrine later termed "minimal deterrence." This was stated with uncompromising clarity by Blackett in 1956:

> I think we should act as if atomic and hydrogen bombs have abolished total war and concentrate our efforts on working out how few atomic bombs and their carriers are required to keep it abolished. In the next few years I see the problem not as how many atomic bombs we can afford but as how few we need. For every hundred million pounds spent on offensive and defensive preparations for global war, which almost certainly will not happen, is so much less for limited and colonial wars, which well may.[21]

British strategic thinkers in fact— even Slessor after his retirement— tended to take the existence of stable deterrence very much for granted. In view of the highly classified nature of all information relating to Bomber Command and the absence of any serious intercourse at that time between Ministry of Defence officials and free-lance strategic thinkers, this was not altogether surprising. It enabled them to concentrate, not only on problems of limited wars (Liddell Hart) but on graduated deterrence and restraints on war (Buzzard) and, in the atmosphere of *détente* which followed the Geneva Summit Meeting of 1955, on "disengagement," disarmament and arms control (Blackett and Healey). When a few years later American thinkers questioned the validity of the doctrine of "minimal deterrence" they evoked from Blackett a forceful rejoinder,[22] in which he expressed the fear that to depart from such a policy would only lead to an endless and increasing arms race. But by the end of the 1950s it was becoming clear that any doctrine of deterrence depended for its validity on technical calculations which stretched far beyond the orthodox boundaries of strategic thinking; and on which it was difficult for thinkers who did not enjoy access to the facilities available in the United States to pronounce with any degree of authority.

III

Within the United States the controversy was now well under way. It had been got off to an excellent start by Mr. John Foster Dulles, whose definition of the doctrine of "massive retaliation" in January 1954 had been far more precise and dogmatic than the statements emanating from Whitehall to the same effect during the past two years. This, it will be remembered, announced the intention of the United States Administration to place its military dependence "primarily upon a great capacity to retaliate, instantly, by means and at places of our own choosing," thereby gaining "more basic security at less cost."[23] The rationale behind this policy was of course political and economic: American weariness with the Korean War, and the desire of the Republican Party to return to financial "normalcy" after what they regarded as the ruinous spending spree of the last four years.[24] It should perhaps be judged, not as a coherent strategic doctrine, but as a political expedient— or even as a diplomatic communication, itself a manœuvre in a politico-military strategy of "deterrence." By these criteria the policy must be pronounced not ineffective. But its logical fallacies were too glaring to be overlooked. The assumption of American invulnerability to a pre-emptive or a retaliatory strike was unconvincing in the year in which the Soviet Union first unveiled her inter-continental bombers. Even when that assumption had been justifiable four years earlier, American nuclear monopoly had not deterred the Korean conflict; and in that very year American nuclear power was to prove irrelevant to the conflict in Indo-China. These, and other points, were rapidly made with force and relish by Democrat politicians and sympathizers out of office, by academic specialists, and by members of the armed services which were being cut back to provide greater resources for the Strategic Air Command.

There has perhaps never been a strategic controversy which has not been fuelled by political passions and service interests. It is entirely understandable, and for our purposes quite unimportant, that the U.S. Air Force should have sought every argument to justify the doctrine of massive retaliation while the U.S. Army powerfully supported its opponents. What is significant, however, is that the latter included every strategic thinker of any consequence in the United States; and the failure of the present writer to find any serious academic defence of the doctrine may not be entirely due to unfamiliarity with the literature. Among the first critics was that pioneer of deterrence theory, Bernard Brodie, who published in November 1954 one of the earliest analyses of the place of "limited war" in national policy;[25] but the first really formidable public broadside was fired by a group of scholars at the Princeton Center of International Studies under the leadership of William W. Kaufmann, in a collection of essays published in 1956 under the innocuous-sounding title *Military Policy and National Security*. In this work Kaufmann himself stressed the need for the United States to have the capacity to meet, and therefore deter, Communist aggression at every level;[26] that "spectrum of deterrence," in fact, which Mr. Robert McNamara was to develop, not without some assistance from Dr. Kaufmann himself, when he became Secretary for Defense four years later. In the same work Dr. Roger Hilsman discussed the actual conduct of nuclear war; both making the distinction between counter-force and counter-value targets in total war, and considering the tactics of war with nuclear weapons fought on the ground;[27] and Professor Klaus Knorr gave one of the earliest published estimates of the kind of civil defence policy which might be feasible and necessary if the United States were really to employ the kind of nuclear strategy implied in Mr. Dulles's statement.[28] Finally Mr. Kaufmann emphasized the necessity for ensuring that military force should be tailored to the actual requirements of foreign policy: a point which was to be expanded more fully in two important books published the following year.

These were Dr. Robert Osgood's study of *Limited War* and Dr. Henry Kissinger's *Nuclear Weapons and Foreign Policy*.[29] Neither author had any significant experience of military operations or operational research. Their intellectual training was in the disciplines of history and political science; but with the shift of strategic thinking from the problem of waging war to that of its prevention, this background was at least as relevant as any more directly concerned with military affairs. Both analysed the traditional rigidity of the American attitude towards war and peace, contrasting it with the flexibility of Communist theory and, as they saw it, practice. Both emphasized the irrelevance of strategic nuclear weapons to the conduct of foreign policy in peripheral areas. Both stressed, as had Kaufmann, the need to provide the appropriate forces for the fighting of limited wars; and both considered that tactical nuclear weapons should be re-

garded as appropriate for this purpose —a view shared by Mr. Dulles himself,[30] and by the Joint Chiefs of Staff under the Chairmanship of Admiral Radford.

Osgood based his belief in the need to use nuclear weapons in limited wars largely on the difficulty of preparing troops to fight with both nuclear and conventional weapons.[31] Kissinger, whose study developed out of panel discussions at the Council on Foreign Relations in which a number of professional soldiers took part, went into the question more deeply, discussing both the possible *modus operandi* of tactical nuclear forces and the kind of limitations which might be agreed between two belligerents anxious not to allow their military confrontation to get out of hand.[32] In doing so he aligned himself with the views of Rear-Admiral Sir Anthony Buzzard, who was energetically canvassing before British audiences both the value of tactical nuclear weapons in making possible graduated deterrence at acceptable cost, and the feasibility of negotiating agreed limitations on the conduct of war.[33] But Buzzard's views were hotly contested in England. Slessor gave them general support, but Liddell Hart was highly sceptical (believing the capabilities of conventional forces to be unnecessarily underrated) and Blackett, after some hesitation, came out flatly against them.[34] In the United States the same controversy blew up. Brodie, writing in 1959, was prepared to admit only that there might be *some* circumstances in which tactical nuclear weapons might be appropriate, but considered that "The conclusion that nuclear weapons *must* be used in limited wars has been reached by too many people, too quickly, on the basis of too little analysis of the problem." Schelling the following year suggested that the break between conventional and nuclear weapons was one of the rare "natural" distinctions which made tacit bargaining possible in limiting war.[35] By this time Kissinger himself had had second thoughts, and agreed that, though tactical nuclear weapons were a necessary element in the spectrum of deterrence, they could not take the place of conventional forces.[36] Within a year Mr. McNamara was to take the debate into the council chambers of NATO, where the advocates of tactical nuclear weapons had already found staunch allies among officials grimly conscious of the unpopularity and expense of large conventional forces. Throughout the 1960s the debate was to continue, in three major languages, about the place of tactical nuclear weapons in the defence of Europe.[37] Only the sheer exhaustion of the participants keeps it from continuing still.

It will be seen that the major American contributions to strategic thinking published in 1956–67 were distinguished by two main characteristics. They attempted to reintegrate military power with foreign policy, stressing, in contradiction to the doctrine of massive retaliation, the need for "a strategy of options." And they tended to be the work of academic institutions; Kaufmann's group at Princeton, Osgood from Chicago, Kissinger working with the Council on Foreign Relations. Their authors were thus concerned less with the technicalities of

defence (Hilsman at Princeton, a former West Pointer, was an interesting exception) than with its political objectives. Over what those objectives should be, they had no quarrel with John Foster Dulles. Although British thinkers, like British statesmen, had been exploring possibilities of *détente* ever since 1954, in the United States the cold war was still blowing at full blast. The Soviet Union was still, in the works of these scholars, considered to be implacably aggressive, pursuing its objectives of conquest in every quarter of the globe, its machinations visible behind every disturbance which threatened world stability. As Gordon Dean put it in his introduction to Kissinger's book, "Abhorrent of war but unwilling to accept gradual Russian enslavement of other peoples around the world, which we know will eventually lead to our own enslavement, we are forced to adopt a posture that, despite Russian military capabilities and despite their long-range intentions, freedom shall be preserved to us."[38] The strategy of options which they urged had as its object, not the reduction of tensions, but the provision of additional and appropriate weapons to deal with a subtle adversary who might otherwise get under the American guard.

IV

Two years later in 1959–60, the major works on strategy in the United States showed a slight but perceptible change of emphasis. As it happened, the most significant of these were the work, not of full-time academics in universities, but of men drawn from a wide variety of disciplines—physicists, engineers, mathematicians, economists and systems analysts—who had been working in defence research institutes on classified information, particularly at RAND Corporation. As a result they analysed the technical problems of de-

terrence with an expertise which earlier works had naturally lacked. These problems appeared all the more urgent to the general public after the launching of the *Sputnik* satellite in 1957; which revealed the full extent of the challenge which the United States had to meet from Soviet technology. For the first time in its history the United States felt itself in danger of physical attack, and the question of civil defence, which had for some time agitated academic specialists, became one of public concern. Yet at the same time there was beginning to emerge in some quarters a new attitude to the Soviet Union. This saw in that power not simply a threat to be countered, but a partner whose collaboration was essential if nuclear war through accident or miscalculation was to be avoided. It recognized that Soviet policy and intentions might have certain elements in common with those of the United States, and that its leaders faced comparable problems. This attitude was by no means general. For scholars such as Robert Strausz-Hupé and William Kintner the conflict still resembled that between the Archangel Michael and Lucifer rather than that between Tweedledum and Tweedledee. But the concept, not only of a common interest between antagonists but of a joint responsibility for the avoidance of nuclear holocaust became increasingly evident after the new Administration came into power in 1961.[39]

The view which commanded growing support among American strategic thinkers was, therefore, that the "balance of terror" was a great deal less stable than had hitherto been assumed, but that if it could be stabilized (which involved a certain reciprocity from the Soviet Union) there would be reasonable prospects of lasting peace. The technical instability of the balance was described by Albert Wohlstetter in the famous article which appeared in *Foreign Affairs* at the beginning of 1958, describing on the basis of his classified studies at RAND Corporation, the full requirements of an invulnerable retaliatory force: a stable "steady-state" peace-time operation within feasible budgets, the capacity to survive enemy attacks, to make and communicate the decision to retaliate, to reach enemy territory, penetrate all defences and destroy the target; each phase demanding technical preparations of very considerable complexity and expense.[40]

The following year the mathematician Oskar Morgenstern was to sug-gest, in *The Question of National Defense,* that the best answer to the problem as defined by Wohlstetter, and the best safeguard against accidental war, was to be found in the development of seaborne missiles; and that it would be in the best interests of the United States if such a system could be developed by both sides. "In view of modern technology of speedy weapons-delivery from any point on earth to any other," he wrote, "it is in the interest of the United States for Russia to have an invulnerable retaliatory force and vice versa."[41] Whether Morgenstern reached this conclusion entirely through applying the game-theory in which he had made so outstanding a reputation is not entirely clear. Professor Thomas Schelling, who also brought the discipline of game-theory to bear on strategy, reached the same conclusion at approximately the same time;[42] but even by cruder calculations its validity seemed evident, and the concept of a "stable balance" was central to Bernard Brodie's *Strategy in the Missile Age,* which also appeared in 1959.[43] This study pulled together all the threads of strategic thinking of the past five years and set them in their historical context. Brodie reduced the requirements of strategy in the missile age to three: an invulnerable retaliatory force; "a real and substantial capability for coping with local and limited aggression by local application of force"; and provision for saving life "on a vast scale" if the worst came to the worst.[44] About how, if the worst did come to the worst, nuclear war should be conducted, he did not attempt to offer any guidance beyond suggesting that the most important problem to study was not so much how to conduct the war, but how to stop it.

Not all of Brodie's colleagues at the RAND Corporation were so modest. The following year, 1960, saw the publication of Herman Kahn's huge and baroque study *On Thermonuclear*

War;[45] the first published attempt by any thinker with access to classified material to discuss the action which should be taken if deterrence *did* fail. The horrible nature of the subject, the broad brush-strokes with which the author treated it, his somewhat selective approach to scientific data and the grim jocularity of the style, all combined to ensure for this study a reception which ranged from the cool to the hysterically vitriolic. Many of the criticisms, however, appear to arise rather from a sense of moral outrage that the subject should be examined at all than from serious disagreement with Kahn's actual views. In fact Kahn basically made only two new contributions to the strategic debate. The first, based on the classified RAND *Study of Non-Military Defense* for which he had been largely responsible, was that a substantial proportion of the American population could survive a nuclear strike, and that this proportion might be considerably increased if the necessary preparations were made. The second was that the United States should equip itself with the capacity to choose among a range of options in nuclear as well as in non-nuclear war; that rather than relying on a single spasm reaction (von Schlieffen's *Schlacht ohne Morgen* brought up to date) the United States should be able to conduct a controlled nuclear strategy, suiting its targets to its political intentions—which would normally be, not to destroy the enemy, but to "coerce" him.[46] Kahn in fact reintroduced the concept of an operational strategy which had been almost entirely missing, at least from public discussion, since the thermonuclear age had dawned ten years earlier. For smaller nuclear powers any such notion, as applied to a conflict with the Soviet Union, was self-evidently absurd. Between the super-powers it was—and remains—a perfectly legitimate matter for analysis. Kahn may have exaggerated the capacity of the social and political

structure of the United States to survive a nuclear holocaust; certainly many of his comments and calculations were oversimplified to the point of naïveté. But it is hard to quarrel with his assumption that that capacity, whatever its true dimensions, could be increased by appropriate preliminary measures; while the position adopted by some of his critics, that even to contemplate the possibility of deterrence failing might increase the possibility of such failure, is hardly one that stands up to dispassionate analysis.

At the beginning of 1961 President Kennedy's new Administration took office and Mr. Robert McNamara became Secretary of Defense. Not entirely coincidentally, the great period of American intellectual strategic speculation came to an end, after five astonishingly fruitful years. The military intellectuals were either drawn, like Kaufmann and Hilsman, into government, or returned to more orthodox studies on university campuses. Most of them continued to write. Kahn has produced two further works refining some of the views expounded in *On Thermonuclear War*.[47] Kissinger has remained a sage observer of and a prolific commentator on the political scene, and is at the moment of writing President Nixon's adviser on international security affairs. Osgood, Wohlstetter and Brodie have all produced notable works of synthesis or criticism. Perhaps the most interesting work has been that of Knorr and Schelling, who have broadened their studies to embrace the whole question of the role of military power in international relations;[48] a remarkably little-explored field in which a great deal of work remains to be done. It would be absurdly premature to suggest that any of these scholars—many of them still comparatively young men—have no more substantial contributions to make to strategic studies; but they are unlikely to surpass the intellectual achievement for which they were individually and jointly responsible in the 1950s. Between them they have done what Clausewitz and Mahan did in the last century, during times of no less bewildering political and technological change: laid down clear principles to guide the men who have to make decisions. Like Clausewitz and Mahan they are children of their time, and their views are formed by historical and technological conditions whose transformation may well render them out of date. Like those of Clausewitz and Mahan, their principles are likely to be misunderstood, abused, or applied incorrectly, and must be subjected by each generation to searching examination and criticism. Debate will certainly continue; but at least we now have certain solid issues to debate about.

The principles established by the thinkers of the 1950s were to guide Mr. McNamara in his work of remoulding American defence policy during the eight years of his period of office in the Department of Defense. "The McNamara Strategy" had a logical coherence —almost an elegance—which may have commanded rather more admiration among academics than it did in the world of affairs.[49] An invulnerable second-strike force was built up on a considerably larger scale than that considered adequate by the believers in "minimal deterrence." These forces were endowed with the capability, even after a surprise attack, of retaliating selectively against enemy forces rather than against his civilian population, so that "a possible opponent" would have "the strongest imaginable incentive to refrain from striking our own cities."[50] Forces for "limited wars" at all levels were created, armed both with nuclear and with conventional weapons. This involved an increase in expenditure, but it was an increase which was not grudged by Congressmen alarmed by an alleged "missile gap" and happy to see fat defence contracts being placed

within their home states; and the techniques of systems analysis which had also been developed at RAND Corporation were employed to keep this increase within bounds.[51] Overtures were made, official and unofficial, to the Soviet Union to establish arms-control agreements based on the principle of a stable balance resting on invulnerable second-strike forces on either side. And plans were put in hand for civil defence projects on a massive scale.

McNamara was able to carry out much of his programme, but not all. The Russians were remarkably slow to absorb the reasoning which appeared so self-evident to American academics. The American public was even slower to co-operate in the sweeping measures necessary to provide effective insurance against holocaust. The ideal of a second-strike counter-force strategy seemed to many critics to be one almost intrinsically impossible of realization. And America's European allies flatly refused McNamara's requests that they should increase their conventional forces to provide the necessary "spectrum of deterrence." The Germans saw this as a diminution of the deterrent to any invasion of their own narrow land, and besides had their own not particularly enjoyable memories of "conventional war." The British, struggling to maintain a world presence on their obstinately stagnant economy, could not afford it; while the French had ideas of their own. None of them, perhaps, could produce a coherent theoretical framework to sustain them in their arguments, but they remained unconvinced. Several of Mr. McNamara's emissaries received, in consequence, a somewhat gruelling introduction to the refractory world of international affairs.

For the American strategic programme was based on two assumptions which were not accepted by all the major allies of the United States; first, that America was the leader of "the

Free World" and had both the right and the power to shape its strategy; and second, it was in the interests of the world as a whole that the United States and the Soviet Union should enter into an ever closer dialogue. Neither of these assumptions was challenged by the British; though not all their countrymen admired the assiduity with which successive British Prime Ministers set themselves up as "honest brokers" between the super-powers the moment they set foot inside Downing Street. Indeed the most substantial British contribution to the strategic debate in the early 1960s, John Strachey's *On the Prevention of War,* quite explicitly advocated a Russo–American diarchy as the best guarantee of world peace.[52] But on the Continent reactions were different. The Chancellor of the Federal German Republic took a glum view of a Russo–American *détente* which could only, in his view, confirm the division of his country and might even threaten the position of Berlin; and long before Mr. McNamara had appeared on the scene the President of the French Fifth Republic had made clear his own attitude to the American claim to act as leader and the spokesman of "The Free World."

V

Too much should not be made of the personality of General de Gaulle in shaping the French contribution to the strategic debate which began to gain in importance towards the end of the 1950s. French military experience during the past twenty years had been distinctive and disagreeable. They had their own views on the reliability of overseas allies as protectors against powerful continental neighbours—neighbours who might in future comprise not only Russia but a revived Germany, or in moments of sheer nightmare, both. The decision to develop their own nuclear weapons had been taken before De Gaulle came into power, though perhaps it took De Gaulle to ensure that they would not be integrated, like the British, in a common Western targeting system. General Pierre Gallois, the first French writer to develop a distinctive theory of nuclear strategy,[53] advanced the thesis that nuclear weapons rendered traditional alliance systems totally out of date since no state, however powerful, would risk nuclear retaliation on behalf of an ally when it really came to the point. In a world thus atomized (in the traditional sense of the word) the security of every state lay in its capacity to provide its own minimal deterrence. The more states that did, indeed, the greater the stability of the international system was likely to be.

Extreme as Gallois's logic was, it probably reflected the sentiments of a large number of his countrymen and a substantial section of the French Armed Forces. In spite of innumerable official expressions to the contrary, there is every reason to suppose that many influential members of the British governing establishment felt very much the same about their own nuclear force. A more subtle variant of this doctrine was presented by General André Beaufre, who argued powerfully in his work, *Deterrence and Strategy,* that a multipolar nuclear balance in fact provided greater stability than a bipolar, since it reduced the area of uncertainty which an aggressor might exploit. So far from atomizing alliances, argued Beaufre, independent nuclear forces cemented them, "necessarily covering the whole range of their vital interests."[54] He was careful to distinguish between multipolarity and proliferation. "The stability provided by the nuclear weapon," he argued, "is attainable only between *reasonable* powers. Boxes of matches should not be given to children;"[55] a sentiment which one can endorse while wondering what Beaufre would define, in international relations, as the age of consent. As for the Russo–American diarchy welcomed by Strachey, Beaufre specifically identified this as a danger to be avoided. "The prospect of a world controlled by a *de facto* Russo–American 'condominium' is one of the possible—and menacing—results of nuclear evolution," he wrote. "Looked at from this point of view, the existence of independent nuclear forces should constitute a guarantee that the interests of the other nuclear powers will not be sacrificed through some agreement between the two superpowers."[56]

The doctrine of "multipolarity" was thus one distinctive contribution by French theorists to the study of strategy in the nuclear age. The second was their analysis of revolutionary war: a subject virtually ignored by American strategic thinkers until the Vietnam involvement brutally forced it on their attention. For the French it had been inescapable. For nearly ten years after World War II the flower of their armies had been involved, in Indo-China, in operations of far larger scope than the various "imperial policing" activities which absorbed so much of the attention of the British Armed Forces, and one which imposed on the French nation a longer and perhaps even more severe a strain than the Korean War imposed on the United States. The war in Indo-China was lost. It was followed by six years of struggle in Algeria which ended, for the French Armed Forces, no less tragically. The outcome of these wars significantly altered the balance of power in the world, but the strategic concepts being developed in the United States appeared as irrelevant to their conduct as those which guided—or misguided—the French armies during the two world wars. The concepts which *were* relevant of course were those of Mao Tse-tung; those precepts evolved during the Sino–Japanese struggles of

the 1930s and developed into a full theory of revolutionary warfare whereby a strongly motivated cadre operating from a position of total weakness could defeat a government controlling the entire apparatus of the state.

The theories of Mao lie outside the scope of this study, though there is little doubt that he is among the outstanding strategic thinkers of our day. Certainly the French paid him the compliment of trying to imitate him. The literature on the subject is so considerable that it may be only by hazard that the earliest French study to receive widespread recognition was Colonel Bonnet's historical analysis, *Les guerres insurrectionnelles et révolutionnaires*.[57] Bonnet in this work gave a definition which has since been generally accepted: "Guerre de partisans + guerre psychologique = guerre révolutionnaire." "Poser cette équation," he went on to claim, "c'est formuler une loi valable pour tous les mouvements révolutionnaires qui, aujourd'hui, agitent le monde."[58] On the basis of this definition and their own experiences, French military thinkers, true to their national intellectual traditions, attempted to formulate *une doctrine*. (It is interesting to note that the pragmatic British, whose cumulative experience in counter-insurgency campaigning was certainly no less than that of the French, thought more modestly in terms of "techniques.")[59] As worked out by such writers as Bonnet himself, Hogard, Lacheroy, Nemo, and Trinquier,[60] this *doctrine* set out the object, both of revolutionary and counter-revolutionary war, as the gaining of the confidence and support of the people, by a mixture of violent and non-violent means directed both at "military" and at "non-military" targets. It was not enough to suppress guerrillas: it was necessary to destroy the basis of their support among the population by eliminating the grievances which they exploited, by giving protection against their terroristic activities and, insisted the French writers, by a process of intensive indoctrination to combat that of the revolutionary cadres themselves.

It would be painful to record in detail where and why these excellent recommendations went wrong. The use of undifferentiated violence by legitimate authority undermines the basis of consent which is its strongest weapon against revolutionary opponents. Indoctrination of a population can be done only by men who are themselves indoctrinated; and since the whole essence of the "open societies" of the West is virtually incompatible with the concept of ideological indoctrination, the men thus indoctrinated rapidly found themselves almost as much at odds with their own society as the revolutionaries they were trying to combat. In Algeria the French Army applied its doctrines with a fair measure of at least short-term success, but in so doing it alienated the sympathies of its own countrymen. The main fault of its theorists—and of their imitators in the United States—was to overlook the element of simple *nationalism* which provided such strength for the insurgent forces: a curious failing in the country which was the original home of that immensely powerful force. They accepted the propaganda of their adversaries, and saw the conflict simply in terms of a global struggle against the forces of world Communist revolution. Marxist categories of thought make it impossible for their theorists even to consider that the most potent revolutionary force in the world may be not the class struggle but old-fashioned "bourgeois" nationalism. The French theorists were no doubt equally unwilling to take into account a consideration which boded so ill for their own side. But there is good reason to suppose that the FLN won in Algeria, not because they were Marxist but because they were *Algerian,* and the French were not. *Mutatis mutandis* the

same applied—and applies still—in Indo-China. Marx and Lenin may provide the rationale of insurgency warfare; Mao Tse-tung may provide the techniques; but the driving power is furnished by the ideas of Mazzini. It is therefore difficult for foreign troops, however well-intentioned, to apply counter-insurgency techniques among a people which has awoken to a consciousness of its national identity with any chance of success.

In addition to the doctrines of multipolarity and revolutionary war, France has produced yet a third contribution to strategic thinking: the doctrine of indirect strategy. This was not totally novel. A group of American thinkers based on the Center for Foreign Policy Research at the University of Pennsylvania had long been working on the assumption that "The Free World" and the Communists were locked in a protracted conflict which could end only in the victory of one side or the other and in which force was only one element out of many which might be used.[61] It was an assumption that could certainly be justified by reference to the works of Marx–Leninist theoreticians. But the publications of these writers tended to be as emotional and tendentious as those of the Marxists themselves. Certainly they had never formulated their theories with the clarity, reasonableness and dispassionate precision of General André Beaufre and his colleagues at the Institut d'Études Stratégiques in Paris.[62] For Beaufre the whole field of international relations constituted a battlefield in which the Communist powers, thwarted in the use of force by the nuclear stalemate, were attacking the West by indirect means. Strategy had progressed from the "operational" (Clausewitz and Jomini) through the "logistic" (the great build-ups of World War II) to the "indirect." Political manœuvres should therefore be seen as strategic manœuvres. The adversary attacked, withdrew, feinted, outflanked, or dug in, using direct force where he could and infiltration where he could not. The West should respond accordingly, devise a single overall political strategy and use economic, political, and military means to implement it.

The trouble with this is that it is not simply a theory of strategy but also a theory of international relations. If it is correct, Beaufre's recommendations follow naturally enough; but Beaufre states his assumptions rather than argues them, and to most students of international relations they are not self-evident. Such a view leaves too many factors out of account. The world is not really polarized so simply. Communist leaders do not control events so firmly. Whatever the ideologues may say, in practice interests are not so implacably opposed. Strategy must certainly be shaped by the needs of policy; but policy cannot be made to fit quite so easily into the Procrustean concepts of the professional strategist.

Perhaps the most significant conclusion to be drawn from this survey is the extent to which the quality of strategic thinking in the nuclear age is related to an understanding of international relations, on the one hand, and of weapons technology on the other. There is of course nothing new in this dependence. Clausewitz emphasized the first, though he never fully adjusted his purely strategic thinking to take account of the political environment whose overriding importance he quite rightly stressed. The second has been evident, particularly in naval and air operations, at least since the beginning of the twentieth century. But strategic thinkers, from the pioneers of the eighteenth century to Liddell Hart in his earlier writings, were able to assume a fairly simple model of international relations within which armed conflict might occur, as well as a basically stable technological environment. Neither assumption can now be made. No thinking about deterrence is likely to be of value unless it is based on a thorough understanding of "the state of the art" in weapons technology. Any thinking about limited war, revolutionary war, or indirect strategy must take as its starting point an understanding of the political—including the social and economic—context out of which these conflicts arise or are likely to arise. Inevitably the interaction works both ways. Strategic factors themselves constitute an important element in international relations: the statesman can never be a purely despotic lawgiver to the strategist. Similarly, strategic requirements have inspired scientists and technologists to achievements they would normally consider impossible. Increasingly the three fields overlap. That is why strategic studies owe at least as much to the work of political scientists at one end of the spectrum, and of physical scientists, systems analysts and mathematical economists at the other, as they do to the classical strategist. One may indeed wonder whether "classical strategy," as a self-sufficient study, has no longer a valid claim to exist.

NOTES

1. B. H. Liddell Hart, *Strategy: The Indirect Approach* (London: Faber, 1967), p. 335.

2. André Beaufre, *An Introduction to Strategy* (London: Faber, 1965), *passim*, esp. pp. 107–130.

3. *Ibid.*, p. 22.

4. The term seems appropriate. Strategy deals with too many imponderables to merit the description "science." It remains, as Voltaire described it two hundred years ago, "murderous and conjectural."

5. P. M. S. Blackett, *Studies of War* (London: Oliver & Boyd, 1962), p. 128.

6. Sir John Slessor, "Air Power and the Future of War," *Journal of the Royal United Service Institution*, August 1954.

7. P. M. S. Blackett, *The Military and*

Political Consequences of Atomic Energy (London: The Turnstile Press, 1948), p. 56.

8. Vannevar Bush, *Modern Arms and Free Men* (New York: Simon & Schuster, 1949), pp. 115–16.

9. As for example Jacob Viner's paper on "The Implications of the Atomic Bomb for East–West Relations," the influence of which is acknowledged by Brodie and many others. Albert Wohlstetter gave an impromptu account at the ISS Conference, of the main lines along which these discussions ran. Some account will also be found in Richard G. Hewlett and Oscar E. Anderson, *The New World* (Vol. I of the History of the United States Atomic Energy Commission, Pennsylvania, 1962), and in the early issues of the *Bulletin of the Atomic Scientists*.

10. B. H. Liddell Hart, *The Revolution in Warfare* (London: Faber, 1946), p. 87.

11. Bernard Brodie, ed., *The Absolute Weapon* (New York: Harcourt, Brace, 1946), p. 89.

12. Brodie, *op. cit.*, pp. 75–76. He did not, however, deal with the problem of vulnerability of retaliatory forces, and the consequent dependence of stability on an effective second-strike capability.

13. Richard N. Rosecrance, *The Defense of the Realm* (New York: Columbia University Press, 1968), p. 159.

14. "The Place of the Bomber in British Policy." Reprinted in *The Great Deterrent* (London: Cassell, 1957), p. 123.

15. B. H. Liddell Hart, *The Defence of the West* (London: Cassell, 1950), pp. 97, 134, 139, 140.

16. Sir John Slessor, *Strategy for the West* (London: Cassell, 1954), p. 108.

17. Lt.-Gen. Sir John Cowley, "Future Trends in Warfare," *Journal of the Royal United Service Institution*, February 1960, p. 13.

18. Rosecrance, *op. cit.*, pp. 160–61.

19. This of course begs the whole question so carefully examined by Stephen Maxwell in Adelphi Paper No. 50: *Rationality in Deterrence* (London: ISS).

20. Slessor, Lecture at Oxford University, April 1955, reprinted in *The Great Deterrent*, p. 181.

21. P. M. S. Blackett, *Atomic Energy and East–West Relations* (Cambridge: Cambridge University Press, 1956), p. 100.

22. P. M. S. Blackett, "Critique of Some Contemporary Defence Thinking." First published in *Encounter* in 1961, this article is reprinted in *Studies of War, op. cit.*, pp. 128–46. See also Blackett's dissenting note in Alastair Buchan: *NATO in the 1960s* (London: Chatto & Windus, 1960).

23. Text in the *New York Times*, 13 January 1954.

24. See the analysis " 'The New Look' of 1953" by Glenn H. Snyder, in Warner R. Schilling, Paul Y. Hammond and Glen H. Snyder, *Strategy, Politics, and Defense Budgets* (New York: Columbia University Press, 1962), pp. 379–524.

25. Bernard Brodie, "Unlimited Weapons and Limited War," *The Reporter*, 18 November 1954. For an indispensable annotated bibliography of the whole controversy, see Morton H. Halperin, *Limited War in the Nuclear Age* (New York: John Wiley, 1963).

26. William W. Kaufmann, ed., *Military Policy and National Security* (Princeton, N.J.: Princeton University Press, 1956), pp. 28, 38, 257.

27. *Ibid.*, pp. 53–57, 60–72.

28. *Ibid.*, pp. 75–101.

29. Robert E. Osgood: *Limited War: the Challenge to American Strategy* (Chicago: University of Chicago Press, 1957). Henry A. Kissinger, *Nuclear Weapons and Foreign Policy* (New York: Houghton Mifflin, 1957).

30. J. F. Dulles, "Challenge and Response in United States' Policy," *Foreign Affairs*, October 1957.

31. Osgood, *op. cit.*, p. 258.

32. Kissinger, *op. cit.*, pp. 174–202.

33. Anthony Buzzard, *et al.*, *On Limiting Atomic War* (London: Royal Institute of International Affairs, 1956); and "The H-Bomb: Massive Retaliation or Graduated Deterrence," *International Affairs*, 1956.

34. Slessor, "Total or Limited War?" in *The Great Deterrent*, pp. 262–84. Liddell Hart, *Deterrent or Defence: A Fresh Look at the West's Military Position* (London: Stevens, 1960), pp. 74–81. Blackett, "Nuclear Weapons and Defence," *International Affairs*, October 1958.

35. Brodie, *Strategy in the Missile Age* (Princeton, N.J.: Princeton University Press, 1959), p. 330. Thomas C. Schelling, *The Strategy of Conflict* (Cambridge, Mass.: Harvard University Press, 1960), pp. 262–66. But the debate continued. Brodie in *Escalation and the Nuclear Option* (Princeton, N.J.: Princeton University Press, 1966) was to argue strongly against what had by then become known as the "firebreak" theory, and emphasize the deterrent value of tactical nuclear weapons.

36. Kissinger, *The Necessity for Choice* (New York: Harper & Brothers, 1960), pp. 81–98.

37. The literature is enormous, but three outstanding contributions are Helmuth Schmidt, *Verteidigung oder Vergeltung* (Stuttgart, 1961); Alastair Buchan and Philip Windsor, *Arms and Stability in Europe* (London: Chatto & Windus, 1963); and Raymond Aron, *Le Grand Débat* (Paris: Calmann-Lévy, 1963).

38. Kissinger, *Nuclear Weapons, op. cit.,* p. vii.

39. For an analysis of the various attitudes of American strategic thinkers to the question of *détente* see Robert A. Levine, *The Arms Debate* (Cambridge, Mass.: Harvard University Press, 1963), *passim.*

40. Albert Wohlstetter, "The Delicate Balance of Terror," *Foreign Affairs,* January 1958. The article is reprinted in Henry A. Kissinger (ed.), *Problems of National Strategy* (New York: Praeger, 1966). The principal relevant studies were *Selection and Use of Air Bases* (R–266, April 1954) and *Protecting US Power to Strike Back in the 1950s & 1960s* (R–290, April 1956) by Albert Wohlstetter, F. S. Hoffman, and H. S. Rowen. Wohlstetter in a private communication to the present writer has stressed also the significant part played in these studies by experts in systems-analysis such as J. F. Pigby, E. J. Barlow, and R. J. Lutz.

41. Oskar Morgenstern, *The Question of National Defense* (New York: Random House, 1959), p. 75.

42. See particularly his "Surprise Attack and Disarmament" in Klaus Knorr (ed.), *NATO and American Security* (Princeton, N.J.: Princeton University Press, 1959). Schelling's whole work on the problem of dialogue in conflict situations is of major importance. His principal articles are collected in *The Strategy of Conflict* (Cambridge, Mass.: Harvard University Press, 1960).

43. Brodie, *Strategy in the Missile Age, op. cit.,* Chapter 8. Brodie, and Schelling, like Wohlstetter, were at the time working at RAND Corporation, as also was Herman Kahn. All have acknowledged their mutual indebtedness during this formative period in their thinking.

44. *Ibid.,* pp. 294–97.

45. Herman Kahn, *On Thermonuclear War* (Princeton, N.J.: Princeton University Press, 1960).

46. *Ibid.,* pp. 301–2.

47. *Thinking about the Unthinkable* (New York: Horizon Press, 1962). *On Escalation: Metaphors and Scenarios* (New York: Praeger, 1965).

48. Knorr, *On the Uses of Military Power in the Nuclear Age* (Princeton, N.J.: Princeton University Press, 1966). Schelling, *Arms and Influence* (New Haven: Yale University Press, 1966).

49. William W. Kaufmann, *The McNa-mara Strategy* (New York: Harper & Row, 1964) provides a useful if uncritical account. It should be read in association with Bernard Brodie's dry commentary "The McNamara Phenomenon," *World Politics,* July 1965.

50. McNamara's speech at the University of Michigan at Ann Arbor, 16 June 1962. Kaufmann, *op. cit.,* p. 116.

51. See Charles Hitch and Roland McKean, *The Economics of Defense in the Nuclear Age* (Cambridge, Mass.: Harvard University Press, 1960) for the promise. The performance was examined in *Planning—Programming—Budgeting: Hearings before the Subcommittee on National Security and International Operations of the Committee on Government Operations,* United States Senate, 90th Congress, 1st Session (US Government Printing Office, 1967).

52. John Strachey, *On the Prevention of War* (London: Macmillan, 1962).

53. Pierre Gallois, *Stratégie de l'Age nucléaire* (Paris: Calmann-Lévy, 1960).

54. André Beaufre, *Deterrence and Strategy* (London: Faber, 1965), p. 93.

55. *Ibid.,* p. 97.

56. *Ibid.,* p. 140. Beaufre's experience as commander of the French land forces in the Suez operation of 1956 may have had some relevance to his views on this point.

57. Gabriel Bonnet, *Les guerres insurrectionnelles et révolutionnaires de l'antiquité a'nos jours* (Paris: Payot, 1955). Important unpublished studies by Colonel Lacheroy were in circulation at the same time.

58. *Ibid.,* p. 60.

59. See, for example, Julian Paget, *Counter-Insurgency Campaigning* (London: Faber, 1967) and Sir Robert Thompson, *Defeating Communist Insurgency* (London: Chatto & Windus, 1966).

60. For a good select bibliography see the excellent and highly critical study by Peter Paret, *French Revolutionary Warfare from Indo-China to Algeria* (New York: Praeger, 1964).

61. Robert Strausz-Hupé, *et al., Protracted Conflict; A Challenging Study of Communist Strategy* (New York: Harper & Brothers, 1959) and *A Forward Strategy for America* (New York: Harper & Brothers, 1961).

62. André Beaufre, *An Introduction to Strategy* (London: Faber, 1965); *Deterrence and Strategy* (London: Faber, 1965); *Strategy of Action* (London: Faber, 1967).

A General Survey of Strategy

ANDRÉ BEAUFRE

ANALYSIS OF STRATEGY

THE MEANING OF THE WORD

What does the word strategy mean?

According to the traditional concept of military strategy it should mean the art of employing military forces to achieve the ends set by political policy. This definition was formulated by Liddell Hart in 1929 and it hardly differs from that of Clausewitz. Raymond Aron in his recent book follows it almost word for word.

In my view this definition is too restrictive because it deals with military forces only. I would put it as follows: the art of applying force so that it makes the most effective contribution towards achieving the ends set by political policy. This definition, however, is applicable to the whole art of war—awkward because by tradition the art of war is divided into strategy and tactics and a third sub-division has recently appeared—logistics. If strategy is neither tactics nor logistics, what is it? Tactics is obviously the art of using weapons in battle in such a way that they make the maximum impact. Logistics is the science of supply and movement. Both are concerned with the "interplay of material factors"; both are therefore more in the nature of a material science, like engineering for instance.

Lloyd has drawn the contrast between "the divine spark" and the "interplay of material factors" and in Napoleon's vocabulary the "divine spark"

was strategy. From this it is but a step (and a step often taken) to equate strategy with the spark of genius. But genius is said to be an infinite capacity for taking pains, so whether the divine spark is there or not, strategy must be based on thought and reasoning. If therefore it is neither a material science nor an aspect of policy, what is it?

In my view the essence of strategy is the abstract interplay which, to use Foch's phrase, springs from the clash between two opposing wills. It is the art which enables a man, no matter what the techniques employed, to master the problems set by any clash of wills and as a result to employ the techniques available with maximum efficiency. It is therefore the art of the dialectic of force or, more precisely, *the art of the dialectic of two opposing wills using force to resolve their dispute.*

This definition will justifiably be characterized as highly abstract and very general in terms. But it is on this plane that strategy must be considered if we are to understand the thought processes involved and the rules which emerge therefrom.

THE AIM OF STRATEGY

As soon as one begins to examine the aim of strategy, the importance of the definition given above becomes clear.

It will be agreed that the aim of strategy is to fulfil the objectives laid down by policy, making the best use of the resources available. Now the objective may be offensive in character (e.g. conquest or the imposition of severe terms), it may be defensive (e.g. the protection of certain areas or interests) or it may merely be the maintenance of the political *status quo*. It is therefore obvious straight away that formulae such as that attributed to Clausewitz, "decision as a result of victory in battle," are not applicable to all types of objective. There is only one general rule applicable to all: disregard the method by which the decision is to be reached and consider only the outcome which it is desired to achieve. The outcome desired is to force the enemy to accept the terms we wish to impose on him. In this dialectic of wills *a decision is achieved when a certain psychological effect* has been produced on the enemy: when he becomes convinced that it is useless to start or alternatively to continue the struggle.

Naturally this outcome may be achieved by military victory but it is by no means the only way. Military victory may be unattainable (e.g. against the rebels in Algeria); other methods may be more effective, as has frequently been proved. If the problem is looked at from the right angle, that of the enemy's psychological reaction, a correct appreciation can be made of what the decisive factors are—and by the same token, we shall have embarked upon a thought process applicable equally to straightforward military victory in the field and to the (so-called) new strategy of nuclear deterrence.

In his analysis of Clausewitz, Lenin produced a much-quoted dictum which shows clearly that the decisive factor is the psychological; he said: "the soundest strategy in war is to postpone operations until the moral disintegration of the enemy renders a mortal blow both possible and easy." He was, however, thinking as a revolutionary and regarded political action as a sort of psy-

chological artillery preparation—the exact opposite of Clausewitz's classical military concept in which the morale of the enemy was to be broken by military victory. A general rule can therefore, in my view, be formulated as follows: *the decision is obtained by creating and then exploiting a situation resulting in sufficient moral disintegration of the enemy to cause him to accept the conditions it is desired to impose on him.*

That is the guiding principle in the dialectic of opposing wills.

MEANS AVAILABLE TO STRATEGY

The correct process of reasoning becomes even clearer when we come to consider the means to be employed by strategy.

To reach the decision required, strategy will have available a whole gamut of means, both material and moral, ranging from nuclear bombardment to propaganda or a trade agreement. The art of strategy consists in choosing the most suitable means from those available and so orchestrating their results that they combine to produce a psychological pressure sufficient to achieve the moral effect required.

To choose the most suitable means the enemy's vulnerable points must be set against our own capabilities. To do this it is necessary to analyse the decisive moral effect required. Whom do we wish to convince? Ultimately it must be the enemy Government but in some cases it may be easier to work on leading personalities (e.g. Chamberlain at Bad Godesberg or Munich), choosing the arguments to which they are most susceptible. Alternatively it may be best to work directly on a certain section of public opinion which has some hold over the Government or on an influential Allied Government or through UNO. If the issue at stake is minor, pressures of this nature may be enough. If the stake is more important, action involving the use of force may be necessary; but here again the choice of means must take full account of the enemy's vulnerable points and of our own capabilities; for instance a military victory of the traditional kind may be either unattainable or involve too great a risk. If this is so, there are numerous alternatives available: a revolutionary uprising with the object of bringing about international action (e.g. the Sudeten Germans prior to Munich): a revolutionary uprising with the object of bringing down the Government (e.g. Prague in 1948): economic pressure (e.g. economic sanctions against Italy in 1935): a prolonged guerrilla campaign combined with international pressure (e.g. the Viet Minh or the Algerian rebels). Which of all the possible alternatives are those best calculated to exert a decisive influence on the thinking of the enemy leaders? If finally military action has to be undertaken, what is its objective to be? "Destruction of the enemy armed forces" according to Clausewitz' doctrine? Will this be possible? If not, would some local success (e.g. the Crimea in 1854) be enough? If so, where? What parts of his armed forces are vital to the enemy (e.g. the navy and air force in England, the army in France)? What geographical area is vital to him? Will it be essential to capture his capital or will that be valueless? Will it be enough to threaten to destroy it? And so on and so on. This type of analysis must continue until we have isolated those means which we have the capacity to use and which at the same time are adequate to produce the decision we require.

THE STRATEGIC PLAN

The strategic plan can now be worked out. We are dealing with a problem of dialectics; for every action proposed, therefore, the possible enemy reactions must be calculated and provision made to guard against them. His reaction may be international or national, psychological, political, economic or military. Each successive action planned, together with the counter to the corresponding enemy reaction, must be built up into a coherent whole, the object being to retain the ability to pursue the plan in spite of the resistance of the enemy. If the plan is a good one, there should be no risk of setbacks. The result will be a "risk-proof" strategy, the object of which will be to preserve our own liberty of action. Naturally strategy must have a clear picture of the whole chain of events leading up to the final decision—which, be it noted in passing, was not the case with us in France either in 1870 or in 1939 or in Indo-China or in Algeria. It must also be remembered that the dialectic struggle between two opponents will be further complicated by the fact that it will be played out on an international stage. Pressure by allies or even neutrals may prove decisive (as at Suez). Germany has lost two wars as a result of failure to grasp this point; she brought England in against her by the invasion of Belgium and the United States by the U-boat war. A correct appreciation of the influence of the international situation upon our own liberty of action is therefore a vital element of strategy; this is all the more important now that the advent of the nuclear weapon has so strikingly emphasized the interdependence of all nations.

PATTERNS OF STRATEGY

Strategic plans can in general be classified into a number of differing patterns depending on the relative resources available to the opposing sides and the importance of the issue at stake. The following are the most typical:

(1) If the objective is only of moderate importance and the resources available are large (or if the action proposed is likely to bring into operation powerful allied resources), the mere threat of the use of these resources may lead the enemy to accept the conditions

it is desired to impose on him; it will be even easier to force him to abandon some effort to modify the established *status quo.* This pattern of strategy, *the direct threat,* is much in vogue at the moment as a result of the advent of the nuclear weapon; it is the basis of the imposing structure of deterrent strategy.

(2) If the objective is still of only moderate importance but the resources available are inadequate to exert a decisive threat, an attempt to attain the objective desired must be made by more insidious methods; these may be political, diplomatic or economic. This pattern of strategy, *indirect pressure,* has been frequently used both by Hitler and the Soviet Union, not so much because they lacked the resources necessary for coercion but primarily because of the deterrent effect of the direct threat from their opponents' forces. This pattern of strategy is most suitable in cases where freedom of action is limited.

(3) If freedom of action is restricted and the resources available limited but the objective of major importance, an attempt will be made to attain the objective by a series of successive actions in which the direct threat and indirect pressure will be combined with a limited application of force. This pattern of strategy, *a series of successive actions,* was employed by Hitler from 1935 to 1939; he only succeeded, however, so long as his objective was apparently of minor importance. As soon as the "nibbling process" appeared likely to affect vital objectives, he found himself inevitably launched into major conflict. Her insular position has in general led Great Britain to adopt this strategy of the indirect approach; it has been very clearly restated by Liddell Hart. It is particularly suited to those nations which are in a strong defensive position (or well protected by nature) and which desire to achieve important re-

sults without committing more than minor offensive resources and are content to proceed slowly. This method of the indirect approach by successive stages was frequently a feature of the eighteenth-century wars in Europe owing to the fact that resources employed were relatively small.

(4) If freedom of action is large but the resources available inadequate to secure a military decision, recourse may be had to a strategy of protracted conflict; the object here is to wear down the enemy's morale and tire him out. To ensure that the struggle can be maintained over a long period, the resources employed will be extremely primitive but the technique by which they are applied (usually total war employing primarily widespread guerrilla tactics) will force the enemy to deploy an effort so great that he cannot maintain it indefinitely. This pattern of strategy, *a protracted struggle, but at a low level of military intensity,* has in general been employed with success in the wars of colonial liberation. Its chief theorist is Mao Tse-tung. It is worth noting that this strategy demands considerable moral endurance on the part of those initiating it and that its prerequisites are a strong emotional element in the struggle and a highly developed sentiment of national solidarity. It is therefore most suitable for wars of liberation. But it can only succeed if the issue at stake is of far greater importance to one side than to the other (as in the wars of colonial liberation) or if it receives assistance from regular armed forces to which it acts as an auxiliary (e.g. the wars of liberation in Europe in 1944–5 and Spain in 1813–14).

(5) If the military resources available are of sufficient strength, a decision will be sought through military victory; the clash will be violent but an attempt will be made to keep it short. The destruction of the enemy armed forces in battle may be enough, partic-

ularly if the issue at stake is not completely vital to the enemy. If not, the whole or part of his territory will have to be occupied in order to bring the fact of defeat home to public opinion and cause it to accept the conditions imposed. Naturally the loser is all the more likely to admit defeat if the victor has a fifth column on his side, as was the case with the French Revolutionary and Napoleonic victories. A fifth column can of course also play an important role in assisting military operations. This pattern of strategy, *violent conflict aiming at military victory*, is the classic strategy of the Napoleonic era. Its principal theorist is Clausewitz, though the well-nigh Wagnerian romanticism of many of his disciples has frequently distorted his theories. This was the dominant European strategy of the nineteenth and the first half of the twentieth centuries. Wrongly it was held to be the only orthodox strategy and therefore gave birth to the two great World Wars of 1914–18 and 1939–45, both of which showed up the limitations of the Clausewitz-Napoleon strategy. The surgical operation which is military victory can only be successful in obtaining a decision if the military capabilities of the time make it possible for that military victory to be both rapid and complete. This situation (as we shall see later when dealing with operational strategy) obtains only for limited periods in the tactical and operational evolutionary process. Apart from these exceptional periods the Clausewitz strategy can result only in the opponents being ranged opposite one another in a gigantic military struggle leading to stalemate (e.g. the position warfare from the end of 1914; Germany in 1940 failing, in spite of victory on the Continent, to cross the Channel and getting bogged down in a hopeless campaign in Russia). In this event a decision is reached only after a prolonged period of mutual attrition out of all proportion to the issue at stake, at the conclusion of which both victor and vanquished emerge from the conflict completely exhausted. It is of interest to note that this sequence of events had already been seen in the case of Napoleon, who failed in face of both England and Russia. Clausewitz and his disciples, however, were so blinded by the Emperor's victories that they failed to recognize the limitations of his strategy. It was in all probability this error of reasoning which cost Europe its world hegemony.

CONCLUSIONS

The five patterns of strategy described above should be considered more as examples than as an exhaustive categorization.

They are of interest mainly as showing the variety of possible courses of action from which strategy has to choose; they should therefore help towards a better understanding of the *nature and originality of the process of strategic thinking*. The thought processes applicable to tactics or logistics are almost entirely methodistic, their object being the rational employment of the military resources available in order to produce a given result; the political thought process must be capable of appreciating what public opinion wants or can be made to accept; both psychology and intuition will therefore play a considerable part. Strategic thinking, however, is a mental process, at once abstract and rational, which must be capable of synthesizing both psychological and material data. The strategist must have a great capacity both for analysis and for synthesis; analysis is necessary to assemble the data on which he makes his diagnosis, synthesis in order to produce from these data the diagnosis itself— and the diagnosis in fact amounts to a choice between alternative courses of action.

Our five examples also serve to show how wrong the numerous strategists have been who prescribe only one form of strategy. Each of the patterns referred to above has its protagonist and has been built up into a theory propounded as the sole, or at any rate the best, solution; in fact each of them may be the best solution, but only in certain defined circumstances. Without adequate analysis of the factors governing strategy, the choice of a course of action has all too often been made out of habit or following the fashion of the moment. As a result governments have not been in control of events and clashes of purpose have led to fearful international catastrophes. The world of today is passing through an unparalleled crisis of readjustment and at the same time science, industrialization and psychological action are making an increasing impact on the military art. More than ever before, therefore, is it vital that we should develop a method of thinking which will enable us to control, rather than be at the mercy of, events. That is why strategy is of such importance and such a problem of the moment.

SUB-DIVISIONS OF STRATEGY

Strategy may be a single entity in so far as object and method are concerned but when it comes to applying it, it must necessarily be sub-divided into specialized categories of strategy each applicable only to a certain field of conflict. The fact is that strategy must to a large extent be governed by material factors and the material factors characteristic of each field of activity differ, producing therefore a different chain of consequences applicable only to that field; for instance, naval strategy has always been distinct from land strategy.

We are therefore faced with a veritable pyramid of differing, though interdependent, forms of strategy; these must be clearly defined if they are to be welded into the best series of co-ordinated actions, all aimed at the same overall object.

At the top of the pyramid and under the direct control of the Government—i.e. of the political authority—is *total strategy*, whose task is to define how total war should be conducted.[1] Its task is to lay down the object for each specialized category of strategy and the manner in which all—political, economic, diplomatic and military—should be woven in together.

This level of strategy is clearly the prerogative of Heads of Government assisted by a Chief of the Defence Staff and some high-level Defence Committee or committees. The five patterns of strategy discussed above were all at the "total strategy" level; it was there shown that the relative importance of the different fields (political, economic, diplomatic or military) may vary considerably according to the circumstances. The military aspect was in fact only in the lead in one of the patterns discussed (No. 5).

Below the level of total strategy there must in each field (military, political, economic or diplomatic) be an *overall strategy*, the function of which is to allot tasks and co-ordinate the various forms of activity within the field concerned. It should be noted here that in the military field the notion of overall strategy already exists; its object is to co-ordinate action on land, in the air and on the sea. There is however no such thing as overall strategy in the political field (e.g. co-ordination of general political policy, internal policy, external policy and propaganda) nor in the economic field (e.g. co-ordination of production, financial policy and overseas trade) nor in the diplomatic field. Yet in these fields of activity strategy is employed almost daily—without anyone realizing it. Because people do not realize this, actions are not based on any concept worked out through any orderly process of reasoning and many opportunities are therefore missed. In fact for every field of activity there should be an overall strategy implemented by the Minister concerned assisted by his Chief of Staff or Permanent Secretary.

Within each main field each branch of activity will have its own distinct category of strategy. This is the level at which concept and implementation meet, when the optimum must be adjusted to the possible in the light of technical limitations. In the military field this vital process of articulation has been termed by the Germans *operational strategy* (operativ). Whether it is realized or not, each branch of activity does in fact have an operational strategy. Its purpose is not only to harmonize the objectives laid down by overall strategy with the capabilities of the tactics and techniques in use in the branch concerned, but also to ensure that those tactics and techniques are developed in the directions which will best fit them to meet future strategic requirements. Operational strategy therefore has a vital part to play; it is one about which there have often been misconceptions. Take for instance the classic strategy of land warfare; it is at this level that the tactical and logistic factors must be taken into account (e.g. the size of force in relation to the area of operations, strategic and tactical mobility, offensive and defensive capacity). It is the impact of these factors which will dictate the form the war will take (static warfare or war of movement, a rapid military decision or a battle of attrition, etc.); it is therefore these factors which determine what the strategic possibilities are. Because neither the importance nor the mechanics of this aspect of strategy were understood, we were taken by surprise by the static warfare of 1914 and by our defeat in 1940; it should have been possible to foresee and so to avoid both. There is, moreover, a peace-time strategy at the operational level; it is primarily concerned with the production of new equipment to outdate that of an opponent. With the advent of the nuclear weapon this form of strategy has become of almost vital importance; it has been termed "logistic" strategy. Until it is accepted as a true strategy (rather than a conglomeration of budgetary and financial programmes) and until it has been accorded its rightful place in the strategic pyramid, it will not be conducted efficiently and we shall therefore not pay the lowest price for the maintenance of our deterrent.

The foregoing analysis of the different categories of strategy clearly does not simplify the problem; rather it illustrates the complexity of the subject. It must be admitted, however, that, although strategy is necessarily an abstract art, it leads to practical conclusions and that these conclusions, as they are unearthed, make it easier to understand the interplay between the various factors. Unless we do understand, we shall be incapable either of making war or keeping the peace.

THE PRINCIPLES OF STRATEGY

Are there rules of strategy which can be used as guide-lines for thought when choosing a course of action? Classic military strategy formulated such rules; they were even thought to be laws of general application and lasting validity; strategy was consequently considered to be an unchanging art in contradistinction to the continual changes in tactics resulting from the evolution of equipment. Today there are good reasons for doubting whether strategy is unchanging. Nevertheless if rules could be evolved they would form a fixed point around which strategic thinking could revolve and only the method of application of the rules would be subject to the evolutionary process.

It is very difficult to deal with this important subject concisely. I propose however to try to run over quickly the main ideas on this question but the reader will soon see that the conclusions which can be drawn are somewhat meagre.

THEORY

The rules put forward by the best-known writers on strategy differ considerably. The résumé of them which follows is so short that I may in some instances have distorted them; at least, however, it shows that they fall into three classes. According to *Clausewitz* there are three primary rules: concentration of effort, action in strength against the main enemy forces and decision in battle in the main theatre of operations, the tactics being defensive-offensive if possible. These rules relate both to overall strategy and operational strategy—military in each case. They are applicable principally to my Pattern No. 5 above. As against this *Liddell Hart* puts forward six positive and two negative rules, the substance of which can be reduced to the following four: force the enemy to disperse by an indirect approach, achieve surprise by selecting unforeseen courses of action, action in strength against the enemy's weak points, achievement of a decision by action in secondary theatres if necessary. These rules relate to the same levels of strategy as those of Clausewitz but in general they are applicable to Pattern No. 3 above. *Mao Tse-tung* laid down six rules: concentric withdrawal in face of an enemy advance; advance if the enemy withdraws; strategically one to five suffices; tactically five to one is needed; live off the enemy; close cohesion between the army and the civil population. These still relate to overall and operational military strategy but in this case are relevant to Pattern No. 4. *Lenin and Stalin* laid down three main rules: in total war the country and the army must be closely knit together psychologically; the rear areas are of vital importance; psychological action must pave the way for military action. These relate to total strategy, a level which means that they are applicable to a number of patterns of strategy. *Modern American strategic thinking* has at the moment evolved two rules: those of the graduated deterrent and the flexible response. This again is total strategy but the emphasis on deterrence and limitation of armed conflict makes them primarily applicable to Pattern No. 1. Going further back, *Mahan* evolved his well-known rule of the overriding importance of the high seas. *Mackinder* on the other hand gave pride of place to the continental theatres. During the thirties *Douhet* forecast that air power would be decisive. Lastly the French school of traditional strategic thought represented by *Foch* summarized strategy in two highly abstract rules: economy of force and freedom of action. These are so abstract that they may be applied to all patterns of strategy.

THE MAIN CONCEPT

It will be seen that these rules are more in the nature of general guidelines for particular situations than laws of universal applicability; this explains their diversity. The only real strategic rules are those of Foch but they are in such general terms that at first sight it is difficult to draw concrete conclusions from them. As we shall see, however, they are no bad framework for an analysis of strategic problems.

But first we must be clear as to exactly what they mean. As a start it is worth reverting to our definition of strategy: "the art of the dialectic of two opposing wills using force to resolve their dispute." In this battle of wills two broadly similar systems will confront each other; each will try to reach the other's vitals by a preparatory process, the object of which will be to strike terror, to paralyse and to surprise—all these objects are psychological, be it noted in passing. In any strategy, therefore, there are two distinct but equally vital components: 1. *Selection of the decisive point* to be attacked (this depends on the enemy's vulnerable points). 2. *Selection of the preparatory manœuvre* which will enable this decisive point to be reached. Since each of the opposing sides will be doing the same thing, there will be a clash between the two preparatory manœuvres. Victory will go to the side which succeeds in blocking his enemy's manœuvre and carrying his own through to its objective. This is what Foch in classic strategic terms called "preservation of freedom of action." The battle of wills therefore comes down to a struggle for freedom of action, each side trying to preserve freedom of action for itself and deny it to the enemy.

If we are much stronger than the enemy, preservation of freedom of action will be easy; we merely have to use sufficient force to paralyse the enemy's manœuvre, while keeping in reserve adequate resources to strike the decisive blow. But this is an extreme case and will occur only very seldom. As a rule it will be necessary to divide our resources intelligently between protecting ourselves against the enemy's preparatory manœuvre, carrying out our own preparatory manœuvre and the decisive blow. This optimum allocation of resources is known in classical strategic terms as *economy of force*.

This analysis in abstract terms of the anatomy of conflict can therefore be reduced to the following formula for the object to be achieved: "to reach the decisive point thanks to the freedom of action gained by sound economy of force." To be useful this somewhat el-liptical expression must be broken down and we must discover by what methods economy of force and freedom of action can be achieved.

This opens up a field of inquiry which has seldom been approached systematically—the explanation perhaps why these problems have remained shrouded in a kind of mysticism. What we now have to do is to *analyse the various possibilities which are the raw material of a strategic decision.*

COMPONENTS OF A STRATEGIC DECISION

It may be accepted that any strategic decision must be taken within the framework set by the three "main co-ordinates" governing any situation at any given moment—time, space and the size and morale of forces available. There is in addition a more complex factor which I shall call "manœuvre"; it is this which governs the order and inter-relationship of successive situations:

(a) *The Factor of Manœuvre.* To some extent this governs the other factors; it is the direct product of the dialectic of the conflict, or in other words of the abstract counterplay between the two opponents. Taking fencing as an analogy, it is clear that there are a number of possible forms of action and reaction: *offensively* there are eight postures—"attack" which may be preceded or followed by "threat," "surprise," "feint," "deceive," "thrust," "wear down," "follow-up." *Defensively* there are six postures—"on guard," "parry," "riposte," "disengage," "retire," "break-off." As far as the actual forces are concerned there are five possible types of decision—"concentrate," "disperse," "economize," "increase," "reduce."

This gives a total of nineteen components to be arranged and combined in the light of the time and space factors. They constitute the keyboard on which the game of strategy is played.

Table 1 . . . sets out each of these types of action, defines them, gives the situations to which they are applicable and an indication of the results to be expected. It will be seen that all are aimed ultimately at *freedom of action,* the object being either to gain it, regain it or deprive the enemy of it. It will also be clear that to ensure freedom of action it is essential to retain the *initia-*

TABLE 1. Fencing Analogy

Action	Definition	Conditions and Comments	Possible Results	
Attack	Attempt to reach enemy vulnerable point.	The vulnerable point must be of vital or near-vital importance. Adequate resources must be available.	Decision or capture of the initiative.	With object of gaining freedom of action.
Surprise	Attack an undefended vulnerable point.	The vulnerable point must be undefended and sufficiently sensitive.	Disorganization of the enemy's dispositions and break in his morale. Capture of the initiative.	As above.
Feint	Threaten a vulnerable point chosen so as to ensure that the enemy's parry uncovers the true object of attack.	The vulnerable point threatened must be ill protected and of great importance to the enemy.	Force the enemy to protect the vulnerable point threatened. Capture of the initiative.	As above.
Deceive	In the narrow sense: Appear to threaten one vulnerable point and then attack another.	As above but the object of the threat is not to elicit a certain parry but to keep up the atmosphere of uncertainty.	Preparatory measure to capture of the initiative.	As above.
	In the broad sense: Appear to be in a posture which is not the real one.	Uncertainty may be so increased as to generate a false sense of security.	As above.	As above.
Thrust	Reach a vulnerable point in spite of the opposition of the enemy.	Resources must be adequate to enable sufficient force to be used. A method of exploiting the initiative once gained.	Deprives the enemy of his freedom of action or wears him down.	As above.
Wear Down	Force the enemy to expend his energy and resources in defending vulnerable points.	As above but the wearing down process is always reciprocal. Of value only for the side which has greater resources or can wear the enemy down quicker than it is worn down itself.	Object to deprive the enemy of his reserves of energy and resources and therefore of the possibility of seizing the initiative.	As above.
Follow-up	Return to a position to attack enemy vulnerable points.	To be carried out if the enemy disengages in order to regain the freedom of action he has lost.	Retention of the initiative.	As above.
On Guard	Be in a position which enables one to defend vulnerable points in good time.	Depends on an estimate of forces available and timing.	Object is to secure oneself against seizure of the initiative by the enemy.	As above.
Disengage	Change dispositions in order to draw the enemy into attacking defended vulnerable points.	Adequate resources must be available. Disengagement changes the direction of the conflict.	Object is to re-establish security.	As above.

TABLE 1. Fencing Analogy (Cont.)

Action	Definition	Conditions and Comments	Possible Results	
Parry	Protect a vulnerable point being attacked.	Protection must be effective and must not entail uncovering other vulnerable points.	Object is to re-establish security.	With object of gaining freedom of action.
Riposte	Strike a vulnerable point thus forcing the enemy to abandon his attack.	The vulnerable point must be vital or at least highly important to the enemy.	Object is to regain the initiative.	As above.
Retire	Move the vulnerable point being attacked out of range of the enemy.	Must force the enemy to make fresh dispositions. Must not uncover other vulnerable points.	Re-establishment of security.	As above.
Break-off	General withdrawal involving abandonment of some limited objective.	The objective abandoned must not be vital.	Re-establishment of security.	As above.
Threaten	Take up dispositions which make it possible to attack an enemy vulnerable point.	Adequate resources must be available. The vulnerable point threatened must be of sufficient importance.	Objective is to reduce the enemy's freedom of action.	As above.

tive which is a fundamental factor in manœuvre.

This analogy with fencing may at first sight appear to have little to do with modern strategy. But not at all! Table 2 . . . gives a series of examples of the types of action resulting from each of these decisions, those in one column being taken from the military strategy of the 1939–45 war and those in the next from the present-day deterrent strategy. A similar table could be made for total strategy, "indirect" strategy and even for the strategy of finance, diplomacy and politics. For instance, from this table it emerges that the Ardennes offensive in 1944 is, in deterrent strategy, analogous to the Soviet inter-continental rocket programme and that Allied naval operations in the Mediterranean in 1943–44 are analogous to the development of the tactical atomic weapon. Security, which in classic strategy implies a judicious distribution of forces, in deterrent strategy means the gaining of some technical advantage over the enemy. Liberty of action, which in classic strategy springs from the possession of the initiative, in deterrent strategy depends on superiority of potential (= security) together with survival capacity and uncertainty regarding the likelihood of escalation (= threat).

It is of the utmost importance that we should realize that these analogies exist if we are to conduct our strategy with a clear idea both of what the manœuvre in progress is and what the possible reactions are.

(b) *Doctrine of Manœuvre.* When faced with a choice as to how to react, we are equally faced by a number of conflicting doctrines.

The first I shall call the doctrine of "the rational application of force"; it takes as its starting point the strength of the forces available and chooses the solution which will permit those forces to exert their maximum effect. The object will be to concentrate effort on the defeat of the enemy's main forces which itself will automatically entail the defeat of the remainder. The main body of our forces will be concentrated against the enemy's strongest point and

TABLE 2. Parallels Between Types of Strategy

Action	Parallel from Military Strategy 1939–45	Parallel from Deterrent Strategy	
		Definition	Examples
Attack	Overlord 1944. Ardennes 1940.	Achieve some technical breakthrough which outdates the enemy defense system.	US followed by Soviet thermonuclear weapons. Soviet rocket programme for Cuba 1962.
Surprise	German Ardennes offensive 1944. Allied landing in North Africa.	Achieve some technical breakthrough far greater than anticipated.	Soviet rockets, atomic and thermonuclear weapons.
Feint	German attack in Holland 1940.	Lead the enemy on in the technological race in a direction different from that one is oneself in fact following.	Soviet bombers in 1955(?).
Deceive	Allied threat against Straits area before the landing in 1944.	Lead the enemy to believe that one has made some breakthrough or conceal some technical advance actually made.	Outer space (?).
Thrust	Battles in Normandy, St. Lô, El Alamein.	Outstrip the enemy in some field in which he is making a major effort.	Increase in the speed and ceiling of US aircraft in 1955.
Wear Down	Verdun (1916). Stalingrad and the Russian campaign. Air bombardment of Germany.	Force the enemy into vast expenditure, greater than one's own, in an important field in the arms race.	The whole technological race.
Follow-up	German campaign in France 1940. The seesaw in Libya.	Exploit some technical advance to gain a limited political advantage.	Soviet protection of Egypt and Cuba. The Lebanon operation.
Parry	German operations in Normandy 1944.	Re-establish the effectiveness of some defensive system by readjustment or technical achievement.	DEW Line. Atomic submarines and Polaris. Reinforcement of shield forces.
Riposte	German Ardennes offensive 1944.	Trump some technical advance by the enemy by a similar advance which outdates his.	US response to the Soviet rocket programme in Cuba.
Retire	German withdrawal to Lorraine after the battle of Normandy.		
Break-off	French Armistice 1940.	Arms agreement or political withdrawal to avoid a showdown.	Soviet withdrawal from Cuba 1962.
On Guard	Defence of Great Britain 1940.	To be ahead of the enemy.	The technological and intelligence race.
Disengage	Naval operations in Mediterranean 1942 in order to isolate Rommel in Libya.	Achieve a breakthrough which forces the enemy to change his posture.	Tactical atomic weapons.
Threat	Allied threats of landings in France prior to 1944.	A measure which could lead to the start of escalation.	The *force de frappe*. Tactical atomic weapons. Survival tactics.

the decisive battle will take place in the main theatre of operations. This is the strategy which emerged from Clausewitz' theories at the end of the nineteenth century; it was the basis of the famous French Plan 17 in 1914.

The second doctrine I shall call the doctrine of *guile*. Its basis is the psychological effect of the action proposed. The solution chosen should be that best calculated to throw the enemy off balance, disorientate him and deceive him. It will usually be necessary to disperse our own forces (or effort) in order to induce the enemy to do likewise. The object will be to gain victory by acting in strength against the enemy's weak points, if necessary in secondary, perhaps even remote, theatres of war. This strategy has been brilliantly expounded in our time by Liddell Hart in *The British Way in Warfare and Strategy*; he there puts it forward as an antidote to the Clausewitz strategy and as something typically and traditionally British.

There are other doctrines, now outdated; for instance the *"geometric"* which the Prussians evolved from Frederick II's echelon order of battle, or Jomini's *"geographic"* doctrine based on an interpretation of Napoleon's victories.

In fact none of these doctrines are of universal validity. Leaving out of account the geometric doctrine which really is dead (though some may ask whether the French theories in the thirties had not resurrected it in another guise), each of these doctrines may lead to a course of action which will be the best possible in some circumstances and the worst conceivable in others. The "application of force" doctrine fits the case where we are stronger than the enemy (though in that case why bother about theory?), or the case where the enemy is the stronger but is dangerously dispersed. The "guile" doctrine is imperative if we are the weaker and will invariably be of value in gaining

local superiority, provided of course that we do not succeed in dispersing ourselves more than the enemy. The "geographic" doctrine is of much importance in military strategy if communications in the theatre of operations are poor (as was the case in Europe in Napoleon's day) and therefore form a well-defined chessboard. (Nowadays the chessboard consists of continents and oceans.)

The choice of the course of action must therefore be based solely upon study of the situation at the time. It will frequently be necessary to follow several of these doctrines one after the other.

(c) *"Modes" of Strategy.*[2] When studying a plan of operations it will usually be necessary to decide upon a *general posture*; this will emerge from whichever doctrine is most closely applicable to the relative position of the two sides. This brings us back to the problem of choosing one of the "patterns" dealt with above . . . ; in the light of the doctrines we have examined these "patterns" fall into two "modes" —direct strategy and indirect strategy.

In the *direct strategy* "mode" are Patterns Nos. 1, 3 and 5, the basic concept being that military force is the principal weapon and that victory or deterrence will be achieved by its use or maintenance. This is the Clausewitz strategy which in fact was no more than a statement in general terms of the concept on which the "rational application of force" doctrine is based. It was the strategy on which commanders of the 1914–18 war worked and it was that followed by the German and American leaders in 1939–45. It is the strategy which now governs the potential clash of nuclear forces. Direct strategy may also make use of the "guile" doctrine particularly if employing the indirect approach.

In the *indirect strategy* "mode" are Patterns 2, 3 and 4. This is the strategy on which are based all forms of conflict in which a decision is sought, not directly by means of a clash between military forces but by less direct methods. These may be political or economic in nature (e.g. a revolutionary war) or they may use military force but proceed in a series of bounds interspersed with political negotiations (e.g. Hitler's strategy from 1936 to 1939). This strategy is coming increasingly into fashion now that any possibility of all-out war as postulated by direct strategy seems likely to lead to an unacceptable level of mutual destruction. This theory is both complex and subtle and is still little understood. It is continuously being employed in the cold war and it may be that it is the only feasible strategy now that direct strategy has been paralysed by the threat of the nuclear weapon.

In fact both "modes" of strategy still exist and are complementary. There are two facets to the dialectic struggle in the world today; in the direct strategy "mode" is the nuclear dialectic, the result of which is to neutralize the great economic and industrial potentials on each side; at the same time in the indirect strategy "mode" the political dialectic in progress, with all its multifarious manifestations, seeps through the cracks in the system of deterrence. Strategy, like music, can be played in either a major or a minor key.

(d) *The Variability Factor.* But this is not all. There is a further factor of great importance in working out a strategic concept—the variability both of resources available and the circumstances surrounding their employment.

The world is evolving very rapidly, particularly in this day and age. Everything is subject to a continual process of transformation. Germany in 1963 for instance has nothing approaching the same prospects as the Germany of 1938. World opinion is not inspired by the same beliefs and does not react in the same way. The tools which strategy must use are also changing with frightening rapidity; the aeroplane of 1945 was obsolete by 1950, that of 1950 by 1960, etc.

As a result the strategist can place no reliance on precedent and has no permanent unit of measure to hand. Strategic thought must continuously take the facts of change into account, not only those of the foreseeable future but probable changes many years ahead. Strategy can no longer proceed by a process of firmly based objective deduction; it must work on hypotheses and produce solutions by truly *original thought.*

This aspect of strategy is one which was hardly grasped at all up to recent years. For a long time evolution was so slow that it seemed reasonable to base decisions on past experience. History still has value today but alone it is inadequate; Paul Valéry was far-sighted enough to appreciate its dangers some time ago. Now that it has been driven back upon hypothesis, strategy must play with time as it has come to do with space; it must discard rigid and dangerous hypotheses like some recent theories, mostly of American origin, which are based on a mathematical evaluation of *probabilities.* Instead it must be based on a whole gamut of *possibilities* and there must be organization to ensure that these possibilities are kept under review so as to sort out in good time those which are growing and turning into fact from those which are disappearing. Here is another factor in manœuvre; there must be forecasts to guard against surprise and keep us abreast of evolution.

There can be no rules for the inventive ability required to work out a future solution to meet an estimated future situation using new or readapted tools. All that can be said is that there must be no routine about it (military existence, being governed by "regulations," is unfortunately rooted in routine). It must draw on imagination and be the fruit of meditation.

These are undeniable facts. Modern strategy, like our civilization, is being carried along by the galloping advance of science. The consequence must be a fundamental change in our thinking habits. It is the future, not the present, which matters. The time-lag for any operation (whether production of new equipment, change in the psychological climate, or alteration of the international balance of power) must now be reckoned in terms of years; yet these are the factors which will govern the future.

Preparation is now of more consequence than execution. In other words it is useless to spend millions on a defence system, the future effectiveness of which is doubtful, whereas it is essential to be *well informed* and *exercise foresight*. These two requirements imply that emphasis (and expenditure) today should be concentrated upon the creation of highly effective intelligence and research organizations. It is through them that it will be possible to follow developments and to control the process of evolution of force by fully-thought-out decisions arrived at in good time.

To conclude this short examination, here is a simple analogy, not over-drawn: the strategist is like a surgeon called upon to operate upon a sick person who is growing continuously and with extreme rapidity and of whose detailed anatomy he is not sure; his operating-table is in a state of perpetual motion and he must have ordered the instruments he is to use five years beforehand.

NOTES

1. The term total strategy as applied to "total war" seems to me clearer than "grand strategy" as sometimes used by the British (particularly Liddell Hart) or "national strategy" as used by the Americans. The term "national defence" means nothing and achieves nothing except confusion of thought.

2. The word "mode" is used here in its musical sense.

Policy and Strategy

André Beaufre

To my considerable surprise, no immediate objection was raised to the definition of "total strategy" given in *Introduction to Strategy*;[1] one reason no doubt was that the approach to the problem was logical but it was also certainly due to the fact that the consequences of my definition were not as first perceived. During my subsequent studies, however, as soon as I embarked upon analysis of indirect strategy, I was faced by numerous objections all tending to question whether problems concerning the use of methods of persuasion or coercion unconnected with military methods could be "strategic." Reverting to the old definition, my critics hold that strategy is a military matter and that what is not military is the concern of "policy." So we were back where we started.

In my view this argument raises a delimitation question of prime importance. It must therefore be dealt with exhaustively in order to avoid any misunderstanding and clarify our ideas sufficiently to overcome the instinctive prejudices which still hold sway in this field.

In the first place it should be emphasized that the extension of strategy which the evolution of international relationships now demands and will increasingly demand, in no way implies an extension of the *military* field to that traditionally considered the concern of the *political*. On the contrary the implication of "total strategy" is to reduce the autonomous character of strictly military strategy and subordinate it closely to an overall strategic concept, which itself will be directly governed by the political concept worked out and implemented by politicians.

The extension of strategy to cover the entire phenomenon of coercion results from the necessity to unite in one single system of thought all the highly diverse procedures employed, whether military or not. Only by such a system of thought is it possible to explain and therefore to understand manœuvres of the type employed by Hitler from 1936 to 1939 or to analyse problems such as those presented by Indo-China, Algeria and now Vietnam. Only by starting from this overall standpoint is it possible to define the exact role of military force and the limits within which it can be used; we shall at the same time avoid falling victim once more to the serious misconceptions of the two great world wars when military force was let loose uncontrolled and used on a scale far exceeding that which proper understanding of the problem would have shown to be necessary to achieve the political objective sought.

Some people, while accepting this point, raise an argument of semantics: in their view the question is not one of "total strategy" but of "total policy." To begin with, however, as I emphasized in *Introduction to Strategy*, policy —or rather "high policy" or "total policy"—consists primarily of the choice of ends and of the framework within which action will take place; its ingredients are therefore to a large extent subjective. Implementation of the policy decision, however, is the result of a process of reasoning which must be basically objective and is the product of the methods used by strategy.

Moreover the term "total policy" as understood by those who wish to use it in place of "total strategy," is in fact what the early twentieth-century theorists called "the conduct of war," traditionally a governmental function. Quite apart from the fact that in these days the "conduct of war" should be a continuous function and should be being used during what we are still in the habit of calling peacetime, refusal to label it "strategic" leads to disregard or underestimation of the importance of the methods worked out by military strategy to deal with problems of this nature. The major innovation, today a necessity, is to inject into the "conduct of war" (and of the peace) the greatest possible measure of strategic exactitude in place of the intuitions and approximations which have so far been the rule in the traditional conduct of that which has served as strategy during the first half of the twentieth century. Provided this is done, it does not matter in the least what label is used, in particular whether it is called "total policy" instead of "total strategy." My only fear is that in refusing to accept the word "strategy" we may equally be tempted to refuse to accept the method and that we may end by failing to appreciate the importance of the revolution in the form of international conflict which has taken place in the last thirty years. For my part I would hope that we could do away with this play of words; it is a legacy from the nineteenth century when people tried to establish an artificial distinction between the political and military fields; in our day this distinction has less and less meaning; I would hope therefore that without beating about the bush we could bring ourselves to state that the

conduct of policy is a function of total strategy.

I am well aware that by putting the matter so baldly I shall be scaring certain of the diplomats. They will ask whether by openly introducing the methods of strategy into a traditionally political field, we shall not be giving international relations a "totalitarian" aspect, a brutal twist savouring of coercion. Are we going to abandon the usual delicate methods and make what may be no more than the perennial minor differences of opinion appear as conflicts? Moreover where does a simple difference of opinion end and conflict begin? Shall we conduct "strategy" between allies? And so on and so on. This seems to me a valid criticism which calls for explanation, all the more so since the fact that I am a military man may justifiably lead to confusion. Moreover certain instances (in America) of exaggerated use of technical analysis may throw doubt upon the possibility of dealing rationally with problems as complex as those of international relationships.

I believe that there are three categories of reply to these objections. In the first place throughout the Marxist-Leninist system of thought no distinction is drawn between the political field and that of total strategy. Rightly or wrongly, the Soviets have achieved complete synthesis between these two fields, a synthesis far more complete than that which I am advocating; they make no distinction between the superior level, that of "high policy" which chooses the ends to be achieved, and the subordinate level, that of "total strategy" which chooses the means capable of achieving these ends. It is essential therefore that we should ourselves be familiar with the system of thought with which we are confronted (just as we were forced to familiarize ourselves with Hitler's "extended strategy").

In the second place adoption of

the methods of total strategy does not necessarily involve extension to mere differences of opinion of the procedure applicable to conflict. On the contrary, systematic study of the procedure known as "political" may in many cases show that far more delicately shaded solutions are available than recourse to military force, all too often used in the past because a suitable political concept was lacking. The recent example of Vietnam, coming after so many others, has proved that nothing is more dangerous than an inadequate political analysis followed by an attempt to mitigate its effects by "calling in the soldiers." In this [chapter] I shall do my best to show that the problems termed "political," particularly those which must be dealt with at the level of policy decision, can be dissected and that thereby extremely interesting possibilities of non-violent action are opened up. These, it seems to me, are entirely in line with present-day evolution which tends to restrict the use of force to the indispensable minimum.

The third category of reply to the objections referred to above is that we are trying to clear the ground in an inadequately explored field; at the present stage I do not claim to be doing more. It would be a great pity, however, if this intellectual pioneering were brought to a halt by semantics and prejudice unless and until it is proved that the general direction which we have chosen for research is leading us into an impasse.

For all these reasons I consider that the concept of total strategy should be thought through right down to its ultimate consequences, until we have some clear idea of the possibilities which it offers; in doing so we should not worry too much about what has hitherto been labelled "policy." Moreover I believe that one of the results of this study will be to clarify and codify the extraordinary junkheap of ideas

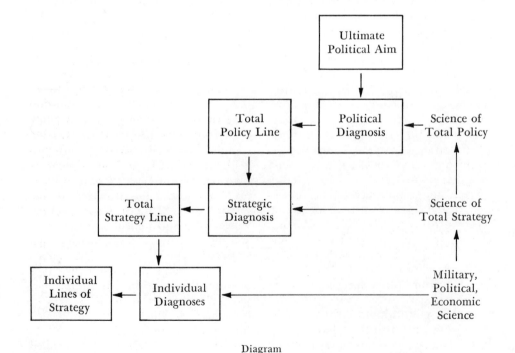

Diagram

Lay-out, Relationship and Interplay of the Basic Strategic Concepts and procedures accumulated under the vague title of policy. In that event terminology will matter very little; perhaps it will be necessary to adopt a new title, neither "policy" nor "strategy" (Raymond Aron has already proposed "praxeology"); this might possibly set at rest some of the more obstinate prejudices.

An interesting suggestion was put forward during our strategic conference of May 1965. This was that strategy should be regarded as applicable to international problems when there was a clearly defined aim of outstanding priority (national survival as a rule), compared to which all other aims were of secondary importance; when on the other hand there were a number of aims of approximately equal and variable priority, the problem would fall into the field of policy.

. . . [T]he "level of policy decision," . . . in my view is *the* political level *par excellence* and governs the entire strategy of implementation. I fear, however, that an attempt to restrict strategy to cases with a clear priority aim might end by confining it to conflicts of the major world war type involving the paroxysm of unrestricted use of military force; to give the word this twist, therefore, would imply reversion to a total strategy of an almost exclusively military nature. Furthermore and even more important, I believe that only by a pseudo-Clausewitzian aberration have we been led to believe that cases existed where one aim was clearly predominant over all the others. "Winning the war" is not a political aim; as Liddell Hart has so clearly demonstrated, the real political aim is the type of peace to follow the war. "Winning the war" means nothing unless the corresponding "war aims" are set out at the same time. Even during the most intense form of military struggle, therefore, thought must always be given to the political

aims; these are likely to be complex and their priority to vary continuously, for history moves quickly during a conflict; if you think of the examples of France, Poland and Italy between 1939 and 1945 (to cite only the most characteristic examples), it will be seen that the British and American set ideas of the time were ill-adapted to these events. It is impossible to confine total strategy within such narrow limits.

Another more finely differentiated suggestion has been made—that strategy should be concerned only with the strictly coercive aspect of international relations and should therefore only be brought into play at intervals when policy decides to have recourse to coercive action. The transition from policy to strategy would therefore constitute the first step in escalation and, apart from periods when such action was in progress, strategy would be dormant and relations solely "political." As we shall see later, however, such a concept ill accords with present-day realities when international relations are of numerous finely graded shades and involve a continuous overlap between relations which may properly be termed political and considerations of security or even measures of coercion. Any attempt to draw too definite a distinction between these various types of relationship risks giving rise to serious misconceptions concerning the very nature of international relations. Conclusions on this subject, however, are premature at this early stage of our analysis of the strategy of action. We must first dig deeper into this difficult subject.

To conclude, I believe that the concept of total strategy defined as the choice of means likely to achieve the ends laid down by policy constitutes a *working hypothesis* which it is worth pursuing through to its ultimate consequences in order to see to what extent the methods of strategic analysis are suitable for a study of the problems now facing us. . . . We shall then be in a position to form some opinion on whatever sub-divisions between policy and strategy may appear necessary.

NOTES

1. "The art of applying force so that it makes the most effective contribution towards achieving the ends set by political policy" and "The art of the dialectic of two opposing wills using force to resolve their dispute" (*Introduction to Strategy*, p. 22).

Strategy

HENRY E. ECCLES

Strategy and tactics and logistics are different aspects of the same thing. If completely separated they become meaningless . . .[1]

JAMES A. HUSTON

THE CONCEPT

*　　*　　*

If we are to understand strategy, we must see it not only in relation to broad concepts of human conflict, to objectives, to policy, and to expectations, but also in relation to its direct military associates, the arts of tactics and logistics. These are intertwined in every major military problem. At the highest levels of planning, logistics, in its role of military economics, seems at times almost indistinguishable from strategy. In the area of active operations, logistics and tactics must work together to serve the interests of strategy. As one looks at strategy and tactics from different levels of command, they seem to shift and at times to blend.

Unless one starts with clear concepts of strategy these matters can be confusing, for the concepts of strategy are the heart of military understanding and open the way to a grasp of the other military concepts. When clearly expressed, they help to place all other military theory and terminology in perspective. Therefore, in this work I have sought to find harmony of concept rather than identity amidst the diversity of ideas and language found in the literature of strategy. At the same time I have looked for the concepts of strat-

egy that would have a coherent relation to the other elements of military thought. While the authors would not necessarily agree with me in detail, I find this harmony and special coherence in the works of two profound and creative military thinkers, Basil Liddell Hart and Herbert Rosinski.

In his book *Strategy*, Liddell Hart devoted the last forty pages to the theory of strategy and to grand strategy. Here, in developing "a new dwelling-house for strategic thought," he discussed the ideas of Clausewitz and Moltke and then wrote:

> We can now arrive at a shorter definition of strategy as—"the art of distributing and applying military means to fulfill the ends of policy." For strategy is concerned not merely with the movement of forces—as its role is often defined—but with the effect. When the application of the military instrument merges into actual fighting, the disposition for and control of such direct action are "tactics." The two categories, although convenient for discussion can never be truly divided into separate compartments because each not only influences but merges into the other.
>
> As tactics is an application of strategy on a lower plane, so strategy is an application on a lower plane of "grand strategy." While practically synonymous with the policy which guides the conduct of war, as

distinct from the more fundamental policy which should govern its object, the term "grand strategy" serves to bring out the sense of policy in execution. For the role of grand strategy—higher strategy—is to co-ordinate and direct all the resources of a nation, or band of nations, toward the political objective of the war—the goal defined by fundamental policy.[2]

This places strategy, grand strategy, tactics, policy, and objectives in a clear perspective.

The element of policy stressed by Liddell Hart here and elsewhere was clearly brought out in the Naval War College publication, *Sound Military Decision,* which said:

> Understanding between the civil representatives of the State and the leaders of the armed forces is manifestly essential to the coordination of national policy with the power to enforce it. While military strategy may determine whether the aims of policy are possible of attainment, policy may, beforehand, determine largely the success or failure of military strategy. Therefore, it behooves policy to ensure not only that military strategy pursue appropriate aims, but that the work of strategy be allotted adequate power, and be undertaken under the most favorable conditions.[3]

These thoughts, together with the Rosinski concept of strategy's being the art of control, provide the foundation for the conceptual unity and coherence essential to military theory. Rosinski wrote:

> For the past 150 years there has been a continuous effort to arrive at satisfactory and illuminating definitions of strategy and tactics. This effort has so far been greatly hampered by the fact that the definitions have been verbal enumerations rather than analytical definitions. The situation is further complicated by the widely differing meanings of the terms as used in the German and Russian as opposed to the French, British and American schools of military thought.
>
> As a result of the work done on a paper on the Evolution of Warfare and Strategy, the following definition is hereby suggested as a formulation which bridges the gap between these two schools of thought and brings into better perspective and focus the ideas of the military thinkers of the past 150 years. *Strategy is the com-*
> *prehensive direction of power; Tactics is its immediate application.*

This definition requires the recognition that there is much more to strategy than mere direction of action. It is a type of direction which takes into account the multitude of possible enemy counteractions and thus it becomes a means of control. *It is this element of control which is the essence of strategy: Control being the element which differentiates true strategic action from a haphazard series of improvisations.*

Thus, strategy in contrast to haphazard action, is that direction of action which aims at the control of a field of activity be it military, social, or, even intellectual. It must be comprehensive in order to control every possible counteraction or factor.

Therefore, except where there is absolutely overwhelming superiority, strategy must be selective in order to achieve economy of force. Comprehensive control of a field of action means a concentration upon those minimum key lines of action or key positions from which the entire field can be positively controlled. This is well illustrated by the concept of control or command of a sea area.

This concept of strategy as a comprehensive control has the advantage that it applies equally to the offensive and to the defensive. On the offensive, the aim of strategy is to break down the enemy's control while simultaneously preventing him from interfering with our attack. On the defensive, strategy similarly seeks to constrain the enemy attack to such a form and degree that, while the defense may be forced back, it still maintains control of its actions and avoids collapse. As long as it can manage to do so; as long as it can continue to parry all decisive thrusts of the enemy, it may suffer a series of defeats but it will still be a coherent strategy and avoid wholesale catastrophe.

In this sense a discussion of the strategy of the three services can best be analyzed in terms of their differing capacities for such comprehensive control. Control is easiest in land warfare, has always been more difficult in naval strategy, is still more difficult in the field of air warfare, and is most difficult in that of the combined strategy of all three forces.

This definition has the advantage that it can be transposed from the military field in which it originated to any of the other fields to which, in the course of the years, it has been increasingly applied by analogy, such as, for instance, the strategy and tactics of science.

This definition has the further advantage that tactics very simply is defined as the immediate action beyond which comprehensive control of the entire field is not necessary.4

IMPLICATIONS OF THE CONCEPT OF STRATEGY

Many discussions of strategy suffer from the semantic confusion arising from the two commonly used meanings of the word "strategic." The first meaning evolves from defining strategy as the art and science of using political, economic, psychological, and military forces of a nation to support national policy. Thus, in this sense, strategic refers to the plan or scheme for such use.

The second meaning defines "strategic" action as the physical destruction of an enemy's warmaking capacity. This second meaning refers primarily to economic, agricultural, and military targets.

The fallacy that strategy and destruction are synonymous and the consequent development of a "weapon strategy," both come from the careless use of the second meaning of "strategic."

The Rosinski concept of "comprehensive control" has certain specific implications of tremendous importance. In particular, it establishes the primacy of strategy in the conduct of national affairs as opposed to the emphasis on destruction that is implicit in any "weapon strategy." The idea that the weapon should determine the strategy to be used is based on the implied assumption that strategy and destruction are synonymous. This simply is not true. Naturally, strategy will be influenced by the availability of weapons, but strategy should use destruction only when there is no other way of gaining or exercising control. The concentration of thought on control naturally leads to a reexamination and better understanding of the objectives whose attainment is the purpose of the attempt to exercise control.

The concept of continuing control

prepares the mind for shifting the emphasis from weapon to weapon or from tool to tool in accordance with changing situations or with the changing capabilities or application of the weapon or weapon systems involved. Thus, the intellectual concept of strategy as "comprehensive control" naturally leads to the intellectual concept of flexibility.

At this point, a terse summary of the concept of strategy leads to other important concepts:

Strategy is the *art* of *comprehensive direction of power to control situations* and *areas* in order to attain *objectives.*

Putting this in context of its associated military terms: A strategic concept is best expressed in specific statements of

> What to control,
> What is the purpose of this control,
> What is the nature of the control,
> What degree of control is necessary,
> When the control is to be initiated,
> How long the control is to be maintained,
> What general method or scheme of control is to be used.

The fundamental concept of strategy clearly states that strategy is the *comprehensive* employment of power, whereas tactics is the *immediate* employment of forces and weapons. *Thus the immediate employment of any force or weapon is tactical regardless of its name or title.* While the employment is tactical, the *ultimate effect,* considered in conjunction with the employment of other forces and elements of power, *is strategic.* The size or power of any weapon should not be considered as the criteria that determine its proprietary right to "strategy" or the term "strategic." Such semantic confusion inevitably leads to confused thinking.

Colonel George C. Thorpe's description of logistics, slightly rephrased, will help us better to understand the relationship: "Strategy and tactics determine the scheme for the conduct of military operations, logistics provides the means therefor."[5] The virtue of this description lies in its logic and simplicity.

Strategy gives the comprehensive scheme, tactics the immediate scheme. Regardless of whether it is comprehensive or immediate, logistics provides the means.

Admiral Robert B. Carney speaks of strategy as "a plan to employ resources to attain objectives."

What is strategy, and what is tactics, will tend to vary with the level of command. The operations of a task group will generally tend to be regarded as tactical by a fleet commander, whereas these same operations may be considered almost as strategic by the commander of one of the ships of one of the task units that combine to make up the group.

Similarly, an army commander would consider a division's operations almost as tactical, while a platoon commander in one of the regimental combat teams or battalions would think of his own operation as immediate or tactical and the division's operations as comprehensive or strategic.

Further important concepts can now be developed.

Common sense, supported by the history of every important military operation, tells us: The practical *application* of a *strategic concept* consists of a group of *specific tactical operations* that *must* be *preceded* by *logistical operations.*

In other words, *operations* are a *combination* of *tactical* and *logistic action* blended to *serve* the *purposes of strategy.*

Operations are conducted by a military commander who employs weapons and forces created by logistic effort and supported by logistic action. The operations themselves are controlled by a complex group of activities of different sorts. Under a great variety of names, these activities blend and overlap. The commander must organize, plan, and supervise these activities. In so doing he is served by communications and by intelligence. The commander also manages, using various techniques of management that include budgeting and financial control. Actions are governed by management policy, by directives, and by plans. There must always be a feedback of information in order that there may be "supervision of the planned action." *But always the inspiration of command,* regardless of how command is exercised, *comes from a sense of strategic purpose.*

This statement of the basic concept of strategy as control and the brief treatment of some of the related concepts open the way for a further discussion of objectives, for just as strategy is the paramount military concept, so *the objective* is the paramount issue in the development of any strategy.

NOTES

1. James A. Huston, "A History of Army Logistics, 1775–1953" (manuscript written for Office of Chief of Military History, Department of the Army, 1962, waiting publication), Part IV.

2. B. H. Liddell Hart, *Strategy, The In-*

direct Approach (New York: Frederick A. Praeger, 1954), pp. 335–336. Part IV (pp. 333–372) is the culmination of his many years of analysis of strategy.

3. *Sound Military Decision*, p. 9. This work, written primarily by Admiral Edward C. Kalbfus, U.S. Navy, who was twice President of the Naval War College, was for many years classified as restricted and was reduced to official use only in 1953. This book was the outgrowth of many years of study of the military estimate of the situation. It has always been controversial. It is abstruse and suffers from the failure of its authors to supply historical examples to illustrate the points made. Nevertheless, it has stood the test of time and in my opinion is still the best single analysis of military decision.

4. This was written by Dr. Herbert Rosinski in September, 1955, following informal discussions with the President of the Naval War College, Vice Admiral Lynde McCormick, and his chief of staff, Rear Admiral Thomas H. Robbins, Jr.

5. George C. Thorpe, *Pure Logistics—The Science of War Preparation* (Kansas City, Mo.: Franklin Hudson, 1917), p. 9.

The Anatomy of Deterrence

BERNARD BRODIE

DETERRENCE OLD AND NEW

Deterrence as an element in national strategy or diplomacy is nothing new. Since the development of nuclear weapons, however, the term has acquired not only a special emphasis but also a distinctive connotation. It is usually the new and distinctive connotation that we have in mind when we speak nowadays of the "strategy of deterrence."

The threat of war, open or implied, has always been an instrument of diplomacy by which one state deterred another from doing something of a military or political nature which the former deemed undesirable. Frequently the threat was completely latent, the position of the monitoring state being so obvious and so strong that no one thought of challenging it. Governments, like individuals, were usually aware of hazard in provoking powerful neighbors and governed themselves accordingly. Because avoidance of wars and even of crises hardly makes good copy for historians, we may infer that the past successes of some nations in deterring unwanted action by others add up to much more than one might gather from a casual reading of history. Nevertheless the large number of wars that have occurred in modern times prove that the threat to use force, even what sometimes looked like superior force, has often failed to deter.

We should notice, however, the positive function played by the failures.

The very frequency with which wars occurred contributed importantly to the credibility inherent in any threat. In diplomatic correspondence, the statement that a specified kind of conduct would be deemed "an unfriendly act" was regarded as tantamount to an ultimatum and to be taken without question as seriously intended.

Bluffing, in the sense of deliberately trying to sound more determined or bellicose than one actually felt, was by no means as common a phenomenon in diplomacy as latter-day journalistic interpretations of events would have one believe. In any case, it tended to be confined to the more implicit kinds of threat. In short, the operation of deterrence was dynamic; it acquired relevance and strength from its failures as well as its successes.

Today, however, the policy of deterrence in relation to all-out war is markedly different in several respects. For one thing, it uses a kind of threat which we feel must be absolutely effective, allowing for no breakdowns ever. The sanction is, to say the least, not designed for repeating action. One use of it will be fatally too many. Deterrence now means something as a strategic policy only when we are fairly confident that the retaliatory instrument upon which it relies will not be called upon to function at all. Nevertheless, that instrument has to be maintained at a high pitch of efficiency and readi-

From Bernard Brodie, *Strategy in the Missile Age.* (Copyright © 1959, 1965 by the RAND Corporation, published by Princeton University Press; Princeton Paperback 1965.) Reprinted by permission of the RAND Corporation and Princeton University Press.

324

ness and constantly improved, which can be done only at high cost to the community and great dedication on the part of the personnel directly involved.

In short, we expect the system to be always ready to spring while going permanently unused. Surely there is something almost unreal about all this.

THE PROBLEM OF CREDIBILITY

The unreality is minimal when we are talking about what we shall henceforward call "basic deterrence," that is, deterrence of direct, strategic, nuclear attack upon targets within the home territories of the United States. In that instance there is little or no problem of credibility as concerns our reactions, for the enemy has little reason to doubt that if he strikes us we will try to hit back. But the great and terrible apparatus which we must set up to fulfill our needs for basic deterrence and the state of readiness at which we have to maintain it create a condition of almost embarrassing availability of huge power. The problem of linking this power to a reasonable conception of its utility has thus far proved a considerable strain.... One of the first things wrong with the doctrine [of massive retaliation as a response to less than massive aggression] is that in many instances the

enemy may find it hard to believe that we mean it.[1]

On the other hand, it would be tactically and factually wrong to assure the enemy in advance (as we tend to do by constantly assuring ourselves) that we would in no case move against him until we had already felt some bombs on our cities and airfields. We have, as we have seen, treaty obligations which forbid so far-reaching a commitment to restraint. It is also impossible for us to predict with absolute assurance our own behavior in extremely tense and provocative circumstances. If we make the wrong prediction about ourselves, we encourage the enemy also to make the wrong prediction about us. The outbreak of war in Korea in 1950 followed exactly that pattern. The wrong kind of prediction in this regard might precipitate that total nuclear war which too many persons have lightly concluded is now impossible.

DETERRENCE STRATEGY VERSUS WIN-THE-WAR STRATEGIES: THE SLIDING SCALE OF DETERRENCE

To return now to the simpler problem of basic deterrence. The capacity to deter is usually confused with the capacity to win a war. At present, capacity to win a total or unrestricted war requires either a decisive and *completely secure* superiority in strategic air power or success in seizing the initiative. Inasmuch as mere superiority in numbers of vehicles looks like a good thing to have anyway, the confusion between deterring and winning has method in it. But deterrence *per se* does not depend on superiority.

Prior to the nuclear age, a force which was clearly inferior to a rival's

might or might not have some real deterrent value. One may surmise that if Stalin in late 1939 had had a better estimate of the capability of the Finns to defend themselves he would have been less eager to attack them. If we can deduce his incentive to attack from the peace terms he ultimately laid down, it seems not to have been a desire to conquer and absorb some extra territories, let alone the whole Finnish nation, but rather the wish to administer to them and to others a sharp diplomatic "lesson." That object was compromised by the successes of the Finnish resistance, despite their final defeat. What this example suggests is that deterrence was and remains relative, not absolute; its effectiveness must be measured not only according to the amount of power that it holds in check, but also according to the incentives to aggression which form the pressure behind that power.

Now that we are in a nuclear age, the potential deterrence value of an admittedly inferior force may be sharply greater than it has ever been before. Let us assume that a menaced small nation could threaten the Soviet Union with only a single thermonuclear bomb, which, however, it could and would certainly deliver on Moscow if attacked. This would be a retaliatory capability sufficient to give the Soviet government pause. Certainly they would not provoke the destruction of Moscow for trivial gains, even if warning enabled the people of the city to save themselves by evacuation or resort to shelters. Naturally, the effect is greater if warning can be ruled out.

Ten such missiles aimed at ten major cities would be even more effective, and fifty aimed at that number of different cities would no doubt work still greater deterrent effect, though of course the cities diminish in size as the number included goes up. However, even when we make allowance for the latter fact, it is a fair surmise that the increase in deterrent effect is less than proportional to the increase in magnitude of potential destruction. We make that surmise on the basis of our everyday experience with human beings and their responses to punishment or deprivation. The human imagination can encompass just so much pain, anguish, or horror. The intrusion of numbers by which to multiply given sums of such feelings is likely to have on the average human mind a rather dull effect—except insofar as the increase in the threatened amount of harm affects the individual's statistical

expectation of himself being involved in it.

Governments, it may be suggested, do not think like ordinary human beings, and one has to concede that the *maximum possible deterrence* which can be attained by the threat of retaliatory damage must involve a power which guarantees not only vast losses but also utter defeat. On the other hand, governments, including communistic ones, also comprise human beings, whose departure from the mold of ordinary mortals is not markedly in the direction of greater intellectualism or detachment. It is therefore likely that considerably less retaliatory destruction than that conceived under "maximum possible deterrence" will buy only slightly less deterrence. If we wish to visualize the situation graphically, we will think of a curve of "deterrence effect" in which each unit of additional damage threatened brings progressively diminishing increments of deterrence. Obviously and unfortunately, we lack all the data which would enable us to fill in the values for such a curve and thus to draw it.

If our surmises are in general correct, we are underlining the sharp differences in character between a deterrence capability and strategy on the one hand, and a win-the-war strategy and capability on the other. We have to remember too that since the winning of a war presupposes certain limitations on the quantity of destruction to one's own country and especially to one's population, a win-the-war strategy could quite conceivably be an utter impossibility to a nation striking second, and is by no means guaranteed to a nation striking first. Too much depends on what the other fellow does—how accessible or inaccessible he makes his own retaliatory force and how he makes his attack if he decides to launch one. However much we dislike the thought, a win-the-war strategy may be impossible because of circumstances outside our control.

Lest we conclude from these remarks that we can be content with a modest retaliatory capability—what some have called "minimum deterrence"—we have to mention at once four qualifying considerations, which we shall amplify later: (a) it may require a large force in hand to guarantee even a modest retaliation; (b) deterrence must always be conceived as a relative thing, which is to say it must be adequate to the variable but generally high degree of motivation which the enemy feels for our destruction; (c) if deterrence fails we shall want enough forces to fight a total war effectively; and (d) our retaliatory force must also be capable of striking first, and if it does so its attack had better be, as nearly as possible, overwhelming to the enemy's retaliatory force. Finally, we have to bear in mind that in their responses to threat or menace, people (including heads of government) do not spontaneously act according to a scrupulous weighing of objective facts. Large forces look more impressive than small ones—for reasons which are by no means entirely irrational—and in some circumstances such impressiveness may be important to us. Human beings, differing widely as they do in temperamental and psychic make-up, nevertheless generally have in common the fact that they make their most momentous decisions by what is fundamentally intuition.

Besides, we have to bear in mind that, especially under a technology where each bomb can destroy a city, deterrence is affected also by the element of great *uncertainty* in the potential aggressor's mind concerning the number of bombs the retaliating enemy will succeed in delivering. It makes a very large difference whether he delivers ten or a hundred, though both may be very small numbers in comparison with his original capability. In

this connection too, the fact that a nation has in the past undergone and successfully recovered from great injury does not mean that it will be blasé about a possible repetition of such a catastrophe. The Soviet leaders are not eager to see 1941–1942 repeated, let alone run the risk of having the damage and casualties of those years greatly exceeded.

All this is not to suggest that we have no interest in "win the war" capabilities and strategies. *So long as there is a finite chance of war, we have to be interested in outcomes; and although all outcomes would be bad, some would be very much worse than others.* Also, if we could imagine a conspicuous capability for winning wars which was able to survive even a surprise attack by the enemy, we should have the ultimate in deterrence. But we have to be ready to recognize that deterrence philosophies and win-the-war philosophies may diverge in important respects. We can say in advance that they are likely to diverge in terms of priority. The objective of erecting a high degree of deterrence takes a higher priority than the objective of assuring ourselves of a win-the-war capability, if for no other reason than the first is likely to be prerequisite to the second anyway. It is likely also to be a good deal more feasible to attain, especially for a country which has rejected preventive war. We are also likely to feel a divergence between the two philosophies when it comes to considering alternative military policies in terms of comparative degrees of provocativeness. For the sake of deterrence we want usually to choose the less provocative of two security policies, even where it might mean some sacrifice of efficiency. But if we were in fact interested primarily in winning and only secondarily in deterrence, we should be extremely loath to make any such sacrifices.

We must notice also that when we say that "maximum possible deterrence" probably depends on ability to win, we are implying, for the first time in the discussion, a *comparison* in the degree of damage likely to be suffered by each side. Prior to this point we were talking of deterrence as something resulting from a *unilateral* consideration of damage, that is, enemy estimate of damage likely to be suffered by himself. This is one of the issues that seems to provoke much confusion about deterrence. It is a truistic statement that by deterrence we mean obliging the opponent to consider, in an environment of great uncertainty, the probably high cost of attacking us against the expected gain thereof. It is only a shade less obvious that his cost has to be measured in terms of damage to himself. But what seems very difficult to grasp is that his gain cannot be measured simply in terms of damage to us, except insofar as that damage provokes an act or condition (i.e., surrender or military obliteration) which terminates the threat to him. Damage to us, however large, which fails to have such an effect may be no gain to him at all.

To be willing to accept enormous destruction only for the sake of inflicting greater destruction on the enemy (which may be all that some mean by "winning") argues a kind of desperation at the moment of decision which rules out reason. We have to expect that at certain extreme conditions of excitement, which may involve erroneous conviction that an enemy attack upon oneself is imminent, the deterrent posture will tend to collapse or be discarded without further regard to estimates of damage or gain to either side. All that means, however, is that the rationality upon which deterrence must be based is ultimately frangible—a conclusion of which history has already given us ample indication.

Another attitude that gets in the way of understanding deterrence is the one which alleges that Soviet leaders, when faced with issues of peace and war, would be indifferent to the loss of individual cities and certainly of the populations (as distinguished from the production capital) within those cities. The implication of this view is that a government or leadership imbued with that kind of indifference can be deterred not by considerations of loss in any graduated sense of the term, but only by the prospect of *losing a war*. This is hardly the place to attempt to weigh the evidence for and against such an attribution of indifference. But as this writer sees it, the view just described grossly distorts and exaggerates some undeniable and important differences between the Soviet system and our own.

Certainly insensibility to human suffering among subject populations, especially when it can be rationalized as a necessary price for alleged future benefits, is much more characteristic of the Soviet system than of our own. This fact probably affects significantly the dynamics of deterrence as described in the preceding paragraphs. But it is not enough to subvert those dynamics. The Soviet leaders might be appreciably less shocked and distressed than our own leaders would be in comparable circumstances by the loss through nuclear bombing of one or more of their large cities, but they certainly would not be indifferent to it—either on humanitarian or prestige grounds.

We have to remember, of course, that the Soviets have a very high incentive for destroying us, or at least our military power, if they can do so—the incentive of eliminating what is to them a great threat. As we emphasized earlier, the degree of incentive to aggression governs the magnitude of the deterrence problem. Under some circumstances the Soviet leaders might be willing to pay a very considerable price for that victory which our destruction would mean for them. But the price must be within their ultimate capacity to pay—i.e., fall well short of threatening the collapse of their own power, internally and externally—and they must have a *high degree of assurance* that (a) we will be destroyed, and (b) they will not be. Also, their incentives to destroy us, while always high, are probably not invariable. They are likely to change significantly with changes in the political and especially the military technological environment.

NOTES

1. See William W. Kaufmann, "The Requirements of Deterrence," in the book edited by him under the title: *Military Policy and National Security,* Princeton University Press, 1956. See also Bernard Brodie, "Unlimited Weapons and Limited War," *The Reporter,* 11 (November 18, 1954), 16 ff.

Alternative Strategies

Raymond D. Gastil

FINITE DETERRENCE

In addition to deterring an opponent, to what extent should we be concerned with reducing destruction in the United States should war occur? Those who advocate concentration on the "assured destruction" mission, on offensive forces directed ultimately against cities, believe that through simplifying the equation of nuclear war in this way, they have directly reduced the chance of war, and increased the chance of cooperation between the United States and the Soviet Union. They see this as the only ultimate guarantee of world peace. They do not worry about the fact that the Soviet Union has the capability of destroying the United States, for as long as the Soviets have this invulnerable capability, Soviet leaders will not be nervous about our actions. They can rest assured that we will never attack them. As the Soviets become assured of our intentions, they will come to de-emphasize the further development of their own strategic capabilities. This will provide the context for future agreements to limit arms. Even if important agreements are not signed, there will then develop a tacit arms limitation relationship between the superpowers.

Those who would advocate de-emphasizing efforts to reduce casualties from Soviet attack, or continued de-emphasis in this area, believe that the alternative to the assured destruction focus is a continued arms race. They reason as follows: Neither side knows the capabilities of the other in detail. If the Soviets develop what might be an effective defense against missiles, we will feel we must maintain our destructive capability. Using conservative calculations we are then likely to develop a much larger and more complex offensive delivery capability than we have today. If we build ballistic missile or other defenses at the same time, the Soviets may well decide that to maintain their deterrent they must also upgrade their forces both quantitatively and qualitatively more than they would otherwise. The building up of forces rapidly on both sides will necessarily leave recurrent gaps or opportunities for one or the other side, and will raise questions about the intentions of both parties. The end result may well be that the offensive forces developed by both sides would in fact be at least as destructive in an actual war as today's forces would be, for both countries would tend to overestimate their competitor's defenses in making offensive calculations.

The foregoing is one vision of a world without nuclear war, and how to get there. Emphasizing assured destruction, this position is often called basic deterrence or *finite deterrence*. (The required finite size of the deterrent has been officially seen as quite large—theoretically, under some conditions it could be much smaller than the current force.)

BALANCED DETERRENCE

Many believe that a more complex or balanced nuclear force than that for finite deterrence should be developed for both offense and defense, for both counterforce and countervalue missions. Offensively this force would strive for largely invulnerable forces, with a capability for careful and detailed targeting. Such a force might be either "superior" or "equal" to Soviet forces, depending on judgments of what these terms mean and judgments of strategic requirements. This approach might be referred to as a *balanced deterrence* strategy emphasizing damage limitation. In view of the destructiveness of nuclear weapons and the reluctance of any nation to strike first, a balanced deterrence posture may well be one of *defensive emphasis* in which superiority or parity is achieved through defensive systems rather than offenses. This is particularly true if BMD technology makes this seem feasible in the future.

If we look at Soviet weapons procurement since the early 1950's, it would appear that the Soviets have either not reacted to our policies in a direct manner or have reacted in a way that did not mirror-image the assured destruction vision. In the 1950's we built a large defensive system against planes, but the Soviets did not go on to build up their bomber fleet. In fact, they developed few offensive forces in the early 1960's. Then in the mid-sixties they started to rapidly build up both offensive and defensive forces. This emplacement was at a time when our budgets were in a trough (although it is not inconsistent with a decision made in response to the McNamara increase in U.S. strategic force budget and the Cuban crisis). Threats to use incomparably smaller forces, such as the Chinese will probably have in the 1970's, will be felt to be quite deterring in the absence of U.S. and Soviet BMD.

This raises the question as to whether the defenses the Soviets have built or may build actually threaten our deterrence capabilities in the near future. If they really do not, then if we build BMD defenses would the Soviets necessarily feel threatened? Or wouldn't it be possible for both sides to let the level of potential destruction go down as defenses were built?

Deterrence can be measured in terms of many capabilities other than the capability to reliably destroy a society. Historically, leaders of nations have been deterred from inaugurating war primarily because they thought that their opponents were stronger in forces or will or both. They did not need to feel that their women and children were at risk. Indeed, it would appear that they have often felt that it was worthwhile losing civilian "values" if victory were possible—without victory there can be little worthwhile in a war. Churchill writes:

> Far more important to us than the protection of London from terror bombing was the functioning and articulation of these airfields and the squadrons working from them. In the life and death struggle of the two forces, this was the decisive phase. We never thought of the struggle in terms of the defence of London or any other place, but only who won in the air . . .
>
> It was therefore with a sense of relief that Fighter Command felt the German attack turn on to London Sept. 7, and concluded that the enemy had changed his plan.[1]

This does not mean that leaders cannot be deterred from beginning wars in the nuclear age by the massive destructive capabilities of a potential opponent. It does suggest that there is an alternative basis for deterrence. Reducing the expectations of Soviet or Chinese leaders that they might achieve political or military victories through either nuclear blackmail or nuclear war is probably as important in preventing war as proving to them the certainty of widespread destruction. It would appear from the record of World War II that Hitler and many Japanese leaders would at the end have sacrificed half of the population of their nations for a good chance at victory. Even the Japanese people were briefly encouraged after Hiroshima by the rumor that the Japanese had used a similar device on Los Angeles.[2] The war ended because from a military point of view the losers did not have any capability to fight. Deterrence that emphasizes preventing an opponent from hoping to win a nuclear war also has the further advantage that deterrence based on this approach is credible. It would seem reasonable to friend and foe that our leaders would be much more likely to actually stand up to an opponent in a crisis if they appear to have prepared for America's survival, and are interested in relative outcome, rather than only in our absolute ability to destroy an opponent's society.

If we accept balanced deterrence, then we will look on Soviet defensive capabilities as being matched at least as well by U.S. defenses as by ensuring our capability to negate what the Soviets might do to defend themselves. Today, a full-scale nuclear war might mean one hundred million fatalities on each side. This looks like a good deterrent balance, but is it? Would we use it to defend Taiwan? Or Berlin? Or West Germany? Would we use it even if the Soviets initiated nuclear use and as a result conquered Western Europe, or helped the Arabs defeat Israel? On the other hand, if we had offensive *and* defensive forces that looked equal or superior to the Soviet forces, and if expected fatalities on both sides were more like twenty to forty million instead of one hundred million, would not the Soviets be just as deterred? Many would judge deterrence would be stronger. In crises a simple capability to kill one hundred million would appear superficially to be more

terrifying to the Soviets. But since it would obviously also terrify us, it might suggest to them that it might pay to press, to threaten, to talk a tough line. An American policy oriented to competitive American advantage or at least survival would be more likely to discourage crisis generation and nuclear blackmail by, instead of against, an aggressor.[3]

The main argument against a more complex or balanced deterrent is that it will encourage continuation of the arms race. The case for this view has been sketched above, but the case against it is at least equally convincing. Political conflicts lead to both wars and arms races. It is hard to show cases in which arms races have themselves made wars more likely, although certain ways of structuring forces may, e.g., accident-prone forces, or the inflexibility of German plans before World War I. Arms races are undesirable primarily because weapons are expensive, and in the nuclear age increase the potential destruction of society. Those arms races of the past that did not precede a war ended because neither side saw much point in them, and both eventually reduced their efforts. A reduction may come about either because two states have no further cause of conflict or because neither state gains a useful advantage. This is particularly true when a challenging state that is trying to catch up or go ahead cannot see any chance of surpassing the wealthier or more technologically advanced state. In the nineteenth century France tried several times to race British naval procurement, but each time it quit when its efforts merely encouraged the British to greater efforts. Thus, not procuring weapons at a level consistently higher than a poorer opponent may encourage that opponent to an effort it would not otherwise make. It may be that our declining strategic budgets in the mid-1960's have incited the Russians to try harder. It may be that if in the future we show willingness to allow the Soviets to build defenses without competing with them, we may inspire the Russians to procure more rather than less in the strategic area.

Two questions stand in the way of most potential disarmament agreements: what to do about states that do not come in, and how to provide inspection adequate enough that the parties can trust the agreements. These questions are particularly important if weapons levels are to be reduced to ten to twenty percent of what is now programmed, and only such reductions would achieve large reductions in potential destruction. At these weapons levels and without complex defenses protecting the superpowers, much less wealthy states can rapidly become the nuclear equals of the United States and the Soviet Union. Thus, with primarily offensive weapons for the urban destruction mission, it is unlikely that the superpowers can, or should, agree to significant arms reductions. Turning to the second question, if the inspection arrangements are not what we would hope for, and they are not likely to be, at low weapons levels each hidden weapon would be of considerable significance without defenses. On the other hand, with defenses on both sides a small amount of hiding of offensive weapons would be of much less significance, for most would be negated in any case. These arguments suggest the theoretical contribution BMD could make to arms reduction. Past Soviet interest in arms limitations on offensive and not defensive systems suggests that reducing ICBM's in the presence of maintained or enhanced BMD is a feasible form of agreement.

Several objections to balanced deterrence were suggested by the arguments in favor of a policy emphasizing assured destruction discussed above. We might add here only the objection that balanced deterrence seems capable of bringing back the option to initiate first strikes by the United States, and therefore may give an opponent a motive in a deep crisis to strike first. Implicitly, we have argued the pros and cons of this position. There seems to be no realistic hope of making sense of the first strike for either party in the next decade. While an estimated outcome of twenty to forty million dead is very different from one hundred million, our leaders could never be sure they could reduce fatalities to the former level. Even if they were sure, an expected result in this range would look so horrendous that it is not likely to give us a realistic first-strike force in the thinking of the leaders of either party. At any rate, from the point of view of war prevention, eliminating the hope of "winning" from future opponent calculations, and giving them less reason to believe we will back down under pressure should more than balance the slight increase this picture might give to the likelihood of American leaders initiating nuclear use in a severe crisis. It should also be remembered that we are a status quo power, and peace is most assured when the status quo power is least afraid and others have greatest regard for its strength and will.

FINITE DETERRENCE AND BALANCED DETERRENCE

We have now distinguished two approaches to nuclear strategy. Finite deterrence is based on preserving an offensive nuclear deterrent, currently at quite high levels, and threatening mutual suicide if war occurs.[4] The bal-anced deterrence policy would emphasize defenses in the current context in which offensive weapons are overbuilt. It would hope to provide America with a "theory of survival," including a hope for fewer casualties if war occurs. The second approach is not preferable because of the strength of the rather sophistic argument on both sides as to the influence of policy on the likelihood of war. These arguments have been developed on a subject with which there is too little directly applicable human experience to be of much use. The testing of the "soft arguments" for both positions suggests only that balanced deterrence offers about as good a chance for nuclear peace and arms reductions as other approaches. The edge that balanced deterrence has is that it may reduce the effects of nuclear war if it occurs.

Analysts often get carried away, and come to put more faith in their argument than it will bear. It does not appear that anyone can guarantee that nuclear weapons will not be used in war, or that any particular policy will lead to this result. The movement of Bertrand Russell's suggestions from preventive war to unilateral disarmament was a kind of hysterical affirmation of this view. Thus, those who are most interested in arms control often want simple deterrence without defenses—yet their further suggestions clearly imply that they do not trust the strategic system they support; their real goal is arms reduction.[5]

NOTES

1. *The Second World War*, Vol. II, pp. 330–31, quoted in George Quester, Bargaining and Bombing During World War II in Europe, *World Politics*, April 1963, XV, pp. 417–37 (428).

2. In source quoted by Fred C. Iklé, *The Social Impact of Bomb Destruction*, Univ. of Oklahoma Press, 1958, p. 180.

3. Thus, while deterrence is usually considered as defensive, there is also "offensive deterrence," the deterrence of a response to a provocation; in the jargon this is now often called nuclear compellence.

4. This is the current contrast of positions. Of course, many of those who want only offensive systems would be willing to go down to a much lower level at which nuclear war would not be suicide. This has other problems . . . , although it may be preferable to our present course.

5. The author further suggests adoption of a third possible alternative—the anti-nuclear strategy. See pp. 55–60 of *Why ABM?*

The Deployment of Defensive Weapons Systems and the Structure of Deterrence

Jerome Rothenberg

WITHOUT ARMS CONTROL

CETERIS PARIBUS SITUATIONS

In discussing the effect of defensive postures on the balance of deterrence without arms control we must distinguish among three types of situations. One is where one side has deployed nontrivial packages of active and passive defense systems and the other has not yet had time to respond: *ceteris paribus* situations. A second is where the noninitiator has had the opportunity to react to the initial deployment, but has chosen to do so without resort to a defensive package: asymmetric *mutatis mutandis* situations. The third is where the response involves defensive deployments as well: symmetric *mutatis mutandis* situations. I begin with the first.

Any first deployment of a defensive package imparts an immediate military advantage to the deployer, regardless of the composition of the package. But the events leading to deployment, and the precise nature of the advantage depends on the characteristics of the defense package. The first refers to the lead time required for procurement and deployment, and the proportion of this time during which the initiator can achieve, or wishes to achieve, secrecy about his action. Given equal initial capabilities on the part of both parties, the higher the values for the two elements, the larger is the po-

tential military advantage to be obtained by deploying first; but also, therefore, the greater is the incentive for the noninitiating party to try to offset this with additions to short lead-time offensive capacity or an actual preemptive strike. Indeed, a very high value combination of the two generates instability: neither party can afford to be second in such deployment. A party engages in deployment as soon as R-and-D progress promises successful deployment. There is no mutual deterrence in deployment. The absence of secrecy reverses this: the longer is the lead-time for procurement and deployment, and the more visible are its early stages, the greater is the likelihood that each side can wait to see whether the other has begun before deciding to respond in kind. Shorter lead-times combined with lack of secrecy require quicker responses, since the noninitiator may reason that systems which are expected to confer only brief advantage are likely to be planned for use in that brief period.

Secrecy during the deployment process is thus of real importance in determining the extent and duration of the advantage conferred by deployment. But secrecy has a different function to play after deployment. Its worth then depends on whether the defense deployment is intended more

From *Issues in Defense Economics*, edited by Roland N. McKean. Copyright © 1967 by the National Bureau of Economic Research. Reprinted by permission of the publisher.

to enhance deterrence or to improve effectiveness in waging war. In the former context the deploying party *wants* the other to know that his weapons will have less impact than he could heretofore expect—and wants him to know this *before* he decides to use them. So secrecy here would be dysfunctional. In the latter context secrecy can succeed in tricking the enemy into using unexpectedly ineffective weapons. It can indeed trick him into *starting a war* which he might not have begun if he knew his offensive weapons were going to be blunted.

The characteristics of the defensive package deployed helps determine the nature and extent of military advantage conferred, partly because they determine lead-time and secrecy, and also for reasons to be noted below. Realistically, given something like present technology, most elements of a defensive package have long lead-times and are grossly visible. This is most nearly so with respect to ABM for cities, and fallout- and blast-sheltering, especially the latter, for urban populations. ABM to protect offensive weapons—airfields and missile silos, for example—has similar lead-times but is susceptible of greater secrecy. ASW is probably amenable to the greatest secrecy. Moreover, the lead-time involved depends on the nature of the technological breakthroughs that make ASW a truly effective instrumentality. Bomber defense systems already exist in the posture of both the U.S. and Soviet Union at a level of effectiveness deemed adequate to meet the prospective bomber threat. So no important new deployment need be considered.

Thus, in the large, one should expect that first deployment of a defensive package will not give rise to long-lasting *ceteris paribus* advantages.

The specifics of deployment will affect what kind of advantage is possible. ASW, for example, can serve as an adjunct to ICBM in a counterforce

first strike, whether preemptive or otherwise. ABM for hardpoint defense is a way of decreasing the vulnerability of retaliatory weapons and therefore enhances deterrence of a first strike. Population-sheltering can improve the stakes for making a counterforce first strike, since the total damage-limitation impact of the counterforce strike and of sheltering against a weakened retaliatory blow could reduce the expected damage from a first-strike policy to a tolerable level. Actually, sheltering alone (unless it is of the current politically unrealistic blast variety) is unlikely to have this much damage-limiting effectiveness against even moderate countercity attacks unless combined with ABM capacity. Its chief *solo* effectiveness is likely to come as fallout protection against counterforce attacks. The combination of fallout-sheltering of populations with city ABM is a natural one. Each enhances the effectiveness of the other. Indeed, city ABM without fallout-sheltering would produce heavy casualties because of the radiation by-products of its "successful" use, and the possibility of enemy bypass attacks to waft radioactivity into the unprotected city.

If combined, active and passive city defenses could enhance the attractiveness of a first strike. But it might also detract from the need for making a first strike. So long as the nation's retaliatory weapons are reasonably secure against a first strike, the ability to limit population damage as well in an enemy strike gives the nation an ability to wait out a crisis without having to resort to a preemptive strike.

The deterrence effects of such first deployment depend in good measure on the credibility of the threats that may be made under its umbrella. With respect to central nuclear war, the key threat is: "If you attack me, I'll attack you and impose intolerable casualties." It is *not*: "If you attack me, I'll attack you and impose greater casualties on you than you impose on me." The distinction is important. If side A attacks side B in a counterforce blow, side B must now decide what it should do. If it should retaliate against side A—instead of perhaps suing for peace—it would have to expect an additional, and this time countervalue, blow. Now the difference in expected casualties from such a retaliation before and after it has deployed a defense package may be large enough to convert intolerable into "tolerable" casualties. Country B would have the incentive with defense deployment but not without such deployment, to retaliate even after a counterforce first strike by country A. This retaliatory attack could always be a countervalue blow unless some alternative target complex promised more effective impact. So B could threaten in advance of any first counterforce strike by A that it would surely retaliate and impose damage upon A in the event of such a strike, because it would have rational grounds for retaliating even after such a strike.

If A's first strike is countervalue, however, B's subsequent choice is different. The deployed defensive package having already been employed to decrease damage in the first strike, the consequences of a retaliatory strike now would be less affected—if at all—by the presence of the defense package. Consequently, the presence or absence of defense no longer has as much chance of making the difference between a rationally justified or unjustified retaliation. Retaliation by B now has to be threatened in advance on grounds of nonrational loss of control under crisis —the basic case of deterrence without defense. And the deterrent effect of the defense package rests on A's belief that the countervalue damage that it can impose in its *first strike* will not be large enough to be decisive because of the defense package.

The defense package decreases the number of hostages to any strike. But its differential effect would seem to be greater where the initial aggressor's first strike would leave the other's defensive capability still essentially intact. Thus, it would appear to enhance deterrence of a central nuclear war primarily where the potential aggressor found initiation of such a war rational on counterforce but not on countervalue terms. Given the nuclear postures of the United States and Soviet Union at present and in the foreseeable future, a *deliberate* first strike against population centers seems unreasonable indeed. Only an initiating counterforce strike—which at present does not look reasonable either—would seem at all likely to commend itself "rationally" to either party. So defense probably enhances deterrence of central nuclear war.

Is any other form of deterrence enhanced? In this asymmetric situation of one-sided defense additional deterrence *is* possible. Say that side A is not seen likely to initiate a central nuclear strike but simply a nonnuclear, but serious, provocation. Side B, possessing the defense package, may indeed be able to threaten nuclear retaliation on grounds that its enemy's lack of comparable defenses and its own ability to blunt an enemy subsequent retaliation would *rationally* warrant such a nuclear first strike as a winning strategy. Such a threat is not incredible. Consequently, a significant range of nonnuclear provocations—lesser armed conflicts and threats, and political aggressions—may be deterred in the *ceteris paribus* situation.

Let us examine how this notion applies to the actual situation. Short of a military provocation technically relevant to U.S. defense, the area where a military provocation by the Soviet Union would be most likely to evoke a U.S. threat of central nuclear retaliation is Europe. The situation of Europe is importantly asymmetrical for the U.S. and Soviet Union. The significance of Europe as ally or prize, as military asset or threat, differs for the two. Its differential location vis-à-vis the two has substantial strategic implications. The Soviet Union has internal land links with Europe; the U.S. requires external, far more distant, sea links. For the Soviet Union, home-based intermediate and even short-range weapons have a potential offensive function against Europe; they do not for the U.S.: only foreign-based intermediate weapons have a comparable function. Finally, the relative military postures of the two vis-à-vis Europe, nuclear and conventional, differ markedly. The Soviet Union can bring a far more overwhelming attack against Western Europe than the U.S. and Western Europe can offset or can bring against the Soviet Union.

One of the problems of the developing strategic nuclear standoff between the two countries is that if the Soviet Union chose to invade Western Europe on a large, conventional scale, NATO would not be able to defend itself with conventional forces alone and, given the contingent use of Russian intermediate and shorter range nuclear weapons, not with tactical nuclear weapons either. Under these circumstances, only a U.S. threat to offer strategic nuclear retaliation might succeed. But because of strategic nuclear stalemate (parity), such a threat would not be especially credible to the Soviet, since even a counterforce first strike could not guarantee only "tolerable" U.S. destruction under a retaliatory countervalue nuclear strike by the Soviets. The increasing lack of credibility of this threat to the Soviet Union as they have increased their assured destruction capability toward "parity" has spread to the NATO allies. These feel less assured that the U.S. would in fact retaliate centrally. A noncentral tactical nuclear response is far less satisfactory to them, since it makes of Europe a nuclear battlefield. And the

overwhelming Russian nuclear capability in this limited arena would cause so much destruction as to make a mockery of Europe being "defended." Thus, in both Soviet and NATO eyes the U.S. strategic deterrent of limited aggression in Europe is seriously degraded. One response to this is the French desire for a national nuclear capability whose retaliatory use has higher credibility, especially when seen as a trigger to provoke U.S.-Soviet Union nuclear exchanges and therefore, in some respects, to enhance U.S. deterrent power again.

In this context, if the U.S. had first deployment of a significant defense package, it might substantially reestablish an effective deterrent against Soviet provocation in Europe. It would again make credible that the U.S. could rationally retaliate even if not directly attacked. Thus, it could perform a most important function. But we must remember that the military advantage that confers this virtue is a short-lasting transitional one. After Soviet response has been allowed for, and subsequent dynamic interplay, the story is quite different. And since defense of Western Europe is a long-term goal of American policy, it *is* long-run deterrence that is wanted. As we shall see below, this may nullify the profitability of first deployment of a defense package, except insofar as U.S. long-run interests suggest that a U.S. first strike, made temporarily tolerable by the umbrella of asymmetrical defense, would be desirable. So, despite the fact that first deployment would augment deterrence, its only practical advantage under the circumstances might be to make a first-strike strategy rational. Moreover, if the Soviet Union duplicated this reasoning, they would see in a U.S. first deployment of defense, not a defensive, deterrent purpose, but an aggressive first-strike one. They might be driven to desperate aggressive countermeasures, perhaps even a preemptive nuclear strike. Thus, if the advantages of first deployment are in reality very short lasting, this could impart important instability into the relative postures. This will be discussed below.

Deterrence against provocations elsewhere is not likely to be much enhanced by first deployment, even in the short-run. While expected damage from a retaliatory interplay might be decreased nontrivially, and to an "acceptable" level with respect to the goal of defending Europe, this damage is still enormous by any human standard, and is likely to be unacceptably high for any U.S. interest less important than Europe (and probably Latin America). Consequently, the defense deployment would not markedly increase the credibility of threats relating to lesser provocations. Indeed, it is not likely even to lead to the making of such threats.

One last point. I have been treating the credibility of threats as essentially unitary: whatever an opponent would believe (disbelieve) our allies would believe (disbelieve) and vice versa. This is probably a good approximation, but at times significant discrepancies may creep in. The general closeness of the approximation is due not only to the fact that both enemies and friends are reading the same objective evidence, but that each group reads the actions of the other as evidence on how well *they* believe certain threats. Thus, the Soviet Union may well read France's efforts to establish an independent nuclear deterrent as disbelief in the threats on which U.S. deterrence depends, and its own belief in the U.S. threats may be thereby affected (since an ally can be assumed to be privy to information not available to an enemy).

Discrepancies arise because the information available to allies and enemies *is* different. Moreover, the vantage is different, and this introduces a strategic variable. Allies have an in-

centive to *act as though* they believe a threat made by one of them to bolster its credibility for the common enemy. On the other hand, an ally may act in a way that appears to be relevant to belief of a threat, but in reality is part of an attempt to improve its bargaining position within the alliance. A motivation of this sort has sometimes been attributed to the French.

ASYMMETRIC MUTATIS MUTANDIS SITUATIONS

I can be quite brief, since most of the basic elements have been treated. The act of deploying a defensive package will be responded to insofar as the other party expects it to have military effectiveness *or* believes that the deployer expects it to have effectiveness. Given anything like present technology the exchange rate greatly favors offense over defense. A reasonable response may well involve adapting and/or augmenting offensive capacity, with no attempt to institute a direct defensive capability. Offensive adaptation includes, for example, retrofitting penetration aids against ABM and submarine performance changes against ASW. Augmentation includes simply increasing the number of offensive weapons. Both measures are designed to offset directly (by saturation or performance or operational tactics) the defensive weaponry on its own terms and thus replace the operational effectiveness of the offense to a level comparable to the pre-defense deployment situation. Since the responding country would wish to achieve this replacement at a given level of confidence in the face of an increased uncertainty about actual effectiveness, such would require an adaptation augmentation objectively greater than what would be necessary to impose the predeployment level of damage.[1]

A response of this sort has every likelihood of being able in fact to offset the military advantage imparted by the defense deployment. Indeed, as suggested, in actual use it would probably more than offset such advantage. Since under anything like present technology the possibility of such offset seems generally appreciated, a known response in offensive capability would wipe out the defense deployer's felt advantage. It would cancel out any enhanced deterrence. On the other hand, for reasons to be discussed below and having to do with uncertainty levels, even a slightly more than exact offset through enhanced offense is not likely to establish increased deterrence for the responding country. The defensive package is likely to increase the threshold of disparity in military capabilities, which is necessary if the opposing side is to have *significant* advantage.

If country A deployed a defensive package, and country B responded with enhanced offensive capability, the interaction might continue in the form of an arms race of the same character—that is, a further defense buildup by A, triggering a further offensive buildup by B, and so on. But this is unlikely. The initial defense deployment would probably have been associated with R-and-D successes. The temporary advantage rendered might or might not have seemed worth the expense and resulting postures. But a new significant technological achievement is not likely to be so conveniently available just in time for A to respond with a new round. And in the absence of such an achievement, the fact that a simple extension of measures involved in the first deployment would have had lesser returns even before B's offsetting response, together with the demonstration that B could respond advantageously to offset A's defense (because of the current technological imbalance between offense and defense), would very likely deter A from initiating a new round as response. The dynamic interaction unit therefore seems to be one round at

a time. Each round is a *new* episode, initiated in its own special terms.

SYMMETRIC MUTATIS MUTANDIS SITUATIONS

Here it is envisaged that country B would respond to A's deployment of a defense package by itself deploying a comparable defense package. In view of the advantage of offense over defense this kind of response has to be motivated. It is likely to come about where both countries have comparable defense technologies available, but where B has been hitherto deterred from deploying its own defense package by the desire to keep A from such deployment. Deterrence having failed with respect to A, it now fails for B as well.

By responding with a defense package, despite the advantages of offense over defense, B is not committing an irrelevancy. It will be recalled that one of the options for A which was enhanced by the defense deployment was a first strike. Insofar as this is so, defense deployment by B has a direct defensive function: it can save lives in the event of attack. But there is a deterrent function as well—exactly the same as for A. If already subject to attack (counterforce especially) by A, the possession of some population defense, for example, could make the difference for B between a rational incentive to retaliate and to surrender. Thus, its presence will tend to deter A from attack.

But the presence of a defense capability on both sides complicates deterrence for both. By decreasing the number of hostages subject to the enemy's attack, it decreases the amount of assured destruction which that enemy can count on in a retaliatory attack. Thus, it decreases the ability of each to deter the other's attack. Each has reason to believe that if it attacks the other, the other will probably retaliate; but if the first attack is counterforce and one's own defenses are not inconsiderable, the combination can reduce over-all damage to oneself to within tolerable limits relative to the possibility of victory. An initiatory counterforce blow bypasses the enemy's *defenses,* while one's own defenses function to absorb the evoked retaliation. The enemy's defenses ultimately enter consideration in that the initiator, having degraded the enemy's offensive capacity by his initial attack and the absorbed retaliation, can obtain victory only by finally threatening a countervalue blow. The impact of this threat depends on the efficacy of defense against the remaining offensive capability of the aggressor. If the willingness to terminate the war depends more on one's *relative defenselessness* vis-à-vis the enemy at some point in the hostilities, rather than on the relative casualties so far inflicted—a not unlikely circumstance—then the mutual possession of a defensive capability can symmetrically weaken deterrence. The defensive packages on both sides do not simply cancel one another out; they can operate almost independently to unhinge a balance of mutual deterrence (except for the effect of uncertainty, as will be discussed below).

Indeed, it is partly for this reason that the mutual postures we have just considered are incomplete. It is very unlikely that B will respond to A's defense capability simply by deploying its own defense. It will in addition attempt to offset the enemy's defense, as we saw in the last section. It will enhance its offensive capability. And the enemy will similarly respond to the defensive capability induced. Thus, if A deploys a defense package, B will probably do likewise and augment offense as well. A, in turn, will offset B's new defense by augmenting its offensive capability. Thus, a defensive and offensive arms race is the likely outcome.

The consequences of this balanced interplay differ from the preceding case. Offensive capability having increased something like proportionally for both sides, and in like form,[2] an initial counterforce blow by A cannot, given approximately the relevant exchange rates obtaining today, reduce expected retaliatory damage to itself much—if at all—below the level obtaining before any defense deployment, despite the presence of that defensive capability.

Thus, with additional offense offsetting defense, no degradation of deterrence occurs for either side—unless, of course, the arms buildup is disproportionate for the two (a different case). The result is similar to the status quo ante in relative strengths, and almost the same in terms of deterrence. A standoff has been purchased at a higher level of armaments—and at great expense—so that in case of war by accident a higher total level of destruction is possible. Moreover, the dynamics of such arms procurement can lead to instability, as will be noted below. The only useful thing which has been purchased is an increased uncertainty as to outcomes of actual operations. This enhances the stability of deterrence somewhat, by increasing the margin of superiority which either side must believe it has in order to be willing to initiate hostilities. But much the same effect is obtainable by increasing the absolute level of offensive capability alone. The higher is this level, the greater the proportion of superiority which one side must possess in order to be able to initiate a counterforce strike and reduce retaliatory damage to a preassigned level. Even the stability bought through uncertainty should not be exaggerated. As long as there are no constraints on offensive capabilities, the induced augmentation is likely to be great enough to prevent any very significant increase in operational uncertainty. It is primarily where offensive constraints exist that this may be an important factor. I shall return to this below.

In sum, where there are no agreed-upon constraints in force structure, deployment of defense packages can confer short-term advantages on the initiator—translated in part into primary and secondary deterrence—but these are largely or wholly offset when the other side responds. The most likely outcome is an expensive cancelling-out of advantage, worsened by an induced dynamic arms acquisition process which can destabilize whatever balance of deterrence existed before defense deployment began.

WITH ARMS CONTROL

The analysis differs if arms control measures are in force. If they are, defensive commitments come at the expense of offensive options, or at least cannot be freely offset by offensive augmentation. The *ceteris paribus* case is the same. Only the *mutatis mutandis* case must be reconsidered.

The situation depends on what kind of arms control obtains. The two main types for this issue are: (1) limitations on offensive weapons systems but not on defensive systems (an approximation to a Soviet preference), (2) over-all force limitations which allow for substitutions between defense and offense. (Limitations specifying particular offensive *and* defensive force levels would not permit us to consider defensive force levels as a decision variable for the two participants.)

Under the first, it is not unlikely that a parallel defensive arms buildup will ensue since, offensive levels being fixed by agreement, every increment of defense for either side decreases expected damage from a war (accidental or not). The incremental reduction of expected damage for each is not undermined by the other's similar defensive additions. With respect to this factor, then, a defense buildup represents an atomistic, nonstrategic choice limited only by the nonmilitary opportunity cost of resources.

But a strategic factor does enter in as well. I noted earlier that defensive deployment may have either a defensive *or* an offensive strategic impact, or a combination of both. By decreasing its own expected damage, defensive deployment decreases the other side's basic ingredient for deterrence. Thus, the parallel defense buildup can be played for aggressive intent and become an arms race—as offensive in character as if offensive and not defensive weapons were being acquired. In such an eventuality the arms agreement itself would be endangered. Thus, both sides would have to realize that the pace and extent of their defensive buildups were constrained by their strategic valuation of the offensive weapons arms control agreement. It is likely, therefore, that a viable, purely offensive weapons-systems limitation would impose indirect limitations on defensive systems as well.[3]

The situation resembles the symmetric *mutatis mutandis* case without arms control except that: (1) offensive levels are prevented from rising to offset the defensive deployment (2) the mutual defensive buildup can proceed much further here before being discouraged by arms control viability and nonmilitary opportunity costs. Together, these mean that the assured destruction arm of deterrence can be substantially degraded. Taken by itself, this could be seriously destabilizing, and war might be initiated before even the telltale warning of a breakdown in the arms control agreement into upward spiralling offensive buildups. But another factor assuages this possibility of instability. Deterrence does not simply depend on what an attacker will lose if he attacks his enemy, but also on what he will gain by making such an attack. It is a question of the *difference* in outcomes between attacking and not attacking. Despite his standing to lose little by an attack, the attractiveness of such a course will be weakened as the potential attacker stands to *gain* less and less. Parallel defensive buildups decrease the assured gains just as they decrease the expected losses. The net effect is not clear.

There are really two effects on the gains from attack: a decrease in the expected level of destruction to one's enemy, and an increase in the variance of possible outcomes. Both make a first strike strategy—and a first strike itself— less attractive. The effect of expected level is obvious. The effect of variance (uncertainty) is somewhat less obvious, but probably compelling none the less. For one thing, the simple inability to be sure of what will happen when the stakes are fantastically high and the knowledge that what is done cannot be undone and that all humanity would pay the cost of a miscalculation would seem to exert strong deterrence against central nuclear attack. For another, there are measures a potential attacker can take to offset some of the effects of this uncertainty—reconnaissance capabilities, flexibility of targeting, salvo capabilities, etc. But all of these are expensive and, under some arms control agreements of the type I am considering, are either limited in quantity or are obtainable only by sacrificing the absolute level of offensive capability. Really effective countering of the enhanced uncertainty—an offensive build-up—is prevented by the arms control agreement.

One may guess at the over-all consequences on deterrence. Both the expected gains and retaliatory losses from an initial attack are decreased. But attached to *both* is an increased variance of outcome. Not only may one's attack prove to be singularly ineffective but also one's defenses against retalia-

tion. The increased uncertainty of both work against a potential attack: he will wish both a high probability that *at least* a specified amount of damage will be done to his enemy, and a high probability (possibly higher) that *no more than* a specified amount of damage be done to him in return. Both require overcompensating for variance —the larger the variance the greater the degree of overcompensation. Again, the critical constraints imposed by the arms control agreement prevent effective insurance. One could easily predict that deterrence against central nuclear war will be enhanced under these conditions: only extreme inadvertent exacerbation of political tensions would seem likely to make an attack worth considering.

Much the same would seem to characterize the second type of arms control—over-all force limitations with substitutability between offensive and defensive weapons systems. The main difference is that the opportunity cost of defensive capability is offensive capability. Given something like present technology, and force levels not very dissimilar from present U.S. and Soviet levels, not much defensive capability will be deliberately acquired at the cost of offensive capability. It is possible that more will be purchased, however, than in the no arms control situation, since the over-all force level constraint will prevent the opponent from easily augmenting his offensive to offset any defensive deployment. Thus, when some R-and-D achievement in defensive systems promises reasonable performance against the current offensive posture, a nontrivial acquisition and deployment of a defensive package may well occur. There is less reason to expect symmetrical (parallel) defensive deployment by both parties under the present case than under previous cases. The over-all constraint puts a heavy premium on each side's *relative* valuation of the different elements in its posture. The over-all situation of the U.S. and Soviet Union (resources, relative costs, preferences) differs in important respects. It is likely that they differ with respect to the usefulness of defense capability. Certainly the past weapons acquisition experience of the two nations supports this presumption. Under over-all force level constraints, the Soviets are likely to buy considerably more defense than the U.S.

The consequences of asymmetric defense deployment will be a pastiche of effects that we have already considered. The constraints against easy offset policies will prevent the strategic interplay from cancelling out. Some decrease in assured destructiveness will be "suffered" by both sides, and some increase in operational uncertainty. As in the case just discussed, these may result in a net enhancement of mutual deterrence against central nuclear war.

For both types of arms control, we may now ask whether deterrence against nonnuclear provocation will also be enhanced, as under the *ceteris paribus* no arms control situation. It is true that possession of some defensive capability makes either a first or second strike more conceivable, and therefore

makes it all the more important to prevent an uncontrolled escalation to the point of central nuclear attack. But such possession can also be looked on as conferring a kind of insurance against error. A nation with considerable defense might believe that it can dabble in non-nuclear provocations—limited wars with some escalation—taking the risk that if it has miscalculated the costs will not be horrendous. A conservative, essentially status quo power might be more influenced by the former consideration—that nuclear war is not unthinkable to a nation willing to take risks (i.e., to gamble within the broader sea of operational uncertainty)—and be deterred from infranuclear provocations. An adventurous, but not necessarily implacably aggressive, nation might be more influenced by its damage-limiting insurance and be led to probe provocatively. Thus, despite what may well be an enhancement of mutual deterrence against central nuclear war, one cannot gauge the effect on deterrence against infranuclear provocation. The difficulty is not due to the weakness of the over-all effect, but to the opposing direction of influences of its components.

NOTES

1. A qualification is necessary. The enemy's defense deployment raises the cost of inflicting any given degree of damage on him. Resources available for national security are not free to the nation: they have as opportunity cost the nonmilitary resource uses foregone. Since national security and other goals are to some extent substitutive, a substantial increase in the cost of the former relative to the latter could well induce some diminution in the level of security sought. This means that the level of assured destruction sought (at given degree of confidence)—i.e., the extent of direct offset to defense deployment—could fall below that of the predeployment situation. In the present example, the cost change is too small to justify serious attention to this qualification.

2. Like form is specified—and assumed—

because if A augmented offense in terms of numbers and accuracy, while B solely in terms of penetration against ABM, a counterforce blow by A would be more effective after such proportional augmentation than before.

3. This is not to say that such an initial agreement might not be amended to allow for an ultimately complete supersession of defensive posture for deterrence. But such supersession is likely to come about by explicit agreement rather than atomistically or even tacitly, because the pathway involves serious strategic instabilities. If progress toward the goal is made possible by an easing of international tensions, then this is more likely to be brought about by a decrease in allowable offensive force levels than by an increase in defensive levels. The former is far cheaper and probably less dangerous.

The Reappraisal of Limited War

ROBERT E. OSGOOD

I

On the most general grounds the conception of limited war surely remains relevant—indeed, imperative. On grounds of morality and expediency alike, it is essential that states—especially nuclear states—systematically endeavour to control and limit the use of force where force is unavoidable. The fact that American public officials and spokesmen now generally take this for granted, while little over a decade ago high government officials commonly asserted that once war occurs it has no limits save those determined by the capacity to gain a military victory, must be regarded as a major and, hopefully, lasting triumph of reason over viscera.

But little about the feasibility and utility of particular limitations in specific conflicts, whether with respect to deterring or fighting a war, can be deduced from the general rationale of limited war. Nor can feasibility and utility be deduced simply by applying the logic derived from abstract models of conflict, although these may sometimes aid rational calculation. Judgments about the feasibility and utility of particular methods of limitation must, of course, take account of objective technical and physical facts, but these facts do not speak for themselves in strategic terms. Such judgments must depend largely on disciplined intuitions, informed and qualified by experience, about the way states actually behave when they are faced with war or the threat of war.

Yet experience is likely to be an inconclusive and misleading guide. If the test of a particular strategy lies in the results of actual warfare, how can one be sure whether the outcome is due to the characteristics of that strategy, to the way it was carried out, or to factors unrelated to strategy? If the test is deterrence, how can one know whether either the occurrence or non-occurrence of the act that one intended to deter was due to the strategy or to other circumstances? At best, experience is a partial representation of the full range of circumstances that might affect the feasibility and utility of strategies of limited war. Nevertheless, because strategy has no self-contained logic like mathematics, experience of one kind or another has been and must be the primary shaper of strategy in thought and action.

It is significant, in this respect, that limited-war thinking has been conditioned by the perspectives common to a particular phase of the cold war, when the cold war expanded to Asia and the Soviet Union achieved the capacity to inflict terrible damage on the United States in any nuclear exchange. Limited-war strategy first blossomed in response to the Korean war (although the implications of nuclear weapons had led Bernard Brodie, Sir Basil Liddell Hart, and a few others to adumbrate concepts of limited war before). It flourished, especially among those out of office, during the Eisen-

From *Problems of Modern Strategy, Part I* in *Adelphi Papers* No. 54. Copyright © 1969 by the International Institute for Strategic Studies. Reprinted by permission.

hower–Dulles Administration. The appeal of limited-war strategy in this period was basically two-fold: on the one hand, the desire to mitigate the danger of nuclear war; on the other hand, the desire to support the policy of containment more effectively. The underlying disposition in both respects was to bring force under control as a rational instrument of policy, but the motive for control has been a combination of fear and determination in different admixtures at different times and in different minds.

In the course of applying the concept of limited war to changing international circumstances, it has become apparent that these two objectives may lead to different policy conclusions, depending on whether one emphasizes effective containment or the avoidance of nuclear war. They may lead to different conclusions not only about particular strategies, which have been copiously examined and discussed, but also about two issues that have scarcely been discussed at all by proponents of limited war: (1) when or whether to intervene in a local war; and (2) the proper intensity and scale of intervention within existing restrictions.

But even more important than the two objectives of limitation in shaping views on these questions are certain premises about the international and domestic political environment which have been relatively neglected in limited-war thinking. These premises concern (1) the nature of the Communist threat and its bearing upon American security; (2) the willingness of the American government and people to sustain the costs of fighting aggression;

and (3) the identity and behaviour of potential adversaries.

It is not difficult to understand why the issues of intervention and the premises about the objectives and the political environment of limited warfare have received far less attention than strategies of limited war. The explanation lies partly in the familiar limits to man's ability to foresee basic changes in his environment or to imagine how new events and conditions might affect his outlook. Strategies, on the other hand, are adaptations to foreign policy in the light of realities and trends that are perceived at the moment. They are frequently rationalizations of existing military capabilities and domestic constraints. Man's political imagination is constrained by what is familiar, but his strategic imagination is relatively free to draw its inferences and design its plans until some unforeseen war tests its propositions—and most strategic propositions fortunately remain untested in the nuclear age.

But the explanation for the relative neglect of political premises in strategic thought also lies in the propensity of American civilian strategists to propound their ideas, often with brilliant ingenuity, as revelations of an esoteric body of learning (which to some extent they were) that would rescue military thinking from conventional wisdom and put it on a rational basis. In this respect, however, the deference of the uninitiated, overawed by the secrets and rituals of the strategic priesthood, has been more important than the pretensions of the priests.

II

Limited-war thinking has been conditioned by a period in which the over-riding objective of American policy was to contain international Communism by preventing or punishing external and internal aggression. According to the prevailing consensus, a local Communist aggression even in an intrinsically unimportant place could jeopardize American security by encouraging further aggressions in more important places, leading to a chain of aggressions that might eventually cause World War III. This view, fortified by the lessons of Fascist aggression, did not, as critics contended, depend on the assumption that international Communism was under the monolithic control of the Soviet Union—an assumption that the proponents of the consensus qualified as soon as its critics—but it did depend on an assumption that amounted to the same thing in practice: that a successful aggression by one Communist state would enhance the power of the Soviet Union, China, and other Communist states, *vis-à-vis* the United States and the free world. By this reasoning American security interests were extended from Western Europe to Korea and, by implication, to virtually anywhere aggression threatened.

Proponents of limited-war strategy sought to strengthen containment. They hoped to make deterrence more credible and to bolster allied will and nerve in crises, like the one arising over access to Berlin. They argued their case as strategic revisionists seeking to save American military policies from the thralldom of misguided budgetary restrictions imposed at the expense of security needs. Conscious of America's superior economic strength and military potential, they rejected the thesis of the Eisenhower–Dulles Administration that the United States would spend itself into bankruptcy if it prepared to fight local aggression locally at places and with weapons of the enemy's choosing.

With the advent of the Kennedy Administration the revisionists came into office. Responding to a dominant theme in Kennedy's compaign, they were determined to fill the military gaps in containment. The United States, according to this theme, was in danger of losing the cold war because the government had not responded to

new conditions—particularly to the rise of Soviet economic power and nuclear strength but also to the shift of Communist efforts to the Third World. The most dramatic evidence of America's threatened decline of power and prestige was the Soviet Union's prospect of gaining the lead in long-range missile striking power, but the missile gap was thought to be part of a wider threat encouraged by misguided American political and military policies that had allegedly alienated potential nationalist resistance to Communist subversion in the Third World and forfeited America's capacity to deter or resist local aggression. To safeguard American security and restore American prestige it would be necessary, among other measures (reinvigorating the domestic base of American power, adopting policies better suited to the aspirations of the underdeveloped countries, and ensuring America's strategic nuclear superiority), to build up the United States capacity to fight limited wars without resorting to nuclear weapons. If the Communists could be contained at the level of strategic war and overt local aggression, the new administration reasoned, the Third World would be the most active arena of the cold war and guerrilla war would be the greatest military threat.

In office, the Kennedy Administration not only increased the United States' lead in long-range missile power; it also built up her capacity to intervene quickly with mobile forces against local aggression at great distances, and it emphasized a strategy of "controlled and flexible response." Identifying the most dangerous form of Communist expansionism as "wars of national liberation," it created special forces to help combat aggression by guerrillas and concerned itself intensively with methods of counter-insurgency.

By 1964, after the Cuban missile crisis and before large numbers of American forces got bogged down in

Vietnam, the United States looked so powerful that not only some Americans but others too (particularly Frenchmen) began to think of the world as virtually monopolar and of America's position in the world as comparable to that of a global imperial power. The only remaining gap in military containment might be closed if the United States could demonstrate in Vietnam that wars of national liberation must fail. To achieve that demonstration was America's responsibility to world order as well as to its immediate interests. In this atmosphere of confidence and determination there was no inducement to question the premises about the wisdom and efficacy of intervention that underlay the prevailing American approach to limited war. The tendency was, rather, to complete the confirmation of a decade of limited-war thinking by proving the latest and most sophisticated conceptions in action.[1]

We shall return to the impact of the adversities of Vietnam on American conceptions of limited war, but first let us review the development of limited-war thinking that had taken place in the meantime.

III

Apart from the fascination with counter-insurgency in the early 1960s, the great outpouring strategic imagination in the United States was inspired by efforts to deter or fight hypothetical conflicts in Western Europe. But these conflicts, in contrast to wars in the Third World seemed less and less likely as *détente* set in. So in this area it was not the discipline of war that impinged upon strategic thought but rather the discipline of restrictions on defence expenditures and changes in the international political atmosphere. Moreover, in the absence of war, merely the passage of time caused a certain attrition of ambitious strategic ideas, as the inherent implausibility of limited war in Europe and the difficulty of gaining agreement on how to meet such unlikely contingencies dampened successive sparks of strategic innovation.

In Europe, as in the Third World, the dominant objective of limited-war strategy was, first, to enhance the credibility of deterrence; second, to strengthen conventional resistance to local non-nuclear aggression; and, no less important, to bolster the West's bargaining position in crises on the brink of war. These three objectives were integrally related. But the objective of effective resistance was far more difficult to achieve in Europe because of the greater physical and political obstacles to limitation and the greater strength of potential adversaries.

The effort to formulate a strategy that would combine effective resistance with reliable limitations reached its logical extreme in 1957 with the theories of limited tactical nuclear war propounded by Henry Kissinger, Rear-Admiral Sir Anthony Buzzard, and others. But these strategies soon died from indifference and incredulity. The difficulty of settling upon a convincing strategy for integrating tactical nuclear weapons into limited warfare in Europe evidently remains overwhelming, and the interest in doing so has declined as the credibility of the West using any kind of nuclear weapons first, except in circumstances warranting the risks of general war, has declined.

While the cold war was still relatively warm the search for a strategy of limited war in Europe enriched the post-war history of military strategy with ingenious ideas, some of which now seem strangely irrelevant. Strategies for fighting large-scale limited wars (endorsed by Alain Enthoven and, apparently, by McNamara in the early 1960s) were condemned to irrelevance by the unwillingness of an ally to support them with the necessary expenditures and manpower, by the unlikelihood that a war involving such powerful adversaries in such a vital area would remain limited, and by the fear of allied governments that emphasizing large-scale conventional resistance would undermine the efficacy of nuclear deterrence. That left strategies (1) to enforce short conventional pauses and raise the threshold between conventional and nuclear war (first publicized by General Norstad); (2) to combine static with mobile, and conventional with tactical nuclear, resistance in limited wars resulting from accident and miscalculation (most notably formulated by F. O. Miksche and Malcolm Hoag); and (3) to control escalation as a bargaining process using non-nuclear and nuclear reprisals and demonstrations (chiefly identified with Herman Kahn and Thomas Schelling).

All of these latter three strategies were attempts to accommodate the logic of limited war to the realities of limited conventional means. They were also responses to perceived security needs in an international political environment in which it was assumed that the threat of Soviet-supported limited aggression was undiminished—and even rising, according to many who foresaw the Soviet achievement of virtual parity with the United States in the capacity to inflict unacceptable second-strike damage. But this assumption became much less compelling or was abandoned altogether with the onset of *détente,* although the conception of raising the threshold of conventional resistance continued to gain adherents and in 1967 was finally embodied in NATO's official strategic position. Consequently, although the logic of flexible and controlled response prevailed on paper and in strategic pronouncements, the means to withstand anything more than the most limited attack for longer than a week were not forthcoming. France's

withdrawal from most arrangements for collective defence only made this predicament more conspicuous.

Only the French government rejected the objective of avoiding an automatic nuclear response to a local non-nuclear incursion; but for all governments the objective of deterrence increasingly overshadowed the objective of defence. Yet despite the declining concern with strategies of limited resistance, the allies were less worried than ever about their security. This was not because nuclear deterrence was more credible. Indeed, one might suppose that Secretary of Defense McNamara's open admission that the United States could not prevent the Soviet Union from devastating the United States even if the United States struck first, would have undermined confidence in America's will to use the ultimate deterrent to defend its European allies. The allies felt secure because even a low degree of credibility was regarded as sufficient for deterrence under the new political conditions of *détente*.

In this atmosphere there was a tendency of strategic thought to revert to the conceptions of the Eisenhower–Dulles period. Proponents of limited-war strategy now took comfort in pointing to the deterrent effect of the danger that any small conflict in Europe might escalate out of control. Considering the nature of Soviet intentions, the value of the stakes, and the integration of tactical nuclear weapons into American and Soviet forces, they were prepared to rely more on this danger and less on a credible capacity to fight a limited war effectively. It is symptomatic that this view found support from Bernard Brodie, an outstanding former champion of local conventional resistance in Europe, who now saw the official emphasis on stressing the conventional-nuclear "firebreak" and increasing conventional capabilities as unfeasible, unnecessary, and politically disadvantageous in America's relations with its allies.[2]

In one respect, the limited-war strategy of the Kennedy–McNamara Administration underwent a modification that was tantamount to official abandonment. The most far-reaching application of the idea of contrived reciprocal limitation of warfare was the counter-force or non-cities strategy, which was intended to make possible the option of a controlled and limited Soviet–American nuclear exchange by holding the American assured-destruction forces (that is, the forces capable of delivering unacceptable damage on a retaliatory strike) in reserve and inducing the Soviets reciprocally to confine nuclear strikes to military targets.[3] When McNamara first publicly announced this strategy at Ann Arbor in June 1962, critics charged that it was intended to enhance the credibility of extended deterrence. This inference was not unwarranted, since McNamara's statement did reflect his view at the time that a strategic deterrent, to be useful, had to be rational to use. In a few years, however, McNamara came to view the strategy as no more than an option for keeping as limited as possible a nuclear war that might result from accident or miscalculation, not as a means of deterring or fighting such a war more effectively. In subsequent statements McNamara explained the objective of a counter-force strategy as exclusively damage limitation. He also explained the difficulties of inducing the Soviets to fight a limited strategic war in such a way as to cast doubt upon its feasibility.[4] Finally, in successive annual reports on the nation's defence posture he indicated that cost-effectiveness considerations dictated a relatively increased allocation of money and resources to maintaining a capability for assured destruction, as compared to the objective of damage limitation.

Summing up the fortunes of limited-war strategy with respect to Europe and central war, we can say that the basic rationale of limited war seems firmly established in the United States and in allied countries, with the possible exception of France, and that this rationale is to some extent implemented in operational plans, military policies, and weapons. But the high-point of limited-war theory—in terms of the inventiveness, thoroughness, and energy with which it was carried out in strategic thought and actual policies—was roughly in the period from 1957 to 1963. Since then economic restrictions and diminished fear of Soviet military action, together with the inroads of time upon novel plans for hypothetical contingencies that never occur, have nullified some of the most ingenious strategies and eroded others, so that limited-war thinking is left somewhere between the initial Kennedy–McNamara views and the approach of the Eisenhower–Dulles administration.

In military affairs, as in international politics, one senses that an era has ended but finds little intimation of the era that will replace it. Meanwhile, strategic imagination seems to have reached a rather flat plateau surrounded by a bland atmosphere in which all military concerns tend to dissolve into the background.

IV

This was the state of limited-war thinking in 1965 when American forces became the dominant element in fighting Communist forces in Vietnam. At that time the only really lively ideas were counter-insurgent warfare and controlled escalation.

Some regarded the war as a testing ground for strategies of counter-insurgency. When the United States began bombing selected targets in North Vietnam, ostensibly in retaliation for attacks on American units at Pleiku and elsewhere in the South, some regarded this as a test of theories of controlled escalation. When American forces in South Vietnam engaged regular units of the North Vietnamese army in large numbers, a host of new strategic-tactical issues arose, such as the issue, which was surely oversimplified by polemics, between search-and-destroy and seize-and-hold methods and the equally over-drawn issue between a mobile and an enclave strategy.

The war in Vietnam should have been a great boon to strategic innovation, since it fitted none of the existing models of limited war, although it contained elements of several. But the lessons derived from the strategies that were tried have been either negative or inconclusive, yet it is not apparent that alternative strategies would have worked any better. Some critics of the conduct (as opposed to the justification) of the war assert that different political or military strategies and tactics, executed more skilfully, might have enabled the United States to gain its political objectives—primarily, the security of an independent non-Communist government in South Vietnam—more readily. Others assert that those objectives were either unattainable because of the lack of a suitable political environment in South Vietnam or attainable only at an unacceptable cost, no matter what methods had been adopted.

If it is difficult to make confident judgments about the efficacy of various strategies and tactics in Vietnam, it is even more difficult to draw lessons applicable to other local wars in which the United States may become involved, since the war in Vietnam is almost surely unique in its salient characteristics: the large size and effectiveness of North Vietnam's combat forces, the organizing genius of Ho Chi Minh, the North's appeal to the South on nationalist grounds stemming from the postwar independence movement, and the weak and fragmented nature of South

Vietnam. Yet lessons will, and probably must, be drawn. Many have already been offered before the war has ended.

The most general lessons concern the political and other conditions under which the United States should intervene in revolutionary or quasi-revolutionary wars, and the proper scale of intervention. It is asserted, for example, that the lesson of Vietnam is that no regime too weak to defend itself against revolution or subversion without American military intervention will be able to defend itself with American intervention.[5] This may turn out to be true in Vietnam, although it is too early to tell. But even so, can one conclude from this single, sad experience that no kind of American intervention under any circumstances, regardless of the nature of external support for revolutionary forces and the characteristics of the defending government and nation, could provide the necessary margin of assistance to enable a besieged regime to survive? No such categorical rule is warranted. And if it were, what would be its utility? The rule does not tell one how to determine whether a regime can defend itself, and it may be impossible to tell in time for American assistance to be useful.

Rejecting any such sweeping rules of abstention, Hanson Baldwin draws a no less sweeping lesson of intervention. Future interventions against insurgency, he says, must be undertaken "under carefully chosen conditions and at times and places of our own choosing," and they must avoid the sin of "gradualism" by applying overwhelming force (including tactical nuclear weapons, if necessary) at an early stage.[6] Walter Lippmann, on the other hand, sees the lesson of Vietnam in such negative terms as virtually to preclude successful intervention in wars of insurrection under any circumstances. Impressed by the unsuitability of such wars for American genius and power, he asserts that Vietnam simply demonstrates that elephants cannot kill swarms of mosquitoes.[7]

Given the general disaffection with the war, Lippmann's conclusion is likely to be more persuasive than Baldwin's. Indeed, although overstated, it contains an important kernel of truth. Once the United States becomes involved in any local war with its own troops, it will tend to use its modern military logistics, organization, and technology (short of nuclear weapons) to whatever extent is needed to achieve the desired political and military objectives, as long as its military operations are consistent with the localization of the war. For every military establishment fights with the capabilities best suited to its national resources, experience, and ethos. In practice, this means that American armed forces (and the large non-fighting contingents that accompany them), when engaged in a protracted revolutionary war on the scale of the Vietnamese war, tend to saturate and overwhelm the country they are defending. If the war were principally an American operation, as the long counter-insurgency war in Malaya was a British operation, the elephant might nevertheless prevail over the mosquitoes in time, even if it had to stamp out in the crudest way every infested spot and occupy the country. But the war in Vietnam, like every other local war in which the United States has or will become engaged, has been fought for the independence of the country under siege—in this case the country nominally represented by various South Vietnamese governments. Therefore, despite South Vietnam's great dependence on the United States, the United States is also dependent on South Vietnam. The chief trouble with this situation is that in some of the most crucial aspects of counter-insurgency South Vietnamese forces and officials have been ineffective and the United States could do nothing about it. Moreover, where American pressure on South Vietnam might have been useful the very scale of the United States' involvement has deprived it of leverage, since its direct involvement gave it a stake in the war that militated against the sanctions of reducing or withdrawing assistance.

In one respect Lippmann's metaphorical proposition may understate the difficulty the United States must encounter in trying to apply containment to a situation like the Vietnam conflict. If South Vietnam lacks the minimum requisites of a viable polity, then no amount of leverage or control could succeed in establishing the independence of a country, even if the organized insurrection and its external support were defeated. In this case, the incapacity of the elephant would be more profound than its inability to kill mosquitoes. In this case, when the adversary were defeated, the task of establishing an independent country would have just begun.

The lesson—although it is not universally applicable—seems to be that if a country cannot defend itself from insurrection with assistance short of American regular forces, the United States can probably defend it only at a level of involvement that will contravene its objective of securing the sovereignty of that country; so that even if the United States should defeat the insurgents, it will be burdened with an unviable protectorate. To oversimplify the proposition: either the United States, under these internal circumstances, must virtually take over the country and run the war itself at the risk of acquiring a troublesome dependent, or it must keep its role limited at least to guerrilla operations and probably to technical and staff assistance at the risk of letting the besieged country fall.

Hanson Baldwin is probably right in thinking that an early massive intervention can, in some circumstances, achieve a limited objective more effectively than a sustained war of gradually increasing scale, but following this generality as a rule of action would entail great risks of over-involvement in quasi-revolutionary wars. Consequently, to condition American support of a besieged country on its ability to survive at a low threshold of direct American involvement seems like the more prudent strategy. This proposition, however, like others concerning the conduct of local wars, implicitly contains a consideration more basic than strategy and tactics: how important are the interests for which the United States may intervene? For if they are truly vital, a high-risk strategy is justified, and even under the most unpromising conditions intervention may be imperative.

America's intervention in Vietnam has suffered from ambiguity on this question of interests. South Vietnam was evidently not considered important enough to justify the costs and risks of a scale of intervention that, if undertaken early enough, might (or might not) have led to a more successful outcome. Indeed, probably no American leader would have considered the eventual scale of war worth the costs if he had known the costs in advance. The reason the United States got so heavily involved in Vietnam lies, not in its estimate of South Vietnam's importance to American vital interests, but in the United States' inability to limit an expanding involvement after it had drifted beyond a certain scale of intervention. Hence, the United States found itself fighting a small version of World War II without undertaking a commensurate mobilization of its resources and manpower—or of its moral energy. In this sense, the scale and costs of the war were greater than the nation was prepared to sustain.

If the larger lessons of Vietnam concerning the efficacy and scale of intervention are ambiguous, the validity and utility of subordinate lessons concerning the strategy of limited warfare are no less inconclusive. Perhaps the strategy that has come closest to a clear-cut failure is controlled escalation, as applied by means of selective bombing in North Vietnam. But even in this case it would be misleading to generalize about the efficacy of the same methods under other conditions. Controlled escalation is a strategy developed principally to apply to direct or indirect confrontations between the United States and the Soviet Union.[8] It envisages influencing the adversary's will to fight and his willingness to settle a conflict by means of a process of "bargaining" during a "competition in risk-taking" on ascending—and, hopefully, on the lower—levels of violence, which would culminate in a mutually unacceptable nuclear war at the top of the escalation "ladder." In the spring of 1965 the American Government, frustrated and provoked by Hanoi's incursions in the South and anxious to strike back with its preferred weapons, put into effect a version of controlled escalation, borrowing language and style from the latest thinking on the subject.[9] Through highly selective and gradually intensified bombing of targets on lists authorized by the President—incidentally, a notable application of one of the tenets of limited-war theory: strict political control of military operations—the United States hoped to convince Hanoi that it would have to pay an increasing price for aggression in the South. By the graduated application of violence, the government hoped through tacit "signaling" and "bargaining" to bring Hanoi to reasonable terms. But Hanoi, alas, did not play the game.

Perhaps the experiment was not a true test of escalation, since the punitive purpose of the bombing was ambiguous. Indeed, in deference to public protests throughout the world, the United States explicitly stressed the purely military nature of the targets as though to deny their bargaining function. Perhaps the escalation was not undertaken soon enough or in large enough increments, thereby sparing the North Vietnamese a decisive dose of punishment and enabling them to make material and tactical adjustments. But it seems more likely that the failure of controlled escalation lay in inherent deficiencies of bombing as a punitive device. In any case, there are special difficulties in applying to an under-developed country a strategy that presupposes a set of values and calculations found only in the most advanced countries. Yet even in an under-developed country there must be some level of bombing damage that would bend the government's will to fight. Perhaps controlled escalation exerts the desired political effect only when there is a convincing prospect of nuclear war at the top of the ladder. Or perhaps it works only against a country fighting for limited objectives. Hanoi had unlimited ends in the South, but the United States had quite limited ends in the North. Whatever the explanation, controlled escalation failed to achieve its intended political effect; and that should be sobering to its enthusiasts, if any remain. None the less, the experience does not prove much about the efficacy of a different strategy of escalation against a different adversary in different circumstances.

Nor does the war carry any clear lesson about the wisdom of granting or denying impunity from attack to a country supporting insurrection in an adjacent country. Critics contend that carrying the war to the north violated one of the few clear-cut rules of the game on which limitation might be reliably based, alienated world and domestic opinion, fortified North Vietnam's determination to fight for an unconditional victory, and distracted attention from the real war—the civil war—in the south, without substantially affecting that war. But advocates of

carrying the war to the North argue that the attrition against North Vietnamese units and logistics was significant and might have been decisive but for self-imposed restrictions that were unnecessarily confining, that these operations were necessary to South Vietnamese morale and provided a valuable bargaining counter for mutual de-escalation, and that the denial of sanctuary is a valuable precedent for avoiding disadvantageous rules of the game in the future and may be a useful deterrent against other states who may contemplate waging wars against their neighbours. Moreover, it can be argued that when a local war cannot be won at a tolerable cost within the country under attack, the only reasonable alternative to a dishonourable withdrawal is to engage the source of external support directly, and charge it with a greater share of the costs, in order to secure a satisfactory diplomatic termination of hostilities.

Both the Korean and the Vietnamese wars indicate that the particular restrictions on military operations will be determined by such a variety of conditions and considerations that it is almost fruitless to try to anticipate them in advance. In some conceivable future circumstances, one can even imagine a sensible case being made for crossing the threshold that bars the United States from using tactical nuclear weapons. It is unlikely, however, that the prevailing reaction to Vietnam will be in the direction that Hanson Baldwin advocates when he condemns the constraints of gradualism and the "cult" of self-imposed limitations. For Vietnam does at least indicate that the United States will go a long and frustrating way to observe significant self-imposed restrictions on a war, rather than insist on obtaining a military victory by all means available.[10] It indicates that even when the nation is "locked in" to an unpromising local war with its own troops, it will prefer to follow the rule of proportionate response to enemy initiatives rather than incur the immediate risks of massive escalation.

It is significant how weak and ineffectual American "all-or-nothing" sentiment has been in the Vietnamese as compared to the Korean war. The idea of the United States confining itself to a limited war, which was novel and antithetical in Korea, has been widely taken for granted in Vietnam. Indeed, the most influential American critics have urged more, not less, stringent restrictions on combat despite the fact that the danger of nuclear war or of Chinese or Russian intervention never seemed nearly as great as in Korea.[11] Those (including some prominent conservative Senators and Congressmen) who took the position that the United States ought either to escalate the war drastically in order to win it or else disengage, clearly preferred the latter course. But their frustration did not manifest a general rejection of the conception of limited war but only opposition to the particular way of applying that conception in Vietnam.

Thus the popular disaffection with the Vietnamese war does not indicate a reversion to pre-Korean attitudes toward limited war. Rather, it indicates serious questioning of the premises about the utility of limited war as an instrument of American policy, the premises that originally moved the proponents of limited-war strategy and that underlay the original confidence

of the Kennedy Administration in America's power to cope with local Communist incursions of all kinds. In Vietnam the deliberate limitation of war has been accepted by Americans simply from the standpoint of keeping the war from expanding, or from the standpoint of de-escalating it, whereas in Korea the desire to keep the war limited had to contend with a strong sentiment to win it for the sake of containment. In Korea the principal motive for limitation was the fear that an expanding war might lead to general war with China or nuclear war with the Soviet Union, but in Vietnam the limits were motivated as much by the sense that the political objective was not sufficiently promising to warrant the costs of expansion. This change of emphasis reflects more than the unpopularity of the war in Vietnam. It also reflects the domestication, as it were, of limited war—that is, of the deliberate, calculated restriction of the ends and means of fighting—as an operational concept in American foreign policy.

Some of the reasons for the strength of sentiment for keeping the war limited, however, bear upon the political question of whether to intervene in local wars at all. They suggest that the specific lessons about the strategy and constraints of limited war that one might derive from Vietnam are likely to be less important than the war's impact on the political premises that underlay American intervention.

V

The political premises that Vietnam has called into question are more profound, yet more limited, and at the same time less explicit than the sentiment embodied in the popular refrain "no more Vietnams." If Vietnam exerts a fundamental impact on American policy with respect to limited-war interventions, it will not be merely because

of the national determination to avoid future Vietnams and to restrict American commitments to a scope more compatible with American power and the will to use it. The whole history of the expansion of American commitments and involvements is pervaded with the longing to avoid new commitments and involvements. Yet a succession of unanticipated crises and wars has led the nation to contravene that longing. Sometimes the desire to avoid the repetition of unpleasant involvements had only led to a further extension of commitments, which in turn has led to further involvements. That is what happened when the Eisenhower–Dulles Administration formed deterrent alliances (including SEATO) to avoid another Korean war.

The reason for this contradiction is not really a sublimated national longing for power—at least not power for its own sake—but rather the nation's persistent pursuit of a policy of containment, which under the prevailing international conditions has repeatedly confronted it with predicaments in which the least objectionable course has seemed to be the exercise and extension, rather than the abstention or retraction, of American power. If a fundamental change in America's use of limited-war strategy as an instrument of policy takes place, it will be because the premises of containment are no longer convincing to the nation and Vietnam has acted as the catalyst to enforce this realization.

In effect, the United States has equated Communist aggression with a threat to American security. Although the relationship of Communist aggression in Asia or Africa to American security is quite indirect and increasingly far-fetched, this equation was plausible enough if one assumed—as Americans generally did assume until after the Korean war and the Sino–Soviet split in the late 1950s—that the cold war was essentially a zero-sum contest between the two super-powers and that a successful aggression by any small Communist state would shift the world balance of power towards the Communist bloc. Moreover, there was no need to question this view of American security as long as American efforts to counter aggression were successful at a tolerable cost.

But *détente* with the Soviet Union and the increasing divergencies of interest among Communist states and parties are changing the American view of international reality, and of the nature and intensity of the Communist threat in particular. Thus, a gain for China or even North Vietnam is not automatically seen as a gain for the Soviet Union or a loss for the United States, and opportunities for limited cooperation with the Soviet Union occasionally appear attractive. Moreover, the accentuation of national and subnational particularism outside the Communist world may have diminished what capacity the Soviet Union or China ever had to extend their control and influence through diplomacy, subversion, or revolution. In Africa, most notably, Americans are becoming accustomed to a great deal of disorder and Communist meddling without jumping to the conclusion that the balance of power or American security is jeopardized. To some extent China emerges as a new object of containment; but despite the long strand of American obsession with China, the Chinese do not yet—and may never—have the strength to pose the kind of threat to Asia that the Soviet Union could have posed to Western Europe, and Asia is simply not valued as highly on the United States' scale of interests as Western Europe.

American involvement in the Vietnamese war began on a limited scale at a time of national self-confidence and self-assertion in the Third World. The United States applied forceful containment there according to familiar premises about America's general interest in stopping Communist aggression without questioning the precise relevance of the war to the balance of power and American security.[12] The scope of American involvement grew in an effort to defeat North Vietnam's "war of national liberation" and to establish a secure non-Communist government

in the South. But during this period
the familiar American image of the
Communist world and its threat to
American security was changing. Furthermore, in contrast to the Korean
war, the Vietnamese war never seemed
to pose a threat to the security of
Western Europe or Japan.

None the less, if American objectives could have been achieved with no
greater pain and effort than the Korean
war, which was also unpopular but not
beyond being resolved on satisfactory
terms, the nation might have accepted
the Vietnamese war as another vindica-
tion of containment—troublesome and
frustrating but not so costly or unsuccessful as to call into question the premises of American intervention. In reality, however, the war became so costly
and unpromising that, given its remote
relationship to American security,
Americans began to doubt the validity
of the premises on which the government intervened. So, whereas the
"never-again" reaction against the Korean war fostered the effort of the
Eisenhower–Dulles Administration to
apply containment more effectively to
Asia at less cost by strengthening deterrence, the "no-more-Vietnams" spirit

seems to challenge the necessity, if not
the basic rationale, of strengthening
military containment in any way that
would increase American commitments.

At the least, these doubts seem
likely to lead to a marked differentiation of interests in the application of
containment—a downgrading of interests in the Third World and a greater
distinction between these interests, and
those pertaining to the security of the
advanced democratic countries. Possibly, they will lead to abandonment of
containment in Asia altogether, in so
far as containment requires armed intervention against local aggression on
the mainland. More likely, they will
simply lead to a sharper distinction in
practice between supporting present
security commitments and not forming
new ones, and between supporting
present commitments with American
armed forces when aggression is overt,
and abstaining from armed intervention in largely internal conflicts. What
they seem to preclude, at least for a
while, is any renewed effort to strength-
en military deterrence and resistance in
the Third World by actively developing and projecting the United States'
capacity to fight local wars.

VI

On the other hand, it is misleading
to reach conclusions about future
American limited-war policies and actions on the basis of the nation's desire
to avoid quasi-revolutionary wars like
the one in South Vietnam, since the
threat of local wars impinging on
American interests could arise in many
different forms. Thus, while the war in
Vietnam seems to be waning and the
prospect of similar national liberation
wars in Asia is uncertain, the capacity
and perhaps the incentive of the Soviet
Union to support local wars that might
spring from quite different circumstances is increasing. The Soviet will to
exploit this capacity will depend, in

part, on the American position. If
Soviet leaders were to gain the impression that the United States is firmly set
upon a course of neo-isolationism and
the absolute avoidance of intervention
in local wars, they might become dangerously adventurous in the Middle
East and elsewhere. The United States
would almost surely regard Soviet exploitation of local conflicts more seriously, than it would regard another war
like Vietnam. So one of the military-
political issues facing the United States
in the late 1960s is how to respond to
the growing capacity of Soviet mobile
overseas forces.

Current trends seem destined to

provide the Soviet Union with a significantly enlarged capacity to intervene in local conflicts overseas, a capacity of which the United States has hitherto enjoyed a virtual monopoly.[13] The build-up of Soviet naval, amphibious, air and land forces in this direction has been accompanied by a substantial expansion of Soviet arms deliveries and technical assistance to Middle Eastern countries, as well as to North Vietnam, and the acquisition of technical facilities (although not permanent bases) in several Mediterranean ports. The experience of observing America's large-scale support of South Vietnam and providing North Vietnam with weapons and logistics support has given Soviet leaders a new appreciation of overseas local-war forces.

At the same time, Soviet strategic doctrine has assigned a greater role to supporting Soviet interests overseas, both on the sea and in local wars on land.

These developments do not portend a mobile overseas capacity that can compete with America's capacity in an armed conflict, but they do provide Soviet leaders with new options for intervening in local wars. They provide new levers of influence in the Middle East and elsewhere. And they impose new constraints on American intervention. The greatest danger they pose is that the super-powers will unintentionally become involved in competitive interventions in local conflicts, where they lack control, and where the *modus operandi* of avoiding a direct clash has not been established.[14]

VII

The history of limited-war thought and practice in the last decade or so provides little basis for confidently generalizing about the feasibility, and utility of particular strategies. Many strategies have never really been put to the test; and where they have been tested, either in deterrence or war, the results have been inconclusive. Moreover, strategies are very much the product of particular circumstances—not only of technological developments, but also of domestic and international political developments. This political environment is always changing. Developments that have made some strategies seem obsolete—for example, the impact of *détente,* domestic constraints, and the balance of payments on strategies of conventional resistance in Europe— might change in such a way as to revive abandoned strategies or evoke new ones. The limited-war strategies appropriate to the international environment of the 1970s—especially if there should be a significant increase in the number and severity of local wars, a more active Soviet policy of intervention in local wars, a more aggressive Chinese military posture, or new nuclear powers—might contain some interesting variations on strategic notions that were born in past periods of intense concern with military security. Changes in military technology, such as forthcoming increases in long-range air- and sea-lift capabilities, will also affect the strategies and political uses of limited-war capabilities.[15]

Yet one has the feeling, which may not spring entirely from a lack of imagination, that in the nature of international conflict and technology in the latter half of the twentieth century there are only a limited number of basic strategic ideas pertaining to limited war, and that we have seen most of these emerge in the remarkable strategic renaissance of the past decade or so. These ideas can be combined in countless permutations and combinations and implemented by a great variety of means, but we shall still recognize trip-wires, pauses, reprisals, denials, thresholds, sanctuaries, bargaining, demonstrations, escalation, Mao's three stages, enclaves, seize-and-hold, search-and-destroy, and all the rest.

What we are almost certain not to witness is the perfection of limited-war conceptions and practice in accordance with some predictable, rational calculus and reliable, universal rules of the game. The conditions and modalities of international conflict are too varied, dynamic, and subjective for limited war to be that determinate. Any search for the strategic equivalent of economic man on the basis of which a grand theory of military behaviour might be erected is bound to be ephemeral and unproductive. On the other hand, I think it is equally clear that military conceptions and practices among the advanced states are not going to revert to romantic styles of the past that glorified the offensive spirit, war *à l'outrance*, the national will to victory, and overwhelming the enemy. If counterparts of the stylized limited warfare of the eighteenth century are unrealistic, counterparts of the total wars of the following centuries would be catastrophic.

The nuclear age has not made armed conflict obsolete, nor has it excluded the possibility of catastrophic war. It has, however, inculcated a novel respect for the deliberate control and limitation of warfare. That respect is a more significant and enduring achievement of limited-war strategists than any of their strategies.

NOTES

1. Beyond proving the efficacy of any particular strategy, a successful war in Vietnam would demonstrate America's psychological and political capacity to cope with limited war. As Secretary McNamara put it, "If you read Toynbee, you realize the importance of a democracy learning to cope with a limited war. The greatest contribution Vietnam is making—right or wrong is beside the point—is that it is developing in the United States an ability to fight a limited war, to go to war without the necessity of arousing the public ire. In that sense, Vietnam is almost a necessity in our history, because this is the kind of war we'll most likely be facing for the next fifty years." Quoted by Douglas Kiker, "The Education of Robert McNamara," *Atlantic Monthly*, March 1967, p. 53.

2. See Bernard Brodie, *Escalation and the Nuclear Option* (Princeton, N.J.: Princeton University Press, 1966). Brodie's differences with the official position (which, incidentally, he exaggerated in attributing to it the objective of resisting conventionally a large-scale Soviet aggression) were no less significant for being differences of degree. For they were intended as an antidote to a strategic tendency, just as his earlier advocacy of preparedness for limited conventional defence was intended as an antidote to the Eisenhower-Dulles emphasis on nuclear deterrence in Europe. See, for example, *Strategy in the Missile Age* (Princeton, N.J.: Princeton University Press, 1959), pp. 335 ff.

3. An even more radical, but not necessarily less plausible, strategy for limited strategic nuclear war, based on striking cities selectively rather than sparing them had already attracted some academic attention. Klaus Knorr and Thornton Read, eds., *Limited Strategic War* (New York: Praeger, 1962).

4. On the one hand, he explained, the Soviet Union would be unlikely to withhold its counter-city capability as long as its missiles were relatively scarce and vulnerable; but on the other hand, he acknowledged that as Soviet missiles became more numerous and less vulnerable, the prospects of confining retaliatory damage from them would vanish completely. In any event, in each annual "posture statement" he stated in progressively more categorical terms that there was no way the United States could win a strategic nuclear war at a tolerable cost.

5. Former Ambassador Edwin O. Reischauer reaches the following "simple rule of thumb" on the basis of the Vietnam experience: "Any regime that is not strong enough to defend itself against its internal enemies probably could not be defended by us either and may not be worth defending anyway." See *Beyond Vietnam: The United States and Asia* (New York: Knopf, 1967), p. 188.

6. "After Vietnam—What Military Strategy in the Far East?," *New York Times Magazine*, 9 June 1968.

7. "Elephants Can't Beat Mosquitoes in Vietnam," *Washington Post*, 3 December 1967.

8. The concept and strategy of controlled escalation are set forth most fully in Herman Kahn, *On Escalation* (New York: Praeger, 1965), and Thomas C. Schelling, *Arms and*

Influence (New Haven: Yale University Press, 1966), although both authors developed the idea in earlier writings. Needless to say, neither author believes that controlled escalation was properly applied in Vietnam.

9. Punitive bargaining, however, was only one of the objectives of the bombing. Two other principal objectives were to raise the morale of South Vietnamese and to impede the infiltration of men and supplies to the South. See General Maxwell D. Taylor, *Responsibility and Response* (New York: Harper and Row, 1967), pp. 26–28; Thomas C. Schelling, *Arms and Influence* (New Haven: Yale University Press, 1966), pp. 170 ff.; and Tom Wicker, "The Wrong Rubicon," *Atlantic Monthly*, May 1968, pp. 81 ff.

10. One indication of the magnitude of self-imposed restrictions is the number and kinds of military actions that the United States refrained from taking that it might have taken to defeat Communist forces. In Vietnam as in Korea a major restriction was on the number of armed forces mobilized and deployed. In both wars the United States reached an upper limit on these forces—higher in Vietnam than in Korea—beyond which it would not go even if it meant ending the war on less advantageous terms. Perhaps the most obvious restrictions—such as not bombing civilian targets and not invading the enemy's homeland—were in North Vietnam. Correspondingly, the most obvious limitations of political objectives have applied to North, not to South, Vietnam. Of North Vietnam the American Government has asked, essentially, only that it stop supporting the war in the South materially and with its regular units. But in the South, too, the American Government has become willing to settle for something considerably less than a total victory without arousing popular protest in the nation.

11. It should be noted, however, that one of the reasons that the danger of nuclear war did not seem so great was that the United States refrained from taking actions, like bombing Haiphong, which seemed to carry too great a risk of Chinese or Soviet intervention compared to their military or political value.

12. One indication of the generalized and unquestioned anti-Communist purpose of America's intervention is that, according to Bill Moyers, President Johnson's special assistant and White House Press Secretary, the containment of China was rarely discussed even as late as the deliberations about the escalation decisions of 1965. Rather, these decisions were taken simply to prevent a Communist (that is, Viet Cong) victory. See, "Bill Moyers Talks About LBJ, Power, Poverty, War and the Young," *Atlantic Monthly*, July 1968, pp. 30–31.

13. Thomas W. Wolfe, "The Projection of Soviet Power," *Survival*, May 1968, pp. 159–65 (reprinted from *Interplay*, March 1968); Curt Gasteyger, "Moscow and the Mediterranean," *Foreign Affairs*, July 1968, pp. 676–87; Claire Sterling, "The Soviet Fleet in the Mediterranean," *Reporter*, 14 December 1967, pp. 14–18. Since the Cuban missile crisis the Russians have made new investments in large long-range air transports and have built up the naval, infantry and amphibious forces, enlarged the merchant marine (including ships configured for military cargo) to put the Soviet Union among the two or three leading maritime powers, and established a greatly augmented naval presence in the Mediterranean, including two helicopter carriers for support of landing operations or anti-submarine warfare. There are no signs, however, that the Soviet Government intends to create what the United States regards as a balanced naval force capable of coping with American naval forces.

14. Gasteyger, *op. cit.*, p. 687.

15. In particular, the C-5A air transports now coming into operation, and fast-deployment logistics ships, not yet appropriated, will greatly increase the amount of troops, equipment, and supplies that can be lifted from the United States overseas in a short time. Such improvements in air- and sea-lift will provide increased capabilities and flexibility in supporting many different kinds of military tasks in remote places at all levels of conflict, and in varied physical and political conditions. By reducing or eliminating the need for a standing American presence overseas they will enable the United States to be more selective in establishing and maintaining bases and commitments. See Robert E. Osgood, *Alliances and American Foreign Policy* (Baltimore: The Johns Hopkins Press, 1968), pp. 137–43.

Counterinsurgency in the
Hot Revolutionary War

David Galula

Force, when it comes into play in a revolutionary war, has the singular virtue of clearing away many difficulties for the counterinsurgent, notably the matter of the issue. The moral fog dissipates sooner or later, the enemy stands out more conspicuously, repressive measures are easier to justify. But force adds, of course, its own difficulties.

At our point of departure in the study of the hot revolutionary war—that is, the moment when the armed forces have been ordered to step in—the situation usually conforms to the following pattern:

The insurgent has succeeded in building his political organization. He directs either an elite party leading a united front, or a large revolutionary movement bound to the cause. Although his actions other than subversion are overt, he operates clandestinely.

The country's map reveals three sorts of areas:

The "red" areas, where the insurgent effectively controls the population and carries out guerrilla warfare.

The "pink" areas, in which he attempts to expand; there are some efforts at organizing the populations and some guerrilla activity.

The "white" areas, not yet affected but nevertheless threatened; they are subjected to the insurgent's subversion but all seems quiet.

Confusion is prevalent in the counterinsurgent's camp. There is a realization that an emergency exists, but the feeling of crisis is more widely spread in government circles than among the population of the white and even the pink areas. The true allegiance of every citizen is open to doubt. The leadership and its policy are questioned. The political, the judicial, the military structures geared for ordinary days have not yet been adapted to the requirements of the situation. The economy is rapidly deteriorating: the government's expenses are rising while its income is declining. In the psychological field, the insurgent has the edge since he exploits a cause without which he would not have been able to develop so far as to engage in guerrilla warfare or terrorism. The counterinsurgent forces are torn between the necessity of guarding key areas and fixed installations, of protecting lives and property, and the urge to track the insurgent forces.

With this general picture in mind, we shall now discuss the various avenues open to the counterinsurgent.

LAWS AND PRINCIPLES OF COUNTERINSURGENCY WARFARE

LIMITS OF CONVENTIONAL WARFARE

Let us assume that the political and economic difficulties have been magically solved or have proved manageable,[1] and that only one problem remains, the military one—how to suppress the insurgent forces. It is not a problem of means since the counterinsurgent forces are still largely superior to the insurgent's, even though they may be dispersed. It is primarily a problem of strategy and tactics, of methods and organization.

The strategy of conventional warfare prescribes the conquest of the enemy's territory, the destruction of his forces. The trouble here is that the enemy holds no territory and refuses to fight for it. He is everywhere and nowhere. By concentrating sufficient forces, the counterinsurgent can at any time penetrate and garrison a red area. Such an operation, if well sustained, may reduce guerrilla activity, but if the situation becomes untenable for the guerrillas, they will transfer their activity to another area and the problem remains unsolved. It may even be aggravated if the counterinsurgent's concentration was made at too great risk for the other areas.

The destruction of the insurgent forces requires that they be localized and immediately encircled. But they are too small to be spotted easily by the counterinsurgent's direct means of observation. Intelligence is the principal source of information on guerrillas, and intelligence has to come from the population, but the population will not talk unless it feels safe, and it does not feel safe until the insurgent's power has been broken.

The insurgent forces are also too mobile to be encircled and annihilated easily. If the counterinsurgent, on receiving news that guerrillas have been spotted, uses his ready forces immediately, chances are they will be too small for the task. If he gathers larger forces, he will have lost time and probably the benefit of surprise.

True, modern means of transportation—particularly helicopters, when available—allow the counterinsurgent to combine strength with swiftness. True, systematic large-scale operations, because of their very size, alleviate somewhat the intelligence and mobility deficiency of the counterinsurgent. Nevertheless, conventional operations by themselves have at best no more effect than a fly swatter. Some guerrillas are bound to be caught, but new recruits will replace them as fast as they are lost. If the counterinsurgent operations are sustained over a period of months, the guerrilla losses may not be so easily replaced. The question is, can the counterinsurgent operations be so sustained?

If the counterinsurgent is so strong as to be able to saturate the entire country with garrisons, military operations along conventional lines will, of course, work. The insurgent, unable to grow beyond a certain level, will slowly wither away. But saturation can seldom be afforded.

WHY INSURGENCY WARFARE DOES NOT WORK FOR THE COUNTERINSURGENT

Insurgency warfare is specifically designed to allow the camp afflicted with congenital weakness to acquire strength progressively while fighting. The counterinsurgent is endowed with congenital strength; for him to adopt the insurgent's warfare would be the same as for a giant to try to fit into a dwarf's clothing. How, against whom, for instance, could he use his enemy's tactics? He alone offers targets for guerrilla operations. Were he to operate as a guerrilla, he would have to have the effective support of the population guaranteed by his own political organization among the masses; if so, then the insurgent would not have it and consequently could not exist; there would be no need for the counterinsurgent's guerrilla operations. This is not to say that there is no place in counterinsurgency warfare for small commando-type operations. They cannot, however, represent the main form of the counterinsurgent's warfare.

Is it possible for the counterinsurgent to organize a clandestine force able to defeat the insurgent on his own terms? Clandestinity seems to be another of those obligations-turned-into-assets of the insurgent. How could the counterinsurgent, whose strength derives precisely from his open physical assets, build up a clandestine force except as a minor and secondary adjunct? Furthermore, room for clandestine organizations is very limited in revolutionary war. Experience shows that no rival—not to speak of hostile—clandestine movements can coexist for long; one is always absorbed by the other. The Chinese Communist maquis succeeded in suppressing almost entirely their Nationalist counterparts in the Japanese-occupied areas of north and central China. Later on, during the final round of the revolutionary war in China, ordinary bandits (almost a regular and codified profession in some parts of China) disappeared as soon as Communist guerrillas came. Tito eliminated Mikhailovitch. If the Greek Communist ELAS did not eliminate the Nationalist resistance groups, it was due to the restraint they had to show since they were entirely dependent on the Western Allies' support. More recently, the FLN in Algeria eliminated, for all practical purposes, the rival and older MNA group. Because the insurgent has first occupied the available room, attempts to introduce another clandestine movement have little chance to succeed.

Can the counterinsurgent use terrorism too? It would be self-defeating since terrorism is a source of disorder, which is precisely what the counterinsurgent aims to stop.

If conventional warfare does not work, if insurgency warfare cannot work, the inescapable conclusion is that the counterinsurgent must apply a warfare of his own that takes into account not only the nature and characteristics of the revolutionary war, but also the laws that are peculiar to counterinsurgency and the principles deriving from them.

THE FIRST LAW: THE SUPPORT OF THE POPULATION IS AS NECESSARY FOR THE COUNTERINSURGENT AS FOR THE INSURGENT

What is the crux of the problem for the counterinsurgent? It is not how to clean an area. We have seen that he can always concentrate enough forces to do it, even if he has to take some risk in order to achieve the necessary concentration. The problem is, how to keep an area clean so that the counterinsurgent forces will be free to operate elsewhere.

This can be achieved only with the support of the population. If it is relatively easy to disperse and to expel the insurgent forces from a given area by purely military action, if it is possible to destroy the insurgent political organizations by intensive police action, it is impossible to prevent the return of the guerrilla units and the rebuilding of the political cells unless the population cooperates.

The population, therefore, becomes the objective for the counterinsurgent as it was for his enemy. Its tacit support, its submission to law and order, its consensus—taken for granted in normal times—have been undermined by the insurgent's activity. And the truth is that the insurgent, with his organization at the grass roots, is tactically the strongest of opponents where it counts, at the population level.

This is where the fight has to be conducted, in spite of the counterinsurgent's ideological handicap and in spite of the head start gained by the insurgent in organizing the population.

THE SECOND LAW: SUPPORT IS GAINED THROUGH AN ACTIVE MINORITY

The original problem becomes now: how to obtain the support of the population—support not only in the form of sympathy and approval but also in active participation in the fight against the insurgent.

The answer lies in the following proposition, which simply expresses the basic tenet of the exercise of political power:

In any situation, whatever the cause, there will be an active minority for the cause, a neutral majority, and an active minority against the cause.

The technique of power consists in relying on the favorable minority in order to rally the neutral majority and to neutralize or eliminate the hostile minority.

In extreme cases, when the cause and the circumstances are extraordinarily good or bad, one of the minorities disappears or becomes negligible, and there may even be a solid unanimity for or against among the population. But such cases are obviously rare.

This holds true for every political regime, from the harshest dictatorship to the mildest democracy. What varies is the degree and the purpose to which it is applied. Mores and the constitution may impose limitations, the purpose may be good or bad, but the law remains essentially valid whatever the variations, and they can indeed be great, for the law is applied unconsciously in most countries.

It can no longer be ignored or applied unconsciously in a country beset by a revolutionary war, when what is at stake is precisely the counterinsurgent's power directly challenged by an active minority through the use of subversion and force. The counterinsurgent who refuses to use this law for his own purposes, who is bound by its peacetime limitations, tends to drag the war out without getting closer to victory.

How far to extend the limitations is a matter of ethics, and a very serious one, but no more so than bombing the civilian population in a conventional war. All wars are cruel, the revolutionary war perhaps most of all because every citizen, whatever his wish, is or will be directly and actively involved in it by the insurgent who needs him and cannot afford to let him remain neutral. The cruelty of the revolutionary war is not a mass, anonymous cruelty but a highly personalized, individual one. No greater crime can be committed by the counterinsurgent than accepting, or resigning himself to, the protraction of the war. He would do as well to give up early.

The strategic problem of the counterinsurgent may be defined now as follows: "To find the favorable minority, to organize it in order to mobilize the population against the insurgent minority." Every operation, whether in the military field or in the political, social, economic, and psychological fields, must be geared to that end.

To be sure, the better the cause and the situation, the larger will be the active minority favorable to the counterinsurgent and the easier its task. This truism dictates the main goal of the propaganda—to show that the cause and the situation of the counterinsurgent are better than the insurgent's. More important, it underlines the necessity for the counterinsurgent to come out with an acceptable countercause.

VICTORY IN COUNTER-INSURGENCY WARFARE

We can now define negatively and positively what is a victory for the counterinsurgent.

A victory is not the destruction in a given area of the insurgent's forces and his political organization. If one is destroyed, it will be locally re-created by the other; if both are destroyed, they will both be re-created by a new fusion of insurgents from the outside. A negative example: the numerous mopping-up operations by the French in the Plain of Reeds in Cochinchina all through the Indochina War.

A victory is that plus the permanent isolation of the insurgent from the population, isolation not enforced upon the population but maintained by and with the population. A positive example: the defeat of the FLN in the Oran region in Algeria in 1959–60. In this region, which covers at least a third of the Algerian territory, FLN actions—counting everything from a grenade thrown in a café to cutting a telephone pole—had dwindled to an average of two a day.

Such a victory may be indirect; it is nonetheless decisive (unless of course, as in Algeria, the political goal of the counterinsurgent government changes).

THE THIRD LAW: SUPPORT FROM THE POPULATION IS CONDITIONAL

Once the insurgent has established his hold over the population, the minority that was hostile to him becomes invisible. Some of its members have been eliminated physically, thereby providing an example to the others; others have escaped abroad; most have been cowed into hiding their true feelings and have thus melted within the majority of the population; a few are even making a show of their support for the insurgency. The population, watched by the active supporters of the insurgency, lives under the threat of denunciation to the political cells and prompt punishment by the guerrilla units.

The minority hostile to the insurgent will not and cannot emerge as long as the threat has not been lifted to a reasonable extent. Furthermore, even after the threat has been lifted, the emerging counterinsurgent supporters will not be able to rally the bulk of the population so long as the population is not convinced that the counterinsurgent has the will, the means, and the ability to win. When a man's life is at stake, it takes more than propaganda to budge him.

Four deductions can be made from this law. Effective political action on the population must be preceded by military and police operations against the guerrilla units and the insurgent political organizations.

Political, social, economic, and other reforms, however much they ought to be wanted and popular, are inoperative when offered while the insurgent still controls the population. An attempt at land reform in Algeria in 1957 fell flat when the FLN assassinated some Moslem peasants who had received land.

The counterinsurgent needs a convincing success as early as possible in order to demonstrate that he has the will, the means, and the ability to win.

The counterinsurgent cannot safely enter into negotiations except from a position of strength, or his potential supporters will flock to the insurgent side.

In conventional warfare, strength is assessed according to military or other tangible criteria, such as the number of divisions, the positions they hold, the industrial resources, etc. In revolutionary warfare, strength must be assessed by the extent of support from the population as measured in terms of political organization at the grass roots. The counterinsurgent reaches a position of strength when his power is embodied in a political organization issuing from, and firmly supported by, the population.

THE FOURTH LAW: INTENSITY OF EFFORTS AND VASTNESS OF MEANS ARE ESSENTIAL

The operations needed to relieve the population from the insurgent's threat and to convince it that the counterinsurgent will ultimately win are necessarily of an intensive nature and of long duration. They require a large concentration of efforts, resources, and personnel.

This means that the efforts cannot be diluted all over the country but must be applied successively area by area.

STRATEGY OF THE COUNTERINSURGENCY

Translated into a general strategy, the principles derived from these few laws suggest the following step-by-step procedure:

IN A SELECTED AREA

1. Concentrate enough armed forces to destroy or to expel the main body of armed insurgents.

2. Detach for the area sufficient troops to oppose an insurgent's comeback in strength, install these troops in the hamlets, villages, and towns where the population lives.

3. Establish contact with the population, control its movements in order to cut off its links with the guerrillas.

4. Destroy the local insurgent political organizations.

5. Set up, by means of elections, new provisional local authorities.

6. Test these authorities by assigning them various concrete tasks. Replace the softs and the incompetents, give full support to the active leaders. Organize self-defense units.

7. Group and educate the leaders in a national political movement.

8. Win over or suppress the last insurgent remnants.

Order having been re-established in the area, the process may be repeated elsewhere. It is not necessary, for that matter, to wait until the last point has been completed.

The operations outlined above will be studied in more detail, but let us first discuss this strategy. Like every similar concept, this one may be sound in theory but dangerous when applied rigidly to a specific case. It is difficult, however, to deny its logic because the laws—or shall we say the facts—on which it is based can be easily recognized in everyday political life and in every recent revolutionary war.

This strategy is also designed to cope with the worst case that can confront a counterinsurgent, i.e., suppressing an insurgency in what we have called a "red" area, where the insurgent is already in full control of the population. Some of the operations suggested can obviously be skipped in the "pink" areas, most can be skipped in the "white" ones. However, the general order in which they must be conducted cannot be tampered with under normal conditions without violating the principles of counterinsurgency warfare and of plain common sense. For instance, small detachments of troops cannot be installed in villages so long as the insurgent is able to gather a superior force and to overpower a detachment in a surprise attack; Step 2 obviously has to come after Step 1. Nor can elections be staged when the insurgent cells still exist, for the elections would most likely bring forth the insurgent's stooges.

ECONOMY OF FORCES

Because these operations are spread in time, they can be spread in space. This strategy thus conforms to the principle of economy of forces, a vital one in a war where the insurgent needs so little to achieve so much whereas the counterinsurgent needs so much to achieve so little.

While a main effort is made in the selected area, necessarily at some risk to the other areas, what results can the counterinsurgent legitimately expect from his operations in these other areas? To prevent the insurgent from developing into a higher form of warfare, that is to say, from organizing a regular army. This objective is fulfilled when the insurgent is denied safe bases, and it can be achieved by purely conventional raids that do not tie down large counterinsurgent forces.

Through this strategy, insurgency can be rolled back with increased strength and momentum, for as soon as an area has been made safe, important forces can be withdrawn and transferred to the neighboring areas, swollen with locally recruited loyal and tested personnel. The transfer of troops can begin as soon as the first step is concluded.

IRREVERSIBILITY

The myth of Sisyphus is a recurrent nightmare for the counterinsurgent. By following the strategy just outlined, the counterinsurgent introduces some measure of irreversibility in his operations. When troops live among the population and give it protection until the population is able to protect itself with a minimum of outside support, the insurgent's power cannot easily be rebuilt, and this in itself is no mean achievement. But the turning point really comes when leaders have emerged from the population and have committed themselves on the side of the counterinsurgent. They can be counted upon because they have proved their loyalty in deeds and not in words, and because they have everything to lose from a return of the insurgents.

INITIATIVE

This is an offensive strategy, and it inevitably aims at regaining the initiative from the insurgent. On the national scale, this is so because the counterinsurgent is free to select the area of main effort; as soon as he does

it, he no longer submits himself to the insurgent's will. It is so equally on the local scale because he confronts the insurgent with a dilemma: accepting the challenge, and thus a defensive posture, or leaving the area and being powerless to oppose the counterinsurgent's action on the population.

In conventional warfare, when the Blues attack the Reds on Point A, the Reds can relieve the pressure by attacking the Blues on Point B and the Blues cannot escape the counterpressure. In revolutionary warfare, when the insurgent exerts pressure in Area A, the counterinsurgent cannot relieve the pressure by attacking the insurgent in Area B. The insurgent simply refuses to accept the fight, and he can refuse because of his fluidity. The Chinese Nationalists' offensive against Yenan in 1947 is an example; when the Vietminh started pressing against Dien Bien Phu in northeastern Indochina, the French command launched Operation Atlante against the Vietminh areas in Central Vietnam; Atlante had no effect on the other battle.

However, when the counterinsurgent applies pressure not on the insurgent directly but on the population, which is the insurgent's real source of strength, the insurgent cannot so freely refuse the fight because he courts defeat.

FULL UTILIZATION OF THE COUNTERINSURGENT'S ASSETS

If the insurgent is fluid, the population is not. By concentrating his efforts on the population, the counterinsurgent minimizes his rigidity and makes full use of his assets. His administrative capabilities, his economic resources, his information and propaganda media, his military superiority due to heavy weapons and large units, all of which are cumbersome and relatively useless against the elusive insurgent, recover their full value when applied to the task of obtaining the support of a static population. What does it matter if the counterinsurgent is unable on the whole to run as fast as the insurgent? What counts is the fact that the insurgent cannot dislodge a better-armed detachment of counterinsurgents from a village, or cannot harass it enough to make the counterinsurgent unable to devote most of his energy to the population.

SIMPLICITY

Why is there so little intellectual confusion in conventional warfare while there has been so much in the past counterinsurgencies? Two explanations may be advanced: When a conventional war starts, the abrupt transition from peace to war and the very nature of the war clarify most of the problems for the contending sides, particularly for the defender. The issue, whatever it was, becomes now a matter of defeating the enemy. The objective, insofar as it is essentially military, is the destruction of his forces and the occupation of his territory; such an objective provides clear-cut criteria to assess gains, stagnation, or losses. The way to reach it is by military action supported by diplomacy and economic blockade. The national organization for war is simple: The government directs, the military executes, the nation provides the tools.

We have seen that this cannot be the case in counterinsurgency warfare. Transition from peace to war is very gradual, the issue is never clear, the objective is the population, military and political actions cannot be separated, and military action—essential though it is—cannot be the main form of action.

Conventional warfare has been thoroughly analyzed in the course of centuries—indeed for almost the entire extent of recorded history—and the process of battle has been sliced into distinct phases: march toward the enemy, contact with the enemy, test of the enemy's strength, attack, exploitation of success, eventual retreat, etc. The student learns in military schools what he has to do in each phase, according to the latest doctrine. Field games are staged to give him practical training in the maneuvers he may have to conduct. When he is in the field under actual war conditions, his intellectual problem amounts to determining which phase of the battle he finds himself in; then he applies to his particular situation the general rules governing the phase. His talent, his judgment come into play only here.

This has not yet been done for counterinsurgency warfare. Who indeed has heard of field games involving the task of winning the support of the population when such a task, which, in any event, requires months of continuous effort, has no clear built-in criteria to assess the results of the games? And who is going to play the part of the population?

Simplicity in concept and in execution is an important requirement for any counterinsurgency doctrine. The proposed strategy appears to meet this. For it is not enough to give a broad definition of the goal (to get the support of the population); it is just as necessary to show how to reach it (by finding and organizing the people who are actively in favor of the counterinsurgent), and in such a way as to allow a margin of initiative to the counterinsurgent personnel who implement the strategy—and they are a widely mixed group of politicians, civil servants, economists, social workers, soldiers—yet with enough precision to channel their efforts in a single direction. The division of the over-all action into successive steps following each other in logical order facilitates the tactical tasks of the agents; they know at each step what the intermediate objective is and what they have to do to reach it.

TO COMMAND IS TO CONTROL

With the step-by-step approach, the counterinsurgent provides himself with a way of assessing at any time the situation and the progress made. He can thus exert his control and conduct the war by switching means from an advanced area to a retarded one, by giving larger responsibilities to the subordinate leaders who have proved successful, and by removing those who have failed. In other words, he can command because he can verify.

What could happen in default of control? The general counterinsurgency effort would produce an *accidental* mosaic, a patchwork of pieces with one well pacified, next to it another one not so pacified or perhaps even under the effective insurgent's control: an ideal situation for the insurgent, who will be able to maneuver at will among the pieces, concentrating on some, temporarily vanishing from others. The *intentional* mosaic created by necessity when the counterinsurgent concentrates his efforts in a selected area is in itself a great enough source of difficulties without adding to it in the selected area.

NOTES

1. Except, of course, the psychological handicap, which can be alleviated only by the protraction of the war. To solve it would require that the counterinsurgent espouse the insurgent's cause without losing his power at the same time. If it were possible to do so, then the insurgent's cause was a bad one to start with, tactically speaking.

The Psychological Instrument of Statecraft

ROBERT T. HOLT AND ROBERT W. VAN DE VELDE

As a result of the Second World War the United States found itself on a pinnacle of world power and consequently in a role of world leadership. It was a strange and unfamiliar role, and its acceptance was both reluctant and hesitant. There was little in the history and experience of the nation which provided a basis for understanding and dealing with the crucial decisions that faced its leaders at every turn. Almost immediately it became apparent that the peace for which we had fought was not to be a real peace and that the other Great Power to emerge from the war sought ends quite different from ours. Victory over the Axis did not solve all problems, as many Americans seemed to have believed it would. Indeed, compared with the simple directness of effort necessary to the conduct of actual war, the mounting complexities of the so-called Cold War period presented new problems to the American statesmen almost daily. In retrospect it is remarkable that the United States responded to the challenge with such rapidity and imagination. The Truman Doctrine, the Marshall Plan, and the North Atlantic Treaty Organization were the imaginative foreign policies which marked the abrupt change in more than 150 years of American peacetime isolation.

While new problems arose to plague the government, and as policies were developed to meet the unfolding world situation, students of international affairs were developing new terms and new concepts to describe and help more fully to understand the international circumstances facing the United States. One such concept, developed as part of an effort to provide an intellectual framework for the new policies, was that of "total diplomacy" or "total strategy."[1] The originators of this concept argued that the foreign policy goals of a Great Power could be achieved only if strategies of statecraft were developed which were based on world-wide considerations and included the integrated use of all instruments of statecraft. No major foreign policy goal, they contended, could be achieved efficiently or economically by the use of any one instrument or by the various instruments working independently of one another.

Total strategies have never been fully developed or implemented by the United States. The strategies that have been employed have not provided for the integrated use of the four major instruments of statecraft—the diplomatic, military, economic, and psychological.[2] There are undoubtedly a number of reasons for this. A presidential form of government in which there is a division of power between the executive and the legislature places limitations on the probable amount of integration that can be developed. The "built-in" frictions that exist between Congress and the White House are most evident when the same party does not control both. But even when one party is in firm control, Congress may place budgetary or other restrictions on the implementation of plans developed by the executive. Another reason for the failure to develop total strategies is that the foreign policy decision-making apparatus in the executive branch involves such a multiplicity of agencies with overlapping authority and responsibility. Perhaps less evident, but certainly no less crucial, is the fact that the democratic process itself inhibits the type of central control which can most readily achieve the coordination necessary to actual totality of action in the implementation of a decision.

But in addition to these organizational and constitutional weaknesses, the United States has failed to develop total strategies for another reason. It has never truly understood the nature of the psychological instrument. Because the instrument has not been understood, it has not been fully exploited. It is with this problem that this [chapter] is concerned.

It is not surprising that psychological operations have not been fully appreciated. Traditionally, there have only been three major instruments of statecraft, each with its own distinctive tools, techniques, and modes of operations. The military employs the weapons of physical violence. The economic involves the manipulation of the production and distribution of goods and services in an attempt to achieve certain foreign policy goals. The diplomatic is distinguished by the fact that it is primarily concerned with direct negotiations between official decision-makers from various states. For centuries these were the instruments used by the statesmen of the world. It is not that psychological operations were unknown. Indeed, Linebarger has traced their employment back to antiquity.[3] But two developments which have culminated in the twentieth century have made the psychological instrument one of the major instruments of statecraft. First, the development of mass communications has made it possible to spread information and ideas to great masses of people in countries that have experienced even a small amount of modernization. In the twentieth century for the first time in history, it has become possible for the leaders of one nation to communicate directly with the *peoples* of another nation. Second, and equally important, the twentieth century has seen the expansion of the potential or actual power base of a society. This has been particularly true in democratic states with the continual expansion of the franchise to a larger and larger segment of the population. But even the most totalitarian of the modern dictatorships can be distinguished from its authoritarian predecessor by the fact that the former is apparently forced to solicit the active support of its subjects whereas the latter could exist with mere passive acquiescence. The new-found power of the masses and the ability of a foreign power to speak directly to these masses have now made the psychological instrument of statecraft a major one.[4]

The activities involved in the use of the psychological instrument have been variously named and described. "Political warfare" and "psychological warfare" have been extensively used during and after the Second World War. The British leaned toward the former, and the United States toward the latter. "Propaganda," "The Campaign of Truth," and "war for men's minds," "communications weapon," and many more represent other attempts to define and/or give an emotional stamp to the activity in question.[5] Officially, the U.S. operations in this area have been labeled "information" and that word has appeared in almost every one of the several titles which our national propaganda agency and its ancestors have borne. This superfluity of names indicates general lack of agreement on the exact nature and role of the psychological instrument. One American scholar using the term "psychological warfare" to apply to the use of the psychological instrument generally, paraphrases Mark Twain in commenting, ". . . psychological warfare is neither psychology nor war,"[6] while another, equally astute and experienced, has a more restricted point of view, defining psychological warfare essentially as the "application of parts of the science called psychology to the conduct of war."[7] Another feels that the distinctive characteristic of psychological operations is that they attempt to influence the *will* to conduct policy as distinguished from the *capability* to conduct policy.[8] A fourth emphasizes the more strictly propaganda function of "talking" about the activities carried on by the other instruments of statecraft.[9]

The failure to develop an adequate and widely accepted concept or name for the operation of the psychological instrument has been matched by a tendency in official Washington to shun direct responsibility for its use. Note the successive changes in status as well as in name of this governmental function. Note the succession of heads of the agency charged with the function, and of presidential advisors in the area. . . . Suffice it to say here that there still exists in Washington a peculiar contradiction between an ardent lip service to the objective and a shunning of the tasks necessary to the objective's attainment. Part of this contradiction stems, perhaps, from the terms employed to describe the task. "Propaganda" awakens automatic memories of Herr Doktor Goebbels, and "warfare," whether "political," "psychological," or "communications," is inappropriate and distasteful to those who may be employing this process in an attempt to achieve a real peace.

But not only have some of the words employed been distasteful, they also indicate that the nature and scope of the activities involved have not fully been appreciated. The limits imposed by the use of any term employing the word "warfare" have already been pointed out. But the innocuous word "information," which has gained respectability, if nothing else, also indicates severe limitations in the concept of the nature of the psychological instrument of statecraft.[10] This comes out clearly in an examination of the official purposes of the various information agencies that have been established.

The language of the basic law for the U.S. "foreign information program," Public Law 402 (80 Cong.), *The United States Information and Educational Exchange Act of 1948*,[11] states: "The Congress hereby declares that the objectives of this Act are to enable the Government of the United States to promote a better understanding of the United States in other countries and to increase mutual understanding between the people of the United States and the people of other countries." Five years later, the President in his request[12] for the establishment of a separate United States Information Agency, said that the new agency is to be "for the conduct of our information programs." These, he said, "include, with certain limited exceptions, four programs; the information activities now administered by the International Information Administration of the Department of State; the information programs financed in connection with the government in occupied areas; the information program of the Mutual Security Agency; and the Technical Cooperation Administration information program." The monotonous repetition of the word "information" in agency titles and in describing their functions is representative of the narrow interpretation and lack of understanding of the psychological instrument of statecraft which has made Washington incapable of properly exploiting this twentieth-century tool. A further indication of this lack of grasp of the inherent potentialities of this instrument is the frequency with which "official" Washington as well as the general public for some time confused the entire program with, and gave to all of it the title of, *The Voice of America*.[13] The President and the National Security Council prescribed, late in 1953, that the mission of the newly created United States Information Agency would be ". . . to submit evidence to the peoples of other nations by means of communication techniques that the objectives and policies of the United States are in harmony with and will advance their legitimate aspirations for freedom, progress and peace."

On July 8, 1953, the White House released a statement on a highly classified report of the President's Committee on International Activities.[14] Judging from some of the wording of this statement, the committee seemed to come close to understanding and recommending the use of the psychological instrument. It said, "In reality, there is a psychological aspect or implication to every diplomatic, economic or military policy or action. This implication should receive more careful attention, both in the planning and execution stage of policy, but not to the exclusion of other factors." But then the statement goes on to say that "except for propaganda there are no 'psychological warfare' instruments distinct from traditional instruments of policy." One is tempted to wonder if the committee did not find that the only ready "solution" to an admittedly complex and trying problem was to deny the existence of facts which gave us the problem in the first place. It did bow to the realities of international relations to the extent of saying that the important thing was "to coordinate and time such [day-to-day governmental] actions so as

to derive from them the maximum advantages."

Later in the report the "information" process was treated at some length, but was almost entirely divorced from policy-making. Only a reportorial role was left to the "information" agency. The nation once again missed an opportunity to realize its full potential in the arena of international relations because the government deliberately denied itself the full use of the psychological instrument.

The mandate of the United States Information Agency enables it to report on and explain our foreign policy and its implementation. As a corollary, of course, it should "explain" the United States and "sell America." In other words, its mission is one easily understood by most twentieth-century Americans—that of public relations man and advertising agent for the nation. But at best this is only part of the job. In some parts of the world where the citizens are immune to the blandishments of "institutional advertising" and too closely concerned with vital problems of daily existence to listen to language better suited to say that the United States is "kind to the hands," or glistens because its people use a lanolin hair lotion, something quite different is needed.

It is a basic thesis of this [chapter] that there *is* a "psychological warfare" instrument distinct from the three more traditional instruments; that this instrument *is* as analytically separable, and as operationally inseparable, from those instruments as, say, the diplomatic is from the military. Reporting and explaining government actions is one function of that instrument; helping to coordinate and time "such actions so as to derive from them the maximum advantages" is another of its functions. But to be fully exploited the psychological instrument must also have a part in initiating policy and action. This is not to claim any position of pre-eminence for the psychological instrument; it is to plead for it a status of equality with the diplomatic, economic, and military instruments, each of which will find its role constantly moving up or down a scale of relative importance, reflecting the set of circumstances peculiar to any given world situation in response to which the particular policy must be developed or the particular action taken.

It is on this ground that the present writers find themselves in sharp disagreement with many other writers in this field who appear content with both the limited role thus far ascribed by the United States to "psychological warfare" or "information program," and content also with these self-limiting terms for that role.[15]

In order to introduce our concept of psychological operations it is necessary to discuss briefly here our view of the nature of statecraft. All foreign policies have an objective (or objectives) and a strategy. The objective is an image of a future state of affairs viewed in relationship to some present state of affairs. The strategy is a plan of action which spells out the manner in which the instruments of statecraft with their various tools and techniques are to be used to achieve the objective. The strategy of foreign policy is always aimed at achieving certain desired responses from the state or states being acted upon. For instance, it was apparent that the major objective of the Truman Doctrine was the creation of a state of affairs in Greece and Turkey in which the influence of the Soviet Union was minimal compared to the influence exercised there by the United States. The strategy (which called primarily for the use of military, economic, and technical aid together with some show of the American "flag") was designed to get the Soviet Union, Greece, and Turkey to act in certain ways believed by the United States to be in its national interest.

If one desires to develop a plan of action to influence the behavior of foreign states, he must have an idea of what determines that behavior. Snyder, Bruck, and Sapin point out that the "key to the explanation of why the state behaves as it does lies in the way its decision-makers define their situation."[16]

To influence the behavior of a state it is necessary to develop a strategy aimed at affecting the manner in which its decision-makers define the relevant situations.[17] Traditionally, strategies employing the economic, military, and diplomatic instruments of statecraft have attempted to influence foreign decision-makers' definition of the situation by materially changing the situation. Defense expenditures may be increased, an army may be moved up to a troubled border, an embargo may be placed on the shipment of certain goods. Diplomatic negotiations may lead to the formation of a new alliance. As the situation is changed, decision-makers' definition of the situation will likely change (although there almost certainly will be no one-to-one relationship between changes in the situation and the way in which various decision-makers define these changes).

But it is not only the decision-makers' definition of the foreign situation that affects their formulation of policy. Domestic considerations may also affect foreign policy decisions. Therefore, in analyzing foreign policy decision-making, it is necessary to distinguish between the decision-makers' definition of the domestic and foreign situations and to understand the relationship between them. If one's object is to precipitate certain kinds of behavior, this can be done by affecting the decision-makers' definition of either their internal or their external situation. Historically, emphasis has been placed on the external situation for the simple reason that it has been more difficult to manipulate objects and events within another state. There are, of course, some notable exceptions. The peace-makers at Vienna in 1815 were greatly concerned with the problem of legitimacy and saw as one aspect of their responsibility for keeping the peace the support and maintenance of "legitimate" governments in Europe. Germany very successfully influenced the foreign policy of Russia in 1917 by manipulating the internal situation when it sent Lenin into that faltering country.

But these examples to the contrary notwithstanding, the traditional methods for a state to influence the behavior of a foreign state have been through the manipulation of material objects, usually in the external environment of the state being acted upon. These traditional strategies involved military and/or economic operations and diplomatic negotiations.

The distinctive nature of psychological operations derives from the fact that they do not attempt to manipulate material objects, but rather try to influence the way in which material objects are perceived and interpreted.

To make this distinction more precise, one can differentiate between the world of objects and events and the way in which objects and events appear to individuals and have meaning—in other words, to distinguish between the world as it "is" and the world as it "appears" and has meaning.[18] The former we will call the *material* world and the latter the *apparent* world. They are not necessarily the same. The dramatic experiments in perception carried on by Ames and Cantril have shown that even such familiar objects as a window or a chair can be greatly distorted if they are seen in unusual surroundings, such as in a room with a sloping floor and trapezoidal walls. In such a room men appear to be either giants or pygmies, depending on where

they stand in relation to the viewer's position.

The differences between the material world and the apparent world are increased and complicated if action and time are introduced into a situation. One has only to note the different accounts eyewitnesses give, quite honestly, to an accident at which they were present. Obviously a set of "facts" exists. Two cars of certain make and model, say, approached each other at certain speeds at a certain time on a certain day and collided in a certain manner at a certain spot with certain resultant damage. This is the material world—the world as it is, or was. But both drivers, even assuming complete honesty on the part of each, may have very different versions of what happened. Furthermore, the drivers' accounts may be quite different from those of two witnesses who happened to be standing at the side of the road at the time. What is more, even the accounts of these identically placed, disinterested witnesses may vary markedly in at least some important respects. This simple example shows two things. First, that the material world and almost anyone's apparent world are often not the same and, second, that even in small, familiar situations actually witnessed, apparent worlds may be quite different from person to person.

The differences between the physical world and the apparent world become even greater, of course, if the situation being "viewed" is more abstract or complex. For example, it is highly unlikely that any two members of the President's Cabinet look on the "Middle East situation" in exactly the same terms. Yet it is likely that their apparent worlds in that area are closer to each other than any of them would be to the situation there as seen by a New York City steelworker or a Las Vegas bartender. Again, it is likely that all these Americans' views of the situation would bear more resemblance to each other than any of them would to the views held, for example, by the Deputy Minister of Defense in the Kremlin or by the Prime Minister of Egypt.

This oversimplified discussion is to emphasize that not only do the material and apparent worlds differ, but that each person's apparent world is, in large measure, delineated by his past and present cultural, educational, geographic, and occupational milieu. These two points—that the material and apparent worlds are not the same, and that individual or group apparent worlds may vary greatly—are fundamental to an understanding of the nature and importance of the psychological instrument of statecraft.

Equally important is a realization that while changes in the material world usually cause changes in the apparent world, there may be no one-to-one relationship. It is even quite possible to have a change in the apparent world without any change in the material world. Changes in either can affect behavioral responses. If a man's house is destroyed by an enemy bomb, the material world and most likely his apparent world will be changed and these changes will evoke some response in behavior and attitude. Part of the response will be "caused" by the material change; he will have to find a new place to live. But the meaning he ascribes to that change—or his new apparent world—will also affect his behavior. He may shake his fist in defiance and work doubly hard to help destroy the enemy. Or he may say to himself, "What's the use? We might as well quit before everything is lost." Changes in the apparent world can come about by various means without changes in the material world. The process of education does it daily to children, and it has been said that no one is too old to learn. The stereotypes one has of foreigners and foreign places —a manifestation of one's apparent world—are often very "real" until there

is an opportunity to travel. This is not to say that firsthand observation will cause one's apparent world to coincide with the material world. It almost certainly will not. But travel will often cause a change in the apparent world without any change in the material world at all. Again it must be stressed that the changes caused are not the same, or equal, or even in the same direction, in two persons making the same trip at the same time. What one "sees" is conditioned by what environment he grew up in, how far he went in school, what his interests are, what he *expects* to see, and what he *wants* to see. It cannot be stated too emphatically that it is man's apparent world, *not* the material world, which determines his attitude and his behavioral response to any given situation.

This discussion provides the basis for distinguishing the various instruments of statecraft and establishing the unique characteristics of the psychological. The diplomatic instrument is identified by the fact that it involves direct contact between the officials of one state with the officials of another. Many times these contacts are negotiations that lead to changes in the material world. The economic and military instruments of statecraft involve direct manipulation of the material world. The psychological instrument involves manipulation of the apparent world.

The question [is] "Whose apparent world? . . . [U]ltimately it must be the apparent world of the foreign decision-makers or what we have called their definition of the situation. But this may be achieved indirectly. Propaganda broadcasts to a foreign population might cause many people to change their attitudes toward their government's policy, which in turn might be instrumental in the decision-makers' estimation of their domestic support, which in turn could lead to a policy change. Psychological operations in a third country might contribute to a change in leadership, which in turn requires the decision-makers in other states to redefine the external situation. But whenever the initial operation involves an attempt to manipulate peoples' views of the world rather than material objects and events, one is dealing with the psychological instrument of statecraft. . . . [T]his concept of psychological operations involves something more than information, or "talk-ing" about policies, or "influencing the will to conduct policy."

One further point should be made. Obviously diplomatic, economic, and military operations do have psychological implications and in many cases it is most difficult to label an operation as *purely* economic or *purely* psychological. It is more useful to think of operations that are woven together in a strategy to affect the behavior of foreign states as *primarily* economic, *primarily* psychological, etc.

NOTES

1. E. M. Earle, "Political and Military Strategy for the U.S.," *Proceedings of the Academy of Political Science,* January, 1941, pp. 112–19; F. S. Dunn, "Peace Strategies in an Unstable World," *Yale Review,* Winter, 1948, pp. 226–40; H. and M. Sprout, *Foundations of National Power* (New York, 1951), p. 70; H. D. Lasswell, "Psychological Policy Research and Total Strategy," *Public Opinion Quarterly,* Winter, 1952–53, pp. 491–500.

2. H. and M. Sprout, pp. 40–42, include a fifth: subversion and sabotage. We would argue that this is not on the same level as the others. Subversion is more likely to be the result of the psychological and/or economic instruments, sabotage to stem from psychological and/or military factors.

3. See Paul M. A. Linebarger, *Psychological Warfare* (Washington, 1954), pp. 1–24. Philip Davidson, *Propaganda and the American Revolution* (Chapel Hill, N.C., 1941), gives a thorough account of the use of the psychological instrument of statecraft in a pre-twentieth-century period. When we talk about the "newness" of psychological operations, we are referring to their conscious, planned, organized, coordinated, and continuing use. The existing broad potential for such use is the result of twentieth-century phenomena.

4. Another point has been made by Lasswell. He argues that one development since the end of the Second World War has further increased the importance of the psychological instrument. The bipolarization of the world, he says, has limited the ". . . grand strategy of encirclement. Instead of the incessant realigning of national blocs in maneuvers of encirclement and counter encirclement, the principal strategy becomes that of penetration, which puts a premium on dividing an elite against itself, and from the rank and file." In this situation psychological operations become even more important while the value of diplomacy is somewhat depreciated. See Lasswell, p. 494.

5. Roland Perusse has listed eighteen terms that are sometimes used synonymously with "psychological warfare." See "Psychological Warfare Reappraised," in William E. Daugherty and Morris Janowitz (eds.), *A Psychological Warfare Casebook* (Baltimore, 1958), pp. 25–34—hereafter referred to as *Casebook.*

6. Saul K. Padover, "Psychological Warfare in an Age of World Revolution," *Columbia Journal of International Affairs,* V, No. 2 (Spring, 1950), 3.

7. Linebarger, p. 25.

8. Hans Speier, "Psychological Warfare Reconsidered," in D. Lerner (ed.), *Propaganda in War and Crisis* (New York, 1951), p. 465.

9. D. Lerner, *Propaganda in War and Crisis,* p. xiii.

10. In 1959 a senior official in USIA in a letter to one of the authors disclaimed for his agency the role "wielder of the psychological instrument of statecraft." And under the present charter, he is quite right.

11. Often referred to as the Smith-Mundt Act.

12. H. R. Document No. 156, 83 Cong., 1 sess., "Message from the President of the United States Relative to the Conduct of Foreign Affairs," referred to the Committee on Government Operations on June 1, 1953, pp. 3–4.

13. Even a State Department witness, claiming eight years service and pleading with a Senate committee not to separate the "information" function from State, repeatedly called it "The Voice of America," when from the context it is quite apparent that he meant the entire program. See H. R. Report 844, Part 2, 83 Cong., 1 sess., "Additional Views of George Meader" (July 16, 1953), establishing U.S. Information Agency (Reorganization Plan No. 8 of 1953), pp. 3–4.

14. Statement published in the *New York Times,* July 9, 1953. The report in question

later came to be known in government circles as "The Jackson Report," named for the committee's chairman, William H. Jackson.

15. There are numerous examples in the Daugherty and Janowitz *Casebook*. And although Daugherty does say, in the article, "Changing Concepts," pp. 12–18, "There is certainly great need for a new term, but before an acceptable one can be coined it is first necessary that there be greater agreement as to scope of the activity that has been described as 'psychological warfare,' " the tone of the editors' introductory chapter is one, if not of acceptance, at least of acquiescence in the role and the term. This really monumental work in the field is, of course, a casebook, and as such may not be appropriate as a vehicle for the editors' ideas. On the other hand, the opening remarks and the title they chose would seem to put them in at least the most recent lead of those with whom we disagree in basic concepts.

16. R. C. Snyder, H. W. Bruck, and B. Sapin, *Decision-making as an Approach to the Study of International Politics* (Princeton, 1954), p. 51—hereafter referred to as Snyder *et al., Decision-making.*

17. We recognize that the strategy to influence the behavior of a foreign state may involve initially an attempt to overthrow the existing decision-makers. The assumption would be, of course, that the new decision-makers would pursue a policy that would be more acceptable than that of the old leaders.

18. Obviously when speaking of the world as it "is" we are not referring to a world which exists apart from any human observation, for that would be a purely metaphysical concept. The distinction we are making is similar to that made by F. H. Allport. (See *Theories of Perception and the Concept of Structure* [New York, 1955], pp. 20–46.) Allport differentiates between phenomenological experience (the world as it appears) and physicalistic experience (or the world as it "is" determined by denotation or encounter).

The Political Use of Strategic Power: Soviet and Western Attitudes

ARNOLD L. HORELICK AND MYRON RUSH

INTRODUCTION

Rulers have always faced the problem of how to employ military force politically to achieve objectives that might otherwise not be achieved at all or only by engaging in hostilities. They have sought to solve the problem by employing military threats and demonstrations in support of their diplomacy. The development of thermonuclear weapons, however, has made the political use of strategic power an acute problem, for the military use of these weapons might entail terrible destruction even to the victor. The requirements, risks, and costs for the political use of strategic power are much lower than for its military use. Hence, the political use of strategic power has never been so attractive.

Since the first demonstration of the military power of the atomic bomb, statesmen have expected the acquisition of nuclear weapons to be politically valuable. Today, leaders of countries aspiring to possess nuclear weapons are more likely to be motivated in their quest by political rather than strictly military considerations. Events of the past decade, however, have also revealed something of the difficulties encountered in trying to make political capital of strategic power. The destructive capacity of the new weapons is so great that even a state which has achieved a measure of strategic superiority may nonetheless so fear the other side's inferior strategic forces as to make resort to general war a last and desperate expedient. To the extent that the weaker side has knowledge of this fear, the stronger side's efforts to extract political advantage from its superiority may be obstructed.

Awareness of these difficulties has convinced many observers that the political worth of nuclear forces has been greatly overrated and that the only purpose they can serve is to defend a state's most "vital interests."[1] Some students of the problem have questioned whether the strategic forces possessed by the United States and the Soviet Union can do much more in time of peace than neutralize the political and diplomatic value of the opposing strategic forces.

No one doubts that the advent of thermonuclear weapons and modern delivery vehicles and their availability to both sides have radically altered the international situation and that even a thermonuclear stalemate may bring some advantage to one side or the other. Nor is there much doubt that if the forces of one side were manifestly capable of launching a highly effective first strike, one that was virtually retaliation-proof, they could be used directly to achieve major political objectives. What is chiefly at issue is the political significance of real or alleged disparities in strategic forces when neither side possesses a manifestly overpowering superiority.

This [chapter] considers the use of strategic power for political ends chiefly from the perspective of Soviet foreign policy. To do so, however, it must first illuminate the general problem of the political use of nuclear forces.

Political use of strategic power does not directly depend on the objective capabilities of the two sides. It depends in the first instance on their beliefs about the strategic balance and on the beliefs of one side about the beliefs of the other and of third parties. Since it involves beliefs, and beliefs about beliefs, it is a highly subjective undertaking, once or twice removed from actual military capabilities.

Of course, it is true that the relevant beliefs are inevitably conditioned by the objective capabilities of the two sides; numerous facts regarding the strategic balance are known to the protagonists and they cannot disregard them in forming their estimates. But there are also great uncertainties in calculating the relative capabilities of revolutionary new strategic weapon systems that have never been employed in combat; these uncertainties may be compounded by incomplete information on the opponent's force structure, by doubt as to the tactics he would employ in the event of hostilities, and especially by the opponent's efforts to widen the area of uncertainty and to manipulate it to his own advantage.

To this inevitable uncertainty, which even the most rigorous analyst or military planner cannot wholly penetrate, is added the imprecision of the statesman's notions regarding strategic matters, which, being influenced by many non-technical factors, may diverge widely from the military planner's refined estimate. Yet the beliefs of statesmen are the stuff of political conflict that rests on strategic forces.

Much of the political struggle involving strategic forces takes place within the limits of this area of uncertainty. Both the calculated "resolution" whereby an inferior power defends its outposts and the bluffs or deceptions that make it possible to win positions from an equal or more powerful opponent are facilitated by the uncertainty that encompasses modern strategic capabilities.

In the era of thermonuclear weapons, uncertainty pervades all military calculations of the strategic balance. Uncertainty, however, may be substantially greater on one side than on the other; moreover, the effects of a given degree of uncertainty on both sides need not always be symmetrical. The successful political employment of strategic power does not require that one's own uncertainties be wholly overcome; it requires that the relevant uncertainties of the opponent be maximized and that the situation be so manipulated as to make the outcome of a given confrontation turn on the opponent's uncertainties rather than on one's own.

In employing their strategic forces for political ends, then, the Soviet leaders must seek to deepen their opponent's uncertainties and anxieties about the strategic balance and to conceal their own; if the required beliefs about Soviet military capabilities do not already exist, the Soviet leaders must try to induce them. This can be an exceedingly difficult undertaking. It is no mere preliminary to the political exploitation of strategic power but lies close to the heart of the enterprise. Various means are available for this purpose:

a) Soviet leaders might *assert* that they possess such capabilities or that they have the military forces that entail them.

b) Soviet leaders might *make threats* that presuppose such capabilities.

c) Soviet leaders might *demonstrate* something of their military capability to induce opponents to credit the U.S.S.R. with the requisite additional capabilities.

d) Soviet leaders might *take actions,*

violent or non-violent, that imply they are confident their strategic capabilities are what they claim them to be; acquiescence or ineffectual resistance by opponents would suggest that they shared the Soviet estimate of the strategic balance.

The first two methods have this limitation: The assertions and threats must themselves be credible. Demonstrations, on the other hand, are often persuasive only to the extent that they reveal secrets; thus they may achieve their object only at the cost of surrendering advantages that secrecy confers. The most effective means available to the U.S.S.R. to induce in an opponent the desired beliefs about the strategic balance is to take actions, backed by strategic threats, that impinge on important interests of that opponent. Such actions might include non-violent measures; for example, the unilateral rescinding of rights, privileges, or immunities created by prior agreements (closing the access routes from West Germany to West Berlin), aggression against countries allied with the United States, and even limited military attacks on the opponent himself. However, if the party whose interests are to be harmed by such actions does not already have the required beliefs regarding Soviet capabilities, the actions may be extremely risky. On the other hand, less risky, more ambiguous actions that only impinge on peripheral interests of the opponent may not significantly influence his beliefs about the strategic balance. Thus far in the cold war, the Soviet leaders have relied chiefly on assertions, threats, demonstrations, and peripheral actions to achieve their ends; they have been reluctant to risk direct action against major Western interests. As we shall see, this reluctance, grounded in the Soviet leaders' sober appraisal of the strategic balance, has had far-reaching effects on the conduct of Soviet foreign policy.

The political use of strategic power poses further requirements. To employ strategic power effectively on behalf of a specific political objective, Soviet leaders also have to make their opponents believe that the alleged correlation of strategic power necessitates conciliation of the Soviet Union *on the question at issue*. It is a little like bringing a queen to bear in chess in order to reconcile one's opponent to defeat in an engagement between pawns. The threat to employ strategic forces militarily in some contingency can be varied as required from a mere rumor of doubtful origin to veiled or implicit threats in the middle range and on upward toward—though it may always fall well short of—the classical ultimatum. For all its flexibility, the threat of strategic attack with nuclear weapons is a dangerous game, pervaded by uncertainty, in which both sides take risks.

The political use of strategic force by the Soviet Union in pursuit of major gains entails major costs and risks. It tends to increase hostility toward and suspicion of the U.S.S.R. in the West and can also lessen Soviet influence among unaligned countries. In such circumstances, policies that are most fruitful in a relatively relaxed international atmosphere may suffer and even have to be abandoned. Moreover, the uncertainty in any direct confrontation between the two chief powers, when intensified by the threatened employment of strategic forces, creates risks that cannot reasonably be assumed in order to achieve a small object and that are greatly amplified if the object sought is weighty.

The difficulties, costs, and risks involved in the political use of strategic forces are formidable; yet, as we shall see, the Soviet leaders have not always been deterred by them. They have tested the efficacy of this political tool in the nuclear age, experiencing some of the benefits as well as the hazards.

Now, after a period of comparative quiescence in the cold war, they must again decide what political role to assign to their strategic forces in the future. The fate of mankind may depend on their choice.

I

Unlike the physical effects of nuclear weapons, which can be calculated without reference to the politics of those who might be destroyed by them, their political effects cannot be analyzed apart from the political character and objectives of the parties possessing them. Few would argue with this statement. Yet many write as if nuclear weapons, which in war "would not distinguish between Communists and non-Communists, between atheists and believers, between Catholics and Protestants,"[2] also reduced to insignificance the political differences between the powers possessing them. This view manifests itself in diverse ways in Western literature on the cold war, military strategy, arms control, and disarmament. The advent of nuclear weapons and the idea of indiscriminate, universal destruction that is associated with them have contributed to the widespread popularity of the thesis of the "mirror image" as the principal cause of international tension: The Soviet leaders perceive (falsely) in the United States a threat to their country's security that is a mirror-image of the threat to American security that we perceive (falsely) in the Soviet Union.[3] In this view, the cold war is chiefly the product of dangerous mutual misperceptions. Some have carried the argument to the point of denying that there are any essential differences in the political character or the goals of the two great powers.[4]

This particular interpretation of the behavior of the parties engaged in the cold war, which emphasizes its symmetrical character, originated for the most part among psychologists. But some strategic analysts, too, are inclined to approach international relations as if the powers contending in the real world were the faceless "Reds" and "Blues" of the war-game room, where each side is equally motivated to maximize its "payoffs," which are defined according to certain objective, hence mutually shared, criteria. In the burgeoning field of arms control and disarmament studies, the assumption, usually implicit, that the political objectives of both sides engaged in the cold war are equally dominated by a desire to avoid thermonuclear war often leads to a preoccupation with technical schemes for breaking the deadlock that fail to cope adequately with the large and crucial area of political disagreement between the two sides, which extends beyond their shared concern over sheer survival.

But the powers confronting one another are not faceless, nor are they simply suffering from hallucinations reciprocally induced by staring at one another through a distorting pane they have mistaken for plate glass. The differences between the two sides are real and substantial, and they intrude themselves into virtually every facet of the interplay between them. To acknowledge this is not necessarily to make moral judgments regarding these differences. Certainly, it does not follow from their existence that they can be resolved only by the annihilation of one side by the other or by their mutual destruction. But to live with these differences in an age of thermonuclear weapons, it is first necessary to recognize that they exist and to understand their implications.

The differences that concern us in this study are those that bear most directly on the political use of strategic power by the two sides. They arise between

1. the foreign policy objectives of the contending powers;

2. the means available to them for pursuing their objectives;

3. the principles that guide their employment of these means and their distinctive styles of political warfare; and

4. the constraints under which they operate in conducting the struggle.

Differences in these areas strongly condition the attitudes of the leaders of the two sides toward the political use of strategic power and, specifically, toward ways of coping with the uncertainties inherent in calculations of the strategic balance.

The political employment of strategic nuclear threats by both the Soviet Union and the United States has become a well-established phenomenon of international life in recent years. There is, however, a fundamental distinction between the purposes for which these threats have been used by the two sides: the Soviet Union has issued such threats principally in support of its efforts to extend Soviet power or influence into non-Communist areas of the world; the United States has resorted to strategic threats for defensive purposes, to preserve allied or friendly non-Communist countries from Communist domination. In other words, United States strategic power has not been brought to bear politically to overthrow Communist regimes. The battlefronts of the cold war have been almost exclusively in non-Communist areas, although military operations, once begun, have sometimes extended to Communist territory, as in North Korea and North Vietnam. In neither instance, however, did the United States even threaten to employ its full military power in order to bring about the elimination of Communist regimes in these countries. During the Cuban crisis of October, 1962, United States strategic power was brought to bear politically but only in pursuit of a limited objective—the removal of Soviet offensive weapons from the island—and not to secure the removal of the Castro regime.

The Soviet Union, on the other hand, has made broad and differentiated use of strategic threats in support of a wide range of offensive foreign policy objectives. "Strategic threats" is used here as a broad term for the expression by one government, verbally or by other means, of an intention to employ its strategic forces against another in certain circumstances. The nature of Soviet strategic threats has varied with the particular situation, the political interest to be served, and the audience to be influenced. Typically, Soviet strategic threats have fallen far short of being ultimatums; often they have been no more than warnings, menacing insinuations, vague predictions of dire consequences, or merely claims of Soviet strategic strength placed in suggestive contexts. Usually the employment of Soviet strategic power was threatened as the *possible ultimate consequence,* not as the *certain and immediate consequence,* of an opponent's failure to satisfy a Soviet demand.

The demands have also varied greatly in kind and in degree as well as in the time period allowed for their satisfaction. Most frequently, the Soviet leaders have required that an opponent refrain from some action that he was allegedly contemplating (for example, a Turkish attack on Syria, 1957; United States attacks on Iraq, 1958, and on Cuba, 1960). Threats covering such demands may be considered "empty threats" if the party threatened is in any case disinclined to carry out the forbidden action. But such threats are not without political value since third parties, or even the threatening side, may interpret failure to act as evidence that the threatened party has yielded to the threat.

On other occasions, the Soviet Union has demanded that an opponent cease activities in which he was already engaged (for example, the Anglo-French-Israeli attack on Egypt, 1956; American U-2 flights over the Soviet Union, 1960). Still other threats have been designed to coerce the opponent into initiating some positive action (for example, withdrawal of allied troops from West Berlin, 1958–62). Since non-compliance is immediately apparent following demands of the last two types, the time period specified for compliance is particularly important.

All these threats, warnings, and menaces emanating from the Soviet leaders have had one thing in common: they have invoked the image of thermonuclear war in support of Soviet political interests. This image has been present in one form or another even though the immediate and direct employment of Soviet strategic forces has rarely been threatened explicitly except in response to a strategic attack on the U.S.S.R. or its allies. Although the sanction threatened is thermonuclear war, precisely when, how, and even by whom such a war might actually be initiated is frequently not spelled out. Only the danger that such a war may occur and the conditions for averting it are specified: if the West fails to acquiesce in Soviet demands war may occur; acquiescence will avert war.

The Soviet *Juridical Dictionary* provides a useful definition of the term "threat" in the broad sense in which it is employed in this [chapter]:

> A threat is a special form of influencing a victim psychologically so as to compel him to commit some action or other, or to refrain from committing it, in the interests of the threatener. This type of threat in certain circumstances . . . may paralyze the will of the victim and lead to the result desired. . . .[5]

The Soviet Union has not attempted to secure changes in the status quo directly by the use of strategic threats. Non-strategic means have been employed as the direct instruments: the use of or threat to use Soviet conventional military strength (as in East-ern Europe, 1945–48; in Iran, 1946; in Berlin since 1948); proxy armies (as in Korea, 1950–53); the export of weapons (as to Egypt and Syria in 1955); support of subversion and guerrilla warfare (as in Greece, 1947–48, and Laos, 1960–61). Strategic threats have typically been employed to enhance the effect of these non-strategic instruments and to limit the West's freedom of action in opposing them.

In their use of strategic threats the Soviet leaders have sought to plant in non-Communist audiences an impression of the great discrepancy between the universally destructive character of thermonuclear war and the seemingly narrow and remote character of the issue of the moment. In effect, they argue: Who wants to die to prevent an East German instead of a Russian from checking Allied documents? Since the West has not pressed for similar "small" changes in the Communist status quo for their own advantage, it has often been made to appear that the danger of thermonuclear war arises from Western intransigence and bellicosity on behalf of a myopic, reactionary defense of the non-Communist status quo. To prevent armed conflict the status quo in the non-Communist world must be adjusted by negotiations and mutual concessions; the status quo in the Communist world need not be changed because it poses no threat to world peace.

In contemporary circumstances, use of strategic threats for offensive political purposes is tantamount to nuclear blackmail. It is calculated to capitalize on mankind's fear of thermonuclear war and on uncertainties regarding Soviet strategic intentions and capabilities, which are fostered by Soviet secrecy. By indulging in this practice, the Soviet leaders have artificially raised international tension in order to advance their political interests. They have relied on the restraint, responsibility, and forbearance of the West, particularly the United States, to prevent the arms race from getting out of control. The evident contrast between the Soviet penchant for using strategic threats and the restraint and responsibility of the American response has at times served Western interests; but it can have this effect only if Soviet threats fail to produce their intended effects. If Soviet threats succeed, United States restraint may be perceived by others as aloofness or fear of commitment.

In taking political advantage of mankind's concern over the danger of thermonuclear war, the Soviet leaders have relied heavily on the great uncertainties that attend calculations of the strategic balance and of the intentions of the powers possessing nuclear weapons. Western leaders have tended to regard the possibility of miscalculations of the strategic balance as a source of great danger; Soviet leaders, on the other hand, have sought to capitalize on such miscalculations. In the past these divergent attitudes toward uncertainty significantly influenced military planning on both sides.

Whereas the United States tended to insure against its own uncertainty or against Soviet miscalculation by acquiring larger strategic forces than might otherwise have been deemed necessary, the U.S.S.R. procured only a limited capability to attack the United States, relying heavily on its ability to convey exaggerated impressions of this capability. Although it is true that the United States is better able than the Soviet Union to pay for "insurance," the difference in attitudes is only partially explicable by the difference in the sizes of the United States and Soviet economies. More fundamental are differences between the *functions* of strategic forces as seen by the two sides and differences in the extent of reliance on *non-strategic means* for deterrence and for the achievement of positive objectives.

The United States strategic force has been designed to deter a Soviet attack on the United States and, in addition, to deter local Soviet military aggression and political aggrandizement. The Soviet strategic force also serves as a deterrent, but essentially as a deterrent to United States and Western responses to its own military and political offensives. From the Soviet point of view, the threat posed by the American strategic force at any given moment is the product of American capabilities multiplied by the provocation offered by Soviet behavior. The former is only partially amenable to Soviet influence, but the latter is essentially under the control of the Soviet leaders, who, enjoying the initiative, may either intensify or moderate their behavior as circumstances require. The United States, on the other hand, tends to see the immediate danger as the product of the relative military capabilities of the rival strategic force coupled with the extent of Western resistance to Soviet pressures. The Soviet leaders can avoid being provocative when circumstances are not favorable; they can always resume the offensive at some later time. But the West feels it must permanently maintain on a high level its capacity to resist encroachment lest temporary slackness be exploited—politically, if not militarily—by the vigilant opponent. Thus, strategic insurance seems necessary because control of tension is judged to reside in Soviet hands. The political yield from Western weapons always seems to lag behind their objective military capabilities. Uncertainty is viewed as tending to work in the opponent's favor, with the result that larger forces recommend themselves as means to reduce potentially dangerous uncertainties, one's own as well as the opponent's.

The Soviet leaders, on the other hand, apparently regard themselves as the beneficiaries of the non-linear relationship between the political and military value of strategic weapons. The advantage they derive is not simply the opportunity to cut costs for strategic forces but also the wider range of options to Soviet decision-makers and strategic planners. Increments in Soviet strategic power, even if they are not large enough to alter significantly the real strategic balance, may have disproportionately large political consequences, because the Soviet leadership is often able to magnify their effects by playing on the anxieties and uncertainties of its opponents.

Western uncertainty regarding Soviet strategic capabilities and intentions has been a prime asset of the Soviet Union throughout most of the cold war. Soviet secrecy, effective in varying degrees over the years, has greatly facilitated the efforts of Soviet leaders to manipulate Western uncertainty. In recent years, technological innovations have greatly improved the West's ability to penetrate Soviet secrecy, and the Soviet leaders have lifted the veil somewhat themselves, but the relative lack of information about Soviet capabilities continues to be an important fact of life in the cold war.

Soviet secrecy embraces not only denial to foreigners of access to facilities in the U.S.S.R. deemed to be of strategic significance but also tight control over the output of Soviet media of communication. It is true that the content of Soviet communications has changed in many significant ways since Joseph Stalin's death, but the ability of Soviet leaders to control what is communicated has not lessened appreciably. The West, by contrast, not only speaks with many voices but listens with many ears. The significance of this difference for the conduct of the cold war by the two sides can hardly be exaggerated. For the cold war, on a day-by-day basis, is to a remarkable extent a war of words. It is largely by verbal means that the intentions, will, and resolution of the adversaries—as well as something of their capabilities—are communicated to one another and to third parties.

Warnings, threats, counterthreats, and ultimatums are the characteristic language of the cold war. Clearly, it is what is believed to be behind the words —the power and will to use it—that determines their credibility. But the West has frequently been highly uncertain in its beliefs about Soviet strategic intentions and capabilities and this uncertainty has often compelled it to weigh carefully the words of the Soviet leaders.

The Soviet leaders are both more strongly inclined and better able to convey exaggerated impressions of their strategic power than are their opponents. They have in fact engaged in deliberate, systematic, and sustained strategic deception against the West. . . . [H]ere it is pertinent to identify another fundamental difference between the two systems that are engaged in the cold war, a difference that makes deceptive practices more feasible for the Soviet Union and vulnerability to their effects more likely in the West.

Governments disposing of nuclear weapons bring them to bear politically in order to influence the policies of other governments in ways that favor their interests. To influence Communist policy in the cold war means to influence the small circle of rulers in Moscow and in Peking, and perhaps the ruling groups in some other Communist capitals; but given the nature of the political process in Western societies and within the Western alliance as a whole, to influence the West's policies means to influence the governments, parties, or peoples allied to the United States as well as important private groups in America itself. The Communists can bring pressure and propaganda to bear at many more points than the West, since all the groups mentioned, as well as articulate opinion in neutral countries, can make their influence felt in Washington. Of course, the most far-reaching and rapid results can be achieved by directly influencing the estimates and beliefs of the top United States and Soviet decision-makers themselves, and both sides have tried repeatedly to do this, with varying degrees of success. But this is far more difficult to accomplish than to exert indirect pressure on them by influencing groups whose opinions they consider important. The top decision-makers, though they lack important information about the capabilities and intentions of their opponents and are therefore uncertain regarding certain crucial strategic matters, are nevertheless far better informed than any other group or party and less vulnerable to the adversary's attempts to mislead. For this reason the strongest Soviet pressures and threats have usually been directed against governments and peoples allied to the United States.

The ability of the Soviet Union to invoke, for self-serving political purposes, the image of a thermonuclear war that would imperil the peoples of distant lands has provided the Soviet leaders with a powerful new instrument of foreign policy. With the aid of this instrument the Soviet Union has become a truly global power, as it was not during Stalin's rule. To exert Soviet influence in distant places, Stalin had at his disposal a world-wide network of disciplined Communist parties and front organizations, but at the time of his death they were largely discredited and increasingly ineffective as instruments of Soviet foreign policy. The chief military means at Stalin's disposal—the large conventional Soviet ground forces—made it necessary for him to limit his active foreign policy interventions to countries in contiguous areas that could be threatened by Soviet bayonets. Of course, Stalin had become so rigid in his strategic thought and so Byzantine in his style of political action that he might have proved incapable of fashioning political strategies and tactics appropriate for exploiting intercontinental nuclear weapons even had he possessed them. In any case, it was left for his successors, and particularly Nikita Khrushchev, who came to power when the U.S.S.R. began to acquire the new weapons, to develop and to test such strategies and tactics. . . .

NOTES

1. Louis J. Halle, for example, contends that "the diplomatic uses of a nuclear panoply are limited largely to situations in which one is defending, against external attack, a *status quo* considered vital" ("Peace in Our Time," *New Republic*, December 25, 1963, p. 17).

2. N. S. Khrushchev, *Sovetsko-frantsuzskaia druzhba: zalog mira* ("Franco-Soviet Friendship: Pledge of Peace") (Moscow: Gosudarstvennoe Izdatel'stvo Politicheskoi Literatury, 1960), p. 35.

3. See, especially, Urie Bronfenbrenner, "The Mirror Image in Soviet-American Relations: A Social Psychologist's Report," *Journal of Social Issues*, XVII (1961), No. 3, 45–56.

4. See, for example, Erich Fromm, *May Man Prevail* (Garden City, N.Y.: Doubleday & Co., 1961), *passim*.

5. *Juridical Dictionary* [*Iuridicheskii slovar'*] (2d ed.: Moscow: Gosudarstvennoe Izdatel'stvo Iuridicheskoi Literatury, 1956), Vol. II, p. 550.

Making Threats Is Not Enough

ROGER FISHER

International conflicts exist because one government is unhappy with what another government is doing or is planning to do. We can therefore at any particular time think of a conflict as an attempt by one government to influence another to do something or not to do something. In international conflict as elsewhere our first reaction to somebody's doing something we don't like is to think of doing something unpleasant to them. In South Africa, we do not like apartheid; we promptly think of stopping future investment in South Africa. We oppose the unilateral declaration of independence by the white minority in Rhodesia, so we plan economic sanctions against Rhodesia. We want North Vietnam to stop the military and political support they are giving to the Vietcong, so we bomb them. Egypt, being opposed to Israel and her policies, decides to block Israeli traffic through the Suez Canal and the Gulf of Aqaba. Our instant reaction is to make it unpleasant for those who are doing or threatening to do what we do not like. We cut off trade, stop aid, stir up public opinion, pass resolutions of censure in the United Nations General Assembly, and institute retaliatory bombing. Whether we think it through or not, the implicit goal of our action is to cause the other government to make some decision. We want to cause them to change their mind. Our action is effective or not depending upon how it affects people's minds.

Raising the cost to an adversary of pursuing the course of action we do not like may not, however, be a good way to exert influence. Imposing pain may not be a good way to produce a desired decision. This is particularly true when the international adversary is a government, which necessarily means a group, a committee, a bureaucracy. Obviously cost is not wholly irrelevant. It is most relevant where we are trying to prevent a decision which has not yet been made. Much of our strategy relates to such potential conflict. We make a highly credible threat in order to deter a government from doing something they had not yet decided to do and perhaps had no intention of doing anyway. The deterrent frequently appears to work. But a present conflict, as contrasted with a potential one, involves an attempt to change a government's mind. We want them to stop doing something they are doing, or to do something they are not doing. As a means of bringing about a change of intention, a foreign policy which concentrates on raising costs to an adversary is likely to prove both ineffective as to them and costly for us.

THE INEFFECTIVENESS OF INFLICTED PAIN

Inflicting pain upon an adversary government is, for a number of reasons, likely to be a poor way of getting them to change their mind. The government

whose mind we want to change anticipated some costs when they decided to
do what we do not like. The costs
which they anticipated were not sufficient to deter them. For us to inflict
pain may simply be to impose costs
which they have already taken into account. To act as they expected is
hardly likely to cause them to reverse
their position.

The theory of inflicting pain upon
another country rests upon the premise
that its government will change their
mind in order to avoid further pain.
Bombing power plants and other targets in North Vietnam, insofar as it was
initiated for the purpose of producing
a political decision, was carried out in
order to make credible the threat of
additional bombing. Present sanctions
exert influence only if they communicate something about the future. They
are intended to convey a convincing
message that unless the decision we desire is made the situation will get worse.
As in a labor strike, each day's infliction of pain is primarily for the purpose of communicating a vivid threat
to inflict additional pain in the future.
If the costs being imposed are no worse
than those that had been feared, a
government is given no reason to reverse their position.

To be sure, pain and costs in actuality may be more impressive than
they were in contemplation. The government we are seeking to influence
may have underestimated the actual
consequences of economic sanctions or
of a bombing program. It is equally
probable, however, and perhaps more
so, that imposed costs will seem less
onerous in actuality than in contemplation. People adapt quickly to adverse circumstances. A future that
might have looked intolerable is proved
to be tolerable. The bombing of North
Vietnam by the United States probably
did more to convince the leaders of
Hanoi that their economy could take it
than it did to make the costs seem im-

possible to bear. The threat of B-52
bombings was perhaps more awe-inspir-
ing than the bombings themselves.

Other considerations also suggest
that inflicting pain upon an adversary
may be worse than useless. There is a
common tendency to treat sunken costs
as invested capital. The greater the
costs we impose upon our adversary,
the greater the amount which they will
regard themselves as having committed
to their present course of action: "Having invested this much in the war of
liberation, we cannot quit now. Having lost so many lives and most of our
power plants, we should not now abandon the effort."

Finally, imposing additional costs
may be like implementing a threat to
kill hostages or prisoners of war: each
cost imposed reduces the amount that
could be saved by yielding to the demand. Suppose an adversary has twenty
power plants. We bomb ten and say,
"Will you quit now to save ten?" They
refuse. We knock out five more and
say, "Will you quit now to save five?"
Although the marginal value of the
remaining plants will have risen, our
adversaries are likely to conclude that
if they would not quit before to save
twenty plants they should not quit now
to save five.

To overcome these difficulties we
are tempted to increase the amount of
pain we impose. "So," we think, "they
thought they could get away cheaply;
we will show them how high the costs
are really going to be." Can we, by
thus imposing unexpectedly high costs,
expect to change their minds?

The first problem is whether the
higher costs are in fact unexpected. Our
adversaries may have foreseen better
than we what we would do. They are
likely to think the worst of us. We are
likely to be optimistic and to hope that
modest efforts will be sufficient. This
appears to have been the situation
during the early stages of the bombing
of North Vietnam. At a time when the

bombing was still light and far removed from Hanoi and Haiphong, the government of North Vietnam spent a great deal of effort on building bomb shelters in Hanoi and on dispersing industry and population. The United States had made no decision to bomb Hanoi and presumably did not expect to do so. While we were presenting them with the vague threat of pain tomorrow if they did not change their mind today, they had in fact already decided not to change their mind even though the level of destruction increased substantially. As the United States stepped up its bombing program, it simply reached levels which had already been anticipated. Although our bombing program changed, the change had been expected. And we knew it had been expected. We should not have been surprised that it was an ineffective way of producing a change in North Vietnam's conduct.

Even where a change has been unexpected, a marginal increase in the costs we are inflicting is not likely to appear to them sufficient to justify reversing their decision. At any one time incurred costs are water over the dam. It is the increase in the threat that matters, and there, too, marginal changes are likely to be insignificant. Everyday experience illustrates the psychological difficulty involved in trying to change a person's mind by increasing the expected cost to him of continuing his actions. If my son is doing something even though I have threatened to spank him ten times for doing it, a threat to spank him twelve times is unlikely to produce better results. If I have decided to build a house at a rather high cost, my contractor knows I will not abandon the enterprise despite marginal increases in that cost.

With a group or a government, the problems are multiplied. First, there is a natural inertia which tends to prevent the reconsideration of decisions already taken—a past decision will continue to govern future conduct even though some of the facts change. Governments cannot reconsider a decision every day. And marginal changes in the cost rarely appear to justify putting a matter back on the agenda at all, since the new problem seems so much like the one already considered and disposed of. We may think that by increasing the pain a little bit every day we have made the adversary reconsider their actions every day. But they may never have seen a new decision as coming up for consideration at all. Their old decision simply continued to govern.

Even if increasing pain puts the matter back on their agenda, making the decision we want will look to them not like a new question but rather like the reversal of a decision already taken. We will be asking them to change their mind and back down because of a little more pain. It is even more difficult for a committee to abandon a course of action to which it has become committed than for an individual to do so, particularly in the face of what is sure to appear as blackmail. No individual in the group wants to be the coward who suggests that the best course might be to yield to pain and give up. Nobody wants to be the one who says, "It didn't work so let's change our policy. We made a mistake. Let's try something else." His status and his reputation among his colleagues are likely to be more important to him than any marginal contribution he might make to the national interest by sticking his neck out. Particularly in response to foreign pressure, any one member of the group may find it personally costly to suggest that the government ought to yield or otherwise to reverse their course. Each may keep his views to himself until it appears that the current of opinion for a change is running strong within the group. Under these circumstances actual support for a change may never be disclosed. If a committee is building a hospital, and the structure has progressed to the third floor when the builder comes in to inform them that the fourth floor will cost $100,000 more than anticipated, the committee is unlikely to abandon the project. The more gradual the escalation of cost the less likely that its increase will cause a change of position.

Discounting renders marginal increases in cost ineffective because an adversary will not be influenced by our doing what they more or less expected us to do. The threat of a drastic increase in pain is likely to be ineffective because it will not be believed. Another government will not be influenced by what they do not expect to happen. The threat of a small increase in bombing is always credible. But verbal threats of drastic escalation are looked at with doubt. Actions speak louder than words, and what we are doing now by way of imposing gradual rising costs suggests what we are likely to do in the future more clearly than can anything we say.

There is another and somewhat peculiar factor which makes it difficult for a government to reverse a decision taken in the face of a risk. A group which has decided to launch a project despite the *chance* that there will be high costs tends to confuse that decision with a decision to complete the project despite the *certainty* that the costs turn out to be high. A decision to start doing something which takes into account certain risks will be confused with a decision to proceed even though the risks materialize. It is impossible to articulate clearly those limited risks which a group of people are taking into account and the risks which they are not.

Examples will illustrate the phenomenon. Suppose a corporation is considering whether to start work excavating for the foundations of a building despite the fact that bids on the

building have not yet come in. It is pointed out that the excavation will cost only $50,000 and that if the building is to be built at all it will be highly desirable to save time. The group discusses the risk that the bids will come in high—so high that the entire plan should be reconsidered. But the group decides to go ahead and start the excavating and to take that chance. Although the operative decision was to risk $50,000 on the high probability that the bids would be acceptable, such a group will almost certainly later believe that they decided to "go ahead with the building" despite high costs— to build even if the lowest bid was much higher than expected. A group decision on Friday to buy groceries for a Sunday picnic despite the possibility of rain will almost inevitably be understood on Sunday morning as a decision to go ahead on the picnic even though the sky now looks threatening indeed.

This process undoubtedly worked on the group in Rhodesia which decided to declare independence despite the small risk that sanctions would impose high costs. Increasing the bite of sanctions did not change their minds even though the costs may have turned out to be much greater than they thought probable. There were no doubt North Vietnamese leaders who were aware of the risk of American bombing when they first decided to step up infiltration. They may later have thought that in deciding to go ahead despite that risk they had decided to persevere after that risk became a demonstrated certainty.

One further reason that increasing a threat, marginally or drastically, does not usually work as well as we hope is that our adversaries see that in carrying out the threat we are hurting ourselves, too. To inflict pain involves a cost to us as well as a cost to them. Carrying out a threat is something we do not want to do except to exert influence. The same thinking which leads us to believe that imposing costs on our adversaries will cause them to change their mind leads them to believe that the costs we are imposing on ourselves are likely to make us change our mind. The bombing of North Vietnam from mid-1965 to mid-1967 cost the United States at least $4 billion in airplane equipment alone. Whatever the monetary value of destruction we inflicted on North Vietnam during that period, it was almost certainly less than that. We looked at the destruction we had caused and could not understand why the rising cost of the war did not influence them to change their mind. They undoubtedly looked at the costs to us and were led to believe that they were so high that we would change our mind. They may have been wrong. But their political logic was as good as ours. Had we considered the net impact of the bombing as it appeared to them—in their eyes it was probably costing us more than it was costing them—we might have better understood the failure of the bombing to exert the kind of influence it was intended to exert.

INCREASING THE PAIN IS COSTLY TO US

Not only is threat making likely to be ineffective in persuading an adversary government to change their mind, it is likely to be unduly costly to us. It may seem as if we pay only modest costs in making a threat. We may look like a bully. Our international reputation as a leader whom others would like to follow may be damaged, and this may undercut our ability to continue to exert influence in the situation. Such immediate costs of our making a threat usually seem small if the threat is merely a verbal one. However, most of the threats we are discussing are "action threats," threats of carrying out future action which are communicated by the actions we are now taking and the pain we are now inflicting. Economic sanctions communicate a credible threat of further sanctions, bombing a threat of further bombing, and the breaking of diplomatic relations the threat of international isolation.

These threats by action involve greater immediate costs to us. First, there are out-of-pocket costs. Economic sanctions cost us lost trade and lost opportunities for future trade. It is expensive to maintain a huge military arsenal at the ready, or to mobilize and transport troops in order to show that we can and will use military force. The program of bombing in North Vietnam cost our economy a great deal. These out-of-pocket costs also represent opportunity costs—there are other useful ways to spend the resources, both at home and abroad. Second, since it is generally regarded as immoral to inflict pain simply to prove that you are willing and able to inflict it, we damage both our reputation and self-esteem. This immorality is so compelling that we will always advance some other justification for an action threat: we refer to it as interdiction, or retaliation, or even self-defense. Deliberate pain whose only justification is to extort a decision too closely resembles torture. If we did not have the interdiction rationale for the bombing of North Vietnam—the contention that our bombing of the North was not only to exert influence but also physically to prevent military supplies from reaching the South—the bombing would have been intolerably immoral both at home and abroad. This necessary gap between our primary motive of threatening future costs and our alleged justification results in a third cost, an almost inevitable "credibility gap," resulting from multiple and inconsistent explanations of military or other measures.

There are other costs of threat

making inherent in the international system. There are styles in international conflict: countries follow the precedents of others in the ways in which they seek to exert influence. A retaliatory raid by Israel may have more impact as an example than as a deterrent. Threats by one become a justification for threats by others. Reciprocal escalation is the consequence of two countries trying to influence each other by threats of demonstrated credibility. This style is costly and destructive to international order. It does not easily lead to solutions.

Another cost of threat making is that it diverts our attention from exactly what it is that we would like to have an adversary do. Britain devoted almost all its attention in the first year after Rhodesian independence to making economic sanctions "effective." Effectiveness was being measured in terms of the extent to which trade was being impeded, not in terms of the extent to which Rhodesians were being influenced to make a decision which Britain wanted. Almost no attention was devoted to the process by which a reduction in Rhodesia's economic welfare was supposed to convert that country into a functioning biracial democracy.

A decision to threaten and the later decision to implement that threat if the adversary fails to respond as we wish are two quite different matters. What exerts influence on an adversary is the risk of unpleasant consequences. They do not need to be certain that we will carry out a threat, nor do we. The fact that it is wise to make a threat does not mean that if our attempt to exert influence fails it will also be wise to carry it out. This is one reason why a decision to threaten is seductively attractive. The postponed costs are not immediately evident. We hope that the threat will be effective, in which case we will get something for very little. If it is not effective, it appears that we

will still have open the choice of what to do then. Since that choice need not be made until later, it is easy at the outset simply to make the threat.

The real costliness of threat making lies in the fact that the postponed bills are likely to be large. If the threat fails, both courses open to us will probably be costly. Failure to implement our threat may reduce our credibility. We can afford to bluff occasionally without ruining our capacity to exert influence. But we cannot bluff every time without making future threats worthless. On the other hand, there are heavy costs in implementing the threat. The out-of-pocket costs are likely to be much larger than the costs of making the threat in the first place. More serious are the costs of doing something we have no reason for doing except that we said we would. There are, of course, some kinds of threats which we would like to carry out anyway: implementing that kind of threat may give us some actual benefit. But most of the threats we make in attempting to influence an adversary are threats of action we do not particularly want to take; such as stopping trade or aid, cutting off diplomatic relations, or taking military action. Once influence has failed it is to nobody's interest that we implement the threat except insofar as we need to in order to retain our credibility. Yet we are likely to take action harmful to both sides and may well accomplish nothing at all.

This problem is particularly acute in the case of our nuclear-deterrent strategy. American nuclear weapons are intended to deter the Soviet Union from using nuclear weapons against the United States. There is an implied demand, "Do not drop bombs on our territory," and an implied threat, "If you do, we will go to war." This may be an appropriate threat, but we should recognize that what we ought to do if a Soviet nuclear missile were in fact to strike Miami is a totally different question.

Presumably we would go to war. But why? "Why" in the sense of historical explanation would be clear, but "why" in the sense of purpose would not be. Would we be seeking to conquer the Soviet Union and occupy its territory? Seeking compensation for Miami? Seeking an apology? Seeking to change their political leadership? Or would we be destroying a substantial part of the world in order to maintain our reputa-

tion as a country willing to do so? Before making threats a government should look ahead to a situation in which the threat has failed to exert the desired influence. Whatever our offer and threat, it is at least possible that influence will fail. We ought to consider the position we would be in, the choices with which we would be faced, and the purposes for which we would then be acting.

A DECISION TO THREATEN BECOMES A DECISION TO IMPLEMENT THE THREAT

There is another reason why threats are costly and why we therefore ought to select with care the threats we make. The future option to bluff or to implement the threat is not as open a choice as it appears. A group tends to treat a decision to threaten as a decision to implement the threat even though analytically these are quite different decisions. We are likely to find ourselves dragged into the implementation of a threat we had no intention at all of implementing.

The bias in favor of implementing threats is another result of the inherent ambiguity of a decision which takes some future risks into account. The decision to make a threat presumably took into account the possibility that the threat would not work and that in such an event we *might* implement it. But a government will tend to treat that decision as a decision not to bluff —as a decision to carry out the threat if the occasion arises. There are a number of reasons for this. The first decision involves a risk within a risk—a risk that the threat will fail and that there will then be the risk of implementing it. This situation is sufficiently ambiguous so that the risks may merge. People will not realize that there is an opportunity for a new decision to be made in the light of new circumstances.

Further, a governmental threat (for example, "If Cuba seizes the oil

refineries we will cut off all trade") sounds like a governmental decision. Subordinate officials will see themselves as having the power to implement such a policy but not to change it. There is no automatic occasion for a new decision. The bureaucracy is likely to proceed day by day toward carrying out the threat. The lack of an equally well-considered alternative to implementing the threat also operates to make any such possibility unlikely.

Confusion between the decision to make a threat and the decision to implement it is particularly costly where the threat is to do something for an indefinite period in response to some one-shot action. An example illustrates how one thing is likely to follow another without re-examination. Suppose a foreign government proposes to nationalize some American-owned property. In an effort to deter them we threaten to cut off all trade if they seize the property. To make the threat credible we suspend trade immediately. If the property is nationalized the initial decision to make the threat will be taken by most people in the government as a decision to cut off, and to keep cut off, all trade. Any official can continue the trade embargo for another day. That appears to be our "policy." A decision *not* to carry out the threat that failed will be regarded as a reversal of a prior decision. It will be difficult for someone to say: "They nationalized the property. That's water over the dam. Our threat failed, and we should now resume trade. We should now try for a different objective, such as compensation or some arrangements to protect other property not yet nationalized, and make threats or offers appropriate to our new purpose." Any termination of the embargo will be left to higher authority within the government. Higher authority will also tend to regard an end of the embargo as a reversal of policy. These open-ended punishments, which include things like nonrecognition and the breaking of diplomatic relations, are likely to continue indefinitely with no real purpose in mind and with no advance consideration of the circumstances in which we would expect to stop imposing them.

Often this kind of policy is justified in terms of teaching our adversaries a lesson. Hurting a country which has failed to do what we want is regarded as rational for educational reasons. Our adversaries and third parties are expected to learn something about us which is worth the investment and the risks: they will have learned that we are not likely to tolerate certain conduct, that if we make a threat we are likely to carry it out, and that there are some things they "can't get away with." History suggests that the value of such lessons tends to be exaggerated.

Perhaps no lesson will be learned at all. On another occasion our adversary is likely to believe that the circumstances are different. There are so many variables in international affairs that one government is unlikely to give much weight to what another government did under different circumstances as an indication of what they are likely to do now. Reputations for toughness are ephemeral. What Khrushchev did in Budapest was not a reliable guide to what he would do in Cuba and even

less reliable as an indication of what Kosygin might do in North Vietnam. Our adversary will place far greater weight on what we will be doing the next time—mobilizing men, moving men, moving planes, calling in congressional leaders—than on what we did before in a different setting.

Our adversary may in fact draw a conclusion directly contrary to the one we wanted. For us to implement a threat involves us both in a painful experience. Rather than learn their lesson, the adversary and third countries may assume that we have learned our lesson: it cost us so much we will not do it again. Looking at the difficulties in which the United States has found itself in Vietnam, would-be aggressors might conclude that the United States would be most reluctant to repeat such an experience and that they could now act with reduced fear of United States intervention.

An action which produces no more constructive result than punishment is likely to look like a failure. The apparent failure of punishing actions—military (as in Vietnam), economic (as with sanctions against Rhodesia), or political (as in the breaking of diplomatic relations with Britain by the African states)—may lead countries to believe that such punishing actions will not be repeated. Further, it is not clear that the failure to take a retaliatory action will teach our adversary that we are soft. They are perhaps as likely to think that having backed down once, we cannot afford to do it again. Retaliation may, it is true, placate the international community and relieve the pressure for vengeance exerted by our domestic population. But it may also aggravate the situation and make our adversary less accommodating. Many of our stubborn international differences result from actions that looked backward instead of forward. Such continuing policies as the nonrecognition of China and restrictions on trade with Cuba and with Eastern Europe involve substantial costs in terms of lost opportunities. Whatever the rationalization, each of these policies was adopted in response to the past action of another government rather than through a rational consideration of how we could best improve the situation in the future. Whenever such responses to the unwanted decision of another government are justified as necessary to maintain our reputation or to teach another nation a lesson, that justification should be examined with skepticism.

If we are trying by a threat to dis-courage another government from engaging in a one-shot bit of conduct, we should probably threaten a one-shot bit of retaliatory action. If the threat fails, at least we can implement it quickly and confront everyone with a *fait accompli*. The single air attack on North Vietnam in August, 1964, following the apparent attacks by North Vietnam on United States ships in the Gulf of Tonkin was retaliatory action of this one-shot kind in response to one-shot action by an adversary. (Unfortunately it also set a precedent for further raids.)

WE SHOULD MAKE THEIR CHOICE PALATABLE

So far I have suggested that governments frequently try to bring about a decision they want by increasing the cost to another government of not making that decision, and that this method of influence is both ineffective and costly. The palatability to an adversary of the choice we want them to make is affected not simply by the pain we threaten to inflict if they do not make the choice, but rather by the total combination of many elements. The set of consequences of doing what we want (including both the benefits and the disadvantages) must be more attractive to them in sum than the set of consequences which will ensue if they do not do what we want. The choice we present them must be palatable. This can be represented by the following map, in which the "offer" designates the entire set of circumstances, both good and bad, which the *adversary* believes will come about if they make the decision we are asking them to make, and the "threat" indicates the set of

MAP

	DEMAND The decision desired by us	OFFER The consequences of making the decision	THREAT The consequences of not making the decision
Who?	Who is to make the decision?	Who benefits if the decision is made?	Who gets hurt if the decision is not made?
What?	Exactly what decision is desired?	If the decision is made, what benefits can be expected?—what costs?	If the decision is not made, —what risks?—what potential benefits?
When?	By what time does the decision have to be made?	When, if ever, will the benefits of making the decision occur?	How soon will the consequences of not making the decision be felt?
Why?	What makes this a right, proper, and lawful decision?	What makes these consequences fair and legitimate?	What makes these consequences fair and legitimate?

Every feature of an influence problem can be located somewhere on this schematic map. The nature of a given problem can be discovered through estimating how the presumed adversary would answer the above questions.

consequences, as they see them, of their not making the decision.

The set of questions we ought to be asking about each of these elements —the decision, the offer, and the threat —will enable us to analyze how the choice we are presenting looks to the country we are trying to influence and what we can do to alter the scheme so as to be more effective in getting them to make a decision. Who is it we are asking? On whom will the consequences fall if they do not make the desired decision? Will they fall on the same "who" as the group we are asking to make the decision? What is the decision we are asking them to make? What is it that we are saying will happen if they do or do not make it? When will these consequences occur? And why are we asking for this decision—is it a legitimate request, a reasonable demand? Are there reasons that they ought to make that choice? If they are "bad," why would implementing the threat be legitimate?

These are questions which the map presents. It does not provide any answers. It is a simple scheme which can be applied to any kind of conflict— marital problems, domestic disputes, or business dealings. It is not unique to international affairs. The proposition of this [chapter] is that by asking about the international conflicts in which we are engaged some of the simple questions indicated by the map—by rigorously asking the simplest questions—a significant improvement can be made upon the present style of foreign policy. The object of our policy is to cause someone else to make a decision. To do so we must alter the decision or the consequences of making it and of not making it so that they will now see the total choice in a favorable light. It is their perception of what is in the boxes on the map that is crucial, not ours. Our task is to change their perception by arranging the desired consequences so that, on the basis of the total attractive-

ness of the combination of all the boxes on the map, they will want to make that decision.

Changing the threat by increasing the threatened pain—military deterrence, damage infliction, weapons development, threats of sanctions—encompasses only half of one box in the threat column. These are the undesirable consequences to the adversary of not making the decision we want. (As they see it, there will of course be desirable consequences, too.) Herman Kahn's book *On Escalation* is essentially forty-two ways to change the way this box looks to an adversary. He suggests how to make the consequences of being "bad" look less attractive, more immediate, or more probable. That entire book is about escalating a threat for the purpose of exerting influence. We need equally detailed books dealing with the problems of whom we are trying to influence, what we want them to do, and how to make that look attractive. Successful influence depends on a consideration of all parts of this map, not just one, and on a consideration of how the various parts ought to be coordinated.

Even when considering only the threat, there may be more effective means of exerting influence than to change the level of threatened pain. One way to change the threat is to make it more immediate, to change the timing. We may not want the threat to appear as an ultimatum, because then its legitimacy would be reduced and the adversary might balk. But we may be able to advance the time at which the disadvantages of their not changing their minds will take effect. Or we might change the threat so that it will fall more directly on those who are being asked to decide. A lunch-counter sit-in is a more effective way to get a business to desegregate than a street march in part because the threat is calculated to fall directly and immediately on those who are being asked to make a decision. We may change the threat so that instead of imposing costs it appears to deprive the decision maker of benefits he had already anticipated. Again, the lunch-counter sit-in is a good example of this technique. Or we may change the nature of the threat for the purpose of getting the decision back on their agenda, so that we present them with what appears to be a choice with quite different dimensions. A more legitimate threat is likely to be more effective. For example, a threat by an international body may exert far more influence than the same threat from an adversary government. Any one of these methods of changing a threat may be more successful in getting an adversary to change their mind than increasing the magnitude of the pain we are promising to inflict on them.

An element which is unimportant to us may be important to an adversary. One of the sticking points of international conflict is that each party thinks that because they regard some issue as unimportant it will be easy for the other party to back down on it. But it is the adversary's perception of what is important which controls their decision, not our perception or some objective standard. No matter how irrational they may be, if we want to influence them, we should deal with them on their own ground; deal rationally with their irrationality. If they prefer prestige to economic welfare, an effective policy will offer them prestige. They may be more influenced by the name attached to a million-dollar aid program than by the fact that it is being offered. The irrationality of an adversary does not make the map irrelevant; it makes all the more important our consciously considering how the various elements may look to them. What do they think we are asking them to decide, what do they think the consequences will be, and how do they value those consequences?

Consider, for example, the choice faced by North Vietnam in May of 1966, as their leaders may have seen it. One of the decisions with which they were faced each day was whether to say that they were willing to negotiate. This was the "demand" of the United States. For this particular decision we can focus our attention on two important boxes: the consequences as they looked to Hanoi of making the decision we wanted and the consequences of not doing so. The table [below] suggests how these may have looked to them.

It is not surprising that given this view of the consequences of the decision we were asking them to make, they did not make it. The task of an effective policy maker would have been to examine this list and decide what *we* could do which would change one or more of the elements that were significant in *their* eyes in order to make it more likely that they would make a decision we wanted.

To arouse maximum support at home we usually insist that a dispute is a conflict of principle. But if we want success we should look for a solution consistent with the principles of our adversary as well as our own. By so arranging matters that an adversary government can go along without abandoning their principles, we make it easier for them to do so. My premise is that most international objectives can be achieved only by something more than our own actions: by having other governments make decisions. If this is so, both we and our adversaries must prefer the decision we want them to make to its alternatives. If only we prefer it, they will not make it; if only they prefer it and want to make it, then it would not be a goal of our policy. Unless there is some common ground there is no hope for influence. We seek to make it appear to them that the sum of the consequences of going along is profitable enough for them to make the decision—that is, it is better than the

THE OFFER (Consequences of saying "We will now negotiate")	THE THREAT (Consequences of *not* saying "We will now negotiate")
BENEFITS *Bombings.* A chance that bombing will stop (but U.S. may insist on continuing until there is a "verified end of infiltration"). *Casualties.* A chance of negotiating a cease-fire (but Saigon and U.S. may insist on continued "pacification" in the South as talks go on). *Negotiations.* A chance of real talks (but they may be frustrated by Saigon or by a dispute over representation of the Liberation Front). COSTS *Ruined morale.* To talk about talks now would undercut our fighting morale while the fighting continues. *Giving in.* To negotiate now is to give in to U.S. blackmail tactics. *No victory.* To negotiate is to abandon the opportunity for an impressive victory over forces of imperialism. *No unification.* To negotiate is almost certainly to abandon the unified Vietnam to which all agreed. *No socialist South Vietnam.* U.S. cannot be expected to agree to a socialist South Vietnam (cf. Dominican Republic). *Foreign-dominated South.* To negotiate means continued domination by neocolonialists against which so many have fought for so long. *Bad precedent.* Successful U.S. blocking of a war of liberation will make imperialist intervention more likely elsewhere.	COSTS *Bombings.* Will increase, with a serious risk to Hanoi and Haiphong. *Casualties.* Our high losses may rise from X per week to Y per week unless we revert to more guerrilla-like tactics. *Negotiations* are postponed for at least one more day. BENEFITS *Possible quick victory.* An excellent chance that Saigon government will completely fall apart or that U.S. will quickly pull out because of criticism at home and abroad. Either would assure us a quick and complete victory. *Certainty of eventual success.* This is a contest of will. The Vietnamese people fighting for their own country, for freedom from foreign domination, and for the socialist society of the future will certainly outlast alien, neocolonialists who try to stop political forces with bombs. We will tolerate high casualty rates longer than they, and thus win. *Loyalty to principle.* To fight on is to adhere to our values and principles. *World-wide respect* for standing up to the American goliath. *Option to negotiate later.* If at any time it seems wise to negotiate, we can do so on terms no less favorable than now.

sum of the consequences of not going along. In game-theory terms this is simply saying that international conflicts are not zero-sum games.

WHO?

The first question on the map is "Who?" Who is it we would like to have make a decision? After Rhodesian independence the British government did not articulate clearly the target of their sanctions, nor was there public discussion of the effect of their policy on the people they claimed to be influencing. Sanctions were intended to make it hard on "Rhodesia." Recognizing that Rhodesia was simply a piece of geography, the British government said that it was the politically responsible community leaders within Rhodesia who were the precise target of influence. The sanctions were presumably aimed at a typical business man in Salisbury—perhaps a banker with political experience.

Put such a man in the upper left-hand box and suppose that he is the "who" we are trying to influence. It is then the consequences to him that are crucial. What is his choice? He gets up in the morning, reads the newspaper, and says to his wife, "I see that Harold Wilson wants us to return to constitutional government, and I suppose he is talking to me. Perhaps I had better go down to Government House and tell them that I am prepared to return to constitutional government.

But if I do, what will happen? I will go in and the British Governor will ask, 'You and who else? Do you have the support of the army? Did you bring others along?' And I will have to say, 'No.' Then he will say, 'When there are enough of you, let me know.' I will walk out and quite likely be picked up and put under house arrest like others of whom the government is suspicious." The consequences to such a man of making the decision Britain was asking him to make were considerably worse than the consequences of not making it. Britain was not offering him any benefits for making the decision.

Making effective policy lies in the coordination of the boxes—the demand, the offer, and the threat—to make an adversary's choice easy and desirable in his eyes. Once we know whom we are trying to influence, we should see whether we are making the offer and threat to the same person or group. In Rhodesia, the first effects of economic sanctions fell on the blacks, who had no voice in any government or private decision making and about whom those with responsibility for changing the course of independence cared little. On the other hand, in Ceylon the government was successfully influenced by the offer of the United States to resume economic aid if the government worked out with a United States oil company a satisfactory arrangement for compensation. Although the offer was directed at the people of the country (no aid, theoretically, would go into the pockets of government officials), the government was deeply interested in the aid. The critical point is the nature of the influence exerted by the offer and by the threat on that group to which we are presenting a choice.

WHAT?

The second question is "What?" What is it we want them to decide? What do they perceive will be the consequences of making that decision (the offer), and what do they perceive will be the consequences of not making it (the threat)? If it is their decision that counts, they must know of the decision we are trying to get them to make. The more mechanically easy it is to make that decision—the more yesable the proposition with which we confront them—the more likely they are to make it.

What is the offer? What do they see as the advantages (and disadvantages) of the situation which they would be in if they went along with us and made the desired decision? In Vietnam, for example, we offered fair elections, economic-aid programs, various levels of American disengagement and withdrawal. There are two questions to be asked about such benefits we are promising to extend to them if they make a desired decision. First, are these benefits things which are really attractive to them? If we are trying to influence a donkey with carrots, it will be important to know if the donkey likes carrots. Equally important is the problem of convincing the donkey that if he performs he will actually get some carrots. The credibility of an offer is just as important as the credibility of a threat. . . . It costs a great deal to make threats credible. It may be that we can exert as much influence by doing things which are easier and less expensive and are designed to convince an adversary that we are in fact committed to our offers. Again, since it is their perception that is important, we should perhaps devote more effort than we now do toward convincing them that we will in fact do what we say we will if they go along with us.

Another way to improve an offer is make the disadvantages of going along appear less costly. This may involve what is called saving face, but the problem is broader than that. In making the decision we want, they will suffer domestic and international costs. We can exert influence by acting to minimize these costs.

WHEN?

The third question is "When?" The decision we are asking them to make will be more palatable if the threat and the offer are well correlated to the time at which the decision is required. When American bombing of North Vietnam began in 1965, there were spokesmen for our government who said, "We do not want their promises, nor do we expect North Vietnam to stop its support for the Vietcong immediately. The decision we want them to make is to taper off over the next three months." If that was true, the message was demonstrably wrong in its timing. It was, "Slow down your support over the next three months or we will bomb you tomorrow." My young son laughs at me when I say, "No television tonight unless you are good next week." He knows that I have to decide before he does.

WHY?

The last question is "Why?" The word is used here in the sense of seeking justification. Is our demand justifiable? How legitimate is it in our adversary's eyes? In terms of morality and humanity, international law, and past actions by ourselves and our adversaries, how justifiable does our demand appear to them?

Legitimacy is usually considered to be icing on the cake. But the legitimacy of our demand as perceived by an adversary is important. They will be more likely to make a decision if it appears legitimate to them. This is true not only because an adversary will see that we can win third-party support for a legitimate demand. Every government must also consider their internal situation. An adversary government must justify their decisions to their own people; they are constrained at least in part by what their own citizens will say about the decision. Also governments and government officials are influenced by what they themselves think is right. Most government officials want to do the right thing by their own standards. No matter how wrong we think our adversary is, we can best see how to influence them by realizing that they think they are on the side of right. Part of exerting influence is convincing them that to make the decision we want them to make would be the right thing to do in terms of the values accepted by them. This is another aspect of the proposition that solving a conflict involves an attempt to get them to make a decision which both is favorable to us and appeals to them.

Similarly, a threat can be legitimate if its implementation would be morally or legally justified. Such a threat is more likely to exert influence than one which appears to be rank blackmail.

WE ARE TRYING TO CHANGE THEIR MIND

Asking such questions should help identify the reasons why our attempts at influence have so often failed. We are not surprised that North Vietnam did not make a decision to indicate that it was willing to negotiate in May,

402 ROGER FISHER

1966. Although the foregoing list is merely descriptive, it provides a base for considering what ought to have been done. It draws attention to consequences we might have tried to change. And if someone proposes a new way of exerting influence, the map provides a way of appraising the new method's chance of success.

In any conflict, we can look at the situation knowing that the balance of consequences has not yet been sufficient to cause the adversary to make the decision we would like him to make; otherwise he would already have made it. At any one time the question is, What aspects of their perceived choice can we change in order to make them change their mind? If it is proposed to induce North Vietnam to agree to negotiate by increasing their casualty rate, we can look at the list and try to guess how North Vietnam would react if they were faced with the prospect that fighting on would increase the rate of casualties not from X to Y but from Y to Z. Could we expect that change to make the decisive difference? What other elements ought to be changed, and how can we do it?

Using the map we can see that threat making is not everything. It is just one of a number of considerations we should be taking into account.

Arms Control for the Late Sixties

James E. Dougherty

The mid-1960's witnessed a remarkable maturing process in the attitude of governments toward the arms problem. It is now widely conceded that both the Soviet Union and the United States have, since the early part of 1963, shifted their attention in international negotiations away from general and complete disarmament toward partial arms control and limitation measures. Less animated today is the discussion over such issues as inspection for total disarmament, the economics of large-scale arms reductions, and the strengthening of international peacekeeping machinery during the transition to a disarmed world. These issues, which had always sounded somewhat abstract, have been replaced by more immediate and realistic problems—the impact of arms negotiations on the Atlantic alliance and the future status of Germany, decisions to be made in respect to ballistic missile defense, the proliferation of nuclear weapons, and the applicability of arms control concepts to the conduct of limited conflict in Vietnam and elsewhere. . . .

GENERAL DISARMAMENT

In retrospect, it is difficult to believe that any government could have looked upon the blueprints for complete disarmament tabled by the Soviet Union in 1959 and by the United States in 1961 as representing a feasible policy goal to be achieved within the foreseeable future. A few years of negotiations at Geneva and of study by Western specialists served the useful purpose of demonstrating the profound difficulties involved—difficulties of a technological, strategic, and political character. It soon became clear that the geostrategic situation of the two superpowers is quite asymmetrical, a fact that compels them to adopt divergent perspectives of their security requirements. (Ocean-based deterrent systems, for example, are more important for the United States than for the Soviet Union.) The task of reaching agreement on first-stage reductions in conformity with the McCloy-Zorin principle that neither side should be placed at an unfair disadvantage thus proved to be much more complex than had been originally thought by the advocates of total disarmament.

The longer the negotiators and the experts grappled with the subject of general and complete disarmament, the more they realized that modern military technology does not lend itself easily to regulation by the traditional diplomatic device of the written treaty. Despite the coincident interest of the superpowers in avoiding a mutually destructive nuclear cataclysm, the dispute since 1964 over the financing of United Nations peace forces and voting in the General Assembly showed that Soviet-Western differences over the development of international organization and order are still sufficiently wide to bar progress toward a disarmed world. The Sino-Soviet split seemed to dispose Moscow toward a rapprochement with the West, at least across the intermediate terrain of Europe. But if the Soviets are genuinely apprehensive over China's long-range foreign policy objectives, then they are hardly likely to embrace plans for substantial disarmament which do not apply effectively to the Peking regime.

Probably none of the five existing nuclear weapon States wants nuclear war now or within the foreseeable future. Yet not one of them has consistently acted as if it regards total disarmament as the only way or the best way of safeguarding its security. Perhaps all five would agree that disarmament is a desirable ultimate goal. But none appears willing to move away from an international political-military environment in which the conditions of equilibrium are relatively familiar toward a radically transformed kind of international politics, except on terms so patently designed to produce unilateral advantage as to be unacceptable to the adversary side. At the present time, each nuclear power attaches a higher priority to policy objectives other than general disarmament. In the long view of history, this may or may not prove to have been a myopic attitude. No one can say for sure. But the current posture of the powers is not a mere matter of stubbornness or ill will. Rather it results from the nature of governments, the nation-state system, and international diplomacy; from the characteristics of contemporary advanced weap-

ons technology, which makes disarmament both more desirable and more difficult to achieve; and from the intensity of the political, ideological, and other value conflicts which mark the twentieth century world.[1]

Fortunately, the fact that total disarmament is perceived as lying beyond man's present reach has not led to despair on the part of governments. The nuclear powers in varying degrees have manifested some awareness of the need for managing military power wisely and cautiously. All five powers at present seem to shun nuclear war as a means of accomplishing their foreign policy objectives. Thomas W. Wolfe, while adopting a prudently cautious interpretation of the significance and extent of the changes which have occurred in Soviet society since the time of Stalin, expresses the opinion that the two superpowers will probably continue to steer clear of a frontal collision. China, according to Harold C. Hinton, recognizes its own vulnerability to nuclear attack and pursues a course of "strategic boldness and tactical caution." In a world where such dangerous crises as the Middle East War of June 1967 can occur at any time, no one would predict that the self-restraint of the five nuclear powers—all of them—will prevail indefinitely. Strategic circumstances might be altered in the future. . . . But for the time being at least, most if not all of the nuclear powers share, in varying degrees, an interest in arms control, despite the fact that at present formal agreements among all five lie beyond the art of what is politically possible.

ARMS CONTROL

In contrast to disarmament, which entails the elimination of armaments, arms control as a theoretical concept reflects a strategic philosophy which accepts the continued existence of national military establishments. Fre-

quently but not always the notion of arms control implies some form of collaboration between adversary States— whether it involve formal agreement, tacit cooperation, or unilateral decisions taken with the expectation of reciprocal action—in those areas of military policy that are thought to be of common or coincident interest to the parties concerned. (We say "not always" because arms control also embraces those unilateral decisions which are deemed worthwhile because they enhance controllability, stability, and security against war even if the adversary does not reciprocate or respond.) The purpose of arms control is generally at least twofold: first, to improve the safety of the international environment against the occurrence of dangerous wars by reducing certain risks inherent in the present military situation; and second, to increase the chances that if military conflicts do occur, as they are likely to from time to time, governments will pursue policies of intelligent restraint rather than engage in operations which lead to uncontrolled escalation, uninhibited violence, and unlimited damage to civilian populations. Many advocates of arms control would insist upon a third purpose—to support policies that will be conducive eventually to disarmament agreements and the growth of peacekeeping institutions in a world where all nation-states have been persuaded to set aside the rule of force in favor of the rule of law. Whether or not this third purpose is "realistic" or "utopian" remains a matter of considerable debate among students of international relations.

The term "arms control," looked at theoretically, is an extremely permissive one and may refer to such diverse measures as the following: 1) administrative, technical, or political arrangements calculated to minimize the risk of nuclear accident, unauthorized use of nuclear weapons, precipitate response to an ambiguous warning, or strategic miscalculation of the adversary's intentions; 2) a program of weapons research, development, and deployment, as well as a strategic doctrine, which stresses the nonprovocative and defensive aspects of national security postures, especially those associated with an "invulnerable second-strike capability"; 3) regional tension-reaching arrangements, such as disengagement, "thinning out" of forces, or the creation of demilitarized or nuclear-free zones; 4) decisions to hold quantitative rates of weapons production below those levels which a nation is economically and technically capable of sustaining in a genuine "arms race"; 5) tension-reducing declarations such as a "no-first-use" pledge or a "nonaggression pact"; 6) the improvement of facilities for emergency communications and prolonged arms control dialogues between adversaries; 7) efforts to separate nuclear forces and strategies from conventional forces and strategies through the utilization of various "firebreaks"—e.g., time, geography, and command; 8) the prohibition of certain activities, such as the sale of conventional arms and delivery systems to countries in "tinderbox areas," nuclear weapons testing in proscribed environments, the emplacement of weapons of mass destruction in orbit, or the establishment of spheres of influence in outer space; 9) a formal verified freeze on the production of specified items, such as fissionable materials for weapons purposes or strategic delivery vehicles; 10) efforts to prevent or retard the proliferation of nuclear weapons to nations not already in possession of them; and 11) the prudent management of crisis diplomacy and limited conflict strategy. This may be, both from a literary and logical standpoint, an unaesthetic inventory, but it serves to illustrate the variety of measures that can be comprehended under the rubrics of "arms control" as this term has been employed in the recent literature.[2]

NOTES

1. In a study undertaken for the United States Arms Control and Disarmament Agency, Arnold Wolfers suggests that a world balance of power, based upon mutual deterrence, constitutes a highly rational goal for the United States, both as the minimum and maximum objective of its military effort. He points out that whereas proportionate reductions in armaments are attractive in theory, they are extremely difficult to attain in practice, and that complete disarmament can usually be expected to prove disadvantageous to the side which originally enjoyed military superiority. Finally, he questions whether an international peacekeeping force of the kind proposed in the U.S. Outline Plan for General and Complete Disarmament could really be relied upon by this country where matters of security and other important interests were concerned, or whether "American vital interests could become exposed to new threats emanating from such a force, instead of being protected by it." "Disarmament, Peacekeeping and the National Interest," in *The United States in a Disarmed World*, prepared at The Washington Center of Foreign Policy Research, Baltimore: The Johns Hopkins Press, 1966, pp. 3–32. See especially pp. 12, 25, and 32. For an exposition of the present author's views concerning the impracticability of general disarmament under the prevailing circumstances of the international system, see the Editor's Introduction to *The Prospects for Arms Control*, New York: Macfadden-Bartell, 1965; "The Status of the Arms Negotiations," *Orbis*, Vol. IX, Spring 1965; "Soviet Disarmament Policy: Illusion and Reality," Chapter 7 in *Détente: Cold War Strategies in Transition*, edited by Eleanor L. Dulles and Robert D. Crane, New York: Praeger, 1965; and *Arms Control and Disarmament: The Critical Issues*, Special Report Series, Washington: The Center for Strategic Studies, Georgetown University, 1966.

2. See, e.g., Donald G. Brennan, ed., *Arms Control, Disarmament and National Security*, New York: George Braziller, 1961; Hedley Bull, *The Control of the Arms Race*, for the Institute for Strategic Studies, New York: Frederick A. Praeger, 1961; David H. Frisch, ed., *Arms Reduction: Program and Issues*, New York: Twentieth Century Fund, 1961; Louis Henkin, ed., *Arms Control: Issues for the Public*, Englewood Cliffs: Prentice-Hall, 1961; Ernest Lefever, ed., *Arms and Arms Control*, New York: Frederick A. Praeger, 1962; Thomas C. Schelling and Morton H. Halperin, *Strategy and Arms Control*, New York: Twentieth Century Fund, 1961; J. David Singer, ed., *Weapons Management in World Politics*, Proceedings of the International Arms Control Symposium, Ann Arbor, Michigan, December 1962 (Joint Issue of *The Journal of Conflict Resolution*, Vol. VII, September 1963, and *Journal of Arms Control*, Vol. I, October 1963); Alastair Buchan and Philip Windsor, *Arms and Stability in Europe*, for the Institute for Strategic Studies, New York: Frederick A. Praeger, 1963; and James E. Dougherty with John F. Lehman, Jr., eds., *The Prospects for Arms Control, op. cit.*, 1965.

Arms Control in the 1970's

James E. Dougherty

I

Just a decade ago, spokesmen of the United States and the Soviet Union publicly discussed general and complete disarmament as though their governments regarded it as a feasible policy goal to be achieved within, say, four to twelve years. A few years of analysis and negotiation demonstrated: (1) that the gulf between rhetoric and reality was wide and deep; (2) that the nature of the arms problem was complex; (3) that the superpowers had no choice but to shift the diplomatic effort from rapid total disarmament to a series of limited arms control measures. Agreements with the purpose of improving the safety of the international environment and moderating the pace of continued armaments competition will, it is hoped, gradually create conditions in which negotiations for substantial arms limitations might be realistically undertaken on a worldwide scale at some future time.

As a result of the Leninist theoretical heritage, large numbers of intellectuals, students and journalists both in the Western and non-Western worlds harbor the suspicion that economics is at the bottom of the disarmament impasse. They trace the lack of progress in negotiating disarmament to that sinister cluster known as the "military-industrial complex," with its "vested interest in perpetuating the arms race." Such an attitude represents a modernized and somewhat more so-phisticated version of the older "devil theory of war" in which U.S. entry into World War I was blamed on the profit-seeking motives of munitions-makers. This *neo-diabolus* theory, accorded the status of religious dogma within the ranks of the American New Left, is admittedly more subtle and comprehensive than its predecessor, which social scientists have long since discredited. But it can never transcend its limitations as a mere corollary of the Leninist theory of imperialism, which is itself a simplistic explanation of the complex phenomena of international relations.

Undoubtedly general disarmament would cause serious economic dislocations. But purely on economic grounds, the problem should prove no more intractable for a capitalist system than for a socialist one—indeed, the former might well adjust more easily to the new environment.[1] The profoundest obstacles to general disarmament, far from being economic, are technical, strategic and political. In the final analysis they are rooted in man's psychological, sociological, technological and cultural structures.

Ever since the onset of the atomic era, countless leaders and concerned citizens have warned that nuclear war is inevitable unless nations achieve complete nuclear disarmament. Yet more than twenty-five years after Hiroshima and Nagasaki, it is unthinkable

From "Arms Control in the 1970's" by James E. Dougherty in *Orbis, A Quarterly Journal of World Affairs* (Vol. XV, Spring 1971). Copyright © 1971 by Foreign Policy Research Institute, Inc. Reprinted by permission.

that any one of the five existing nuclear states—not even China, perhaps especially not China—hopes to achieve any political purpose by initiating nuclear war. Paradoxically, despite the terrors of the thermonuclear age, not one of the five—not even Britain—has acted consistently during the last decade as if she looks upon total nuclear disarmament as the only way, or necessarily the best way, of safeguarding her security. In all five countries we would find intellectuals, government officials, military leaders and others who, in moments of philosophical reflection, regard general disarmament as a desirable goal. But it would seem that in all five most political leaders conclude that the same advanced weapons technology that makes disarmament more ethically imperative than ever before also makes it more difficult than ever to attain technically, strategically and politically.

The United States and the Soviet Union never solved to their mutual satisfaction the technical problems inherent in implementing the 1961 McCloy-Zorin principle that the disarming process should place neither side at an unfair disadvantage. Given the different geostrategic requirements of the two superpowers and the different weapons systems at their disposal, it was impossible even to agree on where to begin the dismantling of arms. (Now, a decade later in the Helsinki-Vienna negotiations we are arguing the same question of where to start "freezing.") Back in the early 1960's U.S. analysts demonstrated their creative imagination by devising a remarkable variety of physical and nonphysical inspection and control schemes to insure either compliance with the disarmament agreement or effective sanctions in case of violation. But that intellectual exercise remained rather theoretical. Virtually all the proposed schemes

were vulnerable to serious criticism: they could be circumvented; they were politically obnoxious to the Soviets; or they were so bizarre that they would be unacceptable even in the more permissive framework of American politics.[2] One crucial inspection problem—that of "hidden stockpiles" sufficiently large to threaten a disarmed power's survival —was never overcome. Governments do not like to discuss those facts that inhibit their ability to engage in public rhetoric concerning persistent foreign policy themes.

The strategic obstacles to general disarmament can be simply put. Essentially they involve the issue of security and the propensity of governments in the nation-state system to seek that security through some form of power balancing and, when possible, deterring war by threatening to make it too costly. All five nuclear powers appear to assume, as John H. Herz has suggested in a revision of his earlier estimate concerning the "demise of the territorial state," that nuclear weapons for all practical purposes have become "unavailable" for any use except deterrence and that, despite lingering ambiguities, they now constitute a safeguard rather than a threat to national security.[3] The two superpowers cannot but wonder, both in their mutual strategic relations and with an eye to other powers, how fast and how far they could dare carry out reductions down the strategic scale before encountering the danger that mutual deterrence might give way to renascent incentives for surprise nuclear attack, based on the expectation of achieving a decisive advantage. This is the central strategic problem in all planning for nuclear disarmament.[4] It would be more accurate to say that we have forgotten it than that we have solved it.

II

The political obstacles to general disarmament were, and remain, insuperable. Essentially, Soviet opposition to Western proposals for inspection and control has been political. There are no signs that the Soviets are more ready today than a decade ago to permit international on-site inspection. (Whatever limited-risk arms control measures we and the Soviets agree upon—such as the Partial Nuclear Test Ban Treaty, the Outer Space Treaty, or the Seabed Treaty and the proposed Strategic Arms Limitation Agreement—require that the United States depend on its own national detection and verification capabilities.) Furthermore, there still exist serious political disagreements between the Western and the communist states over the development of an international peacekeeping organization (especially the United Nations) in lieu of national military establishments. Generally speaking, the nuclear powers appear unwilling to forsake an international environment in which the conditions of precarious stalemate have become relatively familiar for a radically transformed international system in which none of the great powers would be free to invoke either force or the threat of force to protect its interests and pursue its objectives. At present, each nuclear power attaches higher priority to policy objectives other than general disarmament. None of them is ready to start talking seriously about disarmament—this for several reasons.

First of all, because among the five there are serious asymmetries of situation and power, two of the nuclear-weapon states, France and China, are unwilling to enter into serious negotiations at this time. Both have continued to conduct nuclear tests in the atmosphere. Neither power has signed the Nonproliferation Treaty, but neither indicates being motivated to encourage the diffusion of nuclear weapons to additional nations. France has given public assurances of an intention to "behave in this area exactly as do those States that decide to adhere to the nonproliferation treaty."[5] Now that the

de Gaulle era is over, France may be able to return to the international conference table during the 1970's. But for China the strategic security situation is more difficult than it ever was for France. China's position vis-à-vis the superpowers is still quite weak, and she has a long way to go before she possesses the bargaining leverage that would make her feel comfortable about negotiating arms limitations, assuming that she will ever be willing to enter into such a process. Moreover, if China were to be invited some day to a world disarmament conference, in virtue of the fact that she is one of the nuclear *beati possedentes,* and thereby have her international political prestige enhanced, India's incentive to acquire nuclear weapons would probably increase and the prospects for inhibiting the further proliferation of national deterrent forces would be correspondingly diminished. Thus even the timing and the form of international disarmament negotiations can be a tricky business. For now, "pentagonal" negotiations are untimely, and it is impossible to predict confidently whether circumstances would permit them to begin before the end of this decade. Perhaps they should appear no more remote than did such U.S.-USSR agreements as the test ban and the nonproliferation treaty at the height of the Cold War.

The superpowers are still constrained in respect to arms limitation policies by consideration of the effects various types of agreements might have on their alliance systems and on the future behavior of other great powers, notably Germany, China and Japan. In the past, West Germany and other NATO allies have become extremely nervous at the prospect of any substantial alterations in the European political-military situation. The Brandt government's *Ostpolitik* apparently reflects some diminution of West German cautiousness, conservatism and apprehensiveness in the realm of foreign and defense policies—a willingness to strike out on a bolder course looking toward some vaguely defined change. There is now more talk in Western Europe about a European security conference. The adverse security implications of the 1968 invasion of Czechoslovakia have been all but forgotten by Western public opinion, but responsible policy-makers in NATO capitals are still compelled to remember them. Most West European politicians cannot yet see any practical alternative to NATO as a method of preserving the present condition of continental strategic equilibrium; they are generally supported by those people who perceive that the U.S. defense guarantee enables the European countries to enjoy the benefits of lower levels of military expenditure than they might otherwise have to sustain.

Throughout most of the 1960's, any effort by the United States and the Soviet Union to reach even the most limited arms control agreements (such as the establishment of the Washington-Moscow "hot line," the Partial Nuclear Test Ban Treaty and the Nonproliferation Treaty) invariably aroused suspicion on the part of some of the NATO allies. It was perhaps inevitable that an ambiguous détente should be greeted with mixed emotions. On the one hand, many Europeans welcomed the superpowers' willingness to tone down the hostility of their confrontation and to enter a new era of mutually advantageous negotiation; on the other hand, there was some fear (not entirely unjustified) that the two giants might try to strike a few bargains over the heads of, and at the expense of, the Europeans in between. They insisted that, if the premier partner of the Western alliance intended to undertake negotiations with the major adversary, it should also intensify the consultative process within NATO. Henceforth the Atlantic alliance had to conceive its role in terms

of managing both defense and disarmament.[6]

During recent years, intra-NATO consultation has markedly improved. The scrapping of the ill-conceived NATO Multilateral Force (MLF) was accompanied by the creation of a Nuclear Planning Group through which the allies were admitted to a greater share in formulating defense strategy. This apparently has helped to strengthen the impression that alliance strategy is a transatlantic affair, and that even though nuclear command and control must remain in Washington, the development of political guidelines and contingency planning requires a much broader base.[7] Moreover, the need for better consultation on East-West arms negotiations has been recognized. A new Disarmament and Arms Control Section within the Secretariat has carried on discussions concerning the Seabed Treaty (which prohibits placing nuclear weapons on the ocean floor), the control of biological and chemical weapons, and the concept of mutual balanced force reductions (MBFR) in Europe.[8] On this latter point, the allies contend that symmetrical troop withdrawals, negotiated by East and West, are vastly preferable to the kind of unilateral American pullback proposed by the Mansfield Resolution. Faced with a growing neo-isolationist sentiment in the United States, the West Europeans now seem more disposed, publicly if not privately, to make favorable references to the notion of a "carefully planned" European security conference. But the NATO allies wisely insist upon making progress toward a guaranteed Berlin settlement a precondition of such a conference.[9] They also insist that MBFR must be on the agenda.[10] Thus far, however, the Soviets have shown little incentive to negotiate balanced force reductions, probably because they regard domestic political pressures within the United

States for unilateral troop withdrawals as eventually irresistible.

The Soviets have been preoccupied for the last decade and more with the behavior of Germany and China—which causes them the greater worry, Western observers have been unable to decide. During the years of negotiating the Nonproliferation Treaty in the mid-1960's, it was sometimes suggested in the West that when Soviet propagandists inveighed against the militant revolutionism of the Chinese communists, this was really intended to disguise their deep-rooted fear of the Germans. It was also sometimes suggested that when Soviet diplomats at Geneva and elsewhere declaimed against the desire of the "West German revanchists" to acquire nuclear arms, they were only trying to tell us in Aesopian language how worried they were about the Chinese nuclear capability. It is quite possible that Moscow is seriously afraid of both Peking and Bonn. It is also possible, and perhaps more likely, that the Soviet leaders are rational enough to perceive that both Germany and China are at present decidedly inferior in total military capabilities to the USSR; neither by itself can pose a serious threat to Soviet security. Possibly, too, they are more concerned about the one than the other at any given time, depending upon the circumstances—including, e.g., the political character of the government in West Germany and the degree of tension or conflict along the Sino-Soviet border.

III

It has become commonplace for Western observers to analyze the Soviet-American détente following the Cuban missile crisis as a function of two basic assumptions: (1) The Soviets recognized that NATO's political determination, backed by the strategic military power of the United States, made it impossible for the USSR to think any fundamental change in the political situation of Europe could be brought about by the threat of coercive action. (2) As the Sino-Soviet dispute became more publicly acrimonious, Moscow grew anxious to "mend its fences" with the West and thus "safeguard its rear" while preparing to deal with the increasingly ominous threat from China. As we look ahead to the 1970's, these two assumptions will no longer prove adequate for the interpretation of U.S.-USSR relations.

Undoubtedly it was U.S. strategic superiority which enabled the Kennedy Administration to make the response it did in the Cuban missile crisis, to stand fast on Berlin, and to adhere to a nuclear strategy for Europe despite all the talk of "flexible response." That same superiority prompted the Johnson Administration to think it could take a strategic initiative in Asia and "up the ante" in Viet Nam. But in recent years the international strategic equation has been substantially modified, especially in respect to the number of land-based launchers.[11] The significance of quantitative and qualitative changes in the strategic military-technological capabilities of the superpowers is mentioned here merely to indicate that a shift *may* be occurring which could undermine one of the two major assumptions on which the détente has hitherto rested. This is a crucial issue for the Strategic Arms Limitation Talks (SALT) in Helsinki and Vienna.

Western observers have assumed that the dispute with China figured prominently in Soviet motivations for entering the SALT in late 1969. But we should not discount the possibility that Soviet apprehensions over China may have been exaggerated in the past by Soviet policymakers, or by Western observers, or by both. If the Soviets were mistaken, they might now be revising their assessment. The real threat from China, if there is to be one, probably lies in the future. The Peking leadership must certainly recognize its country's strategic vulnerability in this early nuclear phase of its history. There is no reason to believe that a generation nurtured on Maoist doctrine will risk everything by plunging into strategic adventurism.[12]

As the 1960's gave way to the new decade, the British journalist Victor Zorza expressed the opinion that the Soviet military, under Kremlin orders, was preparing to mount a preventive attack on the Chinese nuclear installations at Lop Nor, while the Chinese were increasing their war preparations against the Soviets.[13] Chinese propagandists asserted that Soviet-American negotiations in the SALT were designed to concert a policy of nuclear blackmail against China. Neo-Machiavellians in the West might be tempted to think that the West could derive strategic profit from a Sino-Soviet war. But anyone who is seriously interested in improving the quality of human life on earth as well as the prospects for international arms control and political order is bound to reject such a proposition as morally and politically abhorrent. A war between the USSR and China, regardless of which side started it, would constitute a wild leap into the historic unknown. It might lead to incalculably tragic consequences not only for the protagonists but for their neighbors and for other countries as well, whether they try to remain aloof from the conflict, exploit it from the sidelines, or eventually find themselves drawn into it for one reason or another. A war between any two nuclear powers, even though one be technologically far "smaller" than the other, could become catastrophically destructive of human life, the fruits of civilization, the economic potential for future development, and even the rationality of that

political intelligence on which the survival of mankind depends.

Once the SALT was under way, mutual hostility between China and the Soviet Union lessened considerably. By the end of 1970, one heard little of the Sino-Soviet dispute, or of the earlier speculation that the superpowers were using the SALT to rationalize their acquisition of a missile defense capability against China. On the one hand, the U.S. move into Cambodia may have prompted Moscow and Peking to attenuate their animosity, lest the United States take advantage of it. On the other hand, recent developments, including the recognition of the Peking government by Canada and Italy, along with a perceptible softening of the U.S. position toward the Chinese People's Republic in respect to travel, trade and United Nations diplomacy, helped the CPR to inch toward international respectability, and also served to demonstrate that the triangular Washington-Moscow-Peking relationship is a highly complex phenomenon, comparable to the "three body" problem in physics.[14] It will complicate the arms control picture throughout the 1970's, and the three principals can be expected to try to make capital of it.

A French analyst, Michel Tatu, has recently suggested that it may be less appropriate to interpret the current détente in terms of the Soviets' desire to "safeguard their western rear" while coping with China than in terms of their interest in "safeguarding their eastern rear" while pursuing a more active diplomatic policy in Europe.[15] Such 1970 developments as the Bonn-Moscow treaty (whereby the USSR obtained much of what it sought to gain through a European security conference) should make us wary of any simplistic explanations of Soviet negotiating behavior vis-à-vis China and the West.

Nevertheless, in the future the Soviets will usually have reason, because of geographical factors, to be more worried than the United States about China's nuclear capability. Moreover, because of the population imbalance, the Soviets would not contemplate Sino-Soviet nuclear disarmament negotiations with much enthusiasm. As Peking's nuclear arsenal grows, it will become increasingly difficult for the Soviet political-military leadership to entertain the idea of a pre-emptive attack upon China. Historical-psychological factors rooted in the Russian character and culture, as well as the rationalist dictates of communist ideology, already militate in favor of caution and nonviolent conflict resolution. Perhaps the Soviets realize that, as a sheer matter of coldly calculated *Machtpolitik*, they have passed the point where they could deliberately opt for war with China, and that they must look forward to the inevitable development of conditions of mutual deterrence in Asia. But if so, they will probably strive to maintain a margin of strategic superiority over China as long as possible. There is no reason to think that the leaders in Moscow, in working out an arms limitation policy, would be willing to take the "down escalator" while the Chinese (still a few floors below) are on the "up escalator."

Why, then, are the Soviet Union and the United States involved in the Helsinki-Vienna negotiations? There is a variety of motives, not necessarily similar or of equal intensity on both sides. Both nations are beset by uncertainties. Decision-makers in each country cannot help wondering at times whether things are really going as well as they might, domestically and abroad. As a nation, the United States has become frustrated by the Viet Nam war and by her effort to establish some sort of equilibrium in Asia (despite a degree of success). She has experienced internal social disorders arising from urban crises, racial conflicts and campus unrest, as well as a pervading infla-

tion which has contributed to general discontent with the existing institutional structure. The intelligentsia and youth have fed on one another's alienation from the nation's political, economic and technical culture. All of these factors have generated a demand, led by youth and responded to by some politicians, for a reordering of national priorities from defense and outer space to the environment and the inner city. There is an ambiguous mixture here of futility and hope on the part of those who expect a democratic system that they despise to transform itself by moving in what they deem more ethical directions. (The New Left finds it hard to believe that the "war machine" or the "death economy" can reform itself or carry on serious arms limitation negotiations with the Soviet Union.)

The Soviets, too, have had their problems, quite apart from China. Their counterpart of America's student rebels is the minority of scientists, artists, writers and intellectuals—the Sakharovs and Solzhenitzyns—who in a more restrained way embarrass the communist leaders with their criticisms. Tens of thousands of Soviet Jews, unable to appreciate the subtle distinction that Moscow tries to draw between anti-Zionism and old-fashioned anti-Semitism, would like to depart from the socialist fatherland, and if this were permitted it might lead to unflattering comparisons between the USSR and Nazi Germany. The Soviet leaders, when they look toward Eastern Europe, are probably aware that the Common Market exercises a powerful attraction upon East Europeans, and to an extent even upon themselves. They must also realize that the sobering effects of the invasion of Czechoslovakia may wear off in Eastern as well as in Western Europe. Some East Europeans may still hope to exploit for their own gains the tension on the Amur-Ussuri rivers. A series of repeated applications of the "Brezhnev Doctrine" (in Rumania, Poland and elsewhere) is not something to be anticipated enthusiastically, although Moscow can be expected to apply the doctrine whenever necessary. In other words, the search for limited agreements with the West may either reduce the necessity of further applications of the Brezhnev Doctrine or increase the readiness of Western intellectuals and governments to excuse such "counterrevolutionary interventions" as may yet occur.

IV

Neither the Soviet Union nor the United States appears seriously worried today about a deliberately planned surprise attack by the other. Neither side seems greatly concerned over mild disturbances in the prevailing equilibrium of mutual deterrence caused by fluctuating, marginal differences in particular weapons sectors. Most policymakers in both countries are probably convinced that, for all practical decision-making purposes, there exists at least a temporary, crude parity based on compensating offensive and defensive asymmetries. These asymmetries involve different numbers of bombers, land-based missiles and sea-based missiles, all of differing ranges; different numbers of deliverable warheads and total "throw-weight" (measured in megatons); differences in hardening and dispersal (which affect vulnerability), firing reliability, guidance accuracy, reentry speeds, penetration aids, detonation altitudes, and other weapons-design characteristics known only to the experts; and differences in warning systems, strategic intelligence, attack and defense strategies, offensive and defensive weapons mixes, and ability to overcome the unknowns of large-scale nuclear war (such as the operation of command and control systems under circumstances affecting electronic communications).

Given the present levels in numbers of strategic launchers (with growing numbers carrying multiple warheads), the case can be made that the uncertainties inherent in the calculus of a nuclear exchange are, on the whole, more stabilizing than destabilizing.

Military strategists may continue to worry, as they must, about the numbers game, about the possibility of decisive technological breakthroughs, and about the "worst possible case" in which *our* systems fail to perform well while *theirs* work perfectly. But McGeorge Bundy was probably close to the mark when he said that the political leadership in Moscow and Washington cannot under existing circumstances conceive of any rational purpose to be served by a deliberately planned first strike, because the risks of retaliation are much too great.[16] This need not always be so, although it seems plausible now. The political leadership may be naïve in assessing the intentions of their counterparts in the opposite capital, or they may become so in the future, or they may at some time lose control over the first-strike decision to military leaders who have a different perception of the situation—but these are all possibilities political leaders are understandably reluctant to think about.

The widespread assumption of a U.S.-USSR crude parity of assured sufficiency is important because it is the first time in the twenty-five years of nuclear history that such a condition has been thought to exist. One might infer that American decision-makers have been virtually "marking time" for nearly a decade with respect to deploying strategic military capabilities, as if they were waiting for the Soviets to "catch up" to the point where serious negotiations for arms limitations could begin. But it is recognized that the USSR has been coming abreast at a disturbingly rapid rate within the last two years (and surpassing the United States in land-based missiles by nearly 50 per cent). The United States has sought to reinsure its own security position by preparing to deploy the Safeguard system (around four out of twelve missile sites) and to arm half its land-based Minuteman missiles and three-quarters of its submarine missiles with multiple-warhead weapons.[17]

There are apprehensions on both sides. The Soviets are not happy at the prospect of the Safeguard deployment around even a few sites, for they know that once ABM and radar technology has been produced on a small scale it could be extended rather quickly. They are probably also concerned over the U.S. ability to upgrade the quality of weapons by MIRV-ing them more rapidly than the Soviets can. Conversely, U.S. defense and arms control planners wonder whether the Soviets will be content to level off at crude parity, or whether they might try to sustain and increase their recent momentum in an effort to achieve the kind of strategic superiority the United States has for all practical purposes renounced. The fear is that the Soviets will try to gain a substantial edge by deploying large numbers of SS-9's or other large vehicles with warheads or megatonnage greater than those in U.S. missiles.[18] During 1970, U.S. spokesmen speculated about the possible upgrading of low-performance Soviet anti-aircraft missiles into an effective ABM system; the possibility that the Soviets were developing a satellite-destroyer capability which could seriously hamper U.S. strategic reconnaissance efforts; and the significance of the buildup of the Soviet navy, including the submarine fleet.[19] All of these developments created suspicions that one side or the other was trying to take advantage of the SALT to gain a military margin over its rival, as well as misgivings that ongoing quantitative

and qualitative developments in advanced military technology may quickly render obsolete or irrelevant any precisely formulated clauses of treaties on which the superpowers might reach agreement at Helsinki and Vienna.[20]

But beyond the uncertainties that make it so difficult for the superpowers to reach agreement, there are other uncertainties which motivate them to continue the negotiations. It is possible that both the United States and the Soviet Union see the SALT more in the framework of what may lie beyond 1975 than of presently projected deployments of familiar weapons systems during the next two or three years. The Soviets would probably like to use the SALT to inhibit the deployment of an operational ABM system in the United States (and under certain circumstances they might accomplish this objective). But even if they prove unable to obtain such a bonus, there are other reasons why they would not wish to withdraw from the effort to arrive at some limited-risk, limited-cost, mutual interest agreements. Some of these reasons also serve to explain, in varying degrees, U.S. motivations.

Both are aware that there might be technological breakthroughs in the future. If the SALT were to collapse, competition in military research, development and deployment could well be stepped up. The familiar action-reaction process, marked by occasional overreactions, might end the existing condition of crude parity, creating new military-technological imbalances, perhaps leading to imprudent decision-making in a future international crisis. Both sides share an interest in moderating the rate of competition between themselves as they watch China. (The term "arms race," insofar as it implies a hectic rush to pile up or to improve weapons as rapidly as possible, is not an apt one for describing the present situation. The United States is preparing to deploy a limited ABM system only after ten years of debate.) Both sides must ponder at times the "economics of futility," that is, indefinitely expanding their nuclear missile capabilities and investing in costly new weapons systems throughout the 1970's, only to find at the end of the decade that such programs have had a reciprocal canceling effect, and that neither side has thereby improved its security or its ability to deter, much less gain any meaningful superiority.

Curious contrasts can be drawn here. The Soviets have reason to be worried about the total productive capabilities of the American economic-technological system whether measured in time, quantitative or qualitative factors. In a prolonged and unbridled arms race, the U.S. system, theoretically speaking, should still perform better. Soviet planners may realize this. Moreover, Soviet leaders undoubtedly feel economic pressures to limit spending for strategic arms—pressures for increased investment in agriculture and consumer industries, for narrowing the "technological gap" with the West in nondefense sectors, and for a reallocation of defense resources to the army and navy.[21] But in actuality, the purely economic incentive to reach agreement in the SALT is probably stronger in the United States than in the Soviet Union, because domestic political pressures to reallocate national budgetary resources to nondefense purposes are considerably stronger on Washington than on Moscow. Soviet leaders are undoubtedly aware of such domestic U.S. constraints.

In the final analysis, the logic of the economist is not likely to be the ultimate determinant of defense choices in any country where the leaders are worried about security. Both superpowers will do what they think they must do in the military sector. But economic rationality prompts the leadership groups in the two countries to carry out communications and negotia-tions designed to hold armaments competition to manageable rates, lower than they would be in a more suspicious, fearful climate.

Another important set of shared motives for negotiating strategic arms limitations arises out of the connection between the SALT and the Nonproliferation Treaty. The superpowers definitely prefer a world of five nuclear powers to a world of ten or fifteen, and hence they must consider the implications of SALT's outcome for the viability of the NPT. This is not the central issue, yet it is by no means negligible. Whether or not India or Israel or another country decides to go nuclear will probably not be determined solely by the success or failure of SALT. But if the SALT should collapse entirely or drag on without even producing what the Swedish neutrals call a "cosmetic" or face-saving agreement, it will become easier for several countries to justify decisions to move in directions that contravene the provisions of the Nonproliferation Treaty.

The diffusion of peaceful reactor technology during the last decade has considerably compounded the difficulty of halting the spread of nuclear weapons. "Atoms for peace" are not easily separated from "atoms for war." Despite a growing uneasiness about the dangers of environmental pollution from nuclear reactors, the fact that nuclear energy is becoming economically competitive ensures that it will become more common as a source of power throughout the globe.[22] Thus, the growth of reactor technology will render it easier in the decade ahead for several countries to divert fissionable materials into weapons production if they are determined to do so. The intimate relationship between military potential and the nuclear power industry makes it difficult to prevent the proliferation of weapons without at least seeming to jeopardize the freedom of such countries as West Germany,

Japan, India and Brazil to exploit the atom's peaceful uses. The International Atomic Energy Agency will probably not be able to perform the desired control function for two or three more years.[23] By that time, the possibilities for manufacturing nuclear weapons through centrifuge technology and through the even more esoteric ruby laser or argon technologies may have further compounded the problem of thwarting proliferation through technical controls on international exports.

The superpowers acted out of a combination of self-interest and a sense of international responsibility in agreeing to a Nonproliferation Treaty at the height of the Viet Nam war. But it must be recognized that they can do no more than discourage proliferation, by providing disincentives and compensations; they cannot absolutely prevent it. Their shipment of conventional arms into regions of local conflict, such as between the Arabs and Israel or between India and Pakistan, may under some circumstances decrease incentives, and under other circumstances increase incentives, to acquire nuclear weapons for deterrence or defense. For several years the United States sought to persuade new aspirants to the nuclear club that the game is not worth the candle because small deterrents are costly, provocative, accident-prone, non-credible, subject to rapid obsolescence and highly dangerous because young nuclear powers are vulnerable to preemptive attack. But none of these arguments has proved overwhelmingly convincing and some have often seemed irrelevant to countries worried not about the superpowers but about their immediate neighbors.

It is a sobering thought that the list of countries which have not yet signed the NPT includes Argentina, Brazil, India, Israel, Pakistan, the Republic of Korea, South Africa and Spain. Those that have signed but not yet ratified are Australia, Belgium, the Federal Republic of Germany, Italy, Japan, the Netherlands and Switzerland. During the last three years, the treaty has been criticized on several different grounds. It is a device for "disarming the unarmed." Virtually all of its burdens fall on the nonnuclear weapons states; thus it fails to provide an acceptable balance of mutual responsibilities and obligations. It perpetuates the nuclear hegemony of the five. It prohibits peaceful nuclear explosions by nonweapon countries. It limits the rights of nonweapon countries to develop an export business in civilian reactor technology. It will facilitate industrial espionage. It could inhibit the movement toward European integration. It infringes upon the sovereign prerogatives of nonweapon states by requiring them to submit to international inspection and other forms of "intervention" or "bondage." It limits the choice of nations in respect to vital questions of defense without providing adequate compensations in the security field. Steady if undramatic progress has been made toward reducing some of the foregoing bases of objection to the Nonproliferation Treaty, but several misgivings remain in a number of countries—especially in regard to security—and these are sufficient to make governments reluctant to close off the nuclear weapons option.[24]

The principal question concerning the danger of proliferation is whether the United States, Britain and the Soviet Union can offer credible security guarantees to nonweapon states which adhere to the treaty. At present the three "nuclear arms control powers" are committed to do no more than concert action through the United Nations Security Council in the event of a nuclear attack upon a nonnuclear signatory (and one can argue that the members of the Security Council always had such an obligation under the Charter). We must remember that a nonweapon state such as India is also concerned about the threat of conventional aggression. Indians have no reason to expect that, if their northeast frontier should again come under Chinese attack, they will receive help from the British (who have withdrawn irreversibly from "east of Suez"), from the Americans (who, according to the Nixon Doctrine, plan to reduce their Asian commitments in the post-Viet Nam era) or from the Soviets (who have to worry about their own troop commitments both in Eastern Europe and along the Chinese border).

Any nonnuclear weapon state confronted with either a serious conventional or nuclear threat will naturally fear that as the crisis mounts it will find itself under pressure from the superpowers to make substantial concessions in the interests of peace, so that they need not become involved in its defense. More than that, a nonnuclear weapon state has to worry about the possibility that, in a future defense crisis, the superpowers might be in an adversary rather than a détente relationship with each other. Thus it is understandable that a country in India's position should temporarily adopt the anomalous policy characterized as the "three negatives": No bomb, no treaty, no guarantees.[25] This enables India to defy the superpowers in their efforts to pressure her to sign, while moving steadily in the direction of reducing (perhaps to a matter of days) the leadtime problem between a decision to acquire nuclear weapons (if it should become vitally necessary) and their actual acquisition.

India's decision-making process is of crucial importance to international arms control efforts. Obviously, if she were to become a sixth nuclear power (whether for defense reasons or from a political desire to be guaranteed a place at the international negotiating table at least as early as China is seated

there), pressures would quickly mount for several other states to pursue the nuclear weapons path. Indian officials may perceive that their country is not without political leverage vis-à-vis the delicate triangular relationship of the United States, the Soviet Union and China. During the years when the NPT was being negotiated, Indian spokesmen argued trenchantly that the treaty could be justified as equitable only if it eventually paved the way for nuclear disarmament, or at least a reduction of the symbolic importance of nuclear weapons in international politics. It was largely at the insistence of India that the superpowers agreed to insert Article VI into the treaty: "Each of the Parties to the Treaty undertakes to pursue negotiations in good faith on effective measures relating to cessation of the nuclear arms race at an early date and to nuclear disarmament, and on a Treaty on general and complete disarmament under strict and effective international control." Yet precisely because of India's dependence for security on the continued ability of the superpowers to deter Peking's aggressive behavior by maintaining a wide margin of strategic superiority over China, her leaders are forced to adopt an ambivalent attitude toward strategic arms limitation talks between the United States and the Soviet Union. At present, the New Delhi government is not berating the superpowers for talking about a "freeze" rather than about arms reductions. At the same time, Indian leaders probably take some comfort from the thought that international circumstances are scarcely propitious for a Chinese onslaught against India. Indeed, New Delhi's policy of abstention from nuclear weapons may depend as much upon China's prudent restraint as upon any hope that India could count on assistance from the superpowers *in extremis*.

V

We can see, then, that the prospects for significant progress toward arms control in the 1970's will depend on such a variety of factors as to render prediction difficult even if they do not make hope meaningless. Each of the major world powers suffers under its own unique set of problems, demands, supports, commitments, apprehensions, dilemmas, assets and liabilities. Certainly one of the important tasks of U.S. diplomacy in the Helsinki-Vienna talks is to find out whether the Soviets will be satisfied to accept the condition of crude strategic parity as a permanent part of the superpower relationship, or whether they seem determined to go beyond mild and temporary disturbances of the existing equilibrium (which need not cause panic) toward a more fundamental alteration of the strategic equation to the disadvantage of the United States. If the Soviets should opt for the second course, it will not augur well either for the superpowers or for the world.

What would happen if Moscow should try to seek a decisive superiority in the realm of strategic military technology? One possibility is that the United States, preoccupied with other problems, might allow the Soviets to take a commanding lead. In recent years U.S. defense policies have encountered a rising chorus of domestic criticism. Probably at present a majority of U.S. Senators would evaluate the issue of additional ABM, MIRV and other weapons deployment, regardless of whether they are for or against them, less on grounds of sheer national security requirements than on grounds of the estimated positive or negative impact they would have on the chances of progress in the SALT. This reflects a legitimate theoretical disagreement in the present situation—i.e., whether the further deployment of weapons at this time, which is not seen as urgently

necessary to safeguard national security in a period of rough strategic parity, would have a favorable or an unfavorable effect upon U.S.-USSR negotiations. Put differently, should the United States contemplate recent Soviet deployment rates with equanimity, and even make unilateral concessions in respect to its own deployment policy for the sake of creating a climate favorable to negotiations, or should the United States display a determination to deploy Safeguard and MIRV as may be necessary to perpetuate the condition of parity and to enhance its bargaining leverage for the SALT while remaining ready to reverse decisions on projected but as yet unfulfilled deployments as soon as an equitable agreement is reached?

Perhaps the greatest danger is that the Soviet Union will misinterpret the contemporary American mood and seek to achieve an impressive mathematical superiority that might be exploited psychopolitically in future confrontations with American power. In this undesirable event the possibility of nuclear war might well increase beyond the levels that prevailed when the United States enjoyed strategic superiority, simply because Soviet communist ideology is more dynamically expansionist. It is doubtful, however, despite current uncertainties and ambiguities, that the American political system will acquiesce in the creation of such a situation (just as it is doubtful that the Soviet political system is capable of subscribing to any agreement calling for the destruction of substantial quantities of arms that might some day be useful for the defense of the Russian homeland against attack and invasion).

The American people, accustomed to the concept of planned obsolescence, can readily adjust to the notion of weapons destruction if they think this will lead to enhanced security and peace. With greater difficulty they can be persuaded—as they have been—to set aside the notion of strategic superiority and to think of national security primarily in terms of balance, mutual restraint, parity, equitableness, fair play and reciprocal respect, and negotiated settlements advantageous to both parties. These concepts are not inconsistent with either the American ethos or the American national character. Yet, regarding strategic weaponry, we have in recent years played down our traditional competitiveness and our compulsive desire to be "first in the field." Even this adjustment has not been achieved without political strains, including a tolerable amount of domestic polarization. But if those enduring national cultural traits which the anthropologists assure us cannot be easily changed are still significant in international politics, we should remember that never in their history have the American people shown themselves willing to accept a subordinate role to an external dominant power, particularly one disposed to exhibit any political hostility. It would therefore be unwise for Soviet policymakers to expect that the USSR, having moved abreast of America in strategic military power, could now substantially surpass her and achieve such a strategic preponderance as to pose a psychopolitical threat. That development would not be tolerated by the American political system, regardless of how much polarization or how many drastic political changes within that system the counteractive process would require. Perhaps Soviet policymakers understand the foregoing comments better than do certain segments of the U.S. intelligentsia.

Finally, neither the United States nor the Soviet Union can afford to adopt an exclusively technological, weapons-oriented approach to the SALT. Although a limitation on offensive and defensive strategic delivery vehicles might have a beneficent effect on the international political climate, at least for a time, we also must bear in mind that the existence of long-range nuclear missiles is the necessary but not the sufficient condition of nuclear war. The SALT, as one important dimension of U.S.-USSR functional negotiation, is related to specific geographic-political areas of controversy where superpower interests often conflict—Berlin, the Middle East, Cuba, Eastern Europe, Southeast Asia and Korea. Obviously, there cannot be a complete and close linkage between the SALT and the "conflict temperature" of Soviet-American relations in regions where the two countries are seeking objectives perceived as incompatible. The Soviets may be partly correct in warning that the SALT should be insulated against the adverse effects of ongoing international conflicts. But the United States is right in contending that arms negotiations cannot be entirely separated from those confrontations in which one superpower attempts to apply or support coercive tactics against the other, or against a state to which the other is committed. Such attempts will inevitably have an adverse effect upon the climate of superpower relations and hence upon the prospects for the SALT.[26]

It can be interesting to speculate on what precise type of agreement might come from the SALT. Will there be, as the United States was reported to have proposed in mid-1970, a numerical limit on the total number of strategic delivery vehicles, with each side free to vary the offensive-defensive "mix" to its own needs, except for such stipulated limits as the permissible quantity of SS-9's?[27] Or will there be a five-year agreement, such as the one reported to be advanced by the Soviets, restricting any further deployment of anti-missile defenses except around the two command centers in Moscow and Washington?[28] The American proposal involves a definitional question as to what constitutes a "strategic weapon." The Soviets wish to include the 500 U.S. planes based in NATO Europe and aboard Sixth Fleet carriers in the Mediterranean. The United States argues that if NATO's "tactical aircraft" are to be counted in on the grounds that they are capable of reaching targets in the Soviet Union, then the 700 medium- and intermediate-range missiles based in western Russia and targeted on Western Europe must also be included.[29] The Soviet proposal for a ban on ABM except around the two capitals could give rise to political criticism within the United States, and it would not appear to be an attractive agreement with which the Nixon Administration could enter a presidential election campaign in 1972. Election politics will inevitably play a part. Unless the United States can achieve an agreement before the election campaign moves into high gear in the spring of 1972, it will probably be better for Washington to suspend negotiations until after the election.

But although these questions are important, they are in a sense peripheral to the central question concerning the future of Soviet-American rela-

tions. After a long era of containment, the United States is now preparing to carry out a selective reduction of its global commitments as "policeman of the world." It is hoped that such a reduction can be carried out responsibly, without ushering in a period of dangerous instability in which such powers as China, Germany and Japan might be tempted to embark upon policy courses that will in the long run seem imprudent not only to American policymakers but to their Soviet counterparts as well. To expect the two superpowers to enter into some sort of world condominium arrangement is grossly premature.[30] But perhaps it is not too much to expect the Soviet Union, as a superpower, to assume a stabilizing and peace-strengthening rather than a destabilizing and peace-jeopardizing role. Although the United States and the USSR are a long way from a community of interest based on common political, social and cultural values, they might be compelled to recognize a coincidence of interest, based on a fear of what might happen if they squander this opportunity for at least a minimum of cooperation designed to hold a volatile world together.

NOTES

1. The literature of the 1960's on this point was ample and never really controverted. See Gerard Piel, "The Economics of Disarmament," *Bulletin of the Atomic Scientists,* April 1960, pp. 117-122, 126; *Economic Impacts of Disarmament,* United States Arms Control and Disarmament Agency Publication No. 2 (Washington: GPO, 1962); *Economic and Social Consequences of Disarmament,* Report of a Study by the United Nations Economic and Social Council E/3593/Rev. 1 (New York: United Nations, 1962); Emile Benoit and Kenneth Boulding, editors, *Disarmament and the Economy* (New York: Harper & Row, 1963); Otto Feinstein, "Disarmament: Economic Effects," *Current History,* August 1964, pp. 81–87; *Report of the Committee on the Economic Impact of Defense and Disarmament,* Submitted to President Johnson July 30, 1965 (Washington: GPO, 1965); *United States Report to*

Secretary-General Thant on the Economic and Social Consequences of Disarmament, March 26, 1968, in *Documents on Disarmament 1968,* United States Arms Control and Disarmament Publication 52, September 1969 (Washington: GPO, 1969), pp. 196-203.

2. The author has dealt in detail with these technical problems in "The Disarmament Debate: A Review of Current Literature" (Parts One and Two), ORBIS, Fall 1961 and Winter 1962; "Nuclear Weapons Control," *Current History,* July 1964; "The Status of the Arms Negotiations," ORBIS, Spring 1965; and *Arms Control and Disarmament: The Critical Issues* (Washington: Center for Strategic Studies, Special Report Series, 1966), especially Chapters 6 and 7.

3. John H. Herz, "The Territorial State Revisited: Reflections on the Future of the Nation-State," reprinted from *Polity,* I, 1, 1968

in James N. Rosenau, editor, *International Politics and Foreign Policy: A Reader in Research and Theory* (New York: The Free Press, 1969), pp. 76–89.

4. See Thomas C. Schelling, "Surprise Attack and Disarmament," Chapter 10 of his *The Strategy of Conflict* (New York: Oxford University Press, 1963), especially pp. 235–236; Henry A. Kissinger, "Arms Control, Inspection and Surprise Attack," *Foreign Affairs,* July 1960, pp. 559–561; Hedley Bull, *The Control of the Arms Race* (New York: Praeger, 1961), pp. 168–169; Glenn H. Snyder, *Deterrence and Defense* (Princeton: Princeton University Press, 1961), pp. 97–103.

5. *Documents on Disarmament 1969,* United States Arms Control and Disarmament Agency Publication 55, August 1970 (Washington: GPO, 1970), p. 579.

6. Throughout the decade of the 1960's, the ORBIS "Reflections on the Quarter" were replete with editorial pieces on the misgivings various NATO allies expressed on such subjects as East-West negotiations for general and complete disarmament; the credibility of the Western deterrent; NATO's nuclear strategy; the ideas of "flexible response" and "conventional pause"; the implications of summit diplomacy for Western security and alliance solidarity; proposals for a NATO deterrent and for a European deterrent; the Rapacki Plan for denuclearization of Central Europe; Skybolt and Nassau; the negotiation of the Partial Nuclear Test Ban Treaty; German apprehensions that arms control treaties would become devices for the "backdoor" recognition of East Germany; the effort first to create a NATO multilateral force (MLF) and later to scuttle it in order to attenuate Soviet opposition to the Nonproliferation Treaty; complaints by the West Germans that the NPT would not safeguard their interests in peaceful nuclear reactors; and criticisms by other Europeans that the NPT would have adverse consequences for Euratom and for the whole European unity movement.

7. See Walter Schutze, "European Defense Cooperation and NATO," *NATO Letter,* January 1970, p. 22; W. F. van Eekelen, "Development of NATO's Nuclear Consultation," *ibid.,* July/August 1970, pp. 2-6. Within recent years, the January and the July/August issues of the *NATO Letter* have also carried the texts of the communiqués emanating from the semiannual meetings of the Nuclear Planning Group.

8. See A. G. Kuhn, "NATO and Disarmament," *NATO Letter,* January 1969, pp. 17–19, and "Active Disarmament Consultations in NATO," *ibid.,* March 1970, pp. 20–23.

9. *New York Times,* December 5, 1970. See also Dieter Mahncke, "A Modus Vivendi for Berlin," *The World Today,* April 1970.

10. See the Declaration on Mutual and Balanced Force Reductions issued by the Ministerial Session of the North Atlantic Council, meeting in Rome May 26–27, 1970. *NATO Letter,* June 1970, pp. 24–25.

11. Virtually all published sources of strategic estimates indicate that the Soviet Union has substantially passed the United States during the last two years in the number of land-based missiles, while the United States retains a wide lead in submarine-based launchers. See Stockholm International Peace Research Institute, *SIPRI Yearbook of World Armaments and Disarmament, 1969/70* (Stockholm: Almqvist and Wiksell, 1970), pp. 41–58; *Strategic Survey 1970* (London: Institute for Strategic Studies, 1971), p. 12.

12. For an analysis of Chinese attitudes towards arms control, see A. Doak Barnett, "A Nuclear China and U.S. Arms Policy," *Foreign Affairs,* April 1970.

13. The reader is referred to the following articles by Victor Zorza: "Is Russia Planning War on China?," *Manchester Guardian Weekly,* October 4, 1969; "Chinese War Buildup Worries Kremlin," *ibid.,* December 13, 1969; "Polemics on a Powder Keg," *ibid.,* January 17, 1970. In "Spectre of War on Two Fronts," *ibid.,* January 24, 1970, Zorza presented the following analysis of Moscow's concern: "The United States does not expect to be bothered by China's nuclear capability until the mid-seventies, if then, and not seriously at that. But the threat to Russia, from missiles with a much shorter range, from much cruder nuclear weapons, which might even be carried by aircraft, could materialize much earlier. There is some reason to believe that the threat exists already. Of course, the Soviet Union would be able to respond to a Chinese strike, however small, with a massive salvo that would lay the whole country waste. But even a small Chinese strike is obviously more than the Soviet Union is now prepared to accept, and its policy is to prevent it, rather than to retaliate."

14. For a discussion of the complexities of this relationship, see Pierre Maillard, "The Effect of China on Soviet-American Relations," in *Soviet-American Relations and World Order: The Two and the Many* (London: Institute for Strategic Studies, Adelphi Papers No. 66, March 1970).

15. Michel Tatu, *The Great Power Triangle: Washington-Moscow-Peking* (Paris: The Atlantic Institute, Atlantic Papers No. 3, 1970).

16. McGeorge Bundy, "To Cap the Volcano," *Foreign Affairs,* October 1969, p. 9.

17. See *New York Times,* December 6, 1970, December 20, 1970 and February 27, 1971.

18. Secretary of Defense Melvin R. Laird on more than one occasion has warned against

the threat of a rapid Soviet missile buildup, which could produce a capability to destroy most of the U.S. Minuteman force before 1974. (*New York Times*, January 8 and February 21, 1970.) He said that during the previous five years the USSR had virtually quadrupled the total megatonnage in its strategic offensive force, while the United States had reduced its megatonnage by more than 40 per cent, and was "literally at the edge of prudent risk." (*Ibid.*, April 21, 1970.)

19. See *New York Times*, January 11, February 5, October 4 and October 18, 1970 and April 29, 1971.

20. Anyone interested in pursuing a highly sophisticated debate over the implications of quantitative and qualitative changes in U.S. and Soviet strategic forces for the continuation of mutual balanced deterrence and for arms limitation talks should refer to the following works: William C. Foster, "Prospects for Arms Control," Harold Brown, "Security through Limitations" and D. G. Brennan, "The Case for Missile Defense," all in *Foreign Affairs*, April 1969; George W. Rathjens, *The Future of the Strategic Arms Race: Options for the 1970's* (New York: Carnegie Endowment for International Peace, 1969); Matthew P. Gallagher, "The Uneasy Balance: Soviet Attitudes toward the Missile Talks," *Interplay*, December 1969/January 1970; William R. Kintner, "The Uncertain Strategic Balance in the 1970's," *Arms Control and National Security*, I, 1969; Jeremy J. Stone, "When and How to Use SALT," *Foreign Affairs*, January 1970; J. I. Coffey, "The Soviet ABM and Arms Control," *Bulletin of the Atomic Scientists*, January 1970; Alexander De Volpi, "Expectations from SALT," *ibid.*, April 1970; Jerome B. Wiesner, "Arms Control: Current Prospects and Problems," *ibid.*, May 1970; and J. I. Coffey, "Strategic Superiority, Deterrence and Arms Control," ORBIS, Winter 1970.

21. An excellent analysis of conflicting economic, technological and strategic pressures upon Soviet decision-makers can be found in Thomas W. Wolfe, "Soviet Approaches to SALT," *Problems of Communism*, September/October 1970, pp. 1-10.

22. See Lord Ritchie-Calder, "Mortgaging the Old Homestead," *Foreign Affairs*, January 1970, especially pp. 210–212; Sheldon Novick, *The Careless Atom* (Boston: Houghton Mifflin, 1969); Richard Curtis and Elizabeth Hogan, *The Perils of the Peaceful Atom* (New York: Doubleday, 1969); Philip E. Gustafson, "Nuclear Power and Thermal Pollution: Zion, Illinois," *Bulletin of the Atomic Scientists*, March 1970, pp. 17–23; Alvin M. Weinberg, "Nuclear Energy and the Environment," *ibid.*, June 1970, pp. 69–74.

23. See the author's "The Treaty and the Nonnuclear States," ORBIS, Summer 1967 and Frank Barnaby, "Limits on the Nuclear Club," reprinted from *New Scientist*, 19 March 1970, in *Survival*, May 1970.

24. See Elizabeth Young, *The Control of Proliferation: The 1968 Treaty in Hindsight and Forecast* (London: Institute for Strategic Studies, Adelphi Papers No. 56, April 1969); Ryukichi Imai, "The Non-Proliferation Treaty and Japan," *Bulletin of the Atomic Scientists*, May 1969, pp. 2-7; George Schwab, "Switzerland's Tactical Nuclear Weapons Policy," ORBIS, Fall 1969, pp. 900-914; Shelton L. Williams, *The U.S., India and the Bomb* (Baltimore: The Johns Hopkins Press, 1969); George H. Quester, "India Contemplates the Bomb," *Bulletin of the Atomic Scientists*, January 1970, pp. 13–16; H. Jon Rosenbaum and Glenn M. Cooper, "Brazil and the Non-Proliferation Treaty," *International Affairs* (London), January 1970; George H. Quester, "Israel and the Non-Proliferation Treaty," *Bulletin of the Atomic Scientists*, June 1969, pp. 7–9, 44–45.

25. Hans R. Vohra, "India's Nuclear Policy of Three Negatives," *Bulletin of the Atomic Scientists*, April 1970, pp. 25–27.

26. See James E. Dougherty, "A Nuclear Arms Agreement: What Shape Might It Take?," *War/Peace Report*, December 1969, especially pp. 11 and 16.

27. *New York Times*, August 17, 1970; Chalmers M. Roberts, "Arms Talks: Progress and Prospects," *Washington Post*, August 17, 1970.

28. *New York Times*, January 9, 1971 and April 29, 1971.

29. Hedrick Smith, "After the Helsinki Arms Talks, New Complications," *New York Times*, December 24, 1970.

30. Hedley Bull asserts that, although the United States and the Soviet Union have some common objectives, there is no evidence emanating from the superpowers to "justify speculations that they might agree to establish, or to work towards, some kind of joint hegemony of the globe." "The Scope for Super-Power Agreements," *Arms Control and National Security*, I, 1969, p. 6.

Selected Additional Readings

Beaufre, André. *Deterrence and Strategy*. New York: Praeger, 1966.
  A good description of strategic nuclear deterrence; points out that nuclear weapons are not militarily useful but can be employed as powerful political weapons.

Brennan, Donald G., ed. *Arms Control, Disarmament, and National Security*. New York: George Brazilier, 1961.
  A comprehensive survey of the field of arms control with special attention to the political problems of disarmament.

Calder, Nigel, ed. *Unless Peace Comes: A Scientific Forecast of New Weapons*. New York: Viking Press, 1968.
  A discussion of current trends in development of nuclear weapons, military space vehicles, conventional weapons, military computers, chemical weapons, and other possible additions to future arsenals.

Deitchman, Seymour J. *Limited War and American Defense Policy: Building and Using Military Power in a World at War*. Sec. rev. ed. Cambridge, Mass.: MIT Press, 1969.
  An overview of the nature, organization, and administration of limited war, stressing the need for America to create adequate forces to fight limited wars.

Earle, Edward Mead, ed. *Makers of Modern Strategy: Military Thought from Machiavelli to Hitler*. Princeton: Princeton University Press, 1941.
  A selection of excellent essays on the principal "classical" military thinkers, including Frederick the Great, Clausewitz, Jomini, Moltke, Ludendorff, Mahan, and others.

Green, Philip. *Deadly Logic: The Theory of Nuclear Deterrence*. Columbus: Ohio State University Press, 1966.
  Argues that the strategic theory of Kahn, Schelling, Wohlstetter, and others is methodologically unsound and is based on certain unstated political assumptions which may not hold up under analysis.

Howe, Jonathan Trumbull. *Multicrises: Sea Power and Global Politics in the Machine Age*. Cambridge, Mass.: MIT Press, 1971.
  An analysis of great power confrontation in the context of naval policies in two crises: Middle East, 1967 and Quemoy, 1958.

Kahn, Herman. *On Thermonuclear War*. Princeton: Princeton University Press, 1961.
  Argues that if deterrence fails we must be prepared to fight a nuclear war and win; this is possible if adequate defensive measures are taken.

———. *Thinking about the Unthinkable*. New York: Horizon Press, 1962.
  Argues that we must think about problems of nuclear war even though they are unpleasant; analyzes the nature of nuclear deterrence, international bargaining, and alternative national strategies for dealing with the nuclear war problem.

Kissinger, Henry A. *Nuclear Weapons and Foreign Policy*. New York: Harper and Brothers, 1957.
  Describes the impact of nuclear weapons on military and political problems and argues for tactical use of nuclear weapons in otherwise "conventional" wars.

Leites, Nathan, and Charles Wolf, Jr. *Rebellion and Authority: An Analytic Essay on Insurgent Conflicts*. Chicago: Markham, 1970.
  Uses economic and systems analysis to describe insurgencies and the methods that might be used to overcome them; rejects the concept that allegiance of the people is the basic issue in insurgencies.

Liddell Hart, Sir B. H. *Strategy*. Sec. rev. ed. New York: Praeger, 1967.
  A classic in strategic theory, this volume is the clearest exposition of Lidell Hart's concept of the "indirect approach" to military problems.

Quester, George H. *Nuclear Diplomacy: The First Twenty-Five Years*. New York: Dunellen, 1970.
  Examines international relations in terms of decisions on strategic weapons deployment; argues that U.S. weapons decisions since 1945 have been the result of realistic analysis of concrete situations and practical problems.

Schelling, Thomas C. *Arms and Influence*. New Haven: Yale University Press, 1966.
  Describes the non-military use of strategic weapons for political purpose; the threat to use force—to *hurt* an opponent—has become the essence of a new "diplomacy of violence."

———. *The Strategy of Conflict.* Cambridge: Harvard University Press, 1960.

An abstract treatment of strategy for all conflict situations based on the theory of games and stressing the exploitation of potential force rather than the actual application of force in a military sense.

Scott, Andrew M. *The Revolution in Statecraft: Informal Penetration.* New York: Random House, 1965.

An excellent analysis of the non-military methods states use to gain access to other states, including propaganda, economic aid, technical assistance, cultural exchange, and sub-governmental political contacts.

Snyder, Glenn H. *Deterrence and Defense: Toward a Theory of National Security.* Princeton: Princeton University Press, 1961.

A theoretical analysis of nuclear deterrence policy; demonstrates that in some instances the requirements for deterrence and defense may be contradictory.

Taber, Robert. *The War of the Flea: A Study of Guerrilla Warfare Theory and Practice.* New York: Citadel Press, 1969.

An analysis of guerrilla tactics which stresses the contradiction between desired objectives and available means on the part of the counterinsurgent.

Wohlstetter, Albert. "The Delicate Balance of Terror," *Foreign Affairs,* Vol. XXXVII, No. 2 (January 1958).

One of the early classics of deterrence theory; argues that it is possible for one side to develop a first strike capability and that, therefore, we will have to work continuously to maintain the deterrence balance.

5 | SOCIETAL IMPACTS OF THE NATIONAL SECURITY PROCESS

Introduction

The role of strategy and the implementation of national security policy were treated in Section IV. Section V is concerned with the societal impacts—the principal consequences—of the operation of the national security process for American social, political, and economic institutions.

In the first essay, "The Garrison-State Hypothesis Today," Harold D. Lasswell considers the contemporary significance of his garrison-state concept which was first published in 1937. At that time Lasswell argued that world politics was evolving toward domination or control by specialists in violence. The present article concludes that the garrison-state is still an accurate model of the past and future of our epoch. The author suggests that the only alternative to dominance by specialists in violence is for societies to pursue policies of "civilianism."

The next two selections probe some of the economic implications of national security policy. Bruce M. Russett, in "Who Pays for Defense?" is concerned with the opportunity costs of defense spending: what social programs must be sacrificed in order to achieve given levels of military expenditures; who bears the burdens of the social benefits thereby denied? The second selection, "The Military-Industrial Complex and the New Industrial State" by Walter Adams, offers an explanation of growing industrial concentration in the United States, particularly in defense industries. Adams argues that industrial concentration and the "military-industrial complex" are often the result of imprudent and discriminatory governmental action rather than a consequence of economic

and technical factors or natural selection.

The next two selections consider the issue of secrecy and its meaning for an open society. Harry Howe Ransom assesses the counterpressures against government secrecy in American society in "Secrecy vs. Disclosure: Conflicting Pressures." The sources of reaction against secrecy in national security affairs which he examines are Congress, the mass media, industry, the scientific and technological community, and the military services themselves. Anatol Rapoport assesses the university's relationship to classified military research and evokes the reactions of Alfred de Grazia, Henry M. Pachter, Ernest Van Den Haag, and Raoul Naroll in "Classified Military Research and the University." Their comments focus upon the effects of classified research upon academic freedom and the institutional identity of the university.

The next three selections examine some broad issues affecting the shape and quality of social relations in the United States. Morton Kaplan, in "Loyalty and Dissent," deals with conflicting domestic and international interests in choosing policy, the problems of deciding how to determine and apply values, and the social role of the right to dissent. Adam Yarmolinsky raises a broad set of issues in "The Military Establishment and Social Values." His analysis illuminates points of conflict between the style and traditions of the military and the operative norms of the civilian society. He concludes that the military has become an important source of divisiveness in American society, especially among youth. "Racial Relations in the Armed Forces" by

Charles C. Moskos, Jr., traces the de-segregation of the U.S. military, examines the role of the black soldier, and identifies certain discrepancies between official policy and actual practice. He concludes that military experience probably will contribute to an activist posture among black servicemen as they return to civilian life.

The final set of selections is concerned with military professionalism and the nature of civil-military relations in the United States. "The Emergent Military: Civil, Traditional, or Plural?" by Charles C. Moskos, Jr., explores the extent to which the armed forces are differentiated from American society. He offers three possible models of military-civilian social development —civilianized, traditional, and pluralistic. It is the pluralistic model, in which different segments of the military are more or less "civilianized" depending on their internal needs, that offers the best hope of maintaining both an effective defense mechanism and an overall allegiance of the military to the democratic values of civilian society. Samuel P. Huntington's "Power, Professionalism, and Ideology: Civil-Military Relations in Theory" provides that society can approach civilian control of the military in two ways. Subjective civilian control minimizes military power by maximizing the power of civilian groups in relation to the military. Objective civilian control achieves civilian superiority by maximizing military professionalism which makes the military the tool of the state. "Professionalism: The Hard Choice" by Frederick C. Thayer weighs the contrasting arguments for fusion of civilian and military perspectives within the military against increased professional autonomy for the military. Thayer prescribes the need for awareness by the military that they must maintain a delicate balance between autonomy and fusion. Robert G. Gard, Jr., in "The Military and American Society," assesses the "identity crisis" of the U.S. military profession from his perspective as a young general officer. He is concerned particularly with the process of adapting traditional values of military professionalism to radical new demands. The final selection, "Volunteer Armed Forces and Military Purpose" by Morris Janowitz, is a sweeping analysis of the implications of an all-volunteer military system for U.S. defense requirements. Janowitz sees the all-volunteer armed force as marking the end of a phase of history which has been characterized by the mass army. Janowitz speculates on the meaning of these changes for strategic policy and civil-military relations.

The Garrison-State Hypothesis Today

Harold D. Lasswell

The garrison-state hypothesis was first published about a quarter of a century ago.[1] The object of the present exercise is to consider the significance of the hypothesis in the light of scholarship and of the flow of history to date. The plan of discussion is this: (1) to consider certain points of method and terminology; (2) to examine the prospects for the continuation or discontinuation of the expectation of violence, which is a fundamental factor assumed by the garrison construct; (3) to explore the internal structure of decision within the several nation-states during future years; and (4) to draw implications for the guidance of science and policy.

I

The simplest version of the garrison-state hypothesis is that the arena of world politics is moving toward the domination of specialists on violence. The hypothesis offers a characterization of significant patterns of the past and future, thereby providing a provisional orientation within the flow of events "from what" "toward what." If we take the mid-nineteenth-century nation-states of European culture as the point of departure, it is meaningful to say that the most important elites were specialized in the exercise of business skills, and skills of symbol management, official administration, and party organization. Skills in the management of violence (or, more generally, of extreme coercion) continued to play a prominent role. Nevertheless, their subordination is indicated by the degree to which spokesmen for armies, navies, and police forces justified their appropriations by emphasizing power as a base of wealth, rather than wealth as a base of military-diplomatic power. Post-Napoleonic Europe was progressively absorbed in enrichment through the expansion of industrial society and the further decline of feudal values and institutions. The garrison-state construct proposes a model in which the sequence marches from the relatively mixed elite pattern of the nineteenth century to military-police dominance in the impending future.

With regard to method, the garrison-state formulation exemplifies one of the five intellectual tasks common to all problem solving and hence to the solution of problems of politics. The five tasks are the clarification of goal, the description of trend in the realization of goal, the analysis of conditioning factors, the projection of future development, and the invention and evaluation of policy alternatives. The garrison-state construct obviously belongs primarily to the third and fourth of the intellectual tasks, since it deals directly with trend and projection.

It is worth noting, perhaps, that the garrison-state conception was originally put forward for the purpose, in part, of emphasizing a methodological position which had been outlined by the writer in *World Politics and Personal Insecurity*.[2] I was underlining the fruitfulness of comprehensive hypotheses about the manifold of future as well as past events—after the manner of Marx and other evolutionists—while rejecting the claim of such comprehensive formulations to be called scientific. A "developmental construct" is not limited to the extrapolation of trend curves, nor does it fail to take into account the available supply of scientific data or generalization. A construct such as the garrison state is a means of orientation *in time* toward the most significant features of the total configuration of events. Although comprehensive propositions about past-future configurations have often been labeled "scientific," as Marx and Engels called their bourgeois-proletariat formulation, it is misleading to do so, since their current degree of confirmation in regard to future events is too low to justify the use of the symbol of "science." Hence the word "construct."

Problems of policy are oriented toward the future, and part of the technique of rational decision is to adopt procedures that expose all assumptions about the future to the discipline of explicit consideration. To formulate or to evaluate a developmental construct is to engage in the use of problem-solving procedures.[3] Among political thinkers the developmental method can be most effectively employed in choosing problems of study, in the clarification of goals, and in the invention and evaluation of policy.[4]

In devising constructs, care must be taken to adhere to the distinction between expectation and preference. The garrison-state hypothesis is put forward as a matter-of-fact statement of expectation. The contingencies referred to, however, are perceived as welcome opportunities by some and as catastrophic challenges by others. In

estimating the likelihood of future events, every candid person knows that there is a strong tendency to exaggerate the probability or the improbability of whatever contradicts his conscious or unconscious value orientation. Part of the procedure of problem solving is to search for covert as well as overt preferences and to give explicit consideration to the possibility of bias. In my case this precaution is of no little importance, since my preferred goal is to participate in activities that have promise for the eventual success of a universal order consonant with the requirements of human dignity.[5] Hence I have always regarded the possible coming of a garrisoned world with apprehension. I would like to help prevent this outcome by suitable policies —or, failing this, to encourage policies that humanize the garrison as completely as it can be.

Concerning terminology, a few points are worth mentioning. I use "state" in the conventional sense of jurisprudence and political science to designate a body politic that, when viewed in the context of the world arena, possesses a high degree of formal authority and effective control. Some scholars define terms so that "totalitarian" political systems are not entitled to be regarded as possessing true legal order. To the extent that garrison "states" are totalitarian, on these definitions, the proper terminology, following *Power and Society,* is garrison "rule."[6] I adhere to the earlier label partly because it is well established, and partly because, as presently will be seen, I do not limit the construct so drastically.

Many terms were, and are, available in place of "garrison." Among the considerations that led me to choose "garrison" was that I wanted to include "military" and "police," leaving the two words available as subcategories. Since in common usage, "garrison" has strong military connotations, the expression "garrison police state" is sometimes employed to emphasize that all coercive specialists are included.

The present review of the construct must begin with an outline of the equilibrium conditions of a garrison system. Enough knowledge of the past is at hand to enable us to devise at least a rough working model of this kind. We formulate the fundamental conditions of a garrison system as follows: (1) the power elites value power enough to resort to large-scale coercion when they regard such coercive strategies as useful to the maintenance of their ascendancy; and (2) the elites accept the expectation that the retention of power during at least the immediate and middle-range future depends upon capability and willingness to coerce external or internal challengers.

Since the garrison construct is an aggregate hypothesis, it refers to the dominant characteristics of the entire arena of world politics, thereby going beyond the circumstances of a particular body politic. A garrisoned world is a military arena—not a civic arena—in which resort to extreme measures of coercion is regarded as a persisting state of affairs, or as a chronic danger.

We shall work within the frame of reference provided by these abbreviated models despite the disadvantage that they do not include definite specifications concerning the degree to which demands and expectations regarding power are affected by such factors as civilization, class, interest, personality, or level of crisis. To present a detailed model would involve the discussion with many more categories and formulations than we can touch upon within the limits of the present inquiry. We shall first concentrate upon the examination of the variables likely to affect the expectation of violence, the broad factor whose crucial role is stressed in the highly generalized model sketched above.

Note that the garrison-state construct does not stipulate whether the decision process internal to the state is characterized by narrow or wide participation in the making of important decisions. Hence the garrison is not "by definition" nondemocratic. This is left to empirical inquiry. However, my initial concern for the garrison system grew out of apprehension regarding the future of democracy and of large-scale violence. Although it was not my intention to assert that democracy and military activity are always and everywhere incompatible with one another, I did not intend to suggest that in the light of historical and analytic knowledge there were ample grounds for concern about the viability of democracy under conditions of chronic war and threat of war or violent revolution. My concern was heightened by new factors in the environment of democratic systems—namely, the explosive growth of modern science and technology and the connection of these developments with the control of large population and resource basins suitable for huge capital accumulation. It seemed probable that the dynamism of Germany and Russia was largely to be understood in terms of the destructive implication of the introduction of scientific and technological factors into a divided world arena.

The rise of totalitarian or near-totalitarian systems in Russia, Germany, Italy, and Japan was confronting the traditional strongholds of relatively free government and society with challenges of enormous gravity. Regardless of the immediate outcome of the rivalries and conflicts that were in the foreground twenty-five years ago, I was impressed by the cumulative impact of profound transformations in the structure of world societies, transformations that were not likely to be reversed by short-range wins or losses sustained by particular coalitions in the world arena. My hypothesis was that the Marx-Engels construct of universal felicity after an epoch of world war and revolution is dangerously over-sanguine, the more probable outcome being a world of ruling castes (or a single caste) learning how to maintain ascendancy against internal challenge by the ruthless exploitation of hitherto unapplied instruments of modern sci-ence and technology. My view is the same today, though, as indicated above, I continue to regard it as in-admissible to use the term "inevitable" in referring to comprehensive future developments and regard preventive measures of policy with some confi-dence.

II

It is apparent that the garrison-state construct depends in large part upon the assumption that the expecta-tion of violence (of extreme coercion) will continue, either in the form of a divided and mutually apprehensive arena in world politics or, in the case of a universal state, within the internal arena of the new order. We begin, therefore, by examining the prospects for the continuation or discontinuation of the expectation of violence.

Will the possibility of mutual de-struction provide sufficiently strong in-centive to bring about world unifica-tion by consent? If it is more widely recognized that politics as at present organized precipitates coerciveness, will identifications with the nation-state sys-tem grow weaker, enabling movements toward world unity to succeed? On balance is it probable that the expecta-tion of violence will increase, decrease, or remain the same?

THE SHADOW OF DESTRUCTION

A recurring ground for hope of world unity and peace among advocates of a voluntarily unified world com-munity is the destructiveness of con-temporary weapons. In the last 200 years the appearance of new scientific and technological advances has been ac-companied by a fresh round of predic-tion that war has now at last become so awesome that no thinking man could possibly take the risk of involving his people in a new conflict. Pacifists thought they saw the handwriting on the wall for humanity when balloons soared into the sky, carrying the pos-sibility of a new and overwhelming front against armies, military bases, and cities. In turn, the airplane, long-range artillery, and especially poison gas seemed to hold the key to frighten-ing men into a better world. Today it is commonplace to hear—and to hear from some heads of states—that nuclear war is unthinkable.

No one denies that mankind *can* be destroyed by bombs or gas. But the problems that confront responsible of-ficials are couched in less simple terms. They are not faced with a single button marked "To destroy humanity, push here." The many policy alternatives available at any given moment blur the picture. The following questions serve to indicate the complexity of the "choice map" of top leaders:

Since we and our opponents both recognize the ultimate disaster that can befall us, is it likely that anyone will take the irrevocable step?

Is it not probable that the measures adopted in any immediate crisis will be designed, not for total, but for partial destruction?

Is it not likely that whatever meas-ures are initially launched will be less effective than expected owing to equip-ment failures and human error, as well as to sabotage and instantaneous coun-teraction?

If we continue to hold out a little longer in our negotiations to reduce and limit the most destructive cate-gories of weapon and weapon use, is it not likely that we will obtain better terms of agreement, in the sense that the arrangements agreed upon will provide more security, and also that we have a greater voice in inclusive administrative bodies?

If I seem too eager to agree now will it not weaken my power position at home by suggesting that I am willing to give too much in return for concessions whose true worth cannot be accurately appraised in advance?

POSSIBLE CHANGES IN IDENTIFICATION

The scope of action available to a political leader at a given time depends in part upon the intensity of identification with the established order that prevails at various levels. Is it likely that identifications will be affected by the perpetual mobilization to a degree that makes it "good politics" for leaders to reorganize the existing structure of the arena of world politics in the direction of a united world order attained by consent rather than by coercion?

Analysts of modern civilization have called attention to a phenomenon that is practically unheard of in folk societies although found in some city-centered civilizations of the past.[7] The phenomenon is alienation, by which is meant nonparticipation in the perspectives and behaviors appropriate to nation-states, and the carrying of nonparticipation to the ultimate of self-destruction. Included among nonparticipation patterns are practices which may be part of traditional culture, as when worldly things are abandoned in order to live the life of a recluse for the purpose of meditating upon trans-empirical matters.

Many scholars have been impressed by the evidence of alienation in the modern history of Western Europe.[8] A principal factor is alleged to be the breakdown in the ideological unity of Christendom, a breakup traumatically expressed by the willingness of Chris-

tian powers to form coalitions with the infidel and by the Protestant Reformation. It is conjectured that an additional factor is the unsettling impact of scientific knowledge upon man's image of himself and the world in which he lives. A "personal" God has dissolved into macrodistances or microphenomena equally alien to the cosmologies of the prescientific age. Mass and energy distributions are not yet integrated with the "subjective events" that seem so near yet so remarkably private and unique in human experience.

Investigators point to a variety of factors connected with social change that confront adults with problems of adaptation with which they are unable to cope by reason of the failure of childhood environments to provide the equipment required to enter the adult world with appropriate problem-solving capabilities. This failure to cope, reflected especially in the phenomenon of suicide, has been the focal point of many researches.[9] Investigators have examined the consequences of geographical mobility, which often fails to provide adults or children with a steady "supporting" configuration. Studies have also directed attention to social mobility, the rise or fall of individuals and groups in the class structure of society. Here again exposure to cross-pressure frequently works havoc with the minimum of stability required for early socialization or later continuation.

It is also recognized that our civilization specializes in the rapid obsolescing of old interests and the rapid rise of new ways of thinking, talking, and doing. Within the same ideological and territorial unit, and at the same class level, individuals are perpetually shifting occupations and leisure-time activities. New scientific and technological innovations draw attention to new sources of raw material and energy, or stimulate the invention of novel goods and services and of modified modes of production, merchandising, and utilization. Or the lead is taken by a new control device that makes it seem advantageous to merge plants, to revamp organizational structures, and to reassign personnel. The point of innovation may be a new accounting technique that alters the tax vulnerability of an organization and favors its survival. In any case, the social environment is complicated by operational networks that confront individuals with new patterns of attention and perspective.

The phenomenon called alienation is an extreme form of response precipitated by the clash of norm with norm or of norm with normlessness. It is possible that the spread of schooling, of travel, and of mass media of communication is having results quite different from that sought by the manipulators of communication as an instrument of policy. For instance, despite great apparent differences in the key symbols, slogans, and doctrines of socialism, Communism, and capitalism, the impression may be gathering strength that in all essentials everybody is talking about the same basic pattern of life.[10] Among articulate spokesmen for contemporary nation-states everyone seems to profess human dignity and freedom as an ultimate goal. Everyone favors peace and security, and everyone fosters the sciences and the technologies of production and destruction. Practically everyone endorses a rising standard of living, including social security against unemployment, accident and illness, old age, and related vicissitudes. Almost everyone seems to endorse the recognition of individual merit and to deplore discriminations based upon caste. Nearly everyone appears to advocate freedom to choose friends and intimates and to found a family. In the face of those overwhelming harmonies of goal, differences seem opportunistic, related to the timing of various stages in meeting the problems that arise in modernizing and industrializing peoples of various degrees of backwardness.

I summarize these points because they indicate why it is to be expected that in some states individuals will withdraw their willingness to fight for the preservation of the traditional autonomy of the nation-states or blocs to which they belong. Is it likely that these developments will be important enough to put an end to world rivalry and in so doing to weaken the forces that foster garrison states?

It is probable that the perspective referred to will be more frequent in the industrial countries of the non-Soviet than the Soviet world. The Soviet world has leaped ahead sensationally in ways that strengthen the sway of its central myth. More prosperity in the older countries is welcome, but it is "old hat." It evokes less pride than it once did.

We do not expect "peace at any price" movements to gain influence quickly in the United States in view of the likelihood that most alienated individuals will be recruited from among Americans who are least motivated to join active political programs of pressure-group and party agitation and organization.[11] Furthermore, any new movement will be obstructed by the opposition of established leaders who sense that such movements are potential threats. It is perceived that if "peace at any price" groups were to obtain the support of the Soviet leadership—as they undoubtedly would—Soviet leaders would work with and through them to the disadvantage of other elements.

If in the older industrial nations "peace at any price" movements begin to win significant support, it is safe to predict that police measures will be strengthened against "subversion." The "political vacuum" created by withdrawals of identification may be occupied, therefore, not by anticoercive elements, but rather by persons and programs having a militantly nationalistic coloration. As a means of heightening differentiation from the Soviet-centered world, nationalistic symbols would probably be elaborated and embellished by "religious" symbols (such as "atheistic communism").

It is probable that liberal political leaders would respond to future evidence of general disenchantment by seeking policies capable of firing the imagination of the rising generation at home and abroad. But foreign aid programs, for instance, suffer from the doubts and scruples of liberal regard for autonomy. By raising the cry of foreign interference the established elites of receiving countries are able to obtain exemption from effective supervision. American leaders, for instance, have been embarrassed by this strategy and have tended to leave local cliques of landlords, officers, and officials free to enrich themselves without making a commensurate contribution to economic and social development. By perpetuating sources of discontent that can be exploited by rival world political elements the growth of stable and responsible government is precluded.[12]

The conclusion is that withdrawals of identification with politics, insofar as they gain enough initial strength to threaten the unity of older non-Soviet powers, will provoke policies of the garrison-police-state type.

THE OVER-ALL EXPECTATION OF VIOLENCE

We turn to the future of the overall expectation of violence, recognizing that some points made in the preceding analysis of alienation are also pertinent here. We begin by replying to the question: By what broad paths of change is it conceivable that the world military arena can be transmuted into a civic arena? (1) By a general war that establishes the supremacy of one of the polar powers without damaging the victor to a degree that leaves him unable to hold the dominant position

against a coalition of the remaining powers; (2) by limited wars that expand one of the polar powers without precipitating a general war and that establish such a position of supremacy that the other polar power throws in the sponge and becomes a satellite; (3) by policies short of active war that expand the effective domain of one polar power with the results outlined in (2) above; (4) by a fusion of the effective elites of the polar powers in order to protect themselves from further weakening their position for the benefit of other powers (the fusion could be effective if implemented by ultimatum and active pressure); and (5) by a fusion of effective elites, recruited from many powers in addition to the polar powers, who would establish unity largely by consent.

From past experience we know that one limitation of forecasters is their inability to free themselves from the assumption that the conspicuous scientific and technological features of their time are permanent. Recognizing that a major characteristic of science to date is the tremendous advantage of world powers that have great concentrations of capital at their disposal, we now ask whether technology can change so drastically that instruments of production and destruction are likely to be produced with small-scale outlays? Further, will the tremendous advantage of offensive weapons be nullified by the perfecting of defense? At present there are no convincing signs of basic revolutionary innovations.[13]

It is not to be overlooked that the growth of vast administrative networks under centralized and even largely automatized direction may have the seemingly paradoxical result of making top control spots more vulnerable than before to individual and small-group strategies of power seizure.[14] The patterns of control are continually transformed as new activities require more prompt and refined means of linkage with established and emerging operations. The networks of communication and decision become more elaborate— that is, more centered and subcentered. If small platoons are prepared to make simultaneous assaults upon key panels of control, the chances of success are good enough to risk, especially in times of general stress. Far from relaxing garrison-police conditions, such possibilities confirm the importance of eternal vigilance as the price of maintaining established elites in power.

In considering the future, we do not underestimate emerging technologies connected with "brain machines" and with experimental embryology and genetics. Mechanized robots are not only of potential importance as defensive guards or offensive elements. We are on the verge of producing machines that are capable of devising complex strategies of action and possibly—as Norbert Weiner suggests—of relegating mankind to a subordinate role.[15] At present it appears equally likely that a machine-run globe would be divided along present-day lines or that it would achieve unity. The same point applies to advanced forms of life that may be developed by experimental biology. And we do not dismiss as absurd the possibility that living forms which have developed elsewhere impose themselves here and inaugurate the "discipline from without" that mankind has been unable to attain from within.[16]

Can a communications revolution occur in which world elites voluntarily subject themselves to an ethico-political training that motivates the self-regulating, cooperative efforts necessary to actualize a global order of human dignity? Can such a reconstruction begin at the top (or with mid-elite elements) and lay the foundation for voluntary unification of demand, expectation, and identification?[17] Desirable as these developments are, we cannot at present view their chances with much hope.

III

The preceding examination of the prospects of terrifying the world into voluntary unity, of weakening local identifications for the benefit of an effective universal allegiance, and of weakening the expectations of violence points to one conclusion: the outlook is dim. Hence the precondition of the garrison-state outcome is likely to be fulfilled.

The garrison construct goes further: it characterizes the principal changes in intrastate power that are likely to result from factor combinations that tip the internal equilibrium toward narrow rather than wide power sharing and that favor the self-perpetuation of an elite specialized to the planning and implementation of coercive strategies of power.

Within the Soviet bloc of totalitarian powers the garrison-police construct is highly approximated, though it cannot yet be said with certainty that the ruling families have as yet consolidated themselves into a self-perpetuating caste. I shall not enter into a detailed discussion of the excellent literature now available for estimating the future course of development within the Soviet bloc as it relates to the wider sharing of effective power. I assert only that the garrison construct is more in harmony with the dynamics of totalitarian systems than are alternative hypotheses.

More critical for the future is the course of evolution within advanced industrial nations having traditions and customs of popular government. In previous expositions of the garrison conception we have projected the sequence of change that results when emphasis moves from wealth or other values and is placed upon power.

Perpetual apprehension of war

keeps the accent upon the consideration of power measured as fighting potential. The common goal of maintaining national freedom from external dictation is perceived as requiring the appraisal of all social values and institutional practices with state-power considerations in view. Economic values and institutions are drawn into the preparation of weapons and thereby subordinated to power. Scientific skill and education are requisitioned for research and development. Public enlightenment is limited in the name of military secrecy. Public health is fostered by programs designed to conserve the human resources that figure in military potential. Family and ecclesiastical institutions are given encouragement so long as they interpose no ideological or behavioral obstacles to national security. Institutions of social class and caste are remodeled to the extent that national vulnerability is believed to be at stake.

THE FUNCTIONAL PHASES OF DECISION

In this connection a distinction is to be drawn between those individuals, groups, and structures that are functionally specialized to violence and those that, at any given time, are conventionally recognized as military or police. The growing accent upon power and the institutions of power that occurs in periods of chronic mobilization typically works to improve the position of the uniformed professionals (when the base line of comparison is the precrisis period). At the same time, the comprehensiveness of the problems relating to modern war and war preparation tends to bring about a different result. Party politicians and other group leaders make themselves felt in the planning and execution of strategy; and scientists, engineers, and managers with nonmilitary backgrounds move into the complex and often high-level activities of state and society. The total decision process is carried on with a shifting balance between old and new elements at every phase. In examining the seven functions, we are guided to some extent by occurrences to date,[18] supplemented by the expectation of high levels of continuing and intermittent crisis that we have justified in the earlier part of the paper. In the final part of the present discussion we shall draw some policy implications from the interpenetration of old and new elements in the decision process.

The *intelligence* function is the obtaining and interpretation of information pertinent to decision. In a mobilized world the specialist on violence is in a preferred position, since he seems professionally more qualified than anybody else to give the estimates required in making the translation of "change in general" into "fighting potential." Laymen can listen with understanding to scientists and engineers who discuss the state of research and development at home and abroad, but for policy purposes this testimony must be fused with knowledge of how these activities and results are integrated with military resources organized in particular ways and affected by specific traditions of strategy. War games and exercises provide the specialist on weapons with a basis for making inferences that must be accepted in the last resort as the equations to be built into computing machines engaged in simulation programs. Also, we must depend upon these specialists to guide the delicate operations by which it is sought to penetrate the enemy's wall of secrecy for the sake of uncovering clues to intention and capability.

Perpetual mobilization makes it plausible to extend the scope of the function of the political police to include more thorough investigations of the present loyalty of personnel and of personnel vulnerability under hypothetical future contingencies. These contingencies include inducements offered by opposing powers and the more subtle effects of deprivations connected with a fluctuating state of tension and combat. The political-police function at home merges with the work of those who are seeking to find vulnerable spots in the personnel of foreign powers.

The intelligence function includes the invention and evaluation of strategic programs in the light of formulated goals and of the available body of trend and scientific knowledge, critically projected into the future. All questions of goal, no matter how seemingly trivial at first glance, can be plausibly shown to have a bearing upon the security position of the community.

The *recommending* (promoting) function in the decision process includes the advocacy of courses of action. Hence it goes beyond the presentation of plans to the bringing of pressure to bear upon critical points of action. In the United States, as in many other countries, specialists on violence are traditionally accepted as professional advisors rather than advocates. Hence in the rough-and-tumble of party and pressure politics specialists tend to be looked upon as special pleaders for high expenditure on behalf of provocative policies from which they obtain special benefits. While world crisis continues, however, this evaluation is likely to be modified, as the community comes to believe that proposals relating to strategy have little weight unless they have some measure of professional support. Hence, party leaders find it wise to align themselves with military figures, who are initially treated as advisors but who gradually intervene in public debate as policy advocates in their own right. Thus the scope of permissible participation by the military increases, and the path is cleared for confidence-inspiring personalities among the violence specialists to become candidates for nomination and

election. Since the making of military policy evokes interservice differences, struggling factions reach out for elements in the community at large with which they can join in tacit coalitions to support controverted positions. Party and pressure-group leaders, journalists, scholars, and others will be drawn into these blocs.

Another decision function is *prescription*. At this stage, rules, whether constitutional, statutory, or administrative, are made for the guidance of policy. In Western countries the bodies charged with the prescribing function have been overwhelmingly civilian, subject to the modification that "veterans" are at an advantage after a war has vanished into the distance and the veterans are somewhat obsolete as soldiers. Perpetual crisis now brings older military specialists and newer specialists who are scientists into regular advisory contact with prescribers, and it is safe to say that the deliberations of political bodies are likely to be regarded with some disdain. They have much evidence of time-serving, ignorance, evasion, and general irresponsibility; and this provides a "moral" basis for the possible assumption of authority by the military during moments of severe crisis.

The *invocation* stage of decision is of very direct importance to police specialists, since they are traditionally regarded as the principal agents of the community in performing this function. To invoke is to characterize conduct provisionally as a deviation from prescribed norms. During times of crisis loyalty norms are added to the standards of intercrisis peacetime society. Hence the political-police function flourishes, affording opportunities for specialists in investigation to multiply their numbers and to extend their influence upon personnel selection. The casting of doubt upon the integrity of individuals becomes an instrument by which unscrupulous or credulous members of the political police are often able to rise in power and to appear indispensable to the central elite nucleus.

After invocation comes *application,* which is a final, not a provisional, judgment of conduct. Courts, for example, are organs of government that are highly adapted to the applying function. Whenever police evidence is turned down, courts cause some frustration among the police and often become targets of cumulative resentment. Political police officials are continually edging toward the pre-emption of judicial functions.

The *appraisal* stage of decision is the conducting of "autopsies" on the connection between policy goals, the means employed, and the results achieved. Those who obtain facts pertinent to appraisal are strategically situated, since they control many of the inferences upon which judgment depends. Since policy groups do not like criticism, they exert continual pressure to insure exemption from adverse appraisal by controlling the appraisers. The point is not only to escape criticism, but to do so by providing a scapegoat. For instance, the effort is often made to show that alleged military failures are not failures by the military but are properly attributable to legislative limitation, civilian administrative confusion, and the like.

Finally, we speak of the *terminating* function, which puts an end to arrangements which apply the prescriptive framework, and also to prescriptions themselves. Termination is often a matter of freeing individuals from obligation (or refusing to do so) and hence provides many points of leverage in the social process, especially in civilizations rather than folk societies where contract takes the place of custom.

Glancing over the seven functions, it is clear that specialists on violence are already located at strategic phases of intelligence, invocation, and application, providing bases from which they are in a position to edge toward wider spheres of effective control of crisis continues.[19]

POLITICAL SOCIALIZATION

The foregoing examination of the decision process has indicated how crisis accentuation of state power tends to subordinate all social values and institutions to considerations of military potential, and how as a result, military and police specialists are placed in advantageous positions within the decision process. We cannot terminate the analysis without giving more direct attention to the socialization process (the process of political education). Can we foresee any connection between changes in the perspectives entertained by young citizens as they move toward full participation in the body politic and the rise or fall of garrison states?

The idea that the future of politics depends in part upon the success or failure of political education is no novelty among political thinkers.[20] Many of the generalizations put forward by Plato have been confirmed, broadened, or modified by modern social and behavioral sciences. Plato was explicit in assigning the chief role in bringing about altered perspectives to the parental generation. He spoke, for example, of the "exaggeration" of an accepted ideal by the elders and sketched the political cycles that result therefrom. Assume, for instance, a community whose chief preferred value is wealth; Plato's proposition is that exaggerated stress on wealth—as in the encouragement of saving and investment—provokes a demand on the part of youth to enjoy life by greater consumption, leading in turn to self-indulgence in superfluities, and in a later generation to self-indulgence of the antisocial lusts characteristic of unconscious sexuality and aggression. The end of the cycle is tyranny.

In modern civilization specific sequences similar to these have often been described. Families which focus upon material accumulation are confronted by the rebellious potential of the young, which often leads to rejection of the family-wide goal in order to obtain more egocentric gratification in the form of expenditures on immediate enjoyment. Since a life pattern of egocentricity provides no generalizable norm of responsible conduct for the young, the next generation achieves no superego or ego ideal strong enough to enable the individual to "contain" the extremes of sexual and aggressive conduct referred to above.

Affluent "economies" appear to favor expenditures for egocentric enjoyment. Thus, in industrialized societies the family loses many functions connected with the transmission of cultural norms, which are left to such auxiliary institutions as schools, neighborhoods, and the mass media. The communications industry is particularly dominated by economic considerations and encourages consumption expenditure by exploiting the most exciting appeals, which are largely sexual and aggressive. Owing to the growth of economic concentration, these merchandising appeals spread to the local retailer and penetrate deeply into the body politic.

We sum up these tendencies by saying that the passage from group involvement to egocentricity fosters subsequent passage from "superfluous" enjoyment to sexual and assaultive excesses. These trends are furthered by *failure of superego formation* from (1) *absence of models who are group-oriented* toward such goals as accumulation for family wealth, political power, religious eminence, or medical distinction and (2) *conflict of models as a result of geographical and social mobility.* (These factors often support one another.)

Having recognized the strength of the forces working toward ego indulgence, we must not overlook the possible improvement of educational technique when a problem is fully perceived. Many elements are then stirred into intense activity in the direction of restoring a former equilibrium or of bringing a new and more satisfactory state of affairs into existence. It is true that the subdividing, mobile, and affluent civilization which we know in the United States has not mastered the technique of socialization; hence, uncounted millions of young people are as yet ineffectively challenged to lead significant lives that are contributory to the good of the commonwealth. But we have formidable instruments of communication at our disposal, and there are great reservoirs of aspiration and competence in our civilization. Possibly we can reverse trends toward egocentricity and successfully cultivate personality systems in which identifications are effectively oriented to include the larger community.[21]

A danger in such programs is that they will try to rebuild social consciences by encouraging militancy directed against the stranger (the "other"). Undoubtedly the most ancient and successful means of integrating an individual ego into a more comprehensive self-system is by using the traditional syndrome that includes the expectation of violence, the ethical demand to sacrifice for the common good, and identification with a community less comprehensive than all mankind. Perpetual crisis puts a premium upon appeals of this character and upon acquiring the social discipline symbolized by the folklore that presents the soldier at his best. In this way political power is renewable as a primary social value in rivalry with affection (family), well-being (comfort), skill and enlightenment, and wealth and respect when these values are pursued through the institutional forms of civilian life.

We have recently been reminded,

if such reminders are needed, that young people are predisposed toward the submersion of the narrow ego into the larger self of great social movements that foster action and sacrifice.[22] It is also evident from psychiatric and psychological knowledge how deep are the demands to escape from guilt, "self-contempt," feelings of weakness and related deprivations by plunging into social programs of vast scope. But it is never to be forgotten that everyone does not become sexually or aggressively ego-indulgent all at once; on the contrary, increases in a counter-mores direction generate tendencies toward restoration of the mores. With rare exceptions, the completely egocentric personality is not met with in fact. He is a "theoretical limit." No matter how flamboyantly ego-indulgent the individual may be, intimate investigation almost always shows evidence of conflict with less egocentric tendencies within the personality as a whole.[23] These considerations strengthen the chances that movements on behalf of social responsibility will succeed after periods of drift in the opposite direction.

Can the specialist on violence provide the model of social responsibility capable of mobilizing the latent propensities of the young in modern societies? It is already evident that in industrial society the specialist on violence is not condemned to the role of thug as he was in some of the disdainful images perpetuated by the scholars of China. The professional preparation of the military is not frozen in a sacrosanct mold. On the contrary the curriculum of training has been greatly transformed under the pressure of changes that stem from modern science, technology, and ideology.[24] Despite the cleavages generated within the armed services by the rapid tempo of professional renovation, it is possible to point to officers who have attained distinction in their own right as contributors to the new technologies. A far larger number has achieved enough competence to establish easy working relations with outstanding men of science and scholarship.

IV

CIVILIANISM VS. MILITARISM

We come finally to the point of asking by what policies we can maintain as many as possible of the effective institutions of a free society despite the improbability of moving soon into a world relatively free of the chronic threat of serious coercion. From the point of view of the strategy of human dignity the most promising trends to encourage are "civilianism," the movement that to a degree we can say is developing counter to "militarism." If we understand by "militarism" the permeation of an entire society by the self-serving ideology of the officer and soldier,[25] we can speak of "civilianism" as the absorption of the military by the multivalued orientation of a society in which violent coercion is deglamorized as an end in itself and is perceived as a regrettable concession to the persistence of variables whose magnitudes we have not as yet been able to control without paying what appears to be an excessive cost in terms of such autonomy as is possible under the cloud of chronic peril. As the perspectives of society become adapted to contemporary levels of risk, together with a common acceptance of the fruits of science, can the culture of science itself be more widely understood and applied to problem-solving *procedures* throughout society, including the decision process?[26]

The perception that scientific model building and data processing, when adapted to any recurring set of problems, call for the suspension of final commitment until appropriate assumptions have been explored in disciplined fashion, pertinent data obtained by appropriate methods, and interpretations evaluated by a rigorous procedure—all this indicates the diffusion of the scientific pattern throughout civilization. One implication is that physical scientists, for example, will never betray the culture of science by committing themselves to opinions on political and social matters without having examined the pertinent context with proper discipline.

However Utopian this may be, in the visible future the dynamic equilibrium of politics will work in favor of civilianism to the extent that people— that is, large populations, including the lower classes—continue to be positively valued for military purposes. Hitherto the dependence of arms production upon a huge labor force has been a factor making for a degree of democratization. This trend has gained importance as a result of the modern socialization of risk among all members of the population, whether military or civilian. However, in a technology run by automation the labor force may begin to appear redundant as the disadvantages of a human labor force become more obvious, especially its vulnerability to discontent and hence to the appeal of ideologies counter to the established system of public order. To the extent that mere numbers are perceived as endangering the resource base of a nation-state, demands will be furthered for such policies as effective birth control and the substitution of robots for people.[27]

Up to the present the huge techno-scientific advance in the United States during recent years has greatly retarded the factors making for a police polity of internal repression. It has been possible to supply consumer goods in increasing abundance and to introduce automation at a rate compatible with existing techniques of expansion, re-education, and relocation. In the absence of sudden peaks of crisis the forum providing news and debate has been open to movements to protect civil liberty against disastrous assault or erosion. Despite revelations of the thinness of our subculture of civil liberty,[28] the forces of infringements have been rolled back on some fronts.

The process by which a garrison is civilianized is likely to make rather subtle transformations in the "nucleus elites" of the future. The following questions point toward new elite patterns through a fusion of the skills which are representative of the highly developed specialties of modern civilization:

Is it likely that effective elites will be recruited somewhat outside, though partly inside, the traditional framework of the armed forces? For example, will a new elite emerge that is initially composed of officers, physical scientists and engineers, administrators, party and pressure-group leaders, public relations specialists and lawyers, who gain acceptance as the most realistic and creative individuals in coping with the total decision problem?

Will the traditional services contribute to, while failing to dominate, the new class that emerges in the interstitial positions created within our ever complicating social process?

Will the culmination be a truly civil garrison where anyone resembling the traditional soldier or policeman is as out of date as horse cavalry?

Pertinent to these queries is the evidence brought together in the contemporary study of elites in large-scale industrial societies. The modern decision process appears to function through shifting coalitions composed of formal and tacit representatives of the plurality of groups and persons formed by exposure to and interaction with the complex symbolic and material subdivisions of our civilization. Persons rise to top eliteship who have the personality structure and skill patterns adapted to the task of maintaining internal acceptance within a constituency while engaging in coalitional activities with persons of corresponding aptitude and position. For example, data are now available for distinguishing the "nuclear elite" within the broad elite structure of the armed services of the United States. The problems that arise in operating large-scale organizations in our techno-scientific age tend to converge as one nears the center of formal authority and effective control, and hence to reduce the differences in perspective and operational strategy from one top level to another.[29]

The structure of the elite differs in nations of low industrialization and modernization from the pattern described for the United States; it also diverges in totalitarian polities. In many contemporary nations it is possible to recognize legacies of myth and technique from political systems formed under pre-industrial conditions, such as "oriental despotisms,"[30] in which centralized bureaucracies leaned heavily upon coercive instruments of power. It is also possible to identify political institutions dating from the period in which, under an umbrella of formal centralization, the effective control usually resided with rulers of component territories, who also depended upon coercive means of maintaining their rule against the center and against further dispersion to subcenters.[31] Similarly, we perceive the survival of patterns once current in a feudal society in which rule was not neatly articulated with large contiguous territory, although power relations were fundamental features of the whole society.[32] Furthermore, we sometimes become aware of perspectives persisting from brief or long experience of city-states.[33] In the latter we recognize the close connection between banditry and trade, but we also perceive the strength of the urban subdivision of the social en-

vironment as a factor in shaping civilizations in place of folk societies. In peasant villages—and these are spread over a sizable part of the globe—we now see, not a folk society cut off from wider arenas, but social formations resulting from the centralizing consequences of expanding urban-based civilizations.[34] Among the active folk societies of today—in various stages of disorganization and reintegration in civilization—it is rewarding to trace the extremes of emphasis or de-emphasis upon central authority and control.[35]

Wherever we examine the situation thoroughly, we find that a potent influence is the tendency to introject the standards set by the largest and most successful bodies politic in the arena of global politics. Often the focal point of local discontent is among the military, some of whom are pace-setters in comprehending the technology, science, and total culture of the principal powers. In view of the tendency toward "diffusion by partial incorporation" of the pattern of the top powers, we are justified in saying that it is by no means out of the question that military education may aid in producing a generation of top professional elements who are multivalue-oriented.

Within the Soviet world the elite structure has remained tenaciously in favor of the formal principle of civilian supremacy; hence, the Party continues to be the principal ladder up the authority and control pyramid. Within the Party, of course, it is the specialist upon the political-police function who has an advantage, since central power elements look to the police to protect them from the challenges that arise in a totalitarian system. Established elites in such a system typically consider themselves endangered by decentralization, deconcentration, democratization, pluralization, and deregimentation. It has been indicated above why it is unlikely that existing top-elite components will regard it as advantageous to put an immediate end to the present divided structure of world politics.[36]

In the light of our previous discussion, we conclude, however reluctantly, that the garrison hypothesis provides a probable image of the past and future of our epoch. We would prefer it to be a self-disconfirming hypothesis. The master challenge of modern politics, therefore, is to civilianize a garrisoning world, thereby cultivating the conditions for its eventual dissolution.[37] The discipline acquired in the process may make it possible for mankind to accomplish what it has never been able to achieve before—namely, to create and perpetuate a universal public order of human dignity. So long as there is a gleam of hope for this culminating outcome of man's history, there is hope for life itself.

NOTES

1. My first publications employing the term were in 1937 and 1941. A summary and critique is to be found in Samuel P. Huntington, *The Soldier and the State* (Cambridge, Mass., 1957), pp. 346-350.

2. Harold D. Lasswell, *World Politics and Personal Insecurity* (New York, 1935), ch. 1. For a compendium of my characterizations of the construct, see H. Eulau, "H. D. Lasswell's Developmental Analysis," *Western Political Quarterly*, 11 (June, 1958), 229–242.

3. The allusion here is to the distinction between principles of content and of procedure. The first may be illustrated by the proposition that all rational thought requires goal clarification; the latter by the statement that in a problem-solving process it is important to find a place on the agenda for the clarification of goal.

4. See my discussion of "Strategies of Inquiry: The Rational Use of Observation," in Daniel Lerner (ed.), *The Human Meaning of the Social Sciences* (New York, 1959), ch. 4.

5. Compare M. S. McDougal, "Perspectives for an International Law of Human Dignity," *Proceedings American Society of International Law* (1959), 107–132.

6. Consult Carl J. Friedrich and Zbigniew K. Brzezinski, *Totalitarian Dictatorship and Autocracy* (Cambridge, Mass., 1956). For the definition of "rule," see Harold D. Lasswell and Abraham Kaplan, *Power and Society* (New Haven, 1950), p. 208; "regime" is defined at p. 130. The latter refers to formal authority, the former to effective control. "Law" is both authoritative and controlling.

7. V. Gordon Childe emphasizes the fundamental importance of the invention of cities for the emergence of civilization. The invention is tentatively located in a few river valleys about 7,000 years ago. See his *New Light on the Most Ancient East* (London, 1935) and later publications. Also Robert Redfield, *The Primitive World and Its Transformations* (Ithaca, 1953).

8. Tomás G. Masaryk, *Der Selbstmord als sociale Massenerscheinung der modernen civilisation* (Vienna, 1881); Emile Durkheim, *Suicide* (Glencoe, Ill., tr. 1951).

9. Andrew F. Henry and James F. Short, *Suicide and Homicide* (Glencoe, Ill., 1954).

10. The impression is supported by such official acts as proposing and ratifying the Universal Declaration of the Rights of Man, and by the results of content analysis of the language of politics. For background see Herschel C. Baker, *The Dignity of Man* (Cambridge, Mass., 1947) and the data reported in the Stanford studies of political symbols by Lasswell, Pool, Lerner and others.

11. Indications of the connection between alienation and political participation are found in Robert E. Lane, *Political Life; Why People Get Involved in Politics* (Glencoe, Ill., 1959). See also William Kornhauser, *The Politics of Mass Society* (Glencoe, Ill., 1959); Eugene Burdick and Arthur J. Brodbeck (eds.), *American Voting Behavior* (Glencoe, Ill., 1959).

12. The complications of economic development are shown in studies such as Berthold F. Hoselitz (ed.), *The Progress of Underdeveloped Areas* (Chicago, 1952); Simon S. Kuznets *et al.*, *Economic Growth: Brazil, India, Japan* (Durham, N.C., 1955); Gunnar Myrdal, *An International Economy: Problems and Prospects* (New York, 1956); Albert O. Hirschman, *The Strategy of Economic Development* (New Haven, 1958).

13. The reference is to more sweeping transformations than the spread of nuclear technology although this gives rise to complications. See *The Nth Country Problem and Arms Control* by the National Planning Association (Washington, 1960), which includes a technical annex by W. Davidon and others.

14. A theme that occurs in some writings on strategy; for example, Ferdinand O. Miksche, *Atomic Weapons and Armies* (New York, 1955).

15. The current developments in the science and technology of machines are sum-

marized at intervals in *Science* and *Scientific American*.

16. See my projections in "Men in Space," *Annals of the New York Academy of Sciences*, 72 (April, 1958), 180–194.

17. Attention should be called to new techniques of training that, if used for parochial purposes, may work against more comprehensive perspectives. Consult F. Skinner's novel, *Walden Two* (New York, 1948), and his *Science and Human Behavior* (New York, 1953).

18. For indications see: Ralph S. Brown, *Loyalty and Security; Employment Tests in the U.S.* (New Haven, 1958); Comment, "School Boards, School Books, and the Freedom to Learn," *Yale Law Journal*, 59 (April, 1950), 928-954; Note, "Government Exclusion of Foreign Political Propaganda," *Harvard Law Review*, 68 (1955), 1393-1409; Robert K. Carr, *The House Committee on Un-American Activities* (Ithaca, 1952); Walter Gellhorn, *Security, Loyalty and Science* (Ithaca, 1950); Eleanor Bontecou, *The Federal Loyalty-Security Program* (Ithaca, 1953); Edward A. Shils, *The Torment of Secrecy* (Glencoe, Ill., 1956); Charles V. Kidd, *American Universities and Federal Research* (Cambridge, Mass., 1959); Solomon Fabricant, *The Trend of Government Activity in the U.S. Since 1900* (New York, 1952); F. S. Hoffman, "The Economic Analysis of Defense: Choice Without Markets," *American Economic Review*, 49 (May, 1959), 368, and discussion; James R. Schlesinger, *The Political Economy of National Security* (New York, 1960); Eli Ginzberg and Associates, *The Ineffective Soldier* (New York, 1959), 3 v.; Huntington, *op. cit.*, Part III; National Manpower Council, *A Policy for Scientific and Professional Manpower* (New York, 1953).

19. Existing data concerning participation by coercive specialists in official elites are fragmentary not only in regard to composition but, more importantly, in perspective. The Second *International Yearbook of Political Behavior Research*, edited by H. Eulau and D. Marvick, is devoted to the methods and results of elite research to date.

20. Herbert H. Hyman, *Political Socialization* (Glencoe, Ill., 1959); Lasswell, "Political Constitution and Character," *Psychoanalysis and the Psychoanalytic Review*, 46 (Winter, 1959), 3-18.

21. The systematic study of juvenile delinquency has led to the invention of group as well as individual strategies for dealing with the problems involved—e.g., Fritz Redl and David Wineman, *Children Who Hate* (Glencoe, Ill., 1951)—and the strategies involved in capturing gangs for socially approved activities.

22. Friedrich and Brzezinski, *op. cit.*, ch. 4.

23. Consult *American Handbook of Psychiatry*, especially vol. 1 (New York, 1959).

24. Gene M. Lyons and John W. Masland, *Education and Military Leadership: A Study of the ROTC* (Princeton, 1959).

25. This is the conception employed by Alfred Vagts in *A History of Militarism* (New York, 1937).

26. The task of integrating the scientific outlook with our total civilization appears more urgent and formidable than ever. See C. P. Snow, the physicist-novelist, whose phrase "the two cultures" stirred up lively discussion. Note his "Reply to my critics" in *Encounter*, 14 (February, 1960), 64–68. Also see *Daedalus*, *Journal of the American Academy of Arts and Sciences*, 89 (Winter, 1959), the issue devoted to "Education in the Age of Science."

27. Lurking in the background is the threat of "Machiavelli, M. D.," to which I referred in *World Politics and Personal Insecurity*. Luckily the top elite in Nazi Berlin and Communist Moscow was not recruited from individuals possessing enough knowledge of science and technology to discover the more destructive potentials. See also my "Political Science of Science: An Inquiry into the Possible Reconciliation of Mastery and Freedom," *American Political Science Review*, 50 (December, 1956), 961–979.

28. Notably Samuel A. Stouffer, *Communism, Conformity and Civil Liberties* (Garden City, N.Y., 1955).

29. Morris Janowitz, *The Professional Soldier; A Social and Political Portrait* (Glencoe, Ill., 1960), especially ch. 8 and Part VII.

30. Karl A. Wittfogel, *Oriental Despotism: A Comparative Study of Total Power* (New Haven, 1957).

31. Sally F. Moore, *Power and Property in Inca Peru* (New York, 1958). This book corrects the image of Inca society, law, and politics as a supercentralized system. See also Edwin Lieuwen, *Arms and Politics in Latin America* (New York, 1960).

32. Rushton Coulborn (ed.), *Feudalism in History* (Princeton, 1956).

33. Miriam Beard, *History of the Business Man* (New York, 1938) summarizes the data for the Mediterranean world of the fifth century B.C. and of 1500 A.D.

34. Redfield, *op. cit.*

35. Note especially John Middleton and David Tait (eds.), *Tribes Without Rulers; Studies in African Segmentary Systems* (London, 1958).

36. For details see Simon Wolin and Robert M. Slusser (eds.), *The Soviet Secret Police* (New York, 1957); Merle Fainsod, *Smolensk under Soviet Rule* (Cambridge, Mass., 1958); Nathan C. Leites and Elsa Bernaut, *Ritual of Liquidation* (Glencoe, Ill., 1954); Boris Meissner (and John S. Reshetar), *The Communist Party of the Soviet Union* (New York, 1956).

37. See in this context Huntington, *op. cit.*, and in Janowitz, *op. cit.*, the discussion of "the constabulary concept" in the last chapter. There is a legitimate place for professionals who specialize upon sanctioning policy. I view this as a potential fusion of military, police, correctional, judicial and related skills. See Richard Arens and H. D. Lasswell, *In Defense of Public Order; The Emerging Field of Sanction Law* (New York, 1961).

Who Pays for Defense?

BRUCE M. RUSSETT

THE OPPORTUNITY COSTS OF DEFENSE

Theories of the economic causes of war are at least as old as capitalism, and have in recent years appeared in myriad forms. Around the turn of the last century J. A. Hobson and Lenin developed their famous arguments about the economic driving forces behind imperialist expansion; American opponents of their country's entry into World War I blamed the lobbying of munitions makers; more recently we have had C. Wright Mills and the New Left. The assertions of these theorists are not always susceptible to scientific examination, but to supplement them there have in the past few years been a number of sound and well-documented studies locating in the national economy the groups that benefit most from military expenditures.[1] Such studies show very effectively which industries, and which states, *gain* disproportionately from defense spending and hence develop some special interest in maintaining or increasing those expenditures. One need not accept Marxist or other extreme positions on the causes of war to find such information relevant to identifying political pressure groups that must be countered or compensated in any effort to reduce the level of military spending.

A question closely related to "Who benefits from defense spending?" is, of course, "Who *pays* for it?"; but curiously this second problem has received very little attention. Nothing comes free, and defense is no exception. In this paper we shall examine some evidence about what segments of the economy and society sacrifice disproportionately when defense spending rises. What kinds of public and private expenditure are diminished, or fail to grow at previously established rates, when military expenditures take a larger proportion of a less than infinitely expansible economy? The exercise will use economic data to address some critical political questions. It should point to particular interests, or pressure groups, that are relatively strong (or weak) and able (or unable) to maintain their accustomed standards of living during periods of international adversity, or to seize the pecuniary opportunities presented by the reduced defense effort that may accompany a relaxation of global tensions. Furthermore, it will enable us, in a sense, to do a "cost-benefit" analysis of war or preparedness, to identify the opportunity costs in the kind and amount of social benefits that are likely to be foregone. Such costs may be entirely in the form of current benefits foregone or, if the nation's resource base is eroded, they

From the *American Political Science Review*, vol. LXIII (June 1969). Copyright © 1969 by the American Political Science Association. Reprinted by permission of the author and publisher.

Research for this paper was supported by the World Data Analysis Program of Yale University under grant #GS-614 from the National Science Foundation, and the comparative sections were done under contract #N–0014–67–A–0097–0007 from ARPA, Behavioral Sciences, monitored by the Office of Naval Research. I am grateful to Kenneth Boulding, Peter Busch, John Sullivan, and Murray Weidenbaum for comments. Of course no person or agency is responsible for errors or for the opinions expressed.

may be paid largely by future generations.

The basic question has two prongs, of which only one can be considered here. One part would require detailed data on tax incidences and on wage and price changes. Expanded defense needs are usually financed by a combination of increased taxation and deficit spending. Tax rates would tell us what income or occupational groups suffered disproportionately from assessment increases. Deficit spending in the absence of adequate tax increases normally produces inflation. The wage and price data would show which groups saw inflationary pressures diminishing their real income more sharply than was happening to the average consumer. Generally, one would expect owners of common stocks and land, and union laborers with cost-of-living clauses in their contracts, to suffer least. White collar workers and, especially, pensioners and poor unorganized laborers, have the most nearly fixed incomes and the greatest vulnerability.

While there is some information on these matters, a high degree of precision and specificity is required before the data can yield reliable answers, and I have chosen not to develop that side of the problem here. What I have done is to examine information on *expenditures* by G.N.P. categories, by function, and by governmental unit to see what kinds of alternative spending bear the brunt of heavy military spending. For the United States we have this data for the period 1939–1968 or 1938–1967. This allows us to see the effects of two earlier wars (World War II and the Korean War) as well as the burdens of the current Vietnam venture. Toward the end of the paper we shall compare the American experience with that of several other developed Western states, albeit for a shorter time span.

First, an overview of the changing level of defense expenditures may be helpful. For 1939, in what was in many ways the last peacetime year this nation has experienced, defense expenditures were under $1.3 billion. They rose rapidly with the new preparedness, to a still-unsurpassed peak of $87.4 billion in 1944. The 1968 figure (annual estimate based on the first three quarters) was by contrast $78.4 billion, reflecting a build-up, for the Vietnam war, from levels of around $50 billion in the early-to-mid 1960's. The raw dollar figures, however, are deceptive because they reflect neither inflation nor the steady growth in the economy's productive capacity that makes a constant defense budget, even in price-adjusted dollars, a diminishing burden. Figure 1 shows the trend of military expenditures as a percentage of gross national product over the past 30 years.

We immediately see the great burdens of World War II, followed by a drop to a floor considerably above that of the 1930's. The cold war, and particularly the Korean action, produced another upsurge in the early 1950's to a level that, while substantial, was by no means the equal of that in the Second World War. This too trailed downward after the immediate emergency was past, though again it did not retreat to the previous floor. Not since the beginning of the cold war has the military accounted for notably less than five per cent of this country's G.N.P.; not since Korea has it had as little as seven per cent.[2] Finally, we see the effect of the Vietnam build-up, moving from a recent low of 7.3 per cent in 1965 to 9.2 per cent in 1968. This last looks modest enough, and is, when compared to the effects of this nation's two previous major wars. At the same time, it also represents a real sacrifice by other portions of the economy. The 1968 G.N.P. of the United States was well in excess of $800 billion; if we were to assume that the current war effort accounts for about 2 per cent of that (roughly the difference between

7.3 per cent and 9.2 per cent) the dollar amount is approximately $16 billion. That is in fact too low a figure, since some billions were already being devoted to the war in 1965, and direct estimates of the war's cost are typically about $25 to $30 billion.[3] The amounts in question, representing scarce resources which might be put to alternative uses, are not trivial.

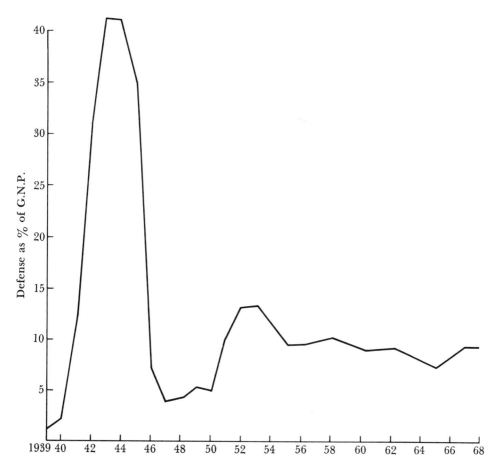

Fig. 1. Defense Expenditures as a Percentage of U.S. G.N.P., 1939–1968.
Source: See Table 1.

CRITERIA FOR EVALUATION

The method of analysis is straightforward. I have computed various kinds of private and public expenditures as proportions of G.N.P., and regressed them against the proportion of G.N.P. represented by defense spending. Both linear and curvilinear regressions (second order curves) were tried, but the curvilinear fit will be reported only when it improves notably on the results of the linear model. Defense is the independent variable, with the implication that the others are dependent upon it; that is, that increases in civil expenditures are made possible by relative reductions in defense spending, and that increases in defense must force relative reductions, whether deliberate or unintended, in nonmilitary items.[4] The causal chain is of course not fully demonstrable with regression analysis, but seems generally plausible.

I assume that defense spending has to come *at the expense* of something else. In the formal sense of G.N.P. proportions that is surely true, but it is usually true in a more interesting sense as well. Economics is said to be the study of the allocation of scarce resources; despite some periods of slack at the beginning of war-time periods (1940–41 and 1950) resources have generally been truly scarce during America's wars. Major civilian expenditures have not only lost ground proportionately (as would nevertheless happen from a military spending program financed entirely out of slack) but have failed to grow at their accustomed rates, have lost ground in constant dollars as a result of inflation, or even have declined absolutely in current dollars. During World War II, for example, such major categories as personal consumption of durable goods, all fixed investment, federal purchases of non-military goods and services, and state and local expenditures all declined sharply in absolute dollar amounts despite an inflation of nearly 8 per cent a year.

Some observers might argue that high levels of military spending are introduced to take up the slack and maintain demand in an otherwise depression-prone economy. If this were the case, opportunity costs would be minimal. But there is little evidence for that proposition in the American experience of recent decades. Certainly the Vietnam experience does not support it. I assume, *pace* "Iron Mountain," that with the demonstrable public and private needs of this society, and with modern tools of economic analysis and manipulation, full or near-full employment of resources would be maintained even in the face of major cuts in military spending.[5] Because of the

skills with which economic systems are now managed, in modern economies defense expenditures are much more likely to force tradeoffs than they were some 30 years ago. Thus the original formulation, "Who pays for defense?" is not inappropriate.

Defense expenditures are not necessarily without broader social utility. Spending for military research and development produces important technological spill-overs into the civilian sector. The education, skills, and physical conditioning that young men obtain during service in the armed forces are likely to benefit them and their society, when they return to civilian life. Rarely, however, is the achievement of such benefits as spillovers the most efficient way to obtain them. While scientific research may be serendipitous, the odds are better that a new treatment for cancer will come from medical research than from work on missile systems. Hence we must still consider the tradeoffs that appear in the official functional categories as real costs, though not quite as heavy costs as a literal interpretation of the dollar amounts would imply.

Finally, we must recognize that some civilian expenditures, for health, for education, and for research, have been stimulated by cold war and ultimately military requirements. Various programs of the 1950's fit this characterization, when a need more for long-run girding of the loins than for more immediate military capabilities was widely seen. Still, this is appropriate to precisely the kind of question we shall be asking. If the civilian and military expenditures consistently compete for scarce resources, they will be highly negatively correlated; if they both are driven by the same demands, they will be positively correlated. If they generally compete but sometimes are viewed as complementary, the negative correlation will be fairly low.

An evaluation of the experience of

this and other nations requires some explicit criteria. There is room for serious argument about what those criteria should be, but I will suggest the following:

1) It is bad to sacrifice future productivity and resources for current defense or war-fighting activities; insofar as possible such activities "should" be financed out of current consumption. Such an assumption might be easily challenged if it were offered as a universal, but for the developed countries of North America and Western Europe in recent years it seems defensible. All of them are now, relative to their own past and other nations' present, extremely affluent with a high proportion of their resources flowing into consumption in the private sector. Furthermore, for the years being analyzed the demands of defense have not usually been terribly great. Since World War II ended, none of these countries has had to devote more than about 10 per cent of its G.N.P. to military needs, save for the United States during the Korean War when the figure rose to just over 13 per cent. It surely is arguable that such needs rarely require substantial mortgaging of a nation's future.

a) By this criterion one would hope to see periodic *up-swings* in defense requirements financed largely out of personal consumption, with capital formation and such social investment in the public sector as health and education being insensitive to military demands.

b) Another aspect of our criterion, however, is the anticipation that in periods of *declining* military needs the released resources would largely be *kept* for investment and education rather than returned to private consumption. In a strong form the criterion calls for a long-term secular increase in the proportion of G.N.P. devoted to various forms of investment, and with this secular trend realized through a fluctuating line made up of a series of upward slopes followed by plateaus, insensitive to rising defense needs but responsive to the opportunities provided by relaxations in the armament pace.

2) Another point of view, partially in conflict with the last comment, would stress the need for a high degree of *insulation from political shocks*. A constant and enlarging commitment to the system's social resources is necessary for the most orderly and efficient growth of the system, avoiding the digestive problems produced by alternate feast and famine. Some spending, for instance capital expenditures for buildings, may be only temporarily postponed in periods of fiscal stringency, and may bounce back to a higher level when the pressure of defense needs is eased. To that degree the damage would be reduced, but not eliminated. In the first place, school construction that is "merely" postponed four years will come in time to help some students, but one age cohort simply loses out. Secondly, boom and bust fluctuations, even if they do average out to the socially desired dollar level, are likely to be inefficient and produce less real output than would a steadier effort.

GUNS, BUTTER, AND STRUCTURES

Calculation of a nation's G.N.P. is an exercise in accounting; economists define the gross national product as the sum of expenditures for personal consumption, investment or capital formation, government purchases of goods and services, and net foreign trade (exports minus imports). Each of these categories can be broken down further. Private consumption is summed from expenditures on durable goods (e.g., automobiles, furniture, appliances), non-durables (e.g., food, clothing, fuel) and services (airline tickets, haircuts, entertainment); investment includes fixed investment in non-residential structures, producers' durable equipment (e.g., machinery), residential structures, and the accumulation or drawing down of stocks (inventories); government purchases include both civil and military expenditures of the federal government, and spending by state and local units of government. Except for inventories (which fluctuate widely in response to current conditions and are of little interest for this study) we shall look at all these, and later at a further breakdown of public expenditures by level and function. Table 1 gives the r^2 (proportion of variance in the dependent variables accounted for by defense), the regression coefficients, and an index of proportionate reduction. The r^2 tells *how closely* the two variables vary together, and the regression coefficient tells *the*

amount in dollars by which the dependent variable changes in response to a one dollar increase in defense. The proportionate reduction index shows the damage suffered by each category relative to its "normal" base. It assumes for illustration a total G.N.P. of $400 billion, an increase of $25 billion in defense spending from the previous period, and that the "dependent" expenditure category had previously been at that level represented by its mean percentage of G.N.P. over the 1939–68 period. This last measure is important for policy purposes, since the *impact* of the same dollar reduction will be far greater to a $100 billion investment program than to a $500 billion total for consumer spending.[6]

In general, the American experience has been that the consumer pays most. Guns do come at the expense of butter. Changes in defense expenditure account for 84% of the variance in total personal *consumption,* and the regression coefficient is a relatively high —.420 (that is, a one dollar rise in defense expenditures will, all else being equal, result in a decline of $.420 in private consumption).

Of the sub-categories, sales of consumer durables are most vulnerable, with 78 per cent of their variance accounted for by defense. Spending on services is also fairly vulnerable to defense expenditures, with the latter accounting for 54 per cent of the variance. But the *linear* regression between defense and non-durables is not nearly so high, with an r^2 of but .04. This is not surprising, as needs for non-durables are virtually by definition the least easily postponed. The low r^2 from the linear model is deceptive, however, because a look at the plot of defense against non-durable consumer goods purchases shows that the proportion of G.N.P. spent on the latter *increased* somewhat in the early 1940's, when war costs were reaching their peak; it was as high in 1942–45 as in many prewar

TABLE 1. The Effect of Defense Spending on Civilian Activities in the United States, 1939–68

	r^2 (linear reg.)	Regression Coefficient	Index of Proportionate Reduction
Personal Consumption (Total)	.84	—.420	—.041
Durable Goods	.78	—.163	—.123
Nondurable Goods	.04	—.071	—.014
Services	.54	—.187	—.050
Fixed Investment (Total)	.72	—.292	—.144
Nonresidential Structures	.62	—.068	—.140
Producers' Durable Equipment	.71	—.110	—.123
Residential Structures	.60	—.114	—.176
Exports	.67	—.097	—.115
Imports	.19	—.025	—.037
Federal Civil Purchases	.38	—.048	—.159
State & Local Gov't Consumption	.38	—.128	—.105

Source: *Survey of Current Business,* 45, 8 (August 1965), pp. 24–25, 46, 11 (November 1966), p. S–1, and 47, 11 (November 1968), p. S–1. Data for 1968 are provisional figures for first three quarters only.

and postwar years. Using a curvilinear regression with a second-degree curve adds another 22 per cent of the total variance to the 4 per cent accounted for by the linear model. The explanation is fairly simple: During the war years new consumer durables such as automobiles and appliances were virtually unavailable, since the factories that normally produced them were then turning out war materiel. Similarly, due to manpower shortages almost all services were expensive and in short supply, and long-distance travel was particularly discouraged ("Is this trip necessary?"). Hence, to the degree consumers' spending power was not mopped up by taxes, or saved, an unusually high proportion was likely to go into non-durables.

Investment (fixed capital formation) also is typically hard-hit by American war efforts and, with its consequence of a smaller productive capacity in later years, diminished investment is a particularly costly loss. The r^2 of .72 is only a little less than that for defense on consumption, and the regression coefficient is a substantial —.292.[7] The slope is of course much flatter than that for defense and consumption (with a coefficient of —.420) but that is very deceptive considering the "normal" base from which each starts. Over the 30 years for which we have data, the mean percentage of G.N.P. consumption typically was about five times as great as investment. Thus in our hypothetical illustration a $25 billion increase in defense costs in a G.N.P. of $400 billion would, ceteris paribus, result in a drop in consumption from approximately $256 billion to roughly $245, or only a little over 4 per cent of total consumption. Investment on the other hand would typically fall from $51 billion to about $44 billion, or more than 14 per cent. *Proportionately,* therefore, investment is much *harder* hit by an expansion of the military establishment than is consumption.

Since future production is dependent upon current investment, the economy's *future* resources and power base are thus in a very real sense much more severely damaged by the decision to build or employ current military power than is current indulgence. According to some rough estimates, the marginal productivity of capital in the United States is between 20 and 25 per cent; that is, an additional dollar of investment in any single year will produce 20–25 cents of annual additional production in perpetuity.[8] Hence if an extra billion dollars of defense in one year reduced investment by $292 million, thenceforth the level of output in the economy would be *permanently* diminished by on the order of $65 million per year.

This position is modified slightly by the detailed breakdown of investment categories. Residential structures (housing) shows the lowest r^2 of the three, but its regression coefficient is the strongest and it takes the greatest proportionate damage. Within the general category of investment, therefore, non-residential structures and equipment usually hold up somewhat better proportionately than does housing. Doubtless this is the result of deliberate public policy which raises home interest rates and limits the availability of mortgages while trying at the same time to maintain an adequate flow of capital to those firms needing to convert or expand into military production. One other feature should be noticed, however. The curvilinear model (second order curve) adds as much as 43 per cent of the remaining variance with non-residential structures. Relative spending goes *up* with increments to very low levels of defense spending to where defense equals about 9 per cent of G.N.P. It then flattens out until, by around the 13 per cent mark, it begins to fall off sharply. This phenomenon is probably the result of construction of new factories for war production and, especially, facilities for military bases and camps when a large army must be mustered quickly from low manpower levels.

The nation's international *balance of payments* is often a major casualty of sharp increases in military expenditures; the present situation is not unusual. Some potential exports are diverted to satisfy internal demand, others are lost because domestic inflation raises costs to the point that the goods are priced out of the world market. *Imports* may rise directly to meet the armed forces' procurement needs—goods purchased abroad to fill local American military requirements show up as imports to the national economy—and other imports rise indirectly because of domestic demand. Some goods normally purchased from domestic suppliers are not available in sufficient quantities; others, because of inflation, become priced above imported goods. If the present situation is "typical," the Vietnam war's cost to the civilian economy would be responsible for a loss of more than one and one-half billion dollars in exports.

The import picture is more complicated. According to the sketch above, imports should *rise* with defense spending, but the r^2 in the table is very low and the slope of the regression line is actually *negative*. This, however, is deceptive and gives a conclusion quickly reversed by a curvilinear regression. The second order curve shows the expectable sharp *positive* relation between defense and imports up to a level of defense more or less equal to 13 per cent of G.N.P. Only then does it flatten out and then turn down dramatically. The four years of World War II show unusually low importation activity, and the reasons are obvious. A combination of enemy occupation of normal sources of goods for the U.S., enemy surface and submarine activity in the sea lanes, and the diversion of our allies' normal export industries to serve *their* war needs drastically reduced America's opportunity to import. To assess the impact of defense expenditures on imports in a less than global war one must omit the World War II data from the analysis. Doing so produces the expected positive regression coefficient, on the order of +.060. This suggests that the current effect of Vietnam may be to add, directly and indirectly, over $1 billion to the nation's annual import bill.[9] Coupled with the loss of exports, the total damage to the balance of payments on current account (excluding capital transfers) is in the range $2.5–$3.0 billion. That still does not account for the entire balance of payments deficit that the United States has experienced (recently as high as 3.4 billion annually) but it goes a long way to explain it.

THE PUBLIC SECTOR

In the *aggregate* there is no very strong impact of defense on *civil public expenditures*. The linear r^2's are a comparatively low .38; the regression coefficients only —.048 for federal civil purchases and —.013 for state and local governments. For the federal government a curvilinear regression helps, however, adding approximately one-sixth of the variance left unexplained by the linear model. During the four peak years of World War II changes in federal civil expenditures were essentially unrelated to changes in defense spending, hence the curve at that end is flattened out. But it is simultaneously steepened, from the linear model, for the 1 per cent to 15 per cent defense range.[10] Samuel P. Huntington notes that "Many programs in agriculture, natural resources, labor and welfare dated back to the 1930's or middle

1940's. By the mid-1950's they had become accepted responsibilities of the government," and hence politically resistant to the arms squeeze. If so, the overall inverse relationship we do find may be masking sharper changes in some of the less well-entrenched subcategories of central government budgeting. We shall investigate this below.[11]

Some restraint is required when relating state and local government expenditures to defense. There really is no relationship except *between* the points above and below the 15 per cent mark for defense. During World War II state and local government units did have their spending activities curtailed, but overall they have not been noticeably affected by defense purchases. Quite to the contrary, spending by state and local political units has risen steadily, in an almost unbroken line, since 1944. The rise, from 3.6 per cent of the G.N.P. to 11.2 per cent in 1968, has continued essentially heedless of increases or diminution in the military's demands on the economy.[12]

When we look at the breakdowns by function, however, it becomes clear that the effect of defense fluctuations is serious, if less distinct than for G.N.P. categories. Three major items—education, health, and welfare—were selected for further analysis, on the grounds that one might reasonably hypothesize for each that expenditure levels would be sensitive to military needs, and, for the first two, that a neglect of them would do serious long-term damage to the economy and social system of the nation.

All three are sensitive to defense spending, with *welfare* somewhat more than the others as is not surprising. In most of this analysis reductions in expenditure levels that are forced by expanded defense activities represent a *cost* to the economic and social system, but welfare is different. Insofar as the *needs* for welfare, rather than simply the resources allocated to it, are re-

TABLE 2. The Effect of Defense Spending on Public Civil Activities in the United States, Fiscal Years 1938–67

	r^2 (linear reg.)	Regression Coefficient	Index of Proportionate Reduction
Education—Total	.35	—.077	—.139
Institutions of			
Higher Ed.	.12	—.013	—.146
Local Schools	.34	—.053	—.125
Other Ed.	.19	—.014	—.265
Federal Direct			
to Ed.	.16	—.013	—.309
Federal Aid to			
State & Local			
Gov'ts for Ed. ..	.08	—.004	—.140
State & Local			
Gov't for Ed.	.24	—.060	—.124
Health & Hospitals—			
Total	.32	—.017	—.113
Total Hospitals	.30	—.014	—.123
Fed. for			
Hospitals	.25	—.004	—.130
State & Local for			
Hospitals	.29	—.011	—.120
Total Other Health	.22	—.003	—.087
Fed. for Health	.06	—.001	—.101
State & Local			
for Health	.45	—.002	—.078
Welfare—Total	.54	—.019	—.128
Fed. Direct for			
Welfare	.13	—.003	—.493
Fed. Aid to State			
& Local Gov'ts			
for Welfare	.17	—.005	—.087
State & Local			
for Welfare	.30	—.011	—.134

SOURCE: G.N.P. same as for Table 1, but adjusted for fiscal years. Others: U.S. Bureau of the Census, *Historical Statistics of the United States, Colonial Times to 1957* (Washington: U.S. Government Printing Office, 1960), pp. 719, 723–27; *Statistical Abstract of the United States, 1963* (Washington: U.S. Government Printing Office, 1963), pp. 392, 419, 422; *Statistical Abstract of the United States, 1967* (Washington: U.S. Government Printing Office, 1967), pp. 390, 421, 423; U.S. Bureau of the Census, *Historical Statistics of the United States, Colonial Times to 1957; Continuation to 1962 and Revisions* (Washington: U.S. Government Printing Office, 1965), pp. 98–101, 148–50. Budget data for 1967 from U.S. Bureau of the Census, *Governmental Finances in 1966–67*, Series GF67–No. 3 (Washington: U.S. Government Printing Office, 1968), pp. 15, 17–19. Data for Institutions of Higher Education, Local Schools, Other Education, Total, Federal, and State and Local for both Health and Hospitals include 1938, 1940, 1942, 1944, 1946, 1948, 1950, 1952–67; others same except for addition of 1951.

duced, one cannot properly speak of a cost to the economy. Rather, if one's social preferences are for work rather than welfare, the shift represents a *gain* to the system. Heavy increases in military pay and procurement do mean a reduction in unemployment, and military cutbacks are often associated with at least temporary or local unemployment. The effect seems strongest on state and local governments' welfare spending. In fact, the inverse relationship between defense and welfare at most spending levels is *understated* by the linear regression model. When a second-order curve is applied to the regression of defense on total welfare expenditures, 32 per cent of the variance remaining after the linear regression is added, to make a total of more than two-thirds of the variance. At all but the highest levels of defense spending, achieved in World War II, the inverse relationship is very steep, with small increases in military needs having a very marked dampening effect on welfare costs. But manpower was quite fully employed during *all* the years of major effort in World War II, so ups and downs in defense needs during 1942–45 had little effect, and the curve flattens out.

Both for education and for health and hospitals their relationship to the immediate requirements of national defense is less powerful (lower r^2), but nonetheless important. Furthermore, the regression line is quite steep for education, and since the mean share of G.N.P. going to education is only 3.5 per cent for the period under consideration, the proportionate impact of reductions is severe.

A widespread assumption holds that public expenditures on *education* have experienced a long-term secular growth in the United States. That assumption is correct only with modifications. The proportion of G.N.P. devoted to public education has increased by three quarters over the period, from 3.0 per cent in 1938 to 5.3 per cent in 1967. But it has by no means been a smooth and steady upward climb.

World War II cut deeply into educational resources, dropping the educational percentage of G.N.P. to 1.4 in 1944; only in 1950 did it recover to a level (3.6) notably above that of the 1930's. Just at that point the Korean War intervened, and education once more suffered, not again surpassing the 3.6 level before 1959. Since then, however, it has grown fairly steadily without being adversely affected by the relatively modest rises in defense spending. Actually, educational needs may have benefited somewhat from the overall decline in the military proportion of the economy achieved between the late 1950's and mid 1960's. The sensitivity of educational expenditures to military needs is nevertheless much more marked on the latter's upswings than on its declines. Education usually suffers very immediately when the military needs to expand sharply; it recovers its share only slowly after defense spending has peaked. Surprisingly, *federal* educational expenditures are less related (lower r^2) than is spending by state and local units of government; also, local schools at the primary and secondary level are more sensitive than are public institutions of higher education (whose share has grown in every year since 1953).

Public expenditures for *health* and hospitals are only a little less sensitive to the pressures of defense than are dollars for education. Here again the image of a long-term secular growth deceptively hides an equally significant pattern of swings. They accounted for a total of .77 per cent of G.N.P. in 1938; as with education this was sharply cut by World War II and was not substantially surpassed (at 1.00 per cent) until 1950. Once more they lost out to the exigencies of defense in the early 1950's, and bounced back slowly, at the same rate as did education, to recover the 1950 level in 1958. Since then they have continued growing slowly, with a peak of 1.23 in 1967. Thus, the pattern of health and hospitals is almost identical with that for education—some long-term growth, but great cutbacks in periods of heavy military need and only slow recovery thereafter. In detail by political unit the picture is also much the same—despite reasonable *a priori* expectation, federal spending for this item is less closely tied to the defense budget than is that by state and local governments. It should also be noted that though the r^2 is much the same, the *impact* of defense on health and hospitals is slightly less severe than on education.

It seems fair to conclude from these data that America's most expensive wars have severely hampered the nation in its attempt to build a healthier and better-educated citizenry. (One analyst estimates that what *was* done to strengthen education accounted for nearly half of the United States per capita income growth between 1929 and 1957.)[13] A long-term effort has been made, and with notable results, but typically it has been badly cut back whenever military needs pressed abnormally hard.

It is too soon to know how damaging the Vietnam war will be, but in view of past regularities one would anticipate significant costs. The inability to make "investments" would leave the nation with a smaller resource base of skill and well-being than would otherwise be the case. We can already see the effect of the war on fixed capital formation, discussed earlier in this paper. Consumption absorbed a larger *absolute* decline in its share of G.N.P. between 1965 and 1968 than did fiscal investment—from 63.3 to 62.1 per cent in the first instance, from 14.3 to 13.8 per cent in the second, but given the much smaller base of investment, the *proportionate* damage is about twice as great to the latter. In most of the major categories of public social "investment," nevertheless, the record is creditable. Despite a rise from 7.6 to 9.1 per cent in the defense share between 1965 and 1967, the total public education and health and hospitals expenditure shares went up 4.5 to 5.3 and 1.17 to 1.23 respectively. And even federal spending for education and health, though not hospitals, rose. There are of course other costs involved in the inability to *initiate* needed programs—massive aid to the cities is the obvious example. But on maintaining or expanding established patterns of expenditure the score is not bad at all.

The pattern of federal expenditures for *research and development* indicates some recent but partially hidden costs to education and medicine. From 1955 through 1966 such expenditures rose spectacularly, and every year, from $3.3 billion to $14.9 billion.[14] Obviously such a sky-rocketing growth could not continue indefinitely; not even most of the beneficiary scientists expected it to do so. Still, if one regresses R & D expenditures against G.N.P. over the entire period 1955 to 1968, the r^2 is a very high .93 and the "estimated" level for 1968 is $19.4 billion, instead of the actual level of $16.3 billion. The actual level of expenditures in fact fell below the estimated level for the first time in 1966—the first year since 1961 when the defense share of G.N.P. showed any notable increase.

Finally, we must note a very important sense in which many of these cost estimates are substantially underestimated. The entire analysis has necessarily been done with expenditure data in current prices; that is, not adjusted for inflation. Since we have been dividing each expenditure category by G.N.P. in current dollars that would not matter *providing that price increases were uniform throughout the economy*. But if prices increased faster in say, education or health, than did prices across the board, the *real* level of expenditure would be exaggerated. And as anyone who has paid a hospital bill or college tuition bill recently knows, some prices have increased faster than others. From 1950 through 1967 the cost of medical care, as registered in the consumer price index, rose by 86.2 per cent. Thus even though the health and hospital share of public expenditure rose in *current* prices, the *real share* of national production bought by that spending *fell* slightly, from 1.00 per cent to about .99 per cent. Presumably the difference has been made up in the private sector, and benefits have been heavily dependent upon ability to pay. Comparable data on educational expenses are less easy to obtain, but we do know that the average tuition in private colleges and universities rose 39 per cent, and in public institutions 32 per cent, over the years 1957–1967.[15] This too is faster than the cost of living increase over those years (not more than 20 per cent), but not enough to wipe out a gain for government education expenditures in their share of real G.N.P.

In evaluating the desirability of an expanded defense effort, policy-makers must bear in mind the opportunity costs of defense, the kinds and amounts of expenditures that will be foregone. The relationships we have discovered in past American experience suggest what the costs of future military efforts may be. These relationships are of course not immutable. Should it be concluded, after enlightened discussion, that certain new defense needs must be met, it is possible by careful choice and control to distribute the burdens somewhat differently. If costs cannot be avoided, perhaps they can be borne in such a way as better to protect the nation's future.

NOTES

1. See, for example, Walter Isard and James Ganschow, *Awards of Prime Military Contracts by County, State, and Metropolitan Area of the United States, Fiscal Year 1960* (Philadelphia: Regional Science Research Institute, 1962) and Walter Isard and Gerald Karaska, *Unclassified Defense Contracts: Awards by County, State and Metropolitan Area of the United States, Fiscal Year 1962* (Philadelphia: World Friends Research Center, 1962). Murray L. Weidenbaum, "Problems of Adjustment for Defense Industries," in Emile Benoit and Kenneth E. Boulding (eds.), *Disarmament and the Economy* (New York: Harper & Row, 1963) presents data on the distribution of contracts by industry. See also James L. Clayton, "Defense Spending: Key to California's Growth," *Western Political Quarterly*, 15 (June 1962), 280–293. *Science*, 161 (1968), p. 448 reports the receipts of various universities for Department of Defense-sponsored research in the physical, biological, and social sciences. On Canada, see Gideon Rosenbluth, *The Canadian Economy and Disarmament* (New York: St. Martin's Press, 1967).

2. This repeated failure to shrink the military establishment back to its prewar level is a phenomenon of some interest to students of the dynamics of international arms races and/or Parkinson's Law. It shows up even more clearly in the data on military personnel, and goes back almost a century to demonstrate the virtual doubling of the armed forces after every war. From 1871 to 1898 the American armed forces numbered fewer than 50,000; after the Spanish-American war they never again dropped below 100,000. The aftermath of World War I saw a leveling off to about 250,000, but the World War II mobilization left 1,400,000 as the apparent permanent floor. Since the Korean War the United States military establishment has never numbered fewer than about 2,500,000 men. See Bruce M. Russett (ed.), *Economic Theories of International Politics* (Chicago: Markham, 1968), p. 521. Should the post-Vietnam armed forces and/or defense portion of the G.N.P. prove to be higher than in the early and mid-1960's, that will represent another diversion from private or civil public resources and a major indirect but perhaps very real "cost" of the war.

3. Much of the war's costs are undoubtedly absorbed by other military categories, such as the number of troops kept in other parts of the world, and reductions in new procurement and maintenance of old equipment not being used in the war zone. Even so, it is likely that our method understates the cost of the war to the civilian sectors of the system. President Johnson's State of the Union Message in January 1968 put the annual cost at $25 bil-

lion in 1967. For 1968 it was nearly $29 billion.

4. It must be made clear that this procedure is not the only plausible way of processing these data. For instance, using another theoretical model one might compute the *differences* between spending levels from one year to the next (t_1-t_0) and run the regression on them, giving different results. The procedure I used here assumes that it is a high *level* of defense spending that gets in the way of particular civilian expenditures; the alternative assumes that it is a sharp *increase*, regardless of level, that forces civilian cutbacks. In fact, though I report only the former, I did also process the data by the other method, finding on the whole lower r^2s. In part, I hypothesize that the reason for weaker relationships with the difference model stems from varying time lags for various types of expenditure. For example, many purchases of suppliers may be sharply reduced simultaneously with the new military demands; reductions in tenured personnel, or liquidation of construction commitments, may take one or two years. To the degree that this is true, analysis of the aggregates with any *particular* time relationship specified (e.g., simultaneous differences, or one-year lag) would show only a weak relationship.

Also, the r^2's and regression coefficients are sensitive to the *particular* set of *years* examined. I also analyzed the World War II years and the post-war years separately, producing different and generally lower r^2's than for the entire period. Hence much of the variance found in this paper stems from differences between rather than within those two periods. Furthermore, inclusion of the war-time years with the others produces a distribution of defense percentages that would offend a purist data analyst—those for 1943 and 1944 are clear outliers nearly three standard deviations from the mean, and hence they exert disproportionate weight in the analysis. Excluding 1939–1945, however, would sharply reduce both the number of data points and the range of experience being analyzed. Thus I have left the earlier years in, but have also been careful to examine the scattergrams to be sure that the r^2's were not deceptively high or low because of any inordinate statistical effect of the war-time peaks.

Although I believe my handling of these two problems was appropriate, the caveat that the conclusions depend on these assumptions, and could be modified by others, is a serious one. The data are available on request from the World Data Analysis Program, 89 Trumbull Street, Yale University, New Haven, Connecticut 06520. Further analysis of the methodological problems with these data will appear in my contribution to volume 5 of *Mathematical Applications in Political Science* (1970).

5. This position is adhered to by most economists. See, for example, Benoit and Boulding (eds.), Disarmament and the Economy: U.S. Arms Control and Disarmament Agency, *Economic Impacts of Disarmament* (Washington: U.S. Government Printing Office, 1965); Emile Benoit, "The Monetary and Real Costs of National Defense," *American Economic Review*, 58 (May 1968), 398–416, and Walter Isard and Eugene Schooler, "An Economic Analysis of Local and Regional Impacts of Reduction of Military Expenditures," *Peace Research Society (International) Papers*, I (1964).

6. This index is computed by the formula

$$ IPR = \frac{25 \ (reg. \ coef.)}{400 \ (mean \ prop. \ of \ G.N.P.)} $$

for the dependent variable. This choice of illustrative values for the G.N.P. and defense increases does *not* of course imply that the impact is thus in any *particular* build-up.

7. The high r^2 is nonetheless a bit deceptive, as a close examination of the plot discloses. If one looks at the periods of moderate defense expenditure since 1940 one finds only a mild relationship between the two variables. Most of the variance is concentrated on the differences between the moderate and high defense groups, and *within* the latter.

8. Robert M. Solow, *Capital Theory and the Rate of Return* (Amsterdam: North Holland, 1963).

9. The costs of military procurement abroad can of course be figured more precisely and directly than we have done here, but by missing the indirect effects of inflation and diverted demand such a computation would understate the loss. Defense Department calculations of the direct cost do in fact come to but $1.5 billion; a complex independent analysis that includes the indirect effects suggests $4.0 billion, or that without the war the United States would actually have maintained a balance of payments surplus. See Leonard Dudley and Peter Passell, "The War in Vietnam and the United States Balance of Payments," *Review of Economics and Statistics*, 50 (November 1968), 437–442.

10. Although recent experience may make it seem obvious that public civil expenditures are likely to be inversely related to defense shares, this perception has not always been universal. Several years ago W. Glenn Campbell reported a strong inverse relationship for the 1953–63 period, in "Assuring the Primacy of National Security," in David M. Abshire and Richard V. Allen, *National Security: Political, Military and Economic Strategies in the Decade Ahead* (New York: Praeger, 1963), pp. 963–984. Otto Eckstein, however, noted some

questionable assumptions in Campbell's analysis and followed with a stronger expression of doubt: "I think that historical experience has been that governments are either stingy, or they're spenders. And if they're stingy about defense, they're stingy about everything. I would say that the historical record suggests that the association between civilian spending and military spending is positive, not negative." "Discussion" in *ibid.*, p. 1012.

11. *The Common Defense* (New York: Columbia University Press, 1961), p. 208. Further masking of the impact on actual programs may stem from the inability of government agencies to reduce costs for building maintenance and tenured employees, thus forcing them in dry times to cut other expenses disproportionately.

12. It might be thought that this would be a case where, if there were no immediate effects of defense needs on state and local government finances, defense might nevertheless force some delayed cutbacks by the areal units. But this too is not the case, since an effort to lag local expenditures a year or two behind defense made no improvement in the fit. Apparently the federal and the areal units of government are sufficiently independent in their major revenue sources that fluctuations

in the needs of the former do not seriously hamper the latter.

13. Edward F. Denison, *Sources of Economic Growth in the United States and the Alternatives Before US* (C.E.D., 1962) as cited in Ruth P. Mack, "Ecological Process in Economic Change," *American Economic Review,* 58 (May, 1968), 47. See also Gary S. Becker, *Human Capital: A Theoretical and Empirical Analysis* (New York: National Bureau of Economic Research and Columbia University Press, 1964) and Theodore W. Schultz, "Investment in Human Capital," *American Economic Review,* 51 (March 1961), 1–17. On this idea of educated manpower as a form of national capital see also the chapter by Kenneth Boulding in Walter Adams (ed.), *The Brain Drain* (New York: Macmillan, 1968).

14. U.S. Bureau of the Census, *Statistical Abstract of the United States, 1968* (Washington: U.S. Government Printing Office, 1968), p. 526, and *Statistical Abstract of the United States, 1963* (Washington: U.S. Government Printing Office, 1963), p. 544. Comparable data for earlier years are not available, so this variable was not used in the computations for Table 2.

15. Myron Brenton, "The Higher Cost of Higher Education," *New York Times Magazine,* April 28, 1968, p. 32.

The Military-Industrial Complex and the New Industrial State

Walter Adams

In *The New Industrial State* John K. Galbraith finds that the giant corporation has achieved such dominance of American industry that it can control its environment and immunize itself from the discipline of all exogenous control mechanisms—especially the competitive market. Through separation of ownership from management, it has emancipated itself from the control of stockholders. By reinvestment of profits, it has eliminated the influence of the financier and the capital market. By brainwashing its clientele, it has insulated itself from consumer sovereignty. By possession of market power, it has come to dominate both suppliers and customers. By judicious identification with, and manipulation of, the state, it has achieved autonomy from government control. Whatever it cannot do for itself to assure survival and growth, a compliant government does on its behalf—assuring the maintenance of full employment; eliminating the risk of and subsidizing the investment in research and development; and assuring the supply of scientific and technical skills required by the modern technostructure. In return for this privileged autonomy, the industrial giant performs society's planning function. And this, according to Galbraith, is inevitable because technological imperatives dictate it. The market is dead, we are told; and there is no good reason to regret its passing.

This blueprint for technocracy, private socialism, and the corporate state suffers from three fundamental defects. First, it rests on the unproved premise that corporate giantism is an inevitable product of technological determinism. Second, it rests on the increasingly more dubious assumption that industrial and political powers are confined to separate, distinct, and hermetically sealed compartments. Finally, it offers no policy guidance, and ignores the crucial questions of responsibility and accountability. If industrial giants, freed from all traditional checks and balances, are to perform society's planning function, what standards shall they use and what assurance is there of an automatic convergence between private and public advantage? What are the safeguards—other than the intellectual in politics—against arbitrary abuse of power, capricious or defective decision making? Must society legitimize a self-sustaining, self-serving, self-justifying, and self-perpetuating industrial oligarchy as the price for efficiency and progress?

In this paper, I shall eschew a dreary and repetitive recital of the voluminous evidence that negates the Galbraith version of a crude technological determinism.[1] I shall also spare the reader any comments on the virtues of private planning—the proposition that what is good for General Motors is good for the country. Instead, I shall offer an alternative (and hopefully, more realistic) explanation of the current levels of industrial concentration, in general, and the military-industrial complex, in particular.

I

My hypothesis—the obverse of Galbraith's—holds that industrial concentration is not the inevitable outgrowth of economic and technical forces, nor the product of spontaneous generation or natural selection. In this era of big government, concentration is often the result of unwise, man-made, discriminatory, privilege-creating governmental action. Defense contracts, R and D support, patent policy, tax privileges, stockpiling arrangements, tariffs and quotas, subsidies, etc. have far from a neutral effect on our industrial structure. In all these institutional arrangements, government plays a crucial, if not decisive, role.[2] Government, working through and in alliance with "private enterprise," becomes the keystone in an edifice of neomercantilism and industrial feudalism. In the process, the institutional fabric of society is transformed from economic capitalism to political capitalism.

My hypothesis is best explained in Schumpeterian power terms. According to Schumpeter, the capitalist process was rooted, not in classical price competition, but rather "the competition from the new commodity, the new technology, the new source of supply, the new type of organization—competition which commands a decisive cost or quality advantage and which strikes not at the margin of the profits and outputs of existing firms but at their very foundations and their very lives."[3] The very essence of capitalism, according to Schumpeter, was the "perennial gale of creative destruction" in which existing power positions and entrenched advantage were constantly displaced by new organizations and new power complexes. This gale of creative destruction was to be not only the harbinger of progress but also the built-in safeguard against the vices of monopoly and privilege.

What was obvious to Schumpeter and other analysts of economic power was also apparent to those who might suffer from the gales of change. They quickly and instinctively understood that storm shelters had to be built to protect themselves against this destructive force. The mechanism which was of undoubted public benefit carried with it exorbitant private costs. And, since private storm shelters in the form of cartels and monopolies were unlawful, unfeasible, or inadequate, they turned increasingly to government for succor and support. By manipulation of the state for private ends, the possessors of entrenched power found the most felicitous instrument for insulating themselves against, and immunizing themselves from, the Schumpeterian gale.

It requires no exaggeration to argue that modern technology and the inherent dynamism of Schumpeterian competition are such that, in the absence of governmental interference and protection, some of the bulwarks of concentrated power could be successfully eroded. . . .

Another case in point is the military-industrial complex, where the morganatic alliance between government and business is even clearer, bolder, and more positive. Here government not only permits and facilitates the entrenchment of private power but serves as its fountainhead. It creates and institutionalizes power concentrations which tend to breed on themselves and to defy public control. The scenario of events should be familiar. The "mad momentum" of an international weapons race militates toward large defense expenditures (currently at an annual rate of $75 billion). This generates a demand, not only for traditional, commercial, shelf items like food, clothing, fuel, and ammunition, but also for the development and production of sophisticated weaponry. Lacking a network of government-owned arsenals, such as produced the shot and cannon in the days of American innocence, or having dismantled the arsenals it did have, the government is forced to buy what it no longer can make. It becomes a monopsonistic buyer of products which are not yet designed or for which production experience is lacking. It buys at prices for which there is little precedent and hardly any yardsticks. It deals with contractors, a large percentage of whose business is locked into supplying defense, space, or atomic energy needs. It confronts powerful oligopolists in a market where technical capability rather than price is the controlling variable —in an atmosphere shrouded by multilateral uncertainty and constant warnings about imminent aggression. In the process, government becomes almost totally dependent on the chosen instruments, *i.e.,* creatures of its own making, for effectuating public policy.[4] Lacking any viable in-house capabilities, competitive yardsticks, or the potential for institutional competition, the government becomes—in the extreme—subservient to the private and special interests whose entrenched power bears the governmental seal.

This unique buyer-seller relationship, which defies analysis by conventional economic tools, lies at the root of the military-industrial complex and the new power configurations generated by it. The complex is not a conspiracy between the "merchants of death" and a band of lusty generals, but a natural coalition of interest groups with an economic, political, or professional stake in defense and space. It includes the armed services, the industrial contractors who produce for them, the labor unions that represent their workers, the lobbyists who tout their wares in the name of "free enterprise" and "national security," and the legislators who, for reasons of pork or patriotism, vote the sizable funds to underwrite the show. Every time the Congress authorizes a military appropriation, it creates a new constituency (*i.e.,* propaganda machine) with a vested interest in its perpetuation and aggrandizement. Thus, the current proposal for an anti-ballistic-missile system, the "thin" variety of which would cost $5 billion and the "thick" variety $40 billion, and which would probably be obsolete by the time it was completed, has been estimated to involve twenty-eight private contractors, with plants located in forty-two states (*i.e.,* 84 senators), and 172 congressional districts. Given the political reality of such situations and the economic power of the constituencies involved, there is little hope that an interaction of special interest groups will somehow cancel each other out and that there will emerge some compromise which serves the public interest. There is little assurance that the corporal's guard of auditors in the General Accounting Office or Galbraith's scientific-professional elite or a handful of disinterested university analysts will constitute a dependable and adequate force of countervailing power. The danger remains that the "conjunction of an immense military establishment and a large arms industry," against which President Eisenhower warned, will become a Frankenstein threatening to control the contract state which brought it into being. The danger persists that power will be coalescing, not countervailing—that the political cloakroom will displace the economic market place.

It would be facile to conclude that the military-industrial complex and the new industrial state represent a price which society must pay—and inevitably so—because of national defense considerations or because of technological inexorability. But this would be to miss the point—to ignore the crucial political component in the institutional arrangements at issue. The military-industrial complex is only a special case illustrating the power problems inherent in the new industrial state. Both are created, protected, privileged, and subsidized by the state. Both represent a form of private socialism— a type of social planning through fragmented, special-interest chosen instruments operating in the "private" sector. Both represent a blending of private economic power and public political power. Both are reminiscent of the Elizabethan monopoly system and its abuse, corruption, favoritism, waste, and inefficiency—an *imperium in imperio*, without demonstrable public benefits, and without any built-in safeguards for the public interest. In sum, to the extent that they are creatures of political power and not the product of natural evolution, there is nothing inevitable about their survival and nothing inevitable about the public policies which spawn and preserve them.

II

Let us examine these public policies which lie at the base of the new industrial state, and particularly the military-industrial complex.

DEFENSE AND SPACE CONTRACTS

These contracts, typically awarded on a negotiated rather than a competitive bid basis and as much the result of political as economic bargaining, convert the private contractor into a quasi-governmental, mercantilist corporation, maintained in a privileged position by "royal" franchise. The attendant abuses, especially the creation of entrenched power positions, are not inconsiderable.

In 1965, the U.S. Comptroller General, an Eisenhower appointee, highlighted the following characteristics of the contract system before a congressional committee:

1. Excessive prices in relation to available pricing information.
2. Acceptance and payment by the government for defective equipment.
3. Charges to the government for costs applicable to contractors' commercial work.
4. Contractors' use of government-owned facilities for commercial work for extended periods without payment of rent to the government.
5. Duplicate billings to the government.
6. Unreasonable or excessive costs.
7. Excessive progress payments held by contractors without payment of interest thereon.[5]

To this list could be added the procurement of items that were not needed, or in adequate supply elsewhere in the armed services, or were in fact being sold as surplus by the buying agency; indirect procurement through the prime contractor rather than direct purchase from the actual manufacturer —at far lower prices and without the pyramiding of overhead and profits; awarding of sole-source contracts for which the contractor had no special competency; the refusal by firms with overall systems responsibility to break out components for competitive bidding, or to furnish specifications for such bidding;[6] and finally, according to the Comptroller General, "excessive prices resulting from the failure of the agencies to request, or the contractors to furnish, current, accurate, and complete pricing data or from the failure to adequately evaluate such data when negotiating prices."[7] In quantitative terms, according to a summary of GAO studies covering the period from May, 1963, to May, 1964, there was ascertainable waste of $500 million in a 5 per cent sample of procurements.[8]

Perhaps it is unavoidable that in the procurement of complicated weapons systems, where uncertainty is pervasive and precedents are unavailable, cost estimates will be unduly inflated. As Peck and Scherer found in their study of twelve major weapon-system development programs, actual costs exceeded predicted costs by 3.2 times on the average, with a range of actual versus predicted costs of from 70 to 700 per cent.[9] Recent prediction errors in the F-111 and Apollo programs, Scherer reports, are of the same order of magnitude.

One can sympathize with the contracting officers negotiating for complex and sophisticated weapons technology and still agree with the McClellan Committee's conclusion that the government should not abdicate its responsibilities for program management, nor delegate these responsibilities to private contractors, if it wants to avoid avoidable abuses and flagrant overcharges: "Even the most reputable and ethical contractor is placed in the conflicting position of managing a program where the feasibility, technical, and economic decisions which should be made by the customer-Government are made by the producer-contractor," the Committee observed with charitable understatement. "The absence of competition, coupled with the urgency to get the program underway, removes normal safeguards against large profits and weakens the Government's negotiating position."[10]

On the other hand, one must understand the reluctance to endanger the national security because of excessive delays caused by punctilious bookkeeping. As Charles G. Dawes told a congressional committee investigating World War I procurement scandals:

> Sure we paid. We didn't dicker. Why, man alive, we had to win the war. We would have paid horse prices for sheep if sheep could have pulled artillery to the front. Oh, it's all right now to say we bought too much vinegar and too many cold chisels, but we saved the civilization of the world. Damn it all, the business of an army is to win the war, not to quibble around with a lot of cheap buying. Hell and Maria, we weren't trying to keep a set of books, we were trying to win the war![11]

GOVERNMENT R AND D AND PATENTS

The awarding of government R and D contracts—and the disposition of patent rights thereunder—is another technique of creating, privileging, subsidizing, and entrenching private power. Again, this is a matter of man-made policy, not institutional inevitability.

The importance of federal policy in this area derives from a number of characteristics of federally financed research. Since World War II, the government has generally paid for roughly 65 per cent of the nation's research and development, but performed only 15 per cent of the work. Two agencies, the Department of Defense and NASA, account for about 80 per cent of the government's R and D outlays. The lion's share of these outlays is concentrated in a few industries, notably aerospace, electronics, and communications. The concentration of R and D contracts is even greater than that of production contracts. There is high correlation between companies receiving R and D contracts and those receiving production contracts. Finally, the benefits of military R and D tend to spill over into civilian markets.[12]

The typical R and D contract, it should be noted, is a riskless cost-plus-fixed-fee venture. It usually protects the contractor against increases in labor and materials costs; it provides him with working capital in the form of periodic progress payments; it allows him to use government plant and equipment; in addition, it guarantees him a fee up to 15 per cent of the estimated cost. Nevertheless, some contractors demand additional incentives. With the arrogance characteristic of all privilege recipients, they want to extend and compound such privilege. "We recognize," says the vice-president of the Electronics Industries Association, a prime beneficiary of government-financed R and D, "that the ownership of a patent is a valuable property right entitled to protection against seizure by the Government without just compensation."[13] In this view, the patent is a right, not a privilege voluntarily bestowed by the government to effectuate a public purpose. By a curious perversion of logic, it becomes a vested privilege to which the private contractor is entitled and of which he is not supposed to be deprived without "just" compensation.

Characteristically, both the Department of Defense and NASA have accepted this argument for privilege creation and made it the cornerstone of their patent policies. The principle at issue requires little adumbration. Allowing a contractor to retain patents on research financed by and performed for the government, as Wassily Leontief points out, "is no more reasonable or economically sound than to bestow on contractors, who build a road financed by public funds, the right to collect tolls from the cars that will eventually use it"[14]—or the right to close the road altogether. It is tantamount to socializing the financial support for research while permitting private monopolization of its benefits. Moreover, as Admiral Rickover observed, firms receiving R and D contracts "are relatively few huge corporate entities already possessing great concentrated economic power. They are not ailing segments of the economy in need of public aid or subsidy. Nor are there any real reasons to offer patent give-aways in order to induce them to accept Defense Department research grants or contracts. . . . To claim that agencies cannot get firms to sign such contracts unless patent rights are given away strikes me as fanciful nonsense."[15]

STOCKPILING OF STRATEGIC AND CRITICAL MATERIALS

This is an "ever normal granary" program, ostensibly designed to enable the United States to fight a war of specified duration, determined by the strategic assumptions of the Joint Chiefs of Staff. In reality, it is a price support program, the details of which are buried in secret government files and the "primary purpose" of which is to subsidize selected mining interests in the name of national security.[16] That, at least, was the conclusion of the exhaustive hearings conducted by the Symington Subcommittee of the Senate Armed Services Committee which examined the origin and growth of the national stockpile, the Defense Production Act inventory, and supplemental stockpile, which by 1961 had involved the expenditure of $8.9 billion.[17]

*   *   *

The point need not be belabored. The rules for operating the national stockpiles as articulated by the industries concerned and their protagonists in government are fairly simple: The government must accumulate reserves against the most unthinkable eventualities. It must buy these materials at prices industry considers remunerative, regardless of world market conditions. This subsidy must be adequate to enable industry to operate profitably until such time as its services are required for mobilization in time of war. Finally, regardless of the available stocks, no disposal must ever be made from the stockpile. Such sales would not only endanger national security but also disturb market conditions and hence constitute unwarranted government interference with free enterprise.

ALIENATION OF THE PUBLIC DOMAIN

To achieve or solidify their control over prices and markets, the giants of American industry cannot rely on the imperatives of modern technology. On the contrary, they must live in constant fear of the "creative destruction" wrought by new technology; and they must always be alert to the potential competition of substitute products and processes. Even more important, they must fight to contain, neutralize, and sterilize the "institutional" competition of the public domain which threatens to impose an intolerable regulatory yardstick on their operations. TVA is an embarrassment to the electric power monopoly, the communication satellite to AT&T dominance, navy shipyards to the shipbuilding cartel, and the Army's Redstone Arsenal and Jet Propulsion Laboratory to the condottieri of aerospace. Pressure must be exerted, therefore, to dismantle such operations, or to circumscribe their competitive viability, or to sell their facilities to private enterprise—in a manner which does not disturb the existing power structure and indeed might even entrench it more solidly. Here, again, governmental cooperation is required for implementation of this grand strategy, and this is a matter of political decision, not technological or economic inevitability.

The disposal of government-owned plants at the end of World War II underscores the nature of the power struggle and the availability of public policy alternatives.[18] In aluminum, the disposal program was a qualified success; Alcoa's prewar monopoly was broken, Kaiser and Reynolds sprung like Minerva from Jupiter's brow, and the aluminum industry was converted into a triopoly. Synthetic nitrogen production was also deconcentrated by the infusion of additional sellers. In steel, by contrast, the disposal program served to entrench and extend oligopoly domi-

nance; the Geneva Steel plant, built at a cost of $202.4 million, was sold to the United States Steel Corporation for $47.5 million, and enabled U.S. Steel to increase its regional control over the Pacific Coast and Mountain States market from 17.3 to a commanding 39 per cent. In synthetic rubber, the wartime operation of the government plants gave a handful of large firms enormous patent and know-how advantages for the postwar period, and the subsequent disposal program resulted in the sale of twenty-five plants to three firms controlling 47 per cent of the industry's capacity.

*   *   *

INTERNATIONAL TRADE BARRIERS

No system based on protection, privilege, and subsidy is safe without barriers to foreign competition. Its beneficiaries recognize the rough validity of the Mancunian assumption that "free international trade is the best antimonopoly policy and the best guarantee for the maintenance of a healthy degree of free competition." Action is, therefore, necessary to protect domestic restrictionism against erosion and subversion from abroad. And governmental action is the most reliable technique available.

*   *   *

The point need not be stressed. Tariffs, quotas, "anti-dumping" statutes, "Buy American" regulations, and similar devices are not only a tax on domestic consumers and a subsidy to sheltered industries, but the capstone of any policy to protect entrenched economic power. They are a crucial facet of the *Realpolitik* designed to preserve the discipline of a nation's *Ordnungswirtschaft*.

III

In conclusion, we may note that the problem at hand is not one of technological determinism which would

militate toward fatalistic acceptance of the *status quo*. Nor is it rooted in the ineffectiveness of what Galbraith calls the charade of antitrust. Instead, it is largely a political problem of governmental creation, protection, and subsidization of private privilege. If this diagnosis is indeed correct, then public policy alternatives are available and a reasonably competitive market is more than a utopian policy objective.

Let me offer two general policy recommendations:

1. Most important is government noninterference in markets which in the absence of such interference would be workably competitive. In the words of Adam Smith, it may be difficult to "prevent people of the same trade from sometimes assembling together," but government "ought to do nothing to facilitate such assemblies; much less to render them necessary." While assuring effective enforcement of the antitrust laws, government should abjure the role of the mercantilist state in sanctioning and legitimizing private privilege. One can only speculate on the quantitative benefits of such measures as the abolition of tariffs in concentrated industries, the deregulation of surface transportation from ICC control, or the elimination of the honeycomb of governmental supports for the petroleum price and power structure.

2. In those areas where competition cannot be allowed full sway or where government cannot avoid active participation in the economic game, the basic guidelines point to preserving the maximum amount of power decentralization feasible. This may require positive encouragement of institutional competition from whatever source available and, at the very least, the preservation of effective yardsticks by which to measure and control monopoly performance. In the national defense sector, for example, government must rebuild and preserve its in-house competence for R and D, systems engineering and management, and contract evaluation. As the Bell Report of 1962 concluded, "there are certain [management] functions which should under no circumstances be contracted out."[19] Basic policy and program decisions respecting the research and development effort—relating to "the types of work to be undertaken, when, by whom, and at what cost—must be made by full-time Government officials. Such officials must also be able to supervise the execution of work undertaken, and to evaluate the results."[20] In short, the government cannot surrender the yardsticks essential for the discharge of its responsibilities to the public.[21] And the public must recognize that the servants of the military-industrial state cannot be allowed to become its masters—either in the name of "free enterprise" or under the guise of promoting the "national security."

What I have said here is not likely to please those who rationalize the *status quo* by invoking some deterministic inevitability. I do not claim that what I have said is particularly new or startling. I do believe, however, that it is true and that, as Dr. Johnson said, men need not so much to be informed as reminded.

NOTES

1. See U.S. Senate Select Committee on Small Business, *Planning, Regulation, and Competition, Hearings*, 90th Cong., 1st Sess., 1967, pp. 11, 27, 53, 66; and U.S. Senate Subcommittee on Antitrust and Monopoly, *Economic Concentration, Hearings*, Parts 3 and 6, Washington, 1965 and 1967.

2. See Walter Adams and Horace M. Gray, *Monopoly in America: The Government as promoter* (New York, 1955).

3. Joseph A. Schumpeter, *Capitalism, Socialism, and Democracy* (New York, 1942), p. 84.

4. See David E. Bell, "Report to the President on Government R&D Contracting," April, 1962, printed in House Committee on Government Operations, *Systems Development and Management Hearings*, Part 1, Appendix I, 87th Cong., 2d Sess., 1962, pp. 191–337; Clark R. Mollenhoff, *The Pentagon* (New York,

1967); and H. L. Nieburg, *In the Name of Science* (Chicago, 1966).

5. U.S. House Committee on Government Operations, *Comptroller General Reports to Congress on Audits of Defense Contracts, Hearings*, 89th Cong., 1st Sess., 1965, p. 46.

6. See *ibid.*, and U.S. Joint Economic Committee, *Background Materials on Economic Impact of Federal Procurement*, Washington, various years 1964–67; appendices contain lists and digests of General Accounting Office reports on defense activities to Congress.

7. *Comptroller General Reports*, p. 46.

8. Nieburg, *op. cit.*, p. 269.

9. Merton J. Peck and Frederic M. Scherer, *The Weapons Acquisition Process: An Economic Analysis* (Harvard Bus. Sch. Div. of Res., 1962), pp. 19–25.

10. U.S. Senate Committee on Government Operations, *Pyramiding of Profits and Costs in the Missile Procurement Program, Re-port No. 970*, 88th Cong., 2d Sess., 1964, p. 141.

11. Mollenhoff, *op. cit.*, pp. 53–54.

12. Richard J. Barber, *The Politics of Research* (Washington, 1966), pp. 71–90.

13. U.S. Senate Select Committee on Small Business, *Economic Aspects of Government Patent Policies, Hearings*, 88th Cong., 1st Sess., 1963, p. 132.

14. *Ibid.*, p. 234.

15. Nieburg, *op. cit.*, p. 294.

16. U.S. Senate Committee on Armed Services, Draft Report of the National Stockpile and Naval Petroleum Reserves Subcommittee, *Inquiry into the Strategic and Critical Material Stockpiles of the United States*, 88th Cong., 1st Sess., 1963, pp. 36–45.

17. *Ibid.*, p. 4.

18. Adams and Gray, *op. cit.*, pp. 117–41.

19. David E. Bell, *op. cit.*, p. 213.

20. *Ibid.*, pp. 214–15.

21. Nieburg, *op. cit.*, pp. 334–50.

Secrecy vs. Disclosure: Conflicting Pressures

Harry Howe Ransom

Among the counterpressures against government secrecy in American society the most important are: (1) the pressure of Congress; (2) a confederated armed services structure . . . characterized by rivalry among its various organizations; (3) a mass media press with energetic competition among its various components for acquiring "firsts" with the news; (4) a competitive industrial system that is a source of much information and in which information is a pivotal element; and (5) a scientific and technological community with its own sources of information and an insatiable appetite for knowledge, in which the free flow of information is an absolute prerequisite.

I

Congress, by its very nature in the American Constitutional system, acts as a catalyst for the flow of information about government. Much Congressional activity involves procuring and interpreting information from the Executive branch. The source of most Executive-Legislative conflict is the Executive claim for secrecy and the Congressional claim for disclosure, even though, ironically, about one-third of all Congressional hearings over the past ten years have been held in secret. Let us consider one broadly illustrative example, the House Subcommittee on Government Information.

An extensive Congressional probe of Executive information policy began on June 9, 1955 when the House Committee on Government Operations created this special subcommittee, headed by Representative John E. Moss, to publicize secrecy policies in all sectors of the Executive branch. Studies by the subcommittee, pursued through the 87th Congress (1962), included detailed questionnaires, hearings, and special studies and produced thousands of pages of reports.[1] The Moss committee became an unremovable thorn in the side of many government public information officers, particularly those responsible for information policies in the Department of Defense.

In an intermediate report on July 27, 1956, the subcommittee stated that the informational practices of the Department of Defense were the most restrictive in any major branch of the Federal Government. In a 1960 report the Moss committee was highly critical of the rate of declassification of documents in the Department:

The Defense Department and its component branches are classifying documents at such a rate that the Pentagon may some day become no more than a huge storage bin protected by triple-combination safes and a few security guards. Millions of documents each year are being added to the Defense Department's classified files, and only a small fraction are being declassified annually. . . . Unless some operative system of declassification is developed in the near future, we may find ourselves completely walled off from our past historical achievements as well as from future progress in basic science.[2]

But, as usual, the many voices in Congress have not been in harmony on this issue. Congressman George H. Mahon, Democrat, Texas, in appropriations hearings for 1955, expressed a contrasting view:

> I think the damage that has been done to this country by the spies and subversives is just a tiny drop in the bucket compared to the damage that has been done by the release of public information as to national defense procedures and programs, and developments, through the Department of Defense, through the Congress and through industry, and through trade journals and so forth.[3]

In its Report on the Department of Defense Appropriations Bill for 1956, the House Committee on Appropriations complained that "Too much information has been released which is of no benefit to the American public but which is of tremendous value to our [Communist] opponents."[4] In its report on the appropriations bill for 1957, however, the same committee warned Defense not to use Congressional concern for unauthorized leaks as an excuse for "withholding legitimate information from the press and public nor as a cover-up for inefficiencies and weaknesses of administration."

Defense Secretary Charles E. Wilson's views were more in harmony with Congressman Mahon and the Appropriations Committee than with the Moss subcommittee. On August 13, 1956, Wilson, reacting to contradictory Congressional and press criticisms of Pentagon information policies, appointed a special Committee on Classified Information, headed by Charles A. Coolidge, a Boston attorney and former Assistant Secretary of Defense, and composed of a senior retired officer from each of the armed services. "I am seriously concerned over the unauthorized disclosure of classified military information," Wilson wrote Coolidge.

He requested that the committee make an examination of laws and regulations, organization and procedures, and adequacy and effectiveness of the Department of Defense system in protecting security information.

After a three-month study, which included interviews with some fifty persons concerned with defense information, the Coolidge Committee issued a report on November 8, 1956, that demonstrated the fundamental secrecy-disclosure paradox by reaching the contradictory conclusions that there had been too much secrecy in the Pentagon in the past and that those who violate secrecy in the future should be more severely punished. The committee criticized overclassification of information by the Pentagon but was at the same time critical of unauthorized disclosure of classified information by high-ranking military men and civilians in the Pentagon. Some twenty-eight recommendations were detailed to cope with this dual problem.

These included: restricting visits to defense plants by reporters for trade and technical journals and requiring that officials of private industry discuss only unclassified information with them; insisting that all press interviews with Pentagon personnel be arranged through the Office of Public Information, with a representative of that office sitting in; creating a special unit within the Office of the Secretary of Defense to investigate and "prosecute" security leaks; holding the commanding officer of the service, office, or unit responsible when the source of improper disclosure cannot be discovered; taking disciplinary action against individuals who disclose information regarding interservice disputes; warning industry against disclosure of classified information in advertisements and withholding contracts in extreme cases; summoning newsmen before grand juries to disclose their sources of published classified information; and issuing a statement from the Pentagon to explain the differences between ordinary peace and Cold War.

Secretary Wilson appointed a three-man committee to study the implementation of those recommendations "found to be constructive." No doubt aware that the Moss committee was watching his every move, he expressed specific reservations about the last two recommendations, indicating at once they would not be followed. They were subsequently ignored, while various parts of the committee's other recommendations were incorporated in administrative regulations.[5]

The "constructive contribution" directive was, however, one of the early casualties of the Moss committee investigations. In August 1957, Secretary of Defense Wilson signed a revised directive (Department of Defense Directive No. 5230.9) which prescribed new criteria for publicly releasing material originating within the Department. Such material, read the new directive in part:

> . . . shall not be cleared for public release until it is reviewed for violations of security and for conflict with established policies or programs of the Department of Defense, or those of the National Government, since such material may have national or international significance. Nothing in this directive shall be deemed to authorize the refusal to clear material, otherwise releasable, because its release might tend to reveal administrative error or inefficiency.

The spirit in which the new directive was to be administered was the important element. Even the new requirement that releasable information must not "conflict with established policies and programs" left wide discretion to the information policy administrator. That is, it allowed the Office of Security Review to suppress dissent or unpleasant information by broad interpretation of this phrase.

Another change attributable to the Moss and Coolidge committees—and to the high money costs of storing and guarding classified documents—was the establishment in 1958 of an Office of Declassification Policy in the Pentagon. Since that time, thousands of cubic feet of secret documents have been declassified. More recently, in July 1960, this office announced an enlightened declassification system by which secrecy labels on many categories of information expire automatically at twelve-year intervals. And on September 20, 1961, President Kennedy issued an Executive Order (10-964) liberally amending this procedure. Except for certain materials from foreign governments or international organizations and those stamped secret by specific statute, such as the Atomic Energy Act, classified information is given a lower label every three years and is completely declassified at the end of twelve years. Seeking to improve the system, the Defense Department in January 1963 announced the formation of a Directorate of Classification management to speed up further the declassification process. But the arbitrary power of secrecy remains in the background, because "extremely sensitive information"—at the discretion of the head of an administrative agency—can be put outside of the declassification procedure.

Prompted by Congressional and press criticism, the Executive branch has at least become self-conscious about secrecy. Various units of the government have begun informational campaigns to eliminate the tendency to overclassify. A persuasive note is that papers classified *Confidential* could be stored at smaller cost than those marked *Secret*. However, while these new policies will benefit future historians and researchers, they have little effect on contemporary secrecy policies.

The political party competition which issues from Congress is another counterpressure against secrecy. During the Truman years, Republicans in Congress complained loud and long at the unnecessary secrecy imposed by the

Executive branch, as did Congressional Democrats under the 1953–60 Republican Administration. Senators who were particularly vocal in this period included Stuart Symington and Hubert Humphrey. "No careful reader of our press can doubt that this country is menaced by a deliberate policy on the part of our Government to withhold information from the American people," said Senator Symington in 1955.[6] Senator Humphrey, inserting into the *Congressional Record* a long dissertation on the problem, stated in the same year: "This shroud of silence which has descended over the Government prevents not only the American people from knowing what it is doing, but prevents the Government itself from functioning as it should."[7] Democratic campaigners in the 1960 Presidential campaign stressed repeatedly the charge that the American people were not being adequately or honestly informed by the Republican Administration about America's relative power position in the world.

When the Kennedy Administration assumed office in January 1961 and attempted to tighten control over the public statements of subordinate officials, particularly in the military services, the cycle began again. Senator Barry Goldwater, on January 30, 1961, asked whether the new Administration was to be "a Dictaphone type of 'gag rule' government bent on its own prestige or . . . a government of free speech which holds the people's interest paramount?"[8] The late Styles Bridges, Senate Republican Policy Committee chairman, resumed—after an eight-year interval—his role as guardian of the free flow of information by denouncing what he called a new "gag policy" of the Kennedy Administration. Former Vice President Nixon told the Detroit Press Club on May 9, 1961: "The whole concept of a return to secrecy in peacetime demonstrates a profound misunderstanding of the role of a free press as opposed to that of a controlled press." The President's plea for press self-restraint would "inevitably encourage government officials to further withhold information to which the public is entitled," Nixon said, and "the plea for security could well become a cloak for errors, misjudgments and other failings of government."

After the attempted Cuban invasion in April 1961, Republican Senator Hugh Scott, Pennsylvania, accused the Administration of trying to "suppress, manage, and regulate the flow of news that should be going to the American public." He charged that government information policies had taken a "drastic and dangerous turn" since Kennedy took office.[9] And in its 1961 report, Sigma Delta Chi's Freedom of Information Committee joined in these sentiments by describing the Washington information picture as "for the most part about what it was under the Eisenhower Administration, with most records and actions of the Federal Government hidden by bureaucratic secrecy."[10]

II

Congress and the competitive party politics therein will continue to serve as the most important counterpressure against government secrecy, but service differences of opinion also play a part. Competition among the Army, Navy, and Air Force fosters "end runs" to Congress and a steady leakage to the press of much officially restricted military information. An end run, in Pentagon parlance, means an attempt by an armed service to curry favor with Congressional committees by informally communicating their dissents over budgetary decisions, often by supplying secret information ("leaks") or detailed opinions that did not survive budget-making procedures within the Executive branch. As one Washington reporter has observed: "Inside the Pentagon, where a sizable chunk of the federal budget is divided up, the highest classifications of military secrecy often go out the window in the rivalry among the services."[11]

Disclosures of this type, involving opinions as well as facts, have produced some of the Department of Defense information security administrators' biggest headaches, and have instilled in many officers a disrespectful or cynical attitude toward official secrets. In testimony before the Congressional Joint Atomic Energy Committee in 1960, Admiral Hyman Rickover reported that a toy manufacturer had marketed a $2.98 model of a Polaris submarine complete with printed instructions based upon official Navy blueprints, thereby disclosing information worth millions of dollars to foreign intelligence services. Said Rickover: "I personally am aghast that this was done, but our internal military controversy is so great there is a tendency for each service wholeheartedly to fight the others in order to achieve its own objectives."[12]

Each of the armed services or units can be expected to have friends on Capitol Hill and among the Washington press corps who are eager to publicize the views of "parochial" experts on particular defense needs, or to kill unwanted policies by premature or misrepresentative disclosure. Presidents and their budget directors have always been equally eager to discourage such discussion as might encourage Congress to untie the strings of the budget package.

The strength and pervasiveness of the "end run" and "leak" tactics is indicated by the vigorous Presidential attempts to contain them. Such attempts are usually at the heart of "news management" controversies. The following memoranda illustrate one way in which the Truman and the Eisenhower Administrations attempted to deal with them.

This memorandum was issued by President Truman on November 15, 1946:

Memorandum for the Director of the Bureau of the Budget

I have noticed that on several occasions certain department and agency officials have shown a tendency to seek from Congress larger appropriations than were contemplated in official budget estimates.

The estimates which I transmit to Congress reflect a balanced program for the executive branch as a whole, and each individual estimate is considered in the light of this program, its relationship to other estimates, and the fiscal position of the Government. While agency witnesses before congressional committees must feel free to supply facts in answer to questions of committee members, I cannot condone the practice of seizing upon any opportunity which presents itself to indicate an opinion, either directly or indirectly, that my estimates are insufficient.

When you notify the heads of the various departments and agencies of the amounts to be included in the 1948 budget for their activities, I wish you would include a reminder that I shall expect them and their subordinates to support only the President's estimates in hearings and discussions with Members of Congress.

On December 31, 1958, President Eisenhower's Budget Director, Maurice Stans, issued the following:

Memorandum for the Honorable Neil A. McElroy

The President will shortly present his budget for the fiscal year 1960 to the Congress. As you know, the normal process of budgeting results in recommended amounts that in many cases are less than the agency head had requested.

It is understandable that officials and employees will feel strongly about the importance of their own agency's work, and will sometimes believe that a larger budget might be in order. Such feelings, however, must be related to an awareness that our budget resources are not adequate to accommodate in any one year all of the things that might be desired. The President is responsible for reviewing the total needs of the executive branch in the light of tax and debt policy and for deciding among competing requests for priorities. Executive branch personnel are expected to support the President in his budget recommendations. . . . It is expected that witnesses will carefully avoid volunteering views differing from the budget, either on the record or off the record. While direct questions at hearings must be answered frankly, it is expected that a witness who feels that he must set forth a personal view inconsistent with the President's budget will also point out that the President's judgment on the matter was reached from his overall perspective as the head of the Government, and in the light of overriding national policy. The witness should make it clear that his personal comments are not to be construed as a request for additional funds. . . .[13]

Similar moves were visible when a new Administration came into office in 1961. Testifying on the question of secrecy on missile projects before the Senate Armed Services Committee in 1961, Defense Secretary McNamara asked: "Why should we tell Russia that the Zeus [anti-missile system] developments may be unsatisfactory? What we ought to be saying is that we have the most perfect anti-ICBM system that the human mind will ever devise." The Secretary observed that he thought it "absurd" to release the contrary truth. Critics were quick to point out the implication that he favored releasing false information, which would probably mislead the American people more than the Russians. The Secretary later denied that he favored this; rather he was concerned about the danger of letting our adversaries know of our difficulties.[14] The distinction he makes is impossible to comprehend.

The public airing of controversy as well as the actual dissents on budgetary decisions have been a main source of trouble for Defense Secretaries. Secretary of Defense Neil McElroy's announcement on April 25, 1958, that promotions to three- and four-star rank in all of the armed services would thereafter be made only after approval by the Joint Chiefs of Staff and the Secretary of Defense and that they would be based in part upon "capacity for dealing objectively—without extreme partisanship—with matters of the broadest significance to our national security"[15] was a move to give the Secretary additional power in his continuing efforts to reduce the pressures for disclosure. At the same time McElroy announced that informational and public relations activities would be integrated through policies established by a Joint Informational Council and by the Office of Plans and Programs in the Office of the Secretary of Defense, bringing the statements and opinions of defense officials, civilian and military, under stricter surveillance before they were released to the public.

Such censorship, which could be subtly applied, caused deep concern in Congress. Congressmen knew that if they were to be partially cut off from the dissenting views about organization and strategy, they would lose still more of their power to influence policy and programs.

A minor crisis occurred when Admiral Arleigh Burke, as Chief of Naval Operations, in June 1958, made clear his disagreement with certain centralizing provisions of the defense organization bill, in testimony to the Senate Armed Services Committee. Shortly thereafter, Secretary McElroy stated publicly that he was "disappointed" in Burke, and regarded the Navy Chief's Senate testimony as "regrettable." He added, "there is too much damn foot dragging" in the armed services when the Secretary of Defense sends down orders.[16]

At this point, the Chairman of the Senate Armed Services Committee, Richard B. Russell, Democrat, Georgia, suspended hearings on the defense organization bill, commenting that Pentagon witnesses apparently could testify "only under duress." Hearings would not be resumed until he was assured that witnesses could testify "in complete candor without being threatened overtly or covertly."[17] Secretary McElroy felt obliged to guarantee Chairman

Russell by letter that Pentagon witnesses would be allowed to give their honest opinions, without reprisal. The Secretary reserved the right, however, to be "disappointed or regretful that an official of the department does not support fully the recommendations of the President."[18] The Senate hearings were quickly resumed.

The controversy could hardly fail to be noticed by other Pentagon witnesses. It is not possible to say how much witnesses would be inhibited in the future by the knowledge that the Defense Secretary or the President might be "disappointed" or "regretful" if their testimony were out of line.

Secretary McElroy's successor, Thomas S. Gates, Jr., expressed the view that criticism of the nation's defense program should be limited to only those expressions of opinion that would not impair "confidence in our armed forces," thereby implicitly including not only officials of the armed services but the general citizenry as well. He declared, in a public speech in August 1960: "Constructive criticism of our methods is helpful and essential to the improvement of our defense program, but this should be within the boundaries, understanding, and belief that our defenses are strong and will be able to meet our heavy responsibilities."[19] Under the Gates formula, anyone bold enough to assume that our defenses were *not* strong forfeited the right to speak out.

Shortly after becoming Defense Secretary in 1961, Robert S. McNamara stated his rules on the subject. During policy development, he expected free and full debate. "Once a decision has been reached and a policy established representing the decisions of the President and other appropriate authorities, then all members of the department, civilian and military, will be expected to support that decision, publicly or otherwise."[20] The Secretary explained that this did not preclude honest answers by officials when queried by Congress. The trouble here, as with earlier rules, is that decisions can seldom be "finally" made. It is likely that the pressures for disclosure will continue, as in the past, to thwart bureaucratic efforts to impose secrecy or a "party line."[21]

III

As the main vehicle for mass communication in a democracy, a free press is another principal opponent of government secrecy. The press is a central problem for administrators and leaders of the policy process because it is, as Douglass Cater has called it, in a very important way a fourth branch of government. "Press" as used here refers to all the mass media. The daily newspaper, in fact, is becoming less important as a news source than television and radio and the weekly news magazines.

The press is not usually directly active in national policy debates. With the exception of minor participation through editorial columns and by a few widely read columnists, the newspapers serve primarily as the arena in which policy debates occur. But press canons of what constitutes news, and the large band of Washington newsmen who apply these canons, figure prominently in the national policy process. The press is recognized by the competing elements in the Executive and Legislative struggle as an often decisive weapon.

A President's usual reaction to this fact is to try to control the flow of information on important policy matters emanating from within the Executive hierarchy. Motivated by the twin news criteria of being "first" and grinding his publisher's ax, the newsman will do his utmost to circumvent Presidentially imposed controls. Because of the vast size of the bureaucracy and the many competitive interests within it, the newsman is often successful in achieving his multiple aims. But in the Cold War, national security crises confront the nation with special problems and dilemmas.

These were acutely plain in the Cuban crisis in the fall of 1962 when the Kennedy Administration moved, amidst a barrage of criticism, to control all government information on the crisis and to regulate the contacts between newsmen and lower echelon officials in the Departments of Defense and State. The purpose was to guarantee that the government spoke "as one voice." Assistant Secretary of Defense for Public Affairs Arthur Sylvester, on October 29, 1962, bluntly described news as a "part of the weaponry" that a President must apply in international affairs, when newsmen complained that they had not only been denied information about the Cuban crisis but deliberately misled—"used" as some put it—by the government.

During this period rules were promulgated requiring State and Defense Department officials to keep a record of contacts with newsmen and a "diary" of their conversations. This aroused strong press protests, and Congressman John Moss began to organize his House Subcommittee on Government Information for a Congressional probe of the government's behavior.

When the crisis subsided, the rules were relaxed, but the central problem of the role and conduct of a free press in the Cold War remains. On October 31, 1962, *The New York Times* editorialized: "A democratic government cannot work if news of and about the government is long suppressed or managed or manipulated or controlled." This is true; but it is also true that a democratic government cannot survive if it cannot provide for the common defense.

In more normal situations, an official, unless he is issuing information for some tactical advantage in the policy struggle, wants to avoid premature publicity of policy, while newsmen are eager to report on policy still in the making. It is not only that it is more newsworthy at this stage; the thoughtful journalist is convinced that a major policy change should be subjected to long public debate.[22] The great mass of information flowing from Washington each day allows the reporter, by applying his own criteria to "news," to set the standards that determine what the public is to know about government.

If the ideals of democratic government are to be attained, the press must favor neither the government's interests nor the interests of special publics, including the Congress, which sometimes itself resorts to unwarranted secrecy. Any tendency of the United States to move even indirectly in the direction of a government-controlled press is to be viewed as a signal that the health of the democracy is in jeopardy. Too much control by the government of too many kinds of news at the source is incompatible with democratic principles. Obversely, an irresponsible press threatens both the viability of democracy and the capability of the nation to provide for the common defense. The years since World War II give cause for alarm on both these scores. Not only has there been an increasing obsession with secrecy by the giant Federal bureaucracy, but the press itself has not lived up to its responsibility to report the truly significant news available. With several notable exceptions, American newspapers continue to headline superficial "news" of fires, robberies, and rapes while giving short shrift to significant trends— as opposed to spectacular events—in world and national affairs.

By all odds the press is among the freest of institutions in the United

States. It ranks with the churches and the Congress in its freedom from restraint against saying what it pleases. Our Constitutional system places as few restraints upon the freedom of the press as upon individuals. With this freedom, and with an unequalled power to inform and persuade, goes great responsibility. The press appears to be performing its role of providing counterpressure against secrecy[23] better than it is assuming its broader responsibility. The press must share the blame that the mass public remains badly informed on the great issues in world affairs and on the nature of the threats to defense and democracy. The public would be well served if the press were to expend on these significant issues at least as much energy as it applies to shouting "right to know."

IV

In competing for government defense contracts private industries are continually involved in the secrecy-versus-disclosure problem. Defense contractors need general information about defense plans, requirements, and programs, and intelligence information about the military programs, capabilities, and plans of potential foreign adversaries. Yet they often must shape their policies and plans without this essential information.

Industrial firms are also often the source of important data on weapons production and the capabilities of new weapons systems. These data are distributed through elaborate public relations programs and can easily be found in reports to stockholders, general advertisements, popular and technical magazines, business conferences and trade conventions, and in technical and trade journals.

As the Coolidge Committee reported to the Defense Secretary in 1956, "some companies give out damaging [to national security] technical information . . . this is especially true in connection with the production of new weapons, and it applies both to prime and subcontractors."[24] Even the casual reader of certain magazines and journals is aware of the large amount of advertising done by commercial firms boasting of their manufacturing "achievements" with defense equipment. Few if any cases can be cited in which this kind of public relations has harmfully or prematurely disclosed information of value to a potential enemy, although the Coolidge Committee on Classified Information detected what it termed "compelling evidence of the real harm caused by information published in trade and technical journals." Some of the data disclosed in such journals represented nearly complete specifications and detailed performance information on new weapons systems. These data were said to be of great help in assisting a potential enemy in attaining superiority in some fields by possession of such information. Knowing our progress, it was argued, enabled the potential adversary to concentrate on the required countermeasures.

R. Karl Honaman, who attempted to administer the Eisenhower Administration's "Strategic Information" program, used to claim that a skillful piecing together of published industrial news, normally disclosed in great abundance in the United States, can result in a highly accurate military-industrial profile. He illustrated his case with the story of an engineer who had applied to a defense contractor for a job and while awaiting security clearance decided to survey what could be learned of the United States military missile program. As Honaman told the story:

He consulted published information available in a public library. This included daily newspapers, technical magazines, and government publications . . . for three months . . . and wrote a report on the U.S. guided missile program. His report, forty-five pages . . . included detailed information which gave for each weapon its name, model designation, manufacturer, guidance system, method of propulsion, length, diameter, range, and maximum altitude. He also included certain reasonable deductions concerning the high level plans and policies of our whole guided missile program. The report was accurate and reasonably complete. It contained so much that it was necessary to classify it.25

Placing a security stamp on the engineer's report was obviously useless, since large numbers of intelligence specialists in Russia can put together even more complete information from similar sources. One critic rightly argued that the new restrictions would not work "unless most of our industrial magazines and normally published data are to become so blacked out as to be useless to anyone."26

Advertising has been cited as influencing the policy debates over alternative weapons systems. And certainly industries with close ties to one service do join in the policy struggle by supporting propaganda for a particular strategic concept or weapons system. This tends to result in greater public disclosure of information than would occur in a monolithic economic system.

Murray Snyder, Assistant Secretary of Defense for Public Affairs in 1960, drafted a directive under which defense contractors would not be permitted by the Defense Department to make "inappropriate claims of operational availability or operational capability of products" or appraisals of effectiveness or ineffectiveness of weapons systems, where in either case:

> because of timing, content, magnitude, or a combination of any of these elements, release of information could reasonably be interpreted as intended to influence the adoption, revision, or concellation of plans, programs, or policies of the Government, including legislation.27

Representative Moss immediately denounced this directive, which he feared "would do a great deal to prevent intelligent discussion of defense policies which may mean life or death to the United States."28 Claiming that advertisements of defense contractors were a valuable source of information for the public, Moss charged that this move was "another attempt to hide controversy behind a mask of conformity." The real problem at issue here is less the disclosure of sensitive information through advertising than the propriety of defense industry propaganda, usually paid for indirectly by the taxpayer, that promotes a particular weapons system in the name of the manufacturer.

V

Perhaps no professional group is as uncomfortable with a pervasive policy of government security and secrecy as the scientific community. By tradition, scientists report the results of their experimentation so that others can accumulate information for further hypotheses and experimentation. This is so vital to scientific progress that the scientists have made some of the loudest protests against narrow security measures.

Dr. Chauncey D. Leake, chairman of the Committee on the Social Aspects of Science of the American Association for the Advancement of Science, stated in 1958: "American scientists have been particularly harassed by ill-advised security regulations which have hampered their scientific activities, inhibited their scientific interests and given them a serious sense of anxiety and frustration."29

Anyone doubting whether Dr.

Leake spoke for a majority in the scientific community should examine, for confirmation, the testimony and statements of a panel of leading scientists before the Congressional Special House (Moss) Subcommittee on Government Information, in March 1956.[30]

One eloquent witness before this committee was Lloyd V. Berkner, president of Associated Universities and a specialist in geophysics and electronics. Surveying what he believed to be the results of a policy of "excessive military security and restriction on information" in the decade since World War II, he found that "the free flow of knowledge of scientific progress on which really important creative ideas completely depend has been severely hampered." Excessive secrecy, he argued, has boomeranged. Aimed at the potential enemy, secrecy measures have instead restricted American scientific progress.[31]

Either an arms race or programs to limit or control armaments must lean heavily upon the *esprit,* capability, and cooperation of the scientific and technological community. But government-sponsored scientific endeavor since World War II—which includes a vast amount of current research—has been hampered by the restrictive influence of official secrecy, enforced by an often exasperating complex of security regulations. Scientists have clashed head-on with government secrecy policies, including: the excessively secret regulations administered by the Pentagon, the Atomic Energy Commission and other agencies; the multiple-clearance system that seriously inhibits interagency communication; and the "need-to-know" concept, which is insulting to scientists, as well as contrary to the basic needs of scientific progress.

Under recent security policies, a wide range of reports, studies, or other information over which the government has control has been available only on a "need-to-know" basis. Such need, in practice, must be interpreted by thousands of individual custodians of "security" information. The "need-to-know" has little to do with a person's or a company's security clearance. A person may have clearance for *Top Secret* information and yet be refused access to documents because some functionary, who is likely to be overcautious, judges that there is no "need-to-know." This can and has had ludicrous consequences, such as the actual cases in which scientists have submitted reports to government agencies and later have been denied permission to re-examine them.

What has the nation gained scientifically from its secrecy policies? Certainly not any high degree of security. America's relative status in science and technology, compared to Russia's in recent years, seems to suggest that the secrecy mania has been self-defeating. As the head of the Army's Operations Research Office, Ellis Johnson, declared in 1960: "We actually are keeping our secrets so closely [from ourselves] that this has aided the Soviet Union to draw ahead of us."[32]

The concepts of military secrecy and the principles of scientific discovery are incompatible. Charles Kettering has been quoted to the effect that "if he locked the doors of his laboratory to others, he would lock out much more than he would lock in."[33] Many eminent scientists believe that too many locked laboratory doors in recent years have dangerously slowed down American scientific and technological progress. Because of secrecy, we and our allies have expended great effort and monies to discover facts and to develop techniques already known to us, and apparently to our Communist adversaries as well.

It is disquieting to hear eminent scientists suggest that it may be impossible to have great developments in science under existing codes of secrecy. One of them has noted that "great developments in the nuclear field were started as a result of the free exchange of information between scientists, unrestricted information, and that is not now possible."[34] Radar is often used to illustrate the harmful effects of secrecy on military technology. Discovered about 1930, radar saw little major development in the ten years following, largely because of the secrecy that surrounded it.

Government security regulations have resulted in attempts to classify "basic laws of nature." Many have felt that the basic facts on atomic fission and fusion were too long classified as secret. Most scientists scoff at such attempts as not only unwise, from the viewpoint of advancing scientific knowledge, but futile, because the whole body of scientific knowledge

moves forward at about the same pace throughout the industrial world. So, scientists tell us, what is known by a few will eventually be known by all, whether they are told about it or not.

Russia appears to be lessening its own internal secrecy—especially in science. There has been a somewhat freer flow of Russian scientific and technical reports in recent years, and increased communication between Soviet scientists and scholars in other nations. And since our relative positions in military technology have been shifting in favor of the Soviets, it would appear that the time has come for America to take some risks in a freer flow of government information to offset the greater risks of secrecy.

NOTES

1. See the *24th Report*, House Committee on Government Operations, 86th Congress, 2d Session, July 2, 1960, and numerous other documents of the Moss Committee in the 84th Congress through the 87th Congress. In the 84th and 85th Congresses, 1955–58, less publicized studies of "Freedom of Information and Secrecy in Government" were conducted by the Senate Judiciary Subcommittee on Constitutional Rights under the chairmanship of Thomas C. Hennings, Jr., Democrat, Missouri. See its various hearings and reports.

2. *24th Report*, p. 89.

3. *Hearings*, House Subcommittee on Department of Defense Appropriations for 1955, 83rd Congress, 2d Session, March 31, 1954, pp. 558–59.

4. House *Report* No. 493, 84th Congress, 1st Session, May 5, 1955, p. 15.

5. For a detailed report by the Secretary of Defense on implementation of sixteen of the twenty-eight Coolidge Committee Recommendations, see House Government Operations Subcommittee, *Hearings*, Part 9, 85th Congress, 1st Session, April 10–12, 1957, pp. 2321–53.

6. Speech in New York City, July 7, 1955.

7. *Congressional Record*, August 3, 1955, pp. 11319–29.

8. The New York *Herald Tribune*, January 31, 1961.

9. Quoted in *The New York Times*, May 12, 1961.

10. *Freedom of Information (FOI) Digest*, Freedom of Information Center, University of Missouri School of Journalism, November-December 1961, p. 1.

11. Douglass Cater, *The Fourth Branch of Government*, Boston, Houghton Mifflin, 1959, p. 10.

12. Quoted in *The Reporter*, July 6, 1961, p. 28.

13. Both of these memoranda were reprinted in the *Congressional Record*, January 15, 1959, p. 643.

14. Quoted in *The New York Times*, May 12, 1962. For contrasting views on the "news management" controversy in the Kennedy Administration see Lester Markel, "The 'Management' of News," *The Saturday Review*, February 9, 1963, pp. 50–51, 61; Hanson W. Baldwin, "Managed News—Our Peacetime Censorship," *The Atlantic Monthly*, April 1963, pp. 53–59; and Arthur Krock, "Mr. Kennedy's Management of the News," *Fortune*, March 1963.

15. Quoted in *The New York Times*, April 27, 1958.

16. Quoted in *The New York Times*, June 22, 1958.

17. Quoted in *The New York Times*, June 24, 1958.

18. Quoted in *The New York Times*, June 26, 1958.

19. Address to the national convention, Veterans of Foreign Wars, Chicago, August 2, 1960.

20. Press Conference, February 2, 1961.

21. A somewhat separate issue, which came to a head in 1961 in the much-publicized case of Major General Edwin Walker, involved the question of the right of the military to propagandize their political views, or to exercise their independent judgment in explaining to the troops and to the public the nature and dimensions of the Communist threat. Walker was removed from his command in Germany for his questionable activities, and later resigned from the Army.

22. The exact roles of information and public opinion in national policy making involve complex and relatively unexplored questions. See James N. Rosenau, *Public Opinion and Foreign Policy*, New York, Random House, 1961. The concern of journalists regarding secrecy is detailed in the annual reports of the Freedom of Information Committee of Sigma Delta Chi, the national professional journalistic fraternity. See particularly the report submitted by the committee on November 1, 1959; V. M. Newton, Jr., Chairman.

23. For some years, numerous journalistic groups, such as the Freedom of Information Center of the Missouri School of Journalism, and Sigma Delta Chi journalistic fraternity, and individuals, V. M. Newton, Jr., J. R. Wiggins, Herbert Brucker, James S. Pope, Clark R. Mollenhoff, Louis M. Lyons, and the late Harold Cross—to name but a few—have fought a vigorous, uphill battle against government secrecy.

24. Report to the Secretary of Defense, Committee on Classified Information, November 8, 1956, p. 20.

25. Cited in Allen Raymond, Report to the American Civil Liberties Union, October 24, 1955, pp. 48–49.

26. Allen Raymond, *loc. cit.*, p. 50.

27. Quoted in the *Congressional Record*, April 25, 1960, p. A3495.

28. *Congressional Record*, April 25, 1960, p. A3494.

29. "What We Don't Know Hurts Us," *The Saturday Review*, January 4, 1958, p. 38.

30. "Availability of Information from Federal Executive Agencies," Part 4, Panel Discussion on Scientific and Technical Information, *Hearings*, Subcommittee, House Committee on Government Operations, 84th Congress, 2d Session, March 7–9, 1956.

31. *Hearings, loc. cit.*, pp. 752–54.

32. "The Lead-Time Problem," *American Strategy for the Nuclear Age*, eds., Walter F. Hahn and John C. Neff, Garden City, New York, Doubleday Anchor, 1960, p. 246.

33. Quoted by Dr. Wallace Brode, in House Committee on Government Operations, *23rd Report*, House *Report* No. 1619, April 22, 1958, p. 11.

34. Dr. Otto Struve, quoted in House *Report* No. 1619, p. 11.

Classified Military Research and the University

Anatol Rapoport

The university should be a community of scholars dedicated to the pursuit of truth—a hackneyed phrase, perhaps, but a deeply meaningful one to those so dedicated.

Not every socially useful institution can or need be a community. A department store, for example, may be an eminently useful institution, a triumph of marketing techniques, an indispensable adjunct to urban society. But a department store is not, and need not be, designed as a community. The only connection between its various services, from selling furniture to duplicating keys, is geographic proximity for the convenience of the shoppers. Neither the shoppers nor the salespeople at different counters need to have anything to do with each other in order for the department store to fulfill its function properly.

I reject the department-store model of the university, the so-called "multiversity," because it is incompatible with the community model; and, I repeat, this does not in any way reflect any judgment on my part as to which of the institutions is the more important to a society. I do have an opinion, but it is not relevant to my argument. It follows that I reject the notion that the university must serve "society" in whatever way society wants to be served as long as such service does not jeopardize other activities essential to the university's mission. The implication of this notion is that such other activities are not jeopardized by the services rendered by the university, as long as the two functions are kept apart. I argue, however, that if different activities in a university have no effect upon one another, then this is prima facie evidence that the university is not a community and therefore its primary function has already been jeopardized.

My objection to conducting classified research in a university is that such activities jeopardize the community a university ought to be and to which members of the university, faculty and students alike, ought to aspire. The community is jeopardized not so much by the distinction between two classes of faculty, those "in" and those "out." After all, every specialist is privy to knowledge inaccessible to those outside his specialty. The university community is jeopardized by secret military research by virtue of the fact that for the most part those who participate in such research owe allegiance to another community, a loyalty that is, in my opinion, incompatible with the loyalty to the community a university ought to be. Moreover, the defense community (or the "strategic community," as it is sometimes called by some of its prominent members) is now a reality, while the community of scholars is still only an ideal. There are many hindrances to the realization of this ideal, but the overlap between the academy and the defense community is, I believe, one of the most important of these factors.

The intellectual defense community arose in the United States in the

This article first appeared in *The Humanist* (Jan.-Feb., 1969) and is reprinted by permission. Copyright © 1969 by the American Humanist Association.

course of the infiltration of military research into the universities since World War II. The circumstances and some of the effects of that infiltration are well known. It must be kept in mind that actual figures tell little of what has happened. Its most important effects have been not quantitative but qualitative; and they must be considered not only with regard to what is happening to universities but also with regard to what is happening to the war business. Specifically, not only has a large sector of the academy become militarized but the war business has become intellectualized; and because of this it has become highly attractive to many people who work with their brains.

It must be borne in mind that dedication to truth as a way of life is a primary motivating factor to relatively few people. Most of us have absorbed the cultural values around us as a matter of course. Among these is an appetite for prestige in terms of the culturally dominant criteria: being near to the foci of power, being valued for one's expertise by those who possess great social prestige, being asked by the wielders of power to advise on matters of policy, etc. These satisfactions, so long denied to the American scientist and scholar, coupled with considerable intellectual challenge in the design of military technology and of global diplo-military strategy, were, I am sure, an important factor in the creation of the scientific-technical defense community. It is a large community. The director of the Willow Run Laboratories made this point when he refuted the notion that the results of classified research were available to very few (*University of Michigan Record*, October 27, 1967).

"This is not so," wrote Dr. Evaldson. "Witness, for example, the Project Michigan annual radar symposium, attended by 400–700 people." Dr. Evaldson is quite right. The scientific-technical defense community is large. And it is a genuine community, another point

made by Dr. Evaldson when he wrote: "Indeed, in some classified areas of activity the dissemination of results may be more timely and complete in its coverage of the people engaged in the subject than is true in some unclassified research." In other words, what Dr. Evaldson seems to be saying (and I agree) is that the defense community is more of a community than the academic-intellectual community.

But the defense community, it seems to me, is held together by values quite different and essentially incompatible with the values that ought to hold together the academic-intellectual community. I say "ought" because I keep in mind that the latter is still only an ideal, while the former actually exists. Moreover, it seems to me, the intellectual community is hindered from maturing by its infusion of academe with the spirit and aims of the defense community.

The primary value of the would-be intellectual community is the unfettered search for the truth and its free dissemination. Closely allied but, at times, only a derivative value is the use of knowledge in the service of humanity. The primary aim of the defense community, on the other hand, is to put power at the disposal of specific groups of men. Since scientific knowledge is a source of power, the defense community seeks such knowledge; and since this knowledge is genuine only if one is aware of truth, the defense community adheres to standards of scientific truth in matters relevant to its pursuits. But in this scheme the awareness of truth is a derivative, not a primary value. In matters not relevant to its pursuits, the defense community is often indifferent to truth. It either takes for granted the world picture of the power wielders or eschews altogether the task of trying to understand the world in which we live.

Please note that I am not here distinguishing between the degrees of dedication to truth of various individuals. It would be presumptuous to make such judgments. I am merely pointing out that complete dedication to the truth and the whole truth is an integral component in the ethics of the ideal intellectual community, but not of the defense community (defined in terms of its mission), except to the extent that truth must be established in the pursuit of specific knowledge.

It seems to me that this must be so; otherwise I cannot explain the totally uncritical acceptance by the defense community of all the clichés of conventional wisdom whenever it feels called upon to justify or to rationalize its activities. In the language of the defense community, war research is assumed, as a matter of course, to be a "service to society." Preparations for war are blithely assumed to increase the nation's "security." War itself is justified as a regrettable but necessary means in the pursuit of "national interests." Journalistic inanities are freely incorporated by the defense community into the lexicon of political discourse, whenever its members engage in such discourse.

If the members of the defense community were also true members of the intellectual community, then they would, of course, be completely entitled to defend their world picture. The intellectual community is inherently anti-dogmatic; and the views of an Edward Teller or a Herman Kahn would be entitled to be heard and discussed side by side with those of a Linus Pauling, a Kenneth Boulding, or an Erich Fromm. But the defense community is not part of the intellectual community. The loyalties of its members are elsewhere, primarily to power, and to truth only in so far as knowing truth helps in the pursuit of power. The work of the defense community does not, in my opinion, help mankind. It is, on the contrary, a threat to mankind. Now this opinion is, naturally, challengeable;

but it is also a challenge. The defense community is not obliged to respond to this challenge. Under the present arrangements it is able simply to hide behind the cloak of secrecy.

Dr. Evaldson, in his defense of classified research, warns against the tyranny of peers. I should think this term is more appropriate in the context of juvenile groups than in the context of an intellectual community. Secrecy protects the war researcher not from the tyranny of his peers but from the scrutiny of his peers. Clearly the intellectual community could not function if the intellectual products of its members were not at all times subjected to scrupulous, at times merciless, scrutiny of all the members of the community. Certainly the intellectual is responsible to his peers, and not only in matters of careful methodology, scrupulous regard for facts, rigor of reasoning, etc. These are scientific standards. But the intellectual community is not just a scientific community. It is a community dedicated to the growth and the preservation of the spiritual human heritage, of which science is only one component. In a genuine intellectual community, not only the scientific validity but also the significance of findings ought to be subjected to scrutiny, analysis, and prognosis; significance, that is, not only in the sense of relevance to other areas of science, but also of relevance to man's life and, above all, to man's outlook.

Let us, then, consider a biologist who is doing "basic" research instigated by a felt need in the defense community for more knowledge about pathogenic micro-organisms, knowledge that will facilitate the creation of strains more resistant to antibiotics. The work itself may be of fundamental importance to biology and may be pregnant with "spin-offs." However, the identity of the contracting agency and the secrecy attending the research bespeaks the intended use of this knowledge. Now the "academic freedom" of the scientist to seek such knowledge is not at issue. What is at issue is the fact that, if he does his work in secret, he is not obligated to justify it, if challenged on moral grounds. It is irrelevant whether the example chosen is realistic or not, or what particular parts of war research happen to be done in what specific universities at this time. As long as research is done in secret, we do not know what research is done where, and why. I think a member of a university faculty has a right to know what research is being done under the auspices of his institution; not only the titles of contracts and their sources and budgets but also the content of the research, its applications and implications. I think that the fraud perpetrated by the Central Intelligence Agency on Michigan State University is a blot on that university's name, and I know personally that many faculty members of that university felt a deep shame when the unsavory role of their institution was publicly revealed.

In a teach-in held recently, a university vice president pointed out that participation in classified research often broadens the contact of a scientist with the advancing of a science. This is meant, I take it, as a justification for classified research on the ground that such participation fulfills the professional needs of a scientist. In my opinion, this is the only valid point in the defense of classified research. But if the faculty members of a university are to be a community (and I always start from this premise), then the professional needs of some faculty members should be weighed against the moral needs of others. Many faculty members feel strongly that the utilization of man's intellectual faculties and of scientific insights for the purpose of increasing the military might of a war-waging state is degrading and immoral. Again, at the risk of redundancy, I must emphasize that the freedom of

some scientists to engage in an activity regarded as immoral by others is not being questioned here. What is being challenged is their right to do so without their colleagues' knowledge about what these scientists are doing and why.

Recall the controversy concerning subversion on campus of a decade and a half ago. There were those who were genuinely devoted to academic freedom and who staunchly defended the Communist's right to his view as a member of a university faculty. They were most concerned, however, with the alleged secrecy of the Communist's activities and commitments. They felt they had a right to know who their colleagues were, not in order to persecute them but in order to be in a position to dissociate themselves from them if their consciences demanded it. An intellectual should have the opportunity to dissociate himself from colleagues who, by serving a war-waging state, violate his moral sense. He should also have the right to dissociate himself from an institution that has become an adjunct of a war-waging state. He cannot do so if research is cloaked in secrecy.

To summarize, the following arguments have been used in defense of classified research on campuses:

(1) Academic freedom has been invoked. The appeal to academic freedom is, in my opinion, irrelevant. If such freedom means anything, it must include the freedom to disseminate knowledge to everyone, not just to privileged groups. The scientist ought to be free to undertake any research that interests him, but he should be in a position to defend his choice to his colleagues. Secrecy cancels this responsibility and is therefore antithetical to academic freedom.

(2) Service rendered to the military establishment has been equated with service rendered to society. I think it is time to turn a jaundiced eye on the proposition that what is good for

the Pentagon is good for the country, or, for that matter, that what is good for this country is necessarily good for man. A university community ought to be an integral part of a world intellectual community and ought to dissociate itself from the power struggles waged by states, blocs of states, and superstates. In this respect, the goals of the intellectual community ought to resemble the goals of a genuinely dedicated religious community, not, of course, in the sense of shared dogmas but in the sense of shared values.

(3) Unclassified "spin-off" from classified research has been cited in the defense of such research. This is no reason for keeping classified research on campus. Spin-offs would presumably occur wherever such research is done. All in all, it is not likely that science would be impoverished if all military research would suddenly stop, let alone if it were excluded from universities.

(4) I will simply dismiss the defense of classified research on the grounds that it brings in money or helps maintain the interest of the military contracting agencies in the research potential of a university. I reject the idea that a university is an enterprise "in the business" of doing research. I have not heard this conception of the university explicitly defended on all campuses, but I must say in all frankness that it is implicit in many of the arguments that I have heard in defense of classified research.

This orientation has also a broader connotation. In the popular mind, the image of a university as a "research business" and an "education business" has become prevalent. Ironically, it is this image that has "legitimatized" the activity of the intellectual in our culture in which the business enterprise is the universal model of all organized activity, all the way from the theater to war. In the business world, growth, solvency, and success in competition are the imperatives of existence. They have been traditionally the dominant values of our society. It has come about, however, that these values are now not only being questioned but actively rejected by a growing sector of our youth; and I am convinced that the ferment on campuses is an expression of a deep resentment on the part of this sector that expects to find other viable values in what ought to be an intellectual community, but instead finds the predominant values of an outlook it has rejected. The *gleichschaltung* of universities to the needs of the business and military world is the most salient symptom of the university's failure to provide a new source of values. Exclusion of classified military research will not, of course, remake the university into a semblance of an intellectual community, but it is an indispensable step in that direction.

(5) Participation in classified research has been cited as a factor in nurturing the scientific interest and the creative interest of the participants. I concede this argument, but at the same time plead for weighing the benefits so derived against the demoralization of other faculty members. The well-known free market principle embodied in the admonition "If you don't like it here, you can go elsewhere" ought to apply more properly to the members of the scientific-technical defense community than to those who view themselves as members of an incipient world intellectual community. The former already have institutions with aims coinciding with their own—the military research institutes specifically created to serve the needs of the military establishment. The latter should also have the right to build their own communities dedicated exclusively to the pursuit of truth, to the dissemination of truth, unencumbered by the needs of the military establishment for secrecy, and to service rendered to all of humanity rather than to groups engaged in a struggle for power.

IN RESPONSE

ALFRED DE GRAZIA:

I cannot find much of a theory in the eminent theorist's diatribe against classified military research, and therefore comment in kind.

I love an open society and I hate secrets. Some of my best friends keep secrets (the scoundrels!). My own life has unfortunately involved many secrets.

I have met men who carry a secret and they are unpleasant men. Some men are power-hungry and, like professors without ideas, gather secrets so as never to be starved out of their strongholds. Then there are all the secrets that are too banal to be publicized; those who hold them are ashamed to reveal them. One could go on; but the point is that most secrets are not worth keeping—or learning. Most classified research is for the birds.

But professors, unlike the birds, try to supplement their incomes. They feel that they need to get equipment, travel, meet people, blow their minds, etc., and classified research helps them do these things. Why keep them from it?

That's the question? Why? Professor Rapoport elevates the question sky-high. He talks of an academic community that doesn't exist and of a defense community that he says (regretfully) exists. He says secrets spoil the academic community. (I think they also usually spoil the defense community.)

But this academic community that we adore—this womb of pure scholarship—where is it? Peel away all the dependencies of classified military and nonmilitary research, and little is left—maybe some Chaucerian scholars (with their cryptic specialties), cuneiform experts (half-a-dozen vestal virgins), and organ-grinders to whom knowledge is a potpourri that they crank out.

I have news for Professor Rapoport. Practically everything is classified. Eighteen years ago I suggested limited outside access to Survey Research Center punched-card files and heard a lot of tongue-clicking. (The situation is now greatly improved.) Yet here is a group as pure as they come. Move to the condition of the pure astronomers and pure physicists and pure psychologists: They're so open-minded that they squirrel away their ideas and will fight you tooth and nail for the right to date their manuscript ahead of yours. Still they love that word "pure," although, or perhaps because, it is devoid of operational meaning.

Then go on to a hundred departments and schools. In all of them professors hold their secrets—the secrets of many types of clients. Following Rapoport's logic, why shouldn't we know who is being interviewed by a teaching psychiatrist or social worker, and why, and whether he is being paid for the knowledge he is concomitantly gaining? Or why shouldn't we bar all corporate, legal, and foundation consultantships, all studies for school boards, all party politicking, all confidential client and subject relations?

Are 2,000 practicing Democratic political scientists going to be made to spill their party secrets to their Republican students? Do we bar medical-school faculty from practicing? No, even though they return to our halls with green on their hands and secrets in their hearts, for we know from the history of science what can happen when medical teaching is kept from bodily contact. And anyway, they won't let us stop them.

In a strangely limited search for a supporting example, Rapoport says we should demand that Communists reveal their secret red selves, so that we can have the pleasure of shunning them. Why not homosexuals, too? Why not the shadowy informants of deans and trustees? Why not everyone? Let us all confess and do it publicly: we of the great Rapoport Academic Community —no secrets, please!

The wicked secret, of course, is the defense secret. "Purge the academic womb of these wickedly secret men, if not of the others." It is not the secret that is disliked; it is the wicked kind of work involved. Never mind that most nonacademic people think classified military research is more noble than the other kinds of classified work. Why not say it? "Let no true academic womb sustain this martial worm." Very well, then there will be no one who will talk intelligently of what went on in the martial community. We would dance around it like savages about a secret source. Whom would this benefit: scientists, students, public, opposing politicians, pacifists? None of these; no one at all. We should become ignorant victims, paranoid dogmatists, smiling organ-grinders.

It occurs to me that, in the "defense" field as in any other, a man should do his duty by his academic community; he should translate his private knowledge into public form; he should teach the young and old to think; he should do good research. In short, he should be a good professor and scholar. If he can be so, and wants to, or has to keep secrets, that's his business. If he cannot be a good professor, he should be fired.

Pari passu, a university administration that cannot administer classified projects in ways that are congenial to our academic way of life should not allow them in or should be fired if it does. But why blame classified military research for the massive delinquencies of our universities? It is merely a leaking tap in this slum dwelling. If the reason is to help raze the slum, well then, that is another matter.

HENRY M. PACHTER:

Terms such as "secret" and "classi-fied" often apply not to the results of research but to the techniques. During the war I was interested in certain violence the Nazis had done to the German language; but to gain access to monitored transcripts of German broadcasts I had to have "clearance." The results of my studies were shared with the "community of scholars," though their ostensible purpose had been "defense." On the other hand, after Hiroshima I wrote to a dozen nuclear physicists imploring them to go on strike and to deny the military any further knowledge of their ghastly invention— but received unanimous refusals on the ground that science could not be stopped. H. L. Nieburg has shown in *In the Name of Science* how the scientists themselves are pushing projects that place them in a commanding position and how they become research tycoons who milk the public treasury under the pretext of "defense." Other examples point in the opposite direction: "Little black boxes" were to record earth tremors and underground explosions; though invented through classified research, their purpose was to police a nuclear-test-halt agreement, a first step towards disarmament.

Classified research is not necessarily connected with warlike purposes and is not necessarily imposed by a scheming "defense community" on a reluctant "community of scholars." The latter simply does not exist; few departments are even on speaking terms with each other; nor do the denizens of one school understand the language and research methods of the other. It is fortunate if some scholars read outside their field; but the average American professor is no philosophe in pure, disinterested pursuit of eternal truth. If he teaches history and political science, he knows that he is training future diplomats, propagandists, and ideologists—at best —and rarely finds among his graduate students one who is interested in theory. Even in the humanities we cannot be sure that our research will not prove beneficial to some commercial or political interests, and there is practically no discovery in the behavioral sciences that has not been used in advertising.

All of this I regret as much as Mr. Rapoport does, but I don't think it is helpful to close our eyes to the obvious fact (the "truth" that Mr. Rapoport claims to pursue) that the university serves the needs and purposes of the community. The question is: Who determines these purposes? Obviously, as long as we have private universities, they will meet the demand of the institutions that finance them. The state universities, on their side, will follow the educational and other goals that have been set by the people's elected representatives, controlled by a free press and open debate. Whether these purposes of the community are humanitarian and praiseworthy (such as social work, urbanism, engineering in the underdeveloped countries) or whether they are dangerous (wasn't LSD invented by academic research?) and in Mr. Rapoport's eyes detestable (defense-connected research) they are all encroachments on the ideal of pure research, and on principle the academy must defend itself against all such demands of the market and of the community.

It does this by imposing conditions on its services: It must be allowed to follow its own methods of research; it must be allowed to train scholars in the spirit of dispassionate, disinterested science; it does not adjust its curriculum to the day-to-day demands of the community but formulates educational goals for the community—and it fights, or should fight with all its might against the ideal of "committed" science. The ethical judgment on the question of whether a particular project of research should be undertaken must be made before the work is assigned. But this decision has many more ramifications than Professor Rapoport seems to rea-

lize; he casts a "jaundiced eye" only on military research. Why not on certain kinds of business research, too? Much of this business research, incidentally, requires even more secrecy than military research. Moreover, I remember how sorry the Spanish republicans were that so few of them had studied military science; my eye is only half-jaundiced. Finally, in some recent student rebellions the question was asked whether the scholarly ideal of the pure quest for truth (for instance, whether Shakespeare was the thirteenth Earl of Oxford) was not just a bourgeois device to keep good minds from thinking of revolution.

It seems to me that Professor Rapoport is confusing the issues. One is the morality of certain research, whether academic or otherwise; clearly this must be left to the conscience of those who engage in it, and cannot be the concern of anyone who sets himself up as his brother's keeper. Another question is the academic privilege of setting its own standards of research, of communication, and of recruitment. A third is whether the aims of the academy can be preserved if professors jet around as government consultants and promoters of causes or seek positions in nonacademic bodies. As a citizen, of course, each professor should have the right and the duty to give his knowledge and abilities to any cause he chooses—on his own time, however, and not as part of his job. But today business, government, and foundations alienate the professors from their profession. The quest for power is being substituted for the quest for knowledge; they are being called away from their calling. One remedy, of course, would be to seek a strict separation of the academy from purpose-directed projects and service research. Weapons research belongs in army arsenals; professors who accept grants from foundations and other outside agencies should be barred from teaching and publishing. Those who stay in the academy should renounce the advantages in terms of income, secretarial and research help, travel, etc., that have come to them in the last 40 years; they should not write recommendations for their students but educate them in the ideal of purposeless studies. I am prepared to return to the ivory tower but not to a tower of pompous hypocrites who pretend to represent an order that they have long repudiated.

ERNEST VAN DEN HAAG:

Professor Rapoport would expel from universities researchers whose work is secret or puts "power at the disposal of specific groups" or is financed by military agencies. They form the "defense community." What, or who, would be excluded? All defense agency funded research whether or not concerned with weapons? Nonsecret military research and secret nonmilitary research? Does either put "power at the disposal of specific groups" more than, i.e., industrial research, leading to patents? Or does Professor Rapoport dislike the "specific group of men" who, he presumes, would get the power more than others? Anyway, does the "defense community" put "power at the disposal" of the President, of generals, of scientists, or of Americans as distinguished from Russians?

Professor Rapoport cannot know which research will ultimately serve peace or war; which research will deter a Stalin or a Mao, defeat a Hitler, or help attack a Castro. The intent of the research (hard to establish anyway) cannot guide us—Professor Rapoport notwithstanding—to the effect. (For example, research on poison gas—regardless of intent—may be useful for (1) protection, if gas is used by others; (2) industrial protection; (3) medical uses.) A case may be made for pure research for "the community of scholars" and against applied science and "social service." But Professor Rapoport only pre-

tends to make this case in order to attack defense research. He ignores schools of business, education, nursing, home economics, physical education, or journalism, none of which do more—at best—than serve society by providing personnel.

The university community is jeopardized, according to Professor Rapoport, because scholars who participate in secret military research "owe allegiance to another community whose loyalty is, in my opinion, incompatible with loyalty to the community the university ought to be." Yet we all owe allegiance to more than one institution or community, i.e., family, church, university, country, party, profession, research institute, project, etc. Our loyalty to such groups may exceed that to the community of scholars (if they were commensurable). This has never been regarded as objectionable. Professor Rapoport's point thus must be that (a) the loyalty to the defense community is incompatible with loyalty to the university community; (b) that this incompatible loyalty to the defense community necessarily, or usually, prevails over loyalty to the university. Both points must be true if the argument is to make sense—yet Professor Rapoport proves neither. Indeed, he makes no serious attempt—other than by asseveration—to show that the members of the defense community are more loyal to it than to the community of scholars—I suspect that the opposite is more often the case —or to show that the loyalties are in conflict, let alone incompatible. Why is membership in the defense community less compatible with membership in the community of scholars than membership in the Democratic party, the Presbyterian Church, or the Mathematical Association? Why is defense research less compatible with membership in the community of scholars than research in race relations?

According to Professor Rapoport, the university community is devoted to the "search for truth and its free dissemination," and secondarily to "the use of knowledge in the service of man," whereas the defense community is interested primarily in "specific groups of men," and in truth only "in the pursuit of specific knowledge." The incompatibility is factitious. Certainly search for truth or knowledge is what research is about. But it is always specific truth that is sought. How can one seek truth in general? Whether truth is the primary aim or prestige, money, or a particular application—such as getting a man to the moon, saving a child, or deterring an enemy—is hard to establish and irrelevant. As for "knowledge in the service of man," both pacifists and militarists believe that their activities are devoted to it. How can one part of the community of scholars decide that another does not serve man?

Professor Rapoport seems to equate "free dissemination" of knowledge with compulsory immediate dissemination. This is an odd usage. Hasn't it always been the privilege of the researcher to disclose or not to disclose his results whenever he chooses? Isn't any scientist morally free not to disclose his nuclear research to a Nazi or Soviet society that, in his opinion, would misuse it, and to disclose it to a democratic one? What else are our military researchers doing? They hand their results to those whom they trust and exclude those whom they don't trust. Ultimately these results will become, *nolente volente,* available to all, as the history of nuclear research indicates. But I see no objection to withholding such results from those who, in the opinion of the researchers, or of the government they trust, may misuse them, or are not entitled to them. (Similar reasoning applies to any, including industrial, research.) There is no *obligation* to disclose research results to colleagues either.

Professor Rapoport also reproaches

the defense community with being "indifferent to truth . . . in matters not relevant to its pursuits." Is this more true for defense researchers than for others? Some people are exclusively interested in their specialty and others in matters that go beyond. Professor Rapoport feels that his stricture applies to the defense community specifically, because its members believe that "war research is . . . a 'service to society.' Preparations for war are blithely assumed to increase the nation's 'security.' War itself is justified as regrettable but necessary. . . ." These views Professor Rapoport cannot "otherwise explain" unless "complete dedication to the truth" is not part of "the ethics . . . of the defense community." This assertion tells us more about Professor Rapoport's dogmatism than about the ethics of the defense community. The views he disapproves of are held by many scholars no less ethical, intelligent, or truthful than Professor Rapoport. He wishes to expel the members of the defense community from the community of scholars simply because they do not share his views. Many nonmembers don't either. And few members of either community will share his fanaticism.

Professor Rapoport disguises his intolerance by suggesting that the members of the defense community would be entitled to defend their views if only they "were truly members of the intellectual community," in which case "the views of Edward Teller and Herman Kahn would be entitled to be heard." But the defense community is not part of the intellectual community and therefore is "able to hide behind the cloak of secrecy." Actually Teller and Kahn (and many others) have been quite articulate in defense of their work. The secrecy of some of their work has not hindered rational discussion of its justification. The issue of secrecy thus is quite irrelevant.

Elsewhere Professor Rapoport objects to academicians doing research when their colleagues "do not know what research is done, where and why." Disclosure would enable him "to dissociate himself from colleagues who, by serving a war-waging state, violate his moral sense." I think he is able to do so without detailed disclosure.

Most important, I do not think that membership in a university involves, as Professor Rapoport thinks, "shared values (religious schools excepted)." The "community of scholars" can exist if the members feel that each is entitled to his own values unshared by the others. The members need share only one value, a common dedication to the pursuit of truth, not to its dissemination nor to any other "service to mankind," since this "service" may include sincerely pursued but inconsistent values and policies. The community of scholars has never arrogated the authority (nor does it have criteria) to decide what truly serves mankind. Professor Rapoport mentions that those who defended Communists on campus had qualms about "secrecy." But those who opposed them—as I did and do—did not do so because of "the alleged secrecy of the Communist activities and commitments," which is but an aggravating circumstance, but because of the activities and commitments themselves. A Communist cannot be dedicated to the search for truth since he is committed to forsake it for the party line and to be loyal to the party rather than to any academic commitment such as honesty. Professor Rapoport did not ask for expulsion of the people who rendered service to truth and mankind by serving Stalin. He now objects to defense research, which implies no such commitment.

It is quite conceivable to me—but apparently not to him—that true service to mankind may involve research or policies that Professor Rapoport thinks do a disservice. Wherefore we have no business excluding each other.

RAOUL NAROLL:

I oppose classified military research at universities. The university should be a free marketplace for ideas. People engaged in classified research are constrained in their discussions with those without security clearances. Indeed, strictly speaking, classified information must not be withheld only from those who lack security clearances. According to the Defense Department regulations in force when I did classified military research, and which I presume are in force still, classified information must also be withheld from every person, cleared or not, unless he has a need to know. The "need to know" rule naturally defines need as a military need. In short, if you have any classified military information, you must not reveal it to anyone unless he needs it to do his military job properly and has a security clearance.

This need to know rule is a wise rule for military affairs. Actual or potential military rivals are constantly at work trying to gather our military information, just as we are constantly at work trying to gather theirs. Good habits about keeping military secrets save the lives of our soldiers, our sailors, our airmen and—these days, alas!—our civilian population. So mum's the word; and the best way to avoid disclosing classified information is to avoid discussing anything at all connected with your classified research with anyone but your security-cleared fellow workers.

Thus a group of people engaged in classified military research have a duty to avoid discussing their research at all with other people not similarly engaged and properly cleared. In short, with most members of a university community. This avoidance goes directly contrary to the proper policy for the fostering of a university community as a free marketplace of ideas. To introduce classified military research proj-

ects to a university campus is to introduce barriers to the free exchange of
ideas.

In time of war, however, when the
safety of the country is at stake, for a
short time the free marketplace closes
its doors. Then the introduction of
classified research projects is the least
of the barriers. The heavy onus of
public anxiety and the need to unite
the people single-mindedly in their
struggle is felt by most responsible citizens and hushes the voices of dissidents.
Dissident voices are dangerous in wartime; but they are the soul of a free
marketplace for ideas. The best rule of
thumb for our American society is, I
think, that adopted by the American
Anthropological Association. We anthropologists have formally declared
ourselves opposed to any classified military research on university campuses—
except in time of war declared by Congress. (As everyone knows, no such
war has been declared by Congress for
more than 25 years; neither the Korean
nor the Vietnam conflicts were thus
declared.)

We need not justify our need for a
free marketplace for ideas by attacking
the social value of the Department of
Defense. There are armies and navies
and air forces and rocket troops and
hydrogen bombs in this world in the
hands of those who would, if they
could, close down all free marketplaces
for ideas. The recent events in Czechoslovakia reminded many of us of this
fact—many who had forgotten what had
happened in Hungary in 1956. The
armed forces of the United States today
are the chief protecting walls that keep
out of much of the world those who
would always silence dissident voices
and deny everyone the right to disagree
with the gospel according to St. Mark.
Therefore, if it were absolutely necessary for the Defense Department to
make use of universities in order to
carry out its research programs, I would
support such use. But the Defense Department has ample funds and ample
facilities elsewhere. Places like the
Rand Corporation are amply provided
for classified research by the Defense
Department. So at the universities, in
times of formal peace, we should co-
operate in carrying out Defense Department research only when such cooperation does not interfere with our free
marketplace for ideas. Unclassified defense research—yes. Classified defense
research—no.

Loyalty and Dissent

Morton A. Kaplan

Many of the most critical problems in the relationship of the citizen to the polity involve the connections between domestic and foreign policy, the importance of the state in the maintenance of desirable values, the moral role of dissent, bargaining with competitors, and guarding against manifest and potential military threats. These problems assume greater and greater importance as the world becomes more complexly interrelated.

Although the Credit Anstalt failure is believed by some to have set off the worldwide depression of the 1930's, the growth of the modern corporation into an international giant that is hardly controllable within the national political framework is a post-World War II development. Improved logistics, improved means of transportation, worldwide satellite television broadcasting facilities, ICBM's, and the huge impact of even relatively minor military ventures on domestic programs make it extremely difficult to formulate international policies without considering their domestic consequences.

Although it is not true that the Vietnamese War has led to a cutback in the Great Society—contrast the $25.6 billion expenditures for Great Society measures in 1968 compared with $9.9 billion for 1960 and $12.9 billion for 1963, and the 45 domestic social programs of 1960 with the 435 that were in existence in 1968—much more in the way of social legislation and in support for pure science would be possible in the absence of military expenditures for Viet Nam. It is reliably reported that even so surgically swift an operation as the Soviet occupation of Czechoslovakia has imposed a considerable burden on the Russian domestic economy. Some at least of the pressure to negotiate ballistic missile limitations results from budgetary strains in the Soviet Union and the United States. The impact of Department of Defense expenditures on the American balance of payments and rate of domestic inflation constitute a severe restraint on American policy.

Although much of the argument against military expenditure and military ventures stems from a social science myth about the development of a garrison state, there is no substantial evidence to sustain this thesis. Similar arguments were strongly asserted before World War II. Yet American society emerged from that war as a more just society in which civil liberties were strengthened. There has been on balance no substantial evidence of the erosion of civil liberties during the Vietnamese War; the protection of dissent during a time of military conflict by the courts and by the political administration of the United States has been perhaps unprecedented in American history.

Moreover, it is a mistake to believe that the choice between domestic progress and international security is a direct and simple choice. If the Vietnamese War is either counterproductive to American security or of little consequence to it, then the argument as to what could otherwise be done—but not what surely would be done—with the saved monies makes sense. If, on the other hand, our security would be weakened by a contrary policy, much greater subsequent expenditures might be forced upon us. If we were eventually thrust back into a beleaguered position, there would likely result a diminution in our civil liberties and retrogression in our social progress and in civil rights. Even if the resulting regime were leftist in orientation, the radical blacks who pursue this goal would likely find themselves betrayed as badly as the Jews who supported Communism against Czarist anti-Semitism in Russia. The relationship between external and internal policy is real; it is, however, anything but simple.

DOMESTIC CORRELATES OF INTERNATIONAL DECISIONS

At least some of the possible decisions of American statecraft can be fateful for the future of American institutions and also for the maintenance of important values in the world. Let us think back to the forceful debate before World War II in order to explicate this problem. Those who favored aiding the allies talked about the military threat stemming from Nazi hegemony in Europe. Predictions were made about German overlordship in Africa after the conquest of Europe. Military conclusions were drawn from the proximity of Africa to the coast of Brazil.

Conservative isolationists—Herbert Hoover is an example—unlike the liberals who opposed prowar measures, met these arguments directly and successfully refuted them. On the basis of the then known technologies Hoover was able to rebut the argument that the Nazis would constitute a military threat to the United States if they secured hegemony in Europe. Although Hoover did not foresee nuclear weapons and although conceivably the Nazis might have constituted a direct military threat to the United States had they acquired nuclear weapons first, the threat to the United States that could properly have been foreseen at the time—and it was neither a direct military threat nor the danger that we might have been deprived of natural resources—was little discussed in that debate.

The danger the United States faced was neither simple nor easily calculable. The quality of life in the United States would most likely have been irreparably harmed by Nazi victory. Anne Lindbergh was proclaiming a wave of the future, in specific an authoritarian wave. Fascists and protofascist groups were becoming increasingly numerous. To the south of us, fascist and Nazi ideologies were making headway, particularly in Argentina and Bolivia but in other nations of Latin America as well.

A world conquered by the Axis would have been a world hostile to American values. It would have been a world in which our confidence in our own values would have been diminished. The military measures that would have been forced upon us had we been encircled by fascist and authoritarian states might have produced major political change in the United States and the garrison state that liberals feared war would bring.

Although it is unlikely that we would have adopted either fascism or Nazism, we would more likely have found our own American mode of response to what would then have been viewed as an inevitable trend of world history. It would also have been argued that only in that manner could we have become strong enough to withstand the pressures arrayed against us.

Yet this latter projection is not something that can be proved. Perhaps the Nazi regime would have mellowed from within. Perhaps its effort to extend control over the continent of Europe would have overloaded it, leading to its collapse.

PERSPECTIVES ON MORAL QUESTIONS

POSSIBLE CRITERIA FOR CHOICE

How do we make decisions in circumstances so resistant to demonstrated proofs or reasoned judgment? Obviously some of the most important moral problems of our time—and perhaps of history—are raised by the questions related to such decisions. Answers to these questions need to be justified under circumstances of gross uncertainty. Consider just a few of the relevant questions. Was the misery of World War II justified? If resistance to the Nazis led to the deaths directly or indirectly of some forty million people, how do we justify the decision to resist if we assume that this result could have been anticipated by reasonable men? Confronted with the determination of the Nazi regime, would it perhaps have been better for the rest of the world to surrender?

Judgments were necessary; it was necessary for political leaders to act with firmness and swiftness upon those judgments. The men who made the decisions were faced with the moral problem of leaping into the unknown upon the basis of inadequate information—a moral problem that necessarily confronts statesmen when they deal with major problems.

Some possible perspectives on those decisions have been offered in [chapter 3 of *Dissent and the State*]. There obviously must have been some upper limit to the costs that would have been acceptable to prevent Nazi victory. Yet perhaps those costs would not properly

have been set very low. The Nazis might have established a thousand-year Reich. They might have involved those not eliminated in complicities that debased them. They might have developed drugs or psychological or biological controls that would have irreversibly changed and debased man. These projections cannot be known scientifically either, although it is important to be aware that the technological techniques that foreshadow them are developing.

Yet there are vast uncertainties. In situations in which little is known and in which radical changes and radical costs are likely to be introduced regardless of what one does, it is perhaps best to follow the advice of Winston Churchill: to do that which is morally right and to resist that which is morally wrong. Although this advice is only a rebuttable perspective and although it will produce historical ironies, it is perhaps the best advice we have.

Resistance to evil is not a simple matter. It produces its own caricatures of the evils fought but it also provides opportunities for heroism and moral courage, for maintaining human self-esteem, and for re-enforcing civilized values that, through millenia of recorded history, have seemed exceedingly fragile.

Much of the debate over current American foreign policy runs aground on intangibles similar to those of the pre-World War II period. Is the danger to the United States that of monolithic Communism? Perhaps division in the Communist world will strengthen rather than weaken its expansive tendencies; perhaps a world dominated by a Soviet bloc and by a number of independent and semi-independent Communist states would be even more hostile to the United States politically and more dangerous militarily than a world in which Communism was unified.

The most crucial area for the United States is that of Western Europe, with its skilled population and great industrial base. Does American involvement in Southeast Asia detract from its ability to form a stable relationship with Europe and to aid in the protection of Europe, or is the credibility of the American guarantee in Asia, if not a prerequisite, an important ingredient in the credibility of American performance in Europe?

Can questions of this kind be answered in the abstract? Or is it a matter of balancing risks, resources, and uncertainties, in which case evaluation is impossible in an absence of the specific relationship of resource to risk to uncertainty, that is, in the absence of a specific analysis of the particular case? Do the answers, in addition, depend upon the historicity of the case, that is, of the specific sequence of events that lead to decision and to the expectations and interpretations that develop in the context of the decision making process? Although rebuttable perspectives can legitimately and usefully be offered that are relatively independent of resources, specific alternatives, contexts, and interpretations, it is obvious that these must be considered rebuttable, that they can at best provide frameworks for analysis, and that decisions have to be made as the stream of particularities unwinds itself.

POLITICAL LEADERS, STATE AND WORLD

Political leaders, as well as ordinary citizens, have responsibilities that go beyond the nation-state. They are citizens of the world as well as of the nation and, although they have par-

ticular responsibilities to the nation of an order not voluntarily accepted by the ordinary citizen, they ought not to ignore the impact of their actions on life styles and prospects in other nations and on hopes for a better and more viable world order. On the other hand, much of the propaganda that has been directed to young people by at least some to the effect that they should act as citizens of the world rather than as citizens of a particular nation badly misleads young people. Until such time as the nation is superseded by more enlightened and more effective forms of political organization, national values as well as world values must be pursued to a significant extent through national organizations. In this pursuit, some nations are obviously more essential than others. The extinction of Denmark, for instance, would be a cultural tragedy but the impact on humane values elsewhere might well be minimal. A serious decline in the military power and political and economic influence of the United States, however, might well have disastrous implications for many of those more enlightened values that are posited in contradistinction to nationalism. There can be occasions on which it is important for good nations to win bad wars, that is, wars entered into for particular reasons that cannot be justified according to the values of the nation or by prudential considerations. It is possible that the loss even of a bad war might threaten very important human values.

If, on the other hand, the policy of a nation threatens desirable national and international values, not merely in particular actions but in general, there is a general obligation to act against the nation. Many German citizens recognized this obligation during World War II and daringly engaged in sabotage of the activities of the Nazi regime. Precisely because the nation-state is the most effective, although not the exclusive, instrument for implementing policy in the world arena, when the national regime genuinely is a force for bad values, it is extremely important to oppose it in general even in some cases in which its policies might accomplish on balance some good.

Sometimes one hears the argument that if the government can employ force abroad without the sanction of law, it is equally valid for citizens to use force at home against injustices. Many people do believe this argument and act upon it either consciously or implicitly. There may be a relationship between the use of force abroad, at least in support of causes not fully understood by the public at large, and the breakdown of order in the domestic forum. If this is so, wise governments will endure some external risks to avoid domestic consequences injurious to the framework of values that characterizes the American polity. Yet, the argument has no validity from the moral point of view.

Although all governments attempt to suppress domestic violence, this suppression in democracies rests upon the supposition that the opportunity exists for a current minority to transform itself into a majority through persuasion. Unlike the Japanese, Americans have never accepted the notion, as given intellectual stature by John Calhoun, that particularly intense minorities have a right to block what a majority desires unless this entails a destruction of the system of majority rule itself. Although the American system of representative democracy is based upon the notion that majorities should not work their will immediately but only after delay, the underlying consensus is that majorities, if they can sustain themselves, ultimately should have their way, provided they do not attack fundamental constitutional constraints.

The international system has no such underlying consensus. It has no constitutional provisions for change.

Moreover, accretions of strength for one of the actors in the system may fundamentally destabilize the system at the expense of other actors. The Baltic states found their existence destroyed by the pact between the Soviet Union and Nazi Germany. There have been significant changes in the domestic Czechoslovak system since the Soviet invasion of 1968. American intervention in Guatemala and the Dominican Republic have had major impacts upon the domestic institutions of those nations. If the United States had not intervened with great effect in World War II, albeit as the consequence of Japanese attack, we might very well be living in a world in which fascist and racist doctrines governed most of humanity. The American domestic value system is hardly immune from large-scale transformations in world politics. Whatever the wisdom or justice of American involvement in Viet Nam, the generalization that the employment of force abroad legitimatizes it at home is based upon a jejune error in analysis: the application of a generalization that applies to one kind of social system to another of a fundamentally different nature.

It would be wrong to draw the contrary inference: that force is always to be employed in the international arena and never in the domestic. The differences between the two systems, although very great in degree, do not justify such extreme inferences. There are many processes of peaceful change in the international system, including norms of internal law that are much better followed than many laymen understand, and there are sometimes circumstances even in democratic political systems in which the processes of peaceful change break down or in which the opportunity to persuade is largely formal. Yet the latter are extremely unlikely to produce a fundamental transformation of the system or to prevent rather than delay persuasion and peaceful change. The repeated threat of force, and even more the conspicuous use of force, in democratic political systems is almost surely more subversive of the processes of peaceful change than the temporary maintenance of some injustice. On the other hand, it is often only the availability of the threat of force and occasionally of the conspicuous use of force that prevents the transformation of the international system in ways that are inimical to democratic and humane values. For this reason the assertion that the use of force by the government abroad legitimates the domestic employment of force against the government is intellectually mischievous.

One other point deserves mention, although it is strongly implied in what has already been stated. The international system operates on the basis of self-help. Although it is not anarchic or lawless, whatever standards are observed are maintained through the decentralized decision making of states and through international organization. The nation operates most effectively in the international system when it acts as a coordinated and coherent unit. Its capacity to do good (or harm) is decreased to the extent that individuals and groups within the nation attempt to defeat its policies or to substitute their judgments for those of the national government. Since the hobbling of government policy rarely permits the substitution of a different and better (depending on the point of view) policy, it usually works harm even with respect to the aims of those who attack the policy decisions. The legitimation of the failure to abide by the normal methods of changing policy by changing governments at elections would destroy the consensus on the basis of which effective external policy is possible. It seems difficult to justify this, except from an exceptionally arrogant point of view, unless one is willing to make the judgment either that the gov-

ernment in general is evil or that a particular policy is so evil that all these other risks become acceptable. Although either conclusion might be true and although there are historical examples where each has been true, it would seem that this conclusion would not lightly be arrived at by responsible people. This would seem to be particularly true in democracies where governments must periodically submit themselves to the people.

The charge has been made that the popular will is frustrated because, for instance, there was no antiwar candidate in the 1968 elections. However, the polls showed with great consistency that Nixon was the overwhelming choice of those who considered themselves Republicans and that Humphrey was the choice of those who considered themselves Democrats. Although it is far from clear that the national will was not registered by the 1968 election regardless of party politics, this is not really essential. The electoral system is a party system and those who insist on working outside of that framework have little legitimate complaint if their influence on the process is diminished by that fact.

JUSTIFICATION AND CONSCIENTIOUS DECISION

Decisions with respect to state and world involve conflicts of conscience over values of overriding importance. These decisions are so important that we must be concerned not merely with the answers to which we come but with the way in which the answers are arrived at, for the justification of substantive value decisions cannot properly be divorced from the justification of the procedures by means of which they are derived. We live in a world in which information is limited, in which role responsibilities and role capabilities differ from citizen to citizen and from political leader to political leader. Although recognition of the limitation of information and responsibility when conscience genuinely demands action can be used as a rationalization for inaction, the insistence upon infallibility of judgment and the right to individual decision can become an excuse for self-righteous and irresponsible self-indulgence.

The political leader arrives at his decisions under conditions of great uncertainty. The citizen sits in judgment under conditions of great uncertainty. If their conclusions differ in ways of exceptional moral importance and if the citizen desires to consider how or whether to engage in dissent, what criteria does he apply? No set of rules can be proposed that permits an unambiguous answer. Yet, for the citizen torn between the fear that he is neglecting to dissent when moral duty requires it and the fear that he might dissent in a merely self-indulgent manner, there are at least some questions that can be asked in the effort to discover whether procedural justification is present. Does the decision adequately take into account the information that is available or is an answer leaped to on the basis of stereotyped formulas? Is there recognition that decisions are made by decision makers on the basis of information not available to the rest of the citizenry? Was there an attempt fairly to assess the motivations and aims of others and the information that might be available to them? Was the complexity of the considerations that enter into the decision and of the consequences that likely will follow from it fairly taken into account? Was there an attempt fairly to assess the consequences of opposition in situations in which one cannot change the decisions of others but might only be able to interfere with their effective implementation?

There is surely a moral difference between preventing SS storm troopers from killing Jews as efficiently as possible and interfering with the daily operations of a school because one doesn't like the program of a principal. The first genuinely accomplishes a good even though it cannot change the general policy; the latter may, although not invariably, do only harm, even to those whose interests are supposedly being protected by interfering with the educative process without replacing it by a better one.

It is part of ethical responsibility to consider consequences. For instance, much of the public dissent to the Vietnamese War needs to be related to the impact that this dissent has upon continuation of the war. Although some writers, such as Arthur Schlesinger, Jr., have argued that North Vietnamese continuation of the war is entirely unrelated to dissent within the United States and have cited some statements of Hanoi to this effect, this opinion is hardly credible and reflects seriously upon those who make it. The North Vietnamese would hardly desire to argue that their victory, if they ever do obtain one, was produced more by dissent in the United States than by their own activities. Thus they would hardly go out of their way to ascribe their success to dissent in the United States. They have on occasion denigrated the value of dissent but they have also made statements indicating the value they place upon dissent in the United States.

In any event, the North Vietnamese would be stupid indeed if their conduct of the war and of their willingness to negotiate and of the conditions under which they are willing to negotiate were not influenced by their estimate of the impact of dissent upon American official behavior. Obviously dissent is an important element both for the outcome Hanoi hopes to achieve and for the price it will have to pay to achieve it. Indeed, the North Vietnamese have often been quite open about the value they place on dissent. According to the *New York Times*:

A Communist source noted what was called "the realities" of the world situation, and said, "After all, we are not negotiating in a vacuum." The principal reality, this source said, is the "irreversible tide" of public opinion against the war in the United States including popular refusal to accept further casualties. "They are cynical about it," an American diplomat commented. "They are telling us in every meeting and at every news conference that bloodshed hurts you more than it does us. If they lose 4,000 men, no one on their side knows it. If we lose 200, everyone does." The other side also appears to be encouraged by the differences between Washington and Saigon over policy.[1]

A conscientious person might nonetheless engage in major public dissent if, in his judgment, the costs of dissent—for instance, the likely prolongation of the war—were outweighed either by other consequences that might shorten the war or by compensating gains with respect to other values injured by American intervention.

THE TREATMENT OF DISSENT

A number of conflicting values enter into the treatment of dissent. It is important in a society that values autonomous choice to protect dissent. Although dissent ought not to be beyond criticism, excessive criticism of dissent runs the risk that the value of autonomous choice might be injured. However, despite much criticism of the government in this respect, it is far from clear that the latter has been the greater present danger. The factor that has been most remarkable in recent years, at least prior to the intervention of Spiro Agnew, has been the extent to which the government of the United States, with some relatively minor exceptions, has maintained a climate of opinion that protected the exercise of dissent and the extent to which the dissenters engaged in a form of reverse McCarthyism by seeking to make criticism of their activities illegitimate. The President, moreover, did have a responsibility as commander in chief of the armed forces to protect the morale of the forces in the field.

Some argue as if there should be no penalties at all for dissent. Although it is true that one desires to protect the right of reasoned speech, it is entirely unreasonable to expect that individuals will not or should not be held accountable in any way for the consequences of their speech. Sometimes some kinds of speech are genuinely inconsistent with the positions that people hold and the responsibilities that go along with the positions. For instance, if a teacher in a public school announced either in class or outside of it but publicly that Negroes are inherently inferior and cannot learn, his opinion, no matter how conscientiously held, would have an impact upon the psychologies of black youngsters that would be inconsistent with his teaching responsibilities. A similar standard would not as clearly be appropriate at the university level. A professor at a college or university, however, who advises students to come to class with guns *is* behaving in a manner inconsistent with the kind of reasoned discourse that characterizes a university; in the absence of extremely extenuating circumstances, his appointment should be terminated. Sometimes the only appropriately available penalty for speech that is injurious to important values is to hold the guilty individual up to public scorn or disgrace.

There is often a failure to distinguish the right to dissent from the right to get one's way. After the occupation of a building or the shouting down of a speaker, one often hears the argument: "But no one conceded to us when we merely engaged in talk." Yet there is no right to succeed; and it is a truism where controversy exists that some people do not like the outcome. Democracy rests on the supposition that there are appropriate institutional processes for deciding controversial issues.

Suppose the Ku Klux Klan started forcibly ejecting black children from integrated schools. Would the argument that they tried talk, that they tried litigation, and that even the electoral process failed them, justify their effort? Would it really be true that the government was suppressing their dissent if it arrested them for their actions? Would their sincerity or their conscience mitigate their crime? Suppose they lynched blacks as a matter of conscience? Would that be acceptable dissent?

Sometimes speech is confused with activities that are not really speech at all. It is true that the right to dissent is not worth much if one does not have reasonable opportunities to exercise that right. Yet, is the dissenter to be the sole judge of the appropriate opportunity? Does he have the right to seize a radio station? To enter my home against my will to harangue me? Do I not have the right not to listen to him?

Suppose the Ku Klux Klan rides in sheets and on horses through the black section of a city carrying signs reading: "Black monkeys are naturally inferior and should be sent back to Africa"; "Niggers who date white women should be castrated and then lynched"; "We'll be watching every nigger who votes." Suppose a Nazi group goes through a Jewish section of town with a sign reading: "All greasy kikes should be gassed."

Are such activities merely speech? Or are they designed to intimidate and provoke? Are they related in a legitimate way to attempts to convince? Don't people have a right not to be harassed and intimidated?

Surely there is a problem here. If we merely suppress what some people dislike intensely, we may destroy meaningful dissent except within a very narrow range of options. Limitations on dissent can, and in some places will, be misused to undermine it. There is a conflict of principles here for which no perfect solution is possible. Moreover, we should attempt to avoid equating planned group provocations with spontaneous individual quarrels in justifying action against one who takes a provocatory position.

Yet surely it should not be beyond the ingenuity of our legislative and judicial systems to devise rules and regulations reasonably protective of both the right to exercise dissent and the right not to be provocatively harassed. Such extreme provocatory harassment is itself destructive of the civility required for constitutional order. The example it sets is destructive of the political community and poisons democratic consensus. If people have a right to prejudice and to express their prejudices—and I believe they do—they are nonetheless not merely indulging in verbal dissent when they manifest the behavior described above. Any reasonable man knows this and so do those who engage in such provocatory behavior. Such behavior is not in any major or legitimate way part of an effort to communicate a political doctrine. It is designed directly, rather than indirectly, to produce action and likely violence. Whatever the abstract and absolutist interpretation of the first amendment made by the Supreme Court, we have the right—even more, the duty—to protect the polity against this.

There are times, however, when I suspect that many so-called liberals do not really believe in dissent or the value of criticism but instead are merely advocates of particular substantive positions. Was Senator Eugene McCarthy, for instance, merely making a disinterested observation after Secretary of Agriculture Orville Freeman was hooted down at the University of Wisconsin when he said that if administration spokesmen wish to be heard, they should stay away from college campuses? Was he appealing to reason during the New Hampshire primary in 1968 when he accused administration supporters of (Joe) McCarthyism for stating that Moscow would be pleased if he won? "Joe McCarthyism," I had thought, implied a reckless profusion of false charges. Although it would be deplorable if we let Moscow's, likes and dislikes determine America's actions, surely the contention was relevant and, as reports from Russia established after the primary, accurate. Who was guilty of a profusion of false charges? More recently (November 1969), a returned prisoner of war, Major James Rowe, declared that American POW's largely ignored Hanoi's propaganda until late 1967, when Hanoi began citing U.S. Senators by name. "The peace demonstrators and the disheartening words of these Senators made our life more dif-

ficult," said Major Rowe. Although appropriate national interests may require such consequences, surely Major Rowe has a right and a direct personal interest in challenging this. Note, however, the libertarian concern of Senator Stephen Young of Ohio for Major Rowe. "Major Rowe," Young said, "should be silenced or assigned to some other post of duty outside Washington. A tour in the Aleutian Islands or some post in remote Turkey might cause his mouthings to be silenced."[2] Whether the Department of Defense assigned Major Rowe to the Washington area because of his views—an improper action—or whether his assignment was independent of his views, the motives of Senator Young and of his "liberal" cohorts were transparent. They were making a brutal use of the powers of the Senate in an effort to stifle criticism.

NOTES

1. *New York Times* (June 25, 1969).
2. *Chicago Daily News* (November 29-30, 1969).

The Military Establishment and Social Values

ADAM YARMOLINSKY

The impact of the military establishment—as of any other institution—on the nation's value system is not easily measured. Easy stereotypes of authoritarianism, conformity, aggression, and brutality are common. The evidence to support or refute them is less readily come by. What is clear is that the effort to sort out reality from myth is a crucial one. It is useful to survey so far as possible the character and range of military influence, tangible and intangible, on the quality of American life.

The history of the United States can be measured as it can for most nations from war to war, as many textbooks and children's book series bluntly indicate. It took one war to create the Union and another to preserve it. For most Americans, the military continues to be the most obvious manifestation of the federal presence, apart from the Post Office. Its influence extends nationwide more than almost any other institution. Soldiers are trained and serve far from home with comrades from every class, race, and region. Only at the executive level of large corporations—and perhaps not even there—does the pattern of movement begin to match the mobility of the military. During the lifetime of those now in their seventies the nation has engaged in five wars in which the United States was a major participant; those now over thirty have lived through three wars that have covered more than a third of their lives.

Until the time comes, if it ever does, when regional differences within the United States are significantly reduced by national television and the spread of other communications, broadly based educational influences and the architectural uniformity of shopping centers, housing developments, and office buildings—and until wars diminish or cease—the separate influence of the military will continue to serve as a unique and potent common national experience.

The military establishment has come a long way from the eighteenth-century mercenary armies, in which close order drill was instituted so that the men would be within the pistol range of their officers. Cadets at the Military Academy at West Point no longer even march to class. But the uniformed military, nevertheless, is still an island of authority and conformity in an increasingly permissive society. In no profession or calling in American society is tradition so clearly manifest. The military officer rises in the morning and puts on a uniform traditional in cut and color, decorated with badges of valor and insignia of rank. When he goes outdoors he is greeted by his juniors and greets his seniors with the traditional salute. In any headquarters, he encounters the flags of his country, his service, and his unit, often decorated with streamers commemorating past campaigns, and, flanking his own desk, if he is an officer of flag rank, his personal colors. He is frequently a participant in traditional ceremonies, more or less elaborate; if he wishes to avoid them, he must take special pains to do so. The civilian employee in the Defense Department finds himself surrounded by tradition and ceremony, and even the defense contractor feels the weight of the military tradition.

The visible forms of tradition reflect the continuity of the military establishment which adds to its impact on government policy. Among the cabinet departments, only State and Treasury are senior, and these are now tiny, and far weaker, principalities. Few institutions in the United States, governmental or private, excepting church, synagogue and the university, approach the military in established and continuous tradition. The recording that sounds retreat at the Air University at Maxwell Field, Alabama, echoes the notes that sounded over the forts in Indian territory more than a century ago. The music does not change. Small wonder that old words—and old ideas—persist.

"The military mind is no idle phrase," a persistent if sometimes captious critic of the military, C. Wright Mills, wrote. "It points to the results of a system of formal selection and common experiences and friendships and activities—all enclosed within similar routines."[1] The career officer, and to a lesser extent the career noncommissioned officer, is the custodian of the values of the military mind, but the career profession itself is of relatively recent origin in the United States. Samuel P. Huntington, in *The Soldier and the State*, observed that "the Constitution does not envisage a separate class of persons exclusively devoted to military leadership"[2] and traces the development of modern military professionalism in the United States to the post-Civil War period. The importance of the military professional increased through the two world wars and especially during the post-World War II technological revolution.

The initial basic training period is the recruit's introduction to the rigid discipline of the military. The World War II Army humor best seller, *See Here, Private Hargrove*, explained the purposes of basic training to recruits:

> All your persecution is deliberate, calculated, systematic. It is the collegiate practice of hazing, applied to the grim and highly important task of transforming a civilian into a soldier, a boy into a man. It is the Hardening Process. You won't get depressed; you won't feel sorry for yourself. You'll just get mad as hell. You'll be breathing fire before it's over. Believe me or not, at the end of that minor ordeal, you'll be feeling good. You'll be full of spirit and energy and you will have found yourself.[3]

Intentional disruption of civilian patterns of adjustment, replacement of individual gratifications with group goals, inculcation of unquestioning acceptance of authority, development of conformity to official attitudes and conduct—all have been cited by military administrators as goals of basic training.

The function of discipline, according to the military, is that of promoting organized living. All too frequently, however, military discipline in practice involves an arbitrary display of power by those in positions of authority.

Commander Ralph Earle wrote in 1917 of the function of discipline in the military:

> The discipline of the Naval Academy well illustrates the principle that in every community discipline means simply organized living. It is the condition of living right because without right living, civilization cannot exist. Persons who will not live right must be compelled to do so, and upon such misguided individuals there must be placed restraints. To these alone is discipline ever harsh or a form of punishment.[4]

But military discipline is not always a model for organized living. It often seems erratic and arbitrary. Some commanders are particularly concerned with the appearance of their men; for example, one man was court-martialed for failing to get a "white sidewall" haircut (the head shaved bare from ears to crown) because the commander felt "members of the honor guard should look alike."[5] Some commanders emphasize inspection: disciplinary proceedings have resulted from a man's failure to have his towel exactly three fingers' distance from the corner of the bed and from failure to clean inside his toothpaste cap. Some commanders stress military courtesy: the recent order of a general that men who failed to salute properly would be sent to the front in Vietnam was only withdrawn after adverse criticism in the press.[6] These demands of discipline centering on appearance, cleanliness, exactitude of detail, and respect for tradition and rank are viewed by important elements within the military as essential to the maintenance of an effective military force.

When those requirements conflict with other values, conflict arises. Disciplinary rules, for example, may be applied so as to deny First Amendment rights (forbidding the reading of certain newspapers, attendance at a peaceful off-post political meeting, or the expression of opinions which conflict with official policies); or so as to deny individual freedoms involving little discernible military interest (such as ordering a serviceman to refrain from drinking, to attend church, or to pay a disputed bill); or so as to be clearly arbitrary and discriminatory (such as calculated harassment of an individual or a group). Because of the clash between the values of many young recruits and those of the career military in the Vietnam war, the permissible boundaries for regulation of conduct through discipline have become a subject of fervent dispute and a number of courts-martial. . . .

Military training and discipline clash with the democratic and egalitarian values of civilian society in many points. The military's group-oriented value system based on rank consciousness, unit loyalty, desire for combat, unquestioning patriotism, and instant response to command runs counter to the egalitarian, individualistic, inquiring humanistic ideals of American civil society.

There is inevitably a penumbra of restraint surrounding the military establishment that reaches beyond the military. The prospect of military service, or of the need for a security clearance in the civilian sector of the military establishment can and does have a "chilling" effect on dissent in American society. And, despite the fact that dissent is endemic in the civilian sector, dissent in the military often arouses civilian resentment. The harassment by local authorities of coffee-houses established by antiwar groups seems to have at least the tacit approval of the local military. Self-interest may also dampen dissent—workers in California defense plants wear buttons reading "Don't knock the war that feeds you." And as we have seen, the revelation of the extensive files maintained by Army intelligence on citizens who might, in its view, constitute a threat to internal security suggests an ominous potential for restraint of legitimate dissent.

Nevertheless, the basic training of the recruit and sustained military discipline fail to achieve subordination to authority for increasing numbers of young men. Desertions and AWOL's have climbed continuously since 1961, and as Table 1 indicates, have spurted in the last years in response to an increasingly unpopular war.

The monthly averages of desertions and AWOL's in 1970 are running even

TABLE 1. Number of Desertions and AWOL's
Fiscal Years 1967-69

Year	Desertions (Absent without leave more than 30 days)	AWOL (Absent without leave less than 30 days)
1967	40,227	134,668
1968	53,357	155,536
1969	(c. 75,000)	NA

NA—not available.

higher, with a projection of almost 100,000 desertions and 250,000 AWOL's for the year.

The military's explanation for this state of affairs has often been simplistic. A House subcommittee in June 1969 asked the Deputy Chief of Staff for Army Personnel, Lieutenant General Albert O. Connor, why desertion rates had increased. Connor replied, "We are getting more young men who are coming in undisciplined, the product of a society that trains them to resist authority."[7]

Endurance of physical hardships, ability to accept enforced obedience, toleration of stress and group indoctrination are obviously essential to military effectiveness. The military must have sufficient authority to maintain order and discipline among its personnel. Nevertheless, the military itself needs to make further adjustments to the realities of the socialization process for young people today, and perhaps to assess its human resources more shrewdly, in particular different periods of national life. Understaffed psychiatric services should be reinforced to cope with adjustment and identity crises. The principles of adolescent psychology need to be better understood by those in command. Experiments in motivational stimulus, such as the rewarding of recruits for achievement with movie or weekend pass privileges, and in less harsh and more rational uses of authority, seem to be promising efforts in the direction of constructive institutional adaptation.

A logical extension of these developments might be an all-volunteer Army, as has been proposed by the Gates Commission and others. On the other hand, tempting as the concept is to the millions of young men who would thereby be protected from service, except in time of general war, an all-volunteer "professional" Army would deprive the military of the salutary consequences that derive from the presence in its ranks of a large propor-

tion of men who think of themselves as citizens first and soldiers a poor second. Draftees, while somewhat inhibited from complaining to their congressmen for fear of a sergeant's wrath, might be far more inhibited if they had long-term careers to protect. By the same token, the Congress would probably show greater concern about what happens to drafted men, and especially about their being sent overseas into unstable areas, than it would be about what happens to volunteers. In addition to the risk to the man involved, the possibility of military movements triggering greater American involvement abroad might, therefore, be increased with a volunteer Army.[8]

If military service led to heightened authoritarian responses or rigid absolutist military perspectives, this impact should be most effective among long-term career noncommissioned officers. These men must accommodate to the internal pressures of a role that stands between the rank and file of enlisted personnel and the officer corps. The commissioned officer's educational background and skill requirements are linked to the larger society and its values; rank-and-file enlisted men are generally reluctant to leave civilian life for the military term, and their basic ties are non-military.

The impact of prolonged exposure to combat, especially intense combat, has observable and immediately disruptive consequences on recruits.[9] Data on long-term consequences, for example, in aggressiveness, are less adequate. The ideological impact seems relatively weak—the formation of a veteran's ideology depends on his joining other ex-combat soldiers in intimate social and fraternal groups, and most peacetime recruits do not join veterans' groups at all.

The impact of military service on personal social values can be observed from one perspective by examining the success or failure of delinquents, who are often encouraged to join or are informally "paroled" into the armed forces. Since the armed forces are prepared to disregard a young man's previous record once he is admitted into service, he can earn an honorable discharge, which will supersede his past police record. Recruitment policies encourage the induction of personnel with minor criminal records during wartime, though less so at other periods. Hans Mattick has produced evidence that felons paroled into the armed forces during World War II had a much lower recidivism rate than those paroled into civilian life.[10]

The most profound changes, of course, take place in basic training, where the intensity of experience, the sharp contrast with civilian life, and the high sense of social solidarity combine to make an often traumatic impact on the recruit. In his study of forty-eight squads in the basic infantry training cycle at Fort Dix during the summer of 1952,[11] Richard Christie found an improvement in self-esteem and personal adjustment—as measured by the recruit's perception of his own physical and psychological condition—and improvement in positive relations with his peers. The study, interestingly enough, revealed that recruits who remained in contact with their homes and family made the poorest adjustment to military training. In addition, the practice of involving the trainees in the leadership hierarchy on a rotation basis produced a strikingly more positive adjustment than the experience of those who had no such opportunity. Christie found a slight and statistically insignificant increase in authoritarianism during the basic six-week training cycle.[12] At the same time, basic training produced in those studied more negative opinions about officers and noncommissioned officers than before training. In effect, basic training apparently served as a form of prophylaxis against authoritarianism.

According to other research, authoritarianism actually decreases as training becomes more complex and more advanced. Two researchers who set out to prove that air cadet training would increase authoritarian predispositions among the officer candidates found instead a decrease in authoritarian traits among cadets after one year of training.[13] Since a characteristic of the military organization is its authoritarian procedures, and since authoritarian personality tendencies imply the predisposition both to dominate arbitrarily others of lower status and simultaneously to submit to arbitrary higher authority, participation in the military training program, they had reasoned, would heighten authoritarian personality tendencies among those who pass such training successfully. The authors were tempted to conclude that their research tools might have been inadequate. But direct examination of combat flight training indicated an emphasis on group interdependence and a concept of team coordination necessary for survival which should have been cautionary. The military environment has the features of any large-scale bureaucracy, including exercise of authority and the special characteristics of preparation for combat, but a modern managerialism and a pragmatic sense of the limits of authority have come to pervade wide sectors of the military structure. . . .

Military attitudes toward disciplinary rules and their enforcement have undergone some changes in recent years. The military has been affected by the inevitable bureaucratization of its personnel functions, and has discovered that absolute demands for conformity are not always the best method for obtaining high achievement. Morris Janowitz, in his study *The Professional Soldier*, concluded that there has been a gradual change in the twentieth century, and particularly in the post-World War II era, "from authoritarian domination toward a greater reliance on manipulation, persuasion, and group consensus."[14] "Leadership" has become a byword for "command," and some of the rigid authoritarianism of the old military has given way to a consciousness, particularly at high command levels, of public relations, group dynamics, and psychology. As Janowitz observes:

> It is common to point out that military organization is rigidly stratified and authoritarian in character because of the necessities of command. . . . It is not generally recognized, however, that a great deal of the military establishment resembles a civilian bureaucracy, as it deals with problems of research, development, supply, and logistics. Even in those areas of the military establishment which are dedicated primarily to combat or to the maintenance of combat readiness, a central concern of top commanders is not the enforcement of rigid discipline but rather the maintenance of high levels of initiative and morale.[15]

*   *   *

The military establishment has also made attempts to ameliorate some of the harmful effects of military discipline. In 1963, General Westmoreland, then Superintendent of the U.S. Military Academy, proposed to the Association of Military Surgeons that mental hygiene staffs should be brought to commanders' headquarters in order to be more available to the troops.[16] Efforts like the Navy's moral leadership program have attempted to use the chaplains' corps to induce a more sympathetic response within the service hierarchy to servicemen's problems. According to then Secretary of the Navy Thomas Gates:

> "Instead of preaching to the men, the chaplains talked to them and drew them out, and the men preached to them."[17]

These programs indicate an increased awareness in the military that certain qualities in servicemen which are desirable in the modern bureaucracy, such as initiative, high morale, and self-satisfaction, are often difficult to develop in a rigid disciplinary system.

Studies of motivation and morale indicate that the military, even in combat situations, respond to the dynamics of social cohesion as civilian groups do. A study by Roger Little of the Office of Military Psychology and Leadership at West Point[18] has described the "network of interpersonal relationships formed by buddies" which has an impact on morale, efficiency, and operational effectiveness in combat greater than compliance with the formal standards of discipline with which it is often at odds.[19] Janowitz indicates that research has reaffirmed the findings that "group cohesion rather than ideological motivation is the basis for understanding contemporary military 'morale.' "[20]

Technology has transformed the military into a bureaucracy in many ways more like civilian society than the traditional military. Most servicemen work an eight-hour day in jobs that resemble a civil servant's or a corporation employee's, and substantial numbers live off post. In the 1950's the Army created a new category of enlisted men, called specialists, who carry the grade and pay of noncommissioned officers but perform primarily technical tasks and are not in the chain of command. Fifty-four per cent of soldiers have technical specialties (electronics, mechanics, crafts, etc.), 36 per cent have service specialties (administration, clerical, food, etc.),[21] and only 10 per cent specialize in combat skills. The majority never receive specialized combat training. On the contrary about twenty men are now required in support for every combat soldier. The convergence of styles between the civilian and the military, . . . is reflected in the pattern of occupational distribution.

Combat is still, however, a fundamental ingredient of basic training—bayonet drill, and rifle and grenade practice. Janowitz, among others, has questioned the validity of the pervasiveness of this "combat standard,"[22] particularly in view of the changes in functions in the military itself. And Albert D. Biderman, senior research associate of the Bureau of Social Science Research, has described the "many disabling neuroticisms" which afflict the military in a society and in a world that does not regard combat as one of the most honorable and exalted of human activities; he questions whether civilian society should "sustain an institution for which systematic violence is a central and sacred goal."[23] . . . Biderman suggests redefining the central function of the military to involve basically noncombat objectives.

* * *

The military is not only the nation's largest bureaucracy, but it is probably the most entrenched, and the least amenable to confrontation or to change. All established American institutions have felt the shock of alienation of the young, but none more than the military.[24] Perhaps even more seriously, there seems to be growing cynicism among the more moderate youth about the validity of American institutions and their capacity for constructive change. If the military establishment is not to be a continuing source of bitterness and divisiveness within the country, and if it is to be effective even in limited ways, it must assume a lower and more flexible posture, not only in the demands it makes on national resources, but in the justification that it offers for those demands.

The symptoms of student alienation—ostracizing or banishment of college ROTC units and violence directed against ROTC buildings, opposition to defense-supported research, and, for a small but articulate and committed minority, the choice of prison or exile rather than military service—are growing in number and in scope. Even apart from the destructive consequences for individuals, alienation between the military establishment and the minority endangers the political cohesion of the country. Whether the primary target is the war in Vietnam, in which they may be called to serve, the size of the military budget, or the pervasive-

ness of military influence in American life, the disaffection of young people tends to overflow the limits of the military establishment and to poison the attitudes of these youths toward American government in general and American society at large. The military is regarded not as a passive beneficiary of a skewed system of national priorities but as a wicked, greedy aggressor conspiring with other vested interests to subvert the American dream.

Alienation, in a way, begets alienation, for polarization in the nation increases as vehement minority reaction evokes a response from the "silent majority," young and old, which takes criticism of the military and demands for institutional change as an affront and a danger.

A disturbing related question goes to the core of contemporary American values. Many middle Americans have tended to embrace the concepts of authority and conformity that are associated with military life, and have increasingly opposed traditional American liberties. How far this civilian rigidity is a reaction to the disconcerting styles of radical youth, how far a response to the unrest in society generally, and how far an effect of the extensive influence of the military itself is unclear. The evidence suggests that all are relevant. Moreover, the most articulate antimilitary spokesmen are under thirty, and the most articulate defenders are over forty, which only accentuates the gap and hardens the polarization. And since so many of the alienated minority are among the brightest of the young, their disaffection makes more difficult the development of a rational philosophy of public policy, including a rational strategy for the uses of military power at home and overseas.

As citizens of the only nation to employ nuclear weapons to attack human targets, many in the United States have suffered a recurrent sense of guilt, a guilt that may have been prolonged and accentuated by the Dulles doctrine of massive nuclear retaliation.

Many American scientists, particularly, have been greatly troubled at the uses to which their knowledge has been put in the service of war. As recently as February 1970, Dr. Charles Schwartz of the University of California at Berkeley circulated a pledge of conscience among his colleagues of the American Physical Society. It carried a drawing of a mushroom cloud and read: "I pledge that I will not participate in war research or weapons production; I further pledge to counsel my students and urge my colleagues to do the same."[25]

But this burden of conscience probably has escaped the majority of the American people. For those who had guilt feelings, the Kennedy administration's substitution of the doctrine of flexible response, designed to deploy military force at the low end of the spectrum, was a matter of considerable moral relief. The sense of reprieve was soon broken by American action at the Bay of Pigs, and later intervention in the Dominican Republic, producing a moral as well as a political division on the propriety of offensive military action. With the extension of the war in Vietnam, and the gradual revelation of the despoliation of land and villages and the extent of civilian casualties, the moral liability for the use of United States military power impacted on the consciousness of American society with splintering force.

An articulate minority, made up primarily of young students and old liberals, reacted with shock and horror to the delayed revelations of My Lai and other military atrocities. Others either refused to believe the stories, or chose to regard the alleged atrocities as justified by the exigencies of war. The division on the moral issue heightened the political tension between hawks and doves, and polarized the civilian society even further. When a fund-raising campaign to pay for civilian counsel was launched on behalf of one of the military defendants, many responded in defense of the conduct itself, although others perhaps did so in protest against what they regarded as unfair exploitation of a scapegoat for the military establishment as a whole. West Point cadets cheered their commandant, Major General Samuel Koster, when he announced his resignation from the academy, citing the charges against him as the commander of the division involved at My Lai. Many doubtless cheered in affirmation of their loyalty to the Point, at a time when it seemed under attack, but those who read or heard of the event could legitimately raise serious questions about the moral discrimination of young men chosen for military leadership, and the choice they might later make as officers, if called upon to do so, between their loyalty to the military institution and their obligation to hold the institution accountable to the country.

The popular reactions to My Lai stimulated grave reflections about national dedication to fundamental principles of human conduct. One began to hear troubled references to possible parallels, in kind, although certainly not in degree, to the national guilt and the moral indifference of "the good Germans." The apparent cover up of earlier investigations of My Lai at all levels of military command has implicated the system as a whole in the minds of many. Only when a former soldier brought the events to the public, did the military respond and consider indictments. But there was no overwhelming public outcry. Whether the acceptance by a sizable portion of the population of conduct previously considered contrary to the laws of war is a consequence, in part, of the growing public reliance on the military, or a contributing cause, it may well produce a brutalizing effect on the moral sensibilities of the country, extending beyond the immediate precipitating events. Insensitivity to unwarranted police violence and insensitivity to brutality in military actions—abroad and at home—may be unrelated phenomena, but they cannot escape mutual reinforcement.

NOTES

1. C. Wright Mills, *The Power Elite* (New York: Oxford University Press, 1959), p. 195.

2. Samuel P. Huntington, *The Soldier and the State* (Cambridge: Harvard University Press, Belknap Press, 1957), p. 135.

3. Marion Hargrove, *See Here, Private Hargrove* (New York: Henry Holt, 1942), p. 3.

4. Ralph Earle, *Life at the United States Naval Academy* (New York: G. P. Putnam's, 1917), p. 165.

5. *New York Times*, July 29, 1956, p. 5.

6. *New York Times,* October 17, 1968, p. 13.

7. *New York Times,* June 21, 1969, p. 5.

8. But rapid increases in the size of the armed forces can be accomplished with less domestic political friction by increasing draft calls than by calling up Reserves—the only practicable alternative available with an all-volunteer force.

9. Roy R. Grinker and John P. Spiegel, *Men Under Stress* (Philadelphia: Blakiston, 1945).

10. Hans W. Mattick, "Parolees in the Army During World War II," *Federal Probation,* September 1960; see also Peter B. Legins, U.S. Senate Report No. 130, 85th Congress, 1st Session, *Juvenile Delinquency,* "Juvenile Delinquency and the Armed Forces," 1957.

11. The study of the impact of military service on personal values and self-esteem requires panel data on a group of recruits as they pass through basic training and military service, but although millions of men have passed through basic training, only one detailed study has been made on selective aspects of the impact of basic training. Richard Christie, *Transition from Civilian to Army Life* (Washington, D.C.: HumRRO Technical Report No. 13, October 1954).

12. Richard Christie, "Changes in Authoritarianism as Related Situational Factors," *American Psychologist,* Vol. 7, 1962, pp. 307-308.

13. Donald T. Campbell and Thelma H. McCormack, "Military Experiences and Attitudes Toward Authority," *American Journal of Sociology,* Vol. 62, March 1957, pp. 482-490. The California scale was used.

14. Morris Janowitz, *The Professional Soldier: A Social and Political Portrait* (Glencoe, Ill.: The Free Press, 1960), p. 8.

15. Morris Janowitz, *The Military in the Political Development of New Nations* (Chicago: University of Chicago Press, 1964), pp. 119-120.

16. William C. Westmoreland, "Military Medicine," 128 *American Journal of Psychiatry,* 209, 1963.

17. Message to Commanding Officers from Chief, Naval Personnel, NAVPERS 15913, July 1968, "Effective Naval Leadership."

18. The West Point Office of Military Psychology and Leadership was established in 1946. Its principal duties are the teaching of the behavioral sciences, some research in behavioral sciences, and guidance counseling for the undergraduates.

19. Roger W. Little, "Buddy Relations and Combat Performance," in *The New Military,* Morris Janowitz, ed. (New York: Russell Sage Foundation, 1964), p. 195.

20. Productivity levels and job satisfaction are adversely affected by overly authoritarian administration. See Kerner, "Rational and Legal Authority Within Hierarchical and Autonomous Bureaucratic Structures," Ph.D. dissertation, Indiana University, August 1969.

21. J. Shelburne and K. Groves, *Education in the Armed Forces* (1965), p. 37.

22. Janowitz, *The Professional Soldier,* pp. 38-51.

23. Albert D. Biderman, "What Is Military?," in *The Draft: A Handbook of Facts and Alternatives,* Sol Tax, ed. (Chicago: University of Chicago Press, 1967), p. 135.

24. The resistance to conformity has touched the military elite as well. At one of the service academies the students could be divided, according to an informed observer, into three categories: "engineers," who accept the system as necessary, "Eagle Scouts," who accept the system enthusiastically, and "mods" and rebels. See *Administration of the Service Academies, Report and Hearings of the Special Subcommittee on Service Academies of the House Armed Services Committee,* 90th Congress, 1st and 2nd Sessions, 1967–1968, pp. 10912-10913.

25. *New York Times,* February 1, 1970.

Racial Relations in the Armed Forces

Charles C. Moskos, Jr.

On July 28, 1948, President Truman issued an Executive Order abolishing racial segregation in the armed forces of the United States. By the middle 1950s this policy was an accomplished fact. The lessons of the racial integration of the military are many. Within a remarkably short period the makeup of a major American institution underwent a far-reaching transformation.[1] Because of the favorable contrast in the military performance of integrated black servicemen with that of all-Negro units, the integration of the armed forces is a demonstration of how changes in social organization can bring about a marked and rapid improvement in individual and group achievement. The desegregated military, moreover, offers itself as a graphic example of the abilities of both whites and blacks to adjust to egalitarian racial practices albeit with some strain. Further, an examination of the racial situation in the contemporary armed services can serve as a partial guideline as to what one might expect in a racially integrated America. At the same time, the desegregation of the military can also be used to trace some of the mutual permeations between the internal organization of the military and the racial and social cleavages found in the larger American society. For it is also the case that the military establishment—as other areas of American life—will be increasingly subject to the new challenges of black separatism as well as the persistencies of white racism.

DESEGREGATING THE MILITARY[2]

Blacks have taken part in all of this country's wars. An estimated 5,000 blacks, mostly in integrated units, fought on the American side in the War of Independence. (But over 20,000 black slaves—on the promise of manumission—joined the British as soldiers, supply handlers, and scouts.) Several thousand blacks saw service in the War of 1812. During the Civil War 180,000 blacks were recruited into the Union Army and served in segregated regiments. Following the Civil War four Negro regiments were established and were active in the Indian Wars on the Western frontier and later fought with distinction in Cuba during the Spanish-American War. In the early twentieth century, however, owing to a general rise in American racial tensions and specific outbreaks of violence between black troops and whites, official opinion began to turn against the use of black soldiers. Evaluation of black soldiers was further lowered by events in World War I. The combat performance of the all-Negro 92nd Infantry Division, one of its regiments having fled in the German offensive at Meuse-Argonne, came under heavy criticism. Yet it was also observed that black units operating under French command, in a more racially tolerant situation, performed well.

In the interval between the two World Wars, the Army not only remained segregated but also adopted a policy of a Negro quota that was to keep the number of blacks in the Army proportionate to the total population.[3] Never in the pre-World War II period, however, did the number of blacks approach this quota. One the eve of Pearl Harbor, blacks constituted 5.9 per cent of the Army; and there were only five black officers, three of whom were chaplains. During World War II blacks entered the Army in larger numbers, but at no time did they exceed 10 per cent of total personnel. Black soldiers remained in segregated units, and approximately three-quarters served in the quartermaster, engineer, and transportation corps. To make matters worse from the viewpoint of "the right to fight," a slogan loudly echoed by Negro organizations in the United States, even black combat units were frequently used for heavy-duty labor. This was highlighted when the 2nd Cavalry was broken up into service units owing to command apprehension over the combat qualities, as yet untested, of this all-Negro division. The record of those black units that did see combat in World War II was mixed. The performance of the 92nd Infantry Division again came under heavy criticism, this time for alleged unreliability in the Italian campaign.

An important exception to the general pattern of utilization of black troops in World War II occurred in the winter months of 1944–1945 in the Ardennes battle. Desperate shortages of combat personnel resulted in the Army asking for black volunteers. The plan was to have platoons (approximately 40 men) of blacks serve in companies (approximately 200 men) previously all-white. Some 2,500 blacks volunteered for this assignment. Both in terms of black combat performance and white soldiers' reactions, the Ardennes experiment was an unqualified success. This incident would later be used to support arguments for integration.

After World War II, pressure from Negro and liberal groups coupled with an acknowledgment that black soldiers were being poorly utilized led the Army to reexamine its racial policies. A report by an Army board in 1945, while holding racial integration to be a desirable goal and while making recommendations to improve black opportunity in the Army, concluded that practical considerations required a maintenance of segregation and the quota system. In light of World War II experiences, the report further recommended that black personnel be assigned exclusively to support units rather than combat units. Another Army board report came out in 1950 with essentially the same conclusions.[4] Both reports placed heavy stress on the supervisory and disciplinary problems resulting from the disproportionate number of blacks found in the lower mental and aptitude levels as established by Army entrance examinations. In 1950, for example, 60 per cent of the black personnel fell into the Army's lowest categories compared with 29 per cent of the white soldiers. From the standpoint of the performance requirements of the military, such facts could not be dismissed lightly.

After the Truman desegregation order of 1948, however, the die was cast. The President followed his edict by setting up a committee, chaired by Charles Fahy, to pursue the implementation of equal treatment and opportunity for armed forces personnel. Under the impetus of the Fahy committee, the Army abolished the quota system in 1950, and was beginning to integrate some training camps when the conflict in Korea broke out. The Korean conflict was the *coup de grâce* for segregation in the Army. Manpower requirements in the field for combat soldiers resulted in many instances of *ad hoc* integration. As was true in the Ardennes experience, black soldiers in previously all-white units performed well in combat. As integration in Korea became more standard, observers consistently noted that the fighting abilities of blacks differed little from those of whites.[5] This contrasted with the blemished record of the all-Negro 24th Infantry Regiment.[6] Its performance in the Korean conflict was judged to be so poor that its division commander recommended the unit be dissolved as quickly as possible. Concurrent with events in Korea, integration was introduced in the United States. By 1956, three years after the end of the Korean conflict, the remnants of Army Jim Crow disappeared at home and in overseas installations. At the time of the Truman order, blacks constituted 8.8 per cent of Army personnel. In 1970 the figure was 13.2 per cent.

In each of the other services, the history of desegregation varied from the Army pattern. The Army Air Corps, like its parent body, generally assigned blacks to segregated support units. (However, a unique military venture taken during the war was the formation of three all-Negro, including officers, air combat units.) At the end of World War II the proportion of blacks in the Army Air Corps was only 4 per cent, less than half what it was in the Army. Upon its establishment as an independent service in 1947, the Air Force began to take steps toward integration even before the Truman order. By the time of the Fahy committee report in 1950, the Air Force was already largely integrated. Since integration there has been a substantial increase in the proportion of blacks serving in the Air Force, from less than 5 per cent in 1949 to 9.9 per cent in 1970.

Although large numbers of blacks had served in the Navy during the Civil War and for some period afterward, restrictive policies were introduced in the early 1900s, and by the end of World War I only about 1 per cent of Navy personnel were blacks. In 1920 the Navy adopted a policy of total racial exclusion and barred all black enlistments. This policy was slightly changed in 1932 when blacks, along with Filipinos, were again allowed to join the Navy but only as stewards in the messman's branch. Further modifications were made in Navy policy in 1942 when some openings in general service were created. Black sailors in these positions, however, were limited to segregated harbor and shore assignments. In 1944, in the first effort toward desegregation in any of the armed services, a small number of black sailors in general service were integrated on oceangoing vessels. After the end of World War II the Navy, again ahead of the other services, began to take major steps toward elimination of racial barriers. Even in the integrated Navy of today, however, black sailors are still overproportionately concentrated in the messman's branch. Also, despite the early steps toward integration taken by the Navy, the proportion of black sailors has remained fairly constant over the past two decades, averaging between 4 and 5 per cent of total personnel.

The Marine Corps has gone from a policy of exclusion to segregation to integration. Before World War II there were no black Marines. In 1952 blacks were accepted into the Marine Corps but assigned to segregated units where they were heavy-duty laborers, ammunition handlers, and antiaircraft gunners. After the war small-scale integration of black Marines into white units was begun. In 1949 and 1950 Marine Corps training units were integrated, and by 1954 the color line was largely erased throughout the Corps. Since integration began, the proportion of blacks has increased markedly. In 1949 less than 2 per cent of all Marines were black compared with 10.0 per cent in 1970.

Although the various military services are all similar in being formally integrated today, they differ in their proportion of blacks. As shown in Table 1, black membership in the total armed forces in 1967 was 9.0 per cent, lower than the 11–12 per cent constituting the black proportion in the total population. It is certain, however, that among those *eligible*, a higher proportion of blacks than whites enter the armed forces. That is, a much larger number of blacks do not meet the entrance standards required by the military services. For the years 1960 through 1966, about 55 per cent of blacks did not pass the pre-induction mental examinations given to Selective Service registrants, almost four times the approximately 15 per cent of whites who failed these same tests.[7] Because of the relatively low number of blacks obtaining student or occupational deferments, however, it is the Army drawing upon the draft that is the only military service where the percentage of blacks approximates the national proportion. Thus, despite the high number of blacks who fail to meet induction standards, Army statistics for 1960–1967 show blacks constituted about 15 per cent of those drafted.

Even if one takes into account the Army's reliance on the Selective Service for much of its personnel, the figures in Table 1 also show important differences in the number of blacks in those services meeting their manpower requirements solely through voluntary enlistments; in 1967, for example, the 4.3 per cent black in the Navy is lower than 9.6 per cent for the Marine Corps or the 9.1 per cent for the Air Force. Moreover, the Army, besides its drawing upon the draft, also has the highest black initial enlistment rate of any of the services. For the 1961–1966 period, the Army drew 10.9 per cent of its volunteer incoming personnel from blacks as compared with 9.8 per cent for the Air Force, 7.2 per cent for the Marine Corps, and 4.2 per cent for the Navy.

There are also diverse patterns between the individual services as to the rank or grade distribution of blacks. Looking at Table 2, we find the ratio of black to white officers in 1970 was roughly 1 to 30 in the Army, 1 to 60 in the Air Force, 1 to 100 in the Marine Corps, and 1 to 200 in the Navy. Among enlisted men across all four services, blacks are underrepresented in

TABLE 1. Blacks in the Armed Forces as a Percentage of Total Personnel, by Selected Years

Year	Total Armed Forces	Army	Navy	Air Force	Marine Corps
1945	7.3%	9.8%	5.0%	4.0%*	3.6%
1949	5.9	8.6	4.0	4.5	1.9
1954	7.9	11.3	3.2	7.5	5.9
1962	8.2	11.3	4.7	7.8	7.0
1965	9.5	12.8	5.2	9.2	8.3
1967	9.0	11.2	4.3	9.1	9.6

SOURCE: Defense Department statistics.
* 1945 Air Force figures refer to Army Air Corps.

TABLE 2. Blacks as Percentage of Total Personnel by Grade and Service (December 31, 1970)

Grade*	Army	Navy	Air Force	Marine Corps
Officers:				
0–7 and up (generals)	.2	–	.2	–
0–6 (colonel)	1.2	.1	.4	–
0–5 (lt. colonel)	4.7	.3	1.2	.2
0–4 (major)	5.2	.5	1.7	.3
0–3 (captain)	3.7	.6	2.2	1.4
0–2 (1st lt.)	2.5	.6	1.4	1.5
0–1 (2nd lt.)	1.5	1.2	1.2	1.9
Total Officers	3.4	.5	1.7	1.1
Enlisted Men:				
E–9 (sgt. major)	6.0	1.5	3.0	2.3
E–8 (master sgt.)	11.8	3.1	4.4	5.3
E–7 (sgt. 1st class)	17.8	5.3	6.2	10.5
E–6 (staff sgt.)	22.0	6.8	10.1	13.4
E–5 (sergeant)	11.3	4.4	14.7	10.6
E–4 (specialist 4)	10.9	2.8	10.7	8.1
E–3 (pvt. 1st class)	13.4	5.0	11.8	10.4
E–2 (private)	15.0	10.2	14.8	13.6
E–1 (recruit)	13.3	13.0	18.3	14.2
Total Enlisted Men	13.5	5.4	11.7	11.2

SOURCE: Defense Department statistics.
* Army titles given in parentheses have equivalent pay grades in other services.

the very top enlisted ranks (but least so in the Army). We also find a disproportionate concentration of blacks in the lower NCO levels in each of the armed forces. This is especially so in the Army where one out of every five staff sergeants is a black. As assessment of these data reveals that the Army, followed by the Air Force, has not only the largest proportion of blacks in its total personnel, but also the most equitable distribution of blacks throughout its ranks. Although the Navy was the first service to integrate and the Army the last, in a kind of tortoise and hare fashion, it is the Army that has become the most representative service for blacks.

CHANGING MILITARY REQUIREMENTS AND BLACK PARTICIPATION[2]

A pervasive trend within the military establishment singled out by students of this institution is the long-term trend toward greater technical complexity and narrowing of civilian-military occupational skills. An indicator, albeit a crude one, of this trend is the decreasing proportion of men assigned to combat arms. Given in Table 3, along with concomitant white-black distributions, are figures comparing the percentage of Army enlisted personnel in combat arms (e.g., infantry, armor, artillery) for the years 1945, 1962, and 1967. We find that the proportion of men in combat arms—that is, traditional military specialties—drops from 44.5 per cent in 1945 to 26.0 per cent in 1962 and 23.5 per cent in 1967. Also, the percentages of white personnel in traditional military specialties closely approximate the total proportional decrease in the combat arms over the twenty-two-year period.

For black soldiers, however, a different picture emerges. While the percentage of black enlisted men in the Army increased only slightly, the likelihood of a black serving in a combat arm is well over two times greater in the 1960s than it was at the end of World War II. Further, when impressionistic observations are made within the combat arms, the black proportion is noticeably higher in line rather than staff assignments, and in infantry rather than other combat arms. In many airborne and Marine line companies, the number of blacks approaches half the unit strength. Put another way, the direction of assignment of black soldiers in the desegregated military is testimony to the continuing consequences of differential racial opportunity originating in the larger society. That is, even though integration of the military has led to great improvement in the performance of black servicemen, the social and particularly educational deprivations suffered by the black in American society can be mitigated but not eliminated by the racial egalitarian policies of the armed forces.[8]

Yet it is also true that the probabilities of a black being assigned to a combat arm are noticeably greater even when certain control variables are introduced. The data given in Table 4 are derived from complete Department of Defense manpower statistics for the year ending December 31, 1965. To

TABLE 3. White and Black Army Enlisted Personnel in Combat Arms, by Selected Years

Category	1945*	1962	1967
Blacks as percentage of total personnel	10.5%	12.2%	12.1%
Percentage of total personnel in combat arms	44.5	26.0	23.5
Percentage of total white personnel in combat arms	48.2	24.9	22.8
Percentage of total black personnel in combat arms	12.1	33.4	28.6

SOURCE: Defense Department statistics.
* Excludes Army Air Corps.

TABLE 4. Army and Marine Corps Enlisted Personnel (Pay Grade E–4) in Combat Arms, by AFQT Level and Race (December 31, 1965)

Category	Army %	N	Marine Corps %	N
AFQT Level I	9.5	(5,835)	16.3	(1,459)
White	9.4	(5,719)	16.1	(1,426)
Black	15.5	(116)	24.2	(33)
AFQT Level II	13.7	(30,743)	29.9	(8,786)
White	13.5	(29,648)	29.4	(8,438)
Black	20.1	(1,095)	40.2	(348)
AFQT Level III	22.3	(51,156)	45.5	(8,729)
White	21.3	(44,079)	45.1	(7,687)
Black	28.5	(7,077)	54.0	(1,042)
AFQT Level IV and V	30.7	(14,232)	55.3	(2,027)
White	26.2	(8,362)	52.9	(1,616)
Black	37.1	(5,870)	64.5	(411)
Total Grade E–4*	20.1	(102,056)	38.1	(21,001)
White	18.3	(87,898)	36.7	(19,167)
Black	31.3	(14,158)	53.2	(1,834)

SOURCE: Defense Department statistics.
* Pay grade E–4 with under four years of military service.

sharpen the analysis, the grade and cohort that is modal for permanently assigned enlisted men in the Army and Marine Corps is used: servicemen who occupy the pay grade E–4 (corporal or specialist fourth class) with less than four years of military service. These manpower statistics concerning proportional assignment in combat arms, in addition to racial breakdowns, also allow for categorization based on the Armed Forces Qualification Test (AFQT), a prime indicator of civilian socioeducational background.

Table 4 reveals that combat arms assignment is markedly higher for blacks compared to whites even within each of the AFQT levels. It is also the case, however, that regardless of race, the lower the AFQT level, the greater the likelihood of combat assignment. These Department of Defense statistics also show that when AFQT level and race are looked at in unison, there are pronounced effects on assignment

probabilities. Thus, blacks in the lowest AFQT levels (IV and V) are about four times more likely to be assigned to combat arms than are whites in AFQT level I: 37.1 per cent to 9.4 per cent in the Army; and 64.5 per cent to 16.1 per cent in the Marine Corps. These findings, however, need not be interpreted as a reflection on the "status" of the black in the integrated military. Actually there is evidence that higher prestige—but not envy—is generally accorded combat personnel by those in noncombat activities within the military.[9] And taken within the historical context of the "right to fight" voiced by Negro organizations with reference to the segregated military of World War II, the black soldier's current overrepresentation in the combat arms might be construed as a kind of ironic step forward.[10]

As is to be expected, the overconcentration of blacks in combat units is all too obviously shown in the casualty reports from Vietnam. As documented in Table 5, during the 1961–1966 period, blacks constituted 10.6 per cent of military personnel in Southeast Asia while accounting for 16.0 per cent of those killed in action. This reflects the high casualties suffered by the Army and Marine Corps—about 95 per cent of all American losses in Vietnam—compared to the Navy and Air Force. In 1967 and the first six months of 1968, however, the proportion of black combat deaths dropped to between 13 and 14 per cent. Yet even in these later figures, black combat deaths were still about one-third above the proportion of blacks stationed in Southeast Asia, and about one and a half times the total black proportion in the American military.

Despite the greater likelihood for blacks to be assigned to combat arms and their resultant higher casualty rates in wartime, the fact remains that the military at the enlisted ranks has become a major avenue of career mobility for many black men.[11] This state

TABLE 5. Blacks as Percentage of Men Assigned to Southeast Asia* and Killed in Action, for Each Service (1961–June, 1968)

Time Period	Army	Navy	Air Force	Marine Corps	Total Armed Forces
Blacks in Southeast Asia					
1961–1966	12.6%	5.4%	10.3%	8.0%	10.6%
1967	11.1	4.7	10.5	8.2	9.8
January–June, 1968	11.7	4.8	10.5	10.1	10.5
Killed in Action					
1961–1966	20.0	.5	1.5	11.0	16.0
1967	13.5	2.9	5.2	12.8	12.7
January-June, 1968	13.3	2.6	1.5	14.1	13.0
1961–June, 1968	15.1	2.2	2.7	12.8	13.7

SOURCE: Defense Department statistics.
* Vietnam, Thailand, and offshore ships.

of affairs reflects not only the "pull" of the appeals offered by a racially integrated institution, but also the "push" generated by the plight of the black in the American economy. Indeed, there is rather conclusive evidence that the gap between black and white job opportunities in the civilian economy has not significantly altered over the past quarter-century. An insight into the causes underlying volunteer initial enlistments can be gained by looking at reasons given for entering the armed forces. Based on responses elicited in the 1964 NORC survey, the motivations of volunteers were grouped into four categories: (1) *personal*, for example, to get away from home, to travel, for excitement; (2) *patriotic*, for example, to serve one's country; (3) *draft motivated*, for example, to increase options in choice of service and time of entry;

and (4) *self-advancement*, for example, to learn a trade, to receive an education, to make the military a career. As shown in Table 6, reasons for service entry among volunteers are reported by race holding educational level constant. There are only slight differences between whites and blacks with regard to personal or patriotic motivations for service entry. The variation between the races is found almost entirely in their differing mentions of draft-motivated versus self-advancement reasons. Within each educational level, black volunteers mention self-advancement almost twice as often as whites. Conversely, whites are markedly more likely to state they entered the services to avoid the draft. In other words, the draft serves as a major inducement for whites to volunteer, while the belief that self-advancement will be furthered

TABLE 6. Service Entry Reasons of Enlisted Volunteers, by Education and Race

Category	Personal	Patriotic	Draft-Motivated	Self-Advancement	Total	(N)
Less than high school						
White	33.2%	13.5%	27.5%	25.8%	100.0%	(6,913)
Black	26.7	17.8	12.5	43.0	100.0	(911)
High school graduate						
White	27.8	10.9	39.5	21.8	100.0	(20,757)
Black	28.8	7.1	25.5	38.6	100.0	(2,440)
Some college						
White	27.5	10.7	47.2	14.6	100.0	(7,947)
Black	30.8	7.7	34.0	27.5	100.0	(701)
Total white	28.8	11.4	39.1	20.7	100.0	(35,617)
Total black	28.7	9.6	24.5	37.2	100.0	(4,052)

SOURCE: 1964 NORC survey.

in the military is much more typical of black enlistees.

Moreover, once within the military the black serviceman is much more likely than his white counterpart to have "found a home." As noted earlier, in all four services there is an over-representation of black NCOs, especially at the junior levels. The disproportionate concentration of blacks at these grades implies a higher than average reenlistment rate as such ranks are not normally attained until after a second enlistment. This assumption is supported by the data presented in Table 7. We find for the years 1964–1967 that the service-wide black reenlistment rate is approximately twice that of white servicemen. (Data from the 1964 NORC survey also show that 50.0 per cent of blacks who were making a career of military life were initially draftees, as contrasted with 21.3 per cent of the white career soldiers who similarly first entered the service through the draft.)

TABLE 7. First-Term Reenlistment Rates in the Armed Services, by Race, 1964–1967

Race	Army	Navy	Air Force	Marine Corps
1964:				
White	18.5%	20.9%	26.3%	12.9%
Black	49.3	39.9	48.8	25.1
1965:				
White	13.7	24.2	19.1	18.9
Black	49.3	44.8	39.2	38.9
1966:				
White	20.0	17.6	16.0	10.5
Black	66.5	24.7	30.1	19.5
1967:				
White	12.8	16.7	17.3	9.7
Black	31.7	22.5	26.9	15.9

SOURCE: Defense Department statistics.

Indeed, except for 1967, about half of all first-term black servicemen chose to remain in the armed forces for at least a second term. Even in 1967 when there is a sharp (but cross-racial) drop in reenlistments, the black reenlistment rate remains at twice that of whites.[12] The greater likelihood of blacks to select a service career suggests that the military establishment is undergoing a significant change in its NCO core. At the minimum, it is very probable that as the present cohort of black junior NCOs attains seniority there will be much greater black representation in the very top NCO grades. The expansion of the armed forces arising from the war in Vietnam and the resulting "opening up of rank" has undoubtedly accelerated this development.

That black servicemen have a more favorable view of military life than whites is indicated not only in their higher reenlistment rates, but also more directly in the 1964 NORC survey data reported in Table 8. Whether broken down by branch of service, educational level, pay grade, or military occupational specialty, black servicemen compared with whites consistently have a less negative view of life in the military. In fact, there is no category or subgroup in which whites are more favorably disposed toward military service than their black counterparts. It should be reiterated, however, that the relatively benign terms in which black men regard military life speak not only of the racial desegregation of the armed forces, but, more profoundly, of the existing state of affairs for blacks in American society at large.

ATTITUDES OF SOLDIERS

So far the discussion has sought to document the degree of penetration and the kind of distribution characterizing black servicemen in the integrated military establishment. We now turn to certain survey and interview data dealing more directly with the question of soldiers' attitudes toward military desegregation. Commenting on the difficulties of social analysis, the authors of *The American Soldier* wrote that few problems are "more formidable than that of obtaining dependable records of attitudes toward racial sepa-

TABLE 8. Enlisted Personnel Not Liking Military Life, by Race and Selected Groupings

Category	White: %	N	Black: %	N
Service				
Army	51.4	(15,007)	35.2	(2,641)
Navy	44.2	(11,158)	29.6	(699)
Air Force	36.1	(12,593)	27.0	(1,414)
Marine Corps	46.5	(3,262)	35.3	(300)
Total military by education				
Less than high school	42.8	(8,431)	28.5	(1,084)
High school graduate	43.2	(24,027)	31.3	(2,985)
Some college	49.3	(9,562)	38.9	(985)
Army enlisted men by military occupation				
Combat	49.5	(3,192)	36.1	(777)
Technical	52.9	(3,390)	35.6	(556)
Administrative	54.1	(2,976)	35.5	(352)
Service	52.5	(4,221)	33.0	(690)
Army enlisted men by pay grade				
E-1—E-2	54.2	(2,992)	39.9	(571)
E-3—E-4	69.6	(7,183)	48.9	(1,197)
E-5—E-6	25.5	(3,826)	14.7	(797)
E-7—E-9	12.9	(1,016)	4.9	(81)

SOURCE: 1964 NORC Survey.

ration in the Army."[13] Without underestimating the continuing difficulty of this problem, an opportunity exists to compare attitudes toward racial integration held by American soldiers in two different periods. This is done by contrasting responses to equivalent items given in World War II as reported in *The American Soldier* with those reported in Project Clear, a study sponsored by the Defense Department during the Korean War. The Project Clear surveys, conducted by the Operations Research Office (ORO) of Johns Hopkins University, queried several thousand servicemen in both Korea and the United States on a variety of items relating to attitudes toward racial integration in the Army.[14]

In both *The American Soldier* and Project Clear (the surveys under consideration were conducted in 1943 and 1951, respectively) large samples of Army personnel in segregated military settings were categorized as to whether they were favorable, indifferent, or opposed to racial integration in Army units. We find, as presented in Table 9, massive shifts in soldiers' attitudes over the eight-year period, shifts showing a

much more positive disposition toward racial integration among both whites and blacks in the later year. A look at the distribution of attitudes held by white soldiers reveals opposition to integration goes from 84 per cent in 1943 to less than half in 1951. That such a change could occur in less than a decade counters viewpoints that see basic social attitudes in large populations being prone to glacial-like changes.

Yet, an even more remarkable change is found among the black soldiers. Where in 1945, favorable, indifferent, or opposing attitudes were roughly equally distributed among the

TABLE 9. Attitudes of White and Black Soldiers Toward Racial Integration in the Segregated Army, 1943 and 1951

Attitude toward Integration	White Soldiers		Black Soldiers	
	1943	1951	1943	1951
Favorable	12%	25%	37%	90%
Indifferent	4	31	27	6
Oppose	84	44	36	4
Total	100	100	100	100
(N)	(4,800)	(1,983)	(3,000)	(1,384)

SOURCE: 1943 data from Stouffer *et al.*, *The American Soldier*, I, 568; 1951 data from ORO, Project Clear, 1955, 322, 433.

black soldiers, by 1951 opposition or indifference to racial integration had become negligible. Such a finding is strongly indicative of a reformation in black public opinion from traditional acquiescence to Jim Crow to the groundswell that laid the basis for the subsequent civil rights movement. It may be argued, of course, that recent developments—separatist tendencies within the black community in the late 1960s—have eclipsed the 1951 findings. Nevertheless, the data is still convincing that on the eve of integration, black soldiers overwhelmingly rejected a segregated armed forces.

Moreover, while the data on black responses toward integration given in Table 9 were elicited during the segregated military of 1943 and 1951, we also have evidence on how black soldiers react to military integration in a more contemporary setting. As reported in Table 10, the Army is thought to be much more racially egalitarian than civilian life. Only 16 per cent of 67 black soldiers interviewed in 1965 said civilian life was more racially equal or

TABLE 10. Attitudes of Black Soldiers in 1965 Comparing Racial Equality in Military and Civilian Life, Total and by Home Region

Where More Racial Equality	Total	Home Region	
		North	South
Military life	84%	75%	93%
Civilian life	3	6	0
No difference	13	19	7
Total	100	100	100
(N)	(67)	(36)	(31)

no different than the Army. By region, as might be expected, we find southern blacks more likely than northern blacks to take a favorable view of racial relations in the Army when these are compared to civilian life. The data support the proposition that, despite existing deviations from military policy at the level of informal discrimination, the military establishment stands in sharp and favorable contrast to the racial relations prevalent in the larger American society.

One of the most celebrated findings of *The American Soldier* was the discovery that the more contact white soldiers had with black troops, the more favorable was their reaction toward racial integration.[15] This conclusion is consistently supported in the surveys conducted by Project Clear. Again and again, comparisons of white soldiers in integrated units with those in segregated units show the former to be more supportive of desegregation. Illustrative of this pattern are the data shown in Table 11. Among combat infantrymen in Korea, 51 per cent in all-white units prefer segregation compared with 31 per cent in integrated units. For enlisted personnel stationed in the United States, strong objection to integration characterizes 44 per cent serving in segregated units while less than one-fifth of the men in integrated units feel the same way. Seventy-nine per cent of officers on segregated posts rate blacks worse than white soldiers as compared with 28 per cent holding similar beliefs on integrated posts.

OFFICIAL POLICY AND ACTUAL PRACTICE

For the man newly entering the armed forces, it is hard to conceive that the military was one of America's most segregated institutions some two decades ago. Today, color barriers at the formal level are absent throughout the military establishment. Equal treatment regardless of race is official policy in such nonduty facilities as swimming pools, chapels, barbershops, Post Exchanges, movie theaters, snack bars, and dependents' housing as well as in the more strictly military endeavors involved in the assignment, promotion, and living conditions of members of the armed services.[16] Moreover, white personnel are often commanded by black superiors, a situation rarely ob-

TABLE 11. Racial Attitudes of White Soldiers in Segregated and Integrated Military Settings, 1951

Racial Attitudes	All-White Units		Integrated Units	
	%	N	%	N
Combat infantryman in Korea saying segregated outfits better	51	(195)	31	(1,024)
Enlisted personnel in the U.S. strongly objecting to racial integration	44	(1,983)	17	(1,683)
Officers rating Negroes worse than white soldiers	79	(233)	28	(385)

SOURCE: ORO, Project Clear, 141, 322, 333, 356.

taining in civilian life. In brief, military life is characterized by an interracial equalitarianism of a quantity and of a kind that is seldom found in the other major institutions of American society.

Some measure of the extent and thoroughness of military desegregation is found in comparing the 1950 President's Committee ("Fahy committee") report dealing with racial integration and the 1963 and 1964 reports of a second President's Committee ("Gesell committee"). Where the earlier report dealt entirely with internal military organization, the later reports address themselves primarily to off-base discrimination.[17] Thus in order to implement its policy of equal opportunity, the military began to exert pressure on local communities where segregated residential patterns affected military personnel. Since 1963 commanders of military installations have been under instructions to persuade apartment and trailer court owners to end segregation voluntarily. These informal efforts had little or no success. In 1967 an important precedent was set when segregated housing was declared off-limits to all military personnel in the area adjacent to Andrews Air Force Base, Maryland. In 1968 the Defense Department announced a nationwide policy forbid-

ding any serviceman to rent lodgings where racial discrimination was practiced. Whatever one's value priorities —concern over military influence on civilian society versus integrated housing—the ramifications of this policy are significant and deserve careful examination.

In their performance of military duties, whites and blacks work together with little open display of racial animosity. Incidents between the races do occur (and are occurring more frequently), but such confrontations are almost always off-duty, if not off-base. (Excepting, importantly, military stockades where racial strife is compounded by the problems of incarceration.) Additionally it must be stressed that conflict situations stemming from nonracial causes also characterize sources of friction in the military establishment, for example, enlisted men versus officers, lower-ranking enlisted men versus noncommissioned officers, soldiers of middle-class background versus those of the working class, draftees versus volunteers, line units versus staff units, rear echelon versus front echelon, newly arrived units versus earlier stationed units, and so on.

Yet the fact remains that the general pattern of day-to-day relationships *off the job* is usually one of mutual racial exclusivism. As one black soldier put it, "A man can be my best buddy in the Army, but he won't ask me to go to town with him." Closest friendships normally develop within races between individuals of similar educational and social background. Beyond one's hard core of friends there exists a level of friendly acquaintances. Here the pattern seems to be one of educational similarities overriding racial differences. On the whole, racial integration at informal levels works best on-duty vis-à-vis off-duty, on-base vis-à-vis off-base, basic training and maneuvers vis-à-vis garrison, sea duty vis-à-vis shore duty, and—most especially—combat vis-à-vis noncombat. In other words, the behavior of servicemen resembles the racial (and class) separatism of the larger American society, the more they are removed from the military environment.

For nearly all white soldiers the military is a first experience with close and equal contact with a large group of blacks. There has developed what has become practically a military custom: the look over the shoulder, upon the telling of a racial joke, to see if there are any blacks in hearing distance. Some racial animosity is reflected in accusations that black soldiers use the defense of racial discrimination to avoid disciplinary punishment. Many white soldiers claim they like Negroes as individuals but "can't stand them in bunches." In a few extreme cases, white married personnel even live off the military base and pay higher rents rather than live in integrated military housing. On the whole, however, the segregationist-inclined white soldier regards racial integration as something to be accepted pragmatically, if reluctantly, as are so many situations in military life.

The most overt source of racial unrest in military community centers in dancing situations. A commentary on American mores is a finding reported in Project Clear: Three-quarters of a large sample of white soldiers said they would not mind Negro couples on the same dance floor, but approximately the same number strongly disapproved of Negro soldiers dancing with white girls.[18] In many noncommissioned officer (NCO) clubs, the likelihood of interracial dancing partners is a constant producer of tension. In fact, the only major exception to integration within the military community is on a number of large posts where there are two or more NCO clubs. In such situations one of the clubs usually becomes tacitly designated as the black club.

Although there is general support for racial integration by black soldiers,

tensions are also evident among black military personnel. Black officers are sometimes seen as being too strict or "chicken" when it comes to enforcing military discipline on black enlisted men. As one black soldier said, "I'm proud when I see a Negro officer, but not in my company." Similarly, black noncoms are alleged to pick on blacks when it comes time to assign men unpleasant duties. There is also the tendency among some of the lower-ranking black enlisted men, especially draftees, to view black NCOs as "Uncle Toms" or "handkerchief heads." This view may be expected to become somewhat more prevalent in the wake of the growing militancy among black youths in civilian society. In the same vein, self-imposed informal segregation on the part of many blacks will become more overt. Nevertheless, the fact remains, and will indefinitely be so, that the military is a sought-after career choice for many black men.

One black writer, who served in the segregated Army and later had two sons in the integrated military, has proposed that what was thought by soldiers in all-Negro units to be racial discrimination was often nothing more than routine harassment of lower-ranking enlisted personnel.[19] In fact, the analogy between enlisted men vis-à-vis officers in the military and blacks vis-à-vis whites in the larger society has often been noted.[20] It has been less frequently observed, however, that enlisted men's behavior is often similar to many of the stereotypes associated with Negroes, for example, laziness, boisterousness, emphasis on sexual prowess, consciously acting stupid, obsequiousness in front of superiors combined with ridicule of absent superiors, and the like. Placement of white adult males in a subordinate position within a rigidly stratified system appears to produce behavior not all that different from the so-called personality traits commonly held to be an outcome of cultural or psychological patterns unique to Negro life. Indeed, it might be argued that relatively little adjustment on the part of the command structure was required when the infusion of blacks into the enlisted ranks occurred as the military establishment was desegregated. In other words, it is suggested that one factor contributing to the generally smooth racial integration of the military was due to the standard treatment—"like Negroes"—accorded to all lower-ranking enlisted personnel.

THE BLACK SOLDIER OVERSEAS

Some special remarks are needed concerning black servicemen overseas. Suffice it to say for prefatory purposes, the American soldier, be he either white or black, is usually in a place where he does not understand the language, is received with mixed feelings by the local population, spends the greater part of his time in a transplanted American environment, sometimes plays the role of tourist, is relatively affluent in relation to the local economy, takes advantage and is at the mercy of a comprador class, and in comparison with his counterpart at home is more heavily involved in military duties.

In general, the pattern of racial relations observed among soldiers in the United States—integration in the military setting and racial exclusivism off-duty—prevails in overseas assignments as well. This norm is reflected in one of the most characteristic features of American military life overseas, a bifurcation of the vice structure into groups that pander almost exclusively (or assert they do) to only one of the races. A frequent claim of local bar owners is that they discourage racially mixed trade because of the demands of their GI clientele. And, indeed, many of the establishments catering to American personnel that ring most military installations are segregated in practice. To a similar degree this is true of shore towns where Navy personnel take liberty. Violation of these implicit taboos can lead to physical threat and often violence.

The pattern of off-duty separatism is most pronounced in Japan and Germany, and somewhat less so in Korea (though the Sam Gak Chi area in Seoul has long been a gathering point for black servicemen). Combat conditions in Vietnam make the issue of off-duty racial relations academic for those troops in the field. In the cities, however, racial separatism off-duty is readily apparent. It is said that the riverfront district in Saigon, Kanh Hoi, frequented by black American soldiers, was formerly patronized by Senegalese troops during the French occupation. In off-duty areas on Okinawa racial separatism is complicated by interservice rivalries and a four-fold ecological pattern shows up: white-Army, black-Army, white-Marines, and black-Marines. A major exception to the norm of off-duty racial separatism occurred in the Dominican Republic. There all troops were restricted and leaving the military compound necessitated soldiers collaborating if they were not to be detected; such ventures were often as not interracial.

In Germany one impact of that country's economic boom has been to depress the relative position of the American soldier vis-à-vis the German working man. In the Germany of ten or fifteen years ago (or the Korea and Vietnam of today) all American military personnel were affluent by local standards. This was (and is today in Korea and Vietnam) an especially novel experience for the black soldier. The status drop of American soldiers in Germany has particularly affected the black serviceman who has the additional handicap of being black in a country where there are no black women. The old "good duty" days for black soldiers in Germany have come to an end as he finds his previous access to other than prostitutes severely reduced. The German economic boom has affected black soldiers in another way. In recent years there has been some friction between foreign laborers (mostly from Mediterranean countries) and black soldiers. Both groups of men apparently are competing for the same girls. At the same time, the foreign workers have little contact with white American soldiers who move in a different segment of the vice structure.

Nonetheless, overseas duty for the black serviceman, in Germany as well as in the Far East, gives him an opportunity, even if peripheral, to witness societies where racial discrimination is less practiced than it is in his home country. Although the level of black acceptance in societies other than America is usually exaggerated, the black soldier is hard put not to make invidious comparisons with the American scene.[21] In interviews conducted in 1965 with black servicemen in Germany, 64 per cent said there was more racial equality in Germany than America, 30 per cent saw little difference between the two countries, and only 6 per cent believed blacks were treated better in the United States.

Observers of overseas American personnel have told the writer that black soldiers are more likely than whites to learn local languages (though for both groups of servicemen this is a very small number). Evidence for this supposition is given in Table 12. Three German-national barbers, who were permanently hired to cut the hair of all the men in one battalion, were asked by the writer to evaluate the German-language proficiency of the individual

TABLE 12. Command of German Language of White and Black Soldiers in a German-Based U.S. Army Battalion, 1965

Command of German*	White Soldiers	Black Soldiers
Conversational	1.4%	7.4%
Some	3.0	7.4
Little or none	95.6	85.2
Total	100.0	100.0
(N)	(629)	(98)

* Based on evaluations of German-national battalion barbers.

personnel in that battalion.[22] When these evaluations were correlated with race, it was found that black soldiers were five times more likely to know "conversational" German, and three times more likely to know "some" German than were white soldiers.[23] Actually, the likelihood of black soldiers compared with whites in learning the language of the country in which they are stationed may be even greater than indicated. Several of the German-speaking white soldiers were of German ethnic background and acquired some knowledge of the language in their home environments back in the United States.

It is more than coincidence that a widely seen German television commercial in 1965—in which white and black American soldiers were portrayed —only the black soldiers spoke German. Similarly, a study of American troops in Japan reported: "In general, Negro soldiers learned to speak Japanese more quickly and expertly than did the white soldiers (whose efforts in this direction were very halting)."[24] The strong weight of evidence, then, is that black servicemen overseas, perhaps because of the more favorable racial climate, are more willing to take advantage of informal participation and interaction with local populations.

RACE AT HOME AND WAR ABROAD

It is important to remember that the desegregation of the armed forces antedated both the beginnings of the civil rights movement in the late 1950s and the black power movement a decade later. In the light of subsequent developments in the domestic racial picture, it is likely that severe disciplinary problems—if not outright organized mutiny—would have occurred had military integration not come about when it did. The timing of desegregation in the military defused an ingredient—all-black units—that would have been explosive in this nation's current racial strife. One has only to be reminded of the embroilments between black units and whites that were an ever-present problem in the segregated military. On the other hand, the armed forces were remarkably free of racial turmoil from the middle 1950s through the middle 1960s.

Nevertheless, it is also the case that the military establishment—at least into the foreseeable future—will not be immune from the racial and class conflicts occurring in the larger American society. Incidents with racial overtones have become more frequent in recent years. Two of the most dramatic occurred in the summer of 1968. Over 250 black prisoners took part in a race riot in the Long Binh stockade outside Saigon. The stockade was not brought under complete military control for close to a month. At about the same time in the United States, 43 black soldiers at Fort Hood, Texas, refused to leave as part of the force assigned to guard the Democratic Convention. The soldiers feared they might be used to combat Chicago blacks. That black soldiers may find they owe higher fealty to the black community than to the United States Army is a possibility that haunts commanders. The likelihood of such an eventuality, however, will be serious only if the Army is regularly summoned into action in black ghettos. Sensitive to the civil rights issue and specter of black power in the military, the armed forces have been surprisingly mild (up to this writing) in their handling of black servicemen involved in racial incidents. Neither the Long Binh rioters nor the "Fort Hood 43" received anything approaching maximum sentences, many cases being dismissed outright. Such a policy of lenient treatment coupled with internal racially egalitarian practices will most likely be sufficient—barring repeated military interventions in black ghettos—to preclude any widespread black disaffection within the armed forces.[25]

The nature of black participation in the military organization has also become inextricable with broader criticisms of America's politico-military policies. Though originally focusing on the war in Vietnam, radical attacks have come to include a questioning of the very legitimacy of military service.[26] Much attention has been given to the relationship between elements of the black militant movement with the movement against the war in Vietnam. Yet the black movement as a whole has remained largely removed from those white radical groups vociferously attacking the military services. (Ironically enough, the emergence of black separatism has worked against white radicals seeking to appeal to black servicemen.) Indeed, the antiwar movement has aggravated not only the already existing cleavages between black moderate and black militant leaders but has also revealed differences between black demands and the goals of white radicals. The pertinent question appears to be not so much what are the implications of the black movement for the military establishment, but what are the effects of the Vietnam War on internal developments within the black movement itself. Although it would be premature to offer a definite statement on any future interpenetrations between the black movement and anti-military groups, a major turning away of blacks per se from military commitment is viewed as highly doubtful. Most likely, and somewhat paradoxically, we will witness more vocal anti-military sentiment within certain black militant groups at the same time that the armed forces increasingly become a leading avenue of career opportunity for many black men.

Nevertheless, there has usually been and is today a presumption on the part of America's military opponents that blacks should be less committed soldiers than whites. Whether for tactical or ideological reasons, the black serviceman has been frequently defined as a special target for propaganda by forces opposing America in military conflicts. In World War II the Japanese directed radio appeals specifically to Negro servicemen in the Pacific theater. In the Korean conflict the Chinese used racial arguments on Negro prisoners of war. Yet a careful study of American POW behavior in Korea made no mention of differences in black and white behavior except to note that the resegregation of black POWs by the Chinese had a boomerang effect on Communist indoctrination methods.[27]

The recent military interventions of the United States on the international scene raise again the question of the motivation and performance of black soldiers in combat. A spokesman for the National Liberation Front of South Vietnam asserted as early as 1965 that "liberation forces have a special attitude toward American soldiers who happen to be Negroes." In the same vein, upon release of three American POWs (two of them black) in early 1968, the clandestine Viet Cong radio announced it was a gesture of "solidarity and support for American Negroes." My observations as well as those of others found no differences in white or black combat performance in Vietnam. In the Dominican Republic, where the proportion of blacks in line units ran as high as 40 per cent, a pamphlet was distributed to black soldiers exhorting them to "turn your guns on your white oppressors and join your Dominican brothers."[28] Again, my personal observations buttressed by comment from Dominicans revealed no significant differences between white and black military performance.[29]

My appraisal is that among officers and NCOs there was no discernible difference between the races concerning military commitment in either the Dominican Republic or Vietnam. Among black soldiers in the lower enlisted ranks, however, there was a somewhat greater disenchantment compared to white as to the merits of America's recent military ventures. Such unease, however, has little effect on military performance, most especially in the actual combat situation. Close living, strict discipline, and common danger all serve to preclude racial conflict between whites and blacks in field units. The evidence strongly suggests that the racial integration of the armed forces, coming about when it did, effectively precluded any large-scale success on the part of America's military opponents to differentiate black from white soldiers.

It is also probable, however, that military experience will contribute to an activist posture on the part of black servicemen returning to civilian life. The black ex-serviceman, that is, will be less willing to accommodate himself to second-class citizenship after participating in the racially egalitarian military system. Further, especially in situations where blacks are intimidated by physical threat or force, techniques of violence and organizational skills acquired in military service will be a new factor in the black movement. Robert F. Williams, the first leading advocate of armed self-defense for blacks, explicitly states that his Marine Corps experience led to his beliefs.[30] It also seems more than coincidence that the ten founders of the Deacons for Defense and Justice, a paramilitary group organized in 1964 to counter Ku Klux Klan terrorism, were all veterans of Korea or World War II.[31] Moreover, black veterans returning from Vietnam are alleged to be prominent in the membership of newly formed paramilitary groups in urban ghettos (e.g., the Black Panthers in the San Francisco Bay area, the Zulu 1200s in

St. Louis, the Invaders in Memphis, the US organization in Los Angeles). Yet, the future role of the Vietnam veteran in the black movement is hard to assess. Undoubtedly, most black veterans—like most people in general—will eschew politico-revolutionary activity and seek to improve their lives along individual lines. But we can also expect, as was the case after previous American wars, that black veterans will play a leading role in their race's struggle for dignity and equality.

Although the military was until recent times one of America's most segregated institutions, it has leaped into the forefront of racial equality in the past decades. What features of the military establishment can account for this about-face? There is a combination of mutually supporting factors that operate in the generally successful racial integration of the armed forces. For one thing, the military—an institution revolving around techniques of violence —is to an important degree discontinuous from other areas of social life. And this apartness served to allow, once the course had been decided, a rapid and complete racial integration. The path of desegregation was further made easier by characteristics peculiar to or at least more pronounced in the military. With its hierarchical power structure, predicated on stable and patterned relationships, decisions need take relatively little account of the personal desires of service personnel. Additionally, because roles and activities are more defined and specific in the military than in most other social arenas, conflicts that might have ensued within a more diffuse and ambiguous setting were largely absent. Likewise, desegregation was facilitated by the pervasiveness in the military of a bureaucratic ethos, with its concomitant formality and high social distance, that mitigated tensions arising from individual or personal feelings.

At the same time it must also be remembered that the military establishment has means of coercion not readily available in most civilian pursuits. Violations of norms are both more visible and subject to quicker sanctions. The military is premised, moreover, on the accountability of its members for effective performance. Owing to the aptly termed "chain of command," failures in policy implementation can be pinpointed. This in turn means that satisfactory carrying-out of stated policy advances one's own position. In other words, it is to each individual's personal interest, if he anticipates receiving the rewards of a military career, to insure that decisions going through him are executed with minimum difficulty. Or, put another way, whatever the internal policy decided upon, racial integration being a paramount but only one example, the military establishment is uniquely suited to realize its implementation.

What implications does the military integration experience have for civilian society? Although it is certainly true that the means by which racial desegregation was accomplished in the military establishment are not easily transferable to the civilian community, the end result of integration in the contemporary armed forces can suggest some qualities of what an integrated American society would be *within the context of the prevailing structural and value system*. Equality of treatment would be the rule in formal and task-specific relationships. Racial animosity would diminish but not disappear. Primary group ties and informal association would remain largely within one's own racial group. But even at primary group levels, the integrated society would exhibit a much higher interracial intimacy than exists in the nonintegrated society. We would also expect a sharp improvement in black mobility and performance in the occupational sphere, even taking into consideration ongoing social and educational handicaps arising from existing inequities. Yet, because of these inequities, blacks would still be over-concentrated in less skilled and less rewarded positions.

Such a description of the racially integrated society is, of course, what one finds in today's military establishment. Moreover, despite inequities suffered by blacks both in being more likely to be drafted and once in the service being more likely to assignment in combat units, blacks, nevertheless, are still much more favorably disposed toward military life than whites. It is a commentary on our nation that many black youths, by seeking to enter and remain in the armed forces, are saying that it is even worth the risk of being killed in order to have a chance to learn a trade, to make it in a small way, to get away from a dead-end existence, and to become part of the only institution in this society that seems really to be integrated.

NOTES

1. Materials covering racial matters in the military are quite extensive. A primary source are those United States government reports dealing with racial relations in the armed forces: President's Committee on Equality of Treatment and Opportunity in the Armed Forces ("Fahy Committee"), *Freedom to Serve: Equality of Treatment and Opportunity in the Armed Forces* (Washington, D.C.: Government Printing Office, 1950); U.S. Commission on Civil Rights, "The Negro in the Armed Forces," *Civil Rights '63* (Washington, D.C.: Government Printing Office, 1963), 169–224; President's Committee on Equal Opportunity in the Armed Forces ("Gesell Committee"), "Initial Report: Equality of Treatment and Opportunity for Negro Personnel Stationed within the United States" (mimeographed; June, 1963), and "Final Report: Military Personnel Stationed Overseas and Membership and Participation in the National Guard" (mimeographed; November, 1964). An invaluable source of information pertaining to racial composition rates within the armed forces are the statistical breakdowns periodically issued by the office of Civil Rights and Industrial Relations (CR&IR) in the Department of Defense.

Another source of data is found in Operations Research Office (ORO), *Project Clear: The Utilization of Negro Manpower in the Army* (Chevy Chase, Md.: Operations Research Office, Johns Hopkins University, April, 1955). The ORO surveys queried several thousand servicemen during the Korean conflict on a variety of items relating to attitudes toward racial integration in the Army. The findings of Project Clear, classified until 1965, are now available for professional scrutiny. A convenient summary of the Project Clear findings as well as an incisive account of how the survey was planned and carried out is found in Leo Bogart, *Social Research and the Desegregation of the U.S. Army* (Chicago: Markham Press, 1969). Some comparable World War II data were obtained from the section dealing with Negro soldiers in Samuel A. Stouffer *et al., The American Soldier: Adjustment During Army Life* (Princeton: Princeton University Press, 1949), I, 486–599.

Much of the information for the findings presented in this chapter are based on my participant observations while on active duty in the Army (1956–1958), and subsequent field trips as a researcher to various overseas military installations: Germany and Korea in 1965, the Dominican Republic in 1966; and Vietnam in 1965 and 1967. Additionally, 67 formal interviews with black soldiers in Germany were conducted in 1965. These interviews were with soldiers who made up almost all of the total black enlisted personnel in two Army companies.

2. This background of the black serviceman's role in the American military is derived, in addition to the sources cited above, from Seymour J. Schoenfeld, *The Negro in the Armed Forces* (Washington, D.C.: Associated Publishers, 1945); Herbert Aptheker, *Essays in the History of the American Negro* (New York: International Publishers, 1945); Arnold M. Rose, "Army Policies Toward Negro Soldiers," *Annals of the American Academy of Political and Social Science*, 244 (March, 1946), 90–94; Paul C. Davis, "The Negro in the Armed Services," *Virginia Quarterly*, 24 (Autumn, 1948), 499–520; David G. Mandelbaum, *Soldiers Groups and Negro Groups* (Berkeley: University of California Press, 1952); Lee Nichols, *Breakthrough on the Color Front* (New York: Random House, Inc., 1954); Eli Ginzburg, "The Negro Soldier," in his *The Negro Potential* (New York: Columbia University Press, 1956), 61–91; Benjamin Quarles, *The Negro in the Making of America* (New York: Collier Books, 1964), *passim*; Ulysses Lee, *The Employment of Negro Troops*, Special Studies on the United States Army in World War II by the Office of the Chief of Military History (Washington, D.C.: Govern-

ment Printing Office, 1966); and Richard J. Stillman, II, *Integration of the Negro in the U.S. Armed Forces* (New York: Frederick Praeger, 1968).

3. Blacks have not been the only racial or ethnic group to occupy a special position in the American military. Indians served in separate battalions in the Civil War and were used as scouts in the frontier wars. Filipinos have long been a major source of recruitment for stewards in the Navy. The much decorated 442nd ("Go for Broke") Infantry Regiment of World War II was comprised entirely of Japanese-Americans. Also in World War II, a separate battalion of Norwegian-Americans was drawn up for intended service in Scandinavia. The participation of Puerto Ricans in the American military deserves special attention. A recent case of large-scale use of non-American soldiers are the Korean fillers or "Katusas" (from Korean Augmentation to the U.S. Army) who make up roughly one-sixth of the troop strength of the Eighth Army.

4. The 1945 and 1950 Army board reports are commonly referred to by the names of the officers who headed these boards: respectively, Lieutenant General Alvan C. Gillem, Jr., and Lieutenant General S. J. Chamberlin.

5. These evaluations are summarized in ORO, *op. cit.*, 16–19, 47–105, 582–583.

6. The notoriety of the 24th Infantry Regiment was aggravated by a song, "The Bug-Out Boogie," attributed to it: "When them Chinese mortars begin to thud / The old Deuce-Four begin to bug / When they started falling 'round the CP [command post] tent / Everybody wonder where the high brass went /They were buggin' out / Just movin' on."

7. Bernard D. Karpinos, *Supplement to Health of the Army* (Washington, D.C.: Office of the Surgeon General, Department of the Army, 1967), 14–15.

8. World War II evidence shows much of the incidence of psychoneurotic breakdown among Negro soldiers, compared with Caucasions, was associated with psychological handicaps originating before entrance into military service. Arnold M. Rose, "Psychoneurotic Breakdown Among Negro Soldiers," *Phylon*, 17 (1956), 61–73.

9. Stouffer *et al.*, *op. cit.*, II, 242–289; Raymond W. Mack, "The Prestige System of an Air Base," *American Sociological Review*, 19 (June, 1954), 281–287; Morris Janowitz, *The Professional Soldier* (New York: Free Press, 1960), 31–36.

10. There are, as should be expected, differences among black soldiers as to their desire to see combat. From data not shown here, 1965 interviews with black soldiers stationed in Germany revealed reluctance to go to Viet-

nam was greatest among those with high school or better education, and Northern home residence. This is in direct contrast with the findings reported in *The American Soldier*. In the segregated Army of World War II, Northern and more highly educated Negro soldiers were most likely to want to get into combat, an outcome of the onus of inferiority felt to accompany service in support units. Stouffer *et al.*, *op. cit.*, I, 523–524.

11. The emphasis on academic education for officer careers effectively limits most black opportunities to the enlisted levels. On this point, see Kurt Lang, "Technology and Career Management in the Military Establishment," in Morris Janowitz (ed.), *The New Military* (New York: Russell Sage Foundation, 1964), 39–81.

12. Some have attributed the sharp drop in the 1967 reenlistment rate to servicemen seeking to avoid a second tour of duty in Vietnam. Although this factor undoubtedly explains some of the decline, the 1967 reenlistment data is suspect on other grounds. A substantial change in the mix of "first-term enlistees" and "inductees" (i.e., the greater number of draftees making up first-term servicemen) has made comparison of reenlistments for 1967 with earlier years questionable.

13. Stouffer *et al.*, *op. cit.*, 566.

14. What methodological bias exists is that the Korean conflict question was a stronger description of racial integration than the item used in World War II. Compare, "What is your feeling about serving in a platoon containing both whites and colored soldiers, all working and training together, sleeping in the same barracks and eating in the same mess hall?" with "Do you think white and Negro soldiers should be in separate outfits or should they be together in the same outfits?" Respectively, ORO, *op. cit.*, 453, and Stouffer *et al.*, *op. cit.*, 568.

15. *Ibid.*, 594.

16. The comprehensive scope of military integration is found in the official guidelines set forth under "Equal Opportunity and Treatment of Military Personnel," in *Army Regulation 66–21, Air Force Regulation 35–78,* and *Secretary of the Navy Instruction 5350.6.*

17. Cf. the Fahy committee report (1950) with the Gesell committee reports (1963 and 1964).

18. ORO, *op. cit.*, 388.

19. James Anderson, "Father and Sons: An Evaluation of Military Racial Relations in Two Generations" (term paper, University of Michigan, December, 1965).

20. Stouffer and his associates, for example, report enlisted men as compared with officers, as Negro soldiers with white soldiers, were more prone to have "low spirits," to be less desirous of entering combat, and to be

more dissatisfied than perceived by others. Stouffer *et al., op. cit.*, II, 345, and I, 392–394, 506, 521, 538.

21. A social-distance study conducted among Korean college students found the following placement, from near to far: Chinese, Europeans, and white Americans, Filipinos, Indians (from India), and black Americans. Personal communication, Man Gap Lee, Seoul National University.

The less than favorable reception of black soldiers—compared with whites—in overseas locales is also illustrated in the Japanese film *The Saga of Postwar Cruelty* (1968), a portrayal of the American occupation from 1945 to 1952. Made by one of Japan's leading directors, Tetsuji Takechi, the film loses no time in making its point. Even before the titles are completed, a Japanese girl is seized, raped, and killed by a drunken black soldier.

22. These barbers were focal points of much of the battalion's gossip and among them saw every man in the battalion on the average of twice a month.

23. These same data, in tables not shown here, reveal that there is an *inverse* correlation between formal education (as ascertained from battalion personnel records) and likelihood of learning German! This reflects the greater probability of black soldiers, compared with whites, to learn German while averaging fewer years of formal education.

24. William Caudill, "American Soldiers in a Japanese Community" (unpublished manuscript), 34.

25. In the wake of outbreaks of racial violence on or near several military bases in the summer of 1969, the Army and Marine Corps announced new guidelines giving greater leeway for black salutes, "Afro" haircuts, and other manifestations of black solidarity among troops. The Pentagon was also considering establishment of biracial councils consisting of officers and enlisted men on all major bases to minimize racial friction.

26. Even in the Civil War there were black spokesmen who opposed black participation in the Union Army. Frederick Douglass attacked them as follows. "They tell you this is the 'white man's' war; that you will be no 'better off after than before the war'; that the getting of you into the army is to 'sacrifice you on the first opportunity.' Believe them not; cowards themselves, they do not wish to have their cowardice shamed by your brave example. Leave them to their timidity, or to whatever motive may hold them back." Quoted in Ronald Segal, *The Race War* (Bantam Books, Inc., 1967), 198–199.

27. Albert D. Biderman, *March to Calumny* (New York: The Macmillan Company, 1964), 60.

28. A copy of the entire pamphlet is reproduced in the Dominican news magazine *Ahora*, No. 108 (September 18, 1965). Although many whites were unaware of the pamphlet's existence, virtually every black soldier I talked to in Santo Domingo said he had seen the pamphlet. The effectiveness of the pamphlet on black soldiers was minimal, among other reasons, because it asserted black equality existed in the Dominican Republic, a statement belied by brief observation of the Dominican scene.

29. Similarly in an interview with a black reporter, the commandant of "constitutionalist rebel" forces in Santo Domingo stated that to his dismay Negro American soldiers fought no differently than whites. Laurence Harvey, "Report from the Dominican Republic," *Realist* (June, 1965), 18.

30. Robert F. Williams, *Negroes with Guns* (New York: Marzani and Munsell, 1962).

31. *The Militant*, November 22, 1965, 1.

The Emergent Military:
Civil, Traditional, or Plural?

CHARLES C. MOSKOS, JR.

Academic definitions as well as ideological attitudes of the American armed forces fluctuate between two poles. At one end are those who see the military as a reflection of dominant societal values and an instrument entirely dependent upon the lead of civilian decision makers. Conversely, others stress how much military values differ from the larger society and how much independent influence the military has come to exert in civil society. These two emphases differ on whether the armed forces or society is primary. Yet neither conception is wholly wrong nor wholly accurate. Rather, the issue is one of the simultaneous interpenetration and institutional autonomy of the military and civilian spheres.

At the outset, nevertheless, it should be made clear that the conceptual question of the independent versus dependent relationship of the military and civilian orders is not intrinsically a value judgment. Indeed, we find diverse viewpoints on the conceptual question crisscrossing political positions. Thus supporters of the military organization have argued both for and against greater congruence between military and civilian structures. Likewise, the harshest critics of the armed forces have variously claimed the military establishment to be either too isolated or too overlapping with civil society. The point here is that at some level a sociological understanding of the armed forces and American society can be analytically distinguished from a political position. In fact, of course, this is not always so readily apparent when one gets down to concrete cases. But it is my personal statement that an ideological position must ultimately lead to social science analyses. This is especially mandatory in the present period when the American military establishment is undergoing profound changes both in its internal organization and in its relationship to the larger society.

ARMED FORCES AND AMERICAN SOCIETY
IN RECENT RETROSPECT

Even in the single generation which has elapsed since the start of the Second World War one can readily observe that the American military establishment has passed through several distinctive and successive phases. Prior to World War II the military forces of this country constituted less than one percent of the male labor force. Armed forces personnel were exclusively volunteers, most of whom were making a career out of military service. Enlisted men were almost entirely of working-class or rural origin, and officers were overproportionately drawn from Southern Protestant middle-class families.

A slightly different version of this article will appear in the *Pacific Sociological Review*, Spring 1973.

Within the military organization itself, the vast majority of servicemen were assigned to combat or manual labor positions. Socially, the pre-World War II military was a self-contained institution with marked separation from civilian society. In its essential qualities, the "From-Here-To-Eternity" army was a garrison force predicated upon military tradition, ceremony, and hierarchy.

The Second World War was a period of mass mobilization. By 1945 close to 12,000,000 persons were in uniform. Although technical specialization proceeded apace during the war, the large majority of ground forces were still assigned to combat and service units. Even in the Navy and Air Corps—services where specialization was most pronounced—only about one-third of personnel was in technical or administrative specialties. The membership of the World War II forces was largely conscripted or draft-induced volunteers. To put it another way, the military of World War II, while socially representative of American society, was still an institution whose internal organization contrasted sharply with that of civilian structures. At home, nevertheless, there was popular support of the war, and criticism of the military establishment was virtually nonexistent.

Following World War II, there was a sixteen-month period with no conscription at all. By the time of the outbreak of the Korean War in 1950, however, the draft had already been reinstituted. The conflict in Korea was a war of partial mobilization: slightly over 3,600,000 men served at the peak of hostilities. Organizationally and materially, the armed forces of the Korean War closely resembled that of World War II. Unlike World War II, however, the war in Korea ended in stalemate, which in turn contributed to adverse accounts of soldiers' behavior: prisoner-of-war collaboration, the lack of troop motivation, and the deterioration of military discipline.

The Cold War military which took shape after Korea averaged around 2,500,000 men, again relying in great part on the pressures of the draft for manpower. Especially significant, technical specialization became a pervasive trend throughout the military during the 1950s and early 1960s.[1] The proportion of men assigned to combat or service units declined markedly with a corresponding increase in electronic and technical specialists. These trends were most obvious in the Air Force, somewhat less so in the Navy, and least of all in the Army and Marine Corps. Moreover, because of the post-Korea doctrine of nuclear deterrence and massive retaliation, it was also the Air Force which experienced the greatest proportional growth during the 1950s.

Although Cold War policies were generally unquestioned during the 1950s and early 1960s, the military did not escape embroilment in political controversy during the Cold War period. Such controversy was centered on issues of military leadership and the institutional role of the military. Command policies at the highest level were subjected to conservative charges in two major Senate hearings. The military establishment found itself on the defensive in countering charges of being soft on Communism in both the McCarthy-Army hearings of 1954 and in the 1962 hearings resulting from the cause célèbre following Major General Edwin Walker's relief from command (for sponsoring troop information programs with extreme conservative content). During the same period, intellectuals on the Left emerged from their quiescent stance and began critically to attack the military establishment from another direction. Deep concerns about the military-industrial complex in American society were raised—an issue which was to achieve fruition of sorts over a decade later. By and large, however, the Cold War criticisms of the military were relatively weak, and in basic respects the armed forces maintained the high regard of the American public.

The war in Vietnam ushered in another phase of the armed forces in American society. There was the obvious increase in troop strength to a high of 3,500,000 in 1970. At the same time the role of the Air Force and Navy went into relative descendancy as the Army and Marine Corps came to bear the brunt of the conflict in Indochina. The Vietnam War also led to deviations from the Cold War policies of manpower recruitment. In 1966, entrance standards were lowered to allow the induction of persons coming from heretofore disqualified mental levels—overproportionately lower class and black. In 1968 the manpower pool was again enlarged, this time by terminating draft deferments for recent college graduates—largely middle-class whites. For the first time since the Korean conflict, the membership of the armed forces was again bearing some resemblance of the social composition of the larger society.

If the debates concerning the military establishment were generally muted in peacetime, this was not to be the case once America intervened massively in Indochina. Although there was a brief spate of glory attached to the Green Berets, opposition to the war soon led to negative portrayals of the armed forces. As the antiwar movement gained momentum, it began to develop into a frontal attack on the military system itself—particularly within elite cultural and intellectual circles. The 1967 March on the Pentagon crossed a symbolic threshold. Not only was the war in Vietnam opposed, but for a growing number the basic legitimacy of military service was brought into open question. Adding to the passion of the antimilitarists were the revelations of American atrocities in Vietnam and the physical and ecological devastation being perpetuated throughout Indochina. To compound matters, there were a host of other fac-

tors somewhat independent of Vietnam which served to tarnish the image of the American military: the capture of the *Pueblo*, the inequities of the draft, reports of widespread drug abuse among troops, corruption in the operation of post exchanges and service clubs, astounding cost overruns in defense contracts, and military spying on civilian political activists.

Even more telling, there were undeniable signs in the late Vietnam period of disintegration within the military itself. Some numbers of men in uniform—white radicals, disgruntled enlisted men, antiwar officers—were increasingly communicating their feelings to other servicemen as well as to groups in the larger society. Moreover, throughout all locales where U.S. servicemen were stationed racial strife was becoming endemic. The possibility that black troops might owe higher fealty to the black community than to the United States military began to haunt commanders. In Vietnam the American military force by 1971 was plagued by breakdowns in discipline including violent reprisals against unpopular officers and noncoms. Although much of the malaise in the ranks was attributed to changes in youth styles (as manifest in the widespread use of drugs), it was more likely that the military's disciplinary problems reflected in larger part that general weakening of morale which seems always to accompany an army coming to an end of a war. Even the use of sheer coercive power on the part of commanders has limitations once the esprit de corps of an armed force has been so sapped.

The contrast in ideological and public evaluations of the American military establishment over three wars is revealing. In the Second World War, the American military was almost universally held in high esteem in a popularly supported war. Conservative and isolationist sectors of American public opinion were quick to fall in line behind a liberal and interventionist national leadership. In the wake of the Korean War, defamatory images of the American servicemen were propagated by right-wing spokesmen. Liberal commentators, on the other hand, generally defended the qualities of the American armed forces. During the war in Southeast Asia, a still different pattern has emerged. Although initially an outcome of a liberal Administration, the war has come to be defended primarily by political conservatives, while the severest attacks on both the behavior of American soldiers and the military establishment now emanate from the Left.

But even beyond Vietnam and factors unique to armed forces and society in the United States, the decline in status of the American military establishment may well be part of a more pervasive pattern occurring throughout Western parliamentary democracies. Observers of contemporary armed forces in Western Europe, the United Kingdom, Canada, and Australia have all noted the sharp depreciation in the military's standing in these societies. Indeed, although it seems somewhat far afield, the possibility suggests itself that Vietnam may be a minor factor in explaining the lessened prestige of the American military establishment. This is to say that the American military, like its counterparts in other Western post-industrialized societies, is experiencing an historical turning point with regard to its societal legitimacy and public acceptance.

THE SOCIAL COMPOSITION OF AN ALL-VOLUNTEER FORCE

A stated goal of the Nixon Administration is the establishment of an all-volunteer force. Shortly after assuming the Presidency, Nixon appointed a commission to study the implementation of an all-volunteer force. This panel—referred to by the name of its chairman, Thomas S. Gates—published its report in February 1970. It was the unanimous recommendation of the Gates Commission to establish an all-volunteer force with a standby draft. In July 1970, legislation was introduced in the U.S. Senate which would put into effect the recommendations of the Gates Commission. Although yet to be passed, the breadth of support for this legislation was revealed in its sponsorship, which included political figures as diverse as Barry Goldwater and George McGovern. Moreover, a bill was passed and signed by the President in 1971 which substantially increased military salaries especially for servicemen in their first tours. The Department of Defense has set July 1, 1973, as the goal for achieving a "zero draft." Under this plan it is expected that all entering servicemen will by that date be volunteers with the proviso that Congress will retain a two-year extension of induction authority and standby authority thereafter.

It seems fairly certain, then, that sooner rather than later this country's generation-old reliance on the draft for military manpower will come to an end. Before looking at some probable consequences of this change, however, some background data is in order on military procurement and retention rates in the modern era. Over the past two decades, with some variation, about one-third of all age-eligible men fail to meet the mental test standards required for military entrance; this group has been disproportionately poor and/or black. About a quarter of the age-eligible men obtain draft deferments (primarily educational) which result in de facto exemptions; this group is greatly overrepresentative of upper-middle-class youth. (In the most recent period, upper-middle-class youth have also decreased their draft liability by utilizing liberalized conscientious objection procedures and obtaining medical documentation of ersatz physical disabilities.) Thus, only about forty percent of age-eligible young men actually have served in the military in recent years; and these men were overproportionately drawn from the American stable working and lower-middle classes.

Between the wars in Korea and Vietnam, about one-fourth of all incoming military personnel were draftees (in almost all cases these were Army entrants). About another quarter were draft-motivated volunteers, that is, men joining the military to exercise a choice in time of entry or branch of service. Therefore, only about half of all entering servicemen in peacetime were "true" volunteers, i.e., men who would have presumably joined the service without the impetus of the draft. During both the Korean and Vietnam wars the number of draftees and draft-motivated volunteers increased sharply. It was estimated that in 1970 less than 25 percent of incoming servicemen were "true" volunteers.

Once within the military, retention rates vary by manner of service entry. In peacetime years, about 20–25 percent of volunteers reenlist for a second term; among draftees the proportion going on to a second term averages about 10 percent. In the later years of the Vietnam War, however, volunteer reenlistments dropped to 15–20 percent, and draftee reenlistments were less than 5 percent. Once a serviceman has made the transition from first to second term, however, he has usually decided upon a military career. With remarkable consistency about four out of five second-term servicemen remain in the military to complete at least twenty years service (the minimum time required for retirement benefits).

What lessons does the experience of the recent past offer for an understanding of the military establishment which will emerge from the institution of an all-volunteer force? Will the armed forces maintain a membership which resembles in basic respects that which existed prior to the Vietnam War, or will the social composition of the military undergo a fundamental transformation? Not too surprising, as in most controversial issues, social science data has been quoted to assert contrary predictions and conclusions.

CHANGES IN THE ENLISTED RANKS

One of the most telling arguments against the establishment of an all-volunteer force is that such a force will have an enlisted membership overwhelmingly black and poor.[2] Yet the Gates Commission counters: "The frequently heard claim that a volunteer force will be all black or all this or all that simply has no basis in fact. Our research indicates that the composition of the armed forces will not fundamentally change by ending conscription.... Maintenance of current mental, physical, and moral standards for enlistment will ensure that a better paid, volunteer force will not recruit an undue proportion of youths from disadvantaged backgrounds."[3]

Another study, contracted by the Institute for Defense Analyses, differs on virtually all counts from the findings of the Gates Commission.[4] Based on a detailed statistical comparison of civilian and military employment earning potential, the Defense Analyses report concludes: (a) non-high school graduates suffer a financial loss if they choose civilian employment over continued military service; (b) enlisted men who have attended college experience a financial loss if they remain in military service; (c) military and civilian earnings for high school graduates are roughly the same; and (d) military earnings for blacks with a high school education or less will far exceed their earnings in the civilian labor force. In other words, on the assumption that social groups will generally behave in their own economic self-interest, an all-volunteer force would significantly overdraw its membership from the less educated and minority groups of American society.

Reference to the experience of all-volunteer forces in other nations is also inconsistent. Again, in support of the all-volunteer force, the Gates Commission finds: "The recent experience of the British, Australian, and Canadian Armed Forces suggest that competitive wages will attract an adequate quantity and quality of volunteers."[5] Yet an account of the British experience notes that typical recruits are "untrained school-leavers" coming from older and impoverished urban areas.[6] Indeed, over a third of British volunteers now join the armed forces *before* their seventeenth birthday (20 percent of all British volunteers being only fifteen years old!).[7]

With such contradictory findings, what are we to conclude as to the probable future social composition of the enlisted ranks? In all probability an all-volunteer force will be less socially representative than the present military establishment, but, with pay raises, nowhere near exclusively dependent on the lowest social and economic classes. That is, a reasonable expectation is that the rank and file of a non-conscripted military will fall somewhere between the claims of the Gates Commission and the dire predictions of an "all black" or "all poor" force.[8] Which of the two extremes an all-volunteer force will tend toward will largely be determined by the eventual total manpower strength of the armed services. A smaller force—say close to 2,000,000 persons—will be able to afford higher entrance standards, thus precluding overrecruitment from America's underclasses. Conversely, a larger force will have to draw deeper from previously unqualified groups.

CHANGES IN THE OFFICER CORPS

The movement toward an all-volunteer force will be accompanied by significant changes in the social bases of officer recruitment.[9] The ROTC units from which the bulk of the officer corps is now drawn will almost certainly decrease in number and narrow in range. Partly as a result of anti-ROTC agitation at prestige colleges and universities, ROTC recruitment will be increasingly found in educational institutions located in regions where the status of the military profession is highest—rural areas and in the South and Mountain states. It must be candidly acknowledged that such ROTC units will often be at colleges and universities with modest academic standards. Within the larger urban areas themselves, there is a possibility that ROTC units may be removed from campuses and instituted instead on a metropolitan basis. This would most likely further restrict recruitment of ROTC cadets coming from upper-middle-class backgrounds.

Moreover, the armed forces will obtain a growing proportion of its officers from the service academies, a step which has already been taken by substantially increasing the size of the student body at these institutions. Although the system of selection into the service academies is broadly based, there is a strong possibility that military family background will become even more prevalent among academy entrants. Because of the expansion of the armed forces over the past twenty years, the number of such military families and their offspring has increased markedly. Such excessive selection from military families—officers and enlisted —would result in a separation of the officer corps from civilian society by narrowing the basis of social recruitment. Likewise, any increased reliance on government-sponsored military preparatory or even privately-sponsored preparatory schools would similarly narrow the social and geographical background of future officers.

Finally, there is the probability that recruitment from the ranks into the officer corps will decline. With the greater and greater emphasis on a college degree, there will be an acceleration of the trend to recruitment from college graduates rather than promotion from the ranks. Such a decline in the proportion of commissioned officers coming from the ranks has already been the experience of European all-volunteer forces.[10] A countervailing factor, however, may be a stepping up of military programs which offer college educations to highly motivated enlisted personnel.

DEVELOPMENTAL MODELS OF THE EMERGENT MILITARY

Underlying much of social change theory are developmental constructs that are implicit predictions of an emerging social order (for example, a classless society, a bureaucratic society, a garrison state). Most simply, developmental constructs are modes of analyses which entail historical reconstruction, trend specification, and most especially, a model of a future state of affairs toward which actual events are heading.[11] Developmental analysis, that is, emphasizes the "from here to there" sequence of present and hypothetical events. Put in a slightly different way, a developmental construct is an "ideal" or "pure" type placed at some future point by which we may ascertain and order the emergent reality of contemporary social phenomena. Models derived from developmental analysis bridge the empirical world of today and the social forms of the future. It follows that one's reading of current and past reality will vary depending upon which developmental model is constructed.

Our purpose here is to apply developmental analysis to the emergent form of the military establishment in American society. Put plainly, what is the likely shape of the armed forces in the foreseeable future? Initially two opposing developmental models are presented, each of which has currency in military sociology thought. A third model is then introduced which both synthesizes and differs from the two previous models. All three models, however, have in common a reference to a continuum ranging from a military organization highly differentiated from civilian society to a military system highly convergent with civilian structures.

Concretely, of course, America's military forces have never been either entirely separate or entirely coterminous with civilian society. But conceiving of a scale along which the military has been more or less overlapping with civilian society serves the heuristic purposes of highlighting the ever changing interphase between the armed forces and American society. It is also in this way that we can be alerted to emergent trends within the military establishment, trends that appear to augur a fundamental change in the social organization of the armed forces within the near future.

The convergent-divergent formulation of armed forces and society, however, must account for several levels of variation. One variable centers on the way in which the *membership* of the armed forces is representative of the broader society. A second variation is the degree to which there are *institutional* parallels (or discontinuities) in the social organization of military and civilian structures. Difference in required *skills* between military and civilian occupations is a third aspect. A fourth variable refers to *ideological* dissimilarities between civilians and military men. Furthermore, internal distinctions within the armed forces cut across each of the preceding variables: differences between officers and enlisted men; differences between services; differences between branches within the services; differences between echelons within branches.

Needless to add, there are formidable problems in gathering meaningful evidence on the degree of convergence or divergence between the armed forces and society.[12] Some of the more important findings of previous researchers on this issue, as well as new materials, are given in the developmental models presented below.

MODEL I: THE CONVERGENT OR CIVILIANIZED MILITARY

A leitmotif in studies of the military establishment between the wars in Korea and Vietnam was the growing convergence between military and civilian forms of social organization. In large part this convergence was a consequence of changes induced by sophisticated weapons systems. These new technological advances had ramifications on military organization which were particularly manifest in the officer corps. For weapons development gave rise not just to a need for increased technical proficiency, but also for men trained in managerial and modern decision-making skills. This is to say, the broader trend toward technological complexity and increase in organizational scale which was engendering more rationalized and bureaucratic structures throughout American society was also having profound consequences within the military establishment. In the military as in civilian institutions, such a trend involved changes both in the qualifications and sources of leadership.

These changes in military leadership were examined in several landmark studies dealing with the Cold War military establishment. Ironically enough, both sympathetic and hostile observers of the changing military establishment were in accord that there was a convergence in the managerial skills required in both civilian and military organizations. In a highly critical and perceptive appraisal of these trends, C. Wright Mills described the "military warlords" as constituent members of the power elite in American society.[13] Mills highlighted the increasing lateral access of military professionals to top economic and political positions. From a different perspective, other writers—most notably Gene Lyons and John Masland in *Education and Military Leadership*, and Samuel Huntington in *The Soldier and the State*—argued that the complexities of modern warfare and international politics required new formulations of officer professionalization and civil-military relations.[14]

The most comprehensive study of American military leadership in the Cold War era was *The Professional Soldier* by Morris Janowitz.[15] Documentation was given of the broadening of the social origins of officers to include a more representative sampling of America's regions and religious groups, and of the increase in the number of nonacademy graduates at the highest levels of the military establishment. Moreover, the military of that period was seen as increasingly sharing the characteristics typical of any large-scale bureaucracy. In effect Janowitz stated that the military was characterized by a trend away from authority based on "domination" toward a managerial philosophy placing greater stress on persuasion and individual initiative.

The trend toward convergence has in some respects become even more pronounced in the contemporary period of the early 1970s. Significantly differing from the pre-Vietnam military, where convergence was most pronounced at military elite levels, the more recent changes were largely focused—with the accompaniment of much mass media coverage—on the enlisted ranks. Partly as a result of internal disciplinary problems occurring toward the end of the Vietnam War, partly in anticipation of an all-volun-

teer force after Vietnam, the military
command inaugurated a series of programs designed to accommodate civilian youth values and to make the
authority structure more responsive to
enlisted needs.

Starting in late 1969, VOLAR (an
acronym for Volunteer Army) programs
were instituted on a growing number
of Army posts.[16] VOLAR reforms included such changes as greater margin
in hair styles, abolishment of reveille,
minimal personal inspections, and
more privacy in the barracks. Much of
the changed Army outlook was captured in its new recruiting slogan,
"The Army Wants to Join You." The
"Z-grams" of Chief of Naval Operations Admiral Zumwalt similarly
alerted commissioned and petty officers
to concern themselves with enlisted
wants and to show more latitude in
dealing with the personal life styles of
sailors. The Air Force, which has always been the most civilianized of the
armed services, issued a new regulation
in July 1971 (AFR 30-1) which specified a broad set of standards (ranging
from haircuts to political protest) which
was unprecedented in equally applying
to both officers and airmen.

Whether changes such as these are
really fundamental or merely cosmetic
will take time to tell. But there does
seem to be occurring something more
than just "beer-in-the-barracks" innovations. Human relations councils consisting of black and white servicemen
are coming to play an increasing role
in the military's attempt to cope with
racial strife. Even more novel are the
officially sanctioned councils of junior
officers and enlisted men which now
exist on a certain number of bases. The
formal purpose of such councils is to
serve as communication channels between the ranks and the command
structure. But a precedent has been
established which could be an omen of
a major reordering of the traditional
chain-of-command authority structure.

Perhaps the *sine qua non* of a

civilian labor force in advanced industrialized societies is collective bargaining of workers. Although trade union-
ism is hardly more than a cloud on the
horizon, there are indirect signs that
such an eventuality may someday come
to pass. The growing labor militancy
of heretofore quiescent public employees at municipal, state, and federal
levels may be a precursor of like activity within a future military. Already
union membership and military career-
ism have proved compatible in the
military establishments of several
Western European countries, notably
Germany and Sweden. Even in the
United States a precedent of sorts is the
situation of full-time National Guards-
men assigned to antimissile installations
who are members of state-employee
unions. There is also the Trotskyist-
influenced American Serviceman's Union (ASU) founded in 1967.[17] The ASU
claimed in 1971 an enlisted membership of 10,000 with representation on
all major military posts. Extremely
ideological and violently hostile toward
career servicemen ("off the lifers" is an
ASU slogan), the ASU's viability as a
genuine trade union is beset by internal
contradictions. Nevertheless, the very
existence of an organization such as the
ASU is indicative of the incipient potential for unionization of the military.

At the professional level, the trend
toward civilianization is even more
apparent. Among active-duty doctors
and lawyers there are manifold indications of greater identity with civilian
professional standards than with those
consonant with military values. (That
the chaplain corps seems less likely to
use their civilian clerical counterparts
as a reference group is worthy of note,
however.) Most notable, at the service
academies the long-term trend has definitely been away from traditional military instruction and toward civilianization of both student bodies and faculty,
for example, less hazing, reduction of
military discipline, more "academic"

courses, and civilian professionalization of the teaching staff.[18]

In brief, there is ample evidence to support the model of the military moving toward convergence with the structures and values of civilian society.[19] This developmental model anticipates a military establishment which will be sharply different from the traditional armed forces. An all-volunteer membership will be attracted to the services largely on the grounds of monetary inducements and work selection in the pattern now found in the civilian marketplace. Some form of democratization of the armed forces will occur, and life styles of military personnel will basically be that of like civilian groups. The military mystique will diminish as the armed services come to resemble other large-scale bureaucracies. The model of the convergent military foresees the culmination of a civilianizing trend that began at least as early as the Second World War and that was given added impetus by the domestic turbulence of the Vietnam War years.

MODEL II: THE DIVERGENT OR TRADITIONAL MILITARY

The conceptual antithesis of the convergent-military model is the developmental construct which emphasizes the increasing differentiation between American military and civilian social organization.[20] Although the consequences of the military buildup for the war in Vietnam somewhat obscure the issue, persuasive evidence can be presented that the generation-long institutional convergence of the armed forces and American society has begun to reverse itself. It appears highly likely that the military in the post-Vietnam era will markedly diverge along a variety of dimensions from the mainstream of developments in the general society. This emerging apartness of the military will reflect society-wide trends as well as indigenous efforts toward institutional autonomy on the part of the armed forces. Some of the more significant indicators of this growing divergence are summarized here.

First, recent evidence shows that starting around the early 1960s the long-term trend toward recruitment of the officer corps from a representative sample of the American population has been reversed. Three measures of the narrowing social base of the officer corps in the past decade are: (a) the overproportionate number of newly commissioned officers coming from rural and small town backgrounds;[21] (b) the pronounced increase in the number of cadets at service academies who come from career military families;[22] and (c) an increasing monopolization of military elite positions by academy graduates.[23]

Second, although the enlisted ranks have always been overrepresentative of working-class youth, the fact remains that the selective service system, directly or indirectly, infused a component of privileged youth into the military's rank and file. The institution of an all-volunteer force will serve to reduce significantly the degree of upper- and middle-class participation in the enlisted ranks. Since the end of World War II, moreover, there has been a discernible and growing discrepancy between the educational levels of officers and enlisted men.[24] (The 1968 decision to draft a higher proportion of college graduates to meet the manpower needs of the Vietnam War can be regarded as only a temporary fluctuation in this trend.) Very likely an all-volunteer enlisted membership coupled with an almost entirely college-educated officer corps will contribute to a more rigid and sharp definition of the caste-like distinction between officers and enlisted men within the military organization of the 1970s.

Third, the transformation of the armed forces from a racially segregated institution (through World War II) into an integrated organization (around the time of the Korean War) was an impressive achievement in directed social change. Although the military did not become a panacea for race relations, it was remarkably free from racial turmoil from the early 1950s through the middle 1960s.[25] It is also the case that the armed forces—as other areas of American life—are increasingly subject to the new challenges of black separatism as well as to the persistence of white racism. Interracial embroilments have become more frequent in recent years and will almost certainly continue to plague the military. Nevertheless, whatever the racial turn of events within the military, the very integration of the armed forces can be viewed as a kind of divergence from a quasi-apartheid civilian society. The military establishment, albeit with internal strife, will remain into the indefinite future the most racially integrated institution in American society.

Fourth, the well known trend toward increasing technical specialization within the military has already reached its maximal point. The end of this trend clearly implies a lessened transferability between military and civilian skills. A careful and detailed analysis of military occupational trends by Harold Wool reveals that the most pronounced shift away from combat and manual labor occupations occurred between 1945 and 1957.[26] Since that time there has been relative stability in the occupational requirements of the armed forces. Moreover, as Wool points out, it is often the technical jobs (e.g., specialized radio operators, warning systems personnel) that are most likely to be automated, thereby indirectly increasing the proportion of combat personnel. The use of civilians in support-type positions can be expected to increase with the advent of an all-volunteer force; again thereby increasing the proportion of traditional military occupations within the regular military organization.

Fifth, there is an indication of an emerging divergence between family patterns of military personnel and civilians. Before the Second World War, the military at the enlisted levels was glaringly indifferent to family needs. In World War II, except for allotment checks, families of servicemen more or less fended for themselves. Starting with the Cold War, however, the military began to take steps to deal with some of the practical problems faced by married servicemen. An array of on-post privileges (e.g., free medical care, PX and commissary privileges, government quarters for married non-coms) were established or expanded to meet the needs of military families. This greater concern for service families on the part of the military became especially evident in the late 1960s. Activities such as the Army's Community Service and the Air Force's Dependents Assistance Program are recent efforts to make available a wide range of services for military families: legal and real estate advice, family counseling, baby-sitting services, employment opportunities for wives, loans of infant furnishings, linen, china, and the like. At the risk of some overstatement, the pre-World War II military might be seen as a total institution encapsulating bachelors, while the post-Vietnam military may well encapsulate the family along with the serviceman husband-father.

The above five factors are only a partial list of indicators supporting the developmental model of a divergent military. Mention can also be made of other parallel indicators. Thus charging the armed forces with welfare and job training programs—along the lines of Project 100,000 and Project Transition—can only lead to greater social distance between officers and the ranks. The continued downgrading of the National Guard and reserve components implies the final demise of the citizen-soldier concept. The further employment of foreign-national troops under direct American command—such as the South Korean troops who today constitute one-sixth of the "American" Eighth Army—would be a paramount indicator of a military force divergent from civilian society.

Perhaps the ultimate indicator of divergence is on the ideological dimension. There is a widespread mood among career officers and noncoms that the armed forces have been made the convenient scapegoat for the war in Vietnam. The mass media, seaboard intelligentsia, and professors of our leading universities are seen as undermining the honor of military service and fostering dissent within the ranks. Although documentation is elusive, the consequence of this has been a spreading defensive reaction within the military community against the nation's cultural elite.[27]

Suffice it to say, there are convincing indicators that the military is undergoing a fundamental turning inward in its relations to the civilian structures and values of American society. With the arrival of an all-volunteer force, the military will find its enlisted membership more compliant to established procedures and a self-selected officer corps more supportive of traditional forms. Without broadly based civilian representation, the leavening effect of recalcitrant servicemen—drafted enlisted men and ROTC officers from prestige campuses—will be no more. It appears that while our civilian institutions are heading toward more participative definition and control, the post-Vietnam military will follow a more conventional and authoritarian social organization. This reversion to tradition may well be the paradoxical quality of the "new" military of the 1970s.

MODEL III: THE SEGMENTED OR PLURALISTIC MILITARY

In somewhat dialectical fashion the two contradictory developmental constructs of the civilianized versus the traditional military can be incorporated into a third formulation—a model of the emergent military as segmented or pluralistic. Such a pluralistic model of the military establishment accommodates and orders the otherwise opposing sets of empirical indicators associated with the civilianized or traditional models. Simply put, the pluralistic military will be both convergent and divergent with civilian society; it will simultaneously display organizational trends which are civilianized and traditional.

It must be stressed, however, that the pluralistic military will not be an alloy of opposing trends but a compartmentalization of these trends. The pluralistic developmental model, that is, does not foresee a homogeneous military somewhere between the civilianized and traditional poles. Rather, the emergent military will be internally segmented into areas which will be either more convergent or more divergent than the present organization of the armed forces. Such a development already characterizes trends between the services. Thus, while the Air Force continues to move toward civilianization and participative control, the Marine Corps announces that it will uphold traditional training procedures and regimentation of personnel. What will be novel in the emergent military, however, is that developments toward segmentation will increasingly characterize intra- as well as inter-military organization.

Traditional and divergent features in the military will become most pronounced in combat forces, labor-intensive support units, and perhaps at senior command levels. Those in the traditional military will continue to cultivate the ideals of soldierly honor and the mystique of the armed forces. A predilection toward non-civilian values will result from the self-recruitment of the junior membership reinforced by the dominant conservatism of career officers and noncoms. Once beyond the first tour of duty, personnel turnover will be very low. The social isolation of such a traditional military will be compounded by its composition, which will be overrepresentative of rural and Southern regions, men coming from the more deprived groups of American society, and sons of military fathers.

Contrarily, the civilianized or convergent features in the military system will accelerate where functions deal with clerical administration, education, medical care, logistics, transportation, construction, and other technical tasks. Those with specialized education or training will be attracted to the service in a civilian rather than a military capacity and will gauge military employment in terms of marketplace standards. Terms of employment will increasingly correspond to those of strictly civilian enterprises. Lateral entry into the military system, already the case for professionals, will gradually extend to skilled workers and even menial laborers. Concomitantly, there will be a relaxation of procedures required to leave the military. The social composition of such a civilianized military will resemble that of those performing equivalent roles in the larger economy. In all likelihood the present less-than-two percent female representation in the armed forces will increase substantially.

From an institutional standpoint, the segmented or pluralistic military will require new organizational forms. The range of such alternative forms can only be sketched here. But as a minimal requirement there must be some structure which will embrace variegated personnel policies, diverse systems of military justice and discipline, and differing work ethos. Indeed,

the antinomies between the civilianized and traditional conceptions of the military may be so great as to prohibit a conventional armed forces establishment. There may develop "two militaries," each organized along entirely different premises. In this format the civilianized military might come to encompass a host of nonmilitary goals, for example, job training, restoring ecologically devastated resources, performing services of health care.[28] Another possible alternative may follow the Canadian pattern where armed forces unification has resulted in a complete separation of support and administrative functions from the combat arms (now referred to as "land, sea, and air environments," in Canadian nomenclature).

Our task here, however, is not to forecast the precise shape of the pluralistic military but rather to define the constants which will determine the emergent military establishment. Most likely, the armed forces of the United States will keep their overall present framework but will bifurcate internally along civilianized and traditional lines.[29] The traditional or divergent sector will stress customary modes of military organization. In the case of the Army this could entail a revival of the old regimental system. At the same time there will be a convergent sector which operates on principles common to civil administration and corporate structures. Contemporary examples of such organization are metropolitan police forces, the Army Corps of Engineers, and the Coast Guard.

THE EMERGENT MILITARY AND AMERICAN SOCIETY

Developmental analysis serves to steer the social researcher between the Charybdis of unordered data and the Scylla of unsubstantiated conjecture as to future social reality. It was with this purpose that three alternative developmental constructs of the military were

presented—civilianized, traditional, and pluralistic. And it was the pluralistic or segmented model which seemed to correspond most closely with contemporary trends in emergent military organization.

Ultimately, the implications of

each of these models must be assessed for the civil polity and the internal viability of the armed forces. A predominantly civilianized military could easily lose that élan so necessary for the functioning of a military organization. A military force uniformly moving toward more recognition of individual rights and less rigidity in social control would in all likelihood seriously disaffect career personnel while making military service only marginally more palatable to its resistant members. A predominantly traditional military, on the other hand, would most likely be incapable of either maintaining the organization at its required complexity, or attracting the kind of membership necessary for effective performance. More ominous, a traditional military in a rapidly changing society could develop anti-civilian values tearing the basic fabric of democratic ideology.

It is the pluralistic model—with its compartmentalized segments—of the military which seems to offer the best promise of an armed force which will maintain organizational effectiveness as well as consonance in the main with civilian values. Indeed, the model of an emergent military with intra-institutional pluralism may have broader applicability to the framework of the larger social system. Our American society seems to be moving toward a future which is neither a rigid maintenance of the old order, nor an all encompassing bureaucracy, nor a "greening" of the country. Rather, new forms of voluntarism and counter-culture will coexist with persisting large-scale organizations and established values. In the last analysis, the developmental model of a kind of split-level pluralism may well be the defining quality of the emergent American society.

NOTES

1. Kurt Lang, "Technology and Career Management in the Military Establishment," in Morris Janowitz, ed., *The New Military* (New York: Russell Sage Foundation, 1964), pp. 39–81.

2. Harry A. Marmion, *The Case Against a Volunteer Army* (Chicago: Quadrangle Books, 1971).

3. *The Report of the President's Commission on an All-Volunteer Armed Force* ("Gates Commission") (New York: Macmillan, 1970), pp. 15–16.

4. Gary R. Nelson and Catherine Armington, *Military and Civilian Earnings Alternatives for Enlisted Men in the Army*, Research Paper P–662 (Arlington, Va.: Institute for Defense Analyses, 1970). See also K. H. Kim, Susan Farrell, and Ewan Clague, *The All-Volunteer Army: An Analysis of Demand and Supply* (New York: Praeger, 1971).

5. *President's Commission, op. cit.*, p. 168.

6. Gordon Lee, "Britain's Professionals," *Army* (July 1971), pp. 28–33.

7. *Ibid.*, p. 31.

8. In this regard, a 1969 survey based on a representative national sample of high school male students found an amazingly high 16 to 25 percent who said they would volunteer for the armed forces, given no draft and no war. Jerome Johnston and Jerald G. Bachman, *Young Men Look at Military Service* (Ann Arbor, Mich.: Institute for Social Research, June 1970).

9. Most of the discussion given here on the probable changes in the social background of the officer corps in an all-volunteer force is a paraphrase of Morris Janowitz, "The Emergent Military," in Charles C. Moskos, Jr., ed., *Public Opinion and the Military Establishment* (Beverly Hills, Calif.: Sage Publications, 1971), pp. 261–62.

10. Erwin Häckel, "Military Manpower and Political Purpose," *Adelphi Papers*, No. 72 (London: Institute for Strategic Studies, 1970). This is an excellent comparative analysis of recruitment and retention policies in Western military systems.

11. Heinz Eulau, "H. D. Lasswell's Developmental Analysis," *The Western Political Quarterly*, 11 (June 1958), 229–42.

12. For a somewhat different formulation of the variables involved in a convergent-divergent model of the armed forces and society, see Albert D. Biderman and Laure M. Sharp, "The Convergence of Military and Civilian Occupational Structures Evidence from Studies of Military Retired Employment," *American Journal of Sociology*, 73 (January 1968), 383.

13. C. Wright Mills, *The Power Elite* (New York: Oxford University Press, 1956). Similar analyses are found in Fred Cook, *The*

Warfare State (New York: Macmillan, 1962); and Tristram Coffin, *The Armed Society* (Baltimore: Penguin Books, 1964). See also the more recent John Kenneth Galbraith, *How to Control the Military* (New York: Signet, 1969); Sidney Lens, *The Military-Industrial Complex* (Philadelphia: Pilgrim Press, 1970); and Seymour Melman, *Pentagon Capitalism* (New York: McGraw-Hill, 1970).

14. Samuel P. Huntington, *The Soldier and the State* (Cambridge, Mass.: Harvard University Press, 1957); and Gene M. Lyons and John W. Masland, *Education and Military Leadership* (Princeton, N.J.: Princeton University Press, 1959). For more recent statements on changing military roles, see Ritchie P. Lowry, "To Arms: Changing Military Roles and the Military-Industrial Complex," *Social Problems*, 18 (Summer 1970), 3–16; Robert G. Gard, Jr., "The Military and American Society," *Foreign Affairs*, 49 (July 1971), 698–710; and Sam C. Sarkesian, "Political Soldiers: Perspectives on Professionalism in the U.S. Military," paper presented at the annual meetings of the American Political Science Association, 1970, Los Angeles.

15. Morris Janowitz, *The Professional Soldier* (New York: Free Press, 1960).

16. U.S. Department of the Army, *Project Volunteer in Defense of the Nation*, Executive Summary (Washington, D.C.: Office, Deputy Chief of Staff for Personnel, 1969).

17. An account of the founding of the ASU by its chairman is Andy Stapp, *Up Against the Brass* (New York: Simon and Schuster, 1970).

18. Laurence I. Radway, "Recent Trends at American Service Academies," in Moskos, ed., *Public Opinion, op. cit.*, pp. 3–35.

19. For additional references to the thesis that the military system will increasingly converge with civilian society, see Anthony L. Wermuth, *The Impact of Changing Values on Military Organization and Personnel* (Waltham, Mass.: Westinghouse Electric Corporation, Advanced Studies Group, 1970).

20. Among sociologists of the military, the view stressing the divergence of the emergent military from civilian society has perhaps been most forcefully argued in my own previous writings. See Charles C. Moskos, Jr., *The American Enlisted Man* (New York: Russell Sage Foundation, 1970), pp. 166–82. As is apparent in the conclusions of this paper, this is a position I have now come to abandon.

21. Radway, *op. cit.*

22. Janowitz, "The Emergent Military," *op. cit.*

23. David R. Segal, "Selective Promotion in Officer Cohorts," *The Sociological Quarterly*, 8 (Spring 1967), 199–206.

24. Moskos, *American Enlisted Man, op. cit.*, p. 196.

25. *Ibid.*, pp. 108–33.

26. Harold Wool, *The Military Specialist* (Baltimore: Johns Hopkins Press, 1968).

27. For perceptive journalistic accounts of growing military estrangement from civilian political and social attitudes, see Ward Just, *Military Men* (New York: Knopf, 1970); and H. Paul Jeffers and Dick Levitan, *See Parris and Die: Brutality in the U.S. Marines* (New York: Hawthorn, 1971).

28. Such a role expansion of the armed services into nonmilitary endeavors is outlined in Albert D. Biderman, "Transforming Military Forces for Broad National Service," paper presented at the Russell Sage Foundation conference on "Youth and National Service," New York, March 1971.

29. In August 1971, the Department of the Army announced that soldiers will henceforth be unable to "hopscotch" across military occupational specialties. *Army Times*, August 11, 1971, p. 4. Policies such as these are direct indicators of the move toward a more segmented military.

Power, Professionalism, and Ideology: Civil-Military Relations in Theory

SAMUEL P. HUNTINGTON

THE VARIETIES OF CIVILIAN CONTROL

The role of the military in society has been frequently discussed in terms of "civilian control."[1] Yet this concept has never been satisfactorily defined. Presumably, civilian control has something to do with the relative power of civilian and military groups. Presumably, also, civilian control is achieved to the extent to which the power of military groups is reduced. Consequently, the basic problem in defining civilian control is: How can military power be minimized? In general, two broad answers exist.

SUBJECTIVE CIVILIAN CONTROL: MAXIMIZING CIVILIAN POWER

The simplest way of minimizing military power would appear to be the maximizing of the power of civilian groups in relation to the military. The large number, varied character, and conflicting interests of civilian groups, however, make it impossible to maximize their power as a whole with respect to the military. Consequently, the maximizing of civilian power always means the maximizing of the power of some particular civilian group or groups. This is subjective civilian control. The general concept of civilian control is identified with the specific interests of one or more civilian groups. Consequently, subjective civilian control involves the power relations among civilian groups. It is advanced by one civilian group as a means to enhance its power at the expense of other civilian groups. It thus becomes an instrumental slogan like "states' rights" rather than an end in itself. Just as the banner of states' rights is normally raised by economic groups which have more power at the state than at the national level in struggles with other groups which have more power in the national government, so the slogan of civilian control is utilized by groups which lack power over the military forces in struggles with other civilian groups which have such power. Like states' rights, civilian control may cover a variety of sins. It is always necessary to ask which civilians are to do the controlling. Except very recently in western society, civilian control has existed only in this subjective sense. Subjective civilian control is, indeed, the only form of civilian control possible in the absence of a professional officer corps. In its various historical manifestations, subjective civilian control has been identified with the maximization of the power of particular governmental institutions, particular social classes, and particular constitutional forms.

CIVILIAN CONTROL BY GOVERNMENTAL INSTITUTION

In the seventeenth and eighteenth centuries in England and America the military forces were generally under the control of the Crown, and the slogan "civilian control" was adopted by the parliamentary groups as a means of increasing their power vis-à-vis the Crown. Since the king, however, was just as civilian as they were, what they actually wanted was to maximize parliamentary control over the armed forces rather than civilian control in general. And parliamentary control was sought, not as a means of reducing the power of the military but as a way of curtailing the power of the king. At the present time, in the United States, Congress and the President engage in a comparable struggle. The Chief Executive identifies civilian control with presidential control—Congress is too large and poorly organized to control the military forces effectively. Congress, on the other hand, identifies civilian control with congressional control—Congress is closer to the people than the President who is likely to become the prisoner of his military advisers. But both Congress and President are fundamentally concerned with the distribution of power between executive and legislative rather than between civilian and military.

CIVILIAN CONTROL BY SOCIAL CLASS

In the eighteenth and nineteenth centuries the European aristocracy and bourgeoisie struggled for control of the military forces. Each class attempted to identify civilian control with its own interests. Since the aristocracy generally dominated the military forces, however, the liberal bourgeois groups made the greatest use of the slogan and identified aristocratic control with military control. Military institutions merely furnished one battleground for the struggle between the two classes which permeated all areas of society; the issue was simply whether aristocratic or liberal interests were to prevail in the armed forces.

CIVILIAN CONTROL BY CONSTITUTIONAL FORM

A broader application of this same identification of civilian control with a particular civilian interest occurs when the claim is made that only a specific constitutional form—usually democracy—can insure civilian control. Civilian control is identified with democratic government, military control with absolute or totalitarian government. In democratic countries, it is argued, policy is determined by persuasion and compromise; in absolutist countries it is determined by force and coercion (or at least the implied threat of force or coercion). Hence, the military, who control the most powerful instrument of violence, will be more powerful in totalitarian countries than in democratic ones. Actually, however, this argument is not necessarily true. In a democratic country, the military may undermine civilian control and acquire great political power through the legitimate processes and institutions of democratic government and politics (for example, the United States in World War II). In a totalitarian regime, on the other hand, the power of the military may be reduced by breaking the officer corps up into competing units, establishing party armies and special military forces (Waffen-SS and MVD), infiltrating the military hierarchy with independent chains of command (political commissars), and similar techniques. Terror, conspiracy, surveillance, and force are the methods of government in a totalitarian state; terror, conspiracy, surveillance, and force are the means by which the civilians in such a state control their armed forces. If employed sufficiently ruthlessly, these means may virtually eliminate military political power (for example, Germany in World War II). Subjective civilian control thus is not the monopoly of any particular constitutional system.

The rise of the military profession

transformed the problem of civil-military relations, complicating the efforts of civilian groups to maximize their power over the military. Such groups were now confronted not only with other civilian groups with similar goals but also with new, independent, functional military imperatives. The continued assertion of the particular forms of subjective civilian control required that these imperatives be either denied or transformed. If this could not be done, civilian control in the subjective sense became impossible. Some new principle was needed to govern the relations between the functional military imperatives and the rest of society. So long as civilian control was simply an instrumental value of particular civilian groups, it was, of course, impossible to secure general agreement as to its meaning. Each group defined it as a distribution of power favorable to its own interests. This explains the peculiar historical fact that, although civilian control was regularly invoked in politics and frequently written about in the eighteenth and nineteenth centuries, it was, nonetheless, never satisfactorily defined. The rise of the military profession, however, while making the particular forms of subjective civilian control obsolete, also made possible a new and more meaningful definition of civilian control.

OBJECTIVE CIVILIAN CONTROL: MAXIMIZING MILITARY PROFESSIONALISM

Civilian control in the objective sense is the maximizing of military professionalism. More precisely, it is that distribution of political power between military and civilian groups which is most conducive to the emergence of professional attitudes and behavior among the members of the officer corps. Objective civilian control is thus directly opposed to subjective civilian control. Subjective civilian control achieves its end by civilianizing the military, making them the mirror of the state. Objective civilian control achieves its end by militarizing the military, making them the tool of the state. Subjective civilian control exists in a variety of forms, objective civilian control in only one. The antithesis of objective civilian control is military participation in politics: civilian control decreases as the military become progressively involved in institutional, class, and constitutional politics. Subjective civilian control, on the other hand, presupposes this involvement. The essence of objective civilian control is the recognition of autonomous military professionalism; the essence of subjective civilian control is the denial of an independent military sphere. Historically, the demand for objective control has come from the military profession, the demand for subjective control from the multifarious civilian groups anxious to maximize their power in military affairs.

The one prime essential for any system of civilian control is the minimizing of military power. Objective civilian control achieves this reduction by professionalizing the military, by rendering them politically sterile and neutral. This produces the lowest possible level of military political power with respect to all civilian groups. At the same time it preserves that essential element of power which is necessary for the existence of a military profession. A highly professional officer corps stands ready to carry out the wishes of any civilian group which secures legitimate authority within the state. In effect, this sets definite limits to military political power without reference to the distribution of political power among the various civilian groups. Any further reduction of military power beyond the point where professionalism is maximized only redounds to the benefit of some particular civilian group and only serves to enhance the power of that group in its struggles with other civilian groups. The distribution of political power

554 SAMUEL P. HUNTINGTON

which most facilitates military professionalism is thus also the lowest point to which military power can be reduced without playing favorites among civilian groups. Because of this, the objective definition of civilian control furnishes a single concrete standard of civilian control which is politically neutral and which all social groups can recognize. It elevates civilian control from a political slogan masking group interests to an analytical concept independent of group perspectives.

The subjective definition of civilian control presupposes a conflict between civilian control and the needs of military security. This was generally recognized by adherents of particular civilian groups who commonly asserted that continued military insecurity made civilian control impossible. By this they simply meant that intensified security threats result in increased military imperatives against which it becomes more difficult to assert civilian power. The steps necessary to achieve military security are thus viewed as undermining civilian control. On the other hand, the effort to enhance civilian control in the subjective sense frequently undermined military security. Because they did not, for instance, recognize the existence of a separate military profession with its own outlook on national policy, civilian groups frequently assumed that the reduction of military power was necessary to preserve peace. This decrease in the power of the military, however, often resulted in increased power for much more bellicose civilian groups. Consequently those civilian groups which tried to minimize the risks of war by reducing the power of the military frequently encouraged exactly what they were attempting to avoid. It is hardly coincidental that the years immediately prior to World War II saw the systematic reduction of the political power of the military in all the future belligerents except Japan, or that the temperature of the Cold War seems to vary inversely with the political power of the generals in the Soviet Union. If civilian control is defined in the objective sense, however, no conflict exists between it and the goal of military security. Indeed, just the reverse is true. Objective civilian control not only reduces the power of the military to the lowest possible level vis-à-vis all civilian groups, it also maximizes the likelihood of achieving military security.

The achievement of objective civilian control has only been possible, of course, since the emergence of the military profession. Subjective civilian control is fundamentally out of place in any society in which the division of labor has been carried to the point where there emerges a distinct class of specialists in the management of violence. The achievement of objective civilian control, however, has been hampered by the tendency of many civilian groups still to conceive of civilian control in subjective terms. Like nineteenth-century aristocrats and bourgeoisie, or twentieth-century French constitutional factions, they are unwilling simply to accept a politically neutral officer corps. They continue to insist upon the subordination of the officer corps to their own interests and principles. Consequently a high level of objective civilian control has been a rare phenomenon even among modern western societies.

THE TWO LEVELS OF CIVIL-MILITARY RELATIONS

What conditions are likely to maximize military professionalism and objective civilian control? The answer depends upon the relation between the two levels of civil-military relations. On the power level, the key issue is the power of the officer corps relative to civilian groups within society. On the ideological level, the key issue is the compatibility of the professional military ethic with the political ideologies prevailing in society. On the one hand, criteria are needed by which to measure military and civilian power. On the other hand, some notion is required as to where the professional military ethic fits into the spectrum of political opinion.

THE OFFICER CORPS AND POLITICAL POWER

Power is the capacity to control the behavior of other people.[2] A power relationship has at least two dimensions: the degree or amount of power, that is, the extent to which a particular type of behavior of one person is controlled by another; and, secondly, the scope or locus of power, that is, the types of behavior which are influenced by the other individual or group. The relations between any two people or groups normally involve the exercise of power in both directions although in all probability in somewhat different if overlapping loci. Power exists in two forms, formal authority and informal influence, both of which may be measured in terms of their degree and scope. Formal authority involves the control of one person over the behavior of another on the basis of their respective positions in a defined social structure. Authority does not inhere in the individual but is an attribute of status and position. Authority, consequently, is ordered, structured, or legitimate power. It is a continuing pattern of relationships which remains relatively constant through successive changes in the individuals involved in the relationships. Its exercise has the sanction of constitution, statute, bylaws, decree, or long accepted custom. It is a truism of politics that formal authority tells only part of the story of power. Informal relationships also exist where one person, or group of persons, controls the behavior of other persons not because they occupy particular positions in a formal structure, but because they control other sanctions or rewards.

This influence may stem from personality, wealth, knowledge, prestige, friendship, kinship, or a variety of other sources. Its distinguishing characteristic, however, is always that it inheres in specific individuals or groups, not in the roles or statuses which those individuals or groups occupy.

AUTHORITY

In analyzing the pattern of authority in civil-military relations the key criteria are the relative level, the relative unity, and the relative scope of the authority of the military and civilian groups. The higher the level of authority of a group, the greater the unity of its structure, and the broader the scope of its authority, the more powerful it will be.

The level of authority refers to the position which the group occupies in the hierarchy of governmental authority. Vertical control is exercised over the military to the extent that they are reduced to subordinate levels of authority. The level of authority of the officer corps is maximized if it is placed at the peak of the hierarchy and the other institutions of government are subordinate to it: if, in other words, it or its leaders exercise military sovereignty. A level of somewhat less authority exists if the military do not possess authority over other institutions, and no other institutions possess authority over them. In this case, two parallel structures of authority exist; one military and one civil. This situation is military independence. Thirdly, the officer corps may be subordinate to only one other institution possessing effective final authority. In other words, the officer corps has direct access to the sovereign. After this, the officer corps might gradually be further subordinated in the governmental structure. Such subordination, however, is generally not carried very far and usually only one level of authority is interspersed between the officer corps and the sovereign. Since this one level is normally in the form of a civilian departmental minister, this level of military authority may be called ministerial control.

The unity of authority refers to the extent to which a given group is structurally unified with relation to another group. A monopolist possesses advantages in dealing with a large number of firms on the other side of the market place. So also, a group which is structurally united possesses great advantages in dealing with a group which is structurally disunited. If the officer corps is originally divided into land, sea, and air elements, and then is unified under the leadership of a single, overall staff and military commander in chief, this change will tend to increase its authority with regard to other institutions of government. It will speak with one voice instead of three. Other groups will not be able to play off one portion of the officer corps against another.

Thirdly, the scope of authority refers to the variety and type of values with respect to which the group is formally authorized to exercise power. The authority of military groups, for instance, is normally limited to military matters. If the chiefs of staff were also authorized to advise the government with respect to agricultural subsidies, the scope of their authority would be significantly expanded. Horizontal civilian control is exercised against the military to the extent that they are confined within a limited scope by the parallel activities of civilian agencies or groups roughly at the same level of authority in the government.

INFLUENCE

The political influence of a group and its leaders is even more difficult to judge than their formal authority. Four rough indices exist, however, by which the influence of the officer corps may be evaluated.

(1) The group affiliations of the officer corps and its leaders. One test of

the influence of a group is the extent and nature of its affiliations with other powerful groups and individuals. For the officer corps these affiliations are generally of three types. First, preservice affiliations arise from the activities of officers before they enter the officer corps. If the bulk of the officers are drawn from a particular social class or geographical section, this may be assumed to enhance the influence of the corps with that class or section. Secondly, officers may develop inservice affiliations in the course of their military duties, as for example, special ties with congressional committees, or with those industries whose products are consumed by the armed services. Finally, postservice affiliations may reflect a general pattern of officer activities after leaving the corps. If, for instance, officers upon retirement normally entered into a particular type of work, or settled in a particular part of the country, this would also presumably increase the influence of the officer corps in those segments of society.

(2) The economic and human resources subject to the authority of the officer corps and its leaders. The larger the proportion of the national product devoted to military purposes, and the larger the number of individuals serving with the armed services in either a civilian or military capacity, the greater will be the influence of the officer corps and its leaders. An increase or decrease in the resources subject to military authority, however, need not involve any change in that authority itself. The level, unity, and scope of military authority may well remain constant throughout changes in the resources subject to military control.

(3) The hierarchical interpenetration of the officer corps and other groups. Military influence is increased if members of the officer corps assume positions of authority in nonmilitary power structures. Military influence is decreased to the extent that nonmilitary individuals penetrate into positions

within the formally defined officer corps.

(4) Prestige and popularity of the officer corps and its leaders. The standing of the officer corps and its leaders with public opinion and the attitudes of broad sections or categoric groups in society toward the military obviously are key elements in determining military influence.

These four factors will help give some index of the political influence of the military. The more or less quantitative extent of these relationships indicates the degree of military political influence. The specific content and nature of the relationships furnish some idea of the locus of military influence. For instance, an increase in the total number of military men occupying positions of authority in the normally civilian branches of government warrants a conclusion as to an increase in the degree of military influence. The specific type of agency in which the military men are working would lead to conclusions as to the locus of this increased influence: they might all be in the foreign affairs department or they might be scattered generally throughout the government.

THE PROFESSIONAL ETHIC AND POLITICAL IDEOLOGIES

Just as there is a variety of civilian groups engaged in the struggle for power, so also is there a variety of civilian ethics or ideologies. Consequently, it is impossible to assume a continuum stretching from military values at one end to civilian values at the other. The military ethic is concrete, permanent, and universal. The term "civilian" on the other hand, merely refers to what is nonmilitary. No dichotomy exists between the "military mind" and the "civilian mind" because there is no single "civilian mind." There are many "civilian minds," and the difference between any two civilian ethics may be greater than the difference between any one of them and the military ethic.

Consequently, the military ethic can only be compared with particular civilian ethics. In this analysis, it will be compared with four manifestations of one species of civilian ethic—the political ideology. A political ideology is a set of values and attitudes oriented about the problems of the state. The ideologies which will be compared with the military ethic are four which have been among the most significant in western culture: liberalism, fascism, Marxism, and conservatism.[3] Each ideology will be considered generally and abstractly, independent of its specific historical manifestations. The point at issue in each case is the extent to which the ideology, viewed as a system of ideas, is compatible with or hostile to the military ethic.

LIBERALISM

The heart of liberalism is individualism. It emphasizes the reason and moral dignity of the individual and opposes political, economic, and social restraints upon individual liberty. In contrast, the military ethic holds that man is evil, weak, and irrational and that he must be subordinated to the group. The military man claims that the natural relation among men is conflict; the liberal believes that the natural relation is peace. Liberalism holds that the application of reason may produce a harmony of interests. For the liberal, success in any enterprise depends upon the maximum release of individual energies; for the military man it depends upon subordination and specialization. The liberal glorifies self-expression; the military man obedience. Liberalism rejects the organic theory of society. In contrast to the military view, liberalism holds that human nature is pliable and may be improved through education and proper social institutions. The liberal normally believes in progress and minimizes the significance of history. Man is more likely to find solutions to his political problems by consulting his reason than by examining his experience.

The military man emphasizes the importance of power in human relations; liberalism normally either denies the existence of power, minimizes its importance, or castigates it as inherently evil. Liberalism tends to assume the existence of that very national security which the military man considers to be continually threatened. Liberal thinking has been largely concerned with economics and economic welfare and has opposed large military forces, balance of power diplomacy, and military alliances. Liberalism believes that the way to peace is through institutional devices such as international law, international courts, and international organization. Liberalism has many pacifist tendencies, but the liberal will normally support a war waged to further liberal ideals. War as an instrument of national policy is immoral; war on behalf of universally true principles of justice and freedom is not. The liberal thus opposes war in general but frequently supports it in particular, while the military man accepts war in the abstract but opposes its specific manifestations.

Liberalism is generally hostile to armaments and standing armies. They are a threat both to peace and to constitutional government. If military organization is necessary, it must be military organization reflecting liberal principles. Civilian control in liberalism means the embodiment of liberal ideas in military institutions. The military professionals are held to be backward, incompetent, and neglectful of the importance of economics, morale, and ideology. National defense is the responsibility of all, not just a few. If war becomes necessary, the state must fight as a "nation in arms" relying on popular militias and citizen armies.

FASCISM

The military ethic and fascism are similar in some respects but they have one fundamental difference. What the military man accepts as the facts of existence to be wrestled with as effectively as possible, the fascist glorifies as the supreme values of existence. The military man sees struggle inherent in human relations; the fascist glorifies struggle as the highest activity of man. The military ethic accepts the nation state as an independent unit; fascism hails the state or the party as the embodiment of moral virtue, the ultimate source of morality. While military thinking accepts war, fascist thinking romanticizes war and violence. The military man recognizes the necessity and uses of power; the fascist worships power as an end in itself. The military ethic recognizes the necessity of leadership and discipline in human society; fascism emphasizes the supreme power and ability of the leader, and the absolute duty of subordination to his will.

The fascist and the military views on human nature and history differ widely. In opposition to military emphasis upon the universality of human traits, the fascist believes in the natural superiority of a chosen people or race and in the inherent genius and supreme virtue of the leader. Military thinking, on the other hand, is skeptical of everybody. While the military man learns from history and the liberal relies on reason, the fascist stresses intuition. He has little use or need for ordered knowledge and practical, empirical realism. He celebrates the triumph of the Will over external obstacles. In this respect, fascism is more individualistic than liberalism and more removed from the military ethic with its emphasis upon the limitations of human nature.

Unlike liberalism, fascism willingly supports the maintenance of strong military forces. While the liberal will fight for ideals and the military man for the security of the state, the fascist fights in order to fight. War is the end not the instrument of politics. In contrast to the cautious, unbelligerent foreign policy of the military man, the fascist advocates a dynamic, aggressive, revolutionary policy with the avowed aims of conflict and the expansion of the power of the state to its ultimate limit. The fascist believes in the internal subordination of all other social institutions to state or party. The military profession itself must have the proper ideological coloring. While fascism does not go as far as liberalism in imposing extraneous forms on military institutions, it is even more hostile to the existence of any potential sources of power apart from the state. Like liberalism, fascism believes in total war, mass armies, and that it is the duty of every citizen to be a soldier.

MARXISM

The Marxist view of man is fundamentally opposed to the military view of man. For the Marxist, man is basically good and rational; he is corrupted by evil institutions. He is naturally at peace with his fellow men. This was his condition before the beginning of history. This will be his condition when the dialectical processes grind to a halt. While Marxist thought denies the existence of fundamental distinctions among men, at the present stage in history it views the proletarian as more progressive than other classes. Like the military man, the Marxist is a careful student of history. While there is a cyclical element in the constant repetition of thesis, antithesis, and synthesis, the basic course of history is linear and progressive. Like the military man, the Marxist sees struggle throughout, but unlike him he sees only class struggle. While the military man recognizes the role of chance and human freedom in history, the Marxist holds that all significant events are determined by economic forces. The Marxist view of history is monistic, while the military view is pluralistic. The Marxist also differs from the military man in his faith that history will come to an end with the realization of a more or less utopian society.

Both Marxism and the military ethic recognize the importance of power and groups in human affairs. The Marxist, however, stresses the importance of economic power, whereas the military man holds with Machiavelli to the superiority of the sword. For the Marxist the basic group is the class—mankind is cut horizontally; for the military man, the basic group is the nation state—mankind is cut vertically. Indeed, Marxism denies the reality of the state as a reflection of group unity, holding that it is merely an instrument of class warfare. While the military ethic recognizes that states will go to war for many reasons, it stresses the concerns of power and security. To the Marxist economic imperialism is the basis of interstate wars. The only wars which he can sanction are class wars, and the only military forces which he can approve are class instruments. He does not recognize universal military values and forms; the character of every military force is determined by the class interests for which it is fighting. He is favorably disposed towards a military force organized upon "proletarian" lines and opposing capitalist interests. Like liberalism, therefore, Marxism insists upon the patterning of military institutions upon nonmilitary ideas.

CONSERVATISM

Unlike liberalism, Marxism, and fascism, conservatism is basically similar to the military ethic.[4] Indeed, it was found appropriate to designate the military ethic as one of conservative realism. In its theories of man, society, and history, its recognition of the role of power in human relations, its acceptance of existing institutions, its limited goals, and its distrust of grand designs, conservatism is at one with the military ethic. Most importantly, conservatism, unlike the other three ideologies, is not monistic and universalistic. It does not attempt to apply the same ideas to all problems and all human institutions. It permits a variety of goals and values. Consequently, conservatism alone of the four ideologies is not driven by its own logic to an inevitable conflict with the military values which stem from the demands of the military function. It alone has no political-ideological pattern to impose on military institutions. While inherent contrast and conflict exist between the military ethic and liberalism, fascism, and Marxism, inherent similarity and compatibility exist between the military ethic and conservatism.

THE EQUILIBRIUM OF OBJECTIVE CIVILIAN CONTROL

The distribution of power between civilian and military groups which maximizes military professionalism and objective civilian control varies with the compatibility between the ideology prevailing in society and the professional military ethic. If the ideology is inherently antimilitary (such as liberalism, fascism, or Marxism), the military acquire substantial political power only by sacrificing their professionalism and adhering to the values and attitudes dominant within the community. In such an antimilitary society, military professionalism and civilian control are maximized by the military's renouncing authority and influence and leading a weak, isolated existence, divorced from the general life of society. In a society dominated by an ideology favorable to the military viewpoint, on the other hand, military power may be increased to a much greater extent without becoming incompatible with a high level of professionalism. The realization of objective civilian control thus depends upon the achievement of an appropriate equilibrium between the power of the military and the ideology of society.

The concessions which the military make in order to acquire power in an unsympathetic society are just one example of the general phenomenon of the ameliorating and diluting effects of power. It is a truism that power melts principle and that those who hold to definite, dogmatic, and rigid value systems are excluded from power in a pluralistic society. Only he who is flexible, willing to adjust, and ready to compromise can win widespread support: power is always to be purchased for a price. The price which the military have to pay for power depends upon the extent of the gap between the military ethic and the prevailing ideologies of the society. The effect which the acquisition of power in a nonconservative society has upon military men is similar to the sobering effects that the acquisition of power has upon radicals. Michels remarks at one point in his *Political Parties* that "Socialists may triumph but never socialism." The same is true with the military in an unsympathetic society. The generals and admirals may triumph but not the professional military ethic. The taming effect of political power makes them good liberals, good fascists, or good communists, but poor professionals. The satisfactions of professional performance and adherence to the professional code are replaced by the satisfactions of power, office, wealth, popularity, and the approbation of nonmilitary groups.

In most societies the relation among power, professionalism, and ideology is a dynamic one, reflecting shifts in the relative power of groups, changing currents of opinions and thought, and varying threats to national security. The maintenance of that equilibrium between power and ideology which constitutes objective civilian control is obviously difficult at best. Any profession experiences a tension between its inherent professional aspirations and the extraneous politics in which it may become involved. The military profession, because of its crucial significance to society as well as the vast power which it must wield when the state is threatened, manifests this tension to a higher degree than most other professional bodies. An element of tragic necessity exists in this relationship. Professional success breeds its own downfall by stimulating political involvement. Nonetheless, the professional man who pursues the values of professional competence and obedience and the political man who pursues power as an end in itself are two distinct types. Yet elements of both exist in most human beings and in every group. The tension between the two, consequently, can never be removed; it can only be ordered so as to make it more or less endurable.

Antimilitary ideologies have flourished in western societies, and the demands of military security, or simply the desire for power, have forced many military individuals and groups to play dominant roles in their governments. They have only been able to do this, however, by surrendering their professional outlook. Yet because these military individuals and groups have been the most prominent and politically involved military men, their attitudes have frequently been assumed by nonmilitary groups to be typical of military thinking. Thus, deviant, nonmilitary military men such as De Gaulle, Ludendorff, and MacArthur are often considered to be representative examples of the "military mind." Actually, such men in their political roles express values stemming from nonmilitary sources.

THE PATTERNS OF CIVIL-MILITARY RELATIONS

The general relations among power, professionalism, and ideology make possible five different ideal types of civil-military relations.[5] These are, of course, ideals and extremes; in actual practice the civil-military relations of any society combines elements of two or more. Three of the five types permit a high degree of professionalism and objective civilian control; two presuppose low professionalism and subjective civilian control.

(1) Antimilitary ideology, high military political power, and low military professionalism. This type of civil-military relations generally is found in more primitive countries where military professionalism has been retarded or in more advanced countries when security threats are suddenly intensified and the military rapidly increase their political power. The export of the institutions and ethics of military professionalism from western Europe to other countries has been as difficult as the export of the institutions of constitutional democracy. Consequently in the Near East, Asia, and Latin America this type of civil-military relations has tended to prevail. Only with great difficulty have nations such as Turkey removed their officers from politics and cultivated professional behavior and outlook. Japan is the only major power to maintain this pattern of civil-military relations over a long period of time. It was, however, also characteristic of Germany during World War I and of the United States in World War II.

(2) Antimilitary ideology, low military political power, and low military professionalism. This combination of elements only appears where the ideology of society is so intensely pursued that it is impossible for the military to escape its influence no matter how far they reduce their political power. Civil-military relations in modern totalitarian states may tend toward this type, a close approximation to it being achieved in Germany during World War II.

(3) Antimilitary ideology, low military political power, and high military professionalism. A society which suffers few threats to its security is likely to have this type of civil-military rela-

tions. Historically, this pattern prevailed in the United States from the rise of military professionalism after the Civil War until the beginning of World War II.

(4) Promilitary ideology, high military political power, and high military professionalism. A society with continuing security threats and an ideology sympathetic to military values may permit a high level of military political power and yet still maintain military professionalism and objective civilian control. Probably the outstanding achievement of this variety of civil-military relations was by Prussia and Germany during the Bismarckian-Moltkean epoch (1860–1890).

(5) Promilitary ideology, low military political power, and high military professionalism. This type might be expected in a society relatively safe from security threats and dominated by a conservative or other ideology sympathetic to the military viewpoint. Civil-military relations in twentieth-century Britain have, to some extent, tended to be of this type.

NOTES

1. For other theoretical analyses of civil-military relations, see Alexis de Tocqueville, *Democracy in America*, vol. II, bk. 3, chs. 22–26; Gaetano Mosca, *The Ruling Class* (New York, 1939), ch. 9; Karl Mannheim, *Freedom, Power, and Democratic Planning* (New York, 1950), pp. 127–131; Stanislaw Andrzejewski, *Military Organization and Society* (London, 1954); Morris Janowitz, "The Professional Soldier and Political Power: A Theoretical Orientation and Selected Hypotheses" (Bureau of Government, Institute of Public Administration, Univ. of Michigan, 1953; mimeo.); Burton Sapin, Richard C. Snyder, and H. W. Bruck, *An Appropriate Role for the Military in American Foreign Policy-Making: A Research Note* (Foreign Policy Analysis Series No. 4, Organizational Behavior Section, Princeton Univ., 1954).

Friedrich's general distinction between objective functional responsibility and subjective political responsibility in the public service is relevant to the distinctions here made between the varieties of civilian control. Carl J. Friedrich, *et al.*, *Problems of the American Public Service* (New York, 1935), pp. 36–37.

2. The analysis of the concept of "power" goes back, of course, to Machiavelli and Aristotle. Some of the more helpful recent discussions are: Harold D. Lasswell, *Politics: Who Gets What, When, How* (New York, 1936), and *Power and Personality* (New York, 1948); Charles E. Merriam, *Political Power* (New York, 1934), and *Systematic Politics* (Chicago, 1945); Bertrand Russell, *Power: A New Social Analysis* (New York, 1938); Gaetano Mosca, *The Ruling Class* (New York, 1939); Carl J. Friedrich, *Constitutional Government and Democracy* (Boston, 1950); Robert M. MacIver, *The Web of Government* (New York, 1947); Bertrand de Jouvenel, *On Power* (New York, 1949); Karl Mannheim, *Freedom, Power, and Democratic Planning* (New York, 1950); Har-

old D. Lasswell and Abraham Kaplan, *Power and Society* (New Haven, 1950); H. Goldhamer and E. A. Shils, "Types of Power and Status," *Amer. Jour. of Sociology*, XLV (1939), 171–182; Reinhard Bendix, "Bureaucracy and the Problem of Power," *Public Administration Review*, V (1945), 194–209; H. A. Simon, "Notes on the Observation and Measurement of Political Power," *Journal of Politics*, XV (November 1953), 500–516; Robert Bierstedt, "An Analysis of Social Power," *American Sociological Review*, XV (December 1950), 730–738; F. L. Neumann, "Approaches to the Study of Political Power," *Pol. Science Quarterly*, LXV (June 1950), 161–180.

3. Classic statements of the Liberal position will be found in the writings of Locke, the French Enlightenment thinkers, Bentham, Adam Smith, John Stuart Mill, Kant, T. H. Green, and Croce. For analysis of the historical components of liberalism, see Harold J. Laski, *The Rise of Liberalism* (New York, 1936), Guido de Ruggiero, *The History of European Liberalism* (London, 1927), and A. D. Lindsay, *The Modern Democratic State* (New York, vol. I, 1947). The best sources for fascist ideology are Hitler's *Mein Kampf*, Mussolini's *The Doctrine of Fascism*, and Alfred Rosenberg, *Der Mythus des 20. Jahrhunderts*. For analysis of fascist ideas, see W. Y. Elliott, *The Pragmatic Revolt in Politics* (New York, 1928); Hermann Rauschning, *The Revolution of Nihilism* (New York, 1939); Franz L. Neumann, *Behemoth* (New York, 2d ed., 1944); William Ebenstein, *The Nazi State* (New York, 1943). I have attempted to place this analysis of fascist ideas at a sufficiently abstract level so as to include both Italian and German fascism, although there are of course many specific differences between the two. The most useful writings for the political theory of Marxism are Karl Marx and Friedrich Engels,

The Communist Manifesto, and V. I. Lenin, *The State and Revolution* and *Imperialism.* Emile Burns, *Handbook of Marxism* (New York, 1935) is a useful compendium. An excellent brief critical analysis is R. N. Carew Hunt, *The Theory and Practice of Communism* (New York, 1951). The classic statement of conservatism is, of course, by Edmund Burke, particularly in *Reflections on the French Revolution* and *Appeal from the New to the Old Whigs.* For analysis of conservatism as an ideology, see Karl Mannheim, "Conservative Thought," *Essays on Sociology and Social Psychology* (New York, ed. by Paul Kecskemeti, 1953).

4. Conservatism, as used here and here-after . . . , refers to the philosophy of Burke, and not to the meaning given this term in popular political parlance in the United States to refer to the laissez-faire, property-rights form of liberalism as exemplified, for instance, by Herbert Hoover.

5. There are eight conceivable combinations of these three factors, but one (anti-military ideology, high military power, high military professionalism) is impossible given the theoretical premises stated above, and two others (promilitary ideology, low military power, low military professionalism; promilitary ideology, high military power, low professionalism) are unlikely to occur except in the most unusual circumstances.

Professionalism: The Hard Choice

FREDERICK C. THAYER

Sooner or later, all military men must choose, as George C. Marshall and others—the Radfords and the Andersons—had to choose between "fusion," that gray world where political and military expertise are no longer distinguishable, and "autonomy," the lonely world of the professional, wherein political temptations and rewards have to be refused.

There may never be a comprehensive and documented account available of the extraordinary attempts made throughout the 1960s to extend the influence of the military services at a time when civilian control became "civilian command." The phrase . . . captured the atmosphere of the times but, aside from a single example, did not spell it out in detail.[1] As Captain Ingram made clear, the Joint Chiefs and the military as a whole had very limited influence on the content of the Draft Presidential Memoranda (DPMs) which were the source documents for military policies. For some of us, it was saddening to watch the indirect dialogue between McNamara, his systems analysts, and the Services, as they tried to reach agreements on how JCS views would be paraphrased in the DPMs, the rule of the game being that the JCS were not to insert *their own* language.

The operationalization of civil-military relationships in those years seemed to follow prescriptions set forth by Colonel (now Brigadier General) Robert N. Ginsburgh[2] and Dr. Edward L. Katzenbach, Jr.[3] The former argued against a theory of political-military "fusion" which held that political and military factors had become so interlocked that separate military expertise or professionalism was no longer possible. It was both possible and necessary to maintain professional separation, he continued, but only if the military got on with the task of developing an overall expertise which transcended the parochial boundaries of the Services. This led him to argue for more responsibility and authority for the Joint Staff, gradual transformation of the Joint Chiefs into the equivalent of a "D-3" on a civil-military general staff, and widespread acquisition by the military of the special skills and techniques, e.g., systems analysis, then emerging from the "think tanks." Katzenbach's argument was aimed at the military war colleges which had become, so he argued, too "civilian" in their concentration on national and technological trends, and on intra-governmental affairs. His solution was to make the war colleges more "military," in part by adding systems analysis to their curricula, perhaps even by combining the colleges.

The contradictions within these prescriptions seem obvious in retrospect. The Services were to accept "military management" as *the* wave of the future, thus wiping out most professional distinctions between the commanders and staffs of the U.S. Sixth Fleet, the Strategic Air Command, and the U.S. Army Vietnam, and they were asked to make sophisticated analytical techniques a new focus of professionalism. Translated into bureaucratic behavior, this led directly toward the "fusion" that supposedly was being avoided.

The most significant attempts at "fusion" paralleled organizational changes which involved the assistant secretaries of Defense and the specialized defense agencies, both traceable to the statutory revisions of 1958. Given delegations of authority from the Secretary, the assistant secretaries became line operating officials, and the geometrical increase in the number of deputy assistant secretaries in the 1960s reflected that change. The specialized agencies became at least semi-autonomous, as with the communications and intelligence agencies (partly subordinate to the JCS), or almost completely autonomous, as with the Defense Supply Agency (formally subordinate only to the Secretary). Perhaps the most intricate arrangement surrounded the Directorate for Inspection Services (DINS). As integral part of the office of the Assistant Secretary for Administration, the DINS inspected the operational readiness of the combat commands (PACOM, EUCOM) and sent its reports of discrepancies to the JCS—who then had to report back to the Assistant Secretary on corrective action taken. In effect, this made the JCS line subordinates of the Assistant Secretary. The DINS was assigned to a high-ranking general or flag officer; the professional dilemmas which faced him and other officers in similar positions are worth further attention.

As it became clear that the assistant secretaries and the specialized agencies were becoming more important, all of the military services attempted to infiltrate those bureaucratic systems. Anytime it was known that a staff position was coming open, especially a deputy assistantship, each service nominated a military professional in the hope that his assignment to the position would materially increase that service's influence in the decision process. Some of us were charged with maintaining a "score-board" on how well each service had done in the past few years, and with analyzing why our individual

services hadn't done better. It gradually became clear that, despite a number of apparent "successes," overall policy results did not appear notably friendlier, but the military services could not see why.

The individual military professional assigned to such duty, whether on the Joint Staff, in the office of an assistant secretary, or in one of the agencies, found himself in a delicate situation. His service expected him to produce evidence that he had "influenced" certain decisions, but he found that he could best prove his objectivity by pointing out to his new superiors the flaws in arguments being advanced by his own service. If an Air Force officer in charge of the DINS, for example, found too many discrepancies in his inspection of the Strategic Air Command, he found himself in trouble both for criticizing JCS supervision of SAC and for colliding with superiors within the Air Force. If he found no discrepancies, he was in danger of losing his identification as an "objective" member of the OSD staff. Thus, all officers assigned to such positions discovered that the trick was to convince their services that they continued to exert "parochial" influence while convincing their new superiors of their objectivity.

The interactions were even more complex than indicated thus far, and extended far into the service staffs themselves. Each service developed its own group of "experts" in the new analytical techniques and, together with staff members interested in force structure decisions, they attempted to exert influence upon their counterparts on the office of the Secretary of Defense (OSD) staff who prepared the DPMs. While the environment was not one of "take your friendly systems analyst to a two-martini lunch," there was some resemblance, for to convince the analyst that *your* force structure recommendations were sound was to virtually ensure the outcome of the DPM. To put it another way, the interactions involved in the analytical processes increased the budgets they were intended to reduce. Furthermore, it became increasingly attractive to tell OSD what it wanted to hear, even if this tended to vitiate earlier recommendations of the same service.

One crucial case involved the interrogations of prisoners conducted in Vietnam by the RAND Corporation. It was clear, of course, that the military course of the war did not follow recommendations handed up by professionals, and this was nowhere more the case than in bombing. There were those in the Air Force in those years, especially in the field, who expressed concern that inappropriate use of airpower was worse than no use at all, and that this might lead to widespread discrediting of airpower itself. As RAND interviewers produced evidence which seemed to demonstrate the effectiveness of air operations, however, RAND, and the Air Staff could hardly wait to get the evidence as far up the chain of command as possible—including the President. There was considerable euphoria attached to a process whereby long-denied access to high-level officials suddenly became available. It might be postulated that long-term professional objectives lost out in competition with short-term budgetary and bureaucratic objectives.

The faddish expansion of systems analytical capabilities led sometimes to almost ludicrous results. As everyone involved well knew, all the agencies previously charged with "operations analysis" and "operations research" concentrated for the most part on future weapons systems, thus turning away from their original assignments. One outcome was that the Services and the JCS had to set up totally new agencies charged with "old-fashioned" operations analysis, in order to chart the detailed effects of military operations against North Vietnam. Because the titles had been pre-empted, however,

the new agencies had to find new titles. This indicated the dangers inherent in hasty attempts to transform the basis of professionalism. To get at the broadest ramifications, however, it is necessary to look at civil-military relationships at the highest levels.

The extent to which things changed in the 1960s can best be demonstrated by a look at what had happened earlier. We know now that during World War II General George C. Marshall "felt that he had to hold the President at a calculated distance in order to keep his own freedom of action."[4] Thus, Marshall consistently declined to visit President Roosevelt at either Warm Springs or Hyde Park, he attempted to avoid any informal confrontations with him, and he even took care not to laugh at F. D. R.'s jokes.[5] To do any of these, Marshall thought, would compromise his ability to express professional disagreement. Yet it is equally clear that few civil-military relationships ever were more productive than this one, and it did not suffer from Marshall's maintenance of his autonomy.

During the 1950s and through the 1960s, however, there was a pronounced trend toward politicization of the military. Perhaps it began with Roosevelt's use of military officers to staff his economic program, or in Truman's reliance upon military men with foreign policy positions.[6] Marshall himself later held high presidential assignments, a point to be mentioned again. A major turning point seems to have been the stance taken by the JCS in 1951, when they became explainers and defenders of Administration policy in general and the dismissal of General Douglas MacArthur in particular. When Congressional Republicans expressed lack of confidence in the JCS, President Eisenhower apparently chose to replace all of them with appointees cleared personally by Senator Robert Taft.[7] Also during the 1950s, the JCS Chairman became more of a vehicle for relaying Administration views to the other chiefs than for relaying their views to the Administration.[8]

Admiral Arthur Radford was both an example of how the position of JCS Chairman transformed itself and of the rewards that can follow from protesting one Administration's decisions, since he had taken a major role in the Navy's 1949 attempts to increase its budget. During the 1950s, Generals Matthew Ridgway, James Gavin, and Maxwell Taylor led the "generals' revolt," and the latter two openly identified themselves as "liberals" when they retired to publish their dissents.[9] Taylor, of course, advocated a "Single Chief of Staff," although he made it clear he did not have Radford in mind for the position. Thus, professional differences became partisan alignments, and Taylor and Gavin became campaign advisers to John Kennedy. This led to yet another cycle of politicization.

Gavin's assignment as Ambassador to France was in accord with normal political behavior, but it had tangential effects upon professionalism. The recall of Taylor to become JCS Chairman, however, had far-reaching implications; his former JCS colleague, Air Force General Thomas White, labeled him a "political appointee" and added that this viewpoint was widespread among professionals.[10] Taylor, much more than Radford, was the White House representative to the Pentagon; one cannot imagine a harsher criticism than the one implicit in Taylor's appointment—the President had no confidence in anyone on active duty.

Admiral George Anderson may have been appointed Ambassador to Portugal because of his dissent on the TFX/F-111, his confrontation with McNamara during the missile crisis, or both. It was acknowledged publicly that he had to be moved, and it did little for the professionalism of the military or the Foreign Service to send him to Portugal. Gavin's reward was bad enough, but politically traditional; Anderson's transfer was a new departure in how to "fire" military leaders.

To these instances must be added the historic tour of the United States undertaken by General William Westmoreland when he was commander in Vietnam. Apparently advised by Washington that he might accept an invitation, he used as the reason for his tour a speech and press conference involving journalists. He quietly visited the Council on Foreign Relations, addressed a state legislature, and made his three-salute speech to the Congress, but he declined invitations to appear before committees responsible for foreign and military affairs. After his return to Vietnam, the Administration made it known that the visit had *not* been used for an evaluation of manpower requests then being processed through channels, thus serving to emphasize the nonprofessional nature of his absence from his command. Few high-ranking officers have gone to such limits to defend policies which were not in accord with their own recommendations, so it comes as no surprise to see more recent speculation that Westmoreland and others have developed a "stab-in-the-back, or Versailles" complex.[11]

These are only the most obvious examples, of course. All during the 1960s, the common practice was for the JCS to travel as a body to Palm Beach or Johnson City during those weeks in December when the President was finishing his work on the forthcoming budget. Anyone familiar with the process knew full well that all the major issues had been decided and that it was unlikely that the JCS would press their individual claims with great vigor as they partook of the semi-vacation atmosphere. The contrast with Marshall's behavior could not have been more striking.

Whether by accident or design, there have been hopeful recent signs. General Curtis LeMay's abortive alliance with Governor George Wallace seems to have been based at least in part on nonmilitary considerations, and we were spared the suspense of waiting to see if a victorious Senator Barry Goldwater would turn to him as JCS Chairman. Since accession to office, President Richard Nixon and Secretary Melvin Laird seem to have altered management practices a great deal and without wholesale removal of the JCS they found when they arrived.

What should be clear by this time is that professional autonomy is the loser when too much of an attempt is made at fusion. When civilian and military attempt full-scale invasion of each other's domains, the latter cannot win—and on professional grounds. How can a professional systems analyst, for example, be expected to admit that his military counterpart in the service is qualified to deal with him on the terrain of systems analysis? Beyond that, it has become distressingly obvious that whatever failures ultimately are held up to public scorn will be described as military responsibilities. Those who found military professionals to be expedient allies in 1960 later became the shrillest critics of the "military-industrial complex."

The concept of professionalism seems to demand that professionals themselves be constantly aware of the delicate balance they must maintain in their own behavior between autonomy and fusion. They cannot be so totally separated as to become the proverbial "society within a society," but neither can they afford total integration within the civilian overhead. The requirement is a stringent one, for it even runs counter to the notion that any President should be free to appoint to high office those in whom he has confidence —regardless of background. Even in the most defensible case, that of Marshall, military professionalism came out sec-

ond best when Marshall was injected into the 1952 campaign; the issues connected thereto, moreover, led to the later problems involving Senator Joseph McCarthy and the Army. From this perspective, there is little doubt that Gavin, Taylor, Anderson, and Westmoreland should have declined appointments or invitations, or should have been less forthright in their public defense of policies they had not recommended. In other words, professionals may have little choice but to defend professionalism from their presumed friends.

The hallmarks of professionalism remain responsibility, corporateness, and an expertise which need not be as transcendent as Ginsburgh argued in 1964. If it is dangerous to have too much of those qualities, as it is, their abandonment means only the end of any professionalism at all. No matter how enticing, political temptations and rewards have to be refused, and faddish techniques approached with caution. This argument is made in realization of the intricate questions associated with it. To carry it too far is to deny second careers; yet they are more necessary now than ever. Current personnel policies would have forced Marshall into retirement in 1931. Further, the actions and reactions which emanate from high-level relationships and attitudes can carry through the ranks in dangerous ways. Effectiveness reports and promotion systems may become weapons with which "hawks" and "doves" attempt to punish each other, if steps are not taken to prevent it. Finally, academic and operational rebuttals have demonstrated that systems analysis can be a useful supplementary tool, but hardly a focus of military professionalism. Herewith one vote for continuing autonomy and depoliticization.

NOTES

1. Samuel P. Ingram, "Civilian Command or Civilian Control?" U.S. Naval Institute *Proceedings*, May 1968, pp. 26–31.

2. Robert N. Ginsburgh, "The Challenge to Military Professionalism," *Foreign Affairs*, January 1964, p. 225.

3. Edward L. Katzenbach, Jr., "The Demotion of Professionalism at the War Colleges," U.S. Naval Institute *Proceedings*, March 1965, pp. 34–41.

4. Forrest C. Pogue, *George C. Marshall, Education of a General* (New York: Viking, 1963), p. 324.

5. Ibid., *George C. Marshall: Ordeal and Hope* (New York: Viking, 1966), p. 23.

6. Sidney Hyman, *The American President* (New York: Harper, 1954), p. 297.

7. Glenn H. Snyder, "The 'New Look' of 1953," in Warner R. Schilling, Paul Y. Hammond, and Glenn H. Snyder, *Strategy, Politics, and Defense Budgets* (New York: Columbia University Press, 1962), pp. 410–415.

8. Paul Y. Hammond, *Organizing for Defense* (Princeton: Princeton University Press, 1960), pp. 380–81. By statute, the Chairman is the only JCS member not directly involved in defense budgets, which remain the responsibility of the military services and their individual chiefs. Thus, as Hammond puts it, the Chairman was encouraged to become *un*responsible, if not *ir*responsible.

9. Maxwell D. Taylor, *The Uncertain Trumpet* (New York: Harper, 1959), pp. 102–03; James M. Gavin, *War and Peace in the Space Age* (New York: Harper, 1958), pp. 248–53. There is nothing new about the dichotomy of "conservatives" and "liberals" in the military, as it is known there are differences between "hawks" and "doves" at present. The Taylor-Gavin moves, however, went further than any other in recent years.

10. Thomas D. White, "Strategy and the Defense Intellectuals," *Saturday Evening Post*, 4 May 1963, p. 10.

11. *Time*, 12 December 1969.

The Military and American Society

ROBERT G. GARD, JR.

I

The armed forces of the United States are in the throes of what is popularly termed an identity crisis. Alongside daily press reports of anti-war protests, draft resistance and opposition to military spending are accounts of such problems within the uniformed services as discipline, race relations and drug abuse. The concern of the military is apparent in recent institutional reforms, most notably in the Navy, designed to make service more attractive and to remove some of the irritants that no longer appear to serve a useful purpose. Not so well-known, however, is the search to adapt traditional concepts and practices of military professionalism to changing requirements and radically new demands.

Protected as it was by vast oceans until the Soviets acquired a nuclear capability, the United States traditionally sought security in a form of national defense based on a tiny, physically isolated active army and a relatively larger but still small navy which could be expanded in time of emergency. Civilian authorities conducted politics and diplomacy without military participation; the military conducted war to victory without civilian intrusion. In keeping with the American liberal ethic, it was considered dangerous to democratic institutions for the soldier to engage in political activity or the affairs of state. But when diplomacy failed, war was sanctioned as a crusade, and it was considered inefficient and

even immoral for the civilian nonprofessional to meddle in the conduct of military campaigns when American lives were at stake.

Traditional U.S. military professionalism, nurtured in the isolation of frontier posts following the Civil War, reflected this doctrine of mutual exclusion. Its aim was simple: to apply military power to destroy an enemy armed force with the fewest possible casualties to itself. Inherent in the soldier's outlook was the conviction that he would be committed to combat only for causes which justified the ravages of war. The soldier considered himself divorced from politics and politically neutral, with loyalty not to abstract principles but to elected political authority, in the person of the President as Commander in Chief.

Vital to combat operations and therefore a necessary part of traditional military professionalism is a set of values which to some extent are contrary to those held by liberal civilian society. Military organization is hierarchical, not egalitarian, and it is oriented to the group rather than the individual; it stresses discipline and obedience, not freedom of expression; it depends on confidence and trust, not *caveat emptor*. It requires immediate decision and prompt action, not thorough analysis and extensive debate; it relies on training, simplification and predictable behavior, not education, sophistication and empiricism. It offers austerity, not material comforts. Unfortunately, the responsibility of the military professional for the security of the nation and the lives of his men can result in a gravity and moral tone in his pronouncements which most civilians resent.

II

World War II vindicated the traditional concept of national defense but it also established the conditions that led to its downfall. The extent to which mutual exclusion was operative during the War can be illustrated by matching Secretary of State Cordell Hull's comment a few days before Pearl Harbor on the U.S.-Japanese situation —"I have washed my hands of it, and it is now in the hands of . . . the Army and the Navy"—with General Marshall's remark during the War on a British proposal to modify military strategy—"I would be loath to hazard American lives for purely political purposes."

The unconditional surrender of Nazi Germany and the occupation of Japan appeared initially to permit a return to small peacetime active forces. Although the early phases of the cold war gave ample evidence of a fundamental change in the position of the United States in postwar international politics, only hesitant and inconsequential steps were taken to change the outmoded concept of national defense. American armed forces were woefully unprepared when the Korean War began. (The proposed defense budget for the fiscal year beginning July 1, 1950, was about $13 billion.) Early in the war, following the landing at Inchon, the military objective was traditional: destruction of the North Korean armed forces.

It was not until after truce negotiations began in 1951 that a fundamental change occurred in the precepts of mutual military and political exclusion. During these negotiations, armed combat lost its wartime autonomy. The objective of military operations ceased to be solely the destruction of the enemy forces in order to remove their capacity to resist; instead, the employment of force was closely controlled to convey a diplomatic message. In keeping with a basic but long-ignored principle of Clausewitz, combat operations were subordinated to political purposes.

In addition to undermining traditional military supremacy in wartime, the shocks of the Korean conflict also demonstrated graphically what the Soviet explosion of an atomic device in 1949 had forecast: the concept of national defense which relied on lengthy mobilization to flesh out skeletal active-duty military forces was outdated. There evolved a new concept of national security policy and strategy, requiring in both peace and war the orchestration with the military of other instruments of statecraft—political, economic, sociological and psychological. But the development of new precepts and relationships was unsystematic and irregular. Adjustments to the profound changes proved exceedingly difficult, particularly for the military.

Civilian participation in what traditionally had been the province of the military establishment grew swiftly. With the Soviet acquisition of a nuclear arsenal, the deterrence of a devastating holocaust became a matter of the highest national priority. But the soldier's experience was grounded in conventional combat operations, not in deterrence and nuclear war; and interservice rivalry over competing strategies and weapons systems—paradoxically compounded by service unification—had to be resolved by civilian leadership. The result was that the military professional no longer was considered to possess an exclusive expertise; it was accepted that the civilian analyst had a role to play. Centralized budgeting, programming and financial management also called for skills in short supply in the uniformed services. A large civilian bureaucracy evolved, first to control and then increasingly to manage in detail the enlarged and highly complicated defense establishment.

Nor was civilian activity limited to the development of strategic concepts and to peacetime military planning and programming. In order to minimize the possibility that limited war or even military confrontation might escalate into disastrous general war, responsible political authority understandably exercised close control over crisis management. In the Korean War, the Army was subject to specific restrictions although the Navy and Air Force were allowed to conduct operations with minimum interference other than the establishment of a geographical limitation. But in the Cuban missile crisis, the President and Secretary of Defense exercised stringent controls over naval blockade operations; and during the Vietnam war, the air campaign has been subject to detailed civilian direction.

III

Increasing civilian involvement in military affairs proceeded more rapidly than military adjustment to it. Rejection of professional military advice in peacetime for nonmilitary reasons has always been acceptable to the soldier; what was and continues to be frustrating, and even professionally embarrassing, is to be overruled by civilians for military reasons or to have civilians interfere in the conduct of military operations. But civilian intrusion into areas that had been considered exclusively military did not constitute the most perplexing problem. The concept of national security policy and strategy called for fundamental alterations in the traditional military professionalism which had guided policies and procedures in the U.S. armed forces for nearly a century.

The conduct of limited war in the nuclear era requires what Morris Janowitz has termed a "constabulary force," one continuously prepared to act, committed to the minimum use of force, and satisfied with a favorable political outcome rather than military victory in the traditional sense.[1] But even more difficult, it also necessitates the highly complex integration of military operations with political, economic, sociological and psychological measures.

Many military professionals regarded the Korean experience as an aberration and failed to comprehend its politico-military lessons. For example, nearly a year after the armistice was signed, the Army Chief of Staff, General Matthew B. Ridgway, stated in a speech: "The day when wars had limited effects is past. ... War ... will be total in character. ... If we must fight, we must win. There can be no other goal. There must be no other outcome." It was not until the Kennedy Administration emphasized the concepts of flexible response and counterinsurgency that restrictions on the use of force and the need to combine other considerations with military operations became widely accepted in principle within the military institution.

In the search for national security policy, the military professional no longer could remain isolated and restrict his peacetime activities to preparation for war. No longer could he abstain from participation in diplomacy and the formulation of policy; nor could he limit himself to military considerations. In June 1961, President Kennedy found it necessary to state in a memorandum to the Joint Chiefs of Staff that he regarded them as "more than military men" and expected "their help in fitting military requirements into the overall context of any situation. . . ."

Bureaucratic imperatives demanded that the military develop within its ranks new technical, analytical and managerial skills of a high order. But continued military preoccupation with the combat function precluded an adequate response to this requirement. Although a relatively large number of uniformed officers have received graduate education, as Army Chief of Staff General Westmoreland stated in a recent address on problems within the Army: specialization "has only been an extracurricular effort."

The military services had made only preliminary progress toward adjusting to a fusionist national security policy when the conflict in Vietnam became a test case of the new strategy. Difficulties in conducting counterinsurgency and the intense reaction against the whole involvement in Vietnam have significantly complicated the problems of modernizing military professionalism. It is true that in some ways public attitudes are typical of the antimilitary outlook that has followed other wars. But two factors can be considered unique and particularly troublesome.

First, there are fundamental doubts about how effective the military is or can be in attaining political objectives. The Vietnam war is perceived to be inconclusive; according to recent public reports, it appears even to many involved in operations there that the insurgency could persist in much the same form over an extended period. And the nature of the conflict makes it exceptionally difficult to justify to American society the loss of lives in clear-cut moral terms. Beyond this, however, there is for the first time widespread and serious questioning of the morality of the use of armed force, particularly as it affects both friendly and enemy noncombatants. Military force is seen by many as a blunt, insensitive and even immoral instrument. In their minds, not only does this invalidate the rational use of the military in attaining political objectives, but it also impugns the very legitimacy of military service itself.

Secondly, there is, particularly on the part of American youth, a hostility toward large bureaucracy, a general feeling of dissatisfaction with what are considered obsolete bureaucratic structures, insensitive administrators and encumbering procedures. This is coupled with a belief—or perhaps an understanding—that outdated policies and practices are sustained through apathy and inertia. Bureaucracies are seen to be capable of only marginal adjustments, not necessary innovation. While these dissatisfactions and misgivings are by no means focused only on the armed services, they are reinforced by other antimilitary attitudes and nonconformist values to produce a unique challenge to the American military establishment, the largest bureaucracy in the United States. Even within the armed services, the desire for increased influence over bureaucratic decisions by those most directly affected undoubtedly will lead to more widespread discontent and resistance to authority.

An additional complicating factor is a new uncertainty about the U.S. role abroad. The emphasis on domestic problems is coupled with public rejection of a defense policy which has appeared to be tantamount to unilateral containment of communism. Nevertheless, to revert to pre-World War II isolation does not seem possible for a superpower in a world in which international politics has become both more dangerous and more complex. Thus there appears to be little justification for the complacent attitude expressed by some, both within and outside the military, that the armed services after Vietnam can either return to traditional concepts of professionalism or adjust in a leisurely and un-

troubled fashion to requirements which
have evolved during and since the Korean War. Indeed, the military profession faces what is probably the most
difficult challenge in its history in pursuing two key and sometimes conflicting objectives: providing for the military security of the United States, and
accommodating present values of American society.

IV

The military services face complex
problems in their primary task of providing trained forces to support national security policy and strategy.
Costs of both weapons and manpower
are rising rapidly. With shrinking military budgets and reductions in general
purpose forces, there is an inclination
to maintain on active duty more com-
bat-type units than can be supported
adequately or manned at or near full
strength, in order to facilitate mobilization. In addition to creating serious
morale problems, to be discussed later,
this approach to force structuring prevents adequate training and produces
units at a low state of readiness. This
might appear acceptable, since any active commitment of U.S. forces seems
unlikely under present conditions.
However, circumstances of U.S. military involvements since World War II
have proved unpredictable, even in the
short run; they are likely to be less
predictable in the future. Moreover,
the Nixon Doctrine asserts full support
of previous commitments and states
that external assistance to an insurgency, as well as overt conventional
attack, may lead to the involvement of
U.S. general purpose forces. If future
international developments require our
military participation, highly trained
and ready units will be needed, particularly in view of the variety of possible
contingencies and the limited size of
our forces.

Military professionals also must
develop a greater understanding of the
implications of the necessary limitations on the use of force in the nuclear
era. They should provide an institutional capability to understand political objectives and to suggest appropriate applications of military means to
achieve them. Military leaders must
comprehend more fully the relationship
of means and ends, and appreciate the
moral principles that play a vital role
in the success, as well as the acceptabil-
ity, of military operations. Deterrence
of war and the attainment of political
objectives must be recognized as "victory," at even the lowest tactical level.

The military involvement of the
United States in Vietnam may be a
special case, with mistakes never to be
repeated; but a careful and dispassionate examination of military strategy
and tactics in light of political objectives is in order. This is essential not
only because of the intensity of public
criticism of the conduct of military
operations and the resultant misgivings
within the military establishment itself,
but also because such a critique should
prove highly instructive in helping to
bring about the effective integration
of military power with other instruments of statecraft in national security
strategy.

Clearly, the complexity of the military establishment and the demands
of national security require the military to develop a high level of capability in areas which until recently
were not considered principal military
responsibilities. The institutional assumption that an effective tactical
commander possesses the capability or
initiative to cope successfully with
other, more tangential assignments
must be rejected. Reexamination and
overhaul of the extensive education
and training programs of the services
are not enough; also essential is a reassessment of career patterns to permit
the development of applicable skills

and to ensure a reasonable prospect of advancement for those who contribute

effectively in assignments other than troop command.

V

Along with providing a flexible military force relevant to political realities, the armed forces must maintain an organization which is sensitive and responsive to change. This is not to suggest that the discipline essential to combat operations should be sacrificed, but rather to recognize that the gap between the values held by a large percentage of American youth and those required for effective military service is probably larger today than ever before. Traditional antimilitary attitudes and the reaction to the Vietnam conflict are compounded by a general desire for greater informality and personal freedom and by an abhorrence of obedience to what is regarded as arbitrary authority. Also, the lack of privacy and a relatively Spartan life-style do not appeal to many who are accustomed to material comforts in an affluent society.

Traditional values are not outdated; those vital to success in battle still must be inculcated in servicemen who may be required to engage in or support combat, both to ensure operational success and to prevent unnecessary loss of life. And in addition, while the rights of the soldier as an American citizen must be protected, there also must be appropriate sanctions against those who fail to meet required standards of discipline and conduct, especially in combat. (Many believe the latest version of the Military Justice Act has created serious impediments to prompt and effective punishment which exacerbate disciplinary problems.) But at the same time, a rigorous review of traditional procedures is in order. While certain rituals that appear irrational may be necessary to produce an essential level of discipline, reluctance to crack the thick crust of custom should not inhibit appropriate change.

Most destructive to morale in the armed services, however, is a lack of purposeful activity relevant to a legitimate military mission. Careful force planning and programming at the highest echelons are necessary to lay the groundwork for rewarding peacetime service. For extensive administrative and logistical activities are required to support military units and installations, and excessive economizing or arbitrary reductions in the civilian work force and in supporting military manpower require that men be detailed from tactical units to perform support functions. Such diversions of personnel—and what is even more damaging, programmed shortages of manpower, equipment and spare parts in tactical units—not only preclude training and reduce readiness but also create the highly publicized environment of make-work and frustration which discourages enlistments and makes it difficult to retain quality personnel.

A related but more complicated problem is retaining talented professionals while maintaining essential values in today's military establishment. Military installations previously provided both separation from civilian society and amenities that would not have been available for equivalent civilian income. However, larger forces and broader responsibilities have increased military contacts with civilians, diluting some of the values that could be maintained relatively easily within an isolated military community. An increasing number of military assignments are not related directly to the combat function, removing the sustaining motivation of the military mystique. Genteel poverty and the Spartan life become less attractive, and the sense of commitment that engenders a willingness to work long hours is likely to become eroded when soldiers associ-

ate closely with civilians who are fi-
nancially more successful in less demanding occupations.

Furthermore, military participation
in the policy process involves a degree
of political activity inconsistent with
the nonpartisan tenets of traditional
professionalism. This not only causes
strains within the military establishment, but it also leads to charges of
excessive military influence in national
security policy formulation. Many hold
the military responsible for unpopular
national security decisions. There is
even evidence of recent concern that
intensified criticism might alienate the
military sufficiently for it to take action
opposing constituted authority. This
appears farfetched; the concept of civilian control, based on the soldier's unconditional commitment to elected
political leadership, remains firmly
grounded in the U.S. military ethos.
But to prevent mutual suspicion and
recrimination, it is important that
American society draw a distinction
between legitimate participation in
policy deliberations on the one hand
and responsibility for policy decisions
on the other, and recognize and support the military establishment as an
instrument of the state.

At the same time, a difficult question can arise for an individual member
of the armed forces when he disagrees
with a policy decision taken by political authority. While institutions as
such cannot take moral stands, individuals cannot ignore them. Since the
demands of both military service and
morality are based on absolutes, service
to the state must be philosophically
compatible with the soldier's moral
predispositions. Once this is accepted,
moral choices rarely arise as a practical
problem; when they do, they are likely
to concern specific means of carrying
out policy. But the nature and intensity
of public criticism of military operations in Vietnam, highlighted by the
My Lai tragedy, raise fundamental
questions that the military services, and
indeed American society, must face
squarely and objectively in analyzing
the use of the military instrument to
obtain political objectives. Such an
inquiry must include moral considerations, but it must avoid distortion of
the Geneva Conventions to support
unwarranted charges of war crimes.

VI

Solutions to the dilemmas facing
the military profession fall somewhere
between two unacceptable extremes:
returning to traditional professionalism, involving withdrawal from society;
or discarding traditional values and
severely impairing cohesiveness and discipline. Obviously, the two should be
reconciled, but the prescription of preserving essential military values while
maintaining a close relationship with
civilian society is inordinately difficult.

If the draft is discontinued to promote a volunteer armed force, it will
be easier to preserve traditional values
but harder to adapt military professionalism to modern demands. The
uniformed services will become more
self-contained and their separation
from society will be more likely. This
could become particularly serious if
the military feel alienated from society
and if civilians regard the military
establishment as a separate community.
Intensive efforts must be made by both
civilian and military officials to encourage contact and cooperation and to
prevent such unfortunate developments
as the elimination of ROTC from our
major universities. A close association
of the armed forces with civilian society
is necessary to ensure that military resources will be employed in a manner
consistent with American societal
values.

In the antimilitary environment
likely to persist for the foreseeable
future, reliance on volunteers would

probably eliminate, for all practical purposes, the soldier of middle-class background from the enlisted ranks. This will also be true, to a somewhat lesser extent, of those from the working or blue-collar class which has been a prime source of military manpower. As an alternative to personnel shortages, the services probably will be required to lower standards and to rely to a large extent on recruitment from the alienated underclasses. In addition to the resulting disciplinary and racial problems, the military would be faced with a massive task of basic education and social rehabilitation. The uniformed services currently are engaged in a New Standards Program (formerly Project 100,000) designed to absorb annually into their ranks a limited number of men who fail to meet mental criteria or who have minor, correctable physical defects. But to rely primarily on the disadvantaged underclasses for the skilled manpower needed in a modern armed force presents an entirely different problem. Substantial increases in pay and other improvements might produce enough qualified volunteers to alleviate the situation somewhat; but without high levels of unemployment, antipathy to military service probably will override its attractions for the large majority of middle and working-class youth.

To obtain sufficient numbers of adequately qualified personnel, it appears essential to continue the Selective Service Act and to maintain relatively high mental standards. But while reliance on the draft will ensure closer contact of the military establishment with society, it will also increase the difficulty of preserving the traditional values necessary to an effective military force. There may be an escape from this dilemma in the concept of a "zero draft," whereby the Selective Service statute would be maintained, to be used only if necessary; this assumes, however, that sufficient numbers of adequately qualified volunteers will be attracted to a military career. The near-term prospects for this solution do not seem very bright, since it will depend upon a reduction in the extreme antimilitary attitudes currently prevalent in American society, a substantial allocation of resources for pay increases and improved living conditions, and imaginative measures by the military establishment to make service a rewarding professional experience rather than the unattractive occupation it is now perceived to be.

Regardless of the status of the draft, the military services undoubtedly will be expected to play a more direct institutional role in helping to solve domestic social problems. It is important, however, that organized military activities extend beyond the military establishment itself only in unusual circumstances, such as emergency disaster relief, in order to avoid involvement of the armed services in local politics and to prevent an unacceptable diversion of military units from necessary training. It is reasonable to expect a soldier to return to civilian society at the end of his enlistment better prepared for useful employment; Project Transition, designed to provide off-duty civilian job training to military personnel near the end of their service, probably should be expanded. Further, the services should make every effort to eliminate all forms of racial discrimination and provide genuinely equal opportunity for all. Individuals can contribute to local civilian projects, and certain organized activities for the underprivileged can be conducted on military installations.

However, it would be wrong to use military units to engage in civic action projects in American cities, as is frequently suggested, for this would thrust the armed services into sensitive activities for which they are unqualified. Poor performance in these projects, or even controversy over selection of priorities, could lead to further resentment of the military establishment. Indeed, while the services must not become isolated from civilian society, every precaution should be taken to avoid placing military organizations in adversary relationships with civilian communities; for example, regular armed forces should be used only as an absolute last resort in controlling civil disturbances, particularly in minority ghettos.

VII

There is probably a good deal of truth in the adage that a democracy gets the military establishment it deserves. The attitudes of American society will set the tone and general limits within which the armed forces can adjust traditional concepts of professionalism to changing realities in international competition and cooperation, changing conceptions of the role of the United States in world affairs, and changing social values. But a continuing dialogue among civilians and military professionals is essential to elucidate the complex issues involved and increase understanding of them.

An effective military force is vital to U.S. foreign policy. Like the search for national security itself, a continuing effort is required to adapt military professionalism to modern demands. But to paraphrase Montaigne, both the journey and the arrivals at way stations matter. The military services must exercise initiative and imagination in developing institutional changes; in the final analysis, however, civilian leadership and resultant public support will determine the pace and difficulty of the journey.

NOTES

1. Morris Janowitz, *The New Military*. New York: John Wiley & Sons, 1964.

The Impact of a Volunteer Force on Strategic Affairs

MORRIS JANOWITZ

The mass conscript armed force with its vast mobilization reserves is currently being phased out of existence in the NATO nations. This event is certain to have a profound effect upon international relations, as well as internal relations between the civil and military sectors within the NATO countries. In the United States, one campaign appeal that President Nixon sought vigorously to implement after taking office in 1969 was to end the draft as quickly as possible and to create an all-volunteer force. He established his President's Commission on an All-Volunteer Armed Force not with the mandate to explore alternative formats but to make specific recommendations and estimates of costs for ending Selective Service before the next presidential election. Paradoxically, the prolongation of hostilities in Vietnam only served to speed up the end of conscription and to develop congressional support for his campaign promise. The termination of conscription was one issue upon which antiwar congressmen and pressure groups could unite with the Nixon administration. The result was the effective political decision not to extend Selective Service legislation beyond 1 July 1973, and the initiation of planning by military officials to reach the objective of a "zero draft call" by 1 January 1973 so that there would be a six-month period of accommodation and transition.

The ending of the draft in the United States will have a deep impact on military manpower systems in Western Europe. Rather than working to maintain existing conscription systems, it will tend to push NATO nations toward an all-volunteer system or toward new forms of militia systems. Over a decade ago, in 1960, Great Britain introduced an all-volunteer system, and in the 1970s will certainly see further overall reductions in British military manpower because of economic pressure and the sheer difficulties of recruitment. In the last three years NATO countries have either reduced the length of conscript service or are debating such reduction. More radical measures are certain to be examined closely after the end of the draft in the United States. The Netherlands, with its powerful commitment to NATO principles and strategy, is openly debating the conditions under which it will institute an all-volunteer armed force and is actively planning such a system. Norway, with its reserved NATO status, may well continue the draft longer as a demonstration of its emerging detachment. In Germany, Helmut Schmidt, the Socialist minister of defense, has advocated an all-volunteer cadre augmented by a short-term (six-month) conscript militia. In Italy, and to a lesser extent France, the size and nature of the manpower systems are connected not only to international

This paper was originally presented in slightly different form to the Annual Conference of the Inter-University Seminar on Armed Forces and Society, October 1971.

relations but also to internal security, and consequently, debate on shifting toward a more voluntary force has been retarded.

Can an all-volunteer system produce an armed force of sufficient strength and quality for an effective international posture of deterrence? The prospect of an all-volunteer armed force also causes deep concern about civil-military relations, especially with regard to the question of social isolation or even "alienation" of the military from the larger civilian society. In the United States the military establishment, and the ground forces in particular, is experiencing a profound crisis in legitimacy; this is due in part to the impact of the agonies of Vietnam, but it involves also internal race tension, corruption, and extensive drug abuse, disintegration of command and operational effectiveness, widespread antimilitary sentiment, and a continu-

ous reduction in force levels which limits career opportunities.

Many high-ranking military officers in the United States at first viewed the end of the draft with utter dismay. Their outlook, of course, reflected their concern with the prerogatives and resources of the military, but they generally felt also that the draft was essential to maintain required manpower levels and that it was politically and morally undesirable for a democratic society to rely on an all-volunteer force. However, as internal tensions in the armed forces have become progressively more disruptive, the established command has come to look toward an all-volunteer system as an acceptable outcome. Younger and more innovative officers, in fact, see the advent of the all-volunteer force as an essential precondition to massive internal professional reform, a first step in reconstructing the ground forces, regardless of the strategic limitations it will impose.

DECLINE OF MASS ARMIES

The military establishment, in any historical period, is both a reflection of the larger society and an institution in its own right with a distinctive environment and ethos. Thus, the ending of the draft in the United States is a dramatic historical transformation of American society taking place in our own time.

The mass armed force had its origins in both technological and sociopolitical change. On the one hand, the mass army was rooted in an organizational system created by increased firepower of the infantry and artillery plus improved means of transporting personnel and supplies. Historical epochs do not, of course, start or conclude on specific textbook dates. But the technology of the mass army was certainly in operation during the American Civil War and the Franco-Prussian conflict, and essential prototype elements, especially its organizational features, were

already in existence during the Napoleonic wars.

On the other hand, there are strong reasons to trace the origin of the mass armed force to the sociopolitical struggles of the American and French revolutions and the forms of modern nationalism which they produced. These rebellions marked the end of the postfeudal armies as the revolutionary leaders armed the ordinary citizenry. The idea that citizenship involved the right and duty to bear arms —truly a revolutionary notion—came into being. In fact, military service was an essential element in establishing and expanding the scope of modern citizenship. To be a citizen of the nation-state was to have the right and duty to bear arms in defense of the state. (It is striking to recall that during World Wars I and II, elements in the Black community in the United States demanded the right to serve in combat units as an expression of their aspirations to full citizenship.)

In Europe, after the French Revolution, the mass armed forces developed professional cadres which were augmented by a conscript and mobilization system. Although the institution rested on an ethos of citizen participation, the professional officers were in actuality highly distinct from the rest of society. (This was not the first time in the history of political and institutional change that a protest movement produced unanticipated consequences.) In the United States, professional cadres were smaller, and the mass armed force did not become effectively institutionalized until the end of the nineteenth century.

In spite of their revolutionary origins, the armed forces ended by serving the cause of nationalism very well: the officer corps of Western Europe had no difficulty in transferring its feudal-based allegiance to the modern bureaucratic nation-state. A corresponding process took place in the United States. Mass armies supplied an opportunity for the lower classes to participate directly in the national polity in a manner they could readily manage and appreciate. Service in the conscript forces in the nineteenth and twentieth centuries was for a significant segment of the population—even after the slaughter of World War I and up through World War II—an act of political affirmation. In both Europe and the United States it became an expression of popular nationalism, undercutting, in Europe, the countermovements toward internationalism and socialism. The right and duty to participate in the conscript armed force, as much as the extension of the franchise, was at the core of the political transformation of modern nationalism.

The distinctive, professional officer corps of the mass armed force, with its strong sense of separation from civilian society, in due course brought with it its own elements of industrial transformation, including an increase in sheer size. In Europe since the close of the Franco-Prussian War and in the United States since the mobilization of World War I, a dominant trend in the mass armed force has been toward "civilianization" of the military. Preparing for war and making war give the military its distinctive institutional climate. However, the boundary between military forces and civilian society has weakened as total mobilization requires larger and larger segments of the population to become part of the war apparatus. Air warfare has meant that the entire population is a target for military action. Military leaders must share authority with civilian scientists as technology becomes more and more complex, and the influx of civilians into the officer corps during periods of mobilization undermines traditional forms of authority and command. Within the professional military, the source of social recruitment into the officer corps has broadened, the concentration of personnel with civilian-type skills has increased, and the pattern of military authority has shifted from authoritarian command to organizational decision making.

The process of civilianization of the mass military is not simply an outgrowth of technology and organizational control. The vast resources required for military operations and the need to justify prolonged hostilities and massive destruction necessitate an egalitarian ideology, both in democratic and totalitarian societies. Increasingly, men are no longer prepared to fight for nationalist sentiments alone; the cause, rather, must be seen as justified morally. Military institutions require direct civilian control for legitimacy. Although the expanded resources of the military permit it to operate as a very powerful pressure group, the threat in advanced nations of old-fashioned military dictatorship seems remote.

The decline of mass armies in the affluent nation-states of the West started at the end of World War II, although it has taken twenty-five years for the process to become fully self-evident. Again, both technological and sociopolitical factors initiated the change. Deployment of nuclear weapons marked the technological transformation of the armed forces of the NATO nations as the sheer destructive power of these instruments altered the scope of war making. But the introduction of nuclear weapons did not per se make inevitable the gradual erosion of mass armies; it was only a precondition.

In advanced industrialized societies the purpose of military institutions in general has been subjected to massive criticism, and in particular the moral value of conscript service has been shaken. Hedonism, personal expression, opposition to the life style of the military establishment, and resistance to military authority, as well as a pervasive new moral criticism, have become paramount among young people. The destructive potential of nuclear weapons has served not only to produce moral opposition to violence, as well as new forms of pacifism, but to heighten realistic understanding of the effective interdependence of national societies. The use of force has traditionally operated within circumscribed limits; the new moral and political definitions serve to generate a powerful sense of neutralism. Literacy, patterns of mass consumption, and political rhetoric have superseded military service as the hallmark of citizenship. Nationalism itself is muted and mixed with diffuse but powerful feelings of transnationalism. The campaigns of the United States forces in Southeast Asia, of course, supplied in the United States an emotional basis to the emerging popular pacificism. These trends are concentrated among an important minority of young people, but can be found in varying degrees in all parts of the social structure. Thus, in Germany, reluctance to serve in the armed forces

has meant in recent years that up to 10 percent of each age cohort are exempted from service under a broad definition of conscientious objection. The notion of a pluralistic society weakens the very foundation of popular military service.

Comparable trends are at work in the Soviet Union and Eastern Europe, but in vastly different cultural and political settings. Totalitarian control eliminates political and moral debate about conscription. Thus published opinion polls from Poland indicate that young people, while they profess "appropriate" answers to general questions about military service, in specific details reveal strongly negative attitudes toward the realities of conscript service. Only a small minority were positively attracted. Discontent among youth is acknowledged to be widespread in the Soviet Union, and this has its implications for conscript service. In the Soviet military, authorities have to deal with their own forms of social turbulence. They have sought to limit the term of conscripts, have emphasized volunteer recruitment wherever possible, and have closed important branches of the armed forces to all but volunteer personnel. The military has been downgraded as a locus of citizenship training; this function has been transferred to premilitary training in high school, where specially trained military personnel are assigned this task.

In the Soviet Union and the other Warsaw Pact countries the military forces serve as an integral element of the internal security system. These political realities, plus the validity given to the Chinese threat, mean that personal (let alone moral or political) opposition to military service has little or no direct impact on manpower policy. But one should not underestimate the extent to which Soviet authorities are concerned and must take into consideration the attitudes of indifferent youth. In the United States and in

NATO, the equivalent opinions exert strong weight in influencing the balance of political decisions about manpower policies.

The introduction of the all-volunteer armed force in the United States means that manpower—as much as or even more than technology—will influence military strategy in the decade of the 1970s. The president's commission projected an all-volunteer force of approximately 2.6 million, or slightly less than that of the pre-Vietnam buildup. At the time that projection already appeared to be either a major miscalculation or a form of self-deception. In the spring of 1971 civilian officials in the Department of Defense were saying publicly that the post-Selective Service force would be approximately 2.25 million, while privately they indicated a more realistic level of 2.0 million. However, the prospect of a force of 1.75 million is more likely before 1975, and an even smaller force after that date cannot be ruled out. The major reduction, of course, will be in the ground forces.

The reduction in manpower partly reflects deliberate national policy, which does not require so large a force. But equally important are economic concerns. There will be intense political pressure to reduce military expenditures below the 1971–72 figure of approximately 8 percent of the gross national product. Any such reduction, however, will be slow and most difficult to achieve, for at any given level of strength, personnel costs in an all-volunteer force will require a markedly greater percentage of the military budget. In the light of the British experience, United States personnel costs can be expected to rise from more than 40 percent to nearly 60 percent of the military budget during this decade. Likewise, unless there is a drastic alteration in weapons procurement policy, the cost of armaments will also rise, since the weapons requested by the military are becoming more and more complex, automated, and costly. Finally, it is highly doubtful that the United States will be able to meet projected recruitment quotas, whatever pay level is offered, without radical internal reorganization of the military such as that described below.

Thus there are two essential questions: How can the United States forces be redeployed and professionally reorganized so as to articulate with a meaningful and politically responsible foreign policy? How can these all-volunteer forces be recruited, trained, and managed so as to articulate with civilian control and prevent social isolation of the armed forces from the main currents of domestic society? Although there is an element of risk, I firmly believe that a military force of 1.75 million men consuming 8 percent of the gross national product (a percentage that should decline gradually) could support a meaningful defense policy of effective, minimum deterrence —rather than a strategy based upon a delicate balance of terror. Such a military force would undertake a variety of national emergency tasks that cannot be performed by civilian organizations, the performance of which would enhance its military effectiveness.

REDEPLOYMENT OF UNITED STATES MILITARY FORCES

The present decade in the United States military policy is obviously conditioned by the successes and failures of the past twenty-five years. During these years the United States has pursued one global strategy of nuclear force and two increasingly divergent strategies for its conventional forces— one in Western Europe and one in Southeast Asia. The redeployment of conventional American military forces rests upon recognition of this duality —upon the differences in American interests, responsibility, capacities, and achievements in Western Europe and the Far East. This formulation and distinction does not exclude the problematic issues of the Middle East, Africa, or South America, but rather places them in an appropriate perspective for the purposes of the analysis at hand.

During the past twenty-five years the prospects of nuclear war have been very remote indeed, and this was abundantly clear to detached observers immediately after 1945. There has been a vast amount of literature pointing out that during this period nuclear technology developed a delicate balance of terror; the impact of nuclear warfare would be so destructive and so self-destructive that the results would be of little political advantage to either the United States or the Soviet Union, and, therefore, the strategy of mutual deterrence emerged. It has been less widely recognized, however, that the absence of a major war is also to be credited to political leadership and to political accommodation in working out arrangements to control the threat of both accidental and premeditated war. The essential political formula was as follows: (1) the Soviet bloc believed that the United States leaders firmly controlled their military establishment and that the United States, on political and moral grounds alone, had ruled out a pre-emptive nuclear attack on the Soviet Union and (2) the conventional forces of NATO were not to be used to support any movements of national liberation within nations of the eastern bloc.

As the 1960s came to an end, this political formula was strained by the uncertainties introduced by MIRV type weapons and antiballistic missiles. Again, the issue did not involve primarily the technology but the political setting, although these new weapons and counterweapons greatly complicated the search for effective political arrangements. The threat of nuclear confrontation between the United

States and the Soviet Union remains remote during the decade of the 1970s as new channels open for mutual political communications and negotiations, both formal and informal. First, the SALT negotiations have become a central forum: at a minimum, prolonged discussion will inhibit the deployment of new weapons, and more effective negotiations will produce ad hoc and partially formalized settlements. Second, partial resolution of the "German question" and unilateral and bilateral troop reductions will serve as a new setting for political discussions and assurances. As China develops her nuclear potential, the United States is required to extend and adapt the political formula of the past twenty-five years to that country; in these circumstances the threat of nuclear war with China will also remain remote.

The problematic issue, therefore, becomes the deployment and redeployment of conventional weapons and troops as adjuncts to the deterrence strategy. In this respect, the experiences and legacies of the past raise sociopolitical issues, questions of importance to any analysis of the possible impact of volunteer forces during the coming decade.

In Western Europe, the stationing of American troops and the system of defense alliances were compatible with European national and political aspirations. Until 1970, stationing the considerable numbers of United States troops required for the NATO strategy of deterrence created relatively few sociopolitical problems at the community level or even for national sovereignty. In the Far East, too, the stationing of troops and their direct involvement were relatively compatible with local and national aspirations until the end of the Korean War. Progressively, however, the tasks of American troops have become more and more difficult because of the opposition they encounter from national and political forces. Cultural and racial differences between the U.S. and local civilian populations have also been deeply disruptive. Moreover, the fundamental sociopolitical basis of military strategy has been increasingly incompatible with the realities of social change and social structure in Southeast Asia. Finally, there has been the stalemate and atrophying of American military intervention in Southeast Asia, due in part to the overestimation by key civilian and military leaders of the impact of conventional strategic air warfare.

In the ever-quickening redeployment and reduction of overseas American military forces, one is struck with the apparent strategic consensus that has emerged; only in Western Europe does there remain a positive function for any significant numbers of United States ground troops. Even in South Korea, the prospect is for an American military presence limited to air and naval units, without ground troops. A contracting system of naval and air bases, selected training missions, plus an overseas scattering of specialized troops for communications and logistical purposes are the augmenting elements. Thus, the question of military posture focuses on the type and number of ground troops required for deterrence and peace keeping through a military presence in Western Europe.

But to identify a common focus does not obscure fundamental differences within the professional military. Military perspectives and doctrine, as held by professional soldiers, have a strong persistence even as they are adjusted to changing technology and an altered sociopolitical environment. The distinction between the "absolutists" and the "pragmatists" still dominates the debate in the day-to-day struggle over military budgets and missions. The trend, because of the wounds to professional pride from the experience of Vietnam, have been more and more toward an absolutist doctrine. This is especially the case in the absence of

incisive top military leaders like those who managed the military establishment during World War II and the Korean conflict.

Both absolutists and pragmatists believe that they are sensitive to the interplay of political, economic, and military factors in worldwide international relations. The heavy investment of the military in the politicomilitary education of higher officers has spread a new vocabulary through the ranks of the professional soldiers and the contents of the mass media reinforce this rhetoric. The strongest advocates of each school really live in different worlds—but it should be emphasized that most officers in effect lean one way or the other. The crucial difference lies in the degree to which the professional military man accepts the strategy of deterrence with its implications for the military, and abandons the "killing business" as the organizing principle of his profession.

Deeply held notions in the professional ideology of violence are involved in the debate. At the international level, the absolutists maintain an "assault" perspective even though they are cognizant of the inhibitions that nuclear weapons place on the great powers. They feel that the full political impact of our military forces will be lost unless a "forward" military posture is maintained. Such an assault posture implicitly rejects the formulation of President Nixon's "no more Vietnams" as a passing political slogan. Rather, the deployment of aggressive air and naval patrol forces, forward positioning of bases, and a potential for significant intervention outside Western Europe are required. The strategic concept is in effect a continuation of the notion of the inevitability of armed conflict, but in an altered format. At the personal level the absolutists are fearful that a military without combat experience will decline and atrophy; the models of Sweden and Switzerland are rejected as not professional and—by implication—insufficiently "masculine."

By contrast, the pragmatists, while emphasizing combat readiness, see the military force as playing its role under powerful political and moral constraints. They see the possibility of a successful United States foreign and military policy without an overt assault ideology. For them, the function of the military is the political intent it imparts as much as the sheer destructive power it bears. At the professional level, they are prepared (and even hope) for a career as a soldier without combat, and they believe that combat readiness can be maintained without repressive disciplines and without "satanizing" the enemy.

Each orientation leads to differing military contributions to the persistent questions of force levels, structure, and deployment. For any given budget or force level, the absolutists are at odds with the pragmatists, although officers' attachments to their own services also help mold professional perspectives. The issue, however, is never (for instance) merely "army" self-interest versus an "air force" approach. The absolutist assumes the desirability of maintaining the military budget at the current proportion of the gross national product or increasing it to a higher proportion, whereas, the pragmatist is prepared to accept or adjust to a lowering from the contemporary 8 percent. The following excerpts from a hypothetical staff paper on joint planning for a 1.7 million force may afford an insight into contemporary professional debates and struggles.

The absolutist, with an assault concept, would recommend a 200,000–man Marine Corps, equipped with capabilities for tactical nuclear weapons, an Air Force of 500,000, and a Navy of 500,000, which would emphasize attack aircraft carriers to support amphibious or airborne warfare. The ground forces would be limited to 500,000, and most of these would be stationed in the United States, with 50,000 at most in Western Europe. The United States NATO ground troops would be part of a fully automated battlefield with electronic surveillance and highly "modernized" weapons and deployment, and they would operate with tactical nuclear weapons as a trip wire. In addition, 15,000 of the ground troops would be a special force trained for armed reconnaissance and counterinsurgency operations behind enemy lines.

By contrast, the pragmatist would limit the Marines to 100,000, specify smaller naval and air forces of approximately 450,000 each, with naval emphasis upon antisubmarine warfare. Some 700,000 men would be allocated for the ground force, of which 150,000 would be stationed in Western Europe (representing half the 1971 force level), and they would be closely articulated with emerging militia systems of Western European nations. The emphasis on special forces would be limited to a few thousand specialists. The forces stationed in the United States would be heavily involved in national emergency work as well.

RECONSTRUCTING THE ARMED FORCES

The adaptation of the United States armed forces to the end of conscription means that operational procedures that have grown up since the end of World War II require comprehensive review. The armed forces are experiencing a deep "generation gap," in that the cadres of middle-level officers are better prepared for institu-

tional change than older and higher-ranking personnel—although, of course, there are important exceptions. The tension is strongest in the ground forces, which have had to bear the burden of Vietnam and for whom the transition to an all-volunteer force is the most difficult.

An armed force which is smaller,

recruited on an all-volunteer basis, and organized more and more as a force in being reverses or at least halts the historic trend of the United States military establishment toward civil-ianization. South Vietnam drastically delayed the emergence of a new organizational format; in fact, military historians will look back on the Vietnam war as one that extended the life of traditional World War II perspectives and strengthened barriers to change. The transitions to an all-volunteer system, therefore, will take place abruptly and under highly unfavorable circumstances.

In the American environment, it was to be expected that economic incentives and financial rewards would be the main thrust for shifting to an all-volunteer system. In the fall of 1971 Congress passed a comprehensive military bill that raised the base pay of an enlisted recruit to over $260.00 a month. Base pay plus allowances and fringe benefits voted at the same time will bring the annual income of an army private close to the very symbolic figure of $5,000.00. The additional costs of these 1971 increases totaled over 2.5 billion dollars. This figure comes close to the total cost increase for personnel which the President's Commission on an All-Volunteer Force estimated would be required to create an all-volunteer force. In short, the economic incentives approach has been put into operation, but there is every reason to believe that major additional increases will have to be instituted in the future.

Meanwhile, other approaches tend to be neglected. Congress dismissed without any debate a system of volunteer national service which would allow young people to select between military and civilian service. Such a program might have strengthened the social definition of service to the nation, and this in turn would have greatly facilitated recruitment by creating a new legitimacy for governmental, commu-

nity, and military service. Moreover, the needs for basic policy changes in recruitment, career lines, education, and deployment are being faced only very slowly. New operating procedures, especially in the ground forces, have been limited to improving the physical character of barracks for enlisted personnel, new recreational resources, wider freedom in personal appearance, and modification of some aspects of the daily routine of garrison life, particularly early morning reveille. Skeptics have described these steps as a "cosmetic" approach to the problem. Likewise, there is a powerful reluctance to explore options for fundamental "institution building" in the armed forces; it is as if to do so would imply a defect in earlier practices. Nevertheless, some areas of change do hold promise of creating volunteer forces appropriate for a democratic society and a military posture of effective deterrence.

First, an all-volunteer service requires a fundamental redefinition of the tenure of a military career in order to strengthen its civil service basis. A significant proportion of both officers and enlisted men will continue to serve for six years or less; for them, military experience is an interlude is an essentially civilian existence. This type of military service appears to be viable, although there are many attendant issues to resolve.

Another group, however, will serve in the armed forces (as now) for much longer periods of time, often up to twenty years. For this group military service must be redefined as one step in a two-step career—that is, a lifetime career in the public service with a military assignment for the first portion, and a civil service assignment, the second.

For enlisted personnel successful completion of a specified period of service, such as three periods of enlistment, could constitute effective entrance into civil service employment. The United States Civil Service, under the Department of Labor, would have the responsibility for placing the individual in the federal service or, by negotiation, in state or local government service. Such a career system would broaden the basis of recruitment, attract personnel of appropriate quality and eliminate the costly system of reenlistment bonuses and existing pension plans. If an enlisted man transferred to the civil service establishment, he would take with him pension benefits equivalent to those of civil employment, and these would be paid to him on retirement.

An equivalent system would operate for officers but would go into effect only after the size of the officers corps had been reduced. In addition, the length of the term of service for officers would be made more flexible. Exit with appropriate pension benefits after ten to twelve years is essential to have a flow of personnel which will integrate with the rank structure and the military tasks to be performed.

Second, the shift over to an all-volunteer system must deal with the inflated rank structure, which is both wasteful and keeps younger men from obtaining meaningful assignments. Likewise, the services must face the fact that too many general officers have accumulated in the three services. The excessive number of such officers thwarts the assignment to important posts of younger men prepared to adapt to the changing environment. The army, in particular, has a deep division between the junior and mid-career officers who actually fought in South Vietnam and the ranking personnel who flew over the battlefield or were in top command positions. The rapid incorporation of men in their forties into the general officer group is essential to heal the breach and to offer an incentive for able mid-career officers to remain in service. To deal with this problem, generals will have to be retired at a rate faster than normal until their numbers have been significantly

reduced. Needless to say, such an objective will be difficult to attain.

Third, the existing worldwide personnel system which leads to continuous, excessive, expensive, and disruptive rotation can no longer be justified. Instead, the armed forces, and particularly the ground forces, will have to develop a modern version of the British regimental system—or in the present context, a modified brigade system. Each man would have a basic unit and a significant portion of his military career would be spent within that brigade. For the Navy, a home port concept and for the Air Force a home base would serve as the equivalent.

Fourth, the armed services will have to recognize that underemployment is a powerful source of negative attitudes toward a military career, especially among young officers. In the past, military personnel were less sensitive to the stimulus and responsibility of their initial assignments. They assumed that war would "break out" at some future time, and then they would be fully engaged. The heavy reliance of the military on short-term officers and the emergence of the strategy of deterrence make the issue of the intrinsic relevance of the day-to-day job and the avoidance of boredom and a sense of futility very important. Fundamental changes are required in military training so that many training functions may be transferred from specialized and centralized units to operational units. This is needed both to improve training and to reduce the amount of underemployment in operational units.

Fifth, the military services will have to place a stronger emphasis on officer candidate schools for recruitment and training of new officers. The end of conscription will tend to reduce the pool from which qualified officers can be selected. Officer candidates will become less socially representative— they will be predominantly from the south and the southwest and from rural and small-town areas. ROTC units will have to be reorganized so that any college student in the United States either on entrance into college or when he becomes a junior would have access to a collegiate ROTC program. In each of the ten major metropolitan areas there should also be a composite program administered by an existing ROTC group which would enroll students from any accredited college in the metropolitan area.

Sixth, the present system of in-service professional schools needs to be consolidated. The present system is wasteful, repetitive, time-consuming, and often merely mechanical. Military officers require extensive education, but many competent officers consider the present system an excessive diversion from professional service. The system should be reduced to a two-tier system, with the interservice component distributed to the service war colleges. A strong emphasis on brief courses to handle new developments in organization and doctrine would be desirable, as well as permission to substitute civilian schooling for attendance at advanced military schools.

Seventh, the academy programs should permit a one-year attendance at a civilian university, for example, in the junior year. Alternatively the academy program could be a five-year program with one year free for civilian work experience or service in the enlisted ranks.

Eighth, the services must establish a Department of Defense commission to revise the essentials of discipline. Combat-ready forces, fully sensitive to their heroic traditions and under the closest operational control, can be trained and maintained without brutality, personal degradation, or "Mickey Mouse" discipline. The United States Marine Corps may be permitted and able to maintain, as its top commanders insist, its traditional organizational code of repressive basic training, but an all-volunteer military force must face openly and candidly questions of authority and military forms. For example, extensive saluting on military bases serves no purpose but to degrade the act; saluting can have meaning as a part of crucial and selected formations.

Ninth, military justice is being transformed by civilian court decisions and will emerge closer to civilian procedures for non-military offenses.

Tenth, there exists a good deal of concern that under an all-volunteer system the physical concentration of military families on bases will contribute to their social isolation. Moreover, the current trend toward more off-base housing will not necessarily be a positive factor here, since relocation in a civilian community does not automatically produce social integration into the larger society. Where feasible, military families should have an element of choice in their housing, since for most of them access to the facilities of the military base is essential to meet the pressures that the military places on family life.

Instead, the quality of integration into civilian society depends upon personal initiative and membership in voluntary religious and community associations, as well as upon military regulations and concepts about civic participation. In Germany, the idea of the "civilian in uniform" has been pressed to the point where regular military personnel—both officers and enlisted men—are permitted to stand for political election while on active duty. In the American context, the need to maintain a nonpartisan (that is, no-party) affiliation remains essential, but a broader perspective on civic participation is possible. Military personnel should be permitted to serve on local school boards, run in nonpartisan local elections and be members of government advisory boards and public panels when they have qualifications and interests.

It is not the responsibility of military personnel to defend and publicize official military policies; this is the task of elected officials. But the military are not hired mercenaries; they cannot be mechanically deprived of participation in community and public affairs. By law, and particularly by judicial decree, military personnel are exercising their particular forms of free speech and citizen petition. The prospect of trade unions, without the right to strike, is a real possibility in the military. This can be done without interfering with professional responsibilities. In a truly pluralistic society, with dignity and good taste, military personnel, while on active duty, should be able to attend education, community, and public affairs meetings and assemblies and state their views on the legitimacy of their profession.

REDEPLOYMENT OF FORCES

The all-volunteer armed force faces a deep dilemma in the subsequent steps of its strategic redeployment. On the one hand there is the powerful self-fulfilling prophecy which is already at work: each reduction in force serves only to dampen new recruitment, especially officer recruitment. (The massive survey of the British forces carried out in 1969, nine years after the end of conscription, found that concern with future force reductions was the major source of professional discontent and one of the main reasons for planning to leave the forces.) Why enter a profession whose career and promotion opportunities are highly uncertain and declining? The plan for a civil service base for the military profession, as described above, is one device for handling this problem. Therefore, paradoxically, the faster the initial reduction to a long-run troop level, the more readily the adaptation can be made to a volunteer force. The phased withdrawal of troops from South Vietnam from a high point of over 500,000 in 1968 represents the largest single component in the overall reduction of manpower. The next step, and especially in ground troop reductions, will have to come from NATO forces. This, therefore, is the other side of the dilemma: the faster the reduction the greater the political difficulties of adapting Western European defense policy to new realities.

Although plans are projected for negotiations with the Soviet Union on European security and on mutual and balanced reduction of forces, economic pressures have committed the United States to unilateral reduction of United States contingents to NATO. Senator Mike Mansfield has been a persistent advocate of troop reductions in NATO, and there is every reason to believe that President Nixon accepted some direct reduction in return for support from members of the Democratic party for his economic program of 14 August 1971. A reduction of 5 to 10 percent of the 310,000 troops could be made immediately without any diminution of military effectiveness. The United States forces in Europe have become excessively bureaucratized, and such a reduction would in fact serve to increase operational morale and reduce the tensions associated with boredom.

Assuming a transition to an all-volunteer force and accepting the goal of a reduction of United States troops in Western Europe to 150,000 in three to five years, the United States must (1) seek effective negotiations with the Soviet Union and (2) initiate a political strategy of reratifying the basic principles of NATO in the contemporary context. If troop reductions, no matter how limited, are seen as first steps toward a United States neo-isolationism and a withdrawal from Western Europe, the Brandt initiatives will collapse, and there will be a major political crisis in Western Europe, with profound implications for the United States. The actual size of our troop commitment is not more important than the stability of our intention.

Only ratification of a new NATO treaty and simultaneous negotiation with the Soviet Union will suffice. This can be accomplished by dispatching a United States delegation of the highest level—including bipartisan representation from the Senate and House of Representatives—to prepare a new treaty for ratification by the president of the Senate. The essential element would be the restatement of long-term United States troop commitment in Western Europe. Such a declaration would set the minimum force level under various conditions, including successful negotiations at the NATO-Warsaw Pact conference.

Such a reratification of NATO principles would include the following developments for NATO and United States forces. First, the United States could establish the fact that the projected manpower reductions in Europe were linked to an increase in the United States strategic reserve available for airborne redeployment to Europe should the future international situation require it. The Nixon doctrine of "no more Vietnams" implies that NATO requirements will have higher priority on this strategic reserve, which should help reassure Western Europe. Second, a NATO rear headquarters in the United States would be in order. At this headquarters European NATO officers could be assigned for planning and staff work and for direct command with United States strategic reserve forces. Third, it should be possible to alter United States planning and commitment from a year-to-year basis for NATO to a five-year basis. For example, it would be useful to explore the establishment of a NATO mutual security bank into which the United States would make payments as a sign of future commitments. Fourth, the United States and NATO nations should encourage new manpower systems in Western Europe. It makes little or no

political sense for the United States to urge Western Europe to maintain a traditional concept of conscription at a time when it is moving to an all-volunteer force. For Europe, and especially for West Germany, militia systems, including six-month conscript service, need to be developed. For the United States, in addition to the reforms mentioned above, the United States reserve forces need to be fundamentally reorganized into three elements. One major part should be a ready reserve, capable of two-week deployment. Another part would be made up of individuals who, following the Israeli pattern, would serve briefly each year as filler personnel in operational units. A third part might be the traditional inactive reserve—but it would function as a real manpower pool, receiving some limited training and being compensated accordingly.

Fifth, the following guidelines are proposed for the NATO-Warsaw Pact conference of mutual force reduction.

1. The immediate establishment of a hot line between the headquarters of the Warsaw Pact and NATO headquarters and a joint Warsaw Pact-NATO liaison staff for information and communication purposes. These measures would reduce the threat of accidental war and implement the surveillance aspects of mutual security arrangements. The joint NATO-Warsaw Pact liaison staff would be located in neutral Switzerland.

2. A step-by-step negotiation first to a 25 percent and then to a 50 percent balanced reduction of the level of ground forces, taking into consideration the strategic positions, weapons balance, and lines of communication of both NATO and the Warsaw Pact nations.

3. The establishment of an effective system of mutual surveillance both to guarantee compliance with negotiated terms and to monitor deterrence capabilities. On-the-spot inspection is probably not necessary, if aerial and

electronic surveillance is organized on a joint basis.

All these changes in military organization and troop deployment involve shifts in professional ideology and self-conception. It is now more than a decade ago that I offered in *The Professional Soldier*, in assessing alternative futures for the military, a definition of a .constabulary force.[1] The constabulary concept provides a "continuity with past military experiences and traditions, but it offers a basis for radical adaptation of the profession. The military establishment becomes a constabulary force when it is continuously prepared to act, committed to the minimum use of force, and seeks viable international relations, rather than victory, because it has incorporated a protective military posture doctrine."

In the prologue to the new 1971 edition of *The Professional Soldier*, I underline the conclusion that prolonged hostilities in Vietnam have unfortunately diverted the attention and energy of the military from such a goal. A mass of materials have been written about the changing role of the military in contemporary society, the essence of which is widely debated by military officers. The military profession is divided and indecisive about how much of the emerging doctrines it will accept. The notion that the military is mainly in the "killing business" dies slowly. But the vitality of the military depends on the transformation of its self-definition to one in which peace keeping is its legitimate role.

Moreover, it does not appear that the military can renew its vitality unless it comes to see itself employing its facilities in a wide range of national emergency functions. The basic issue is not, as traditionalists hold, that the military should not be diverted from its fundamental mission. The military have long engaged in national emergency functions. But the nature and contents of these functions must change. In reconstructing the military,

it is essential to make effective use of its manpower and vast resources to keep it an active and responsible institution. The notion "deterrence is not enough" does not necessarily imply an assault mentality. It is also an outlook required to attract and retain bright and highly motivated men who wish to avoid underemployment and get on with the job of social change.

Clearly, the military cannot engage in activities or programs which are better performed by civilian agencies. The essential issue is to make use of its standby resources, that is, its ability to respond to emergencies, broadly defined, and to improvise in a nonroutine fashion. The military are already deeply involved in control of the effects of natural disaster—floods, hurricanes, and the like pose emergency situations that require their flexible resources. To natural disasters can be added the increasing scope of man-made disasters; oil spills, power failures, and chemical and atomic accidents are likely to increase rather than decrease. The armed forces are indispensable in a vast array of air and sea rescue work, to which is being added, on an experimental basis, medical evacuation, especially of victims of road accidents, where alternative facilities are not available.

But the major frontier rests in the arena of environmental control, and the handling of particular aspects of pollution and destruction of resources. The Corps of Engineers has moved in this direction, but only the first steps have been taken. Many units in the armed forces have contributions to make and the notion of a military career as part of a civil service career means new patterns of assignment between military and civilian agencies. An armed force of over one and one-half million men offers a significant manpower pool, and one that is urgently needed given the economic pressure of contemporary American society.

The concept of the all-volunteer force does not deny or destroy the difference between the military and the civilian, for to do so runs the risk of creating new forms of tension and unanticipated militarism. On the contrary, it calls for a special sensitivity to the distinction between the civilian and the military, each with its specific responsibilities. But the boundaries between the civilian and the military can be redefined without excessive civilianization of the military. It is not a force composed of men who, on the average, will spend the bulk of their working lives in the military; projections of a highly stable force forecast that the length of service for enlisted men in the army will be no more than five years, with an equivalent figure for officers. In fact, a military which is engaged primarily in deterrence does not have to be a profession with less, but can be one with more civilian contacts.

The all-volunteer armed force marks the end of the historical era of the mass armed force. The rise of the mass armed force was not purely a military development but reflected the sociopolitical trends of nationalism.

The present internal tensions and the crisis in legitimacy within the armed forces have meant that the decline of mass conscription, although delayed by the war in Vietnam, will take place rapidly and without significant resistance in American society. The form and character of the all-volunteer force, again, will not be a purely military phenomenon but will reflect the character of the larger society. The all-volunteer armed force will be rooted especially in those elements of American society which continue to be the carriers of traditional nationalism. But the military can also reflect and incorporate new forms of transnationalism which already exist both in its own ranks and in civilian society. Under these circumstances, it will be the duty of civilian society to assume an active role in directing the military to redefine its professional perspectives and to help it understand that peace keeping through a military presence, deterrence, and participation in the control of national emergencies are the modern definitions of the heroic role.

NOTES

1. *The Professional Soldier: A Social and Political Portrait,* Free Press of Glencoe, 1960; revised 1971.

Selected Additional Readings

Dumhoff, G. William. *Who Rules America?* Englewood Cliffs, N.J.: Prentice-Hall, Inc., 1967.

Assesses American politics as a process of shifting coalitions which are dominated by the upper class. Includes a chapter on the military, CIA and FBI.

Ekirch, Arthur A., Jr. *The Civilian and the Military.* New York: Oxford University Press, 1956.

Describes the traditions of antimilitarism in American history and reflects upon the contemporary inclination toward militarism.

Galbraith, John Kenneth. *How to Control the Military.* New York: New American Library, 1969.

Discusses the responsibility of American institutions for involvement of the U.S. in the Vietnam War and prescribes ways for citizens to assert their dominance over military policies.

Ginsburgh, Col. Robert N. "The Challenge to Military Professionalism," *Foreign Affairs,* 42 (January 1964), 255–268.

Explores the challenge to the military professional ethos by civilian decision-making practices and considers how the military can respond.

Goodman, Walter. *The Committee: The Extraordinary Career of the House Committee on Un-American Activities.* New York: Farrar, Straus and Giroux, 1968.

A case study of the three decades of operation of the Committee on Un-American Activities of the U.S. House of Representatives.

Grodzins, Morton. *The Loyal and the Disloyal: Social Boundaries of Patriotism and Treason.* Cleveland: The World Publishing Co., 1966.

Investigates why people are loyal or disloyal to their country and how these commitments are manifested.

Janowitz, Morris. *The Professional Soldier: A Social and Political Portrait.* New York: The Free Press, 1971.

A revision of the 1960 edition of this sociological study of the career officer corps, its organization, leadership, and professional identity.

Just, Ward. *Military Men.* New York: Knopf, 1970.

A journalistic but interesting portrait of the attitudes and outlooks of U.S. Army personnel at all levels of the hierarchy.

Lapp, Ralph. *The Weapons Culture.* Baltimore: Penguin Books, 1969.

Describes the growth of the "military-industrial complex" subsequent to the Eisenhower Administration.

Lasswell, Harold D. "The Garrison State," *American Journal of Sociology,* XLVI (January 1941), 455–468.

Written prior to World War II, this article asserts that society will become increasingly dominated by specialists in violence in a world of garrison states.

Lyons, Gene M. "The New Civil Military Relations," *American Political Science Review,* LV (March 1961), 53–63.

Assesses changes in the pattern of civil-military relations wherein the "civilians are becoming 'militarized' and the military 'civilianized.' "

Melman, Seymour, ed. *The Defense Economy: Conversion of Industries and Occupations to Civilian Needs.* New York: Praeger, 1970.

A collection of original essays by graduate engineering students about the problems of conversion from defense to civilian industrial production.

Millis, Walter. *Arms and Men: A Study in American Military History.* New York: The New American Library, 1956.

Traces the evolution of the American military since the founding of the Republic in terms of social, political and technological factors.

Mills, C. Wright. *The Power Elite.* New York: Oxford University Press, 1956.

The elaboration of Mills's thesis that a power elite dominates the influence processes of American society. Assesses the role of the military in these processes.

Russett, Bruce M. *What Price Vigilance? The Burdens of National Defense.* New Haven: Yale University Press, 1970.

A very readable quantitative analysis of defense spending with respect to the allocation of economic burdens and their effects on nondefense public programs and private spending.

Stillman, Richard J., II. *Integration of the Negro in the U.S. Armed Forces.* New York: Frederick A. Praeger, 1968.

Describes the changing role of the black man in the American military.

Vagts, Alfred. *A History of Militarism.* Rev. ed. New York: Free Press, 1959.

A historical and comparative account of the phenomenon of militarism since the feudal period. A revision of the 1937 edition.

Wamsley, Gary L. *Selective Service and a Changing America: A Study of Organizational-Environmental Relationships.* Columbus: Charles E. Merrill Publishing Co., 1969.

Studies the evolution of the draft and analyzes the organizational factors which shaped the capacity of the Selective Service System to adapt to changes in its political environment.

Contributors

WALTER ADAMS is President and Professor of Economics at Michigan State University.

RAYMOND ARON is Professor of Sociology at the University of Paris.

ANDRÉ BEAUFRE is Général d'Armée and Director of the Institut Français d'Études Stratégiques.

BERNARD BRODIE is Professor of Political Science at the University of California, Los Angeles.

SEYOM BROWN is a Senior Fellow in the Foreign Policy Division of the Brookings Institution.

KARL VON CLAUSEWITZ, Prussian general and writer, was Director of the Kriegsakademie in Berlin at his death in 1831.

JAMES E. DOUGHERTY is Executive Vice President and Professor of Political Science at St. Joseph's College.

HENRY E. ECCLES, Rear Admiral, U.S. Navy (Ret.), is a Lecturer at the U.S. Naval War College.

ROGER FISHER is Professor of Law at Harvard University.

DAVID GALULA, a former French Army Officer, wrote *Counterinsurgency Warfare: Theory and Practice* at the Center for International Affairs at Harvard in 1962–63. Mr. Galula died in 1967.

ROBERT G. GARD, JR., Brig. General, U.S. Army, is Director of Discipline and Drug Policies in the Department of the Army.

RAYMOND D. GASTIL is a Center Fellow at the Battelle Seattle Research Center and an Employee Member of the Hudson Institute.

PAUL Y. HAMMOND is Associate Department Head of the Social Sciences Department at the RAND Corporation.

ROBERT T. HOLT is Professor of Political Science at the University of Minnesota.

ARNOLD L. HORELICK is a Senior Staff Member in the Social Science Department of the RAND Corporation.

MICHAEL HOWARD is a Fellow in Higher Defence Studies at All Souls College, Oxford University.

SAMUEL P. HUNTINGTON is Frank G. Thomson Professor of Government at Harvard University.

MORRIS JANOWITZ is Professor of Sociology at the University of Chicago.

MORTON A. KAPLAN is Professor of Political Science at the University of Chicago.

KLAUS KNORR is Professor of International Affairs at the Woodrow Wilson School, Princeton University.

PHILIP S. KRONENBERG is Assistant Professor of Political Science at Indiana University.

HAROLD D. LASSWELL is Professor of Law at Yale University.

CHARLES C. MOSKOS, JR., is Chairman of the Department of Sociology at Northwestern University.

ROBERT E. OSGOOD is Professor of American Foreign Policy at the School of Advanced International Studies, Johns Hopkins University.

E. S. QUADE is Head of the Mathematics Department of the RAND Corporation.

LAURENCE I. RADWAY is Professor of Government at Dartmouth College.

HARRY HOWE RANSOM is Professor of Political Science at Vanderbilt University.

ANATOL RAPOPORT is Professor of Mathematical Biology and Senior Research Mathematician at the

597

Mental Health Research Institute, University of Michigan.

JAMES RESTON is Vice President of the *New York Times.*

GERHARD RITTER was formerly Professor Emeritus in History at the University of Freiburg/Breisgau. Professor Ritter died in 1967.

JEROME ROTHENBERG is Professor of Economics at the Massachusetts Institute of Technology.

MYRON RUSH is Professor of Government at Cornell University.

BRUCE M. RUSSETT is Professor of Political Science at Yale University.

JAMES R. SCHLESINGER is Chairman of the Atomic Energy Commission.

FRANK L. SIMONIE is a Research Assistant and Ph.D. Candidate at New York University.

V. D. SOKOLOVSKY, Marshal of the Soviet Union, was formerly Chief of the Soviet General Staff. Marshal Sokolovsky died in 1968.

FREDERICK C. THAYER is an Associate Professor in the Graduate School of Public and International Affairs at the University of Pittsburgh.

ALEXIS DE TOCQUEVILLE was a French writer and political analyst. De Tocqueville died in 1859.

FRANK N. TRAGER is Professor of International Affairs and Director, National Security Program at New York University, and Director of Studies at the National Strategy Information Center.

ROBERT W. VAN DE VELDE is Professor of Public and International Affairs at the Woodrow Wilson School, Princeton University.

RAYMOND VERNON is Herbert F. Johnson Professor of International Business Management at the Harvard Business School.

QUINCY WRIGHT was formerly Professor of International Law at the University of Chicago. Professor Wright died in 1970.

ADAM YARMOLINSKY is Professor of Law at Harvard University.

Index

Acheson, Dean, 72, 140, 175, 233–34, 260, 269
Adams, Walter, 429, *463–71*
advertising, industrial, 481
AFL-CIO, 165–66
Africa, 53, 356, 498, 584
Agnew, Spiro, 271, 504
AID, 139, 143, 144
air bases: location of, 210–11
air warfare: strategy in, 320; effect of, 581
Alcibiades, 115
Alexander, 76, 115
Algeria: insurgency in, 58–59, 300, 301, 363, 365; economic growth in, 250; French in, 294, 295, 301; mentioned, 314
alienation: political effects of, 435–37; in U.S., 513–14
alliances: as means, 46; motivation for, 65; of U.S., 356; and arms limitation, 409
Allison, Graham T., 10, 19
Alsace-Lorraine, 53, 56, 61
Alsop, Stewart, 170
aluminum: multinational production of, 244, 249, 252; industry in U.S., 469
ambassadors, U.S.: role of, 140–41; appointment of, 147–48
American Anthropological Association, 496
American Civil Liberties Union, 28
American Farm Bureau, 164–65
American Physical Society, 514
American Serviceman's Union (ASU), 544
The American Soldier, 523, 524, 525
Anderson, George, 564, 567, 568
Anthony, Robert N., 187
anti-ballistic missile weapons (ABM), 229, 336, 339, 415, 419, 584
antisubmarine warfare (ASW), 336, 339
antiwar movement, 530, 538, 570, 579
Apollo: procurement of, 467
Aqaba, Gulf of, 388
Arab-Israeli conflict, 142, 332, 417
Arab League, 60
Ardennes, battle of, 310, 517
Argentina, 246, 249, 417, 498
aristocracy: officers of, 122–23, 124; control of military by, 552
armed forces, U.S.: civilian control of, 10, 32, 263–64, 551–54, 564–69, 571–72; socioeconomic make-up of, 124, 536–41; attitude of Congress toward, 143; legislation on, 153, 168; professional, 273, 439–40; and McNamara, 292; limits on, 360n10; size of, 460n2, 515n8; competition in, 475–76; tradition in, 507–8, 570; desertions in, 509–10; recruitment policy, 510–11, 519; volunteer,

510, 582–83; desegregation of, 516–20, 532–33, 545–46; differential opportunity in, 520, 525–29; morale in, 538–39, 570, 575–76, 577; civilianized model of, 542–45, 581; traditional model of, 545–47; pluralistic model of, 547–49; and civilian society, 561–62, 564–65; organization of, 570–71; new roles for, 572–75, 592; in domestic problems, 577, 592; decline of mass, 580–83; troop reduction in, 584, 590–91; and civil service, 587–88. *See also* military officers; military personnel; military professionalism; volunteer army
Armed Forces Procurement Act, 153
Armed Forces Qualification Test (AFQT), 521
Armed Forces Reserve Act, 153
arms control: U.S.–U.S.S.R. agreements on, 203; and weapons development, 231, 482; and strategy, 281; emphasis on, 286, 292, 403, 407; deterrence and, 342–44; objectives of, 382, 404–5, 413, 419–21, 497; in garrison-state hypothesis, 407
arms race: and threat of war, 113; in deterrence theory, 330, 332; stimulants to, 340, 341–42; Western restraint in, 385; economic motive for, 407; and government procurement policy, 415–16, 464–65; and needs of science, 482; mentioned, 10, 111
Army and Air Force Authorization Act of 1949, 179n17
Aron, Raymond, *53–62*: his definition of strategy, 299; mentioned, 51, 127, 317
Arrow, Kenneth J., 265
atomic submarine program, 142
atomic weapons. *See* nuclear weapons
Australia, 255, 417, 539, 541
Austria, 38, 40, 83, 286
Austria-Hungary, 53
authoritarianism: in military training, 511–12

Bagehot, Walter, 160
balance of payments, U.S., 456
balance of power: maintaining, 65; as motive, 72–73; and causes of war, 86–87
Baldwin, Hanson: on future intervention, 351, 352–53; theory of, 354
ballistic missile defense (BMD): political effect of, 200; limited effectiveness of, 201–2; justification of, 202–3; in deterrence theory, 331; and arms reduction, 333
bargaining, crisis, 93, 95, 98–99
Barkley, Alben, 146
Bavaria, 48n7
Bay of Pigs, 73, 514

prices: and defense spending, 450; corporate control over, 468–69
Princeton Center of International Studies, 287
problem solving technique, 432
productivity, national: and defense spending, 453
programming, planning, budgeting system (PPBS), 9, 181, 187
Project 100,000, 546
Project Clear, 524, 525, 527
Project Transition, 546, 577
propaganda: as means, 46, 103, 300, 371–72, 373; in strategy concepts, 281, 300; goal of, 364; effect of, 376–77; directed to Blacks, 531. *See also* psychological instrument
Pruitt, Dean G., 127
Prussia, 61, 77, 120, 311, 561, 580
psychological instrument: in strategy, 300, 307, 311; in U.S. policy, 371, 372–73; role of, 373–75; aims of, 376–77; mentioned, 46, 102, 117, 571, 572
psychology, adolescent, 510
psychotherapy, 269
public debate: in policy process, 164–65, 169, 170; and NSC deliberations, 177–78; and press coverage of foreign policy, 234, 236, 237; on Vietnam, 262; mentioned, 32
Pueblo, 538
Puerto Ricans, in U.S. military, 534n3
Punic Wars, 115
Pyrrhus, 58

Quade, E. S., 132, *206–23*
Quemoy, 73

radar, 482
Radford, Arthur, 175, 288, 564, 567
radio. *See* communication, mass media
Radway, Laurence I., 131, *133–51*
RAND Corporation: decision process of, 210–11; *Study of Non-Military Defense*, 291; and Vietnam policy, 566; mentioned, 20, 206, 214, 284, 289, 290, 292, 496
Ransom, Harry Howe, 22, 429, *472–84*
Rapacki Plan, 422n6
Rapoport, Anatol, *485–91*: response to, 491–96; mentioned, 429
raw materials: as vital interest, 59, 66; sources of, and war, 89; U.S. control of, 107; and multinational corporations, 243–44, 248–50, 251; exports of, 245; stockpiling of, 468; mentioned, 60
Rayburn, Sam, 146
Reischauer, Edwin O., 359n5
Republican Party, 287
research: framework for, 18–20; and weapons requirements, 184; and new management techniques, 186–87; industrial, 243, 464; emphasis on, 313; for military power, 439; spillover from military, 452, 487–88; U.S. expenditure for, 459, 470; classified, and

university, 485–96; opposition to defense, 513, 514
reserve forces legislation, 153, 172
resources, national: as goal of state, 56, 57, 59, 60; as limit on military power, 94; bureaucratic competition for, 228, 265, 273, 452, 453, 513; in strategic theory, 282, 301–2, 303; future, 453; stockpiling of, 464
Reston, James, 169, *233–39*
retaliation, massive: force for, 155, 290, 336–37; in deterrence theory, 284–86, 326–28; controversy over, 285; in U.S. policy, 287, 292; for nonnuclear aggression, 337–39; effect of, 395–96; mentioned, 514, 537
revolution: in national security study, 36; socialist, 106, 107, 108; danger of, in democracy, 122, 124; theory of, 294–95, 296; as means of strategy, 301; conditions of intervention in, 351–55, 357–58; strategy in, 361–69. *See also* national liberation, wars of
Rhodesia: economic sanctions on, 388, 391, 393, 395; British strategy in, 399–400
Rickover, Hyman George, 142, 468, 476
Ridgway, Matthew B., 169, 171, 567, 572
Ritter, Gerhard, 52, *114–21*
Rockefeller, Nelson, 141
Roosevelt, Franklin D.: attitude toward internal conflict, 136; and creation of NSC, 137; bipartisan approach of, 141, 142; and Congress, 149; his leadership, 169; and the press, 233; mentioned, 145, 566
Roosevelt, Theodore, 158, 169
Ropp, Theodore, 127–28
Rosenau, James N., 19
Rosinski, Herbert, 319, 320–21
Rostow, Walt, 138
ROTC, 513, 541, 576, 589
Rothenberg, Jerome, 280, *335–44*
Rowe, James, 506
Rumania, 413
Rush, Myron, 280, *379–87*
Rusk, Dean, 145
Russell, Bertrand, 269, 334
Russell, Richard B., 158, 159, 477
Russett, Bruce M., 429, *449–62*
Russia: regimes of, 48; Tsarist, 53, 62, 77, 303. *See* Union of Soviet Socialist Republics

sabotage, 377n2
Safeguard, 415, 419
SALT (Strategic Arms Limitation Talks), 273, 409–20 *passim*, 584
Sandys, Duncan, 285
Sapin, Burton, 374
Saudi Arabia, 245
Schelling, Thomas: and role of will, 263; theory of, 286, 288, 290, 349; recent work of, 291–92; mentioned, 281
Scherer, Frederic M., 467
Schilling, Warner R., 189
Schlesinger, Arthur, Jr., 503

Universal Declaration of the Rights of Man, 446n10
universal military training, 153, 172
universities: intelligentsia of, 267, 268; dissent and, 271, 274n27, 504, 547; objectives of, and secrecy, 485–96; mentioned, 233

Valery, Paul, 312
Vandenburg, Arthur, 141, 233–34
Van den Haag, Ernest, 493–95
Van de Velde, Robert W., 280, *370–78*
Venezuela, 66, 245, 252–53
Vernon, Raymond, 132, *240–59*
Versailles Treaty, 142
veterans, 531–32
Vietnam, North: bombing of, 232, 350, 353–54, 360n9, 383, 388, 389, 391, 392, 396, 401; Soviet support of, 358; and U.S. policy, 398–99
Vietnam War: effects of, on U.S., 47, 190–92, 193, 195, 198–99, 260–62, 272, 514, 523; goals of U.S. in, 64; troop withdrawals, 66–67, 590; decision making on, 139, 146, 229; Fulbright hearings on, 234; press coverage of, 235, 237; U.S. domestic attitudes toward, 263–64, 267–68, 269–71, 575, 576; strategic failure in, 316, 395; lessons of, 350–55, 574; U.S. restraint in, 360n10, 360n11; U.S. policy in, 400, 401, 402, 411, 573; costs of, 450–51, 452, 456, 459, 497–98; and antiwar movement, 503–4, 506, 513, 530; casualties in, 521–22; mentioned *passim*
Voice of America, 373
volunteer army (VOLAR): decision process on, 17–18; effects of, 510; social composition of, 539–42, 576–78, 583, 586–90; model of, 543–45, 547; in Europe, 579–80; redeployment of forces, 590–93

Walker, Edwin, 484n21, 537
Wallace, George, 271, 272, 568
Waltz, Kenneth N., 128
war colleges, U.S., 564, 589
War of 1812, 516
War of Independence, U.S., 516
Warsaw Pact-NATO conference, 591
weapons systems: decision making on, 32, 155, 231; procurement of, 143, 465, 466–67, 583; and Congress, 158–59; Soviet, 171, 384; determining requirements for, 183, 184, 185–86; cost of, 201–2, 439, 449, 574, 583; and strategic theory, 296, 321–22, 335; and disarmament, 408; need for information for,

480–81; research for, 492, 514; influence of, 543. *See also* nuclear weapons
Weiner, Norbert, 438
welfare, spending for, 457–58
Wellington, 1st Duke of, 234
Werner, Herman O., 127
Western Europe: and industrial blackmail, 250–51; defense of, 286, 289, 332, 347, 348–50, 356, 357; vulnerability of, 337–39; and arms limitation, 409–10; troop withdrawal proposals for, 410–11; alienation in, 435; affluence of, 453; U.S. policy toward, 500, 583–84; civil-military relations in, 539, 561; defense of, 584–85; U.S. troops in, 590–91
Westmoreland, William, 512, 567, 568, 573
West Point, Military Academy at, 507, 514, 515n18
White, Thomas, 567
White House staff, 20, 38, 137, 138, 238
Wilensky, Harold L., 29
Williams, Robert F., 531
Wilson, Charles E., 473, 474
Wilson, Harold, 235
Wilson, Woodrow, 149, 162–63, 169
Wise, Sydney F., 127
Wohlstetter, Albert, 290, 291
Wolfe, Thomas W., 404
Wolfers, Arnold, 5, 35, 128, 406n1
Wool, Harold, 546
workers: armaments, 263; technical, 267; professional, 267, 544; defense, 509; white collar, 450
world federation, 90
World War I: goals in, 53; casualties of, 103; strategy in, 311; U.S. entry in, 407, 449; mentioned, 106, 107, 247, 303, 516
World War II: causes of, 88; casualties of, 103; strategy in, 282, 309, 310, 311; civilian populations in, 331, 332; cost of, 450, 452, 456, 457, 458; U.S. entry into, 498–99; mentioned *passim*
Wright, Quincy, 51, *85–91*

Yarmolinsky, Adam, 429, *507–15*
Yenan, 367
Young, Stephen, 506
youth movement: U.S., 268–71, 413, 442–43, 500, 514, 518, 538, 544, 573, 575, 582; Soviet, 582
Yugoslavia, 103, 105

Zorza, Victor, 412
Zumwalt, Elmo R., Jr., 544